I0198823

*Heretics and Politics*

# HERETICS AND POLITICS
Theology, Power, and Perception
in the Last Days of CBC

∾

## THOMAS A. FUDGE
University of New England, Australia

## H
Hewitt Research Foundation
Washougal, Washington
2014

Published in 2014 by Hewitt Research Foundation,
Washougal, Washington 98671

© 2014 Thomas A. Fudge. Except for brief quotations in a review, no part of this publication may be reproduced, stored in or introduced into a retrieval system, or transmitted, in any form, or by any means, electronic, mechanical, photocopying, recording, or otherwise, without the prior permission in writing of Hewitt Research Foundation, or as expressly permitted by law, by license, or under terms agreed with an appropriate reproduction rights organization.

You must not circulate this work in any other form
and you must impose this same condition on any acquirer.

All rights reserved. Published 2014
Printed in the United States of America

20 19 18 17 16 15 14     1 2 3 4 5 6 7

ISBN 13: 978-1-57896-275-4 (hardcover)
ISBN 10: 1-57896-275-7

Library of Congress Cataloguing-in-Publication Data
Fudge, Thomas A.
    Heretics and Politics: Theology, power, and perception in the last days of
    CBC/Thomas A. Fudge
    pages cm
    Includes bibliographical references (pages) and index.
    ISBN 13: 978-1-57896-275-4 (hardcover)
    ISBN 10: 1-57896-275-7

    1. Conquerors Bible College 1953-1983. 2. United Pentecostal Church–20th
    century. 3. Bible colleges–history–20th century. 4. Church and college
    history. 5. Theology, Doctrinal, controversies. 6. Church history–United
    States–20th century. Title.

For Donna Fisher and Esther Peden
who stood by their husbands during the last days of CBC

and for Jerry Dillon and April Purtell
friends for life

# Table of Contents

# List of Figures and Illustrations

General Catalog   1979-1981

## CONQUERORS BIBLE COLLEGE
Portland, Oregon

0.0  College catalog from the last days of CBC. View of Portland and Mt. Hood from the Rose Gardens

# Abbreviations

ABI      Apostolic Bible Institute (St. Paul, Minnesota, 1937–)

CBC      Conquerors (Cascade) Bible College (Portland, Oregon, Vancouver, Washington, 1953-1983)

DOE      Division of Education (1968 –)

FC      The Fudge Collection (private collection of more than 5,600 documents relating to the UPC)

IBC      Indiana Bible College (Indianapolis, Indiana, 1981–)

JCM      Jackson College of Ministries (Jackson, Mississippi, 1975-2004)

LCMS      Lutheran Church, Missouri Synod

Manual      *Manual* [of the] *United Pentecostal Church International* (2014)

Minutes      Minutes of the meetings of the CBC Board of Directors

PAJC      Pentecostal Assemblies of Jesus Christ (1931-1945; 1947–)

PBI      Pentecostal Bible Institute (Tupelo, Mississippi, 1945-1974)

PCI      Pentecostal Church, Incorporated (1932-1945)

PG      *Patrologia Graeca*, ed., Jacques Paul Migne, 161 vols (Paris: Migne/Garnier, 1857-1866)

PL      *Patrologia Latina*, ed., Jacques Paul Migne, 221 vols (Paris: Migne/Garnier, 1844-1865)

SBC      Southern Baptist Convention

UPC      United Pentecostal Church

WA      *D. Martin Luthers Werke. Kritische Gesamtausgabe*, 121 vols (Weimar: Hermann Böhlaus Nachfolger, 1883-2009)

0.1 Conference of the Northwest District, Caldwell, Idaho, 1961. Many important CBC personalities appear including: Edwin Judd, R.V. Reynolds, Orion Gleason, Norman Rutzen, Wayne Nigh, Verneal Crossley, Jet Witherspoon, the Fishers (Harry, Freda, Don and Donna), John Klemin, C.H. Yadon, C.M. Yadon, and Dale Walker

# Acknowledgements

The genesis of *Heretics and Politics* occurred more than fifteen years ago. In 1997, I decided to do a second PhD and elected to work in the field of theology. At that time I was a fully-tenured member of the faculty in the Department of History at the University of Canterbury in Christchurch, New Zealand. I did my doctoral work under the auspices of the Department of Theology and Religion at New Zealand's oldest institution of higher learning, the University of Otago in Dunedin. The resulting dissertation was later expanded, revised, and published as an academic monograph.[1] During the research for the PhD in theology, I identified two other, much smaller, projects within Oneness history which interested me and which I thought deserved attention. The first was an examination of C.H. Yadon (1908-1997), who played a fairly large role in my book on the UPC. The other idea was an exploration of the issues which coalesced to terminate the existence of CBC. Both projects had their initial start in the late 1990s when I produced an outline draft of each subject. During my extensive interviewing and collecting of materials for the eventual book on that chapter of theological history, I engaged in double duty to the extent that I was often able to include in my interviews material related especially to CBC. This proved fortuitous because since I conducted those interviews no fewer than fifty-three of those men and women have died.

The last days of CBC were marked by fraternal fighting and brawling among the brotherhood. Some of it was personal, much of it theological.[2] The last days of CBC reveal a story literally crawling with stark contradiction, muddled by lost or murky memory, characterized by confused chronology, and fraught with a host of

---

[1] Thomas A. Fudge, *Christianity without the Cross: A History of Salvation in Oneness Pentecostalism* (Parkland, FL: Universal, 2003).
[2] Some view this "fratricidal brawling" as endemic in early Pentecostalism. Robert Mapes Anderson, *Vision of the Disinherited: The Making of American Pentecostalism* (New York: Oxford University Press, 1979), p. 222.

non-sustainable assumptions. In this book, I have attempted to eliminate fiction, put to rest unreliable rumor, resolve contradiction, articulate a proper chronology, and test a variety of persistent assumptions about the college and its personnel. In those efforts I am very grateful to those who shared documents and consented to be interviewed concerning the subjects contained in this book, especially the family of Donald W. Fisher, the last president of CBC, who is critically, controversially, and unavoidably, the central figure in this study. These included his parents Harry Fisher (1916-2013) and Freda Fisher (1919-2013), his wife Donna, his three daughters Susan Paynter, Karissa Hopkins and Ronna Russell, his father-in-law Clarence Lewis (1912-2007), and his sister Doris Newman. Those who worked with him at JCM, especially T. L. (Thomas Lynn) Craft, Daniel J. Lewis, Joseph H. Howell, James D. Wilkins, Mark Roberts, Jewel (Yadon) Dillon, and Skip Paynter, and at CBC, especially Jerry and Esther Peden, April Purtell, David Wasmundt, Darline Kantola, and Raymond Sirstad, among others, provided valuable insights. Among his friends and colleagues I learned important details from Jewel Dillon, Paul Adams, Jesse Martin, Wayne Nigh, Norman Rutzen, Jerry B.D. Dillon, and many more. I had the good fortune of substantive and useful input about CBC from former presidents E.G. Moyer (1912-2006), Ralph V. Reynolds (1913-2002), Edwin Judd, and C.H. Yadon. Other leading figures in those last years, such as C.M. Yadon (1922-2003), Paul Dugas (1923-2006), Barry King, and George M. Sponsler (1923-2008) also shared their thoughts and insights on the history and developments in the Northwest and at the college. Among the most useful of my interviewees was Jerry Dillon, who spent a dozen years at CBC, knew every president personally and possesses significant knowledge of the school and its history. Portland area pastors and ministers such as Gary Gleason, Nathaniel Yadon (1953-2009), Leon Brokaw, Ruby Klemin (1919-2012), Clyde Barlow, and Phillip Dugas (1933-2012) were especially helpful. Frank LaCrosse and Dan Satterwhite also contributed to my inquiries. From outside the context of the Northwest, I benefitted greatly from interviews with Nathaniel Urshan (1920-2005), C.M. Becton (1928-2010), Arless Glass, and David Bernard. The latter could speak with insight into matters at JCM in the aftermath of the Fisher administration while the former men had been involved with different aspects of the Northwest and CBC. Thetus Tenney enjoyed a close and unique relationship with Don Fisher over a long period of time (1966-1981) and I am grateful for her willingness to spend three hours in Sydney sharing aspects of that professional and personal friendship. Beyond these, I have had occasion to interview or talk with a good number of Fisher's students either from JCM or CBC. Those perspectives were sometimes deeply insightful. Two individuals stand out for their willingness to correspond and talk with me concerning various details of this research over the course of many months. These were Dan Lewis and Jerry Dillon. Both were enormously helpful for their careful reflections on events at JCM and CBC. Of the faculty teaching at CBC during the very last years, and students studying at the college during both of the last two years, I contacted 85% and 92% respectively. Jules Filipski at the Oregon Historical Society was helpful on the shipyard facilities.

Many of the interviews noted within these pages were recorded, and I have made every effort to present the views of these individuals and others besides with fairness and within the context they made their remarks. More often than not I have judged it prudent to quote the precise words and language of these individuals and for those recorded I have been able to present those comments with the highest degree of accuracy. Some of these interviews spanned several hours, others were relatively short. Less formal conversations have been dated and referenced as an interview. I am grateful to all, even to those who rather reluctantly were persuaded to engage in discussion and wound up answering questions and providing information which contributed in various ways to the development of the following narrative. No one who agreed to answer written or verbal questions can be regarded on that basis as having endorsed any of my arguments, interpretations, or conclusions. I am particularly grateful to Ian C. Campbell (retired Professor of History at the University of Canterbury in New Zealand), Thomas A. Robinson (Professor and Chair of Religious Studies at the University of Lethbridge in Canada), Cole P. Dawson (Vice President for Academic Affairs and Dean of the Faculty at Warner Pacific College in Portland), and Daniel J. Lewis (Senior Pastor of Troy Christian Chapel in Michigan). All four served as referees for the book. Each read earlier versions of the manuscript and wrote extensive written reports towards the improvement of the text. None can be held responsible for remaining errors or for the fact that some of their advice was ignored by the author. Each contributed in several ways to the account that follows. Lucy S.R. Austen undertook the copy-editing process and the text is more readable as a result. April Purtell worked on many of the images and produced an extraordinary dust jacket. Tim Cluley stepped in at the eleventh hour with some much-needed expertise on last minute modifications. Trish Wright, Academic Coordinator for the School of Humanities at the University of New England, provided expert technical assistance, worked very hard on the presentation of the text, assisted with the grueling preparation of the index, and also functioned as a research associate and international liaison, fulfilling each role with panache. Her patience, proficiency, professionalism, consistent enthusiasm, and good humor have been gifts.

The vagaries of memory bedevil any attempt to build an argument on oral sources. Memory is neither fixed nor stable and its reliability is always questionable. To what extent is orality mere hearsay? Does it simply constitute gossip? Detractors of the theses developed in these pages will seize upon that possibility to dismiss the explanatory arguments for the cessation of CBC, while those sympathetic will hardly even notice the preponderance of oral witness. There is no source, whether oral or written, official or ad hoc, which stands beyond question or critique. There are no sacred texts unmediated by time, culture, context, and/or human hand. Historical truths are versions of memory, each of which have been tempered by a myriad of factors. There is always unavoidable bias and distortion, and oral testimony is perhaps more prone to these perilous pitfalls than other forms of witness. I have attempted to compensate for this with the weight of evidence gleaned from several sources. The events discussed in the following pages occurred thirty to forty years ago. Not even the sharpest memory can bring to mind in precise detail all that happened. The politics of memory and historical recollection is built upon shifting sand.

After the closure of CBC, Darline "DK" Kantola (ill.5.20, p. 292) oversaw the preservation of essential documents from the college history, and these were shipped to St. Louis in late 1984 for storage and preservation.[3] I am grateful to David K. Bernard, Robin Johnston, and John Smelser at the headquarters of the United Pentecostal Church in Hazelwood, Missouri for facilitating access to the CBC collection.[4] I have used all sources at my disposal, including but not limited to notes, journals, college yearbooks, sermons, college course syllabi, church materials, letters, official correspondence, tape-recordings, interviews, national and regional publications of the UPC, college catalogues, relevant scholarship, personal memoirs, various unpublished materials, and photographic evidence obtained at the UPC headquarters and elsewhere. The footnotes will reveal the nature and extent of the usage. There were quite a number of interviewees who are not quoted or referred to by name in these pages but this should not be considered a reflection of the quality or usefulness of those contributions.[5] From time to time an interviewee asked to go off-tape. With one exception, I have not included any material that was unrecorded or where the source asked not to be quoted or identified.

There are 162 illustrations which supplement the text. These feature the principle personalities presented in the narrative, or are relevant for understanding the subjects herein. I am grateful to those who supplied pictures, especially Jewel (Yadon) Dillon, Jerry Dillon, April Purtell, and Jesse Martin. Quite a number came from my own collection, while the remainder was culled from the various

3 Darline (Kantola) Royer interview, 15 August 2013, Yuba City, California. Many materials considered unimportant were discarded. Kantola possibly consulted with George Sponsler and Norman Rutzen at the time but she had little guidance in selection. Nevertheless, her work must be regarded as one of significance. Regrettably there does not appear to be an inventory of the existing CBC collection, though prior to its relocation to St. Louis it was described as consisting of "five filing cabinets and one metal shelf cabinet." Darline Kantola, letter to the CBC board, 13 September 1984, p. 1. FC, inv.doc.no 0707-5236-34. There are four filing cabinets in St. Louis.
4 Apart from student records I was assured unrestricted access to all extant CBC materials. David K. Bernard, letter to Thomas A. Fudge, 28 June 2013 (FC, inv.doc.no 0707-5076-33), and confirmed in conversations with John Smelser, Director of the Center for the Study of Oneness Pentecostalism, Hazelwood, Missouri, on 30 and 31 July 2013.
5 Fudge, *Christianity without the Cross: A History of Salvation in Oneness Pentecostalism,* pp. 372-376. Every one of these 204 individuals possessing any knowledge of the themes elaborated in this book were asked to reflect on those topics.

JCM and CBC yearbooks and other periodical publications. Almost all of these are pre-digital and of varying quality, with some rather poor. I am grateful to Norman Rutzen, Edwin Judd, and Jerry Dillon for helping to identify the many people in ill.0.1, p. xviii.

Twenty-two appendices contain various documents I regard as important. It also seems prudent to point out that revelations about Don Fisher's personal life subsequent to the closure of CBC may have had a bearing on the memories of various interviewees and attempts have been made to counterbalance this possibility with active consideration of other sources. The narrative which follows integrates historical research, theological reflection, and personal memoir. All three forms of writing are reflected throughout the pages which follow. Biography, memoir, and ecclesiastical conflict are unavoidably interwoven in the fabric of history and theology which is the story of *Heretics and Politics.*

Thomas A. Fudge
Armidale, NSW
Australia

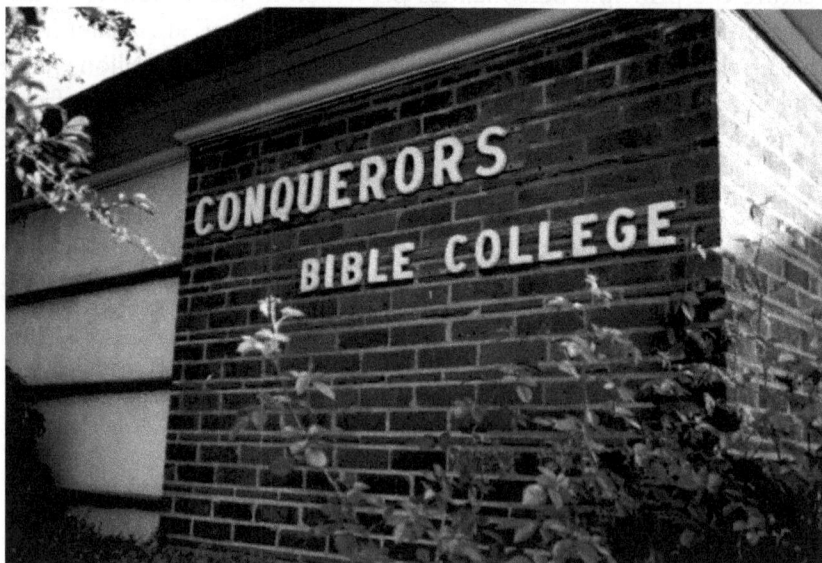

0.2  College sign near the main Lombard Street entrance

# Introduction

*If we must give account for every idle word,*
*let us take care not to have to do so for every idle silence.*[1]

Everything could have been different. The college could have grown, flourished, survived. Instead, a myriad of factors made it defunct. This is a story about power, perception, and the fall of an American educational institution. It is a tale about a failed attempt at reform within an insular religious community. It is an account of how an internecine struggle destroyed an institution. It is a narrative of institutional tragedy and individual triumph. It is a reflection on a theological controversy wherein truth claims were advanced against suspected heretics, and reformers believed they suffered injury and malice at the hands of their own brethren. This book constitutes an argument which situates theology at the core of conflict. It is an examination of the tense drama created by colliding models of educational philosophy. It is the elaboration of an unpopular history about men who strove with each other; men who would not yield. It is a chronicle about hard fought victories overshadowed by crushing defeats whereby those who won the small battles wound up losing the war. It is an analysis of the political uses of theology and a specific exploration of the madness of theology and its often-regrettable outcomes which have frequently been manifested in the history of Christianity. The general theme is not new but this particular version has not previously been recorded.

There are two kinds of people in this book: guards and explorers, who might also be characterized as pilgrims and settlers. They are rather like librarians and archivists. In my scholarly career I have met many of these men and women during extensive research stints at the Bodleian Library in Oxford, the Cambridge

---

[1] "Deinde si pro verbo otioso reddimus rationem, videamus ne reddamus et pro otioso silentio." Ambrose, *De officiis* 1.9. The critical edition is Ivor J. Davidson, *Ambrose: De officiis*, 2 vols (Oxford: Oxford University Press, 2001), vol. 1, p. 122.

University Library, the British Library, the Austrian National Library in Vienna, the National Library of the Czech Republic, the Prague Cathedral Chapter Library, the Vatican Library, numerous university libraries throughout North America, Europe, and the south Pacific, monastic libraries in the United States and Europe, and denominational archives of groups such as the Assemblies of God, the Church of God (Anderson), and the United Pentecostal Church. Librarians and archivists generally consider themselves either as guards protecting books and manuscripts from prying eyes, or as guides facilitating access to the riches of wisdom. The former discourage investigation and conceal certain sources while the latter endeavor to suggest hitherto unknown materials and make everything available. In this book we encounter men who were absolutely convinced that they knew religious truth and wished to enforce its acceptance by others. We encounter other individuals who believed that truth was to be explored and only by asking and fostering hard questions could one hope to arrive at truth. The inescapable confrontation centered in matters of theology and the issues of institutional practice that derived from them.

All things considered, it is certainly not surprising that no one has written anything substantial either about the last years of Conquerors Bible College (CBC) generally or about Don Fisher (1939-1995) specifically. Within the UPC itself, both subjects are characterized by defensiveness and a lack of critical standards. Depending upon the point of view, those respective histories might understandably be considered either much too obscure or too embarrassing to put into print and perhaps are regarded in some quarters as little dramas best forgotten. The college has been shuttered for more than thirty years and Fisher has been dead for over eighteen years. They are ghosts who haunt only a few. There has been sufficient time for reflection on both subjects but it seems unlikely anyone will take up the details of this unfortunate, albeit minor, chapter in American religious history. Besides, *cui bono?* Whom does it benefit? Is there anything edifying in telling a story of decline and destruction? To the outsider, a book such as this may understandably appear as a costume on a farce, a tale hardly to be taken seriously. Even if there are redeeming qualities to this sliver of history, the story is too obscure to attract the attention of historians outside the fraternity of the United Pentecostal Church, and those who might consider it are likely to conclude that the effort would be an unrewarding exercise. Those who might be inclined to investigate such events would have to face the problem of the paucity of source material, and the draconian and secretive policies restricting access to materials in the archives of the UPC.[2] These same obstacles discourage someone within the UPC from turning his or her attention to the matter. Such an individual must be prepared to deal with the unwashed and unholy backsliders who thoughtfully and intentionally abandoned the "one God, Acts 2:38, tongue-talking, Holy Ghost filled, water baptized in Jesus name, come out from among them and be ye separate message." Without dealing with these apostates the story can neither be properly told nor meaningfully evaluated. Alternatively, those comfortable with such dissenters cannot and must not ignore the stalwart defenders of UPC orthodoxy, or "the message" as it is commonly called, who opposed the backsliders and in some cases militated for the status quo.[3] These impediments might also be compounded by a general reluctance to violate the deliberately inculcated principle concerning pastors and ministers within that religious movement known by its biblical shorthand, "touch not mine anointed."

In order to properly assess the last stages in the history of CBC it is virtually impossible not to "touch the anointed." Indeed, the

---

[2] These former policies governing research a few years ago appear to have now been relaxed, and more acceptable conventions adopted. This can only be applauded. However, some issues persist.

[3] In the UPC, the term "the message" refers to the doctrine of Acts 2:38, to wit, repentance, baptism by immersion in the name of Jesus for the remission of sins, the necessity of the gift of the Holy Spirit with the initial evidence of glossolalia, and the insistence on personal holiness which include a rather stringent dress code (especially for women). Sometimes the term almost exclusively implies holiness standards. On this latter point I am indebted to Wallace Leonard interview, 3 August 2013, Boise, Idaho. The UPC "message" is frequently though controversially regarded as the core of the Gospel, comprising the heart of the apostolic proclamation of the early church. Any member, especially ministers, not considered 100% behind the strictest interpretation of this message and regarding each of its aspects as binding on all true Christians, and possessing definitive salvific implications, are routinely denounced as being "weak on the message." The latter phrase is insider shorthand for compromisers and liberals. Confirmed by Clyde Barlow interview, 13 August 2013, St. Helens, Oregon.

"anointed ones" *must* be subjected to careful scrutiny because too often in the history of religion, categories such as these allow certain people to sidestep human responsibility and act in ways inconsistent with the rule of law, human ethics, or indeed the principles of the kingdom of God. Historians are the custodians of the past and there is a duty to appropriate but not obliterate the past. Interpretation, like translation, is either a place of beginning or a place of conclusion. The interpreter is always suspect because like translation, interpretation is always shifting. If the translator is regarded as a traitor, the interpreter runs the risk of alienating. This appears unavoidable. There is no such thing as definitive history, there are only interpretations. The historian must select, interpret, and evaluate. Presuppositions are unavoidable. The best one can do is attempt to come to terms with the values and assumptions each one inevitably brings to the historical discipline and make every effort to avoid confusing those convictions with the evidence.[4] What people call historical facts are more properly judgments about historical events. The historian has the duty to explore and explain the human experience and the forms of anxiety which may have created certain historical events or crises. No proper historian can avoid that challenge even if such undertakings cause discomfort, are unpopular, or are considered ill-advised.

In earlier stages of my work I received a cautionary note. "If the purpose of your work has been, and is, to draw God's people closer together, I say amen, and God use you for such a noble undertaking. If it is to point out the disparity, and places where we can or do differ, then I pray that you will stop and think again ... ."[5] The basic right and duty of open inquiry and critical evaluation cannot entertain arbitrary boundaries. While this right may not be absolute it cannot bow to unfounded accusations of suspect methodology or of agenda-driven research in defiance of church authority (a charge often leveled against scholarship which does not suit the emerging status quo or the existing paradigm). The historian has four duties: first, to investigate the past; second, to

---

[4] Outlined succinctly in Rudolf Bultmann, "Ist voraussetzungslose Exegese möglich?" *Theologische Zeitschrift* 13 (1957), pp. 409-417.
[5] Ruby Klemin, letter to Thomas A. Fudge, 27 June 2001. FC, inv.doc.no 0707-2863-20.

reconstruct what happened; third, to provide an explanation for what happened; and fourth to prepare a record for the generations to come. This book fulfills a debt to posterity by telling a story that might otherwise never be known or eventually forgotten.

What is the task of the historian when setting down a chapter of the past? Histories are precious, for they recover forgotten events of the past, they record ideas of significance, and they can bring to life that which appears dead. Histories reveal how the past was played out, they bring from the shadows into the light how men and women lived, acted, failed to act, and died. Histories are useful, but they are not easily assembled. What is required is an individual with the heart of a lion who is unafraid to write the truth. Too many histories are written to satisfy special interests or political agendas and are prone either to glorify something trivial or vilify something important. Too many are motivated by love or hatred of the subject. Such histories are notoriously unreliable, and the work of God in human affairs is shamefully manipulated. As a result the reader has no idea what to believe. By this crude mistreatment, potentially good and useful histories are ruined and amount to little more than idle gossip. It is not the task of the historian to merely address what he or she wants, to blithely ignore that which is not convenient, to praise one thing or despise another on little more than a careless whim. Histories should be written with great care, honesty, and with unswerving devotion to truthfulness.[6]

My interest and preoccupation with the story of the destruction of CBC is both historical and personal. From the perspective of history, no great truth, whether spoken by Jesus, Buddha, or Zoroaster, should ever be ignored, and nothing that has occurred should ever be lost. Unfortunately, much of human history is indeed lost and forgotten. The more that is lost, the more we are impoverished. The story of CBC is not mentioned in reference works on religion and is unlikely ever to be included.[7] This should

---

[6] This paragraph is a condensed paraphrase of Martin Luther, *Preface to the History of Galeatius Capella* (1538), in *D. Martin Luthers Werke. Kritische Gesamtausgabe*, 121 vols (Weimar: Hermann Böhlaus Nachfolger, 1883-2009), vol. 50, pp. 383-385.

[7] For example, neither Bill J. Leonard and Jill Y. Crainshaw, eds., *Encyclopedia of Religious Controversies in the United States*, 2nd edition (Santa Barbara: ABC-CLIO, 2013), Stanley M. Burgess, ed., *The New International Dictionary of Pentecostal and*

not be taken to mean that its history is unimportant. From an official UPC perspective, "CBC was a tremendous school."[8] On a personal level, I was among the last students who undertook formal studies at CBC and I was still preoccupied in those pursuits when the doors closed for the last time in its thirty-year history.[9]

> One of the major turning points in my life started twenty five years ago next month when I arrived in Portland and was hustled off to the old CBC campus on Lombard by Jerry Peden. It was a Monday evening, 21 September, when I arrived and within minutes of reaching the campus was introduced in turn to you and to Don [Fisher]. I could not possibly anticipate what that encounter would mean for me as the years passed. It is true to say that CBC 1981 was a watershed experience for me. I think you know that I have always regarded Don as one of my mentors and as an individual who eventually exerted a great influence over my life. Funny about that, since I did not particularly like him early on. I am glad I took the opportunity in 1989 to write to him and tell him in some detail what he had meant to me on my own journey ... All I can say for sure is that at various times in my journey I have warmed my hands before the fire of his life and I do not and cannot disparage his memory. In him there were things lost, but also things found, and his dying and death when set next to life is swallowed up by the living and the life (which is Christ). I am glad I knew him.[10]

I owe a debt to Don Fisher. It might be tempting to present an uncritical hagiography of the man and turn him into a sort of modern exemplar of a medieval saint but that would ultimately be unprofitable. He was hardly a saint and some would say he missed sainthood by a rather wide margin. I would not be prepared to contest such an assertion. Writing a wartless narrative would serve little purpose.

---

*Charismatic Movements*, 2nd edition (Grand Rapids: Zondervan, 2002), or George H. Shriver, ed., *Dictionary of Heresy Trials in American Christianity* (Westport, CT: Greenwood Press, 1997) refer to CBC.

[8] Arless Glass interview, 24 September 2013, Pasadena, Texas. Glass served as superintendent of the DOE for thirty years (1976-2006). See ill.4.40 p. 240.

[9] I applied for entrance to CBC in February 1981, received notice of a successful application the following month, and six months later moved from Maritime Canada to Portland. *The Journal of Thomas A. Fudge, 1980-1985*, entries for 6 February, 10 March, and 21 September 1981.

[10] Thomas A. Fudge, letter to Donna Fisher, 22 August 2006. 8

In the compelling introduction to his curious book, Ἀληθῆ
διηγήματα [True History], the second-century writer Lucian of
Samosata (c.125-c.180) hilariously sets forth his methodology which
culminates in the confession that the only true statement in his
entire book is that nothing which follows is true.[11] I have tried to
avoid that counsel of despair. Instead, I have actively endeavored to
comfort the afflicted and afflict the comfortable. Official UPC
histories of CBC, were they ever to be written, would probably
consign Fisher to a footnote, or perhaps a paragraph at best. The
last days of the college would receive short shrift. This is not a
history of CBC. It is not a biography of Don Fisher. Rather, *Heretics
and Politics* is a short analysis of the end of CBC, focusing mainly on
the last two years of its existence between 1981 and 1983. To do so
means dealing with the context of the UPC in the Pacific
Northwest and it also means coming to terms with Fisher, who was
the central figure in those years. In order to understand Fisher, one
is obligated to look carefully at his history prior to assuming the
presidency of CBC. I have essentially limited this exploration to the
five-year period falling between 1976 and 1981 when he served as
Executive Vice President at Jackson College of Ministries in
Mississippi. That drama has been set within the wider framework of
Christian sectarianism wherein strident theological conviction
sometimes produced factionalism, hatred, and violence.

Among first-century Christians at Corinth already we find the
followers of Jesus dividing into groups loyal to Paul or Peter or
Apollos. One of the most misused texts in the entire Bible is the
admonition "come out from among them and be separate" (II
Corinthians 6:17). The text and the context quite clearly refer to

---

[11] διόπερ καὶ αὐτὸς ὑπὸ κενοδοξίας ἀπολιπεῖν τι σπουδάσας τοῖς μεθ᾽ ἡμᾶς,
ἵνα μὴ μόνος ἄμοιρος ὦ τῆς ἐν τῷ μυθολογεῖν ἐλευθερίας, ἐπεὶ μηδὲν ἀληθὲς
ἱστορεῖν εἶχον—οὐδὲν γὰρ ἐπεπόνθειν ἀξιόλογον—ἐπὶ τὸ ψεῦδος ἐτραπόμην πολὺ
τῶν ἄλλων εὐγνωμονέστερον· κἂν ἓν γὰρ δὴ τοῦτο ἀληθεύσω λέγων ὅτι
ψεύδομαι. οὕτω δ᾽ ἄν μοι δοκῶ καὶ τὴν παρὰ τῶν ἄλλων κατηγορίαν ἐκφυγεῖν
αὐτὸς ὁμολογῶν μηδὲν ἀληθὲς λέγειν. γράφω τοίνυν περὶ ὧν μήτε εἶδον μήτε
ἔπαθον μήτε παρ᾽ ἄλλων ἐπυθόμην, ἔτι δὲ μήτε ὅλως ὄντων μήτε τὴν ἀρχὴν
γενέσθαι δυναμένων. διὸ δεῖ τοὺς ἐντυγχάνοντας μηδαμῶς πιστεύειν αὐτοῖς.
A.M. Harmon, ed., *Lucian of Samosata, A True Story* [Loeb Classical Library, no.
14] (London: William Heinemann, 1913), pp. 250-253.

paganism and to hostile anti-Christian influence. The passage has no relation to Christian theology or doctrinal interpretation. Paul neither said separate from those who are with Peter nor did he say avoid the ideas of Apollos. Even where Christian separation might be legitimate, it has rarely been done peaceably. On account of theology and religious practices, officials of Latin Christendom in the thirteenth century marshaled their forces to exterminate communities of Christians in southern France. By the fifteenth century, stalwart descendants of these same persecutors repeatedly preached crusades against other Christians in Bohemia and took up swords in an effort to preserve doctrinal purity. Dissenters throughout the history of the church have been ruthlessly pursued, harassed, persecuted, expelled, exiled, imprisoned, tortured, and burned alive at stakes all in the name of Jesus and for the glory of God. Dissent is rarely permitted amongst dissenters, and for reasons rooted in theology men like Martin Luther signed death warrants against "Anabaptists" and John Calvin gave his consent to the execution of Michael Servetus who perished in the flames at Geneva. Puritans banished certain Christians from Massachusetts Bay Colony and hanged Quakers on Boston Common in the seventeenth century. The trail is long and bloody.

The story of CBC is not unique in the history of Christianity in modern America. There are shades, variations, and parallels of the theme. One example is the controversy over power, control, theology, and politics within the Missouri Synod Lutheran Church which led to the establishment of Seminex in 1974. Such events often are examples of conservative thinkers coming to power and then using that power to suppress ideological variants. Seminex and CBC share that common denominator. There are similarities between the Lutheran J.A.O. (Jacob) Preus II (1920-1994) and the Oregon Pentecostal Barry A. King. Another parallel movement occurred within the Southern Baptist Convention, mainly between 1979 and 1990. Alarmed at the course being charted, especially in the colleges and seminaries, the SBC stressed the notion of biblical inerrancy as the absolutely essential theological principle of the denomination. Moderates were actively marginalized and the SBC successfully placed staunch inerrantists in positions of power and influence, thereby virtually eliminating liberal trends within the convention.[12] The histories of CBC and the Southern Baptist Convention in the 1980s are not that much different. There are useful parallels between the Baptist leader Adrian Rogers (1931-2005) and the UPC pastor Paul Dugas. A protracted struggle at Fuller Theological Seminary in southern California cresting between the 1960s and the 1980s exposed similar currents of discontent.[13]

There are two ways to tell the story of the last days of CBC. The first is from the point of view most accessible to those already aware of the college and the UPC, with a narrative illuminated by reference to larger themes in religious history. The second is treating CBC and the UPC as exemplars of the larger theme of the treatment of truth and deviance in religious history, thought, and practice. This might include the way in which religion is presented to people born into religious households and communities. I have chosen to consistently follow the former approach. It is impossible to meaningfully engage in the great historiographical inquiry "wie es eigentlich gewesen" – what exactly happened as it actually was – without the prior consideration of the issues delineated in chapters one to three.[14] The first three chapters form an essential context to my understanding and interpretation of what happened at CBC and is intentionally a long introduction to the heart of the story which is detailed in the final three chapters. It is essential to note that I have not endeavored to simply chronicle what happened at CBC as much as to explain why those events transpired as they did.

American culture of the 1960s forms an essential context for understanding the developments within the Missouri Synod, the Southern Baptist Convention, and the United Pentecostal Church. The rise of a fundamentalist impulse can be related to wider social and cultural realities. These include but are not limited to the death

---

[12] Sources for the struggles within the LCMS and the SBC are noted on p. 471.

[13] A useful study is George M. Marsden, *Reforming Fundamentalism: Fuller Seminary and the New Evangelicalism* (Grand Rapids: Eerdmans, 1987). See also Rudolph Nelson, *The Making and Unmaking of an Evangelical Mind: The Case of Edward Carnell* (Cambridge: Cambridge University Press, 1987).

[14] Leopold von Ranke, introduction to *History of the Latin and Teutonic Nations* (1824), in Roger Wines, ed., *Leopold von Ranke: The Secret of World History: Selected Writings on the Art and Science of History* (New York: Fordham University Press, 1981), pp. 56-59.

of God theologies associated with Thomas Altizer and others, the Vietnam war, anti-war sentiment, university campus riots, anti-establishment initiatives including the Hippie movement, the "summer of love," widespread recreational drug use, Woodstock, the sexual revolution, feminism, gay rights, other counter-cultural manifestations, the threat of nuclear war, an escalating Cold War with its saber-rattling political bravado, fears about communism, political assassination, the civil rights movement, skyrocketing energy costs, OPEC and the oil crisis, the controversial supreme court decision in *Roe v. Wade*, Watergate, and the widespread rabid attention being paid to an apocalyptic doomsday mentality within conservative Christianity and in American culture reflected in the shrill pronouncements of ideologues such as Hal Lindsey, Jack van Impe, John Hagee, Tim LaHaye, and John Walvoord (1910-2002). While this book makes no effort to connect these ideological and social outcomes in the 1970s and 1980s to the reforms and takeovers evident in a number of conservative religious bodies, they do provide essential aspects of the wider culture. The development of conservative Christian political alliances, the rise of dominion theology and increasing emphases on Christian reconstructionism, the homeschooling movement, the Moral Majority, and evangelical Christian support for the interests of the Israeli state indicated growing concern with many of the dominant aspects of American culture.[15] From an international perspective, the modernist crisis within Roman Catholicism at the turn of the twentieth century (on both sides of the Atlantic) reveals that such alarming theological clashes were not uniquely Protestant.[16]

Don Fisher was a striking paradox. He was clearly a powerful personality within his own church denomination, attaining national

---

[15] See Nancy T. Ammerman, "North American Protestant Fundamentalism," in Martin E. Marty and R. Scott Appleby, eds., *Fundamentalisms Observed* (Chicago: University of Chicago Press, 1991), pp. 1-65.

[16] Sound overviews in Lester R. Kurtz, *The Politics of Heresy: The Modernist Crisis in Roman Catholicism* (Berkeley: University of California Press, 1986) and Joseph F. Kelly, *History and Heresy: How Historical Circumstances can Create Doctrinal Conflicts* (Collegeville, MN: Liturgical Press, 2012), pp. 110-150. The former is marred to some extent by the slavish application of sociological principles to a very specific historical context.

prominence while still in his twenties, yet ended up as a pariah. He inspired deep loyalty and produced many fervent disciples. Former

0.3 Don, Donna, Karissa and Ronna Fisher at Fisher's installation as President of CBC, April 1981

students characterized Fisher as "the first person who ever believed in me. That alone changed my life."[17] Others noted he was someone approachable who always made students feel important, someone they could talk to, someone who genuinely cared.[18] He could be kind and generous one moment but cutting and ruthless the next. "He was full of contradictions."[19] He was a minister of the gospel who spent the last decade of his life earning money, a lot of money, in the secular business world. Don Fisher was a man who took pride in his appearance, yet on one of the last occasions I saw him he was wearing a rather bland house coat, shuffling away from me down a hallway with his underwear around his ankles.[20] These

[17] April Purtell interview, 13 April 2013, Camas, Washington.
[18] Audrey (Zapalac) Greer interview, 22 September 2013, Morton, Washington, and Joe Higgins interview, 4 October 2013, Portland, Oregon.
[19] Lori (Falwell) Callan interview, 23 September 2013, Hugo, Oregon.
[20] This on account of his advanced illness, resulting in debilitating physical weakness which robbed him of the strength to dress himself properly.

are stark contrasts. According to the man generally acknowledged as Fisher's most important mentor, a life cannot be assessed by incidents or impressions but on its whole.[21] I have chosen to draw attention to Don Fisher in the period between 1976 and 1983, while neither ignoring the period before nor events thereafter. By all accounts Fisher was a complex personality. One former colleague wrote "perhaps this will help you understand D.W.F." inside the front cover of an exceptionally surprising book, G. Gordon Liddy's autobiography.[22]

*Heretics and Politics* is a story of tragedy. It is easy to take sides in historical controversies, especially when the stakes are high and issues of truth and theology intrude. In this book I have tried to present nuanced sympathy for the efforts of Don Fisher and his colleagues – at Jackson, Mississippi and in Portland, Oregon – at the respective colleges where Fisher served in administrative capacities. On the other hand, it would be near-sighted to fail to appreciate the other side in the struggles and conflicts which convulsed JCM, especially between 1979 and 1981 and which beset CBC in its last years. There were men on the other side of the equation who opposed Fisher and his ideas and vision for the Bible colleges. They considered him a ringleader within a Trojan horse of heretics and those weak on the message within the fellowship of the United Pentecostal Church. That perspective cannot be ignored.

---

[21] "The worth of a man is measured by his whole life, not by a single failure or success." C.H. Yadon, "Knowing the Worth of a Man" *In Touch* 1 (No. 1, 1986), pp. 1 and 6. *In Touch* was a publication of Christ for the People Community Church established by Don Fisher. It appeared in nine issues between 1986 and 1990, edited successively by Jerry Dillon and April Purtell. In addition to the editors, contributors included former JCM and CBC faculty and students C.H. Yadon, Susan (Fisher) Paynter, Donna Fisher, Skip Paynter, Dan Lewis, Jewel (Yadon) Dillon, Peggy (Yelm) Dougherty, Kris Dillon, Alvin Cobb, and Thomas A. Fudge. See ill.0.1, p. xviii. Alvin Cobb is in the back row, first on the right. Commenting on the publication, Don Fisher wrote, *"In Touch"* was excellent ... thought provoking, meaningful ..." *In Touch* 1 (No. 2, 1986), p. 8.

[22] G. Gordon Liddy, *Will: The Autobiography of G. Gordon Liddy* (New York: Dell Publishing Company, 1980). Fisher owned the book. His signature appears therein. Jewel (Yadon) Dillon later acquired the volume and gave it to April Purtell with the quoted inscription. Purtell later gave the book to the author.

It would be unfair not to recognize that such concern had merit. Don Fisher certainly threatened their ideas. His philosophy of education ultimately ran counter to established tradition. His detractors, in some cases, believed fervently that he and his colleagues in the south and on the west coast not only undermined the denomination but imperilled souls. Once inside the colleges, he emerged with his colleagues from a theological Trojan horse and proceeded to plant weeds which threatened to choke out the life of the wheat. This was intolerable. Believing Fisher and his academic colleagues to be toxic and dangerous heretics teaching heresy to impressionable young students helps in understanding why his detractors took the position they did in wishing to remove Fisher and other theological suspects from college level influence. The Trojan horse and its occupants had to be expelled from the collegiate city, and the walls and gates made secure once more.

In the pages which follow, men such as C.H. Yadon, Jerry Dillon, Dan Lewis, Joseph Howell, and Don Fisher are revealed as men embracing doctrines and theological ideas and methodologies which were not, and could not be, sanctioned by the United Pentecostal Church without that organization altering its essential identity. One of the fundamental questions posed in the book is whether it is possible to be both United Pentecostal and intellectual, with integrity and commitments to both areas, at the same time. Don Fisher, Joseph Howell, Dan Lewis, Jerry Dillon, and to a lesser extent, C.H. Yadon, found that challenge nearly impossible. Others responded differently. Thomas Craft, Doyle Spears, David Bernard, Paul Dugas, Barry King, Winfred Earl Toole (1927-1985), and many of their colleagues were unprepared to allow reformers or heretics to drastically change the doctrines and approaches of their church and religious identity without challenge.

It is also indefensible to suggest that the UPC had no right to censure Fisher, had no justification for attempting to discipline him, or possessed no basis for preferring theological charges against him. Critics of the treatment of Don Fisher have sometimes argued that the UPC had no business scrutinizing his work at the colleges. One must wonder by what definition or criteria that position can be maintained. Surely the United Pentecostal Church possessed the rights of discipline and self-definition in the same manner as the medieval church or the modern Roman Catholic, Southern Baptist, or Missouri Synod Lutheran churches as considered in this book. Belonging to any organization carries with it obligations and expectations that one will abide by the rules of the organization. It is certainly not unreasonable to expect that deviants should remove themselves and go elsewhere. A squash player has no place in a tennis club. Historic church polity such as medieval canon law makes the essential point that officials have a duty to intervene in ecclesiastical or theological irregularities. Sectors of the United Pentecostal Church found themselves at risk from division and dissent in aspects of the histories of JCM and CBC. One may wish to argue the finer points of church doctrine and the history of theology, but opponents of Don Fisher conceived themselves as defenders of truth and the faith once delivered to the saints.

In a parallel, separated by more than five centuries, Jan Hus was accused of heresy, prosecuted, excommunicated four times, tried in ecclesiastical courts and finally burned at the stake in 1415 as a contumacious heretic, who for the sake of the vine of Christ had to be completely cut off and turned out of the community of faith. It is understandable, though ultimately misguided, to denounce the men of the Council of Constance as evil and sinful. I admire the courage, conviction, and integrity of Jan Hus. At the same time, I understand from a theological, ecclesiastical, and legal point of view why the medieval church in the Bohemian province acted as it did with respect to one of its own priests. This is not to argue that Hus' enemies were all men of probity or integrity. Some of them were scoundrels of the worst kind. It is also not an apology for the rightness of the medieval church and the theological wrongness of Jan Hus. It is an acknowledgement that issues such as these are complex, and that both sides in tragic and tumultuous events may have a point, even a justification for acting as they do. In the final analysis, my sympathies lie with Hus, but not to the point of failing to recognize that the courts which tried him and the church authorities that withstood him were neither capricious nor without merit. Accused heretics are rarely blameless and in the narrative analysis which follows I have endeavored to present both sides of the conflict with fairness, even though I have taken up the minority side and have chosen to focus on the merits of that perspective.

The question of nomenclature should be clarified. This book makes numerous references to heresy and heretics. I do not regard the terminology as judgmental or negative. Heresy is a technical category within religious thought, but for the purposes of this study I regard men such as Don Fisher, Joseph Howell, Dan Lewis, Jerry Dillon, C.H. Yadon, and others as heretics because they did deviate in significant ways from the mainstream of the United Pentecostal Church. It will be up to the reader to decide if their theological departures should be condemned or saluted.

When "that frigid, quarrelsome old woman, Theology, ha[s] swollen herself to such a point of vanity" unavoidable clashes occur.[23] What is problematic in these clashes are absolute truth claims. It is exceedingly difficult if not impossible to negotiate around the volatile minefields of absolute truth. This was the issue in medieval Bohemia, among modern Roman Catholics, Southern Baptists, Missouri Synod Lutherans, at Fuller Seminary, and among United Pentecostals. Don Fisher and some of his colleagues fell victim to this situation and in such circumstances there are always tragic and unintended consequences. At Jackson this precipitated the "lost generation," and in Portland the demise of a Bible college and the eventual personal destruction of Don Fisher. Some of his detractors grieved in the wake of these developments but insisted the Trojan horse had to go.

It has been said that if it matters little, one should make little of the matter.[24] The story told in these pages matters a great deal so I have chosen to make a great deal of the matter. "This is a history that needs to be written."[25] Don Fisher and CBC affected the lives of hundreds of students. It will be up to the reader to determine the nature of that influence. There will be a variety of responses, for

---

[23] Erasmus, letter to Ludwig Platz, 31 July 1520. There is a variant reading in *The Correspondence of Erasmus*, trans. R.A.B. Mynors (Toronto: University of Toronto Press, 1988), vol. 8, p. 18.

[24] T.F. Tenney, letters to Thomas A. Fudge, 2 December 1999 and 29 February 2000. FC, inv.doc.no 0707-1028-08, and FC, inv.doc.no 0707-1274-09.

[25] Lewis J. Davies interview, 19 August 2013, Murrieta, California with similar comments made by a number of those interviewed for this book especially Norman Rutzen, Jerry Dillon, Wayne Nigh, Donna Fisher, Raymond Sirstad, George Sponsler, R.V. Reynolds, E.G. Moyer, and C.H. Yadon.

history provokes within each of us admiration and loathing, inspiration and desperation. History has its own impulses. "The past is full of life, eager to irritate us, provoke us and insult us, tempt us to destroy or repaint it."[26] CBC has been praised and criticized, promoted and ignored. Fisher is both hero and villain, holy man and heretic. I have attempted to present Fisher as a man of virtue and vice who equally exemplifies triumph and tragedy. He was despised and loved, reviled and revered. This book is a contribution to his memory and to that of CBC (not one without the other) and a firm reminder of the sum and substance of the theological confessions of St. Paul who insisted he was convinced that nothing was able to separate us from the love of God in Christ Jesus. The words uttered by the thief at Calvary apply to all whose lives once intersected with the history of CBC and also forms a prayer for all of us: "Jesus, remember me when you come into your kingdom."

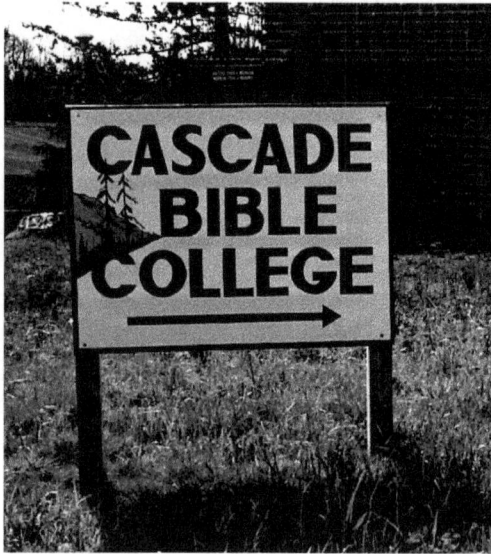

0.4  Sign at the new CBC campus, Vancouver,
Washington, Autumn 1982

---

[26] Milan Kundera, *The Book of Laughter and Forgetting*, trans., Michael Henry Heim (New York: Alfred A. Knopf, 1980), p. 22.

# Prologue

# End of an Era

*Jesus I know, and Paul I know, but who are you?*
*—query of a demon (Acts 19:15)*

A proverbial saying in ancient Greek and Latin texts, with reference to fighting against the will of the gods or opposing more powerful opponents, can also be found in the canonical Acts of the Apostles, when Saul of Tarsus, who had been persecuting Christians, has a dramatic encounter on the road to Damascus. From within a bright light an authoritative voice addresses Saul in the Hebrew language using the familiar words, "it is hard (or painful) for you to kick against the pricks."[1]

A long struggle came to an end one winter morning in 1983. On 11 February, the president of Cascade Bible College (formerly known as Conquerors Bible College) in Vancouver, Washington, Donald W. Fisher, uncharacteristically arrived late for the Friday morning chapel service. Immediately taking the podium he announced to the gathered faculty and student body that he had just contacted a college music group already in Seattle scheduled to perform at a district conference and instructed them to return to campus forthwith. The college choir was at that moment prepared to leave for the same venue immediately following lunch. That trip was cancelled. Fisher then dropped a bombshell by announcing that "in view of prevailing circumstances," he was resigning as president of the institution.[2] He also stated he was turning in his ministerial credentials to the headquarters of the United Pentecostal Church International. Fisher had held ministerial credentials with that

---

[1] Acts 26: 9-14.
[2] Don Fisher, letter to the CBC board, 11 February 1983. FC, inv.doc.no 0707-5221-34. See Appendix 16, p. 454.

denomination since 1958.[3] After twenty-five years, he was walking
away. A shock wave of disbelief rippled across the room. There
were audible gasps. Deborah Beaulieu, a first year student from
Massachusetts ran screaming from the chapel in tears. Moments
later a stunned student body filed silently from the room. Faculty,
students and visitors milled around in the parking lot restively.
Shock registered on a number of faces. There were numerous
questions but few answers. CBC had imploded. What, exactly, were
the "prevailing circumstances" Fisher had alluded to?

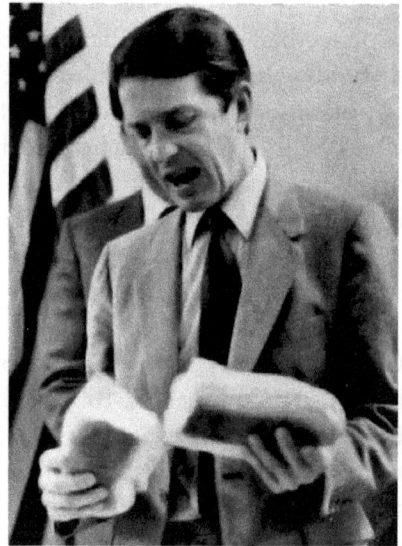

0.5   Don Fisher celebrating Holy Eucharist, CBC chapel, 11 March 1983

One month later, on 11 March, a final service resembling a
requiem, which included a celebration of the eucharist, took place
in the CBC chapel (ill.5.17, p. 285). It was an emotional event but

---

[3] Fisher's resignation from the UPC was not accepted. "I'm not certain where
that had to come from—the district or headquarters. I do remember that when
Don sent in his resignation they would not accept it." Donna Fisher, letter to
Thomas A. Fudge, 18 March 2013, p. 2. FC, inv.doc.no 0707-4957-33. It is
doubtful that Fisher took any note of this. If Fisher's resignation was considered
"under question," this action could only have been taken on the basis of a formal
decision on the part of the relevant District Board. *Manual* (2014), Article vii,
section 7, point 21 (a), pp. 51-52.

no one detected resignation in Fisher. If anything, there was a hint of controlled defiance. Shortly before his death, the sixteenth-century reformer Philip Melanchthon prayed to be delivered from *rabie theologorum* [the madness of the theologians].[4] On 19 April 1560, Melanchthon expired. Though he had more than a dozen years remaining in his life, there is some evidence that Don Fisher experienced that same release on 11 March 1983.

The convocation that morning marked the end of thirty years for an American Bible college. Immediate events were described somewhat prosaically: "I led the chapel service, and then the news came. Our trip to Seattle was cancelled. Bro. Fisher resigned the presidency of the college and also resigned from the UPC and it appears CBC has run its course. It's just about over ... Things have suddenly come to a head."[5] The last comment was a serious understatement. There was nothing sudden about the events of that winter Friday morning in February. There had been a deliberate, gathering momentum against the college for some time and the current had only strengthened in the previous two years. "Don [Fisher] became the scapegoat."[6] It is also untrue to assert as one of Fisher's critics did that the college was "highly esteemed by everyone."[7] The events culminating in 1983 mitigate that view with some rather dramatic evidence. Moreover, national officials said "it was a terrible catastrophe that they [CBC board] ever brought him [Fisher] in."[8] What did all of this mean? How did these currents form a confluence which gathered in greatness against one man and one small college? How should those last days of CBC be evaluated and understood? Is there merit in seeing events culminating at CBC

---

[4] A sheet of paper found on Melanchthon's table after his death included the words "liberaberis ab aerumnis, et a rabie theologorum." *Philippi Melanthonis opera quae supersunt omnia*, ed., Karl Gottlieb Bretschneider, *Corpus reformatorum*, vol. 9, (Halle: Schwetschke, 1842), col. 1098.

[5] *The Journal of Thomas A. Fudge, 1980-1985*, entry for 11 February 1983. Fisher got off the phone with Washington District Superintendent Verneal Crossley, told his secretary April Purtell, "it's all over," and went to the chapel and resigned. April Purtell interview, 16 January 1999, Camas, Washington.

[6] Norman Rutzen interview, 8 February 1999, Caldwell, Idaho. "He became the fall guy." George Sponsler interview, 12 February 1999, Portland, Oregon.

[7] Nathaniel Urshan interview, 23 April 1999, St. Louis, Missouri.

[8] Cleveland Becton interview, 14 April 1999, Dallas, Texas.

as another manifestation of the universal propensity for violence and scapegoating?[9]

What factors brought the college to its dramatic and sudden demise? Was Don Fisher truly a heretic? Had he mismanaged the institution so badly it collapsed? Was there a conspiracy to drive Fisher into exile? Were the woes at CBC financial, theological, or a combination of issues? Did Don Fisher overstep the limits of his ability? Did he attempt to avoid all oversight of his activities? There are supporters for each of these theories. Some board members locate the struggle in issues of conflict between the governing districts, financial challenges, doctrine, and holiness standards.[10]

0.6   Don Fisher with CBC students David Brown and
Melanie Poulsen, Fall 1981

Constitutionally, CBC was designed to be controlled by its Board of Directors. The board limited the power of its president and mandated that presidential decisions and actions be confirmed by the College Board. Once Don Fisher assumed the presidency he

---

[9] The work of René Girard is instructive here especially his *I See Satan Fall Like Lightning*, trans., James G. Williams (Maryknoll: Orbis Books, 2001).
[10] Frank LaCrosse interview, 1 October 2013, Spanaway, Washington.

undertook a revision of the existing college by-laws, wherein the chairmanship of the board was taken from its previous rotation among the superintendents of the Oregon, Washington, and Idaho Districts and placed permanently within the purview of the college president.[11] In some quarters, this action was considered ill-advised in that it appeared to give too much power to the president. The UPC Division of Education attempted to intervene, while some national officials believed the revising of the by-laws and the elevation of the president to the chairmanship of the Board of Directors constituted the beginning of the end for CBC.[12]

This is a rather dramatic suggestion, which advances the claim that Fisher deliberately manipulated the board into granting him more power, whereby allowing him legitimately to do whatever he willed with the college. Provocative as it seems, this thesis tends to overlook two rather important considerations. First, a properly constituted board meeting ratified the revised governing documents of the corporation, and secondly, the documents did not rule out future amendments, and indeed specifically made provision for the by-laws to be "altered, amended or repealed" and new statutes to be implemented at any time by affirmative action of the College Board.[13] Members of the board at the time considered it more prudent to have the president assume chairmanship, inasmuch as the prior arrangement of a revolving chair was not viable in terms of governance.[14] If Fisher's action is to be regarded as detrimental to the survival of the college one is forced to re-evaluate the CBC board itself, and to query especially why the allocation of the board chairmanship was never "altered, amended or repealed" or otherwise replaced by a new by-law as permitted. Regardless of how

---

[11] *Restated Articles of Incorporation of Conquerors Bible College* (1982), Article 5, p. 2 (FC, inv.doc.no 0707-5216-34), and *Restated Corporate By-Laws Conquerors Bible College* (1982), Article 2, section 5, p. 1 (FC, inv.doc.no 0707-5215-34). Both of these documents were adopted by formal motion by the CBC board. *Minutes*, CBC board meeting, 5 June 1982, p. 2. FC, inv.doc.no 0707-5217-34. Norman Rutzen, Frank LaCrosse, and C.H. Yadon were the named board members moving and seconding the two motions.

[12] Arless Glass interview, 24 September 2013.

[13] *Restated Corporate By-Laws Conquerors Bible College* (1982), Article 5, section 1, p. 3. FC, inv.doc.no 0707-5215-34.

[14] Norman Rutzen interview, 27 September 2013, Caldwell, Idaho.

one interprets the restated by-laws, the president of CBC was still answerable to the Board of Directors. Moreover, the increased power of the president in 1982 had nothing to do with the level of opposition to CBC over the years prior to Fisher's appointment.

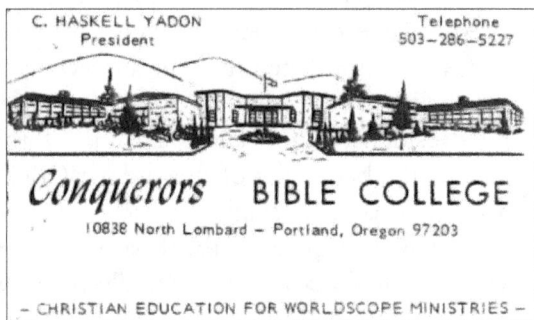

0.7  C.H. Yadon's CBC business card, 1968

The story of the last days of CBC is one of theological differences, power struggles, and perceptions. It is a tiny chapter in the history of the church, in which victories are gained at great cost. One of C.H. Yadon's well-known and insightful stories summarizes the showdown at the college. Yadon once told this tale during a General Board meeting when he was asked his opinion when suggestions were advanced about taking action against individuals maintaining differences of theology. An Idaho farmer was having trouble with a rat in his barn. All attempts to trap the rat failed. At length, the farmer decided to deal more directly with the problem. Armed with a double-barrelled shotgun, the farmer took up a comfortable position in the barn awaiting the rat's appearance. Soon, the rodent appeared on a rafter overhead in the hayloft and paused atop a box. The farmer took careful aim and pulled both triggers. There was an enormous explosion. The farmer was hurled backwards through the open door and landed flat in the yard as the entire barn was blown to smithereens. In his single-minded attention on eliminating the rat, he had forgotten that the box in the hayloft was filled with dynamite. As farmhands rushed to the scene the dazed farmer was heard to mutter aloud, "Boys, I believe I got that rat."

# 1

# History and Heresy Hunters

*When the existence of the Church is threatened, she is released from the commandments of morality. With unity as the end, the use of every means is sanctified, even cunning, treachery, violence, simony, prison, death. For all order is for the sake of the community, and the individual must be sacrificed to the common good.*[1]

It is axiomatic that the problem of heresy is a reflection of the question of authority and competing claims. Before turning to the drama of the last days of CBC, it is both relevant and important to outline one of the most familiar and effective constructs in the history of Christianity. The urge to purge has existed from the beginning. Men like Athanasius, bishop of Alexandria, asked Egyptian monks to remove all non-sanctioned books from their monastic libraries and thereafter read only those books deemed acceptable. That was in the year 367. A relatively newly-discovered fragment of the Coptic text of Athanasius' letter reinforces the argument that Athanasius intended to even more vigorously contain the perceived threat of heresy. The document in question calls for the church to be purged of every form of defilement. The bishop has in mind questionable books used by certain Christians he considered heretical.[2] On either side of the year 367, Cerinthus, Marcion, Montanus, Origen, Sabellius, Paul of Samosata, Mani, Arius, Didymus the Blind, Nestorius, Eutychus, and a hundred others were expelled from the Christian community. Men such as Athanasius and many of his colleagues were not prepared to grant

---

[1] The quotation is based loosely upon the fifteenth-century conciliarist Dietrich Niem (and perhaps the canon lawyer Hostiensis) and quoted as such in Arthur Koestler, *Darkness at Noon*, trans., Daphne Hardy (New York: Scribner, 1941), p. 97.

[2] David Brakke, "A New Fragment of Athanasius's Thirty-Ninth *Festal Letter*: Heresy, Apocrypha, and the Canon" *Harvard Theological Review* 103 (No. 1, 2010), pp. 47-66.

permission to think, to believe, or to explore the faith. Truth was to be protected, not investigated. Suspicion and censure of unofficial ideas evolved into heresy hunting.

Accusations of heresy serve a purpose considered important by the accuser. Such accusations rarely relate to faith or theology specifically, but rather are concerned principally with power and control. Faith, theological ideas, or religious practice are used as the vehicle to advance heresy charges. Thus, in a religious context, an adversary is often denounced as a heretic and a different point of view is frequently labelled heresy. The nomenclature is useful for distinguishing boundaries and for determining identity. It serves to indicate how groups perceive threats or compromises in relation to their basic and essential values.[3] There is nothing abnormal or necessarily negative about determining "heretics" and "heresies." In its briefest of definitions, a heretic is an individual who challenges a closed system of presumed or declared truth.[4] The heretic might be either a stranger to the community or a deviant insider.[5] Doctrine, theological orientation, as well as religious movements are often developed in the struggle with competing ideas. The history of Christianity has often defined its beliefs in relation to heresy. From time to time, religious thinkers have found themselves in tension with established authority. In those clashes, beliefs are re-examined, doctrines are challenged, and relationships are redefined. It is never entirely possible to predict outcomes or consequences, but what is certain is that the clashes involving heretics and politics shape theology and the nature of faith communities.

Within a closed environment, the emergence of a single victim or single group scapegoat mechanism is predictable. When two or more people cultivate the same desire or objective, one encounters an escalation of mimetic desire. This means that the second and subsequent parties attach themselves to the agenda because the first party has taken it up and because the subsequent parties assume the

---

[3] A brief but useful discussion appears in Thomas A. Robinson, "Doing Double Duty: David Reed as Apologist and Critic of Oneness Pentecostalism" *Canadian Journal of Pentecostal-Charismatic Christianity* 1 (2010), pp. 86-87.
[4] There is a good overview in George H. Shriver, ed., *American Religious Heretics: Formal and Informal Trials* (Nashville: Abingdon Press, 1966), pp. 13-17.
[5] Kurtz, *The Politics of Heresy*, pp. 3 and 155.

objective is salutary. Once this mechanism is established and the problem is defined, the victim or target must either be expelled or destroyed. The scapegoat mechanism predictably yields patterns of persecution.[6] Heresy hunting and witch hunting are two examples found within the history of Christianity. The examination of the last days of CBC which follows is an historical sketch and analysis of a particular example wherein boundaries were drawn, identities asserted and firmly established. It shows how one group perceived compromise in relation to its fundamental set of core values.

The construction of heresy sometimes exceeds the definition offered above and historically, reaches back at least as far as early Christianity. Heresy in later medieval Europe took on a notorious element which resulted in demonizing alleged deviants, and the phenomenon of witch-hunting was born. There were actual witch hunts from the fifteenth-century lasting for 300 years, in which men and women across Europe were persecuted, prosecuted, tried, and executed on charges stemming from Satan worship to sexual deviance to undermining society.[7] That most of the victims of these witch-hunts were innocent of the charges manufactured against them is not the point here. Christianity and the church have never been exempt from, and have often participated in and facilitated such repressive measures.

Witch hunts are by definition conducted on the basis of accusations, denunciations or common rumor. They are carried out by zealots generally outside the rule of established law, without regard for the rights of the accused, lacking all semblance of sustainable *prima facie* evidence, and are directly aimed at the total destruction of the suspects. Historically, targets of witch hunts were normally arrested and interrogated, and the relevant authorities would employ all means, including authorized judicial torture, to extract confessions from the accused. Testimony was solicited from

---

[6] See Girard, *I See Satan Fall Like Lightning*, pp. 9-10 and 35 and Girard, *The Scapegoat*, trans., Yvonne Freccero (Baltimore: Johns Hopkins University Press, 1989), pp. 12-24.

[7] Brian Levack, *The Witch-Hunt in Early Modern Europe*, third edition (London: Pearson Longman, 2006) and Thomas A. Fudge, "Traditions and Trajectories in the Historiography of European Witch Hunting" *History Compass* 4 (No. 3, 2006), pp. 488-527.

practically any source with a view to naming the leaders and perpetrators, and identifying their accomplices, supporters, and sympathizers. It was astutely noted long ago that "men never do evil so completely and cheerfully as when they do it from religious conviction."[8] Theology, the "quarrelsome old woman," is often at issue.

The notion of witch hunting seems to be a peculiar feature of modern societies. The term "witch hunt" is of twentieth-century provenance and refers to the often relentless pursuit of an undesirable person or group fuelled largely by contrived charges and artificial accusations motivated by a political agenda.[9] There are many modern examples. The labors of Joseph McCarthy in the 1950s gave rise to the terms "McCarthyism" and "witch hunts."[10] More recently one can point to disturbing parallels in alleged cases of ritual child abuse, supposed holocaust denial, and the so-called "war on terror."[11] All of these are driven by political motivations and by fears that are emotional in origin. The idea of exceptional crimes allows for extraordinary measures, and provides the perfect premise for a witch hunt. The category of exceptionalism allows that practically any act or action could be considered an offence, with the hypothetical provision that the offence might be considered an exceptional crime subject to severe penalty.[12]

---

[8] Blaise Pascal, *Pensées – The Provincial Letters*, trans., W.F. Trotter and Thomas M'Crie (New York: Random House, 1941), p. 314 (no. 894).

[9] Christina Larner, *Witchcraft and Religion: The Politics of Popular Belief* (Oxford: Blackwell, 1984), pp. 88-91.

[10] Ellen Schrecker, "McCarthyism and the Red Scare," in Jean-Christophe Agnew and Ray Rosenzweig, eds., *A Companion to Post-1945 America* (Oxford: Blackwell, 2002), pp. 371-384.

[11] See Debbie Nathan and Michael Snedeker, *Satan's Silence: Ritual Abuse and the Making of a Modern Witch Hunt* (New York: Basic Books, 1995), Thomas A. Fudge, "The Fate of Joel Hayward in New Zealand Hands: From holocaust historian to holocaust" *History Now Te Pae Tawhito o te Wa* 9 (No. 2, May, 2003), pp. 12-21, and Robert Rapley, *Witch Hunts: From Salem to Guantanamo Bay* (Montreal: McGill-Queen's University Press, 2007), pp. 207-273 as three specific introductory studies.

[12] Edward M. Peters, "*Crimen exceptum*: The History of an Idea" in Kenneth Pennington, Stanley Chodorow and Keith H. Kendall, eds., *Proceedings of the Tenth International Congress on Medieval Canon Law* (Vatican City: Bibliotheca Apostolica Vaticana, 2001), pp. 137-194.

The clash of new ideas and established rigid mentalities, coupled with a fear of dissent, and an irrepressible desire for control, cannot abide any encouragement towards critical thinking. "The critical mind is a threat to custom, tradition and the status quo. The more insecure one is about his tradition or belief, the more critical and repressive one is toward the critic."[13] In closed religious communities there is fear that difference can lead to dissent while dissent can result in a loss of identity and autonomy. The threat of difference creates a climate of suspicion, predicated upon rumor, and ultimately based on fear.

Modern day heretics are often labelled as such within a specific culture.[14] The suspect is routinely demonized. He or she is then conceived as an enemy of truth, in opposition to Jesus, a corruptor of youth, an inveterate troublemaker, arrogant and wicked. None of these things may be true, but they are essential components in the hunt for heretics. United Pentecostal Church members tend to talk to themselves in a long-established ideological rut which features unique linguistics. This is not unusual in communities of this type throughout history. At its most rudimentary level, the term heretic is simply applied to people with whom we disagree.[15] Institutions embracing this approach tend to indoctrinate rather than educate. The results are never salutary. "To deny academic freedom is historical suicide."[16] But intellectual freedom and a philosophy remaining open to education potentially imperils essential identities. There are no easy solutions to this dilemma.

The madness of theology is that blind lust for control which assumes it possesses absolute truth and cannot tolerate any deviation, however slight, from doctrinal formulations which are considered divinely sanctioned and the result of revelation. The

---

[13] Don C. Marler, *Imprisoned in the Brotherhood: A Search into the Fundamentalists' Web of Tradition* (Jericho, NY: Exposition Press, 1973), p. 25. Ostensibly there was talk in the UPC about suing Marler over his book. Don C. Marler, letter to Thomas A. Fudge, 21 January 2013. FC, inv.doc.no 0707-4926-33.

[14] David A. Reed, *"In Jesus' Name": The History and Beliefs of Oneness Pentecostals* (Blandford: Deo Publishing, 2008), pp. 338-349.

[15] Sebastian Castellio, *De haereticus* (1554) in Roland H. Bainton, trans., *Concerning Heretics* (New York: Octagon Books, 1965), p. 129.

[16] Arthur F. Holmes, *The Idea of the Christian College*, revised edition (Grand Rapids: William B. Eerdmans, 1987), p. 66.

history of Christianity provides evidence of this mentality. The third-century bishop Cyprian of Carthage argued that "outside the church there is no salvation."[17] Of course, it was his definition of the church which prevailed. The protracted *homoousios* controversy in the patristic era, in one sense, boiled down to a heated dispute over a diphthong. The eventual implications separated faithful Nicene Christians from wicked Arian heretics. Adjectives took on theological significance adjudicating the margin of separation between heresy and truth. Just before the heretic Michael Servetus perished at the stake he was heard to cry out, "O Jesus, son of the eternal God, have mercy on me." The representative of orthodox truth William Farel who heard the cry regretfully concluded that Servetus might have been saved had he called upon the eternal son of God rather than the son of the eternal God. Unfortunately, he was damned to hell because he placed the adjective in the wrong place.[18] The *Quicunque Vult* (Athanasian Creed) brought together a variety of theological declarations, culminating in the assertion that anyone who disagreed was condemned to forfeit salvation.

The madness of the theologians sometimes extends into areas which lack all semblance of scholarly support. Exegesis within the United Pentecostal Church has needlessly argued for splitting hairs on grammatical grounds which cannot be located unambiguously in the Greek text. Is water baptism "for" the remission of sins or

---

[17] Often cited erroneously as "extra ecclesiam nulla salus," the phrase accurately is "salus extra ecclesiam non est." Cyprian, Epistle 73, "To Iubaianus, concerning the baptism of heretics," 21.2, appearing in William Hartel, ed., *Corpus scriptorum ecclesiasticorum latinorum*, vol. 3.2 (Vienna: Friedrich Tempsky, 1871), p. 795. Though most often attributed to Cyprian, the concept appears earlier in Origen, "Homiliae in librum Jesu Nave," in PG, vol. 12, col. 841. The idea caught on and was repeated frequently by Augustine, Chrysostom, Fulgentius, Bede, Innocent III, Thomas Aquinas, Bonaventure and many others. In 1215 the fourth Lateran Council formally adopted the idea. Norman P. Tanner, ed., *Decrees of the Ecumenical Councils*, 2 vols (London: Sheed & Ward, 1990), vol. 1, p. 230. This was repeated by Pope Boniface VIII in his 1302 bull, Extrav. 1.8.1 *Unam sanctam*, in Emil Friedberg, ed., *Corpus iuris canonici*, 2 vols (Leipzig: Tauchnitz, 1879-81), vol. 2, cols. 1245-1246, and then later in the bull of union with Coptic Christians, "Decretum pro Jacobitis," issued by the Council of Florence (1442), in Tanner, ed., *Decrees of the Ecumenical Councils*, vol. 1, p. 578.
[18] Noted in Roland H. Bainton, *Hunted Heretic: The Life and Death of Michael Servetus 1511-1553* (Gloucester, MA: Peter Smith, 1978), p. 214.

"because of" the remission of sins? Are sins forgiven at repentance but only remitted in water baptism?[19] Theologians and grammarians may wish to argue the finer points of biblical interpretation, but it is the madness of theology to suggest that salvation is in some sense predicated upon language or that heaven and hell depends upon the correct placement of an adjective. Defenders of orthodoxy within the Missouri Synod Lutheran Church, the Southern Baptist Convention, Fuller Seminary, and the UPC stressed the proverbial adjectives. The theology programs at Jackson and Portland under the Fisher administration focused on other emphases.[20] Collisions of some magnitude were inevitable. During the crises at JCM and CBC, men in other denominations warned of Orwellian mentalities insisting upon conformity and operating upon the foundations of "suspicion, rumor, criticism, innuendoes, guilt by association, and the rest of that demonic family of forced uniformity."[21]

The confrontation in the Northwest and the crisis at CBC were hardly unique. John Tietjen, president of Concordia Seminary in St. Louis, was suspended from his position in August 1973 and then again in January 1974 after a fact-finding committee, chaired by Paul Zimmerman, carried out an investigation of heresy allegations among the seminary faculty.[22] This was occasioned by the election of Jacob Preus to the presidency of the Missouri Synod Lutheran Church in 1969 and the consistent influential support of Lutheran editor Herman Otten.[23]

Preus took over the Missouri Synod having ridden to election on a platform of opposing the incumbent Oliver Harms (1901-1980), who had been attempting to establish fellowship with the

---

[19] Discussed in Fudge, *Christianity without the Cross*, pp. 115-116, 126-135.
[20] Dan Lewis, course syllabus, TH230 *Systematic Theology I*, JCM, p. 3 actually reads "Discuss inadequacy of question 'When is the Blood Applied'." FC, inv.doc.no 0707-4785-32.
[21] Russell H. Dilday, "On Higher Ground," sermon at the SBC, Kansas City, MO, 13 June 1984, in Shurden and Shepley, eds., *Going for the Jugular: A Documentary History of the SBC Holy War*, pp. 112-121 at pp. 113-114.
[22] Zimmerman, *A Seminary in Crisis: The Inside Story of the Preus Fact Finding Committee* is a generally fair and even-handed account though by no means the only perspective.
[23] Burkee, *Power, Politics, and the Missouri Synod: A Conflict that Changed American Christianity*, pp. 6-9.

American Lutheran Church, a group Missouri regarded as generally weak on the message. The charges of heresy levelled against the Concordia professors were dismissed after an inquiry concluding in February 1973. That outcome did not satisfy Preus. Later that same year the General Convention of the Missouri Synod, meeting at New Orleans, formally condemned the faculty for failing to uphold the authority of scripture and for summarily ignoring a presumptive *sola scriptura* principle.[24] Tietjen did everything he could in an effort to shield the faculty from charges of heretical depravity and the negative implications that produced. All of his efforts were in vain and Tietjen was forced from his position. Once he was removed from office, widespread protests broke out. A full ninety percent of the seminary faculty went on record in pledging support for Tietjen and then called for an immediate moratorium on teaching. Formal instruction at Concordia effectively ground to a halt. By February 1974, a newly constituted and even more conservative Board of Control declared that the seminary faculty were in violation of their contracts and unless they resumed formal classroom instruction they would be fired. The majority chose to resist that directive, and refused to adjust their theological perspectives to suit the Board of Control. With massive student support, on 19 February 1974 the faculty made preparations to abandon the campus en masse.

The students and faculty who refused to conform to the Preus initiative made crosses with their names inscribed thereon and planted these in the main quad of the campus, effectively turning the seminary into a cemetery. Singing the hymn "The Church's One Foundation," they preceded to Walther Arch, which they boarded up with wooden frames upon which the word "exiled" appeared (ill.1.1). Outside the seminary walls and beneath the statue of Martin Luther the group stopped and sang Luther's great hymn "A Mighty Fortress Is Our God." Then they marched away from Concordia Seminary. Tietjen preached a sermon in a nearby park on DeMun Avenue, on Hebrews 13:13-14: "Let us go forth ... for here we have no lasting city." The next day, the heretical exiles founded

---

[24] *Proceedings of the Fiftieth Regular Convention* (New Orleans, Louisiana, July 6-13, 1973) (St. Louis: Concordia Publishing House, 1973), p. 138. The entire text of Resolution 3-09 appears on pp. 133-139.

Concordia Seminary in Exile (Seminex).[25] Five years later, Don Fisher was thrust into the same position as John Tietjen. By then members of Fisher's faculty were sustaining similar charges in Jackson as Tietjen's had in St. Louis.

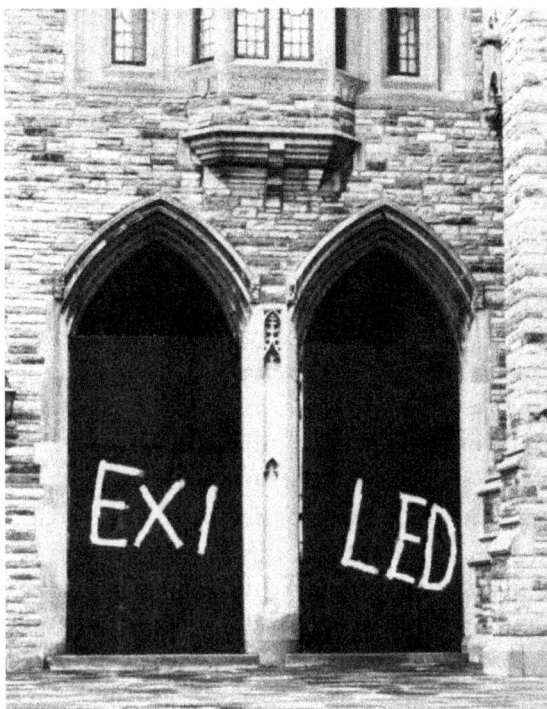

1.1 The barricaded Walther Arch at Concordia Theological Seminary in St. Louis, Missouri, 19 February 1974

At the same time that Jacob Preus and his colleagues were purging the Missouri Synod of heresies facilitated by John Tietjen, and during the same period when theology programs at JCM and CBC were coming under sustained fire on account of faculty like

---

[25] I am grateful to Winfred A. Schroeder (1915-2004), longtime Missouri Synod pastor, and Gary M. Simpson, Professor of Systematic Theology at Luther Seminary in St. Paul, Minnesota (who attended Seminex) for informal discussions and useful insights into the events in St. Louis. See Zimmerman, *A Seminary in Exile*, pp. 126-128, Tietjen, *Memoirs in Exile*, pp. 209-212, Danker, *No Room in the Brotherhood*, pp. 302-323, and Board of Control, *Exodus from Concordia: A Report on the 1974 Walkout* (St. Louis: Concordia College, 1977), pp. 119-128 for accounts of the walkout.

Joseph H. Howell, Dan Lewis, Jerry Dillon, and C.H. Yadon, the Southern Baptist Convention witnessed an intentional movement to rescue the denomination from a widening liberal trajectory, and return to a redefinition of uncontested biblical inerrancy. Fearing apostasy, in 1976 Texas pastor W.A. Criswell (1909-2002), Houston judge Paul Pressler, and college president Paige Patterson, who later became the president of the SBC, drew up a double strategy for eliminating liberals and bringing the SBC back into a clearly conceived theologically conservative focus.[26] This plan included maneuvering Adrian Rogers into a long-term tenure as president of the convention. (Rogers was subsequently elected on the first ballot at the 1979 Houston convention.) Evidently, W.A. Criswell had mentioned in his 11 June conference sermon that delegates had gathered to elect Rogers.[27] With a reliably conservative head of the convention, the SBC began a process of taking control over virtually every level of denominational administration by seeing that fundamentalists maintained a majority.

There were several eventual outcomes. Women were pushed even farther from the role of pastors and the ordained ministry. Education in SBC institutions of higher learning was required to be biblically-based in strict accord with a specifically mandated SBC hermeneutic. Pastoral authority was greatly enhanced. Strident condemnation of all liberal interpretation of scripture and theology coalesced. Those suspected of being weak on the message came under intense scrutiny. One example was Russell H. Dilday (1930–), president of Southwestern Baptist Theological Seminary in Fort Worth, who was fired without notice in 1994 for allegedly holding liberal views of the Bible and for failing to sufficiently support the prevailing fundamentalist ethos within the SBC.[28] Other dissenters or heresy suspects were elsewhere fired.

---

[26] Shurden and Shepley, eds., *Going for the Jugular: A Documentary History of the SBC Holy War*, p. xii and Paige Patterson, *Anatomy of a Reformation*, p. 3 who does not mention Criswell. This might be on account of the fact that Criswell later stepped back from the methods employed by Patterson. Shurden and Shepley, eds., *Going for the Jugular*, p. 3.

[27] Shurden and Shepley, eds., *Going for the Jugular*, p. xi.

[28] "SBC Seminary President Fired" *The Christian Century* (23 March 1994). The vote was 26-7 against Dilday.

The hunt for liberals was predicated upon clear considerations of politics, power, and fear. Three times in the space of nine years

1.2 Adrian P. Rogers, preaching, undated photograph

Adrian P. Rogers was elected to serve as president of the Southern Baptist Convention. His mark on Baptist history was as decisive as it was indelible. Another hero of the SBC takeover was Albert Mohler. When the dust had cleared, the UPC was rid of Don Fisher and his liberal colleagues, the Missouri Synod had seen the last of John Tietjen and most of his supporters, and the Southern Baptist Convention had contained the threat of heresy. In all three cases, theology had been purified, one model of reform had been crushed and another had been firmly established. The reform programs which replaced those syllabi of errors were predicated on solid commitments to evangelism, biblical inerrancy, premillennialism, and separation from the world. That separation included every form of liberal theology together with the several methodologies of historical criticism.[29] One of those in the firing line described the

---

[29] Noted in Ammerman, "North American Protestant Fundamentalism," pp. 4-8. Historical criticism is defined and discussed in Chapter 3, pp. 100-101.

resurgence as "self-destructive," "contentious," and "combative."[30] Similar responses can be identified in the LCMS and in the UPC.

Preceding these acrimonious purges was another example of an intentional effort to reform particular fundamentalisms. Charles Fuller established a seminary in southern California in 1947 with a view to raising the intellectual standards of Fundamentalism. Edward J. Carnell (1919-1967), who served as president of Fuller, came under withering criticism for his defence of the Revised Standard Version of the Bible (RSV) as well as for his progressive theological views. At length, Carnell finally sought healing from what he termed the serious illness of Fundamentalism.[31] He had

1.3   Edward J. Carnell, early 1960s, just after his tenure at Fuller

1.4   Fuller Theological Seminary, Pasadena, California

already in 1955, delivered a controversial inaugural speech which antagonized some of his peers, in which he argued that toleration was a virtue, not a vice, and might be held among the attributes of a proper seminary.[32] Faculty members such as George Eldon Ladd

---

[30] Russell Dilday, *Higher Ground: A Call for Christian Civility* (Macon, GA: Smyth & Helwys, 2007), p. 2.

[31] Harold E. Fey, ed., *How My Mind Has Changed* (Cleveland: Meridian, 1960), pp. 91-93.

[32] Edward J. Carnell, "The Glory of a Theological Seminary," inaugural address, 17 May 1955.

supported Carnell while others openly fumed that he was suggesting a policy of appeasement with heretics.[33] The work of men such as Ladd and Carnell along with Paul K. Jewett (1930-1991) and Béla Vassady (1902-1992), provoked national concerns that Fuller Seminary was backslidden, weak on the message and compromising with heretics. Men such as John R. Rice (1895-1980), Bob Jones, Sr. (1883-1968), Harold Lindsell (1913-1998), and Carl McIntire (1906-2002) were convinced that Fuller was no longer viable as a defender of the faith. Issues such as a lack of robust support for biblical inerrancy, latent tolerance for different doctrinal convictions, and the use of historical-critical methodology produced strident accusations that Fuller was an example of apostasy.[34] The constituency was divided. Even less radical thinkers at Fuller like Carl F. H. Henry (1913-2003), David A. Hubbard (1928-1996), and William S. LaSor (1911-1991), found themselves operating beneath a shadow of suspicion, where issues of absolute truth and fidelity to the faith once delivered to the saints became tests of fellowship and marks of orthodoxy.

These currents of controversy were neither new nor unique to Protestant Christianity. The methods of historical criticism when applied to the Bible provoked a strong reaction within Roman Catholicism in the late nineteenth century which persisted well into the twentieth century. In that context the struggle became known as the modernist crisis. In brief, the work of key figures such as the French priest Alfred Loisy (1857-1940) and the Irish Jesuit George Tyrrell (1861-1909) challenged the scholastic method used by the Roman Church and this presented a threat to Catholic dogma (ill. 6.18, p. 374).[35] Loisy was dismissed from his professorship at the Institut Catholique de Paris in 1893, Tyrrell was expelled from the Jesuit order in 1906, and both men were excommunicated in 1908. Pope Pius X banned Loisy as *vitandibus* meaning an individual who should be avoided. This amounted to major excommunication

---

[33] Surveyed in Marsden, *Reforming Fundamentalism*, pp. 147-150.

[34] See Marsden, *Reforming Fundamentalism*, pp. 172-196.

[35] Gabriel Daly, *Transcendence and Immanence: A Study in Catholic Modernism and Integralism* (New York: Oxford University Press, 1980) provides a provocative study of the history of theology which also sheds important nuance on neo-scholasticism at the turn of the twentieth century.

(ill.1.8, p. 40).[36] The shrill alarm which sounded may be attributed either to the latent mentality of active heresy hunting evident within Roman Catholicism, or to the severe challenges posed by various and diverse theological interpretations.

| 1.5  Fr. Alfred Loisy, undated photograph | 1.6  Pope Pius X, c. 1905 before the sanctions of Loisy and Tyrrell |

The Vatican answered the challenge posed by historical criticism with a barrage of papal encyclicals, lists of banned books, expulsions from all positions of authority and influence, strident condemnations of all contrary persons and points of view, and excommunications. Clerics were forced to take oaths opposing historical criticism as applied to scripture and theology. All of these measures were aimed at the newly defined heretics. Pope Pius X took executive action against the liberalizing tendencies by issuing the Index decree *Lamentabili sane exitu* on 3 July 1907, underscoring that unless the liberals were silenced and contained, the affair would only conclude "with lamentable results."[37] "A lamentable departure indeed" was followed up with the encyclical *Pascendi domini gregis* on

---

[36] Details in Loisy's three-volume autobiography. Alfred Loisy, *Mémoires pour server à l'histoire religieuse de nôtre temps*, 3 vols (Paris: Émile Nourry, 1930-1), vol. 2, pp. 642-643.

[37] Claus Arnold and Giacomo Losito, eds., *"Lamentabili sane exitu" (1907): Les documents préparatoires du Saint Office* [Fontes archivi sancti officii Romani, vol. 6] (Vatican City: Libreria editrice vaticana, 2011).

8 September 1907.[38] "Feeding the Lord's flock" was possible only with the commensurate suppression of dangerous ideas. To solidify and enforce these decisions, three years later Pius X called for all priests and professors to swear an oath against modernism.[39] That requirement lasted six decades until 1967 and included complete agreement with *Lamentabili* and *Pascendi*.

Unwilling to leave any stone unturned, an international group, widely known as *Sodalitum Pianum* [the fellowship of Pius] or "La Sapinière," as it was called in France, was convened by the Italian priest Umberto Benigni (1862-1934) to locate and identify heresy in the church. It is of note that the spy-master Benigni was mostly interested in politics and power and saw theology as a means to an end.[40] Parallels might be identified within the LCMS, the SBC, and the UPC. Even earlier than all these measures, a commission was established in 1902 to ensure that no Roman Catholic scholar promoted any view contrary to doctrines already asserted by the church. Put together, these measures give indication of how seriously the Roman Catholic Church viewed the modernists who represented a "synthesis of all heresies."[41] Similar tensions were vibrating with some intensity within the UPC, and the question of being both United Pentecostal and intellectual at the same time had become a pressing and persistent consideration.

Part of the argument in this book is that between 1981 and 1983 the last of the fervent heresy hunters, in pursuit of Don Fisher, gathered outside the gates of CBC and over the course of two years closed the last chapter in the decline of the college, succeeded in driving Don Fisher into permanent exile, and brought

---

[38] The text appears in *Acta Sanctae Sedis*, vol. 40 (Rome: Libreria Editrice Vaticana, 1907), pp. 593-650. English text in Paul Sabatier, *Modernism: The Jowett Lectures, 1908*, trans., C.A. Miles (New York: Charles Scribner's Sons, 1909), pp. 231-348.

[39] For ease of access, the full text of the decree *Sacrorum antistitum*, which is dated 1 September 1910, can be found archived on the official Vatican website at http://www.vatican.va/holy_father/pius_x/motu_proprio/documents/hf_p-x_motu-proprio_19100901_sacrorum-antistitum_lt.html

[40] Otto Weiß, *Modernismus und Antimodernismus im Dominikanerorden: zugleich ein Beitrag zum "Sodalitium Pianum"* (Regensburg: Friedrich Pustet, 1998), pp. 261-282. On Sapinière, see Émile Poulat, *Intégrisme et catholicisme intégral: un réseau secret international antimoderniste: La "Sapinière" (1909-1921)* (Paris: Casterman, 1969).

[41] Pius X, encyclical *Pascendi domini gregis* in Sabatier, *Modernism*, p. 309.

to an end what they perceived as a dangerous and subversive element within the Pacific Northwest region of the United Pentecostal Church. The question of motivation, on both sides, remains at issue. Heresy hunters throughout history have often exhibited an utter disregard for the ethics of Jesus. The fear of doctrinal difference aroused others. One of the main targets of the heresy hunt put it this way, "There are some folk who have a hard time sleeping at night knowing there are people out there who think differently than they do."[42]

The story of the controversial efforts at educational reform at JCM and CBC reveals men who recognized the value and authority of the past but who also actively strove to find within the past modern applicability. This produced anguished concern on the part of some who felt that Fisher's initiatives invited heresy and came dangerously close to denying doctrines once formulated by early Oneness Pentecostals. The detractors of men such as Don Fisher, C.H. Yadon, Joseph H. Howell, Dan Lewis, and Jerry Dillon were convinced that certain doctrines were above investigation and should simply be followed, believed, and defended and not exposed to unnecessary inquiry. The suspects noted above, disagreed and instead suggested that prior formulations, religious experiences, and truth claims might possibly be improved. They held this conviction with confidence in the process of education, theological reflection, and intellectual progress.[43] Howard A. Goss took the position that the Manual was not sacrosanct and ought to be investigated and where necessary amended. The notion was shocking to many on the grounds that the Manual had been directed by the Holy Spirit. Goss dismissed that perspective. "I know better than that. The Lord had nothing to do with it. I wrote a lot of it myself."[44]

---

[42] C.H. Yadon interview, 27 August 1997, Caldwell, Idaho.

[43] There are numerous historical parallels illuminating the friction between men who took opposite sides on such matters. Most recently, see Clare Monagle, *Orthodoxy and Controversy in Twelfth-Century Religious Discourse: Peter Lombard's Sentences and the Development of Theology* (Turnhout: Brepols, 2013) which admirably sheds light on events more than eight hundred years ago.

[44] Goss made the comments to Kenneth Reeves in Paducah, Kentucky in 1954. Kenneth Reeves interview (with Ruth Goss and Mary Wallace), 1982, St. Louis, audio recording. FC, inv.doc.no 0707-2630-19.

In a similar manner as medieval bishops and inquisitors, modern denominations have often been driven by arrogance with respect to those they might better have striven to understand. By consequence the suspected heretic suffers, as well as the church, which ignores an opportunity to engage in the important task of self-criticism and examination.[45] Challenge or criticism from within a social group is often more offensive than external critique.[46] Was the pursuit of Don Fisher, and by extension the fall of CBC, a witch hunt or another manifestation of heresy hunting? Both sides in the struggle perceived the other as the problem, and as the enemy to be defeated. However one looks at the final stages in the history of CBC, there were strangers at the gate.[47]

1.7 Jerry Dillon and Raymond Sirstad at the 25th anniversary celebration of the founding of CBC, Hilton Hotel, Portland, 9 June 1978. The occasion was noted by the media. "Pentecostal Bible school marks birthday" *The Oregonian*, 3 June 1978, p. 34. See Appendix 4, p. 433

---

[45] Shriver, *American Religious Heretics*, p. 15.

[46] Kurtz, *The Politics of Heresy*, p. 141.

[47] The idea of the voice of the stranger comes from the Gospel of John and was effectively used by C.H. Yadon in 1992 and 1993 with reference to the Westberg Resolution, a General Conference decision requiring all ministers to sign an annual statement of UPC doctrinal loyalty. For references see Fudge, *Christianity without the Cross: A History of Salvation in Oneness Pentecostalism*, pp. 223-224.

1.8 Grave of Alfred Loisy in the cemetery at the village of Ambrières, in Champagne, in the Department of Haute-Marne, in northeast France. The stone reads in French: "Alfred Loisy, priest, retired (or removed) from the ministry and from teaching. Professor at the College of France." Then in Latin: "he who did your will by keeping his solemn promises." Loisy shared a final resting place with Marie Maulandre who had died seventy years earlier and was no relation. By canonical mandate, there was no religious service for Loisy and his burial was witnessed by only three people.

# 2

# Don Fisher, Jackson, and the
# Days before CBC

*His face was like that of one who has made a long journey.*[1]

The two Pentecostal denominations that came together in 1945 to form the United Pentecostal Church each had a well-established tradition of particular doctrinal and empirical attributes. With the merging of the two sects, however closely related, there were bound to be fine points of interpretation which might later become sources of friction or even fission. It is doubtful that this possibility was in the minds of those who banded together in the Northwest to establish a Bible college. (Many of these men and women can be seen in ill.0.1, p. xviii.)

2.1 E.G. Moyer around the
time he founded CBC

2.2 C.H. Yadon at the time
CBC began, early 1950s

---

[1] *The Epic of Gilgamesh*, ed., N.K. Sandars (London: Penguin, 1972), p. 63.

Thus, when Cascade Bible College was founded in Portland, Oregon, in 1953 as Conquerors Bible College, the potential existed for it to become a focus of disputation. Its founder was Ernest Gibson Moyer, an Oregon minister in the United Pentecostal Church (ill.2.1). He had the strong support of prominent Idaho minister C.H. Yadon who served as chairman of the College Board of Directors in the early period and came from the liberal wing of the UPC.[2] The college received formal endorsement from the 1954 General Conference of the UPC which convened at Columbus, Ohio, and this ratification was announced in its official publication.[3] The foundation of the school was generally a welcomed addition to the Northwest. An exception to that widespread enthusiasm was expressed by Emanuel Rohn (1903-1996) in Caldwell, Idaho, who was "grossly disappointed" that the old Northwest District did not offer the same level of support for the Northwest Bible Training School he had started but instead went ahead with the Moyer initiative which resulted in the founding of Conquerors Bible College. (See ill.0.1, p. xviii. Rohn is front row, seventh from left.)[4] Two decades later, Rohn continued to vie for part of the market.[5]

The foundation of CBC occurred a scant eight years after the merger agreement which established the new United Pentecostal Church. The memory of the merger struggle was still green, and throughout its life the school, founded by the moderate wing of the

---

[2] *Conquerors Bible College (Portland, Oregon) General Catalog 1979-1981* (Portland: CBC Press, 1979), p. 7. FC, inv.doc.no 0707-4787-32.

[3] The Minutes of the April, 1954 General Board meeting reflect discussion. The Minutes of the 1954 General Conference passed a motion resolving to endorse CBC. Jerry Jones, letter to Thomas A. Fudge, 5 December 2013 (including extracts from those Minutes). By consequence, the endorsement was formally obtained and announced in the fall of 1954 and published in *The Pentecostal Herald* 30 (No. 1, 1955), p. 18. Between 1945 and 1968 the Board of Christian Education had jurisdiction. At the 1968 General Conference in Atlantic City, New Jersey, the DOE was created to supersede the earlier board and it adopted more specific policies. Arthur L. Clanton and Charles E. Clanton, *United We Stand*, revised edition (Hazelwood: Word Aflame Press, 1995), pp. 273-280.

[4] Edwin Judd interview, 10 April 1999, St. Louis, Missouri.

[5] He proposed starting a six-month intensive Bible course in Caldwell and got his proposal under consideration by the CBC board. However, no action was taken. *Minutes*, CBC board meeting, 14 March 1975, p. 3.

## We hope you like
# Our New Name

### ... in the tradition of the beautiful Northwest!

The Conquerors Bible College label is bowing out so the college (still CBC), which has served our fellowship well since 1953, can be identified locally and regionally with the magnificent Cascade Mountain range which stretches its crest from border to border. Its world famous peaks, including Mount Baker, Mount Rainier, Mount St. Helens, Mount Adams, Mount Hood and Mount Jefferson, all speak of the dynamics of CBC's rich heritage. At this very moment hundreds of her graduates are preaching and teaching the Word of God around the world ... including four members of the Foreign Missions Division team at the World Evangelism Center and 31 alumni under appointment as UPCI missionaries!

Donald W. Fisher • President

The Bible has always been the standard in the Northwest. The Holy Scripture remains our bulwark. There isn't a firmer foundation than the Word and the Lordship of Jesus Christ.

We're not flashy out west ... just solid.

So if it's Bible you're looking for ... you can study it with integrity in a beautiful atmosphere, both spiritually and geographically!

Our new campus in WASHINGTON will be ready when you are ...

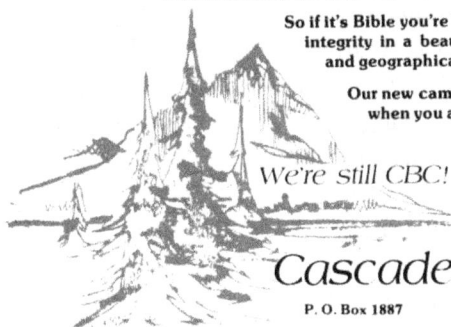

We're still CBC!

*Call our office today, collect, for information ... 503-286-5788.*

# Cascade Bible College

P. O. Box 1887          Vancouver, Washington 98668

2.3   Full page advertisement reflecting CBC's new name, Spring 1982

UPC, was the object of suspicion by the "water and spirit" purists. The nature of that struggle is delineated below. From 1953 until 1982 the college was known by its original name and was located on the same site in Portland. During that last, abbreviated academic year, its name and location changed to Cascade Bible College in the adjacent town of Vancouver, Washington. As history demonstrated through the tumultuous events of 1982 and 1983, the Vancouver period was critical for that controversy which accompanied it. Even some of the principal people at the time acknowledged this, while unwilling to negate the significance of that appendix. "The purest [sic] from the past will never admit that the last two years were as important as any of the rest but in my mind they will always be the most significant."[6] For all intents and purposes, the life, history and importance of CBC was forever linked with Portland.

Located at 10838 North Lombard Street, in the Portland suburb of St. Johns, Conquerors Bible College was not a major player in the Portland higher education circle. Even within the United Pentecostal Church constellation, CBC was never regarded as a premier institution and did not achieve the reputation earned elsewhere among UPC colleges. It was noted in 1974 that CBC was neither as well-known nor as well-publicized as other UPC colleges. New pastors coming into the Northwest seemed to possess little knowledge of CBC.[7] Even official denominational histories are sometimes unclear on basic facts about the college.[8] Apostolic Bible Institute (ABI) in St. Paul, Minnesota, under the direction of S.G. Norris (1901-1990), and later Robert Sabin (ill.6.13, p. 348), enjoyed a reputation for maintaining a strong theological orientation. Indeed, Sabin would exert a formative influence on Joseph Howell and the later critic of the UPC, Gregory Boyd.[9] Howell became one of Fisher's colleagues, exercising a not inconsiderable influence over some of the later events at CBC. All things considered, Joseph Howell is one of the key figures in this tale of heretics and politics. Another UPC college, Jackson College of Ministries (JCM) in Jackson, Mississippi, had a national reputation for excellence in music, especially during the tenure of Lanny Wolfe (1974-1993). By

---

[6] Jerry Peden, letter to Thomas A. Fudge, 27 September 1999.
[7] Loren Yadon, letter to the CBC board, undated [1974], p. 2. Yadon was serving at that time as a college field representative. FC, inv.doc.no 0707-5168-34. CBC was also little known in Portland. "Pentecostal Bible school marks birthday" *The Oregonian*, 3 June 1978, p. 34.
[8] Clanton, *United We Stand*, p. 276 claims CBC closed in 1985.
[9] Joseph Howell interview, 21 April 1999, Pensacola, Florida. Sabin made use of Adolf von Harnack's multi-volume and influential *History of Dogma*, an unusual text in the UPC. The latter's polemic is Gregory A. Boyd, *Oneness Pentecostalism and the Trinity* (Grand Rapids: Baker, 1992).

any calibration, CBC was a small, insignificant, and parochial Bible school.

As with all UPC colleges at the time, CBC was a three-year unaccredited institution granting certificates to graduates but no degrees in any of its six major areas of study, despite the fact that some UPC pastors claim to have earned a degree at CBC.[10] Almost all of its student body over its thirty year existence was drawn from the ranks of the denomination especially from the old Northwest District which comprised the states of Idaho, Oregon, Washington, Montana, Wyoming, along with the Canadian province of British Columbia. After the dissolution of the old Northwest District in 1965, the college was controlled by the newly established Districts of Oregon, Washington, and Idaho. A few students from elsewhere in the United States and Canada attended CBC as well as a handful from overseas. Those in the latter group were almost always the children of UPC foreign missionaries who frequently were CBC graduates themselves. Almost all of the student body were from the ranks of the UPC. In the same vein as wider American culture at the time, there was both concern and uncertainty about admitting Negro students.[11] The college faculty, while not expected to have earned degrees or qualifications in the disciplines they taught, were required to be members of the sponsoring church in good standing with the organization. Lack of academic credentials was sometimes offset by other qualities.[12] In other words, they were required to be strictly orthodox in their theological views and personal morality.

---

[10] *Conquerors Bible College (Portland, Oregon) General Catalog 1979-1981*, 70 pp. Arless Glass, "Our United Pentecostal Church Bible Schools are not Accredited" *The Pentecostal Herald* 57 (No. 8, 1982), p. 4. See also Mary Lois Sleeva, "A History of the Bible Schools Related to the United Pentecostal Church," unpublished MA thesis, Indiana Central College, 1973, 389 pp. ICC is now the University of Indianapolis. The website for the UPC church in Salem, Oregon states that senior pastor James Dillon "holds a degree from Conquerors Bible College." www.cwfsalem.com

[11] See *Minutes*, CBC board meetings, 11 November 1958, 12 January 1959, and 13 November 1962 which reflect the struggle. The chief issue revolved around the possibility of interracial marriage.

[12] Donald M. Carmont, *The Naked Mentor: One Man's Journey, One Man's Journal* (Belleville, ON: Epic Press, 2005), p. 62. Carmont was a former UPC pastor who attended Bible college in New Brunswick.

Needless to say, the administrative personnel, and especially the presidents of CBC, were individuals of exceptional regard and reputation at the national level of the UPC. E.G. Moyer served as its first president from 1953 to 1957 and was followed successively by the Canadian and sometime foreign missionary Ralph Vincent Reynolds (1957-1963), Orion Baker Gleason (1963-1966), Edwin E. Judd (1966-1968), C.H. Yadon (1968-1971), John Eugene Klemin (1971-1978), Ralph Reynolds, for the second time (1978-1981) and finally by Donald W. Fisher (1981-1983).[13] When Reynolds stepped down in 1963, there was pressure on C.H. Yadon to take over CBC.[14] He declined. When Klemin resigned in 1978, the Oregon District put Paul Dugas' name forward for consideration as the next president.[15] The minutes of a CBC board meeting show that upon Klemin's resignation the names of four candidates were advanced in order of preference. These included Ralph V. Reynolds, Paul Dugas, former UPC General Superintendent Stanley W. Chambers, and Arlo Moehlenpah.[16] John Klemin backed Chambers and made formal recommendation to the board.[17] While never elected to the presidency of CBC, Dugas nevertheless played a key role in the history of the college (ill.3.11, p. 127). A number of the men who were CBC presidents, either before or after their tenure in Portland, served in national capacities with the UPC. Reynolds and Klemin were foreign missionaries of sterling reputation and the latter was one of the featured preachers on the UPC's international *Harvestime* radio program. Gleason served as a district superintendent. Judd

---

[13] All are deceased with the exception of Judd who considered C.H. Yadon his mentor. Edwin Judd interview, 10 April 1999. Technically, Moyer was the college superintendent. This title was later discontinued and replaced with the office of president. Minutes of the Annual Northwest District Conference of the United Pentecostal Church, 2 July 1957, Bend, Oregon.

[14] Extant letters to Yadon urging this include C.M. Yadon, 12 March 1963, Carl Adams, 19 March 1963, and Orion Gleason, 20 April 1963. I have read these letters, now in the possession of Jewel (Yadon) Dillon.

[15] Paul Dugas interview, 25 January 1999, Portland, Oregon. Others said that Dugas wanted the school. Leon Brokaw interview, 29 January 2001, West Linn, Oregon, and Harry Fisher interview, 8 December 2000, Bend, Oregon.

[16] *Minutes*, CBC board meeting, 28 August 1978.

[17] John Klemin, letter to the CBC board, 28 August 1978, pp. 1-2. FC, inv.doc.no 0707-5184-34.

was a member of the Foreign Missions Board and a regional field supervisor. Yadon was the national director of home missions and radio director for the *Harvestime* program.

Until the Fisher appointment there had been overall agreement and general consensus on the election of presidents. An exception was the appointment of Edwin Judd in 1966 who was elected by a

2.4  Main CBC campus building as it appeared in the
early 1970s, viewed from the east

unanimous secret ballot vote.[18] In his official letter of resignation to the CBC College Board, Orion Gleason dedicated twenty-six lines of recommendation in favor of Judd. The Idaho District formally protested the ways and means by which Judd attained the office.[19] It is noteworthy that Judd was considered for the presidency in 1963 when Ralph Reynolds resigned (upon the recommendation of Reynolds) but his candidature was defeated on the basis of "hearsay, supposed, doctrinal errors."[20]

The CBC college student body reached its crest during the presidency of John E. Klemin between 1976 and 1978, but never exceeded one hundred and fifty at any given time even though it

---

[18] C.M. Yadon, letter to Idaho ministers, 25 March 1966. FC, inv.doc.no 0707-5146-34.

[19] Orion Gleason, letter to the CBC board, 16 December 1965, and Idaho District, letter to the CBC board, 13 March 1966. FC, inv.doc.no 0707-5146-34.

[20] Orion B. Gleason, letter to Idaho District ministers, 22 March 1966 and C.M. Yadon, letter to Idaho ministers, 25 March 1966. See ill.0.1, p. xviii. Gleason is in the front row, eighth from the left.

was estimated that perhaps 200 on-campus students could be accommodated.[21] The zenith of the college coincided with an unsuccessful effort around 1975 either to extend the Lombard campus or purchase a larger facility. In the former case, plans were drawn up and materials were purchased. The alternative facility was the 3.3 acre Academy of the Holy Child at 5404 N.E. Alameda Street which came available and CBC made a formal offer. Neither initiative was successful.[22] In its thirty years, CBC graduated a total of 351 students, or about twelve per year. The average number of

| 1954 | 3 | 1964 | 16 | 1974 | 15 |
|------|---|------|----|------|----|
| 1955 | 2 | 1965 | 8 | 1975 | 11 |
| 1956 | 8 | 1966 | 5 | 1976 | 13 |
| 1957 | 9 | 1967 | 13 | 1977 | 13 |
| 1958 | 8 | 1968 | 17 | 1978 | 30 |
| 1959 | 10 | 1969 | 14 | 1979 | 11 |
| 1960 | 7 | 1970 | 3 | 1980 | 11 |
| 1961 | 7 | 1971 | 14 | 1981 | 14 |
| 1962 | 6 | 1972 | 21 | 1982 | 6 |
| 1963 | 8 | 1973 | 22 | 1983 | 3 |

2.5  CBC graduates by year (1954-1983)

graduates each year under the eight college presidents was: Moyer: 5.5; Reynolds: 7.5; Gleason: 7; Judd: 15; Yadon: 17; Klemin: 18; Reynolds: 12 and Fisher: 4.5.[23] If the number of graduates was

---

[21] President's Report (John Klemin), meeting of the CBC board, 16 December 1971, p. 2. FC, inv.doc.no 0707-5155-34.

[22] Jerry Dillon interview, 19 April 2013, Camas, Washington. Holy Child Academy operated from 1914 to 1973 and was owned by the Pennsylvania-based Society of the Holy Child Jesus, a Catholic female religious order. *Minutes*, CBC (special) board meeting, 23 June 1973. FC, inv.doc.no 0707-5162-34. The campus consisted of three main buildings totaling approximately 63,000 square feet. The asking price for Holy Child Academy was $650,000. CBC tendered two formal offers. Attorney David C. Swart, letter to C&R Realty Co., 12 July 1973. FC, inv.doc.no 0707-5163-34. Further details in *Minutes*, CBC board meeting, 3 August 1973. FC, inv.doc.no 0707-5164-34. David C. Swart, letter to C&R Realty, 12 March 1974. FC, inv.doc.no 0707-5167-34.

[23] *Ensign*, vol. 30 (1983), p. 8 states that 352 students graduated from CBC and almost 1,200 had studied there. I based my figure on counting the number of

small, a disproportionate number, more than thirty, became foreign missionaries for the United Pentecostal Church and at one time five of the six global missions regional field supervisors were former students. Statistically, this makes CBC a major contributor between 1945 and the 1980s.

Following the pioneering initiative of Moyer, the succession of CBC college presidents was generally predictable, conservative, and orthodox. These several criteria, curiously, seemed almost entirely

2.6 Presidents of CBC (1981). *Left to right:* John Klemin, Edwin Judd, Don Fisher, C.H. Yadon, E.G. Moyer, and Ralph Reynolds. The other former president Orion Gleason (1914-1973) was deceased. With the exception of Moyer, all appear in ill.0.1, p. xviii

lacking in 1981 when Donald W. Fisher, then serving as executive vice-president at Jackson College of Ministries (JCM) in Jackson, Mississippi, was appointed to head CBC as its eighth president.[24]

---

graduates noted in the thirty volumes of *Ensign*. There are 351 names listed as CBC graduates in *Ensign*, vol. 30 (1983), pp. 74-75. The 352nd graduate may have been Franz Bibfeldt but it has proven impossible to determine which year he studied at CBC.

[24] Fisher had been appointed to JCM in 1976 upon the recommendation of Tom Fred Tenney. James Stewart warned Fisher not to go to JCM fearing fallout from residual PCI and PAJC differences and perhaps a cultural clash between the ethos of the deep south and Fisher's Northwest orientation. Mark Roberts interview, 5 May 1999, Nashville, Tennessee. Stewart shared his thoughts and counsel with Roberts. As a result of the move to Mississippi, "personal happiness took a nosedive." Ronna (Fisher) Russell interview, 20 July 2013, Bellingham, Washington.

Fisher was neither predictable nor conservative and had a personal history of being progressive. He was a theological product of the old Northwest District (see ill.0.1, p. xviii) and had a long history with the UPC, though it was at JCM and CBC that he achieved notoriety. His tenure came at a critical point in the history of CBC. The-then academic dean of the school placed his views before the College Board of Directors. These are worth noting.

> FIRST, AND FOREMOST, he must be a man of deep spiritual stature. He must be a man of prayer, a man who walks with God and is spiritually alert. SECOND, CBC needs a man who will resolutely stand, in the face of eroding faith, for the Apostolic doctrine and message. Moreover, he must not only say he believes it, he must teach it! THIRD, he must be a man who believes, teaches, practices, and enforces strong Biblical standards of Bible Holiness, both spiritual and physical. FOURTH, he must be a man who has been loyal to CBC down through the years. He must be a man who primarily has the school at heart, and looks upon the position as more than a job. He must be void of personal interest. AND LAST, he must be a man of progress with a positive mental attitude. There are many other qualities necessary, but these are paramount at this point in our history.[25]

Raymond Sirstad (ill.4.24, p. 206) believed rightly and accurately that CBC had reached a uniquely critical stage in its history at the time Fisher was appointed, especially as viewed against the main stream of thought in the Oregon District.[26]

Just as the famous twelfth-century theologian Bernard of Clairvaux was not always the abbot of a Cistercian house, so Don Fisher was not always a college president though neither man is usually thought of outside those contexts. It is too often the case that important historical personalities are examined only subsequent to their rise to public prominence. Who was Don Fisher before he became vice-president and then president of two UPC Bible colleges? Was Raymond Sirstad's admonition taken seriously? And if so, on what basis? (That consideration noted, there were those who thought that Sirstad himself had been unfairly overlooked in

---

[25] From Raymond A. Sirstad, letter to the CBC board, 8 April 1981, p. 3. FC, inv.doc.no 0707-5195-34.

[26] Raymond A. Sirstad interview, 27 August 2013, Vancouver, Washington.

the development of the college, and that he should have been appointed president of CBC.)[27]

2.7 Don Fisher shortly before he assumed
the presidency of CBC in 1981

Donald Wayne Fisher was born on 16 February 1939, to Harry Benson Fisher and Freda Blanche (Harlan) Fisher in Bend, Oregon. He had one sister Doris who was born in 1935. His grandfather, James Wilder Fisher (1892-1971), was not a Christian and Don had little meaningful contact with him. His paternal grandmother, Sylvia L. Fetty (*c.*1896-1926), died when Harry was only ten. His maternal grandparents, Joshua Vincent Harlan (1881-1968) and Blanche

---

[27] David Reynolds interview, 12 August 2013, Gresham, Oregon. That Ralph V. Reynolds promoted Sirstad for the presidency has been confirmed in Daniel R. Sirstad interview, 26 August 2013, Troutdale, Oregon, and Raymond A. Sirstad interview, 27 August 2013.

Venus Honey (1894-1971), were Christians and the young Don Fisher had positive relationships with them. James Fisher had warned young Harry to stay away from "that Harlan brat." Harry disobeyed. When the two married, James told Harry he suspected the union would not last six months. As it turned out, the marriage lasted into its eightieth year.[28] Harry and Freda Fisher moved to Idaho and lived there between 1941 and 1964 in Idaho Falls, Pocatello and Salmon. Harry Fisher pastored churches in Pocatello and Salmon for twelve years and also worked at farming and in construction. (See ill.0.1, p. xviii. Freda Fisher is in the fourth row, fifth from the left while Harry Fisher is in the back row, wearing a bow tie, ninth from the left.)

Most of Don's public schooling was taken in eastern Idaho. As a boy, he was eager to help with farm work, and his life was typical for boys in the 1940s. He rode bicycles, had playmates, played games, badgered his parents for a dog, and helped take care of rabbits. Don did not cause his parents any trouble as a boy. His church involvement was not extensive as there were few activities for children, predicated mainly on the fact that there were no children at all in the Pocatello church pastored by Harry Fisher. He took considerable interest in drama performing in school plays, and also showed some aptitude in painting. Don wanted to play drums but his father refused to allow that so he chose trumpet and gained sufficient proficiency to play solos in church.[29] He pestered a shopkeeper in Pocatello until he was given a menial job but he soon took the initiative in terms of responsibility. His employer was duly impressed.

Later in life, Harry Fisher believed he had been too strict with Don and would do things differently given the opportunity. Harry Fisher regrets never having seen his son act. Chief among his regrets is the fact that, because he was bi-vocational, the elder Fisher did not spend a lot of time with his son. "I was too tied up with the church." Fisher pastored most of the time during which Don was growing up and in addition to church work had full-time

---

[28] Doris (Fisher) Newman interview, 20 August 2013, Bend, Oregon.
[29] He later played trumpet in the CBC orchestra. There is a photograph in *Ensign*, vol. 1 (1954), p. 33.

responsibilities on his farm. As a consequence, father and son did very little together. There is no indication that the young Don Fisher said much about how he felt, opened up to his parents, or took them into confidence on things he may have been thinking or concerning issues in his own life. Harry Fisher did not attempt to draw his son out into dialogue, a matter he also came to regret in later life. It cannot be said that the young Don Fisher had an overly positive relationship with his father. In many respects, Harry Fisher's relationship with Don was mirrored by the relationship he had with his own father who was likewise very busy with the life of farming and working in sawmills. Considered in retrospect, the lack of love, trust, acceptance, and understanding potentially planted seeds in young Fisher he would later struggle with.[30]

Don Fisher was a small man in height and bulk. As an adult he stood not more than five feet five inches in height and weighed less than 140 pounds. Both parents were aware that this bothered their son. At one stage in his life, Don Fisher consulted a physician in Salem, Oregon in relation with his concerns about being small, though the outcome of that medical inquiry is unknown. As he grew into manhood, Fisher was embarrassed that he could not fit into men's clothing and therefore had to purchase boy's sizes. None of this led to teasing on the part of his peers so far as his parents were aware. The young Don Fisher liked to play basketball but the bigger boys would not often let him play because he was small. No one bullied him and he refused to be bullied or intimidated. Don got his own ball and on one occasion when the bigger boys wanted to use it, young Fisher decided this might be allowed but only if they consented to paying him ten cents per boy for the loan of the ball. It appeared that Fisher had leadership qualities even at a remarkably young age. He was not shy, was always meticulous about his appearance, did not like getting dirty, and always wore a cap.[31] After he attained prominence as a minister,

---

[30] Donna Fisher and Ronna (Fisher) Russell interviews, 7 October/20 July 2013.

[31] Freda Fisher tells a story about Don as a small boy inadvertently stepping in manure on the farm and standing there screaming, holding his fouled foot in the air, refusing to take another step until the offending feces was removed. The cap is mentioned elsewhere. "We visited Pocatello when Harry Fisher pastored there. Don was a little boy wearing an aviator's cap." Noted in Ellis Scism and Harry

Fisher absolutely despised being introduced as a small man with a big message.

When Don Fisher had completed eight grades of education and wanted to proceed to high school, he asked if he could do it in Portland at CBC, which in its early years also had a high school program. His parents were reluctant to hold him back since he was so keen to go and their consent was predicated partly upon the fact that there were no other young people in the Pocatello church. With considerable hesitation, the Fishers allowed their young son to leave home at the age of fourteen and make the 650-mile journey to Oregon. Allene Moyer (1914-2009), wife of CBC president E.G. Moyer, took Don Fisher under her wing and seems to have been a maternal figure for him during those first years away from home. He later told stories of being tormented by the college-age boys who subjected him to various forms of harassment.[32] A handwritten note to Jewel Yadon captures something of Fisher's experiences. "Hi! 'Teach.' I have enjoyed your fellowship this first year of C.B.C. and hope to see you around next year. I know I have been a trial for your faith, but maybe I can be improved by next year. 'Pray for me.' May all of the trials of your faith turn into blessings."[33]

Separated by hundreds of miles, Fisher and his parents stayed in touch chiefly by letter-writing. After he had completed two years of high school in Portland, CBC decided to discontinue the high school program and focus more fully on the college curricula, so Fisher returned to Idaho.[34] By this time his parents had moved from Pocatello to Salmon, a small town 200 miles to the northwest on the Idaho-Montana border between the Lemhi, Bitterroot, and Salmon mountain ranges in one of the most remote areas in the United States. Described by his parents as "very studious and very

---

Scism, *Northwest Passage: The Early Years of Ellis Scism 1909-1949* (Hazelwood: Word Aflame Press, 1994), p.269.

[32] Ronna (Fisher) Russell interview, 20 July 2013, who says her father shared some of these stories. Also Loren Yadon interview, 26 July 2013, Boise, Idaho, based on testimony from the late Ordell Yadon (1937-2001) who was a CBC student with Fisher.

[33] This note appeared alongside his formal portrait in Jewel Yadon's personal copy of *Ensign*, vol. 1 (1954), p. 23.

[34] *Conquerors Bible College (Portland, Oregon) General Catalog 1979-1981*, p. 7.

industrious" and with "not a lazy bone in him," Fisher completed the last two years of high school in a single year in Salmon and earned a 4.0 grade point average. It was sufficient for valedictorian but that honor went to a female classmate who had the same grade point average but had done all four high school years in Salmon.

Don was popular and the Fishers approved of his friends except for one young lady, who did not go to church and who was in the habit of keeping Don out late at night. Harry Fisher seems to have intervened in that budding teenage relationship and soon Don's nightly excursions were curtailed. Committed to returning to CBC, this time as a fully-fledged college student, Fisher turned down a lucrative employment opportunity with a bank. Not to be put off, the bank offered to keep a position open for Don and defer his employment until he completed college. Don was grateful for the confidence, but he had no intention of returning to Salmon, Idaho. His parents noted that Don always seemed to know where he wanted to go and suggested that he may have admired Abraham Lincoln, of whom he had a small statue in his room.[35]

At CBC Fisher met people with whom he formed life-long friendships, including some of the Yadons, Gene Dillon, Norman Rutzen, and Wayne Nigh. Among his boyhood friends were Kenneth and Donna Austin whose father, Donald F. Austin, (1913-2003) pastored a church in Idaho Falls for fifty years (see ill.0.1, p. xviii. Austin is in the back row, fourth from the left). The daughters of Della Olson, Dorothy, Laura, and Joyce, were also friends. Dorothy and Joyce Olson, as well as Donna Austin, attended CBC. The years at the college in Portland seemed to have exerted a positive influence on Fisher and provided the basic formation for a career in ministry. It was at CBC that Fisher met Donna Lewis, another young student from Montana. Fisher wrote to his parents from the college that he was falling in love with Donna Lewis and wrote with conviction that he had never known that love could be so wonderful. Nearly fifty years later Harry Fisher could still vividly recall that letter. Don and Donna married on 14 August 1959. After

---

[35] The comment about Lincoln came in a discussion about influences on Don Fisher as a boy. It may have no particular meaning. For example, it would be specious to suggest Fisher learned anything from Lincoln or was influenced by him. He may simply have admired the statue.

graduating from CBC, Don Fisher attended the liberal arts Cascade College in Portland where he earned the undergraduate B.A. degree and subsequently the necessary qualification for teaching in public schools.[36]

In 1960 and 1961, he was an assistant pastor at the UPC church in Jerome, Idaho, and in the latter year was briefly an assistant pastor in Salem, Oregon. Between 1961 and 1964, he was a home missionary in Hoonah, Alaska. He returned to Portland in 1964 to serve as an assistant pastor to John Klemin at the Killingsworth Street church. During 1964 and 1965, he served as pastor in Vancouver, Washington and taught at CBC. In 1965, he was also the secretary-treasurer for the Youth Department in the Oregon District and his resignation from the college was accepted with some reluctance.[37] In 1966, he was elevated to national prominence in St. Louis at the UPC headquarters. From 1966 to 1968, Fisher was Director of Promotions and Publications for the UPC Youth Division and initiated the national Bible quiz program. From 1968 to 1970, he served as the founder and editor of Word Aflame Publications, where colleagues described him as possessing a brilliant and stimulating mind.[38] Between 1970 and 1976, Fisher was the director of overseas ministries within the Foreign Missions Department, and was directly responsible for coordinating the first international UPC convention convened in Jerusalem in 1976. From 1976 through 1981, he served as the executive vice-president at Jackson College of Ministries. This last appointment is germane to later events in Portland in terms of understanding the harvest that was gathered into history at CBC.

Jackson College of Ministries has a longer history than can be related here, but it began in 1945 as Pentecostal Bible Institute in Tupelo, Mississippi. In 1974, the Mississippi District of the United Pentecostal Church approved transfer of the PBI charter to Thomas L. Craft, pastor of the large First Pentecostal Church in Jackson, and the following year the college was reorganized under the name Jackson College of Ministries. At this time, JCM was

---

[36] The preceding eight paragraphs are based upon an interview with Fisher's parents. Harry and Freda Fisher interview, 13 July 2005, Bend, Oregon.
[37] *Minutes*, CBC board meeting, 10 June 1965, p. 18.
[38] Thetus Tenney interview, 6 June 2013, Sydney, Australia.

intentionally concerned with implementing a more practical dimension to its several programs. Rather than simply employing a traditional faculty to deal with theory, the college determined to bring in regular practitioners of various forms of ministry. Both Thomas Craft and T.F. Tenney were solidly in favor of such an

2.8 Thomas L. Craft, *c.* 1980, as president
of Jackson College of Ministries

approach and this appealed to Fisher as well.[39] As executive vice-president, the implementation of this re-orientation fell to him.

Prior to all of these developments, Don Fisher had graduated from CBC. Among the eight members of the class of 1958 featured in the district paper wearing their caps and gowns was the nineteen-year-old Don Fisher.[40] Despite his fairly impressive UPC pedigree, twenty-three years later in 1981 there were numerous voices questioning his fitness for college presidency. By contrast, Fisher believed his return to the Northwest and to CBC was the will of

---

[39] Thetus Tenney interview, 6 June 2013.
[40] *Pentecostal Northwestern News* 12 (No. 6, 1958), p. 3.

God and some in the Northwest were confident that Fisher could provide "God-directed, competent leadership."[41] Some men in the Northwest with long connections to the college believed that Fisher was the one man with any chance of salvaging CBC.[42] After all, he had built JCM into a powerhouse UPC college.[43] Many disagreed, and a variety of rumors reached as far afield as the Atlantic District (Canada).[44] It should be pointed out that Fisher had decided to resign from JCM, without pressure, on or about 1 January 1981, well before R.V. Reynolds announced his decision to retire from CBC.[45] The eventual assault on Fisher's theological acceptability became well-known and soon a battle in the Northwest was on. His defenders attempted to bring about resolution.

> Brethren, the time has come – is long overdue – for men to behave as Christian gentlemen. Sordid and twisted unnuendos [sic] regarding a fellow minister's doctrine is unbecoming to men of God. Not one shred of evidence has been produced to even imply any doctrinal irregularities, either to me or our General Superintendent. A generous letter of high recommendation from Brother Urshan was sent to all pastors of the Northwest earlier ... An Apostolic approach to our ministry includes much more than just the heart of the Gospel message; it also includes our relationship to each other, our attitudes and our spirits. The facts are evident. Let's get on with the business of the church and Bible training in the Northwest, in unity of spirit and purpose.[46]

---

[41] Open letter from Don Fisher, "We're Coming Home!" published in the CBC annual yearbook *Ensign*, vol. 28 (1981), p. 127 (see Appendix 6) and Raymond Sirstad, "CBC News" *The Oregon District Apostolic Accent* (June 1981), p. 4.

[42] Jerry Dillon interview, 5 January 1999, Portland, Oregon.

[43] Karissa (Fisher) Hopkins interview, 15 August 2013, Vacaville, California.

[44] In the summer of 1981 the author was informed in Saint John, New Brunswick that Fisher "had been run out of Jackson." The assumption lacked evidential merit. Surprise was registered when the informant learned Fisher was on his way to Portland to assume the mantle as CBC's eighth president. *The Journal of Thomas A. Fudge, 1980-1985*, entry for 23 June 1981.

[45] Donna Fisher interview, 3 January 1999, Vancouver, Washington. By contrast Craft says that Fisher simply put his resignation under his door and disappeared. T. L. Craft interview, 20 April 1999, Jackson, Mississippi. The characterization is curious.

[46] Norman Rutzen, letter to the Northwestern Brethren, 13 November 1981, p. 1. FC, inv.doc.no 0707-4808-32. See Appendix 13, pp. 449-450. Urshan later noted

Officials at Jackson College of Ministries went on record as acknowledging that "many rumors have been flying" about concerning Don Fisher including his apparent denial of the inspiration of scripture and allegations that he did not believe the *Fundamental Doctrine* of the UPC. However, these rumors were summarily dismissed as "absolute falsehood."[47] As the incoming president of CBC, Fisher pledged complete allegiance to the word of God.[48]

The president of JCM, Thomas L. Craft, evidently also publicly praised Fisher in the spring of 1981, during the college graduation ceremonies on 15 May, and went so far as to say that Fisher was welcome to remain at JCM.[49] The probity of that sentiment has been widely questioned by those who served on faculty at the college in the School of Theology during the Fisher years with some members finding it hard to imagine that such a statement represented the deepest sentiments of Craft's heart.[50] Elsewhere, Craft said he was very happy to see Fisher go and regarded Fisher's departure as God's blessing.[51] The letter written by Thomas Craft does not seem to have been widely known for national officials later stated that the CBC College Board "did not get the proper

---

that prior to CBC, Fisher had a good reputation. Nathaniel Urshan interview, 23 April 1999. No trace of the Urshan letter mentioned by Rutzen has been found and it is quite possible Rutzen confused this with a similar letter written by Thomas Craft. However, Rutzen continues to maintain that Urshan was involved to the extent of approving CBC's decision to invite Fisher to take the presidency. Norman Rutzen interview, 24 July 2013, Caldwell, Idaho.

[47] Thomas L. Craft, letter to C.M. Yadon, 29 April 1981, p. 1. FC, inv.doc.no 0707-4804-32. Eighteen years later, on four occasions, Craft denied ever writing anything on behalf of Fisher but at length remembered composing a "very generic" letter which he thought he had sent to George Sponsler. Thomas Craft interview, 20 April 1999. I believe the letter to C.M. Yadon is the one Craft refers to. I would contest its characterization as "generic." See Appendix 9, pp. 440-41.

[48] Donald W. Fisher, "An Open Letter from the President-Elect" *CBC Jubilation* 15 (No. 1, 1981), p. 3.

[49] Noted in Norman Rutzen, letter to the Northwestern Brethren, 13 November 1981, p. 1. In the same letter, Rutzen says he confirmed with Craft in late October 1981, the latter's high view of Fisher.

[50] Dan Lewis interview, 6 April 1999, Troy, Michigan.

[51] Thomas L. Craft interview, 20 April 1999. Craft was president until 1997. The college closed in 2004.

recommendation from [JCM] where he [Fisher] had been."[52] As a matter of fact, Craft's letter was sent to all pastors in the Oregon, Washington, and Idaho Districts.[53] Nevertheless, had due diligence been done, the college in Portland might have avoided a Trojan horse.

One of the central planks in the house of opposition to Don Fisher was the conviction that he was not sufficiently committed to the theological orientation of the UPC. Even some CBC faculty were unsure if Fisher truly adhered to UPC doctrine.[54] The rumors have been noted. Thomas Craft put in writing his opposition to such accusations by stating they were baseless. That was in 1981. A number of years later, his memory perhaps colored by subsequent events, Craft reversed himself by stating without qualification that Fisher would utter slurs against the UPC in college classrooms at Jackson and emphatically stated, "I know he didn't" believe UPC theology. Apparently, Fisher told Nathaniel Urshan in Jackson that he did hold to the message as articulated by the UPC. Craft later said, "that was a lie."[55] Were Craft's public comments and written statements in 1981 political posturing, or were his later comments the result of faulty memory? It is difficult to conceive a third option. Moreover, Fisher was on public record in declaring that he was not principally committed to the UPC: "I love this fellowship ... but I have no oblations. I do not kiss the toe of any institution."[56] Statements like this may have generated distrust but they mirrored

---

[52] Cleveland Becton interview, 14 April 1999. Others have suggested that Craft's letter was merely a clever mechanism for getting Fisher out of Mississippi. David Reynolds interview, 12 August 2013. The intended purpose of the Craft letter remains unsolved.

[53] A handwritten note, dated 9 November 1981, from a "planning session" consisting of Fisher, Sirstad, Rutzen, C.H. Yadon, Crossley, and LaCrosse noted the intention (FC, inv.doc.no 0707-5205-34) which was later confirmed in Norman Rutzen, letter to the Northwestern Brethren, 13 November 1981, p. 1. Others doubt that this mailing ever happened. Raymond A. Sirstad interview, 27 August 2013.

[54] Darline (Kantola) Royer interview, 15 August 2013.

[55] Thomas Craft interview, 20 April 1999 for this paragraph and the statement to Urshan has been corroborated in Nathaniel Urshan interview, 23 April 1999.

[56] Don Fisher, "Let Christ be Formed in You," sermon at McCormick's Creek, Indiana, 1974, audio recording. FC, inv.doc.no 0707-5439-35.

the sentiment of his mentor who said, "I hate religious politics and I refuse to bend or bow to that spirit."[57] Fisher and C.H. Yadon subscribed firmly to a perspective articulated nearly 200 years earlier. "He who begins by loving Christianity better than Truth will proceed by loving his own sect or church better than Christianity, and end in loving himself better than all."[58]

What was the sum and substance of the theological orientation at JCM during the Fisher years? One perspective argues that the program was a deliberate effort to educate people beyond the scope of Pentecostalism: Don Fisher and his colleagues, especially Dan Lewis and Joseph Howell, were attempting to turn people from UPC doctrine. Can this argument be sustained? Prominent ministers declared that Fisher, especially, "was turning the students away from our doctrine."[59] Some have argued that the program at Jackson represented a definite progression even beyond the PCI point of view. The PCI (Pentecostal Church Incorporated) was the more liberal of the two movements which merged in 1945 to form the UPC. Were Fisher and his colleagues actively promoting a PCI perspective? One pointed critique posited the following: "Private communion services were held without the knowledge of the college or the sponsoring church so I would say that's a pretty strong indication there was an attempt to create a following."

One faculty member, David Bernard, followed the exodus of the core of the theology teachers at JCM. Based upon his interaction with returning students who had been taught earlier by Howell and Lewis, Bernard was of the opinion that there had been a fairly thorough undermining of certain UPC doctrine. Bernard characterized the teaching approach and methodology of his predecessors as reducing the differences between the Oneness and Trinitarian notions of God to semantics; characterizing the idea of the efficacy of the name of Jesus in baptism as deference to magical

---

[57] C.H. Yadon, "Testimony of a Good Conscience," JCM graduation address, 1978, audio recording. FC, inv.doc.no 0707-5438-35.

[58] Samuel Coleridge Taylor, *Aids to Reflection* (Princeton: Princeton University Press, 1993), p. 107. Originally published in 1825.

[59] Cleveland Becton interview, 14 April 1999. This is refuted by students who have testified they never heard anyone at JCM speak against UPC doctrine. Larry Snyder interview, 5 May 1999, Bowling Green, Kentucky.

formulas; suggesting that healing was not subsumed in the atonement; that tithes were merely an Old Testament custom; that holiness standards constituted sheer legalism; that the baptism of the Holy Spirit was not essential to salvation and tongues had no evidential value for anything spiritual; and that end-time prophecy be either ridiculed or dealt with from an historicist point of view.[60] All of these ideas were alleged to have been promoted in JCM classrooms by means of questions, open-ended discussions, or suggestive hints.[61] In some cases, notions which might seem at variance with UPC theology appeared in print. "The offense of the cross, then, is that one must be saved by faith in Calvary alone."[62] The UPC does not subscribe to a doctrine of *sola fide*, salvation by faith alone, and if the statement above indicates that conviction then a theological departure is evident. Parallel issues can also be found at CBC, even though definitive articulation can ordinarily only be established after the fact. As one former CBC faculty member put it, "it isn't our doctrine that saves us anyway; it's the finished work of Christ that saves ... all else is secondary."[63] This was a central theological principle in the Fisher colleges.

These allegations are serious. It is true that Dan Lewis openly criticized dispensational pre-millennialism in classrooms on the grounds that these were not official UPC doctrines, despite the fact that many considered them unassailably orthodox. Lewis made a significant transition in his own thinking on matters of eschatology while at Jackson. He arrived on the faculty in 1976 from Portland as a confirmed dispensationalist. However, by 1981 he had completely

---

[60] *Manual* (2014), pp. 170-171 notes a later General Board resolution denouncing the historicist or preterist position.

[61] The previous paragraph and these observations are based squarely on thoughtful comments made by David Bernard interview, 16 April 1999, Austin, Texas. Bernard clearly referred to Fisher, Lewis, and Howell but was careful not to use names and indeed never mentioned any of these men by name, preferring to characterize a group rather than impugn an individual.

[62] Dan Lewis, course syllabus, TH231 *Systematic Theology II*, JCM, p. 6. FC, inv.doc.no 0707-4786-32. Several syllabi from Lewis' courses are footnoted herein. None are dated but all may be assigned to the 1980-1 academic year. Dan Lewis, letter to Thomas A. Fudge, 27 July 2013. FC, inv.doc.no 0707-5264-34.

[63] Jerry Dillon, letter to John and Ruby Klemin, 8 January 1984, p.1. FC, inv.doc.no 0707-4796-32.

abandoned that hermeneutical position. He deliberately exposed students to a variety of eschatological options including but not limited to those advanced by many influential twentieth-century theologians such as Albert Schweitzer, Jürgen Moltmann, Rudolf Bultmann and C.H. Dodd. However, Lewis did not attempt to

2.9  Dan Lewis as a member of the     2.10  Dan Lewis, lecturing in a JCM
        JCM faculty, 1976-1981                          classroom, 1977

influence his students to adopt any particular point of view but he did intentionally not emphasize the dispensational model.[64] This perspective was made explicit in the teaching materials which stated "no attempt will be made to force students into acceptance of any particular mode of interpretation nor will there be any favoritism shown to 'pet' systems."[65]

---

[64] Dan Lewis, letter to Thomas A. Fudge, 9 May 2013. FC, inv.doc.no 0707-5025-33. Lewis adopted as a course text Millard Erickson, *Contemporary Options in Eschatology* (Grand Rapids: Baker, 1977).
[65] Dan Lewis, course syllabus for TH224 *Contemporary Eschatology*, JCM, p. 1. FC, inv.doc.no 0707-4784-34.

There were traces of other perspectives within the UPC. Historicism is a methodology applied to Christian eschatology which interprets biblical prophecy with historical events and identifies symbols with persons or societies located within history.[66] The influence of C.H. Yadon, who adopted an historicist position, hypothetically may have been a factor at JCM but it is unlikely that Yadon was particularly influential on this point since he neither taught in that area nor were his views widely known.[67] The theology faculty was solidly opposed to the UPC-endorsed Richard Heard end-time revival campaigns which came to Jackson at least three times during the Fisher years. During one Halloween season, disenchanted JCM students painted "666" on their foreheads as a parody while posters featuring people with flaming heads appeared in classrooms.[68] It is not hard to imagine that Fisher, Lewis, and Howell were secretly delighted. In his *Systematic Theology* class Lewis bluntly said he would not require rebaptism of those previously baptized in the triune formula.[69] On at least one occasion after about six "tongues and interpretations" punctuated a single service, Don Fisher told a student directly that he thought the performance was not only indefensible but ridiculous. Fisher's comment was on the grounds that what had occurred that night was contrary to scripture.[70]

Two further examples illuminate Fisher's independence of mind. The phenomenon of speaking in tongues or glossolalia was doctrinally prescribed and according to the UPC constituted initial

---

[66] Prominent advocates include Joachim of Fiore (*c.* 1135-1202), Martin Luther (1483-1546), Heinrich Bullinger (1505-1575), Thomas Goodwin (1600-1680), Matthew Henry (1662-1714), and William Miller (1782-1849). Within the UPC, one might include C.H. Yadon, Wayne Nigh, and Clinton Brown (ill.4.3, p. 151).

[67] Yadon's views were later condemned under a prohibition of preterism ratified by the General Board in 2005. *Manual* (2014), pp. 170-171.

[68] April Purtell interview 16 January 1999, and Dan Lewis, letter to Thomas A. Fudge, 6 February 2013.

[69] Mark Roberts interview, 5 May 1999.

[70] Larry Snyder interview, 5 May 1999. The Fisher comment came during a music conference in March 1981 at the Jackson Convention Center. During that same service, Howell expressed his discontent, Fisher told Tom Fred Tenney it was wrong, the latter just shook his head, Thomas Craft stood on the stage and made no effort to intervene. Jim Wilkins interview, 1 May 1999, Cleveland, Tennessee.

evidence for spirit baptism. One of the requirements for holding the office of student body president at CBC was spirit baptism with the evidence of other tongues. Eric K. Loy, the last person to hold that position, had never spoken in tongues. Don Fisher was aware of this but did not interfere in Loy's election.[71] CBC students have noted that he taught that an individual was filled with the Holy Spirit at repentance and upon acceptance of Christ as Lord and Savior.[72] Fisher publicly asserted that speaking in other tongues was not the sole or even the most important basis for confirmation or belief in the indwelling of the Holy Spirit and furthermore was not the distinguishing mark of a true Christian.

Around 1973, his oldest daughter struggled with her inability to speak in tongues. Fisher told her that the primary indication or evidence of the Holy Spirit was enumerated in scripture as love, joy, peace, patience, kindness, goodness and so on (Galatians 5:22-3). Since he perceived these in her she did not need to worry about speaking in tongues.[73] Such advice was definitely not sanctioned by the UPC, so Fisher's pastoral approach was unorthodox according to UPC standards. His youngest daughter Ronna also had similar difficulties relating to the spiritual emphases fostered within the UPC and she found the level of emotionalism in the south utterly incomprehensible. This produced a great deal of fear as well as disconnection. Unfortunately, Fisher seems either to have been unaware of this or unable to address the situation with his youngest daughter.[74]

In terms of water baptism and implicit concepts of baptismal regeneration and the idea of remission, C.H. Yadon was adamant: "the blood is not in the water" and neither he nor men like Harry Fisher believed it was necessary for one to be baptized in order for

---

[71] Eric K. Loy interview, 17 July 2005, Spokane, Washington.
[72] Audrey (Zapalac) Greer, letter to Thomas A. Fudge, 24 September 2013. FC, inv.doc.no 0707-5334-34.
[73] Don Fisher, untitled sermon at Christ for the People Community Church, 30 November 1983, Vancouver, Washington and Susan (Fisher) Paynter interview, 24 January 1999, Vancouver, Washington. By extension, Fisher's father testified he received the Holy Ghost when he gave his heart to Christ in 1930 at age 14. Harry Fisher interview, 8 December 2000. There was no reference to tongues or initial evidence doctrine.
[74] Ronna (Fisher) Russell interview, 20 July 2013.

sins to be remitted.[75] That was a theological conviction widely
maintained in the old PCI tradition. Fisher stood in that stream of
thought. It cannot be gainsaid that Fisher and his colleagues,
especially C.H. Yadon, Dan Lewis, and Joseph Howell, believed
that what was distinctive to the UPC was not necessarily essential to
historic Christianity. This failure to identify one with the other was
at the heart of the opposition to Fisher's efforts at Jackson and
Portland.

Reflecting on his tenure at CBC, C.H. Yadon publicly declared
that what frustrated him most were faculty meetings wherein
additional rules and regulations were drawn up.[76] Fisher was also
not much of a defender of some of the more rigid lifestyle rules and
regulations which UPC Bible colleges typically required of students.
For example, at CBC in 1982, practically every previous rule was
eliminated save for curfew (loosely enforced) and students not
being in the housing facilities of the opposite sex, which in practice
was a matter of personal honor as opposed to strict policing and
which became less and less a feature of the college culture. At JCM,
a group of students once went off to see a football game. When this
infraction of college rules was discovered it fell to Don Fisher to
deal with the matter. He gathered the offenders together and gave
them a "good going-over" and finished up by saying, "boy, I wish I
could have been there with you."[77] Examples could be multiplied.
Under his successor's administration at JCM, the policy was to
"catch them in sin" and the attention paid to students was more
concerned with moral surveillance than education of the examined
faith.[78] Fisher did not subscribe to denominational positivism – the
idea that everything endorsed by the UPC must be true or followed
because it is UPC. Instead, he tended to encourage critical thinking
on virtually everything. New faculty members at CBC in 1981 sold
their televisions to avoid causing conflict. Don Fisher later told
them he took no note of trivial matters like televisions and whether

---

[75] Jewel (Yadon) Dillon interview, 2 January 2001, Caldwell, Idaho and Harry
Fisher interview, 8 December 2000.

[76] Noted in C.H. Yadon, "The Will of God Today," sermon in the JCM chapel,
12 November 1980, audio recording. FC, inv.doc.no 0707-5511-35.

[77] Gene Dillon interview, 3 August 2013, Caldwell, Idaho.

[78] Gene Dillon interview, 3 August 2013.

they owned one or not was of no concern to him.[79] There were concerns over Fisher's policy of little to no supervision of college students but he was not only immune to persuasion, he refused to take advice on the matter and accused his detractors of disloyalty.[80]

Another anecdote provides some nuance for questioning the position assumed by Fisher and some of his colleagues with respect

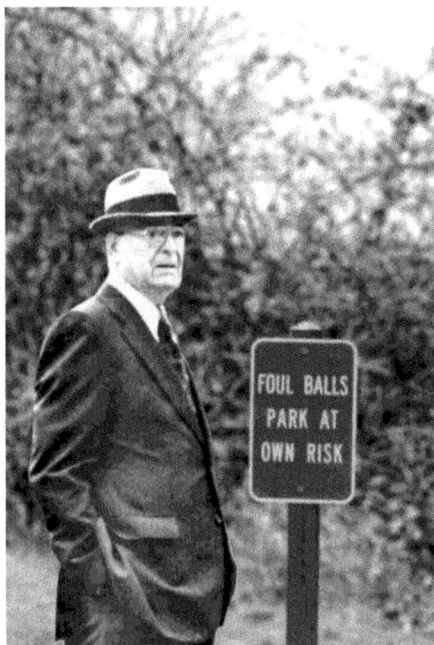

2.11  C.H. Yadon, on Strawberry Island, Washington
around the time he made the "foul ball" comment in 1976

to the prevailing climate within the UPC. In 1986, there was a breakfast gathering of some members of the Yadon family in Caldwell, Idaho at the home of Norman Rutzen. During that breakfast an informal conversation about Pentecostalism in general ensued. In that conversation C.H. Yadon commented drily "we hit

---

[79] Barbara Wasmundt interview, 3 October 2013, Dallas, Oregon.

[80] Both David Reynolds and Wanda Calder met with Fisher to express their reservations but were sharply rebuffed. David Reynolds interview, 12 August 2013. Others had concerns about the lack of regulations. Darline (Kantola) Royer interview, 15 August 2013.

a foul ball and we've been playing out of bounds ever since." The
comment referred to the origins of Pentecostalism going all the way
back to the early revivals at Azusa Street in 1906 Los Angeles, and
Yadon's point was that since the original premise was technically a
foul ball, everything thereafter was doubtful and in fact out of
bounds and until the "game" could be resumed in fair play territory,
there would be continued serious, ongoing, unresolved, theological
challenges.[81] Yadon's point was that Pentecostalism has too often
been woefully short on theology and long on experience. Indeed,
Pentecostalism appears to have built its theology upon experience.
However, experience is subjective and responses to experience are
equally subjective and therefore this constitutes an insecure basis
upon which to theologize. Pentecostalism has too often been
predicated on a self-centered approach to religious practice. This
implies that both God and considerations of truth are secondary.[82]
The notion of the "foul ball" must be understood as an operative
principle or assumption in the approach to theology undertaken by
some at JCM and CBC during the Fisher years. For those on the
other side, it was the Trojan horse (Fisher and friends) that created
the "foul ball," and it was the misguided reformers who needed to
return their game to fair play territory.

It was common knowledge that after three well-reported years,
Fisher's last two years on the Jackson administration, beginning in
1979, had been marked by increasing controversy and conflict.
Faculty members at JCM such as Joseph Howell and Dan Lewis
were suspected (rightly) of deviating from UPC orthodoxy (ill.2.12,
p. 70). Lewis and Howell were interested in the idea of truth rather
than UPC distinctiveness and organizational loyalties. Once again,
we see evidence of a general aversion to denominational positivism.
By consequence, the direction naturally led away from the UPC.
Fisher was well aware of their directions and proclivities and was
the enabler of what happened at Jackson. Howell was a central
character in this drama, noting "I was the devil at Jackson," and
accepts responsibility for what happened there, though he is also

---

[81] Vern Yadon interview, 6 December 2000, Bothell, Washington, who was
present at that gathering and participated in the conversation.
[82] H. Terris Neuman, "Anti-Intellectualism and the Bible College" *Faculty Dialogue*
18 (Fall, 1992), p. 141.

certain he had Fisher's approval and at no time did he operate outside his contractual obligations.[83]

Others were absolutely certain that Don Fisher knew exactly what was going on and approved it.[84] For example, it was Don Fisher who encouraged Lewis and Howell to revise their courses and to reconsider their pedagogical approaches. Under his express direction and approval, professors such as Howell and Lewis rewrote course descriptions, and undertook new emphases in their teaching. Fisher had numerous face-to-face meetings with his faculty members wherein changes in curricula were discussed. By 1979, Fisher was actively fostering and providing direction to the various academic changes which were being implemented. A number of those courses, including *Romans, Church History, Systematic Theology, Hermeneutics,* and *Eschatology,* were completely overhauled at Fisher's direction. He proofread each revised course description and discussed content with Howell and Lewis. Bringing C.H. Yadon on faculty was a deliberately-conceived strategy by Fisher to inculcate a moderate PCI-type ethos into JCM. "Don [Fisher] was never 'led,' he always did the leading."[85]

Fisher did not often go on record theologically, but a measure of his orientation can be gauged from what Lewis and Howell were doing in terms of teaching and educational philosophy.[86] There are several points to be considered.

First, the curriculum of the School of Theology was reviewed and revised. It was Joseph Howell without doubt who provided the

---

[83] Lewis notes that Howell was the academic mind behind the JCM approach and Fisher was the facilitator. Dan Lewis, *The Journey Out of the United Pentecostal Church* (Troy: MI: By the author, 1994), p. 31. FC, inv.doc.no 0707-4800-32. Howell's "radicalism" prompted Lewis to take the theoretical ideas promoted by Howell and apply them to UPC doctrine. In that sense, Howell was a significant catalyst. Joseph Howell interview, 21 April 1999. Howell made the "devil" comment to the author on 19 April 1999 during a telephone conversation.

[84] Jewel (Yadon) Dillon, Jim Wilkins, Dan Lewis, Joseph Howell, April Purtell, Mark Roberts, Larry Snyder, Thomas L. Craft, Donna Fisher, Gene Dillon, and Skip Paynter are among those with Fisher at JCM who have confirmed this statement.

[85] Dan Lewis, letter to Thomas A. Fudge, 13 September 2013. FC, inv.doc.no 0707-5304-34.

[86] Mark Roberts interview, 5 May 1999 and Larry Snyder interview, 5 May 1999.

intellectual basis for a new direction.[87] In retrospective, Howell's formulation was the charter of the Trojan horse within which Don Fisher had boldly ridden into Jackson. Second, in 1979, the college

2.12 JCM faculty, 1979. *Front row:* Sharla Young, Don Fisher, Donna Fisher, Ruby Martin, Charlotte Alford, Mary Francis Craft, Thomas Craft. *Second row:* Jim Wilkins, Judy Anderson, Jewel Dillon, Wayne Goodine, Billie Chisholm, Gene Dillon. *Third row:* Bruce Howell, Lanny Wolfe, Ron Dansby, Dan Lewis, Don Travis, April Purtell. *Back row:* Elizabeth Dumas, Jeff Switzer, Jackie Stricker, Mark Roberts, Denny Hahn, Nancy McCraw. Joseph Howell joined the faculty later that year.

catalogue was restructured and perhaps the most telling indication of direction was spelled out in the written purpose or mission statement of JCM under the title "The Reasoning behind the Reasoning."[88] Several statements therein underscore the direction Fisher had pointed JCM. The most important was the unambiguous declaration that students had to be trained to think for themselves. Fisher deliberately assembled members of the theology faculty who

---

[87] Joseph Howell interview, 21 April 1999. Howell was asked by Fisher to consult on these revisions.

[88] *Jackson College of Ministries Catalogue* (Jackson, MS: JCM, n.d.), p. 4. The year is 1979 and the author, though not noted in any way, was unquestionably Joseph H. Howell. FC, inv.doc.no 0707-4672-34.

were highly regarded with a modicum of theological sophistication. Dan Lewis was a "fantastic teacher" and Joseph Howell was considered "brilliant."[89] Both men were highly respected and widely regarded as equally dynamic and very effective teachers.[90] Third, new courses or newly restructured courses such as *Romans* (taught by Howell), in which he engaged with Reformation thought, and *Systematic Theology* and *Hermeneutics* (both taught by Lewis) did not follow traditional UPC syllabi and therefore raised many questions among students, especially when this was compounded by a sermon preached by Dan Lewis on Galatians wherein Lewis simply concluded one was saved by faith.[91] Lewis ignored the texts normally prescribed for teaching theology in UPC colleges and adopted books that must have surprised those who read them carefully.[92] Howell also taught church history and this, in his own view, was perhaps the most subversive thing he did at JCM because he demonstrated that Oneness Pentecostalism was only one idea within Christian history and something of a johnny-come-lately.[93]

C.H. Yadon taught the same thing with respect to church history. "We Pentecostals ought to inform ourselves a little more about church history. There have been some people on this earth that loved God before we ever showed up. And you read about John Hus. You read about the Waldensians and others ... Martin Luther ... History is full of this."[94] Yadon also lectured on doctrine at Jackson prior to 1979, encouraging similar breadth.

That encouragement was soon active engagement. Joseph Howell had read the works of Karl Barth, Dietrich Bonhoeffer, John Wesley, H.R. Niebuhr, and Martin Luther, was influenced by the thought of Søren Kierkegaard, used the methodology of historical criticism, taught kingdom theology which ran counter to

---

[89] Thomas Craft interview, 20 April 1999.

[90] David Wasmundt interview, 3 October 2013, Dallas, Oregon.

[91] Jim Wilkins interview, 1 May 1999.

[92] For example, Donald G. Bloesch, *Essentials of Evangelical Theology*, 2 vols (San Francisco: Harper & Row, 1978). Useful comments in Dan Lewis interview, 6 April 1999. Bloesch (1928-2010) was an influence on Lewis.

[93] Joseph Howell interview, 21 April 1999.

[94] C.H. Yadon, "Fire That Will Never Go Out," sermon at the Idaho District camp meeting, 22 July 1982, audio recording. FC, inv.doc.no 0707-5512-35.

dispensational thought, and he generally introduced a hitherto
unknown level of scholarship into the UPC. He also admitted he
was actively ignoring apostolic Pentecostal categories in his research

2.13  Joseph H. Howell as a member of the JCM faculty, 1979

and teaching.[95] Howell's acumen was so highly regarded that it was
reported that in his spare time he amused himself by reading
Bultmann![96] Some students found this environment "intellectually
exciting."[97] The acrimonious Missouri Lutheran Seminex affair,
which had erupted publicly just prior to all this in St. Louis, was
also predicated at least partially on discontent over faculty using
historical-critical methodology.[98] Similar concerns were coming to
the surface within the Southern Baptist Convention at the same
time. In all three cases, theology was a catalyst for reform as well as
repression. In some specific episodes, the madness of theology
predominated and tensions escalated. Fourth, and additionally, the
theology faculty proposed the establishment of a new journal which

---

[95] Joseph Howell interview, 21 April 1999.
[96] Larry Snyder interview, 5 May 1999. It is doubtful that a single UPC minister in
the 1970s had read the works of German theologian Rudolf Bultmann (1884-
1976) or could articulate any aspect of his theological system.
[97] Stan Blevins interview, 11 April 1999, Indianapolis, Indiana.
[98] Tietjen, *Memoirs in Exile*, p. 98 and Zimmerman, *A Seminary in Crisis*, pp. 9, 28,
144, 164, 173-186, 280-328.

was to be called *Dialogue VI*. The proposal generated a rumor which one faculty member reported: "I heard lip that things were going to 'blow you out of the saddle.'"[99] Its intended program was so controversial that even C.H. Yadon considered it too provocative, and predicted an unhealthy backlash were it to go forward.[100] In other words, Yadon was sufficiently shrewd to realize the eventual implications of the theological program already in motion at Jackson. The theological implications of the Yadon influence (which Fisher embraced), and the teaching methodologies of Howell, Lewis and some of their colleagues, were bound to result in a collision of significant magnitude not unlike the one that occurred two decades earlier in Mississippi between two quite different cultural approaches and theological schools of thought represented by C.D. Soper (1909-1991) and men such as J.E. Anderson (1905-1981) and M.D. Padfield, Jr.[101] Between Soper and Fisher there were other tensions and conflicts, one of which resulted in the resignation of James Molter (1911-1997) as president of PBI amidst allegations of unfair dealings by the Mississippi District Board.[102]

There is no question that the strongest formative influence on Fisher had been exerted by C.H. Yadon.[103] Some of Fisher's colleagues in education had also been similarly shaped. "Whatever significance the Northwest had on me was largely due to a single man, C.H. Yadon ... I certainly was influenced by Yadon."[104] Many of Fisher's faculty colleagues at Jackson as well as students and

---

[99] *The Diary of Jewel (Yadon) Dillon*, entry for 27 March 1980.

[100] Thomas Craft interview, 20 April 1999 and Lewis, *The Journey Out*, pp. 33-34.

[101] Soper was asked to resign from PBI in 1960 on account of doctrinal weakness and when he offered qualifications was terminated. C.D. Soper, undated letter addressed to "The Board of Trustees Pentecostal Bible Institute" and Resolution of the Board of Trustees, 30 June 1960. FC, inv.doc.no 0707-2272-16 and FC, inv.doc.no 0707-2273-16. Anderson was superintendent of the Mississippi District from 1957 to 1970 and Padfield was later the national Superintendent of Education for the UPC. Padfield's life ended in obscurity.

[102] Reflected in Ruby Martin, letter to Edwin Judd, 10 May 1968. FC, inv.doc.no 0707-5150-34.

[103] Yadon likewise exerted a powerful influence on Fisher's father. Harry Fisher interview, 8 December 2000.

[104] Dan Lewis, letter to Thomas A. Fudge, 9 May 2013. FC, inv.doc.no 0707-5025-34.

other individuals connected to JCM gave witness that Fisher was neither conservative nor a conformist. That character was attributed at least in part to the consistent Yadon influence. Fisher's education

2.14 Dan Lewis, Don Fisher, and C.H. Yadon
in Jackson, Mississippi, late 1970s

at Cascade College in Portland doubtlessly was formative in that it exposed him to a wider evangelical emphasis and the broader scope of Christian history and thought. The prevailing theological orientation at Cascade College was Wesleyan and the school was related to the Evangelical United Brethren.[105] Don Fisher's ideas about education as well as theological convictions were shaped at Cascade College in those post-CBC years. Apropos to the UPC, Fisher was described as a man ahead of his times in terms of vision, ideas, methodology, and practice. In 1982, CBC graduating senior David Brown remarked that Fisher was at least fifteen years ahead of his time. Similar comments could be advanced from the Jackson context.

---

[105] Roderick T. Leupp, letter to Thomas A. Fudge, 16 September 2013. FC, inv.doc.no 0707-5221-34. Leupp's father Thomas A. Leupp (1922-1991) was president of Cascade College from 1961 to 1966.

During Fisher's tenure, a statement was made at JCM that the college intended to become "the Harvard of Pentecostalism."[106] His vision clearly included the raising of academic standards.[107] Fisher attempted to secure the services of CBC graduate Rich Mincer as Dean but this was thwarted by Nathaniel Urshan. Fisher later told Mincer he wanted to shift JCM into a more significant academic orientation based upon intellectual honesty.[108] It was clearly this motivation which guided faculty selection during the Fisher years at JCM.[109] Fisher encouraged questions and allowed boundaries to be challenged to an extent that southern UPC culture simply could not tolerate.[110] He believed fervently that religious organizations were "so fat with theology, religion, creeds, and dogmas" that they were liable to give birth to the Antichrist.[111] That critique included the UPC. Ultimately, JCM became renowned not for its theology program but for its music department. Impatience and arrogance caused mistakes and the failure to achieve the goals envisioned by Fisher, Lewis and Howell prompted one JCM faculty member to conclude "we blew it."[112]

The contemporary rumors that Fisher was quite at odds with many of the UPC's distinctive teachings, while at JCM are given strong support by later anecdotal evidence. On one occasion during the 1979-80 academic year, Ken Ramella, a senior student, preached on the peace of God during one of the regular services in the JCM chapel. By all accounts the sermon was well structured, argued, sound, but was quite uncharacteristically, in the preaching context of the UPC, rather subdued. The usual Pentecostal responses of

---

[106] Loren Yadon interview, 26 July 2013.

[107] Jewel (Yadon) Dillon interview, 24 July 2013, Caldwell, Idaho.

[108] Rich Mincer interview, 27 September 2013, Caldwell, Idaho, reflecting on an April 1979 conversation.

[109] "I am not interested in the traditional 'Bible school' framework. It has outlived its day. I feel JCM has, by and large, put away much of the traditional trappings that became an empty sacrament to one generation of people (my generation)." *The Diary of Jewel (Yadon) Dillon*, typed, supplementary, entry for 29 January 1980. FC, inv.doc.no 0707-5142-34.

[110] Thetus Tenney interview, 6 June 2013.

[111] Don Fisher, "The Will of God is Sanctification," sermon at McCormick's Creek, Indiana, 1975, audio recording. FC, inv.doc.no 0707-5441-35.

[112] Jewel (Yadon) Dillon, letter to Jim Wilkins, 29 September 1981.

clapping hands, holding one's arms up, calling out, saying "Amen" or "preach brother" were not evident. There was apparently little emotion either on the part of the preacher or the gathered congregation. The student concluded the homily and sat down. The chapel was silent. Fisher, who happened to be sitting in the rear of the chapel, suddenly jumped to his feet, tore off his suit jacket, and ran down the aisle swinging his jacket over his head and shouting. He ran to the platform, still swinging his jacket, grabbed the microphone and screamed into it with a deliberately muffled and incoherent voice. The startled audience followed every move. Fisher then stopped, put his jacket back on and calmly asked the congregation, "Now which one of us said anything?" His point, a critique of "anointed" Pentecostal preaching, was lost on no one.[113] Fisher's reaction mirrored that expressed in the sentence C.H. Yadon sometimes said: "the problem with a lot of preachers is they expect a dollar's worth of shout out of a nickel's worth of truth."[114]

At a JCM faculty meeting during the 1980-81 academic year, Thomas Craft, supported by Lanny Wolfe, confronted the faculty with concerns that there was insufficient response during church worship. Don Fisher threw cold water on the inquiry by asking why people were looking at others when they were supposed to be engaged in worship. In a separate meeting involving Craft, Fisher, Howell, Lewis, Mark Roberts, and Jim Wilkins, Craft raised concerns over the lack of enthusiasm for the Richard Heard end-time prophecy revival campaigns, the more subdued nature of the chapel services in the preceding year, and related matters especially, as Craft put it, in light of the fact that the men in that meeting seemed to be raising dozens of questions among students but providing no answers.[115] Pastors complained to T.F. Tenney about the nature and extent of questions that students brought with them from JCM.[116] The differences between services in the JCM chapel and those held at the college church "contrast almost to the point

---

[113] Larry Snyder interview, 5 May 1999 who was in the JCM chapel on that occasion. The story has been corroborated by Skip Paynter interview, 24 January 1999, Vancouver, Washington.
[114] Jerry Peden interview, 19 July 2002, Lincoln, California.
[115] Jim Wilkins interview, 1 May 1999, and Dan Lewis interview, 6 April 1999.
[116] Thetus Tenney interview, 6 June 2013.

of contradiction."[117] Indeed, the point was made that the teachings of the church and those at the college were "totally opposite."[118] The college stressed intellect while the church appeared committed to emotion.[119] The final Richard Heard crusade in 1981 exposed these differences and represented the antithesis of the theological inquiry going on in the college.[120] Student cliques, loyal respectively to Don Fisher or to Thomas Craft, began to develop. There were Craftsmen and Fishermen.[121] Even faculty and staff were caught up in the struggle.[122]

2.15  James K. Stewart, in Columbus,     2.16   Stewart lecturing at CBC,
         Ohio, around 1979                              February 1982

Within the United Pentecostal Church in the 1970s it is possible to identify at least several ministers whose thinking exceeded the

---

[117] Joseph Howell interview, 21 April 1999.
[118] Thomas Craft interview, 20 April 1999. This was especially apparent from 1979 onward.
[119] Karissa (Fisher) Hopkins interview, 15 August 2013.
[120] Stan and Sandra Blevins interview, 11 April 1999, Indianapolis, Indiana.
[121] Mark Roberts interview, 5 May 1999.
[122] "I think someday I'll have to choose between these to [sic] men, I pray not. It's eating them both up alive – me too, and I'm sure others." *The Diary of Jewel (Yadon) Dillon*, entry for 8 October 1980.

boundaries of the denomination. These include James K. Stewart (1935-1986), J.T. (Jesse Truman) Pugh (1923-2010), T.F. Tenney, C.H. Yadon, and Don Fisher. These same men were noted for encouraging others to think, for raising questions, but also for retreating to the security of the church when students or colleagues began to press issues too far. Some of them even warned against asking too many questions. These retreats left the ones challenged to think without direction, guidance, or answers. Some considered this unfair.[123] It is not persuasive to include Fisher among those who raised questions and then withdrew. The program within the School of Theology at JCM and the general ethos at CBC suggests that Fisher provided structure, direction, and guidance to those who chose to engage in the examined faith. This can be argued on the basis of the course work supervised by Joseph Howell and Dan Lewis. This approach ran counter to the general trends in UPC education which consistently encouraged indoctrination rather than open inquiry.[124] As the fifth-century bishop of Auvergne once declared "it is dangerous to tell the truth."[125]

At the same time that Fisher and his colleagues were shaking the foundations in Jackson, there were growing concerns among pastors in Portland about what was being taught in classrooms at CBC.[126] During the crisis in the Missouri Synod Lutheran Church (which led to the establishment of Seminex in 1974), an intentional fact finding committee was convened in 1971, to determine exactly what was being taught at Concordia Seminary in St. Louis.[127] This so-called "Blue Book" played a decisive role in the affairs leading to the creation of Seminex. Over a three-month period, between 11 December 1970, and 6 March 1971, faculty members were formally interviewed and these testimonies were recorded. A summary was then submitted to the church authorities including the seminary's

---

[123] Loren Yadon interview, 26 July 2013.

[124] Anne Wilkins, "The Alternative Christian School Education" *CBC Jubilation* 14 (No. 4, 1980), pp. 1 and 3.

[125] Sidonius Apollinaris, *Epistulae*, ed., W.B. Anderson (London: Heinemann, 1936), 4.22.5.

[126] Gary Gleason interview, 7 January 2000, Oregon City, Oregon.

[127] Known as the "Blue Book" on account of its cover, this lengthy report appears as an appendix in Zimmerman, *A Seminary in Crisis*, pp. 199-444.

appropriately named "board of control."[128] One can only speculate on what might have been revealed had Thomas Craft elected to follow a similar model at Jackson or if the Washington and Idaho Districts had undertaken an investigation of CBC faculty during the Fisher years.

A few years after the height of theological controversies at JCM and CBC, another of the UPC Bible colleges undertook an investigation. They mandated, in terms of salvation, that the concept of grace must conform to the understanding articulated in the UPC's "articles of faith," that only the Acts 2:38 doctrine should be tolerated or taught, that speculation about the possible salvation of non-Oneness people should not be discussed in the college, and that holiness standards were to be fully upheld.[129] That posture stood counter to the philosophy advanced by Fisher and his colleagues which cannot by any calibration be regarded as an *apologia* for the Acts 2:38 doctrine. As Joseph Howell put it, "Our understanding of theology pivots around our key proof text: Acts 2:38. This passage is not only viewed as the final word on New Testament salvation, it is often treated as the only word. But the sermon of Peter on Pentecost is not summarized by his final proclamation of repentance, water baptism, and Holy Spirit indwelling."[130] Don Fisher did not directly challenge the hoary Acts 2:38 hermeneutic but at the same time he was unwilling to force scripture, theology, and history within its narrow parameters. At the heart of the escalating controversy in Portland were definite issues of theology, "the quarrelsome old woman," and the specific model of education endorsed and advanced by Don Fisher and his colleagues. It is to this important second consideration we now turn our attention.

---

[128] The report has been published as an appendix in Zimmerman, *A Seminary in Crisis*, pp. 155-196.

[129] Clearly articulated in an official letter from district superintendent Paul Price to all ministers in the Western District, 7 March 1994. FC, inv.doc.no 0707-0081-01. See Fudge, *Christianity without the Cross*, p. 174.

[130] Joseph Howell, "Essentials of Faith," undated typescript, p. 1. FC, inv.doc.no 0707-3054-21.

2.17 Don Fisher teaching students (Gregg Calder, Daniel Sirstad, Lori Falwell, Kim Simmons, and Ruth Caldwell) in the CBC courtyard, Spring 1982

2.18 Don Fisher with JCM students, *c.* 1979

# 3

# Education and its Enemies in the UPC

*Seeking truth is not a trade capable of supporting a man;*
*for a priest it is the greatest danger.*[1]

The practice of education under Don Fisher actively explored the question of whether it was possible to be both United Pentecostal and intellectual with integrity. That examination produced a crown of thorns which pressed upon the brow of its several wearers and eventually caused splits in two colleges. Efforts to explore questions of history, theology, and truth were routinely dismissed when outcomes strayed from UPC orthodoxy. Church apologists argued the "ultimate conclusions can be rejected on a scholarly yet biblical basis."[2] The crux of conflict in the LCMS and in the SBC was firmly rooted in theology and theological method. Alarm was most pronounced in the colleges and seminaries. Both issues were paralleled at Fuller Seminary and in the United Pentecostal Church.

The seeds of Fisher's later outspoken criticism of certain aspects of Pentecostalism were apparently beginning to sprout an early crop even while he was at Jackson. This critique, as the years at CBC demonstrate, was not limited to emotionalism in worship or what some might call religious enthusiasm. Before the dust had settled over the remains of CBC, Don Fisher was widely considered a heretic for reasons that were rooted in his approach to theological inquiry within the context of formal education. Don Fisher was uncomfortable with the limits of reform maintained within the UPC, first at Jackson and then at Portland. Theological limitations

---

[1] The quote comes from the journal of Alfred Loisy (1857-1940). Loisy, *Choses Passées* (Paris: Nourry, 1913), p. 305; entry for 9 April 1904. For his tumultuous career see Francesco Turvasi, *The Condemnation of Alfred Loisy and the Historical Method* (Rome: Edizioni di storia e letteratura, 1979).

[2] David K. Bernard, letter to Kenneth B. James, 18 September 1985 referring specifically to Dan Lewis' essay "Escape from History" noted below on p. 292.

indicated theological possibilities. For example, what is theologically and practically possible? These questions were predicated upon an *a priori* assumption that theological understanding should not be limited by the opinions of others in past generations, no matter how sacrosanct such views may have been. Howard Goss agreed. Theoretically, nothing was beyond the realm of critical examination. In practical terms, as Hamlet put it, "There are more things in heaven and earth, Horatio, than are dreamt of in your philosophy."[3]

3.1   Gene Dillon and Dan Lewis discussing theology, JCM, *c.* 1978

One of the currents in the initiatives at Jackson and in Portland was that truth was not something to memorize, protect, or even claim. Truth simply could not be fenced, crystallized, or possessed.[4] Instead, truth was direction, something to pursue, a goal to strive for. "The spirit of the gospel is contrary to that ultra-serious arrogance which claims the finality of truth for any of our statements or confessions about truth."[5] Some advised, "Be attentive, be intelligent, be rational, be responsible, develop and, if necessary, change."[6] Part of Fisher's philosophy of education can

---

[3] William Shakespeare, *Hamlet*, Act 1, scene 5, lines 187-188.
[4] Enumerated in C.H. Yadon, "The Will of God Today," sermon in the JCM chapel, 12 November 1980, audio recording.
[5] Don Fisher, sermon "Jesus is a Festival," Christ for the People Community Church, 24 June 1984, audio recording.
[6] Bernard Lonergan, *Method in Theology* (New York: Herder & Herder, 1972), pp. 53-55, 231-232.

be read in official publications. For example, an advertisement titled "Responsible Freedom in a Context of Faith" characterised the college as a place to ask questions. "An education begins with questions, not answers. What do you believe and why? ... At Cascade we encourage questions that lead to discovery. Probing, searching, evaluating are all part of the learning process. Don't let our openness surprise you. Freedom always starts with questions and choices ... Are you ready for the responsibilities of freedom and faith?"[7] The idea of ignoring traditional or established answers and instead beginning with questions situated the approach at CBC on a different plane than elsewhere in the UPC. During the fall term of 1980, Thomas Craft told the JCM faculty that questioning, critical thought, and open inquiry was dangerous.[8] This unmistakable emphasis on questioning and critical thinking later promoted at CBC appears to replicate the ethos evident at JCM.[9] Critical thought implies open-ended inquiry and a willingness to follow the evidence wherever it might lead. Fisher wanted a thoroughly explored and academically vetted faith, based on the results of questioning rather than the uncritical assimilation of pre-packaged church-endorsed answers. The reliance on answers created an impediment to change, eliminated ambiguity, and generally ruled out the imperative of essential disobedience or active compromise when open inquiry encountered aspects of incompatibility within the tradition or structure. Purity was imperilled by curiosity.[10]

The Missouri Synod Lutherans, the Southern Baptists, and some at Fuller Seminary had similar anxieties to those expressed by Craft. By contrast there was an implicit Jeffersonian element in Fisher's philosophy of education. "I have sworn on the altar of God eternal hostility against every form of tyranny over the mind of man."[11] The freedom to think at JCM was not just thinking

---

[7] *The Cascadian* 16 (No. 3, 1982), p. 8. FC, inv.doc.no 0707-4760-32.
[8] Lewis, *The Journey Out*, p. 35.
[9] Lewis, *The Journey Out*, pp. 22-26.
[10] Thomas A. Fudge, "Obrana 'Kacírství': Teoretické pojednámí" *Medievalia Historica Bohemica* 9 (2003), p. 308.
[11] Thomas Jefferson, letter to Benjamin Rush, 23 September 1800 in Dickinson W. Adams, et al., eds., *Jefferson's Extracts from the Gospels: "The Philosophy of Jesus" and "The Life and Morals of Jesus"* (Princeton: Princeton University Press, 1983), p. 320.

about the UPC, or theology, but was rather more holistic and robust aimed at encompassing thinking about attitudes, values, one's own spirituality, and much more.[12] Faith was not knowledge or a certainty of truth which needed protection. Fisher, and his colleagues, including C.H. Yadon, Joseph Howell, Dan Lewis, and Jerry Dillon, were less concerned with defending particular doctrines than they were with hearing the word of God. The educational climate at CBC encouraged the removal of intellectual taboos and cultivated the idea that no subject was too sacred to be examined and intellectual adventure should never be considered too dangerous to undertake. At CBC there was no disconnect between the devotion of faith and intellectual exploration and wide-ranging inquiry. Don Fisher emphasized balance and agreed with United Pentecostals on the matter of accepting Jesus into one's heart as a place for beginning a spiritual life but he went farther in actively urging his students to accept Jesus into their minds as well. He was quite convinced that the life of the spirit could not be developed outside the life of the mind and that the general Pentecostal ethos, which subscribed to the "feeling was believing" point of view, was inadequate.

Don Fisher and C.H. Yadon never accepted an overarching UPC metanarrative and they stood on the conviction that there was an evolving as well as a plural, or diverse, character implicit in the movement. Accordingly, the ethos cultivated by Fisher held that no one could lay legitimate claim to a better, greater, or more comprehensive grasp of theological truth or doctrinal purity. Any attempt to unravel the complexities of UPC psychology must begin with the staunch conviction of doctrinal purity and unquestioned truth which is assumed and asserted throughout the denomination. This assurance tends to blur the distinctions between intellectual inquiry, models of education, and religious practice.[13]

C.H. Yadon was on public record stating that the United Pentecostal Church had no "experts" in the areas of holiness or

---

[12] Skip Paynter interview, 24 January 1999.
[13] The definitive study of the larger themes is George M. Marsden, *Fundamentalism and American Culture* (New York: Oxford University Press, 1980) but see also Nathan O. Hatch, *The Democratization of American Christianity* (New Haven: Yale University Press, 1989).

theology.[14] Fisher agreed. Therefore, the study of theology at CBC was a process to enter into, not a program to be completed. It was a lifelong experience, not a discrete methodology or course to be mastered. It was a holistic approach to God and to spirituality, rather than the robotic mechanical adoption of doctrine. Professors actively taught that it was insufficient to accept Pentecostal doctrines without prior serious investigation.[15] From a theoretical point of view, Fisher and Yadon conceived of education as an essential process wherein all claims to universality were open to challenge.[16] Both men agreed that truth was not knowledge and that the gospel could not be distilled into a system of salvation. They were adamant that it was the gospel which saved. A system cannot save even if the system in question was Acts 2:38. What they advocated was "freedom from ecclesiastical manipulation."[17] Moreover, C.H. Yadon once advised a UPC General Board meeting that it was impossible to discover truth by voting on it. Consensus on General Conference resolutions had nothing to do with truth, per se, and the fact that a majority vote might carry a point of view did not therefore establish the motion as truth. Don Fisher agreed, and his philosophy of education reflected that conviction. Yadon's point of view was often expressed publicly.

> I wish we knew how to deal with our problems other than resolutions. I wish we had the spiritual capacity to rise in the Spirit and move into situations that would liberate the body of Christ from its small entanglements and set us free in the Spirit to flow in the will of God and righteousness. It is a sign of weakness when

---

[14] For example, during a general conference sermon, Yadon said "we have no experts. There are no holiness experts in the United Pentecostal Church. There are no theological experts." C.H. Yadon, sermon "Areas of Ministry that Cannot be Numbered," General Conference, Louisville, Kentucky, 1974, audio recording (FC, inv.doc.no 0707-2581-19), and in a written response paper published in *Symposium on Oneness Pentecostalism 1986* (Hazelwood, MO: Word Aflame Press, 1986), pp. 312-313.
[15] Dan Lewis, course syllabus, TH230 *Systematic Theology I*, JCM, p. 1. FC, inv.doc.no 0707-4785-32.
[16] Joyce Appleby, Lynn Hunt, and Margaret Jacob, *Telling the Truth about History* (New York: Norton, 1994), p. 3.
[17] Don Fisher, sermon "The Resurrection," Christ for the People Community Church, 27 May 1984, audio recording.

every time we have a problem arise we have to try and plug a loop hole. That is not the answer.[18]

It was the perceived answer for the United Pentecostal Church, the Missouri Synod Lutherans, and the Southern Baptists. Nevertheless, Yadon had a point which has too little been seriously considered by movements like the UPC. Should boards comprised of men who are neither scholars nor in possession of an academically informed mind be allowed to decide theological issues? There are unavoidable problems of some gravity when doctrine is subjected to the shifting power of politics. What justification can there be for men without proper theological training to make decisions on theology? The answer can only lie in a misguided assumption that the Holy Ghost will overshadow those men and at the proper moment illuminate their minds and provide knowledge and wisdom ordinarily only achieved through many years of concentrated discipline. An appeal to Luke 12:11-12, wherein one will be aided by the Holy Spirit at any given moment on what to say, is illegitimate, takes the text away from its context, and violates basic principles of interpretation.

Don Fisher was suspected of liberalism at best and heresy at worst on account of his insistence on critical thought, his love of "intellectual challenge," and his Northwest roots, all of which were considered a liability in the south. The PCI/PAJC divide remained at issue.[19] In retrospect, family members considered the decision to go to Mississippi a "huge mistake."[20]

In general, the word liberal is related to the idea of freedom. Intellectually, this means the freedom to think. Educationally, it implies the unrestricted freedom to follow truth wherever it leads. Institutionally, it is freedom from all forms of interference from those in authority who might seek to control or suppress the direction, pace, or end result of such thinking or exploration. (The United Pentecostal Church, the Southern Baptist Convention, and the Missouri Synod Lutheran Church are religious systems to which

---

[18] C.H. Yadon's sermon, "Four Pillars of our Faith," at the annual Idaho District camp meeting, 1980, audio recording, is one example.

[19] Thetus Tenney interview, 6 June 2013.

[20] Ronna (Fisher) Russell interview, 20 July 2013 and Karissa (Fisher) Hopkins interview, 15 August 2013.

conscience is enslaved and by which the spiritual pilgrimage of the human soul is controlled. The freedom encouraged at Jackson and in Portland ran counter to that system.) Theologically, it is freedom from all declared rules and restraints which seek to protect particular ideas or doctrines. The liberal insists upon freedom to inquire and conclude. The liberal approach is to write theology in pencil rather than in pen. Don Fisher promoted the gift of freedom. This was reflected also in his preaching. "When we live by the creeds, and confessions, and the dogmas of a religious system instead of by faith in the transcultural risen Christ, we become pitiful slaves to sectarian bigotry."[21]

Joseph Howell's articulation of the purpose of the college in Mississippi summarized Fisher's philosophy in Portland perfectly.

> Christian education is serious business ... the "right spirit" cannot make up for obvious shortcomings in our academic approach ... *Education* ... is not the filling of an empty vessel with facts, but rather *the training of an individual to think for himself* ... pre-packaged ... "pat answers" and "how to" courses ... never meet the needs ... The responsibility of the Christian educator is to produce students capable of self-criticism, both on individual and corporate levels. We need ministers who can discriminate between cultural baggage and the lifting up of Biblical principle. The *offense* of Christianity is the cross, *not our offensive attitudes or defences* ... The immature Christian may wish to secure himself in the anti-intellectualism of unquestionable beliefs. But today it is essential that we know not only what we belive [sic], but also why we believe it ... demanding the toleration of interpretive differences. The challenge of the Christian educator is to point the student to the path of the "examined life" ...[22]

In other words, the most important work in this life consists in healing the eyes of the heart so that one might see God.[23] The formulation is Augustinian but the goal was evident in the Fisher programs at Jackson and in Portland. Fisher wanted a program of

---

[21] Don Fisher, sermon, "The Resurrection," Christ for the People Community Church, 27 May 1984, audio recording.

[22] From "The Reasoning behind the Reasoning," *Jackson College of Ministries Catalogue*, p. 4. This resonated with Fisher who often referred to "eternal babies" unless Christ was formed within. Don Fisher, "Let Christ be Formed in You," sermon at McCormick's Creek, Indiana, 1974, audio recording.

[23] Augustine, Sermon 88.6 in PL, vol. 38, col. 542.

education, rather than indoctrination, featuring open inquiry rather than blind adherence to prescribed doctrine.[24]

One of the great themes of Fisher's philosophy of education was the idea of balance in the relation of faith and inquiry. This emphasis was stressed both at Jackson and in Portland and students were challenged by the ideal.[25] JCM students once gave Fisher a desk-sized set of scales in recognition of his consistent reference to need for balance. Fisher also recognized the importance of the intellect.[26] He brought these conceptual approaches along with him to Portland and the college advertised its mission with terminology such as "CBC does more than give pat answers. We prepare you for the tough questions."[27] Fisher claimed that the approach at CBC was Biblical before it was denominational, though that distinction carried little weight in the evolving development in the Northwest.[28] This approach did not imply either a pre-determined or intentional jettisoning of tradition or core beliefs. The educational initiative championed at Fisher's CBC was predicated upon giving new life to old texts wherein the process of faith, living, and learning mediates a new message while preserving old truths. Fisher was fond of quoting the New Testament admonition about moving on from basic ideas to maturity and, instead of setting down the foundations time and time again, proceeding onto new ground (Hebrews 6:1). "Let us get out of the dark dungeons and sepulchers of religious tradition and fear and guilt of condemnation."[29] Fisher agreed that confronting and conquering fear led to freedom.[30] Initial experience and fidelity to unexplored ideas is insufficient. Fisher insisted that "some people expose their spiritual immaturity so often they ought

---

[24] Fisher articulated this to Jerry Peden during a private conversation in Hot Springs, Arkansas around 1979. Jerry Peden interview, 19 July 2002.

[25] For example, Daniel R. Sirstad interview, 26 August 2013.

[26] As noted previously, Fisher may have been influenced on this point, in part, by books he read. See, for example, Liddy, *Will*, p. 32.

[27] Full page advertisements in *Ensign*, vol. 29 (1982), p. 173 and *CBC Jubilation* 16 (No. 1, 1982), p. 8.

[28] Lewis J. Davies, letter to Winfred E. Toole, 2 May 1978, pp. 2-5 indicates the futility of that distinction. See Appendix 3, pp. 428-432.

[29] Don Fisher, sermon "The Resurrection," Christ for the People Community Church, 27 May 1984, audio recording.

[30] Liddy, *Will*, pp. 9-11, 138-139.

to be embarrassed."[31] Something of particular depth and substance was required. "The emotional infant is not made emotionally mature by the infilling of the Holy Ghost."[32] Fisher perceived that both history and education, based upon critical thinking, delivered people from the mind-numbing influence of ages past and times present. On the surface it sounded entirely reasonable but the encouragement towards critical thinking contained dangerous bacteria generated by the Trojan horse.[33]

Some of his protégés and colleagues describe Fisher as a "great teacher in terms of prodding students to think," while colleagues characterized him as possessing a singularly brilliant mind capable of profoundly communicating ideas and mounting intellectual challenge.[34] His enemies believed it was their duty to instil answers so thoroughly and so absolutely in their constituencies that there would be no further need for questions at all.[35] This was a modern reflection of a much older and deeply-rooted concern. "Physicians embrace, lawyers value, and philosophers accept whatever leads to the renewal of their disciplines, we theologians alone stubbornly protest and hate what is good for us."[36] Don Fisher was convinced that the UPC concept of training only served to create a certainty and a security that simply did not exist. Regardless of the subject, a true believer will firmly dismiss any evidence or argument which is

---

[31] Don Fisher, "The Will of God is Sanctification," sermon at McCormick's Creek, Indiana, 1975, audio recording.

[32] Don Fisher, "Evangelization of the Subconscious," sermon at McCormick's Creek, Indiana, January 1975, audio recording. FC, inv.doc.no 0707-5440-35. See Appendix 2, pp. 404-427.

[33] Darline Kantola, "Education Can Be Dangerous" *CBC Jubilation* 13 (No. 3, 1979), p. 1 argued that the Bible clearly teaches the importance and necessity of education. FC, inv.doc.no 0707-5099-33.

[34] Mark Roberts interview, 5 May 1999, Cheryl (Johns) Crousser interview, 1 October 2013, Newberg, Oregon, Thetus Tenney interview, 6 June 2013, and Kristi (Eld) Christensen interview, 4 October 2013, Caldwell, Idaho.

[35] Comments to this effect were made to Dan Lewis by Mississippi pastor Doyle Spears anonymously referenced in Lewis, *The Journey Out*, pp. 25-26 and identified in Dan Lewis, letter to Thomas A. Fudge, 17 April 2013.

[36] Erasmus, *"Apologia in Novum Testamentum,"* in Joannes Clericus, ed., *Desiderii Erasmi Roterodami Opera omnia*, 10 vols (Leiden: Petrus van der Aa, 1703-6), vol. 6, p.\*\*2. The translation is cited from István Bejczy, *Erasmus and the Middle Ages: The Historical Consciousness of a Christian Humanist* (Leiden: Brill, 2001), p. 116.

contrary to his or her convictions. It is easier to embrace as true those things one hopes or wishes are true.[37] But is this faith? Applying these principles to education, Fisher was maligned for teaching students to "critique" and allegedly at his suggestion did not involve themselves in worship or in the sermon. The critical spirit was considered quite inappropriate.[38] The relation of faith and inquiry was one of those significant areas wherein Fisher repeatedly underscored balance. Whereas for Don Fisher, anti-intellectualism bordered on sin since God created the human mind,[39] for his detractors, original research became original sin.[40] At the same time that Fisher was coordinating an intensive critical thinking program men in other denominations were calling into question the basis of academic freedom and the ongoing investigation of truth. "The search for truth has ended. I hold truth in my hand and it is the word of God. It is the Bible. We have found the truth. You need search no more. Zero in on it, hide it in your heart that you might not sin against God. That which is not of faith is sin."[41]

Fisher's response to all of this, especially the fear engendered by such openness, was to say, "I believe in the work of the Holy Spirit in the life of the believer." He also refused to tell people what the "truth" was, preferring, instead, to encourage others to search out the truth for themselves. When asked what truth was, Fisher replied that he could state what he believed truth was, but that would be of little value to the questioner. Pilgrims had to come to the truth through their own search and not merely reiterate what someone else declared to be truth.[42] As the CBC college crest boldly proclaimed, truth was mighty and would prevail. Fisher was certain that truth was neither a statement nor a doctrinal position.[43] It was

---

[37] The idea is stimulatingly explored in Chet Raymo, *Skeptics and True Believers: The Exhilarating Connection between Science and Religion* (New York: Walker, 1998).

[38] Thomas L. Craft interview, 20 April 1999.

[39] Neuman, "Anti-Intellectualism and the Bible College," p. 140.

[40] Kelly, *History and Heresy*, p. 148.

[41] From James Robison, "Satan's Subtle Attacks," sermon at the SBC pastors conference, Houston, Texas, 10 June 1979, in Shurden and Shepley, eds., *Going for the Jugular: A Documentary History of the SBC Holy War*, pp. 24-38, at pp. 31-32.

[42] *The Journal of Thomas A. Fudge, 1980-1985*, entry for 19 September 1983.

[43] Don Fisher, sermon "Jesus is a Festival," Christ for the People Community Church, 24 June 1984, audio recording.

infinitely greater than all human formulations. He could harken to the sage advice about learning and faith discovered on the journey.

> He [Jesus] comes to us as one unknown, without a name, as of old, by the lakeside he came to those men who knew him not. He speaks to us the same words, follow me, and sets us to the tasks which he has to fulfil for our time. He commands. And to those who obey him, whether they be wise or simple, he will reveal himself, in the toils, the struggles, the conflicts which they shall pass through in his fellowship. And as an inexpressible mystery they shall learn in their own experience who he is.[44]

3.2 The CBC crest

This was unsettling to some students. After coming to CBC, some students compared Fisher to his predecessor R.V. Reynolds and concluded that the former did not hold strongly enough to certain fundamental beliefs of the UPC. This was based chiefly on Fisher's refusal to provide direct answers in the classroom, especially when pressed on questions about salvation. Dan Sirstad, Dennis Spanner, and especially Tom Winchell considered this tactic evasive and it raised questions about Fisher's commitment to UPC orthodoxy.[45] However, the programs facilitated by Fisher mandated that religion "must inherently leave room for self-criticism. Any faith which refuses to carefully and regularly examine itself is subject to error of

---

[44] Albert Schweitzer, *Geschichte der Leben-Jesu-Forschung* (Tübingen: J.C.B. Mohr (Paul Siebeck), 1906/1984), p. 630. First complete English edition *The Quest of the Historical Jesus*, ed., John Bowden (Minneapolis: Fortress Press, 2001), p. 487.
[45] Joe Higgins interview, 4 October 2013 who had first hand knowledge.

the most disastrous qualities."[46] Elsewhere, Charles Hodge once famously remarked that during his tenure at Princeton of nearly sixty years his colleagues "were not given to new methods or new theories. They were content with the faith once delivered to the saints. I am not afraid to say that a new idea never originated in this Seminary."[47] Don Fisher boldly asserted there was something new at Jackson and also in Portland. What he meant was there were new ideas being considered, new approaches tried, a new quest for truth, new emphases, a new desire for the kingdom of God, and a new commitment. This was not simply a commitment to preserve and conserve the faith as codified by the movement, but a new purpose altogether like that articulated in Fisher's mid-1970s addresses at the campus ministry retreats convened at McCormick's Creek, Indiana coordinated by Tom Hare, Pat O'Pelt, and Rich Mincer (see ill.3.15, p. 138). Here one might think especially of his provocative sermon, "Evangelization of the Subconscious," coupled with the academic methods introduced by Howell and Lewis. He emphasized the necessity of the formation of Christ within the believer but warned that sometimes people thought they were pregnant with God when in fact the growth was simply a tumor. What has been formed in the student or pilgrim? Fisher placed emphasis on Christ formed within not the development of a substitute.[48]

The concept and practice of academic freedom within the traditional American Bible college is fraught with a myriad of difficulties. Within the educational constellation of the United Pentecostal Church, the concept has little currency. The same could be said for Southern Baptist and Missouri Synod Lutheran Church colleges and seminaries. UPC Bible schools exist mainly in a defensive stance, with avowed aims of protecting old truths and keeping new ideas at bay. Academic freedom may be understood as the freedom to explore truth and all topics in a responsible manner. It includes the right of students and faculty to think. In application, teachers have the freedom to inculcate this ethos into the hearts

---

[46] Dan Lewis, course syllabus for TH222 *Bible Introduction and Interpretation*, JCM, p. 1. FC, inv.doc.no 0707-4781-32.

[47] A.A. Hodge, *The Life of Charles Hodge* (New York: Scribner's, 1880), p. 521.

[48] Don Fisher, "Let Christ be Formed in You," sermon at McCormick's Creek, Indiana, 1974, audio recording.

and minds of their students and to actively encourage them in this regard. Teachers have a duty to equip students for the demands of critical thought. Conversely, the student should have the freedom to think for himself or herself and to disagree with the point of view advanced by the teacher or embedded in the curriculum.[49]

Between 1940 and 1970, a major shift could be observed within church-affiliated institutions in the United States. Most religious institutions of higher learning no longer sought exemptions from the principle of academic freedom set out in the 1940 *Statement* of the American Association of University Professors.[50] The United Pentecostal Church could not be included in that number. Within the UPC, there is no statutory obligation incumbent upon any college to promote, defend, or practice academic freedom. The role of the colleges and any accompanying mission statements do not include a commitment to the values of academic and intellectual freedom or indeed of institutional autonomy. A Bible college of the UPC does not accept that, in the exercise of academic freedom, college faculty may sometimes act as critics of prevailing ideas or modes of thought within a larger intellectual constituency. It would be impossible to find evidence which even tacitly acknowledged or affirmed the legitimacy of such activities and certainly there would be neither encouragement nor support for any academic staff engaged in them. For example, theological inquiry involving Biblical criticism and methodology which did not intentionally defend assumptions of inerrancy came under sharp censure in the Missouri Synod and in the Southern Baptist Convention.[51]

Historically, within the United States there have been many controversies over the application of academic freedom. Supreme Court decisions have ruled that institutions may control not only what is taught but how subjects are taught.[52] Federal courts have

---

[49] For conservative elaboration of academic freedom, with reference to religious based institutions, see Holmes, *The Idea of the Christian College*, pp. 61-76.

[50] "1940 Statement of Principles on Academic Freedom and Tenure with 1970 Interpretive Comments," AAUP Policy, Tenth Edition. Interpretive comment no. 3, p. 5 at http://www.aaup.org/report/1940-statement-principles-academic-freedom-and-tenure.

[51] Zimmerman, *A Seminary in Crisis*, pp. 53, 55-60.

[52] Examples include 354 U.S. 234 (1957) and 438 U.S. 265 (1978).

maintained that academic freedom is not the purview of the professor but belongs to the institution.[53] Basic to legal thinking is the conviction that academic freedom should be protected and is considered a special aspect of the First Amendment which opposes laws that impose orthodoxy on classrooms.[54] The UPC agrees that the college, by virtue of its endorsement by the denomination, controls the nature of education, and that they have the exclusive right to determine the curriculum and the scope of inquiry: First Amendment doctrines are inapplicable. It is doubtful that Don Fisher agreed with a strict interpretation of this position although possibly he did not perceive his administration at Jackson or Portland as being antithetical to the aims of the UPC.

It is useful to recognize that orthodoxy is often created or reasserted in confrontations with heresy. The changing of the guard at Jackson in 1981 was not the first time in UPC college history that academic guns and doctrinal mercenaries were hired to settle all issues of uncertainty and diversity, and to nail down all corners of precious truths which may have come loose during previous examinations. The work of such men, though understandable from a denominational point of view, precludes creative thinking and scholarship, and severely impairs academic freedom. Similar impulses characterized both the Missouri Synod and the Southern Baptist Convention. There was considerable fear concerning the openness to questioning which Fisher and his colleagues endorsed. Many of Fisher's detractors, both at Jackson and later at CBC, considered that the role of the UPC Bible College was to instil answers, not to provoke questions. Fisher saw it differently.

A medieval theologian and Augustinian prior once pointed out that Christians have an obligation to make an effort to understand what they believe.[55] There does not seem to be any evidence that Don Fisher claimed any special revelation or made assertions to being led by unique insight. His faith stance was not blind belief in authority or an uncritical acceptance of a previously established doctrine. He does not seem to have retreated into abstract believing

---

[53] One example is civil action no. 3:07-cv-00646-HEH, *Stronach v. Virginia State University*, 2008.

[54] *Keyishian v. Board of Regents*, 385 U.S. 589 (1967).

[55] Richard of St. Victor, *De trinitate*, in PL, vol. 196, col. 889.

in order to avoid thinking. He remained open to argument and was not susceptible to blanket appeals to authority. For Don Fisher, truth and knowledge were better than ignorance. Inquiry was better than dogma. Education led to understanding and the strongest faith was the examined faith. The unexamined faith was worthless and holding to doctrines which had not been subjected to the lamp of critical analysis had nothing to do with authentic spirituality. In this approach to education, history and theological knowledge were not simply a passive acceptance of evidence and doctrinal formulations but an intentional motivation into active critical interpretation. This was reflected in JCM course syllabi. "Faith which is accepted *a priori* is not faith at all, but obtuseness."[56] Fisher's focus was on youth and missions, anchored in education and the examined faith, and coupled with wholeness and a passion for the kingdom of God while carefully preserving the virtue of balance.[57]

If a fifth rider were to join the Four Horsemen of the Apocalypse, it would certainly be ignorance.[58] Fisher must have been disconcerted to discover that by 1981 the Pacific Northwest was under the sway of sectarian orthodoxy. The last years of CBC focused on defeating this fifth horseman, though Fisher could not have been unaware of the ultimate defeat of his previous liberalizing campaign at JCM. It may be telling that Fisher suggested to John Klemin (1926-1995) that he appoint former CBC faculty member Jerry Dillon as the class teacher for college-age attenders in the Vancouver UPC church and that if he did so, Fisher would be keen to recommend students choose Vancouver as their church home.[59] Clearly, Fisher perceived Dillon as a sort of theological ally in much the same sense as the core of the JCM theology department had been. The JCM program had not been, from an institutional perspective, very successful. Even stalwart supporters

---

[56] Dan Lewis, course syllabus for TH222 *Bible Introduction and Interpretation*, JCM, p. 1. FC, inv.doc.no 0707-4781-32.
[57] April Purtell interviews, 16 January 1999 and 13 April 2013.
[58] Jaroslav Pelikan, *The Idea of the University: A Reexamination* (New Haven: Yale University Press, 1992), p. 21.
[59] John Klemin, letter to Jerry Dillon, 8 July 1982, p. 1. FC, inv.doc.no 0707-4792-32. Confirmed in Jerry Peden interview, 19 July 2002. Dillon had enjoyed a close relationship with the college for more than two decades by that time.

considered the theology faculty ill-advised. They did not represent sufficient theological breadth, were very young, and none had deep roots or commitment to UPC doctrine. These factors alone created immediate suspicion and incompatibility in the deep south UPC culture. Don Fisher had been unwise in assembling such a group.[60] There are suggestions that Fisher surreptitiously appointed men such as Lewis and Howell who were notoriously weak on the message, who did not believe (at least sufficiently) UPC doctrine, and who contributed to a serious lowering of standards. The true views of these men were deliberately concealed from Thomas Craft in another manifestation of a theological Trojan horse.[61]

3.3  Mark Roberts as a member
of the JCM faculty, 1980

Eventually, several of those faculty members came under sustained theological suspicion. Dan Lewis resigned. Joseph Howell was so severely censured that he too departed. Mark Roberts lasted less than one additional semester before he was brought up on a "heresy examination of sorts" and fired for maintaining "false doctrine." In the midst of the abrupt exodus, JCM student Robin Wentworth stood up publicly and read aloud Joseph Howell's

---

[60] Thetus Tenney interview, 6 June 2013. There is agreement that Fisher may have erred in striving to accomplish his educational goals in the south. Dan Lewis, letter to Thomas A. Fudge, 17 June 2013. FC, inv.doc.no 0707-5067-33.
[61] Arless Glass interview, 24 September 2013.

charter on the "reasoning behind the reasoning." Critics were silently appalled.[62] Thomas Craft asserted he intended to fire all of them but their resignations pre-empted that plan.[63] David Bernard and Allan Oggs (1935-2007) replaced the heretics and endeavored to re-establish orthodoxy.

The arrival of Allan Oggs was contentious. First, Thomas Craft did not consult with the College Board over the appointment. Men such as John Kershaw and T.F. Tenney expressed concerns.[64] Second, Oggs cultivated a climate of suspicion concerning those who remained whom he considered part of the Fisher regime. "Learn to cover your tracks" was Oggs' philosophy and he enjoined more than one member of the JCM community to do just that. Plausible denial and a lack of transparency began to characterize operations at JCM under Oggs, factors which hitherto had not been evident under Fisher. There were rumors of unethical management, as well as a growing distrust between faculty and administration. David Bernard was generally regarded as trustworthy and a man of integrity but there remained lingering concerns over Oggs.[65]

The departure of Fisher and his colleagues precipitated a veritable sea change at JCM.[66] Not only did classroom content and administrative policy change, visible evidence of the Fisher years disappeared *damnatio memoriae*.[67] Photographs of many graduates from the previous years were removed from their public places never to be seen again.[68] Numerous tape recordings of sermons, seminars, and lectures delivered by Don Fisher and Dan Lewis were destroyed. The college library was purged of questionable texts

---

[62] Lewis, *The Journey Out*, p. 39. Mark Roberts interview, 5 May 1999. Hugh Rose advised Howell to leave JCM. Thomas Craft interview, 20 April 1999.
[63] Thomas Craft interview, 20 April 1999. It has been suggested the Jackson heretics were asked to leave. David Bernard interview, 16 April 1999. This is inaccurate save for the exception of Mark Roberts.
[64] Gene Dillon interview, 3 August 2013.
[65] Much of the opinion about Oggs was reflected in Jewel (Yadon) Dillon interview, 24 July 2013 and Oggs counseled both she and Stan Blevins to cover their tracks. Stan Blevins interview, 11 April 1999.
[66] Joseph Howell interview, 21 April 1999.
[67] Latin phrase originating in the Roman Empire meaning the "condemnation of memory" wherein steps were taken to erase all trace of one from history.
[68] Jewel (Yadon) Dillon interview, 24 July 2013.

added to the collection by Howell and Lewis. Oggs seemed quite determined to get rid of all those faculty and staff members previously associated with Don Fisher.[69]

In principle, Fisher agreed with liberal thinkers such as William Cowper Brann (1855-1898) who deplored the narrow approach of protecting rather than exploring truth claiming that those who discouraged inquiry were the sort who "could look thro' a keyhole with both eyes at once." Brann characterized Baylor University, a Baptist-sponsored institution in Waco, Texas, as a conglomeration of "intellectual eunuchs, who couldn't father an idea if cast bodily into the womb of the goddess of wisdom."[70] The practical application of Fisher's views required that rather than simply denigrating and dismissing the doctrine of the Trinity, for example, classes at CBC featured debates wherein both Oneness and Trinitarian positions were carefully examined and compared.[71] Even earlier, CBC classrooms featured three or four interpretations of doctrines like the new birth.[72] The school of thought within the United Pentecostal Church represented by Fisher, seems to have maintained the view that truth was most likely to be discovered if people were enabled to investigate and debate differences without censure. The perennial question is: who has the right and the authority to determine truth? The church says it has, while the reformers believed this was feasible by means of education. Such views precipitated never-ending struggles and heresy hunting.

JCM and CBC students were introduced to the world of serious academic scholarship by means of assignments which required them to read and analyse works of proper religious thinkers, and thereafter prepare what was referred to as formal theological textual reviews.[73] In these assignments, students were exposed to a wide

---

[69] Gene Dillon interview, 3 August 2013. These exercises in purging JCM were orchestrated with the active support of Allan Oggs and Mary Francis Craft.

[70] William Cowper Brann, *The Complete Works of Brann, the Iconoclast*, 12 vols (New York: The Brann Publishers, 1919), vol. 10, pp. 80 and 82.

[71] *The Journal of Thomas A. Fudge, 1980-1985*, entry for 18 October 1982, referring to the Doctrine III class taught that term by C.H. Yadon.

[72] Edwin Judd interview, 10 April 1999.

[73] *The Journal of Thomas A. Fudge, 1980-1985*, numerous entries including 4, 5, 7, 8 and 30 November 1982.

variety of theological opinions, exegetical methods, and doctrinal formulations across the spectrum of Christian thought. There was no judgment from those teachers about what was heretical, acceptable, or orthodox. Instructors at other UPC colleges insisted they likewise "allowed all views to be expressed" in the classroom.

Upon close examination there were two differences when compared to the open questioning encouraged and permitted by Fisher. The critical difference was that in other UPC colleges instructors would present and affirm the views of the UPC whereas Fisher would leave matters unresolved. The other difference was that Fisher and his colleagues are alleged to have engaged in concerted efforts to make disciples of certain individuals privately and these secret tutorials called into question the ethics of education.[74] *Prima facie* evidence is scarce. It is true that on one occasion two students at Jackson accompanied Joseph Howell to Northminster Baptist Church to hear the renowned John Claypool preach. Those students, however, intercepted Howell on his way and prevailed upon him to take them along. It would be quite disingenuous to suggest that Howell was luring young people into Trinitarian traps. A number of other students, including Robin Wentworth, Jeffrey Derr, Chris Klug, Ed Moehlenpah, Larry Snyder, and Stanley Blevins used to go book-shopping at the Reformed Theological Seminary bookstore with Joseph Howell, who would actively suggest appropriate buying selections. In the spring of 1981, Howell prepared and distributed an annotated reading list for those interested and serious about theological inquiry.[75] Howell's list was comprehensive, balanced, and markedly anomalous for the UPC at that time. His list covered biblical studies (including exegesis, hermeneutics, Greek and Hebrew language guides), theology, church history, ethics, and apologetics. On his list one encounters Robert W. Funk, Otto Eissfeldt, Gerhard von Rad, Martin Noth, Rudolf Bultmann, Albert Schweitzer, Karl Barth, C.H. Dodd, Joachim Jeremias, Dietrich Bonhoeffer, John A.T. Robinson, Søren Kierkegaard, Reinhold and H. Richard Niebuhr,

---

[74] David Bernard interview, 16 April 1999.
[75] Joseph H. Howell, "Suggested Booklist for Theological Students." On page one of this twenty page typescript we find reference to Jackson College of Ministries and the date 12 May 1981. FC, inv.doc.no 0707-4691-32.

Paul Tillich, Emil Brunner, Joseph Fletcher, John Calvin, Martin Luther, introductions to historical critical methodology, form criticism, redaction criticism, and much more. Judged against UPC orthodoxy, Howell's booklist was both utterly incomprehensible and entirely unwholesome. It was a more suitable library for a sophisticated theologian within a heretical Trojan horse. Moreover, he did not include a single Word Aflame Press publication. A hundred years earlier, Howell might have been brought up on heresy charges. There were off-campus Bible studies with Joseph Howell after the latter left JCM but there is no evidence that these occurred while he was a member of the faculty. Similar meetings convened after his departure, were initiated by students.[76] However, neither Howell nor Dan Lewis, as a rule, concluded lectures or classroom discussions with an affirmation of UPC doctrine after presenting alternative theological positions.[77] Nevertheless, it does not seem plausible to argue that Fisher was running an intentional covert operation aimed at undermining the UPC.

Among the issues were theology and the approaches to theological investigation. Concerns over the uses of the historical critical method within conservative branches of Christianity were widespread in the 1970s. The methods of historical criticism subject the topic under investigation to rigorous analysis without dogmatic presuppositions or limitations, and must be predicated on robust impartiality. Since there is clearly no such thing as the disinterested historian or unbiased, objective scholar, the application of these methods is a challenge for all practitioners. The historical critical method cannot accept as *a priori* that the Bible represents a collection of unified or complementary beliefs reflecting infallible truths, or that the history of theology is divine revelation or the codification of absolute truth; rather it begins from the proposition that the Bible is a summary of beliefs held by different traditions or

---

[76] Stan and Sandra Blevins interview, 11 April 1999. The group consisted of up to ten students including the Blevins', Mike Hensen, Sherri Dixon, and others.

[77] Larry Snyder interview, 5 May 1999. Snyder was one of those who went with Howell. Neither Snyder, Howell, nor Lewis recall private studies or communion services which they participated in. As for the latter, "it is something of which I was unaware and about which I am doubtful." Dan Lewis, letter to Thomas A. Fudge, 24 May 2013. FC, inv.doc.no 0707-5036-33.

communities of faith. In practice, when applied to scripture, historical criticism is distinct from the devotional uses of the Bible, does not begin with assumptions about inerrancy, plenary or verbal inspiration, and considers the texts as products of human creation which can be investigated according to scientific principles.[78] In response to the notion that God wrote the Bible, Alfred Loisy dismissed the suggestion as a childish notion and quite absurd.[79] The roots of historical criticism can be located in the work of the Scholiasts in the ancient library of Alexandria.

If many other Bible colleges virtually ignored the methods of historical criticism, or kept such troublesome ideas locked away to save students from irreversible contamination, the theological programs under Fisher at JCM and CBC were prepared to grapple with the implications of such inquiries. One of the set texts at CBC made the matter explicit. "Historical criticism is a necessary Biblical science if we wish a faith that is neither gullible nor obscurantist ... historical criticism ... is not an evil but a necessity" and it is quite impossible to engage in proper scholarship while ignoring these methods.[80] A number of Fisher's colleagues, to greater and lesser degrees, were committed to this methodology, and they brought under the lamp of this scrutiny the texts of the Bible and the foundational texts of UPC doctrine. Joseph Howell and Dan Lewis, especially, strove to practice more responsible hermeneutics and they ventured into areas of historical-critical methodology in their teaching in JCM classrooms. Their utilization of such exegetical methods were not in themselves merely an expression of liberal theology, modernism, postmodernism, or any other ideological commitment. The methods appear to have been utilized primarily to achieve two goals. The first was a better and more responsible understanding of the Bible itself, which Howell and Lewis, together with Fisher, C.H. Yadon, Dillon, and a number of others, felt was irresponsibly handled by so many within the UPC. The second goal

---

[78] See Joseph A. Fitzmyer, *The Interpretation of Scripture: In Defense of the Historical-Critical Method* (New York: Paulist Press, 2008).

[79] Loisy, *Mémoires pour server à l'histoire religieuse de nôtre temps*, vol. 1, p. 306.

[80] Bernard Ramm, *Protestant Biblical Interpretation: A Textbook of Hermeneutics*, third revised edition (Grand Rapids: Baker, 1970), pp. 9-10. Affirmed in George Eldon Ladd, *The New Testament and Criticism* (Grand Rapids: Eerdmans, 1967).

was to locate and establish meaningful connections to historic Christianity. The scholastic research and reflection undertaken and encouraged under Fisher's administrations caused some individuals to arrive eventually at the "uncomfortable conclusion that UPC teaching was theologically inadequate and historically dishonest ... High volume and unrelenting repetition of bad hermeneutics within the UPC only underscored for us the basic conclusion that the historic church was essentially right and our mother denomination was essentially wrong."[81]

With these objectives in mind, the theological premise at Jackson and at CBC suggests something different from the conflicts noted within either the LCMS or the SBC. Inasmuch as these Christian churches already stood within the larger tradition of historic Christianity, these denominations were actively engaged in a struggle of how best to preserve that heritage while at the same time embracing academic integrity. Conservative thinkers among the Southern Baptists and within the Missouri Synod reduced such considerations to their own denominational confessions, while so-called liberals felt the imperative to widen their purview. At JCM and at CBC, the premise was different, in that men such as Howell and Lewis considered the UPC as standing outside this historic continuum and were therefore committed to finding meaningful linkages. The apparent similarities between movements within the SBC, the LCMS, and the UPC cannot be taken as absolute parallels.

Intellectually, Fisher was aware of the devastating impact the Enlightenment had on Christianity. He was not unaware of the alternatives presented by the historical critical method and while he did not personally engage with the principles and methods of historical criticism, since he did not teach theology, he did not attempt to limit its uses by Lewis and Howell. Lewis admits he described such methodology in classrooms but did not actively engage with it.[82] Fisher intentionally supported the role of reason and the intellect, and did not object to any of these methods if they led to a clearer understanding of scripture, theology, and the history of the church. He was committed to the life of the mind. Fisher

---

[81] Dan Lewis, letter to Thomas A. Fudge, 17 June 2013.
[82] Dan Lewis, letter to Thomas A. Fudge, 7 May 2013.

would have agreed with Kant that one must take risks. "Dare to know. Have courage to use your own reason!"[83] That loyalty also helps to explain why he was keen to see Jerry Dillon running the college-age education program at the church in Vancouver. Fisher was convinced that Dillon shared compatible learning values and was unafraid to grapple with difficult questions.

While Fisher may not consciously have been attempting to destroy the UPC, it is quite certain that he was adamant about the need for intellectual progress and reform. This was initiated in several ways. The King James Version was the near-universal preferred Bible in the UPC, but in the fall of 1981 all CBC students were required to purchase a copy of the recently-published New International Version of the Bible (NIV), which the college bookstore stocked. There was some grumbling about this from a few students but the NIV was required and students had no option but to comply. Don Fisher openly read the NIV while in Jackson.[84] He clearly adhered to the notion that God's word, however that should be understood, should be as immediate and fresh as the early texts were to the first Christians, unencumbered by a form of language no longer current.[85] Fisher understood that the idea of biblical inerrancy originated in the seventeenth century as a result of Protestant scholasticism and as such was a hegemonic imposition upon Christianity from the nineteenth century onwards. The Protestant churches of the Reformation had not taught it; indeed, the concept was not notionally part of the worldview embraced by the reformers. The same might be said for the patristic period or the early church. As part of the aftermath of the Enlightenment, many theologians attempted to find intellectual moorings for the faith in principles of human reason. Don Fisher held firmly to the

---

[83] Immanuel Kant, "What is Enlightenment?" in Lewis White Beck, ed., *On History* (Indianapolis: Bobbs-Merrill, 1963), p. 3.
[84] Dan Segraves, "Why I Use the King James Version" *The Pentecostal Herald* 55 (December, 1980), pp. 5-7, 11 and reprinted in his more expansive *The Search for the Word of God: A Defense of the King James Version* (Stockton: Christian Life Press, 1982), pp. 112-113 reflects a basic UPC perspective. Larry Snyder interview, 5 May 1999, notes Fisher's practice.
[85] D.A. Carson, *The King James Version Debate: A Plea for Realism* (Grand Rapids: Baker, 1979), p.102 makes that point.

authority of the Bible but considered inerrancy a modern invention
which claimed more for scripture than scripture did for itself. In
teaching courses in theology, both Fisher and C.H. Yadon reflected
this conviction. There were CBC students who believed they
refined their skills in reading and interpreting the Bible by means of
the educational approach at the college under Don Fisher.[86]

Books by the aforementioned John Claypool (1930-2005),
Bernard Ramm (1916-1992), F.F. Bruce (1910-1990), Bruce Larson
(1925-2008), and Jerry Bridges (1929–) were required course texts at
CBC. Fisher likewise recommended reading Malcolm Muggeridge
(1903-1990) and referred to him in sermons.[87] UPC publications
were markedly absent as class texts. Only books by Jet Witherspoon
(1897-1992) and George Shalm (1925-1988) seemed prominent.[88]
Claypool was a Baptist minister who later became an Episcopal
priest. Ramm was also a Baptist, who questioned flood geology and
did not accept young earth theories. He had studied with Karl Barth
at Basel in the late 1950s and had been heavily influenced by Barth's
theological approach, to the point where Ramm himself could be
considered Barthian.[89] Bruce was affiliated with the Open Brethren
but opposed the idea of dispensationalism, a hermeneutic widely
accepted within the UPC. Additionally, his book was recommended
to students on the subject that salvation was by faith alone.[90] Larson
was Presbyterian, Bridges an interdenominational Evangelical, and
Muggeridge was an agnostic who late in life converted to Roman

---

[86] Lori (Falwell) Callan interview, 23 September 2013.

[87] John R. Claypool, *The Preaching Event* (Waco: Word Books, 1980); Ramm,
*Protestant Biblical Interpretation: A Textbook of Hermeneutics*; F.F. Bruce, *Paul: Apostle
of the Heart Set Free* (Grand Rapids: Eerdmans, 1977); Bruce Larson, *The Meaning
and Mystery of Being Human* (Waco: Word Books, 1978) and Jerry Bridges, *The
Pursuit of Holiness* (Colorado Springs: Navpress, 1978). All five books were
significant texts at CBC. Fisher, sermon "Authentic Freedom," Christ for the
People Community Church, 1 July 1984, audio recording, refers to Muggeridge.
CBC students recall reading some of these authors at the college. Michael Nigh
interview, 18 August 2013, Redondo Beach, California.

[88] Jet Witherspoon, *Acts: The Amazing History of the Early Church* (Hazelwood:
Pentecostal Publishing House, 1972) and George Shalm, *Spiritual Gifts for a
Dynamic Church* (Hazelwood: Word Aflame Press, 1977).

[89] Bernard L. Ramm, *After Fundamentalism: The Future of Evangelical Theology* (San
Francisco: Harper & Row, 1983) reveals this in some detail.

[90] Dan Lewis, course syllabus, TH231 *Systematic Theology II*, JCM, p. 6.

Catholicism. None of these writers could be regarded as endorsing anything remotely United Pentecostal and each held to theological positions quite contrary to UPC doctrine. Their presence in UPC

3.4 Jerry Dillon, Business Manager and member of the CBC faculty, Spring 1977

college curricula indicated the planting of questionable seeds in the minds of students. Not surprisingly, every one of these scholars (save Muggeridge who was not a theological thinker) was on Howell's booklist. Similar materials could be found in the CBC library, which had been greatly expanded under the C.H. Yadon administration (1968-71). During the 1969-70 academic year, CBC purchased more than 6,000 volumes of mainly religious holdings to supplement the college library, increasing its inventory to more than 8,500 titles.[91] During the 1970s, non-heterogeneous theological books were deliberately added to the library.

---

[91] *Conquerors Bible College (Portland, Oregon) General Catalog 1979-1981*, p. 8. These were indirectly acquired from Cascade College (which had operated in Portland between 1918 and June 1969) at a cost of one dollar per volume. The bulk of the 30,000 volume library was acquired by Judson Baptist College on 24 December 1969. Judson was founded in 1956 and closed in 1985. I am grateful to Kris Dillon, librarian from 1969-1978, Donna Fisher, letter to Thomas A. Fudge, 14 April 2013, Darline (Kantola) Royer, letter to Thomas A. Fudge, 15 June 2013 and David Brown, letter to Thomas A. Fudge, 13 August 2013 for information. *Ensign*, vol. 23 (1976), p. 56 claims the library contained 9,000 volumes. A news

Meanwhile, Fisher's request that former CBC faculty member Jerry Dillon be appointed to the Vancouver church was acceded to, and Dillon began teaching a series on the doctrines of election and predestination to the college-age Sunday School class.[92] Based upon a Calvinist hermeneutic, this was predictably controversial, and at least one CBC student, Tom Winchell, refused to continue after a confrontation with Dillon during one of the classes wherein the idea of eternal security was discussed and Dillon quite shockingly suggested that human activity had no bearing on salvation. What was Fisher's response to this? He took the view that the strongest faith is the examined faith and that theological positions which were unable to sustain challenge were probably too frail to be worth defending. In consequence, he made no attempt to muzzle Dillon. At the same time, in doctrine classes on campus, C.H. Yadon provided students with extracts from the controversial work of the Protestant martyr Michael Servetus (1511-1553). While definitely antitrinitarian, Servetus was certainly not Oneness (as some of Paul Dugas' disciples were excitedly proclaiming) and Yadon thought it was useful to consider other points of view on theologies of God.

There were dissenters to these approaches. At Jackson, student Tommy Galloway represented a bloc of opinion which thought the school should be preparing theology students to be good preachers, not exposing them to divergent ideas and forcing them to grapple with difficult questions and rigorous academic scholarship.[93] This corresponds to the ideas set forth by UPC Bible college officials, who asserted that the single primary objective of the school was to instil in students "cardinal truths."[94] The idea of critical thinking was never mentioned. It was clear that Fisher and his colleagues were somewhat less interested in "cardinal truths" than they were in developing minds capable of intellectual discrimination and critical scholarly reflection able to formulate core beliefs. That posture

---

story put the number at 10,000. "Pentecostal Bible school marks birthday" *The Oregonian*, 3 June 1978, p. 34.

[92] *The Journal of Thomas A. Fudge, 1980-1985*, entry for 10 January 1982, notes the commencement of the study.

[93] Larry Snyder interview, 5 May 1999.

[94] For example, see R.A. Beesley, "The Importance of Bible Colleges to our Fellowship" *The Pentecostal Herald* 61 (No. 2, 1986), p. 7.

caused immediate alarm bells to sound throughout the UPC and elsewhere. Conservatives within the Southern Baptist Convention were unambiguous that the movement to eliminate liberal tendencies had no purer motive than to halt the multitudes from falling "across the precipice of eternity and into the chasm of hell."[95] Similar sentiment can be located within the UPC. This does not mean that theology professors at CBC and JCM had no regard for "cardinal truths." But it does suggest a conviction that such values should not trump proper education and critical thought.

3.5   C.H. Yadon and A.T. Morgan, Hoonah, Alaska, 1963

In 1963, A.T. Morgan (1901-1967) told C.H. Yadon and Don Fisher in Hoonah, Alaska that in his early days as a preacher he was encouraged to simply preach against things. After following this principle for some time, Morgan ran out of things to preach against. One night as he stood to deliver another sermon he noticed a man wearing white shoes so he decided to preach against white shoes.[96] C.H. Yadon, Don Fisher, and their colleagues at JCM and CBC thought the proclamation of the gospel, the kingdom of God, and the ethics of Jesus more important than attacking issues which had

---

[95] Patterson, *Anatomy of a Reformation*, p. 18.
[96] Donna Fisher interview, 7 October 2013, Vancouver, Washington.

absolutely no relation to God, salvation, or the gospel. That conviction informed their approach to education.

All of this draws attention to the objectives and role of the Bible college within the UPC. In the period up through the 1980s, there was little evidence that Bible colleges differed to any real degree from churches. It is difficult to avoid the conclusion that Bible colleges sponsored by the UPC were more concerned with appearances and impressions of spirituality than with academic advancement. Daily chapel services where attendance was required, numerous weekly church services, and Bible studies, and a regular devotional schedule were expected features, while commitment to academic formation played a rather distant secondary role.

While not discounting the importance of spiritual development, this is not the purview of a proper college. Spiritual development belongs to the role of pastors, churches, chaplains, and families, particularly parents. It is reasonable to assume that the average UPC student coming to Bible college should have attained considerable spiritual development already. If not apparent, one might question the pastors, churches, and parents which had these young men and women in their hands for close to twenty years on average. Students arriving at college who have not achieved a modicum of spiritual development are indicative of deficiencies in their spiritual formation. All too often pastors, churches, and parents wanted the Bible colleges to do their jobs. This is not a phenomenon unique to the UPC. Many theologically conservative and church-sponsored colleges have historically operated on similar unwritten policies.

When the Bible colleges agreed to take on that responsibility there were two definite outcomes: proper academic education was subordinated to secondary concerns, and the college became a type of Sunday school or Christian day care. In 1981 at Jackson, college life was almost completely swamped by pressure from the church for students to be involved for weeks at a time in the Richard Heard revival crusades. The 1981 crusade began in March and continued until May. Students were expected to go to church for every service. This was not unusual in those days. These on-going revivals were almost always anti-intellectual, embarrassing from an academic point of view, and educationally worthless. Indeed, these protracted church functions served to shelter students from ideas, critical thought, and intellectual exploration. Protracted, emotional church services at Jackson were normative.[97] Fisher considered the approach lacking the essential component of balance.

Writing from within the context of the United Pentecostal Church, Don C. Marler perceptively argued that "creating schools that are just elaborated churches is a duplication of efforts and as such is a waste of time, effort and money."[98] Others noted that in too many UPC college classrooms, students were being exposed to little more than a repetition of what had been presented in Sunday school.[99] It appears that Don Fisher had no interest in duplicating the role of the local church either at JCM or CBC and that posture generated considerable distrust. Marler's little book was read by some of the faculty at Jackson, and it should be numbered among the intellectual stimuli motivating the critical thinking impulse.[100] Likewise, Fisher was determined to greatly expand the horizons of thought. During a JCM faculty retreat, at least some faculty were exposed to "the third force" psychology of Abraham Maslow (1908-1970).[101] "Third Force" psychology relies on the premise that all people are inherently good, and that by means of a conscious evolution of attitudes, beliefs, values, and desire one can achieve a state of self-actualization wherein the individual can guide his or her own life to a meaningful and constructive end.[102] Writing nearly five

---

[97] The following is a contemporary comment from a visitor to the Jackson church. "It was a long drawn out affair. Father Craft babbled on for as long as the speaker did ... it was kind of a long affair as well. Then of course the weeping and wailing which served to elucidate the foolishness." *The Journal of Thomas A. Fudge, 1980-1985*, entries for 17 and 18 May 1984. A perennial problem within American Bible colleges is the clear lack of academic rigor. Neuman, "Anti-Intellectualism and the Bible College," pp. 135-142.

[98] Marler, *Imprisoned in the Brotherhood*, p. 31.

[99] Comments made by M.D. Padfield, UPC superintendent of the DOE, during winter term at CBC. Summarized in John Klemin, letter to the CBC board, 14 March 1974, p. 1.

[100] Dan Lewis, letter to Thomas A. Fudge, 24 January 2013 confirms that members of the JCM faculty read Marler's, *Imprisoned in the Brotherhood* and it appeared on suggested reading lists. FC, inv.doc.no 0707-4716-32. Dan Lewis, course syllabus, TH230 *Systematic Theology I*, JCM, p. 6.

[101] *The Diary of Jewel (Yadon) Dillon*, entry for 31 May 1980.

[102] See Frank G. Goble, *The Third Force: The Psychology of Abraham Maslow* (New York: Grossman, 1970). Maslow later rejected this theory.

hundred years ago, renowned Christian thinkers argued that those responsible for education could not be excused from this duty. The education of young people was considered more important than establishing cities, building castles, or attaining wealth. Without knowledge and wisdom these achievements were meaningless. Education was considered that important. Resolute determination was articulated. "If God is willing, I will deal with this issue more fully in a separate book at another time. I will really go after those shameful, despicable, damnable parents who are not really true parents at all, but instead are despicable pigs and poisonous beasts who eat their own offspring."[103] Hindering proper education was unconscionable. Fisher was not prepared to allow Richard Heard-like activities to distract students from education at CBC. There was not a single instance between 1981 and 1983 when students had to choose between academics and the demands of a local church.

The Fisher program at CBC (adapted from its predecessor model at JCM) embraced several crucial points and questions in embryonic form. These commitments formed the backbone of learning during the final years of CBC. The approach outlines the principles of a rigorous theological critical method. First, there was a deliberate exploration for the central idea of Christianity. This was not assumed to have already been articulated by means of special revelation. Second, an effort was made to explicate the meaning of salvation in the New Testament. Once again, this was not simply a doctrinal point to be adopted without the requisite inquiry and exploration. Fisher's approach always began with questions not answers. That philosophy can be observed in practice in the classes taught by Fisher, Joseph Howell, Dan Lewis, C.H. Yadon, Jerry Dillon, and others. Third, one finds evidence of an effort towards the identification of the main ideas in the New Testament. Theologically, this implied exegetical inquiry extending well beyond the hermeneutical horizon of the Acts of the Apostles. Fourth, there was a commitment to dialogue about whether there are formulas in scripture with relation to salvation, and if so, whether

---

[103] Martin Luther's preface to a German treatise on the proper structure of a Christian household written by Justus Menius, *Oeconomia Christiana* (1529). The preface appears in WA, vol. 30, pt 3, pp. 60-63.

these formulas were to be understood as general descriptions or accepted as prescriptive. Fifth, one discovers evidence of an examination of the relationship between religious practices and salvation. Sixth, there was also a rudimentary approach to a careful application of hermeneutical method. Seventh, in contrast to a great deal of doctrinal formulation within the UPC, there was an insistence upon a unified approach to Biblical theology. The priority of Acts was neither assumed nor adopted. Acts 2:38 formed neither the point of departure nor the mandatory conclusion.

Thus, within the theological approach facilitated by Fisher, the UPC plan of salvation was set aside. "The New Testament knows no 'one – two – three' plan of salvation" but rather the pursuit of salvation was an ongoing pilgrimage.[104] These same principles were applied to UPC doctrinal formulations extending even to the *Fundamental Doctrine*. The results were a remarkable openness and encouragement of theological discourse and research at CBC, and a curriculum which openly advertised "a search for 'the theological roots' of our doctrinal distinctives."[105] Fisher claimed the emphasis was educationally legitimate and balanced. It seems evident that the approach to theology and learning at Jackson and in Portland accepted as axiomatic that the authentic encounter with God preceded doctrine. This approach is consistent with the principle that the "law of prayer" is also the "law of belief." In other words, faith and religious practice precedes and illuminates doctrine, which it helps to formulate and the encounter with God becomes decisive for determining the nature of theology itself, not the other way round. In application, systems of belief should neither shape nor dictate religious experience.[106]

According to Fisher, "the one who dares to teach must never cease to learn." That statement was heard often in CBC classrooms. All of these considerations formed aspects of a commitment to the examined faith which characterized education at Jackson and later in Portland. This may be contrasted with other approaches which

---

[104] Joseph Howell, "Essentials of Faith," undated typescript, pp. 1-2.

[105] *Cascade Bible College 1982-1984 Catalog* (Vancouver, WA: CBC Press, 1982), p. 6. FC, inv.doc.no 0707-5113-34.

[106] The maxim *lex orandi, lex credendi* originates with the fifth-century Augustinian apologist Prosper of Aquitaine. PL, vol. 51, cols. 209-210.

did not regard scholarship as important but instead emphasized coming to the classroom "prayed-up."[107] Fisher "believed in a good solid education" with intentional depth, and critical thinking, and he successfully brought passion and learning together.[108] Colleagues considered Fisher both an excellent teacher and a man possessing exceptional leadership skills.[109] Under his administrations, it was expressly stated that students would be exposed to problematic issues within the UPC. These included but were not limited to discrepancies between truth and logic, ignorance concerning context, bogus typology, improper synthesis, mixed metaphors, the obscurity of Biblical language, lack of documentation for important ideas, untenable interpretations, lack of scholarship, misuse of terminology, and a lack of credibility.[110]

In contrast, UPC Bible college curricula elsewhere might mention scholarship rhetorically but generally without substance.[111] Thoughtful observers noted, even years later, "there still is a suspicion of education" and Pastor Randy Langley, preaching in a Hillsboro, Oregon pulpit declared that the more education one has the less spiritual that person is.[112] Within the SBC, professors "embalmed with the fluid of higher education" were denounced as harmful to the body of Christ.[113] Such convictions doubtlessly lay behind Fisher's comment in a faculty meeting at CBC in the fall of 1982 to the effect that the UPC knew very little about proper education.[114] As this comment reveals, Fisher became more outspoken at CBC than formerly. It was no secret that his style and methods cut across the grain of UPC tradition. His programs at Jackson and in Portland were a reaction against what he perceived

---

[107] Paul Dugas interview, 25 January 1999.

[108] Thetus Tenney interview, 6 June 2013.

[109] Roger Yadon interview, 8 October 2013, Whitehorse, Yukon.

[110] Dan Lewis, course syllabus TH224 *Contemporary Eschatology*, JCM, p. 3.

[111] For example, Harry L. Bowman, "The Aims and Objectives of Pentecostal Bible Colleges" *The Pentecostal Herald* 39 (No. 11, 1964), pp. 3 and 13.

[112] George Sponsler interview, 12 February 1999. The Langley statement was made in 1987. Dale Royce interview, 24 August 2013, Hood River, Oregon.

[113] James Robison, "Satan's Subtle Attacks," sermon at the SBC pastors conference, Houston, Texas, 10 June 1979, in Shurden and Shepley, eds., *Going for the Jugular: A Documentary History of the SBC Holy War*, pp. 24-38, at p. 27.

[114] Nathaniel Yadon interview, 15 December 2000, Vancouver, Washington.

as intellectual sterility in the UPC. He was determined to prevent irresponsible intellectual torpor. In this sense, the more liberal-arts college curriculum approach contrasted with the older traditional Bible Institute philosophy. Later views on the college thought this innovation contributed to the downfall of CBC.[115]

With reference to specific developments at JCM "[Dan] Lewis mentioned that the philosophical gap between the school and the church was widening ... I have been aware of ... an idiological [sic] flow away from the 'Bible school' concept toward a more collegiate, more quasi-seminary status."[116] Some traditionalists feared getting "someone who is all intellect and not much Holy Ghost. I for one can see the trend that is moving our people and school away from Evangelism, into intellectualism."[117] Such strangers the UPC wanted to keep out of their college classrooms. These conflicting models of education could not tolerate each other forever and as a result there was considerable kicking against the pricks. Notwithstanding this, and despite claims to the contrary, the Bible alone was not the sole text in Pentecostal Bible schools.[118] Scripture alone as an ideal is never achieved because scripture can never be alone.

Fisher's philosophy of higher education and his approach to curriculum developed early in his career as can be seen before he became a college administrator. Between 1966 and 1970, he worked at the UPC headquarters with Thetus Tenney, Jewel Dillon, and James K. Stewart in literature and curriculum development. This quartet of writers might be described as intentional dreamers who actively sought out new ways of thinking, who explored new ways of teaching, who experimented with many alternative forms of disseminating knowledge, and whose work appeared to be predicated upon a foundation of asking the type of questions that no one else did. Fisher was characterized as being very progressive in his thinking, and Stewart as possessing a brilliant mind, while

---

[115] Edwin Judd and Raymond Sirstad interviews, 10 April 1999, 27 August 2013.

[116] *The Diary of Jewel (Yadon) Dillon*, typed, supplementary, entry 29 January 1980.

[117] C.M. Yadon, letter to C.H. Yadon, 12 March 1963, which was written after the resignation of Ralph V. Reynolds from CBC, speculating on the next college president. FC, inv.doc.no 0707-1159-08.

[118] Noted in Grant Wacker, *Heaven Below: Early Pentecostalism and American Culture* (Cambridge, MA: Harvard University Press, 2001), p. 150.

Dillon (the daughter of C.H. Yadon) came from the old Northwest and PCI tradition, and Tenney was an independent thinker in her own right. Their work was bound to be controversial. Sometimes this had to do with content, methodology or even presentation. In

3.6  Thetus Tenney, Tioga, Louisiana, *c.* 1979

3.7  Jewel (Yadon) Dillon, 1947. See also ill.2.12, p. 70

the case of the latter, Tenney wrote *The Kingdom Way* at Fisher's behest. This was the first youth camp curriculum in the UPC. The cover of that publication was a psychedelic yellow, orange, green, and purple fleur-de-lis. Someone other than Fisher may have insisted upon a more basic cover design. At a camp meeting soon after publication, the presiding district superintendent publicly ripped the cover from the publication saying it was altogether inappropriate. The content was completely ignored and the work was condemned on the basis of its cover. Ironically, the work Thetus Tenney wrote had, unknown to the minister in question, been inspired by a sermon he had preached. Of course Fisher was disgusted at the failure to examine content and considered the episode another example of the emphasis upon externals and an inability to come to grips with more important matters. Some feared this quartet of thinkers and writers were in danger of being disfellowshipped. Even if overwrought, the four thinkers did generate suspicion in some quarters of the UPC.

Jewel Dillon, James Stewart, Thetus Tenney, and Don Fisher wanted to shed new light on old truths and were willing to explore

# WORD AFLAME PUBLICATIONS

## QUESTIONS AND ANSWERS from the EDITOR

D. W. Fisher

WORD AFLAME PUBLICATIONS

An ambitious program has been under way for months to bring our people a total literature supply which is *strictly Pentecostal.* The name of this new concept in the field of Pentecostal literature is WORD AFLAME PUBLICATIONS.

Our new WORD AFLAME materials are rolling off the presses. Since any new program needs to be fully explained to be understood we have prepared some simple answers to often-asked questions.

If you have other questions, please write to our office. You will receive an immediate reply.

**Q.** What department is this new literature program a part of?

**A.** WORD AFLAME is a part of the Editorial Department, UPC.

**Q.** What basic difference is this new literature going to make?

**A.** The total program, from outlines to lesson content, is prepared by Oneness Pentecostals. That always makes a difference!

**Q.** Are all ideas and plans entirely original?

**A.** Is anything new under the sun? However, you will be pleased at the many unique ways these

materials have been especially created for Pentecostal Sunday schools.

**Q.** Would you recommend switching back to our own materials even if our church is accustomed to using another company's literature?

**A.** Do you use another denomination's evangelists? teachers?

**Q.** Will these new materials be "the best on the market"?

**A.** We try harder. We have witnessed a mighty assistance from the Holy Ghost in preparation and we think you will be pleased. You can help us improve by participation and patience.

**Q.** Are some WORD AFLAME materials already being used?

**A.** No. None will be ready for use until October, 1969.

**Q.** When will we be able to see samples, and place our order for the FALL QUARTER?

**A.** Some samples are available now. Other material is rolling off the presses daily. Place your FALL QUARTER order beginning in July.

Begin planning now to place your Sunday school in *Strictly Pentecostal* hands. Order WORD AFLAME PUBLICATIONS for Fall '69.

Ordering is simple: Place your usual order through the Pentecostal Publishing House, 3645 S. Grand Blvd., St. Louis, Mo. 63118.

3.8   Word Aflame publications announcement, *Forward* 1 (No. 1, 1969), p. 17

boundaries and test new ideas and methods. Instead of simply providing basic lesson outlines which, for example, took students through a book in the Bible, these four writers sought to delineate themes and deeper meanings within the texts, without necessarily, being bound to the text. The first adult literature manual, *God's Heartbeat,* reveals deliberate higher-level thinking. At this time,

Fisher displayed a profound ability to communicate and reach people on an intellectual level. This was foundational for his later career. He strove to achieve depth in his work, advocated critical thinking, and began to demonstrate a passion for education. He began also at this time to exert significant and powerful influence on young people including Tommy and Teri (Spears) Tenney.[119] That impact on UPC youth persisted until 1983. These writers met quarterly in St. Louis, and Don Fisher was the central figure who organized and directed their activities.[120]

There was a certain amount of anxiety around Don Fisher and it seems true that there was some latent danger in what he was doing from a United Pentecostal Church organizational point of view. By way of comparison, in early twelfth-century France, mothers hid their sons, wives distracted their husbands, and companions directed their friends elsewhere when Bernard of Clairvaux came to town preaching. This was on account of his ability to persuade. Mothers, wives, and companions feared that their sons, husbands, and friends might all at once become Cistercian monks.[121] No one really knew for sure what Bernard was preaching or telling those who followed him. He was not a monk at the time and effectively was not under spiritual supervision or answerable to any direct monastic or episcopal authority. This type of successful maverick discipleship caused varying levels of alarm. The same sort of phenomenon surrounded Don Fisher. He was charismatic and effective and possessed powers of persuasion and influence. Some students were convinced "the spirit of God was on him."[122] Pastors, church leaders, and parents maintained suspicion about what he was teaching, what he permitted to be taught, the sort of questioning and inquiry he encouraged, and the influence he exerted over the young people who enrolled at JCM and later at CBC. His public commitment to freedom and openness became increasingly worrisome.

---

[119] The preceding two paragraphs have been greatly informed by Thetus Tenney interview, 6 June 2013. Others confirm Fisher's tremendous ability and creative insights. Arless Glass interview, 24 September 2013.

[120] Jewel (Yadon) Dillon interview, 24 July 2013.

[121] William of Saint Thierry, *Vita prima Bernardi*, 1:3:15 in PL, vol. 185, col. 235.

[122] Audrey (Zapalac) Greer interview, 22 September 2013.

In 1966, A.T. Morgan, then UPC General Superintendent, told Don Fisher to never commit his life to an organization. As if true to this advice, he was never a "yes" man and this created friction and brought Fisher adversaries who "fought him tooth and toenail."[123] Fisher was also unalterably opposed to certain well-worn traditions, within the UPC specifically and American evangelicalism generally. He appeared relatively uninterested in eschatology, at least as it related to the powerful and pervasive emphases of the 1970s. These emphases were summed up in the wider American church world in the wildly speculative and exegetically superficial publications of Hal Lindsey such as *The Late Great Planet Earth* (1970), and in film productions such as the popular *A Thief in the Night* (1972) and its sequels.[124] The phenomenal success of Lindsey's book might be attributed to the fact that so many people confused it with a work of science fiction.[125]

Within the UPC, the preaching campaigns of Richard Heard at Jackson in the spring of 1981 were viewed rather icily by Don Fisher, and described by Joseph Howell as based upon "horrible biblical exegesis."[126] Lewis characterized the revivals as a "mixture of fear tactics, crowd psychology, and exhibitionism."[127] Thomas Craft seems to have made the Heard crusade a litmus test of faculty support. The theology faculty, including Fisher, Lewis, Howell, Roberts, along with others such as Jim Wilkins, not only failed that test but failed spectacularly. During the protracted services, Don Fisher would sit at First Pentecostal Church and open his Bible and read. That was his way of protest.[128] Moreover, he later unofficially

---

[123] Harry Fisher interview, 3 July 2005.

[124] *A Distant Thunder* (1978) was shown at First United Pentecostal Church in Saint John, New Brunswick in the spring of 1981 in what was an unprecedented event. *The Journal of Thomas A. Fudge, 1980-1985*, entry for 18 April 1981. The same films were screened at JCM during the Heard revivals.

[125] James Barr, *Fundamentalism* (Philadelphia: Westminster, 1977), pp. 206-207.

[126] Joseph Howell interview, 21 April 1999, April Purtell interview, 16 January 1999, Skip and Susan (Fisher) Paynter interview, 24 January 1999, and a number of others, consider the Heard revivals a major turning point for Fisher at JCM serving as a major catalyst exposing unbridgeable divergences between the college and the church.

[127] Lewis, *The Journey Out*, p. 38.

[128] Larry Snyder interview, 5 May 1999.

forbade songs at CBC which tended to focus upon or emphasise the second coming of Christ, and he openly voiced his displeasure with traditional songs such as "I'll Fly Away."[129] He considered the emphasis overused, worn-out, and an excuse to sidestep proper education, robust intellectual development, critical thinking, and discipleship, while tending to trivialize the Christian life. Fisher was not about to tolerate any duplication of the Richard Heard theological orientation at CBC. There was some opposition to this general and unwritten prohibition but the matter did not become contentious at the college. There were students who had come up under strident end-time prophecy preaching who came to CBC having drunk deeply from that well but left the college years later skeptical and decidedly uninterested in those types of eschatological speculation, at least as determined by the "strict C.I. Scofield dispensational" model.[130] Fisher gave scant attention to marks of the beast, theories of one-world governments and common global currencies, 666 tattoos, speculation over the identity of the man of sin, physical manifestations of Antichrist, alignments of planetary bodies, or wistful calibrations aimed at determining when the last generation may have commenced. He even suggested leaving the celebrated works of Larkin and Scofield on the shelves.[131] He was no more interested in the apocalyptic significance of the 1947 United Nations General Assembly Resolution 181 which created the modern state of Israel than he was in the possible theological implications of the Balfour Declaration (1917). All of these were elements in UPC preaching at the time. It seems evident that Fisher subscribed neither to creationism, as defined by mainstream Evangelicalism, nor to radical eschatological speculation linked to current affairs as fulfilment of biblical prophecy. Both emphases

---

[129] *The Journal of Thomas A. Fudge, 1980-1985*, entry for 28 September 1981. Later, C.H. Yadon also expressed a mild disapproval with such emphases. C.H. Yadon, sermon "Now and Then," Valley Pentecostal Church, Caldwell, Idaho, 22 June 1997, audio recording. FC, inv.doc.no 0707-3156-22.

[130] Lewis J. Davies interview, 19 August 2013.

[131] Don Fisher, "Let Christ be Formed in You," sermon at McCormick's Creek, Indiana, 1974, audio recording. Clarence Larkin (1859-1924) and C.I. (Cyrus Ingerson) Scofield (1843-1921) were prominent exponents of dispensational and futurist eschatology and their works were widely embraced within the UPC.

have been convincingly exposed by scholars as based upon flawed hermeneutics.[132] He opposed the trivializing of doctrine and fear tactics adopted in such popular UPC teaching and evangelistic tools as the "Search for Truth" program. He rarely referred to perennial ideas such as the tribulation, the millennium, or ideas of a believer's rapture. He preferred to emphasize the mandates of the kingdom of God and the person of Jesus over such unimportant matters. The CBC community may have participated in the Royce D. Elms (1940-2010) Portland revival in the 1970s, wherein Elms postulated that the rapture would occur at midnight and actually counted down to that hour (as Marvin Hicks did elsewhere), but Fisher consistently steered his constituency away from those themes. His personal canon within a canon regarded the epistles as more worthy than the Acts of the Apostles. Much of the foregoing could be said of C.H. Yadon. The "experts" were increasingly suspicious.

While he never attacked the *Fundamental Doctrine* of the UPC, Fisher did preach in the CBC chapel in 1982 calling into question the validity of a one-time Acts 2:38 experience as the high point of one's spiritual pilgrimage.[133] He had articulated this publicly years earlier. "There are other things involved in being a disciple of Jesus Christ than having an initial baptism of excitement."[134] This was foreshadowed at Jackson, where faculty taught in classrooms that "new birth without new life is still birth."[135] Even earlier he had warned his hearers that it was possible to "be impregnated with God and have a spiritual abortion."[136] Fisher and his colleagues appeared to emulate the doctrine of C.H. Yadon who, as we have

---

[132] See Ronald L. Numbers, *The Creationists: From Scientific Creationism to Intelligent Design* (Cambridge, MA: Harvard University Press, 2006) and Paul Boyer, *When Time Shall be no More: Prophecy Belief in Modern American Culture* (Cambridge, MA: Harvard University Press, 1992).

[133] A number of students and colleagues recall Fisher's refusal to emphasize Acts 2:38. These include Cheryl (Johns) Crousser interview, 1 October 2013, David Wasmundt interview, 3 October 2013, and Stan Johnson interview, 5 October 2013, Caldwell, Idaho.

[134] Don Fisher, "Evangelization of the Subconscious," sermon at McCormick's Creek, Indiana, January 1975, audio recording.

[135] Joseph Howell interview, 21 April 1999.

[136] Don Fisher, "Let Christ be Formed in You," sermon at McCormick's Creek, Indiana, 1974, audio recording.

previously seen, stated publicly on many occasions that the UPC
had no "experts" in the areas of holiness or theology. That
sentiment rankled many but Fisher considered it salutary advice. He
was skeptical about absolute truth claims, and from a theological
perspective remained opposed to the encouragement and practice
of blind obedience.[137] He believed both were enemies of education,
and were seductive invitations to a form of spirituality restricted to
the pasture, rather than the experience of God on the pathway.

Fisher was convinced that it was indicative of arrogance and
depravity to believe that one possessed Truth. The theology
programs at Jackson and in Portland quite clearly regarded the work
of doing theology a human task. Fisher never mistook theology for
truth, recognized its undeniable humanity, and avoided the trap of
dealing with theology by means of pathological seriousness. Simply
put, during the last years of CBC there was little evidence of that
fateful identification of doctrine with the word of God. This was a
result of theological critical methodology. The PCI tradition had
long celebrated the toleration of doctrinal differences, and upheld
the merger agreements with respect to the unity clause appended to
that historic document. This allowed the 1945 merger to succeed
when previous efforts at union had foundered on the shoals of
theological difference.[138] Jesus may well have said that in his father's
house were many rooms but too many of his disciples insisted they
should all live in the same one.[139] The general constituency of the
PAJC clearly reflected that conviction, as did the Missouri Synod
Lutherans and the Southern Baptists. Don Fisher stood at the
forefront of a school of thought which opposed the growing trend
to shift everyone into the same room. Others identified these
inflexible differences as divisive and a hindering element.[140]

Typical Pentecostal expressions of worship were noticeably
absent during the Fisher years at CBC. This observation should be
tempered by the fact that the Pacific Northwest historically had
seldom exhibited the emotional sensationalism frequently found in

---

[137] Such characteristics indicate religious corruption. Charles Kimball, *When
Religion Becomes Evil* (New York: HarperSanFrancisco, 2002), pp. 41-99.
[138] See Fudge, *Christianity without the Cross*, pp. 74, 100 for details.
[139] R.I. Moore, *The Origins of European Dissent* (Oxford: Blackwell, 1985), p.1.
[140] Loren A. Yadon, letter to Jerry Dillon, 15 September 1981.

other parts of the country. There were virtually no "spiritual manifestations" at CBC during the Fisher years such as running, jumping, dancing, loud shouting, significant displays of glossolalia, tongues and/or interpretations, "prophesying," or exaggerated emotionalism. Fisher did not place any particular emphasis upon these things and in some ways actually discouraged them.[141]

Prior to Don Fisher's arrival at CBC, Jerry Dillon actively intervened in such activities. On one occasion at First Church on Killingsworth Street, in the revival meeting preached by evangelist Royce D. Elms, during the Jim Roam pastorate, Dillon ordered CBC student Gary Visser to stop slithering along the floor under the pews, to get up and sit down and to ever after cease and desist from such nonsense which some considered worship.[142] The Northwest patriarch C.H. Yadon was described by his parishioners in El Paso, Texas, in the late 1940s, as a man who might have made an excellent Baptist minister and a sermon he preached at a camp meeting in Tennessee in the early 1970s was characterized as the sort of homily one could hear any Sunday at a Baptist church.[143] Other area ministers took firm stands against some of these practices and even resigned from positions in protest. In 1973, Jim Roam (1942-2004) brought to Portland the Texas evangelist A.D. Spears, who promoted the practice of "dancing in the spirit." Roam then fatefully decided to make the practice policy. When there was resistance, C.H. Yadon had to intervene and negotiate a settlement wherein Roam backed down.[144] During a 1975 DOE meeting in Portland, Stanley Chambers condemned the "bunch of playboys ...

---

[141] He reprimanded Nathaniel Yadon for allowing too much "spirit-led" worship on one occasion at Christ for the People Community Church in the fall of 1982. Nathaniel Yadon interview, 15 December 2000, characterized the admonition as "being hauled on the carpet."

[142] Jerry Dillon interview, 19 April 2013.

[143] Clarence W. Lewis interview, 5 January 1999 who stated that Yadon himself had shared that comment. The Tennessee anecdote was Harold Hodge's (1917-2006) opinion. Noted initially in Vern Yadon interview, 6 December 2000, and confirmed in Harold Hodge interview, 5 February 2002, Jackson, Tennessee.

[144] Jerry Dillon resigned as Minister of Music at First Church when the senior pastor asserted that all ministers on his platform were required to participate in or support the dance. Jerry Dillon, letter to James E. Roam, 14 May 1973, (FC, inv.doc.no 0707-4778-32) and Jerry Dillon interview, 5 January 1999.

[in the UPC who] enjoy shouting and jumping more than the preaching of the Word."[145] Students upset by vociferous statements advanced by UPC evangelist Charles Mahaney (1942-2007) during a preaching campaign in Portland in 1982 were advised by Fisher to take no note of such ideas and concentrate rather upon the more balanced approaches being taught and encouraged at the college.[146] Mahaney was a brutish preacher of some renown who was once described as "another Hitler." Mahaney described himself as so narrow-minded that if he fell on a nail he would put out both eyes. He was sufficiently impertinent to declare publicly that he believed only half of United Pentecostals would be saved while the rest of humanity would be lost and go to hell.[147] Fisher, C.H. Yadon, and their colleagues considered such declarations nonsense.

It is noteworthy that during the first week of Fall Term at CBC in 1981, Fisher's first session as president, there was an extensive teaching seminar conducted in the CBC chapel with a focus on the Sermon on the Mount, the Kingdom of God, and the ethics of Jesus.[148] Moreover, during his CBC presidency, Fisher delivered a series of sermons at the Idaho District camp meeting wherein he placed a significant emphasis upon grace.[149] This emphasis on the kingdom of God seemed to accurately characterize the Fisher style, and one looks in vain for similar campus-wide seminars on Acts 2:38, or traditional UPC emphases on holiness and its nominated standards. Fisher's dilatory progress in fully articulating UPC doctrine with respect to salvation, holiness, and the Godhead could only be explained by the fact that either he did not fully believe

---

[145] Quoted in John Klemin, letter to the CBC Board, 14 March 1975, p. 1.

[146] Mahaney did not speak at the CBC campus but many students attended this meeting. The anecdote involved the wife of CBC student Bob Bowker and was communicated at the time by Peggy (Yelm) Dougherty. *The Journal of Thomas A. Fudge, 1980-1985*, entry for 22 January 1982.

[147] Dennis R. Knibb, former principal of Saint John High School in New Brunswick (1965-1992), heard Mahaney, from his office down the hall, preaching at the Atlantic District youth convention (16-18 May 1981) convened in the school auditorium. Knibb was so taken aback by the protracted and bombastic harangue that he asked David Fudge about the speaker: "is he another Hitler?" *The Journal of Thomas A. Fudge, 1980-1985*, entries for 16-18 May 1981.

[148] *The Journal of Thomas A. Fudge, 1980-1985*, entries for 22/23 September 1981.

[149] Norman Rutzen interview, 24 July 2013.

these tenets or that he simply did not regard their propagation as necessary. The latter is certainly true. Students of Fisher have reflected on his emphasis on the alternative kingdom of God point of view.[150] From a more general theological perspective, this underscores the differences between the emphases on the Sermon on the Mount and the Nicene Creed within historic Christianity. The former says nothing about doctrine or what one should believe. The latter says nothing about behavior or ethics but is devoted exclusively to precepts Christians are required to believe. While by no means eschewing theology, the Fisher philosophy placed greater stress on the Sermon than on the Creed. The Sermon became an embarrassment to the Christian church historically and its implementation was increasingly viewed as both impracticable and impossible. The Creed became ascendant. Doctrine replaced ethics. Theology superseded morality.

3.9　Barry King, *c.* 1978, and (3.10) shortly after he assumed the pastorate of the Beaverton church

Northwest ministers such as Barry King and Allen Picklesimer sometimes stressed the UPC manual more than the Bible.[151] They were not alone in this stance. In the 1970s, the Ohio District discussed the feasibility of producing a holiness manual for the

---

[150] April Purtell interview, 13 April 2013.
[151] Wallace Leonard interview, 3 August 2013, and Jerry Dillon interview, 19 April 2013.

entire world delineating appropriate standards. James K. Stewart was so annoyed with the idea that during a board meeting he hurled a copy of the UPC manual against a wall with the retort that there was already a more important manual in existence which was scripture and there was no need for another.[152] By way of emphasis for much of the UPC, holiness standards and Acts 2:38 were considered more essential than the kingdom of God and the ethics of Jesus. This can be adjudicated by an examination of sermons and publications. Fisher's approach to education did not reflect that institutional commitment and once again we find Fisher positioned outside denominational positivism.

Such denominational emphasis is characteristic of many religious bodies. During the Missouri Synod purge in the 1970s, we find evidence for the view that every professor should interpret scripture precisely as the Lutheran Confessions.[153] Within the Southern Baptist Convention, colleges, universities, and seminaries were sometimes required to only appoint faculty, regardless of discipline, who adhered to the *Baptist Faith and Message*, the doctrinal statements of the denomination, a document Adrian Rogers helped to revise. There was pressure on Fuller Seminary faculty to maintain unswerving commitment to Fundamentalism. Reformers within these churches believed that theological paralysis prevented the reign of God from illuminating faith, and generally held to the view that the gospel transcended history and could not be restricted to theology. That noted, it seems too ambitious to claim that there were self-conscious movements to create reform within any of these churches, Roman Catholic, Missouri Synod Lutheran, or Southern Baptist.[154] Was there a challenge to the institutional authority of the UPC? Were there specific theological challenges?

Was there a deliberate attempt to shift the educational paradigm within the Bible colleges? Joseph Howell and Dan Lewis gradually did move towards an intentional reform agenda. Lewis wrote to Episcopal priest, former UPC member, and Oneness scholar, David Reed in July 1980, underscoring the direction they were

---

[152] Wayne Nigh interview, 25 July 2013, Caldwell, Idaho, on Stewart's authority.
[153] One example is Zimmerman, *A Seminary in Crisis: The Inside Story of the Preus Fact Finding Committee*, p. 50.
[154] Kurtz, *The Politics of Heresy*, p. 135.

charting out at JCM and noting an attempt to break free from the current pathway, both in encouraging dialogue, and specifically in adopting a more tolerant perspective on theological differences. From 1979 onwards, both Howell and Lewis especially "were consciously trying to find avenues of connection with evangelical theology and historic Christianity."[155] College course syllabi drew a distinction between "teachings which were purely Pentecostal" and those which were shared with historic Christianity.[156]

Around 1960, a brash UPC evangelist preaching in Morton, Washington at a youth rally told young people that those who did not apply and practice the obligatory appearance standards would go to hell. Turning to the ministers on the platform the evangelist warned them that any pastor allowing such worldliness would go to hell with the offenders. The well-known compromiser Carl Adams was one of the main targets.[157] Many years later, Adams said with mild disgust that he hoped that God had forgotten the incident.[158] In terms of holiness, as understood by the UPC and reflected in its self-described "standards," a protracted exchange between C.H. Yadon and CBC students in a doctrine class tellingly reveals the ethos at the college. During a lecture, Yadon made comments which prompted a student to ask what were appropriate "standards of holiness." Yadon responded that the measure of holiness could only be calibrated by looking at Christ. He intimated that the concept of plural "standards" was unhelpful. "There is only one standard of holiness." For many years, Yadon kept a desk plaque in his office bearing the words "the secret to holy living is living holy in secret." For Yadon that was the essential point, not visible adornments which may not have reflected a core quality, value, or state of being. Unsatisfied, the student wanted to know about women wearing trousers. Was such practice worldly or acceptable? Yadon would not make a censorious judgment. Once again he insisted, "there is only one standard of holiness." The student

---

[155] Lewis, *The Journey Out*, pp. 29-33 which quotes the letter to Reed and also Lewis, letter to Thomas A. Fudge, 7 May 2013. FC, inv.doc.no 0707-5023-33.

[156] Dan Lewis, course syllabus, TH231 *Systematic Theology II*, JCM, p. 1.

[157] Paul Adams interview, 16 August 2013, La Quinta, California.

[158] Carl Adams interview, 17 August 2013, Palm Desert, California. See ill.0.1, p. xviii. Adams is the fourth from the left in the front row.

persisted. What did Yadon think about women cutting their hair? Once again, the professor demurred from agreeing that this constituted sin or a departure from righteousness or indeed had any clear connection to the idea of holiness. Yet again he concluded, "there is only one standard of holiness." Frustrated with Yadon's refusal to publicly support UPC party line doctrine, the student asked the professor pointedly to comment on what "standards of holiness" were and exactly how they should be understood and implemented. C.H. Yadon did not hesitate before replying with the mantra "we have only one standard of holiness, and that is Christ." The example is Christ, his ethics, his conduct, his values, his life. That is the sole standard. The rest are human rules and regulations which have no meaning for the principles of the kingdom of God, cannot be understood as reliably reflecting the nature of God, do not necessarily indicate meaningful separateness from the world, cannot be taken to imply commitment to Christ alone, and are unrelated to matters of sanctification or salvation. In other words, "there are no holiness experts." Follow Christ.[159]

While highly controversial within the context of the UPC, Yadon's point was unmistakable: Christ alone is the standard for holy living. Everything that is known about Don Fisher's thought, teachings, and practice provides no indication that he did not fully subscribe to the position articulated by Yadon. Students at CBC were aware that Fisher and Yadon wished to slowly but deliberately reform aspects of the UPC.[160] CBC students noted that Don Fisher did not seem to be like the majority of UPC pastors.[161] Even earlier, Jerry Dillon caused raised eyebrows when instructing new students about the standards of the college by noting that the college standards were not necessarily biblically mandated.[162] The "experts" were unimpressed. Men such as Barry King, Paul Dugas and some other ministers perceived such theological orientation as evidence

---

[159] *The Journal of Thomas A. Fudge, 1980-1985*, entry for 18 November 1982 and *Symposium on Oneness Pentecostalism 1986*, pp. 312-313. A parallel can be found in a summary of discussions between Lew Davies and Winfred Toole several years earlier. Lewis J. Davies, letter to Winfred E. Toole, 2 May 1978, p. 4.
[160] Kristi (Eld) Christensen interview, 4 October 2013.
[161] Cheryl (Johns) Crousser interview, 1 October 2013.
[162] Jerry Dillon interview, 19 April 2013.

that CBC was weak on the message, that Yadon, Fisher and their supporters were heretical, and out of step with the organization. Moreover, they considered such teaching patently dangerous. They were convinced that a Trojan horse had been brought within the gates at CBC. There is considerable evidence that many of the strident defenders of UPC doctrine despised the Yadon name.[163]

The crisis at CBC was precipitated by an influx of missionaries into the Northwest. The college was convulsed. The hardliners became absolutely convinced that CBC was "disseminating liberal theology" to the students.[164] Outsiders arrived with the assumption

3.11 Paul Dugas, *c.* 1981, while pastoring (3.12) in
St. Johns, just south of the CBC campus

that the Northwest was in need of serious change and recalcitrant liberals had either to be reformed or to be expelled. In the throes of this struggle, "CBC became a pawn."[165] Men such as Paul Dugas were among the militant vanguard leading the charge against the compromisers in the Northwest. Others later confessed they were desperate about the future of the college, and acknowledged that things may not have been handled as well as they could have.[166] Nevertheless, the final crisis at CBC did not arise suddenly. The

---

[163] Wallace Leonard interview, 3 August 2013.
[164] Clyde Barlow interview, 13 August 2013.
[165] Darline (Kantola) Royer interview, 15 August 2013.
[166] David Johnson, letter to Jerry Dillon, 16 February 1984.

conflict had been slowly building, developing, and approaching for years.[167] Its climax was only hastened by the appointment of Don Fisher to the presidency.

Under Fisher's post-UPC ministry, former students undertook research on the idea of justification by faith and the theology of Martin Luther, which Fisher incorporated into his discipleship program. By 1985, the teaching of Reformation theology and justification by faith, by former Fisher students, could be found in some UPC churches.[168] The impact was limited. A number of JCM and CBC students and colleagues also left the UPC. Dan Lewis identified himself with the Evangelical movement. Joseph Howell, Larry Snyder, and Robin Wentworth joined the Methodist tradition. Stephen Graham converted to Roman Catholicism. Jim Wilkins and Thomas A. Fudge became Episcopalians. Jerry Dillon and April Purtell embraced Reformed theology and became Presbyterians. Mark Roberts remained Pentecostal but in a version far removed from the UPC. Of the students at CBC who studied both of the last two years, during the Fisher administration, eighty-three percent left the UPC, and seventy-one percent of teaching faculty over the last two years also ceased affiliation.[169] These are significant statistics.

Some of Fisher's detractors declared they knew something was amiss with him as far back as the 1960s. The clues were often murky but intriguing. "One thing I noticed about him, in my observation, keeping my ear to the ground, he seldom would ever use the name Jesus. It was always Christ ... Christ ... Just between you and me and the good Lord of heaven, I don't think he believed

---

[167] Raymond A. Sirstad interview, 27 August 2013.

[168] *The Journal of Thomas A. Fudge, 1980-1985*, entries for 14 and 17 December 1983, 3 and 29 July 1985. In the latter context, one discussion on Galatians lasted until 3:00 a.m. On the discipleship classes, *The Journal of Thomas A. Fudge, 1980-1985*, entries for 15 and 29 April, 6, 13, 20 and 27 May 1984. Fisher also referred to justification by faith in his own sermons. For example, Don Fisher, "Evangelization of the Subconscious," sermon at McCormick's Creek, Indiana, January 1975, audio recording.

[169] Among the faculty, Raymond Sirstad, John Klemin, Darline Kantola, Roger Yadon, and Nathaniel Yadon remained UPC, while Don Fisher, Donna Fisher, Jerry Peden, Esther Peden, David Wasmundt, Ruth Ann Brokaw, Lyn (Sheets) Johnson (1956-1989), Stan Johnson, April Purtell, C.H. Yadon, Dana P. Rowe, and Kelvin Alexander left the organization.

the new birth."[170] Fisher did not preach the new birth message or talk about holiness standards.[171] In this he followed the stance assumed by C.H. Yadon and his own father. Late in 1951, Harry Fisher preached a sermon on the radio station KEYY, in Pocatello, Idaho on salvation by faith.[172] It is probable that Fisher remained in the older PCI theological stream of thought characterized by some as "accept Jesus Christ as Lord and you are saved."[173]

In other quarters, Fisher was suspected and sometimes accused of being a Trinitarian. Using terminology such as "God the Spirit" in sermons contributed to these assumptions.[174] In the revised CBC college catalogue, drawn up by Don Fisher in 1982, an original sentence in the doctrinal affirmations included the sentence "we believe in the unity of the Godhead." This was later stricken upon the advice of C.H. Yadon, who warned Fisher that while, in his opinion, there was nothing theologically problematic with that formulation, his detractors would use it against him to provide further fuel for the fire. Yadon, Frank Ewart (1876-1947), Harry Morse (1879-1963), Howard A. Goss (1883-1964), and many others of that generation could heartily embrace the idea, but long before the 1980s, it was clearly not sufficiently Oneness.[175]

Yadon would have known this better than anyone given the responses in some sectors of the UPC to the book he had edited thirty years earlier.[176] He believed in the pre-existent Son of God, which ran counter to UPC theology, and he was asked not to

---

[170] Barry King interview, 20 January 1999, Beaverton, Oregon. While others acknowledge Fisher's regular use of the title Christ, they did not detect anything troubling about that. Thetus Tenney interview, 6 June 2013.

[171] Donna Fisher and Joe Higgins interviews, 3 January 1999 and 4 October 2013.

[172] That particular sermon was printed as Harry Fisher, "Salvation by Faith" *Pentecostal Northwestern News* 7 (No. 1, 1952), pp. 3-4.

[173] Raymond A. Sirstad interview, 27 August 2013.

[174] Donna Fisher, interview, 3 January 1999 was aware of rumors originating at JCM that Fisher was a "Trinitarian at heart." Noted also in Jerry Peden interview, 19 July 2002. Don Fisher, "Evangelization of the Subconscious," sermon at McCormick's Creek, Indiana, January 1975, audio recording, utilizes the phrase.

[175] The most recent study of Goss is Robin Johnston, *Howard A. Goss: A Pentecostal Life* (Hazelwood: World Aflame, 2010). There is a review in *Pneuma: The Journal of the Society for Pentecostal Studies* 34 (No. 1, 2012), pp. 109-110.

[176] Peden was present when Yadon reviewed the doctrinal statements and made his recommendation. Jerry Peden interview, 19 July 2002.

preach or promote the idea.[177] Yadon did, however, have students deal with such questions on examinations at CBC.[178] Privately, Yadon asserted that "God was never made flesh," a comment that reveals much about his understanding of the incarnation.[179] Yadon's book was controversial, "but anything that stimulates some people to think outside of their circle of fixation has to be a bone of contention."[180] Indeed, in the year 1969, C.H. Yadon was openly characterized as a Trinitarian by fellow UPC ministers.[181] He stood in the Oneness tradition but for him God was neither a closed subject nor a matter that could not be investigated.[182] His wide-reading habits and forays into various areas of inquiry caused some to refer to him as a "theological meddler."[183] Yadon was not a reformer in the sense that Fisher, Lewis, and Howell were. He was an independent thinker who was fearless in drawing attention to ethical dilemmas or important theological irregularities. His roots in Pentecostalism went back much farther than the 1945 merger which created the United Pentecostal Church. Because he had significant interaction with that generation in the late 1920s up through the mid-1940s, he possessed a more astute grasp of the historic trajectory, especially in terms of the gains made by the proponents of the "water and Spirit" doctrine, which increasingly marginalized everyone else as "weak on the message."[184] He maintained fellowship with the English-born W.H. (William Henry) Offiler (1875-1957), who pastored in Seattle. Offiler was both

---

[177] Nathaniel Urshan interview, 23 April 1999, and Tom Fred Tenney interview, 20 April 1999, Tioga, Louisiana.

[178] A test in his Doctrine class, dated 2 June 1971, posed this query: "What is the basic difference between the doctrine of trinity and oneness on the teaching of the pre-existence of Christ?" FC, inv.doc.no 0707-2091-15.

[179] Hack Yadon interview, 11 December 1999, Tacoma, Washington.

[180] Edwin Judd interview, 10 April 1999. The book in question is C. Haskell Yadon, *Jehovah-Jesus, the Supreme God: Son of God, Son of Man* (Twin Falls, ID: By the author, 1952). J.L. Hall (1933-2011) refused to discuss the book with C.H. Yadon. C.M. Yadon interview, 11 December 1999, Puyallup, Washington.

[181] Jerry Dillon interview, 5 January 1999. Frank LaCrosse showed Dillon a copy of the Yadon book and asserted that Yadon definitely was not Oneness.

[182] Jewel (Yadon) Dillon interview, 2 January 2001.

[183] Vern Yadon interview, 6 December 2000.

[184] Dan Lewis, letter to Thomas A. Fudge, 7 May 2013.

Trinitarian and disinterested in the theological ramifications of the "New Issue" controversy.[185] Neither C.H. Yadon nor Don Fisher were adverse to thinking of God in the manner that earlier Pentecostals had. "God is triune, a trinity. Three manifestations of one God, not three eternally distinct persons or Gods, as that is tritheism."[186] Similar language appears in the work of A.D. Urshan.

Disciples and family members of Yadon came under suspicion. Edwin Judd was viewed with distrust by "water and spirit" advocates. When Vern Yadon (ill.4.36, p. 227) was interviewed by the Idaho District Board in 1968 in Boise, in connection with his application for ministerial license, he was especially grilled by Norman Peter V. Shebley (1909-1995) on his understanding of John 3:5. (See ill.0.1, p. xviii. Shebley is the third from the left in the front row.) Stout defenders of the "water and spirit" doctrine were convinced that being born of water and spirit in John 3:5 was confirmation of baptism in the name of Jesus and the infilling of the Holy Spirit articulated in Acts 2:38. Everyone knew that C.H. Yadon did not consider this a valid understanding of the New Testament. But what was being taught at CBC? Edwin Judd assured Vern Yadon that Shebley's interrogation was aimed to discover what Vern Yadon had been taught in CBC classrooms by Judd and others.[187] None of this concerned some prominent ministers who maintained the view that C.H. Yadon "was General Superintendent material."[188] Students at JCM considered Yadon's ideas and approach surprisingly relevant and he was characterized as "an old-timer who didn't sound like an old-timer."[189] Nevertheless, Yadon remained a target and was always a suspect because of theology.[190] This suspicion had a long history and existed prior to the 1945

---

[185] E.N. Bell, "The Godhead" *Pentecostal Evangel* 370/1 (11 December 1920), p. 9. CBC board member Jim Christensen's father William was converted under Offiler, later pastored in Toppenish, Washington, and associated with C.H. Yadon. Jim Christensen interview, 1 October 2013, Caldwell, Idaho.

[186] *Discipline – The Pentecostal Church, Inc.* (Dallas: The Herald Publishing House, n.d.), p. 3. This is the pre-1945 merger PCI manual.

[187] Vern Yadon interview, 6 December 2000.

[188] W.M. Greer interview, 2 May 1999, Jackson, Tennessee. Greer was district superintendent of Tennessee for thirty years (1949-1978).

[189] Larry Snyder interview, 5 May 1999.

[190] Darline (Kantola) Royer interview, 15 August 2013.

merger. PAJC ministers, for example, warned Nebraska minister Jerry Tiller (1913-1999) that Yadon was subversive, theologically dangerous, and a man to be avoided. Tiller failed to follow this advice and eventually became one of Yadon's supporters.[191]

Competing educational approaches remained at issue. There is an enormous difference between education and indoctrination. The Oxford medievalist R.W. Southern (1912-2001), noted "we learn not by being told but by being puzzled and excited."[192] While education opens possibilities, indoctrination limits options. The Greek historian Plutarch (46-120) argued that the mind is not a container to be filled but a fire to be lit, for this is what creates the impulse for independent thought and the unhindered quest for truth.[193] Indoctrination is content to fill the containers of minds but education seeks rather to light the fires of critical examination. Don Fisher referred to hearts being ignited by truth.[194] Authentic education and the real institution of higher learning seeks to cultivate intellectual exploration. Clarence Darrow said it succinctly. "It is the duty of the university, as I conceive it, to be the great storehouse of the wisdom of the ages, and to let students go there, and learn, and choose."[195] There is no evidence that Fisher opposed such philosophy. The indoctrination approach limits choices and sees its duty to expose students only to certain ideas while arguing towards predetermined and approved answers. The Bible school approach to education in early Pentecostalism consisted chiefly of mastery of the King James Version of the Bible and the doctrines particular to the relevant tradition.[196] Proper education knows no

---

[191] Stan Johnson interview, 5 October 2013. Tiller was Johnson's grandfather.

[192] R.W. Southern, *Medieval Humanism and Other Studies* (New York: Harper & Row, 1970), p. 47.

[193] The expression is found in Plutarch's essay *De auditi* [On Listening to Lectures]. There is an edition. Plutarch, *Moralia*, 7 vols (Cambridge, MA: Harvard University Press, 1927), vol. 1, pp. 201-259. See p. 257.

[194] Don Fisher, "Let Christ be Formed in You," sermon at McCormick's Creek, Indiana, 1974, audio recording.

[195] Statement made by Clarence Darrow in a court trial. *The World's Most Famous Court Trial: A Complete Stenographic Report of the Famous Court Test of the Tennessee Anti-Evolution Act at Dayton, July 10 to 21, 1925, Including Speeches and Arguments of Attorneys* (Cincinnati: National Book Company, 1925), p. 182.

[196] Wacker, *Heaven Below: Early Pentecostalism and American Culture*, p. 151.

limitations, recognizes no exclusive truth claims, and celebrates the questions. Authentic education is unrestrained critical thinking. Some have expressed it this way: "I have no teaching. I only point to something. I point to reality, I point to something in reality that had not or had too little been seen. I take the one who listens to me by the hand and lead them to the window. I open the window and point to what is outside. I have no teaching, but I carry on a conversation."[197] There is no evidence that Fisher ever read Martin Buber, but the philosophy behind the pedagogical approach during the last days of CBC was not incompatible with the non-dogmatic, dialectical model. In other words, theology, that "quarrelsome old woman," was neither fixed nor sacrosanct.

Faith or commitment to doctrinal propositions maintained at the cost of intellectual integrity is not faith at all. The antithesis of faith is fear, whether this is fear of biblical criticism, the scientific method, or theological inquiry. The strongest faith is the examined faith. The UPC, the Missouri Synod Lutherans, and the Southern Baptists maintained very firmly that the idea of the examined faith was dangerous insofar as it involved questioning. Teaching in the Bible college classroom in Stockton, California, Daniel Segraves suggested it was very dangerous to question basic, fundamental truths that one had previously been assured of. Don Fisher wanted to know the basis upon which the prior assurance was based.[198] That anecdote sheds important light upon divergent philosophies of education within the 1970s and 80s UPC. The issue of education versus indoctrination was the subject of robust debate at one of the annual summer meetings of UPC educators in Colorado and the outcome indicated that the UPC favored the latter.[199] Don Fisher was never going to support that approach.

The ideas of education at JCM and CBC can be taken one step farther by drawing attention to the obligations of theological masters in the Middle Ages. In the later twelfth century, we find a cogent outline of the three tasks required of medieval theologians.

---

[197] Martin Buber, "Replies to My Critics," *The Philosophy of Martin Buber*, eds., Paul Schlipp and Maurice Friedman (LaSalle, IL: Open Court, 1967), p. 693.
[198] *The Journal of Thomas A. Fudge, 1980-1985*, entries for 13 and 19 September 1983.
[199] Donna Fisher interview, 3 January 1999.

These were articulated as *lectio*, *disputatio*, and *praedicatio*.[200] In other words, learning consisted of three essential elements. First, reading (*lectio*) formed the foundation and the basis for everything. Second, disputation (*disputatio*) comprised the walls. This was necessary because nothing can be completely understood until it has been subjected to careful examination. Third, proclamation (*praedicatio*) functioned as the roof which then protected the community of the faithful from various and unpredictable storms. Thus the medieval approach to theology meant careful reading and commentary on scripture, critical debate over that which was received or learned, and the proclamation of those critically evaluated truths.

3.13  The new JCM campus, 1979

What was Don Fisher's vision for Christian higher education within the UPC? This is a critical element to understanding a great deal about the man and his work at JCM and at CBC. It also goes some distance towards creating an explanatory model for illuminating aspects of the clash which precipitated the destruction of CBC. It seems unlikely that Fisher knew anything directly about medieval theology and its practice. However, in a discernible sense, that tripartite methodology was attempted in the Bible colleges under the successive Fisher administrations. He placed a keen emphasis upon wide reading and a balanced approach to theological

---

[200] Peter the Chanter, *Verbum abbreviatum* c.1 in PL, vol. 205, col. 25.

inquiry. This has been suggested above with some examples. He also actively encouraged informal disputations, discussion, and intentional dialogue around practically everything. At Fisher's CBC there were no sacred cows or nominated topics beyond debate or question. That included notional concepts of the Godhead, ideas about salvation, and the practice of the faith. A central theme was an application of the Philippian injunction, "work out your own salvation." College students were not left to flounder about without direction but they were not encouraged to rest on the laurels of whatever experience they might have had previously. Fisher was aware that he was dealing with theological puberty. Medieval Latin thought drew a distinction between *id quod est* (that which is) and *id quo est* (that by which something is). Applied in the modern sense, the theological education at CBC was concerned with two types of faith: the faith one believes and the faith by which one believes.

3.14  Russell H. Dilday, preaching at Tallowood Baptist Church, Houston, Texas, 29 July 2012

The UPC focused on the first type, while men like Fisher, C.H. Yadon, Lewis, and Howell emphasized the latter. Parallels can also be found in the LCMS and in the SBC. Seminary presidents John H. Tietjen (1928-2004) and Russell H. Dilday are examples of those with an active interest in both kinds of faith. Another text which gained wide emphasis at CBC was II Timothy 1:7, which noted that God had not sent a spirit of fear, but of power, love, and a sound mind. Fisher suggested the latter was all too little used in UPC culture. He challenged his students to dare to think. If wide reading provided a foundation and the strongest faith was the examined faith, considered, evaluated, and debated, then preaching, teaching, and proclamation could take place with confidence and authority. Don Fisher did not believe in impromptu sermons, traditional Holy Ghost anointing (which frequently amounted to an excuse to avoid the injunction of II Timothy 2:15), and he saw no merit in the sort of widespread superficial proof-texting evident in altogether too much Pentecostal preaching. Before there could be *praedicatio* there had to be *lectio* and *disputatio*. Fisher would have endorsed the German theologian Helmut Thielicke (1908-1986) when the latter firmly insisted, "I do not tolerate sermons by first-semester young theological students... one ought to be able to keep still... during this formative period in the life of the theological student he does not preach."[201] The components of such philosophy and practice were evident in Portland in the last years of CBC.

If Fisher's academic administration and related philosophy of education departed from the *de rigueur* of the UPC, it cannot be described as an aimless foray into a sterile intellectual musing divorced from spirituality, emotion, or the heart. While Fisher was committed to the life of the mind, he was also personally invested in the journey of the Christian pilgrim. Both interests may be subsumed under the rubric of balance. The idea of meaningful transformation emerges as a major theme. One of the whimsical yet profound books that Fisher actively used to explore this idea was a well-known children's tale chronicling how toys become real.[202] Transformation was not limited to acquiring something and possessing it. Fisher drew theological parallels and significance out of such stories. Possessing truth was meaningless if one strove mainly to protect rather than integrate and apply truth.

In the autumn of 1976, Fisher introduced another book dealing with the idea of transformation.[203] This was an allegorical retelling

---

[201] Helmut Thielicke, *A Little Exercise for Young Theologians*, trans., Charles L. Taylor (Grand Rapids: Eerdmans, 1962), p. 12.

[202] Margery Williams, *The Velveteen Rabbit* (New York: Avon Books, 1975), originally published in 1922.

[203] Robert E. Way, *The Garden of the Beloved* (Garden City, NY: Doubleday, 1974).

of the spiritual life. The story follows the path of a young man who gives up all of his goods and worldly accoutrements and endures various tests and trials as he comes to learn, understand, and embrace the art of love which he gleans from the keeper of the garden. Fisher read the story aloud to a group of JCM students and by the time he had reached the end of the tale he was in tears and simply walked out of the classroom overcome with emotion.[204] What are we to make of this and how does it inform our understanding of Fisher's motivation?

Prior to these literary explorations, one of Fisher's favorite books was the fable of a seagull who determines to learn about life regardless of cost.[205] Under pressure, Jonathan Livingston Seagull decides to be a normal gull like the others. However, his thirst for learning propels him to reject the ordinary and he concludes "We can lift ourselves out of ignorance, we can find ourselves as creatures of excellence and intelligence and skill. We can be free."[206] But the discoveries made by Jonathan Livingston Seagull are never known by the gull community because they refuse to listen, they refuse to consider that there might be something other than what they already know. When the experiments with flying persist, Jonathan Livingston Seagull is expelled from the gull community on accusations by the Elder Seagull of "reckless irresponsibility" which leads to "violating the dignity and tradition of the Gull Family." The gull who truly could not conform is banished from the community.[207] Whatever cannot be understood or accepted is demonized, and efforts are made to destroy it.[208] The novella advances a philosophy which discourages surrender to pre-existing categories or expectations. Innovators of tradition and accepted truths will be misunderstood and banished. The willingness to pursue truth and learning is endless and salutary and there will always be a few willing to become disciples of new thinking. In other words, some people are content to live their lives, others

---

[204] April Purtell interview, 13 April 2013.
[205] Richard Bach, *Jonathan Livingston Seagull – A Story* (New York: MacMillan, 1970).
[206] Bach, *Jonathan Livingston Seagull*, p. 27.
[207] Bach, *Jonathan Livingston Seagull*, pp. 34-35.
[208] Bach, *Jonathan Livingston Seagull*, p. 90.

create theirs.[209] Fisher wanted all of his students to be like Jonathan Livingston Seagull. The road taken by those who tell new truths is often difficult. Socrates seated on the steps drinking hemlock. Jesus crucified with criminals. Jan Hus burned alive. Galileo badgered into denouncing his own proven theories. Anne Hutchinson banished from Boston in 1638. Oscar Romero murdered at a San Salvador altar in 1980. The trail of blood can be followed through the corridors of history and especially within the household of faith.

3.15  McCormick's Creek State Park, venue for the
campus ministry retreats in the 1970s

Even before Fisher began his work at Jackson, these themes of transformation and the desire to learn are evident. In the early 1970s during one of the several state-wide weekend campus ministry retreats at McCormick's Creek State Park, a few miles west of Bloomington, Indiana, at which Don Fisher, James Stewart and Wayne Nigh were featured speakers, one of Fisher's addresses ended when he broke down sobbing and saying to the congregation that he needed prayer. He had the young men and women present gather around him and pray.[210] How should this be understood? One of his famous sermons, "Evangelization of the Subconscious," reflected Fisher's passion for the healing of the mind. He called for

---

[209] Fisher recommended the book to others well before he went to Jackson. Dan Lewis, letter to Thomas A. Fudge, 24 May 2013. FC, inv.doc.no 0707-5036-33.
[210] April Purtell, letter to Thomas A. Fudge, 3 April 2013.

a renewal of thinking in general wherein the mind of Christ became the dominant paradigm and Fisher called for "the healing of our memories." He went on to suggest that religious experience was inadequate to address the scope of the human sin problem. "The person who has serious emotional problems and personality difficulties is not automatically healed by either regeneration or sanctification."[211] Another sermon delivered at McCormick's Creek was titled "On to Rome." In this address, Fisher spoke of St. Paul's determination to go to Rome and he urged his hearers to commit themselves in the same manner to truth regardless of cost or consequence. However, these ideas and events are interpreted in light of Fisher's subsequent career, it seems fair to conclude that one of the guiding principles of spirituality and education which Fisher embraced and endeavored to emphasize at JCM and CBC was the idea of transformed life. McCormick's Creek, *The Velveteen Rabbit, Jonathan Livingston Seagull,* and *The Garden of the Beloved* are important clues to understanding Fisher's approach and motivation.

Because of this commitment to transformation, Don Fisher could not support denominational positivism. On this basis it has been suggested that he went to CBC intending to overturn the UPC.[212] Can that assumption bear the weight of inquiry? In 1979, at the behest of the newly elected General Superintendent Nathaniel Urshan, the UPC distributed a document called "The Quest for the Apostolic Key" to all licensed ministers. The focus was evangelism and renewal. Urshan encouraged ministers to submit ideas to the denominational headquarters and the paper was associated with a letter Urshan had written which described the philosophy and intention of the paper.[213] Don Fisher and his associates at JCM took this assignment quite seriously. They concluded that the quest for the apostolic key was not a matter of prayer, fasting, or evangelistic outreach. It certainly had nothing to do with so-called end-time prophecy. Perhaps the program at JCM which Fisher facilitated was a response to Urshan's challenge. Fisher conceived that the quest

---

211 Don Fisher, "Evangelization of the Subconscious," sermon at McCormick's Creek, Indiana, January 1975, audio recording.
212 Thomas Craft interview, 20 April 1999.
213 Nathaniel A. Urshan, "To the beloved ministers of the United Pentecostal Church," 5 November 1979, 2 pp. FC, inv.doc.no 0707-0254-03.

for the apostolic key had to be founded in some meaningful sense upon education. This seems to be the cornerstone of his ministry.[214]

3.16  Thomas Craft and Don Fisher at JCM, 1980

Shortly after the Urshan challenge went out, Fisher met with Jerry Peden (1947-2003) at Hot Springs, Arkansas. Both "The quest for the Apostolic key" and Don Fisher's vision were discussed. According to Peden, Fisher was frustrated at Jackson, feeling that his initiatives for a new approach to education were encountering unmovable resistance, and there was increasing difficulty between he and Thomas Craft. There was pressure on Craft from alarmed ministers in east Texas and Louisiana, the District and College Boards, and even Craft's wife.[215] Mary Francis Craft (1938-2001) exerted considerable influence over her husband and by extension in the college. The friction between President Craft and Don Fisher was exacerbated by the undercurrent of tension between Fisher and the president's wife. These divisions were captured adroitly by a question sometimes posed by JCM students: "Are you a Craftsman or a Fisherman?"[216] These tensions occasionally spilled over in faculty meetings. One staff member noted, "Bro Craft exercised his

---

[214] Donna Fisher interview, 3 January 1999.

[215] Donna Fisher interview, 3 January 1999 and Dan Lewis interview, 6 April 1999.

[216] Gene Dillon interview, 3 August 2013.

pastoral authority to give the faculty some direction. Don [Fisher] took up the defence of the faculty."[217] Power struggles ensued.

Elsewhere, Curtis Young in Baton Rouge was not keen on JCM and was eager to see Fisher dismissed.[218] It seems also manifestly evident that Fisher was not comfortable in southern culture.[219] This prompts the query, what was Fisher trying to do? According to Peden, based upon the Hot Springs discussions, Fisher wanted to turn JCM into more of an advanced theological college, in the general sense of a seminary. In more specific terms, Fisher wanted education rather than indoctrination; open inquiry rather than prescribed doctrine. Fisher had no interest in pouring new wine into old wineskins. He knew very well that the old jugs could not handle the new wine. In specific terms, he deplored having students trace maps of the missionary journeys of Paul as college level projects and was disgusted that prominent ministers could preach such nonsense as declaring that Martin Luther suffered for his faith to the extent of being forced by his persecutors to subsist on a "diet of worms."[220] In the face of such spectacular misunderstandings and gross ignorance of church history, Joseph Howell was observed standing at the rear of the auditorium vigorously shaking his head contemplating the awful thought of Luther's "diet of worms." Such incidents were hardly exceptional. Fisher's philosophy of college administration suggests agreement with Don Marler that Bible colleges were "havens for the mediocre, the frightened, the narrow-minded, the maladjusted ..." where academic standards were so low as to be disgraceful.[221] He determined to remedy the problem. He

---

[217] *The Diary of Jewel (Yadon) Dillon*, entry for 12 February 1980.

[218] Jim Wilkins interview, 1 May 1999.

[219] Thetus Tenney interview, 6 June 2013. T.L. Craft later told Darline Kantola he thought Fisher might be more effective in his own Northwest culture than continuing in the south. Darline (Kantola) Royer interview, 15 August 2013.

[220] The Luther example was noted in a sermon by Anthony Mangun at the Jackson Convention Center before one to two thousand people during the annual music conference in March 1981. Larry Snyder interview, 5 May 1999. Mary Francis Craft had students make maps of Paul's travels in the class on Acts. Stan Blevins interview, 11 April 1999. Blevins made a map which was traced by another student. Craft gave Blevins a grade of "C" for the original drawing while the copy of the Blevins map was awarded a mark of "A".

[221] Marler, *Imprisoned in the Brotherhood*, p. 32.

believed that the person who experiences excellence in learning has thereafter no need to surrender to that which is average.[222]

At Hot Springs, Fisher cogently articulated a balanced vision that encompassed unity, toleration, scholarship, examined faith, a Socratic methodology, and a non-dogmatic posture. Fisher was convinced that JCM was not the type of place which could facilitate his vision. Faith and scholarship need not be divorced and Fisher was keen to consummate that marriage. He agreed whole-heartedly with the assertion that "historical research can neither give nor take away the foundation of the Christian faith ... [but] historical research has influenced and must influence Christian theology."[223]

Fisher thought that the examination of faith could not be examined with intellectual integrity in Jackson. Implicitly at first and then more explicitly, he began to raise the important question of whether it was possible to be both United Pentecostal and intellectual at the same time while maintaining integrity as both. George Eldon Ladd (1911-1982) at Fuller Seminary, and Don Fisher may represent the peril of trying to stand in two worlds simultaneously.[224] Both were eventually forced to choose sides.

During the Hot Springs conversations with Jerry Peden, Fisher expressed his conviction that perhaps in the Northwest there was an ethos in which his vision might prosper. There was direct conversation about assuming the Boise, Idaho facilities formerly used by A.D. Hurt. C.H. Yadon was involved in these discussions. It is Peden's understanding that Yadon approached Hurt on the matter. Outcomes from those conversations are not known.[225] The idea was that Fisher might go to Boise to administer a theological college based upon the principles elaborated above. Fisher also contemplated the idea that such a school might be for men only, though that thought was never a central plank in the program.[226]

---

[222] Bach, *Jonathan Livingston Seagull*, p. 25.
[223] Formulated in Paul Tillich, *Systematic Theology*, vol. 2 (Chicago: University of Chicago Press, 1957), p. 113.
[224] Marsden, *Reforming Fundamentalism*, pp. 248-250.
[225] A. Dale Hurt (1896-1990) had gone to Boise in 1934 and served for many years as president of the International Bible College. He retired in 1985.
[226] The preceding paragraph is based largely upon a four hour interview with Jerry Peden, 19 July 2002. I am likewise indebted to Dan Lewis interview, 6 April

Characteristically, Fisher's vision for CBC was ambitious. The only other president in the history of the school who thought about radically changing the institutional identity of the college was Edwin E. Judd who considered making the school less provincial and more of a regional center, perhaps by relocating CBC to a more centrally situated western city such as Denver or Salt Lake City.[227] The problems and the challenges facing education within the UPC were prominently exposed in the work of Don Fisher in Mississippi and in the Pacific Northwest. The work posited "experts" against non-experts, progressive thinkers against old guard traditionalists, and revealed strangers in the shadows at the gates of the Bible colleges.

3.17  Edwin E. Judd, 1966, as        3.18 Don Fisher and Edwin Judd in the
      president of CBC                      CBC print shop, 1957

It was hard to kick against the pricks. Don Fisher's arrival at CBC signalled the last years of the college. The struggle during that time can only be understood and made intelligible in light of larger developments coming to maturity in the Northwest. We now turn to those momentous events.

---

1999, for discussion of "the quest for the apostolic key" document and its role in developments at JCM. Further comments in Lewis, *The Journey Out*, p. 23.

[227] The idea was never publicly presented and given Judd's relatively short tenure as president was never attempted. Edwin Judd interview, 10 April 1999.

3.19   Red Lion Hotel, Jantzen Beach, Portland,
hosts a CBC event, 5 June 1980

3.20   Aerial view of the CBC campus, around 1970, with Terminal 4 of
the Port of Portland and the Willamette River in the background

# 4

# The Northwest and its Transformations

*Acts of injustice done*
*Between the setting and the rising sun*
*In history lie like bones, each one.*[1]

The closing of CBC marked an important turning point for the
United Pentecostal Church in the Pacific Northwest.[2] The manner
of its demise and destruction was sufficient to cause some ministers
ultimately to cease denominational affiliation.[3] It has been shown
elsewhere that the Northwest historically was a bastion of liberal
theological thinking within the UPC.[4] In that sense, the Northwest
was renowned for openness, toleration, non-dogmatic attitudes, and
less stringent defence of doctrinal propositions in contrast with
other schools of thought and indeed within the mainstream of the
UPC as it had developed by the 1970s. That perception was widely
recognized within the fellowship of the UPC. There were no
"experts," C.H. Yadon had insisted, therefore it was ill-advised to
dogmatize on matters which lay beyond one's purview. Toleration
was preferred.

Against this ethos of open inquiry, some prospective students
were warned that CBC was "weak on the message" even though
since the 1950s the college had publicly declared its fidelity to the

---

[1] W.H. Auden and Christopher Isherwood, *The Ascent of F.6: A Tragedy in Two Acts* (New York: Random House, 1937), Act II, Scene V.

[2] Norman Rutzen interview, 24 July 2013.

[3] Wayne Nigh interview, 25 July 2013 identified this as one of several factors.

[4] Fudge, *Christianity without the Cross* demonstrates in several ways the less strident doctrines articulated in New Brunswick (Canada), Tennessee, and the Pacific Northwest. L.H. Hardwick interview, 22 August 2013, Nashville, Tennessee characterized Oregon and Tennessee as historic "grace districts" as opposed to legalism (Hardwick's term) found elsewhere. Clyde Barlow interview, 13 August 2013, thinks the Northwest was "very liberal."

fundamentals of the UPC.[5] One former president declared that if doctrinal weakness was an accurate description of the college then he likewise was guilty.[6] The first General Superintendent of the UPC Howard A. Goss had always felt at home in the Northwest. The influence of Ellis Scism (1909-1994), the Yadon family, strong currents of old PCI thinking, and a less militant approach in the history of ideas can be located throughout the region. Fisher was a product of CBC and the wider ethos of that part of the country.

By 1981, the province of New Brunswick had long since succumbed to a different approach from that promoted by Sam Steeves (1898-1978), Ed Wickens (1918-), Earl Jacques (1900-1961), and their colleagues. Tennessee was no longer under the influence of W.M. Greer (1906-1999) who once patrolled the boundaries of that district meeting the "radicals" at the state line and directing them to destinations outside Tennessee.[7] Even the Northwest had witnessed a gradual move away from its more moderate stance, largely on account of an infusion of militant missionary mentalities from California and other areas. Historically, CBC avoided student recruitment in California in deference to the fact that a UPC school existed there. By 1976, the college felt obligated to challenge recruitment efforts by the Californians in Idaho, Washington, and Oregon.[8] Outspoken, proud hardliners in California characterized the Northwest as comprised of "grievous wolves" and "smooth operators" without "backbone or guts." C.H. Yadon was singled out as a prime example.[9] Men like Don Fisher and Puyallup pastor Gene Ziemke were viewed with considerable suspicion, if not for doctrinal reasons then because they were insufficiently strident about enforcing the UPC's preoccupation with holiness standards.[10]

---

[5] Lewis, *The Journey Out*, p. 16 tells how he was warned about this when in the late 1960s he announced his intention to study in Portland. *The Pentecostal Herald* 34 (No. 6, 1959), p. 23 for a college announcement.

[6] Ralph Reynolds interview, 13 December 1999, Abbotsford, British Columbia.

[7] This was Greer's own characterization of his practice. Vern Yadon interview, 6 December 2000.

[8] John Klemin, letter to Kenneth Haney, 14 April 1976. FC, inv.doc.no 0707-5174-34. Christian Life College (formerly WABC) began in 1953.

[9] I.H. Terry interview, 13 January 1999, Bakersfield, California.

[10] Wallace Leonard interview, 3 August 2013, Darline (Kantola) Royer interview, 15 August 2013, and also Gene Ziemke interview, 23 September 2013, Milton,

Up until the 1970s, the prevailing attitude in the old Northwest was that "we could really disagree but we didn't have to be disagreeable."[11] CBC exemplified that idea. The college challenged prospective students to "consider carefully the SPIRIT and the ATTITUDE of the students coming from [CBC] ... One well known pastor said of CBC students he had met, 'they have a different spirit about them.'"[12] Men shaped by this philosophy did not apply pressure on issues of theology, especially concerning the new birth and notions of holiness. Evidently they took seriously Yadon's declaration that none were "experts." Friendship and fellowship meant more than doctrinal unanimity. By contrast, much of the UPC, Missouri Synod Lutherans, and Southern Baptists considered theology and notions of truth more important than friendship and fellowship.

The historic ethos associated with CBC began to change with the influx of outsiders which resulted in a "hostile takeover of the Northwest" and this hindered the effectiveness of the college.[13] This drastic change of climate was to some extent deliberately orchestrated and imposed. This intentional urge to purge extended also to foreign territories. UPC missionary Wayne Nigh (ill.4.1) laboring very successfully in Germany, found himself the object of persecution in the late 1970s and early 1980s. Unsurprisingly, one of Nigh's main detractors was John D. Goodwin, whose roots can be located within the aggressive attitudes and strict theological orientation which flourished in California.[14] Goodwin and some of his European colleagues, such as Hulon Myre (1923-1992), John Nowacki in France, Dan Sharp in Augsburg, Rick Collins based in

---

Washington. Others point out that Ziemke had inconsistent policies on holiness standards. Norman Rutzen interview, 27 September 2013.

[11] Norman Rutzen interview, 8 February 1999.

[12] Comments by John Klemin in a CBC advertisement in *The Pentecostal Herald* 53 (No. 6, 1978), p. 22.

[13] E.G. Moyer interview, 27 January 1999, Portland, Oregon. Agreement in Ruby Klemin interview, 13 February 1999, Portland, Oregon, Jerry Dillon comments during an interview with Harry and Freda Fisher, 8 December 2000, and Darline (Kantola) Royer interview, 15 August 2013.

[14] Goodwin is currently listed as a bishop serving on the pastoral staff of the UPC affiliated Two Mile Apostolic Tabernacle in Twentynine Palms, California. www.twomileapostolic.com

southern Germany and Switzerland, along with Jimmy Green in Mannheim, were determined to cast enough question on Nigh's work so as to deprive him of continued UPC endorsement. The reasons for this initiative do not appear to diverge from the agenda

4.1   Wayne and Esther Nigh, at Schloß Freudenberg, Germany, May 1981

operating in the Northwest. Given his PCI roots, CBC education, and reflection of the spirit and emphases of the historic Pacific Northwest, Wayne Nigh was suspected of theological deviance on issues like the new birth and the perennially-significant holiness standards. Moreover, he could not possibly be identified as a fervent defender of the Acts 2:38 doctrine and Jean-Claude (John) Nowacki became convinced that Nigh was deviant on salvation issues and moreover was quite wrong on the interpretation of John 3:5, which the UPC considered evidence for their water and Spirit doctrine. Instead of stressing these points of theology, Nigh, like Fisher and the Yadons, appeared more intent on making disciples of Christ than on producing United Pentecostals. Goodwin found this unpalatable and worked hard to undermine Nigh's credibility, going so far as to allege that Nigh permitted the use of tobacco. This was based upon the sighting of cigarette butts outside Schloß Freudenberg in Wiesbaden where Nigh's ministry was centered. (It should be noted that the Schloß was situated in a public park.) Goodwin arranged for letters of complaint to be sent to the UPC foreign missions board in St. Louis to alert them to the insufferable worldliness being tolerated in Germany.

The criticism of Nigh was so severe and so vitriolic that on one occasion Foreign Missions director Harry Scism publicly rebuked Dan Sharp during a meeting in Europe for his impertinence. As part of the reappointment process, Nigh's last appearance before the Foreign Missions Board in St. Louis in May 1983, according to Edwin Judd, precipitated the lengthiest session of its type, fifteen hours over two days, and prompted Nigh later to remark that "it was like swimming with sharks."[15] During the second day of the hearings, Nathaniel Urshan telephoned Nigh and told him that if he would repent Urshan could guarantee him a missions appointment. When pressed on what the nature of his repentance should be, Urshan told Nigh it related to his need to enforce proper standards of holiness, specifically clean-shaven men. Disputes of this nature disgusted men like C.H. Yadon. During the same time period he preached that men shaved daily to keep from looking natural and publicly declared his desire to grow a beard that reached to his navel.[16] Suspicion, accusation, innuendo, and hypocrisy coalesced to finally bring the UPC foreign missionary board to a decision not to renew Nigh's endorsement and appointment as a missionary. Nigh was simply too rebellious and theologically unreliable. Thus in 1983, Director Harry Scism called Nigh at Schloß Freudenberg in Wiesbaden during a service to announce the verdict (ill.4.2). Nigh was summoned from the platform to take the telephone call. Inexplicably, Scism declined to reveal to Nigh what the determining factors were in bringing the missions board to its decision.[17] Nigh

---

[15] Dale Royce interview, 24 August 2013, who heard the remarks from Judd and Nigh. Confirmed by Wayne Nigh interview, 27 September 2013, Caldwell, Idaho.
[16] C.H. Yadon, "An Old Preacher's Last Words to a Young Man," sermon at the Idaho District camp meeting, 21 July 1982. FC, inv.doc.no 0707-2473-18.
[17] Details confirmed in Wayne Nigh interview, 25 July 2013. I personally witnessed John Goodwin's hypocrisy in Europe during a missions trip between

described the situation in terms of being "shot down" and a period of time constituting the "darkest and hardest time of [his] life." Off the record, Edwin Judd revealed to Nigh what Scism would not.

4.2  Schloß Freudenberg, (more properly a villa) built in 1904 by the architect
Paul Schultz-Naumburg in Wiesbaden-Dotzheim, Germany.
View from the southwest in the summer of 1984

The UPC absolutely could not abide Nigh's doctrinal position on eschatology and the fact that he did not uphold vigorously as requirements certain standards of holiness especially pertaining to facial hair (see ill.5.18, p. 286).[18] Beyond this, Nigh was notoriously suspect on the new birth and absolutely deviant on the matter of end-time prophecy.

Concerning the subject of eschatology, though defying strict categorization, in broad terms Wayne Nigh was a semi-historicist

---

Wiesbaden, Germany and Antwerpen, Belgium. *The Journal of Thomas A. Fudge, 1980-1985*, entry for 16 August 1984.

[18] Wayne Nigh, letter to Jerry Dillon, 15 February 1983. FC, inv.doc.no 0707-4795-32. Elements of Nigh's understanding of eschatology were condemned in summary form in the position paper "The Coming of the Lord" adopted by the General Board in 2005. *Manual* (2014), pp. 170-171. Nigh considers the position paper theologically and historically hopeless.

with "very strong historical leanings" not unlike the position taken by C.H. Yadon and Clinton Brown (1905-1986). On the doctrine of eschatology, Nigh had been influenced by the works of lawyer and writer Philip Mauro (1859-1952), to which he had been introduced

4.3 Itinerant Idaho Bible teacher Clinton Brown with CBC students: Gregg Calder, Peggy Faust, Troy Wasmundt, Peggy Yelm, Thomas A. Fudge, Eric K. Loy and Kim Simmons, 1 April 1982

by Edwin Judd while a CBC student.[19] During the days of dilemma on what to do with the German problem, former CBC president John Klemin was sent to Germany to interrogate Nigh on his eschatological views. Klemin did not detect anything seriously problematic. On a similar mission, Foreign Missions Board member Wayne Rooks (1927-1997) came to Germany on behalf of the UPC to see what Nigh was up to. The Foreign Missions board also sent a committee to Wiesbaden to investigate the various allegations lodged against Nigh by his enemies. In the end, Nigh was stricken from the list of endorsed UPC missionaries. What happened in Germany to Wayne Nigh as an individual was a microcosm of what

---

[19] The book Judd gave Nigh was Mauro's, *The Seventy Weeks of Daniel and the Great Tribulation* (Boston: Hamilton Bros, 1923), a veritable challenge to the theories of C.I. Scofield which were prevalent throughout the UPC.

was occurring institutionally at CBC. Outsiders were determined to correct apparent theological drifts.

Prior to all of this, in the early 1970s the College Board passed a motion to consider seriously establishing a CBC extension campus in Germany upon the request of Wayne Nigh, who had interest in establishing closer ties with the American church. Nigh envisioned students spending time in Europe and faculty members having the opportunity to teach in both locations with Germany also providing a venue for fourth-year interns interested in a career in missions. At one stage, Nigh had as many as a dozen former CBC students in Wiesbaden serving in various capacities. The College Board of Directors went on record as favoring the Nigh proposal. But the proposal failed to come to maturity. European regional field supervisor Hulon Myre had concerns about Nigh's work and there was opposition from a number of other missionaries, including Goodwin. Nigh wished to foster a curriculum which did not simply teach a rote UPC catechism but would expose students to critical thinking and theological exploration.[20] In this sense, he shared common goals with Don Fisher. In 1973, a working German-CBC connection was possible. A few years later the idea of connecting CBC to Nigh's Wiesbaden School of the Bible was unthinkable to the newly-arrived experts.

Ordinarily, in the history of religion, outsiders were the agitators for change not defenders of tradition. The erosion of support for CBC obvious from the 1970s onwards, reflects similar ideological developments elsewhere. The seeds of change started to be sown in 1968 when Jim Roam assumed the pastorate of "First Church" in Portland on Killingworth Street. This marked the beginning of outsiders coming into the Northwest, mainly from California but also from places such as Oklahoma and elsewhere, manifesting the ethos cultivated in the context of the UPC deep south. Roam was followed in that pastorate by Winfred Toole. Roam brought Toole to Portland from California in 1973 without the consent of the church board and the appointment ultimately was disastrous.[21] Paul

---

[20] *Minutes*, CBC board meeting, 3 August 1973, p. 2, FC, inv.doc.no 0707-5164-34, and Wayne Nigh interview, 27 September 2013.

[21] Ron and Wanda Calder interview, 9 August 2013, Oregon City, Oregon, Dwain Hornsby interview, 3 October 2013, Milwaukie, Oregon, Joe Sargent interview, 4

Dugas, Barry King, who was "one of the real main pivots" of these changes, Bill Davies, who idolized Winfred Toole and "became a sort of marionette of Vaughn Morton," and others exerted dramatic change.[22] The hardliners included these men as well as others such as David Knight, Verneal Crossley, Gary Gleason, Phil Dugas, and Clyde Barlow.[23] These changes, first of personnel and then of demography, had a detrimental effect upon the culture and ethos of toleration long established by the old PCI tradition in Oregon, Washington, and Idaho. Toole, Dugas, King, and a number of others considered the Yadon outlook fatal. There *were* definite "experts" in matters of holiness and theology after all and they, the likes of Toole, Dugas, and King, were the self-described "experts." Their influence and interference undermined the college and contributed significantly to its eventual demise.[24]

Even some Northwest men came under the spell of this new ethos. An example is Clyde Barlow who had come to CBC as a student but eventually became a "fervent disciple of Paul Dugas," and was later described as a "clone of Paul Dugas [manifesting] the same rigid, ridiculous, regressive, fundamentalist, narrow, wooden, mindless approach to the things of God as Paul Dugas."[25] Barlow admits he "used to hang on every word" uttered by Dugas and by consequence was very strongly influenced by him.[26]

Fisher may have imagined the Northwest was still in some sense as he had known it. If he did so, he was mistaken.[27] There had

---

October 2013, Vancouver, Washington, and Jerry Dillon interview, 19 April 2013. Sargent was a church board member at the time and attended First Church from 1960 to 1980.

[22] King was from the Northwest but had left at an early age and pastored in Oklahoma for many years. Jerry Dillon interview, 5 January 1999. The description of King is from Leon Brokaw interview, 29 January 2001 while that of Davies is from Lewis J. Davies interview, 19 August 2013. Darline (Kantola) Royer interview, 15 August 2013 believes King and Dugas exerted significant influence.

[23] Clyde Barlow interview, 13 August 2013.

[24] George M. Kelley interview, 23 September 2013, Albion, Idaho.

[25] Jerry Dillon interview, 5 January 1999.

[26] Clyde Barlow interview, 13 August 2013.

[27] Jerry Peden believes that Fisher thought the Northwest still retained something of its vibrant tolerant character which had been part of his earlier experiences in the 1950s and 60s. Jerry Peden interview, 19 July 2002.

been enormous cultural shifts within the UPC between the 1960s and the 1980s.[28] In retrospect, it seems evident that Don Fisher was not sufficiently diligent in assessing the nature of the UPC in the Northwest before agreeing to take on the presidency of CBC. If he had undertaken a comprehensive investigation of the evolving ethos surrounding the college, he either thought he was strong enough to turn the wheel of that history, or failing to do so, he considered CBC and the effort as good a hill to die upon as any other. CBC was his *alma mater* and he believed he could save it from the ruination brought about by the Californicators and other missionaries.[29] It is quite incontestable that Fisher believed in the extraordinary power of the human will.[30] It is also possible that Fisher found merit in the doctrine of Canadian Prime Minister John Diefenbaker who insisted that "the probability of defeat is no justification for surrender to a false principle."[31] By 1981, there were few places left for Fisher within the UPC. Perhaps he regarded Portland as a place to make a last stand.

Winfred Toole, who was elected superintendent of the Oregon District upon the resignation of C.H. Yadon in 1975, was a considerable force in changing the direction of the Northwest away from its historical roots.[32] (ill.4.4) Some regarded him as the saving antidote to the Yadon heresy and believed that Toole saved Oregon from continued error and turned the area from its downward doctrinal spiral.[33] Others were less enthusiastic, merely responding to that idea with the bland comment "oh, that's nonsense."[34] Toole had also been responsible for making a similar impact in the Exeter, California church in the early 1950s.[35] His tenure in Portland was

---

[28] Thetus Tenney interview, 6 June 2013.

[29] Karissa (Fisher) Hopkins interview, 15 August 2013.

[30] Liddy, *Will*, p. 449.

[31] Noted in John G. Diefenbaker, *One Canada*, vol. 3: *The Tumultuous Years 1962-1967* (Toronto: Macmillan, 1977), p. 282.

[32] Norman Rutzen interview, 8 February 1999.

[33] Barry King interview, 20 January 1999.

[34] E.G. Moyer interview, 27 January 1999. Agreed in Frank LaCrosse interview, 16 January 2001, Tacoma, Washington.

[35] Leon Brokaw interview, 29 January 2001. That church had previously been pastored by Odell Cagle (1900-1986) and earlier by W.L. Stallones (†1939), who baptized C.H. Yadon. John Klemin also came out of that church.

unsuccessful inasmuch as there was resistance at First Church to his more strident insistence upon "the message" and rigid standards of holiness.[36] There was no affinity between Winfred Toole and Don Fisher. Indeed, "Toole was absolutely about to die" when Fisher was appointed as president of CBC.[37]

4.4 Winfred E. Toole, preaching in the CBC chapel, 1980

Others saw the appointment of Don Fisher at CBC as "tragic" and a "definite mistake" and "the main one at fault was Ralph Reynolds."[38] Conversely it should be noted that when Reynolds turned the office of CBC president over to Fisher he stated that he had peace in his heart with that decision.[39] Paul Dugas and Barry King were but two of the stalwart supporters of the Toole position which was a consistent and energetic defence and propagation of the Acts 2:38 message, required for salvation. Organizational

---

[36] Ron and Wanda Calder interview, 9 August 2013, Jan Smith interview, 24 September 2013, Milwaukie, Oregon, and Dwain Hornsby interview, 3 October 2013.

[37] Paul Dugas interview, 25 January 1999.

[38] Ralph Reynolds interview, 13 December 1999.

[39] Ralph Vincent Reynolds, "Welcome Back to CBC ..." *CBC Jubilation* 15 (No. 1, 1981), p. 3.

officials described Dugas as a "vicious" personality who "caused a lot of problems" on account of his "hard attitude" when he taught at CBC.[40] When he took on perceived heretics, compromisers, and those weak on the message, Dugas was "unpredictably explosive." He imagined himself in mortal combat and "still thought he was in the Battle of the Bulge." He took no prisoners.[41] Defenders of Dugas suggest he was frequently misunderstood.[42] However one characterizes him, Dugas considered John Klemin insufficiently robust on "the message" and thought that many of his colleagues

4.5  John Klemin and CBC student Eric K. Loy, 1982

were compromisers. An acrimonious appearance before the College Board resulted in flared tempers with Dugas eventually storming

[40] Nathaniel Urshan interview, 23 April 1999. Urshan also noted that Dugas was asked to leave the faculty of Christian Life College by Kenneth Haney and was also "released" from Gateway College of Evangelism in St. Louis. Dugas taught at CBC from 1969-1973. Urshan and Dugas had a longstanding personal quarrel and the former's comments should be understood in that context.

[41] Lewis J. Davies interview, 19 August 2013. Dugas did fight in World War II as a paratrooper and was present during hostilities at the Battle of the Bulge.

[42] Clyde Barlow interview, 13 August 2013. Barlow thinks that because Dugas was so firm in his doctrinal opinions, his detractors effectively stripped him of all compassion and humanity, qualities, Barlow asserted, which Paul Dugas had in abundance.

out in a state of agitation and C.M. Yadon hollering and running after him.[43] According to thoughtful reflections on attitude, "you can drive people away from good food with poor table manners."[44] While this is not the place to explore the matter, it is altogether possible that men like Dugas and King were the more powerful influences in Oregon and that Toole was manipulated by them, inasmuch as Toole lacked the courage of his own convictions. He was of meek temperament until he took to the pulpit where he delivered "thunderous blasting sermons" and became transformed into "Samson and Shamgar all rolled into one."[45] While holding to the more stringent UPC doctrines, Toole might also be described as an ethical man with integrity and gentlemanly qualities, though possessing some insecurity.[46] A similar characterization might be made for his successor, David Johnson who was also a "weak leader" on account of failing to muster the courage to defend his own convictions.[47] Toole later confessed he thought it had been a mistake to withdraw support for the college.[48] Had he not been under pressure from certain elements in the Oregon District, Toole probably would have continued to support CBC.[49] But by the time he came to that position of seeing support for CBC as a salutary posture, the college was a heap of smouldering ruins, Don Fisher had vanished into life beyond the UPC and Toole himself was afflicted with Waldenström's disease which killed him shortly thereafter. None of these men – Toole, King, Dugas or their supporters – had any theological sympathy with the Yadons, the PCI point of view, or the tradition of the Pacific Northwest. That placed them in opposition to CBC.

---

[43] Jerry Dillon interview, 19 April 2013.
[44] Edwin Judd interview, 10 April 1999.
[45] Lewis J. Davies interview, 19 August 2013.
[46] Darline (Kantola) Royer interview, 15 August 2013.
[47] Jerry Dillon interview, 5 January 1999, and Dan Lewis, letter to Thomas A. Fudge, 24 May 2013. FC, inv.doc.no 0707-5036-33. Dillon would go so far as to say that "Winfred Toole was a coward." Jerry Dillon interview, 19 April 2013.
[48] George Sponsler interview, 12 February 1999. Patterson, *Anatomy of a Reformation*, p. 17 points out his own regret over the bellicose confrontations in the SBC. Clyde Barlow interview, 13 August 2013, also regrets his previous stance concerning the college.
[49] Raymond A. Sirstad interview, 27 August 2013.

These observations concerning Winfred Toole have also been advanced with respect to the Washington District Superintendent Ernest Verneal Crossley (1926-1996), who was also subjected to enormous pressure by the militant missionary mentality which had slowly infiltrated the Northwest (ill.5.6, p. 256).[50] Crossley had been converted in Twin Falls, Idaho, under the ministry of C.H. Yadon, but he did not reflect the Yadon influence in his leadership.[51] There are good grounds for assigning Crossley's theological conversion to the influence of his wife (Tiny Anderson) whose thinking had been shaped by the more strident emphases in California (see ill.0.1, p. xviii. Tiny Crossley appears in the third row, fifth from the left).[52] Crossley went along with some Oregon District initiatives which disadvantaged CBC.[53] Some were adamant in their opinion that the entire area had been adversely affected by C.H. Yadon and his supporters, and that fact alone constituted the biggest problem.[54] Conversely, others testified that Yadon "was highly esteemed ... one of the finest men we ever had."[55]

By 1981, the UPC had changed to such an extent from its origins in 1945 that there were few places left for men like Don Fisher. Perhaps he believed there was sufficient space remaining in the Northwest.[56] Fisher associates claim that he believed a more evangelical Bible College approach would have greater success within the UPC in the Northwest.[57] Mississippi was never going to

---

[50] According to colleagues, Crossley was not capable of exercising the type of leadership needed to unite the district and the college. Frank LaCrosse interview, 16 January 2001, and Jerry Dillon interview, 19 April 2013.

[51] Donna Fisher interview, 3 January 1999.

[52] E.W. Yadon interview, 25 July 2013, Nampa, Idaho, and Ron and Wanda Calder interview, 9 August 2013. Repeated efforts to contact Tiny Crossley for confirmation or clarification were unsuccessful.

[53] Winfred Toole, letter to the brethren of the Oregon District, 9 March 1982.

[54] Statement of Robert Bibb reflected in Jerry Peden interview, 19 July 2002.

[55] Nathaniel Urshan interview, 23 April 1999.

[56] "Don [Fisher] went back to the Pacific Northwest thinking it may have been the last bastion of toleration in the UPC. In the years he was away, the radicals from California and elsewhere moved in and one by one the states of Oregon, Washington and Idaho fell prey to their machinations. By the time Don returned in 1981 the handwriting was not just on the wall, but caked in concrete." Thomas A. Fudge, letter to Pamela Hatheway, 24 January 2003.

[57] Lewis, *The Journey Out*, pp. 41-42.

tolerate the emphases of men like Lewis, Howell, and Fisher. Perhaps Oregon would. Not one of the presidents who preceded Don Fisher at CBC can be regarded as hardliners or PAJC sympathizers. This is not to say they did not believe the message but it does imply they refused to adopt the more strident application of its emphases. If John Dearing (1880-1940) had been the teacher *par excellence* for Oneness Pentecostals in the old days, then Paul Dugas represented the new guard and while his proclamations may be characterized as shrill, few even knew of Dearing and the PCI point of view.[58] Men steeped in the old Northwest tradition had begun to voice concerns. For example, we find the sentiment that "Idaho does not need any more 'southern ram-rodders' if you know what I mean."[59] Yadon said there were no "experts." Missionaries to the Northwest were determined to prove him wrong. When the dust settled, the gates of CBC were besieged with "experts." The old guard found it hard to kick against the pricks. According to some local pastors, the invaders did not possess a Christ-like spirit and the changes they introduced had an adverse effect upon the entire region.[60] There was an increasingly deep suspicion of those "experts" claiming to know the answers, men John the Baptist called a "generation of vipers."[61]

Renewed controversy began to swirl around CBC almost from the moment the announcement was released that Don Fisher had resigned from JCM and was on his way to the west coast to take the reins of CBC which had been relinquished by Reynolds. Fisher was

---

[58] Dugas edited the periodical paper, the *Apostolic Contender* for almost thirty years from 1974 until he was stricken with dementia a short time before his death in 2006. While the publication unarguably sat well to the right of the UPC's official periodical publications such as the *Pentecostal Herald*, Dugas' paper represented a new trend prevalent throughout the Northwest.

[59] Wayne Nigh, letter to Jerry and Kris Dillon, 26 March 1984. FC, inv.doc.no 0707-4798-32.

[60] Wallace Leonard interview, 3 August 2013 for the comment about attitude, and Mickey Denny interview, 23 September 2013, Sequim, Washington, for the negative outcome.

[61] C.H. Yadon, "Last Address to the Oregon District," Oregon District Conference, 24-26 April 1975, Eugene, Oregon, audio recording. FC, inv.doc.no 0707-5437-35. At this conference Yadon stepped down from his duties as district superintendent.

aware of dissent. "I accepted the presidency of the college knowing her existence was being challenged (at the April meeting) all the while believing men would be honest, ethical and Biblical in their approach to solving the difficulties of the past."[62] During the second Reynolds era, an apparent (though generally superficial) wide swathe of popular support for the college was evidenced in the Portland metropolitan area. This popular support can be determined largely from the stance taken by local UPC ministers to the college and its administration. The relationship between CBC and area pastors remained a point of ongoing concern.[63] Since the college was located in Portland, the Oregon District formed the first and immediate bastion of support and control. Indeed, the general administrative constituency of the United Pentecostal Church International seldom involved itself in district matters unless specifically asked to do so. Even on such occasions there was often considerable reluctance to assume any other posture than mediation, neutrality, or moral influence.

In legal terms CBC technically was sponsored by the UPC as a denomination, but the more relevant reality was that the college was owned, operated, and controlled jointly by the Districts of Idaho, Washington, and Oregon. Since Idaho lay four hundred miles from Portland at its closest point, in practical terms it had the least immediate control. Notwithstanding the popular support for the college in Reynolds' time, the essential support base in the Oregon District was markedly eroded almost immediately when Fisher was appointed, thanks to the influence of the reformers from California and elsewhere. They had been awaiting the change of presidency as their opportunity to reform the ethos of the college. It is possible that with the departure of R.V. Reynolds, some thought that perhaps Paul Dugas or someone of his theological orientation might be appointed to the presidency of CBC. Those constituting the more hard-line tradition in the Northwest must have been stunned and dismayed when Don Fisher was announced as the successor to Reynolds.

---

[62] Don Fisher, letter to the "friends of CBC," 14 December 1981, p. 1. FC, inv.doc.no 0707-4809-32. See Appendix 14, pp. 451-452.
[63] Ralph V. Reynolds, letter to the CBC board, 8 June 1979. FC, inv.doc.no 0707-5185-34.

Former CBC faculty member and president, Edwin E. Judd spoke for forty-five minutes at the Oregon District conference at Bend in 1981, urging that body of ministers not to withdraw support for the college (ill.3.17, p. 143). Judd's admonition was not heeded. By a three-to-one margin, the Oregon District withdrew from any meaningful association with CBC. Some of the Oregon ministers privately considered Judd to be an unreliable liberal, theologically influenced by C.H. Yadon, and they were unpersuaded by his appeal to support the college.[64] After all, questions about his doctrinal orthodoxy had persisted since the 1960s, and his election to national prominence did little to allay the suspicions held by his detractors. Edwin Judd's advice would never do.

What were the issues? There appear to be two significant factors. The first was financial. One argument explaining Oregon's withdrawal centers on the heavy financial responsibility carried by the three sponsoring districts. By 1981, the Oregon District found the burden too heavy to bear.[65] This argument might carry greater weight were it not for the fact that Oregon had committed its true desire to print and to presentation, to wit that it wanted to control the college and bring it completely under the jurisdiction of the Oregon District. If the weight of one-third financial responsibility for CBC was difficult for Oregon to sustain, how did it propose to singlehandedly support the college? This factor alone calls into question the validity of the argument that Oregon withdrew primarily in the face of mounting fiscal difficulties. Finance may have been at issue but it was hardly the critical point.

The second factor was doctrine. Self-identified hardliners in Oregon are certain that issues of theology contributed mightily to the Oregon action.[66] Quite apart from suspicion over Don Fisher, three additional and concrete points of conflict were identified at the time: the first was over who should control the college, the second centred on whether the college or the local church should have jurisdictional authority over the students, while a third concern focused on whether students should be permitted to attend a

---

[64] Lewis J. Davies interview, 19 August 2013.
[65] Raymond A. Sirstad interview, 27 August 2013 and Jim Christensen interview, 1 October 2013.
[66] Clyde Barlow interview, 13 August 2013.

Portland-area UPC church which did not support CBC.[67] David
Reynolds, then serving as president of the Alumni Association,
feared that CBC was in danger of being destroyed, and in his strong
appeal for support also pondered why the Oregon District felt it
necessary not only to withdraw support but to impose further
sanctions. "Why has the District Board forbidden the giving of
scholarships and recommended against the buying of ads in the
Ensign?"[68] The 1981 *Ensign* featured eleven ads from the district
and eighteen churches bought advertisements. By contrast the 1982
*Ensign* featured no Oregon District ads and only six churches
purchased space in the yearbook. The Oregon District took the
view at its November 1981 meeting that those recommendations
were consistent with its position about the college.[69] However, it is
difficult to avoid concluding that despite official denials Oregon did
attempt actively to interfere and disadvantage CBC. Oregon District
superintendent Winfred Toole admitted as much. "I made a request
at the close of the C.B.C. Board of Directors meeting that in the
interest of peace and harmony that the District Superintendents on
the board [Toole, Crossley, and Rutzen] not attend the C.B.C.
Dinner held in Salem that evening. The Superintendent of
Washington graciously complied. We have expressed our
appreciation to him."[70] Norman Rutzen was obviously unwilling to
acquiesce and both he and former CBC board member Enoch
Hutcheson from Klamath Falls attended the Salem banquet.[71] One
may speculate dimly on the nature of the peace and harmony which
motivated Toole and what his feelings were about Rutzen's refusal
to aid the Oregon District. Nevertheless, Rutzen was not going to
be bullied into withdrawing one iota of support for the college.

---

[67] David Reynolds, letter to CBC Alumni and Friends, 1 December 1981, pp. 1-2.
FC, inv.doc.no 0707-5207-34.
[68] David Reynolds, letter to CBC Alumni and Friends, 1 December 1981, p. 1.
More than three decades later, Reynolds continues to stand behind his letter.
David Reynolds interview, 12 August 2013.
[69] See Winfred Toole, letter to Oregon District pastors, 23 February 1982. FC,
inv.doc.no 0707-5208-34. See Appendix 15, p. 453.
[70] Winfred Toole, letter to the brethren of the Oregon District, 9 March 1982.
FC, inv.doc.no 0707-5214-34.
[71] *CBC Jubilation* 16 (No. 1, 1982), p. 6 published photographs of both men
speaking at the Salem banquet.

There were thirty-seven churches in the Oregon District at the time the resolution to withdraw official support for CBC was ratified. Only seven Oregon ministers out of a total of seventy-six actively opposed that action. The seven included Leon Brokaw, George Sponsler, Raymond A. Sirstad, and Albert Dillon (1932-2007).[72] Sirstad attempted in vain to persuade his colleagues to maintain continuing support for the college.[73] A later resolution, originating from Section One of the district and backed by Paul Dugas and Barry King, called for the establishment of a new Bible college in 1983 based upon obtaining the original CBC charter. The proposal reached the floor of the Oregon District conference in April 1983 but was defeated.[74] Once again, this action calls into question the claim that Oregon withdrew support for the college chiefly on account of unbearable financial exigencies. Faced with the presidency of Don Fisher at CBC, the Oregon District "fought him every inch of the way."[75] At that time, in 1981, Winfred Toole was the superintendent, David Johnson was secretary, and the remainder of the board included George Sponsler (Section One), Albert Dillon (Section Two), David Knight (Section Three), L.N. (Noel) Murphy (Section Four), Titus Duncan (1926-2013) (Section Five), and J.D. Borders (Section Six). The only definite supporters of Fisher on that board were Dillon and Sponsler (ill.5.3, p. 252). Oregon had taken legal advice on the district's position and made a

---

[72] Leon Brokaw interview, 29 January 2001. The other three defenders were Darline Kantola, John Klemin, and a young man from southern Oregon. The latter may have been Raymond Swarringim who pastored in Eugene. Jerry Dillon interview, 19 April 2013. Three of the seven were college employees and Sponsler was a member of the national DOE. This means that only four Oregon pastors supported CBC. I am enormously grateful to John Smelser and Gina Masters for manually counting the seventy-six Oregon ministers from the pages of the 1981 UPC Ministerial Directory and for providing me with that list. John Smelser, letter to Thomas A. Fudge, 22 August 2013. FC, inv.doc.no 0707-5283-34. One must not surmise that all seventy-six ministers attended that conference. The number of churches is based upon *Ensign*, vol. 28 (1981), p. 145 and the 1981 UPC ministerial directory, pp. 243-244.

[73] Raymond A. Sirstad interview, 27 August 2013.

[74] Undated typescript resolution requesting the CBC board to allow Oregon to obtain the charter for the purpose of operating a UPC-endorsed college within Oregon under its sole control. FC, inv.doc.no 0707-5228-34.

[75] Frank LaCrosse interview, 16 January 2001.

presentation to the CBC board. Ralph Reynolds, Edwin Judd, Hugh Rose, George Sponsler, David Johnson, and Barry King were admitted to a board meeting in connection with the Oregon case for a single-district college governance administered by Oregon. Following a lengthy discussion, C.H. Yadon moved that the matter be referred back to Oregon for further clarification. That motion was carried. However, it seems evident that the CBC board was not about to turn control of the college over to Oregon.[76] In a deeply ironic move which must have galled Fisher, both Winfred Toole and Gary Gleason, having withdrawn support for CBC continued to sit on the College Board during the 1981-82 academic year setting up a peculiar administration.

Unlike JCM, Apostolic Bible Institute in St. Paul, Minnesota, Texas Bible College in Houston, Christian Life College in Stockton, California, and other UPC colleges, CBC did not have an officially recognized college church for students to attend during their formal studies.[77] By 1978, this matter had become an acute problem. The background to this development may be found in the changes occurring within the Northwest, which gathered momentum in the 1970s. At CBC there was a fairly solid sense of unity and purpose, despite mounting conflict with a growing number of the Portland-area pastors. The arrival and influence of men such as Paul Dugas and Barry King brought significant challenges to the college. In the opinion of some College Board members both men "were as radical as could be."[78] There were no serious disagreements between local churches or pastors and CBC before the arrival of "southerners and foreigners." The strident claims of such men, which interfered with the goals and work of CBC, became the chief factor prompting the college church initiative.[79] Numerous battlegrounds formed around the "quarrelsome old woman" and men made her, theology, a test of fellowship.

---

[76] *Minutes*, CBC board meeting, 13 June 1981, pp. 2-3. FC, inv.doc.no 0707-5202-34. Rose and Sponsler represented the DOE.

[77] JCM, ABI, TBC (Houston), and CLC (the former Western Apostolic Bible College in Stockton, California) each had a strong home church base pastored by men like Thomas Craft, S.G. Norris, James Kilgore, and Kenneth Haney.

[78] George M. Kelley interview, 23 September 2013.

[79] Jerry Dillon interview, 19 April 2013.

Rivalries formed among students as to which church was more spiritual or doctrinally sound.[80] Thomas R. O'Daniel, a 1973 CBC graduate who had previously been working as a missionary in Ghana, West Africa, was sent to the college in 1978 on account of undefined problems and evidently some thought O'Daniel could help shore things up.[81] John Klemin advanced a proposal, endorsed by the CBC faculty, that a college church be founded. Following a protracted discussion a motion was brought before the board that the idea be ratified. The motion was then voted upon by means of a secret ballot with an eight-to-three outcome in favor of the concept.[82] Proposals for a specific college church had been raised previously and had advanced to the extent of CBC actually filing an application for a college church with the Oregon District Board. With a single abstention, the board unanimously declined the application.[83] Oregon opposition to the initiative was firm. Jerry Dillon was the principle impetus behind the college church initiative. When he resigned in 1978, his decision was discussed by the board. It is noteworthy that the chairman of the board, C.M. Yadon, enlarged the discussion to include the matter of the college church (ill.5.13, p. 270). Inasmuch as Yadon was fiercely opposed to the idea, it is likely that Yadon considered Dillon's resignation as a solution to the perennial debate over the establishment of a college church.[84] The chief concern with the application revolved around the question of pastoral leadership and its immediate corollaries, pastoral authority and control. Local ministers held that they were pastors and CBC faculty were teachers and they drew clear lines of demarcation. CBC faculty members like Jerry Dillon

---

[80] Darline (Kantola) Royer interview, 15 August 2015 who supported the college church idea.

[81] Dale Royce interview, 24 August 2013, notes that O'Daniel made this known to him shortly after arrival. Thomas R. O'Daniel, letter to Thomas A. Fudge, 13 September 2013, characterizes his work at CBC as college promotion and student recruitment. FC, inv.doc.no 0707-5309-34.

[82] *Minutes*, CBC board meeting, 10 March 1978, p. 1. FC, inv.doc.no 0707-5180-34.

[83] Undated letter (*c.* 1977) from John Klemin to the CBC staff. FC, inv.doc.no 0707-4750-32.

[84] *Minutes*, CBC board meeting, 8 June 1978 (FC, inv.doc.no 0707-5183-34), and Jerry Dillon interview, 5 January 1999.

and Darline Kantola considered the categories both mistaken and distorted in the assumption that the college could not provide a pastoral role to students. Despite the opposition there were renewed efforts to establish a college church. These efforts failed.[85] Don Fisher and some of his predecessors supported the idea of a college church.[86] In light of this situation, CBC students were obligated to select one of the supporting area churches as a place to attend regularly during their time in Portland. This was a firm college requirement.[87]

The year before Fisher arrived, no fewer than eight Portland area UPC churches had been designated as options for CBC students to attend. These were frequently referred to with reference to the pastor. Clyde Barlow in St. Helens; Abundant Life Church, pastored by Paul Dugas in St. Johns; Barry King in Beaverton; First United Pentecostal Church (remnant), pastored by Leon Brokaw in Milwaukie; George Sponsler at Neighborhood in the east Portland-Gresham area; John Klemin in Vancouver; Gary Gleason in Oregon City; and Evangel Church pastored by Phillip Dugas on North Killingsworth Street.[88] Once Fisher was ensconced in the president's office at 10838 North Lombard, Barlow, both Dugases, King, and Gleason withdrew their support for the college leaving only Klemin, Sponsler, and Brokaw in active, open support. Their churches constituted the choices for students in terms of a home church for the 1981-82 academic year.[89] Fisher had attempted to establish a working agreement between the college and local churches, wherein area pastors, while having CBC students in their congregations, would agree that the college took precedence over

---

[85] John Klemin, letter to the CBC board, 8 June 1978, p. 1 (FC, inv.doc.no 0707-5182-34) and Klemin, letter to the CBC board, 28 August 1978, p. 1. FC, inv.doc.no 0707-5184-34.

[86] Ralph Reynolds interview, 13 December 1999.

[87] *Conquerors Bible College (Portland, Oregon) General Catalog 1979-1981*, p. 12.

[88] *Ensign*, vol. 28 (1981), pp. 112-113.

[89] There were actually a total of four options for students during that academic year. Nathaniel Yadon had opened a small mission church in Orchards, east of Vancouver in 1981. Pledging his support for Fisher and the college, students were permitted to consider this venue as their church. A very few did. Yadon was appointed to the faculty in the fall of 1982 during that last ill-fated year of CBC's existence, but taught only during Fall Term.

the church.[90] Most of the Portland churches declined to enter into any such contract. It is not surprising that some of these pastors refused to stay in fellowship with the college when it is apparent that Fisher was not the unanimous choice for president to succeed the retiring Reynolds. Presumably, some of the pastors withdrawing support were among those months earlier declining to support Fisher as president-elect. Some vocally admitted this. "I opposed his coming. I very strongly opposed his coming to the president of the school that was going out as well as to the chairman of the Conquerors Bible College Board ..."[91] Paul Dugas was on record as saying much the same thing.[92] National officials adamantly declared that Fisher should never have been appointed as college president.[93] It is possible they suspected a theological Trojan horse and feared its entrance into the Northwest. Even Fisher may have entertained some misgivings as he wondered why the CBC board was interested in him.[94]

The actual vote for Don Fisher apart from the declaration that he was a "large majority selection," does not appear to be a matter of record.[95] In the puzzling absence of any terms of reference governing the election of presidents there is some difference of opinion on whether a simple majority was sufficient, whether the appointment of a president required a two-thirds majority, or if a

---

[90] "Working Agreement" form established by CBC for the 1981-82 academic year. FC, inv.doc.no 0707-5204-34.

[91] Barry King interview, 20 January 1999.

[92] Paul Dugas interview, 25 January 1999. Harry Fisher who worked at CBC between 1975 and 1981 knew all of the area pastors and said he was not surprised at the eventual hostility. Harry Fisher interview, 13 July 2005.

[93] Cleveland Becton interview, 14 April 1999.

[94] Michael Nigh interview, 18 August 2013. Fisher told Nigh the day before he interviewed that he did not know why he was in Portland and wondered why CBC was even considering him for the presidency.

[95] Stated in Norman Rutzen, letter to the Northwestern Brethren, 13 November 1981, p. 1. Others thought Fisher had unanimous support from the CBC board when he interviewed for the presidency. Donna Fisher interview, 3 January 1999. This does not appear to be accurate. Some present in the session which elected Fisher agree with Rutzen's characterization of the vote. Raymond A. Sirstad interview, 27 August 2013, George M. Kelley interview, 23 September 2013, Mickey Denny interview, 23 September 2013, Frank LaCrosse interview, 1 October 2013, and Jim Christensen interview, 1 October 2013.

definite unanimous decision was required.[96] The CBC board which appointed Don Fisher to the college presidency was comprised of representatives from each of the three controlling districts. Idaho

4.6  CBC Board of Directors, 1981. *Back row, left to right:* George Kelley, Enoch Hutcheson, Mickey Denny, Paul Yadon, Paul Dugas, Frank LaCrosse, and Jim Christensen. *Front row, left to right:* Raymond Sirstad, Winfred Toole, C.M. Yadon, Norman Rutzen, and Ralph V. Reynolds

was represented by Norman Rutzen, Paul Yadon (1913-1983), and the laymen George M. Kelley and Jim Christensen. Washington was represented by C.M. (Charlie) Yadon, Frank LaCrosse, and the layman Mickey Denny. Oregon was represented by Winfred Toole, Paul Dugas, and the layman Enoch Hutcheson from Klamath Falls. Ralph Reynolds and Raymond Sirstad also sat on that board as non-

[96] Raymond A. Sirstad interview, 27 August 2013, opined a simple majority was sufficient while Jerry Dillon thought a two-thirds margin was required. Expressed during an interview with Harry and Freda Fisher, 8 December 2000. Arless Glass interview, 24 September 2013, thought there had to be consensus. There is no statement in the 1967 CBC *Corporate By-Laws* (FC, inv.doc.no 0707-4777-32) or in the 1982 *Restated Corporate By-Laws*, 15 October 1982, to resolve the matter. FC, inv.doc.no 0707-5215-34.

voting members representing the college.[97] Some of these men, such as Winfred Toole and Paul Dugas, had also been members of the College Board of Directors or served on the Executive Board at the time Fisher was appointed.[98] Many of these men had a long association with CBC.

The College Board was selected at the district level of the three controlling districts. Each of the superintendents were automatically members of the board. For each term, one licensed minister and two laymen were elected in each district conference, having either previously been nominated by the relevant District Board or sometimes following open nominations from the floor. The college president was an *ex officio* board member. The Executive Board consisted of the three district superintendents and the college president.[99] The normal configuration of two laymen and one minister was sometimes reversed so that at times some districts were in fact represented by two ministers and one layman. While technically noncompliant with the requirements of the by-laws, no one seems to have objected.[100]

Lay representation on the College Board ended abruptly in 1981. Lay membership on the board had historically been a unique feature of the CBC administration. By a vote of six-to-three, the board initially ratified a motion brought by Norman Rutzen and seconded by Paul Yadon that an additional layman from each district be added to the board. However, further discussion prompted a motion to rescind the amendment, which passed even

---

[97] Paul Yadon is mistakenly identified as his older brother C.H. Yadon in the photograph published in *Ensign*, vol. 27 (1981), p. 12. I have been unable to explain why Oregon and Washington seem to be one representative short. Hutcheson had involvement with CBC from the early 1960s, serving on its board for perhaps as many as eight years. Enoch Hutcheson interview, 20 August 2013, Klamath Falls, Oregon.

[98] *Ensign*, vol. 27 (1981), pp. 12-13. The administrative board was made up of Sirstad, C.M. Yadon, Toole, Rutzen, and Reynolds.

[99] *Corporate By-Laws, Conquerors Bible College*, 1967, Article 2, sections 1 and 3, p. 1. FC, inv.doc.no 0707-4777-32.

[100] In 1982, the configuration of the board constituency was altered to include three from Idaho and three from Washington, two of whom were to be ordained ministers, in addition to the superintendents of those districts and the college president. *Restated Corporate By-Laws* (1982), Article 2, section 1, p. 1.

though Norman Rutzen went on record as opposing the new motion. Verneal Crossley supported Rutzen on this point.[101] Jim Christensen, George Kelley, Mickey Denny, and Enoch Hutcheson were the last laymen to serve on the CBC board. At the next meeting no laymen were seated. This action, which occurred prior to Fisher's election as president, may be considered one of the factors in the downfall of CBC.[102] Some members of the board considered the action inappropriate and contrary to the historic tradition of college administration dating back to 1953, when CBC was founded by E.G. Moyer. That year, Moyer spoke at the Northwest District camp meeting in Bend urging that lay representation should be fundamental to the founding and governing of the college.[103] Moyer actually sold shares in the college throughout the old Northwest District, whereby the constituency of the sprawling district owned CBC (see ill.0.1, p. xviii). The dissolution of the lay board possibly had legal implications but no one raised that concern in 1981. The move to eliminate the lay members of the board was not announced prior to the meeting and therefore the matter was "pretty cut and dried" and there was no opportunity to discuss the issue with the laity of the several districts.[104] The matter was potentially divisive. As noted, lay representation was a unique feature of the CBC administration. However, the function of the lay members was curious in that they were sometimes excluded from particular discussions or decisions taken by the board. On a regular basis the lay representatives were asked to vacate the board room while particular matters were vetted. Some members considered the practice intolerable.[105] Behind the scenes, it was apparent that some ministers did not want

---

[101] *Minutes*, CBC board meeting, 8 April 1981, pp. 1-2. FC, inv.doc.no 0707-5196-34. Confirmed in George M. Kelley interview, 23 September 2013. The *Restated Corporate By-Laws* (1982), Article 2, section 1, p. 1 makes no mention of laymen.

[102] David Reynolds interview, 12 August 2013, and Mickey Denny interview, 23 September 2013. Others took a neutral view on the matter. Enoch Hutcheson interview, 20 August 2013.

[103] George M. Kelley interview, 23 September 2013.

[104] Jim Christensen interview, 1 October 2013.

[105] Mickey Denny interview, 23 September 2013. Other individuals regarded the lay representatives as lacking authority to govern the college. Frank LaCrosse interview, 1 October 2013. The statement is curious.

lay representatives privy to the arguments at board level undergirding the private promotion of more radical positions.[106] In 1981, board member Paul Dugas apparently told Fisher that he wanted the president of CBC to maintain a strong position on the essential doctrine of "full salvation."[107] Several of those pastors withdrawing support had also previously served as adjunct teachers at the college. None of them ever again taught on the CBC campus. In a contemporary summary of the situation, Fisher wrote at the end of 1981, "as the last few months have evidenced, some have chosen to disassociate themselves because they have no spirit or desire to cooperate, only to control. This unfortunate move was initiated by men who have no love-roots in the Northwest; no rich heritage in the struggle which gave birth to our college; neither do they share our perspective."[108] (Many of the original supporters are seen in ill.0.1, p. xviii.) That last comment was absolutely correct. Doctrinally, there was very little in common between Don Fisher and Paul Dugas while philosophically there was no fellowship between Fisher and Barry King. This letter may have been a tactical error on Fisher's part, however, especially in the accusation about the newcomers. While its accuracy is hard to dispute, the charge was seized upon with special venom and produced even more hostility even as Fisher publicly urged his detractors that they were obligated to work within the spirit of the early UPC which forbade contending for points of view to the disunity of the organization.[109]

There was more to the matter which appears to have gone unrecorded. Reference to honesty and ethics in this same letter, and noted earlier, suggest a brewing climate of hostility and opposition. Much of the conflict initially centered in Oregon. Winfred Toole charged the college with unbecoming conduct, and complained that

---

[106] Norman Rutzen interview, 27 September 2013. Similar comments in Jim Christensen interview, 1 October 2013.

[107] Paul Dugas interview, 25 January 1999.

[108] Don Fisher, letter to the "friends of CBC," 14 December 1981, p. 1. FC, inv.doc.no 0707-4809-32. Apparently there was a second, similar, letter, dated 16 December, which also raised the ire of some ministers. I have not found this letter but it is referred to in Winfred E. Toole, letter to Don Fisher, 9 March 1982. FC, inv.doc.no 0707-5213-34.

[109] Jerry Peden interview, 19 July 2002, and Don Fisher, "A Point of Interest to Those Who Care" *CBC Jubilation* 15 (No. 4, 1981), p. 2.

CBC fundraising activities within Oregon itself failed to utilise the "proper ethical principles," and went on peevishly to state that he "should have been the first to be consulted and notified." Toole

4.7 Cleveland M. Becton around the time of his involvement in the Oregon District's opposition to CBC in the early 1980s and (4.8) preaching at the Oregon District Conference in Roseburg, 1986

then appealed directly to General Superintendent Nathaniel Urshan to intervene.[110] Don Fisher wasted no time in taking the high road and offering apologies to Toole and other offended ministers in Oregon.[111] It is rather unclear precisely why Toole was upset but Fisher's letter went out "in love and in deep desire for peace so that the work of God and the name of our Lord will not be harmed or hindered." Winfred Toole accepted Fisher's letter in good faith.[112] Meanwhile, Urshan dispatched UPC General Secretary Cleveland Becton to Portland to arbitrate the Oregon District's complaint. Becton later advised the CBC board that it would be expedient in the future for local pastors and district officials to be notified of any

---

[110] Winfred Toole, letter to the Oregon District pastors, 23 February 1982. FC, inv.doc.no 0707-5208-34.

[111] Don Fisher, letter to Winfred Toole, 25 February 1982, and copied to Urshan, C.M. Becton, Arless Glass, and the CBC board. FC, inv.doc.no 0707-5210-34.

[112] Winfred Toole, letter to Don Fisher, 9 March 1982. FC, inv.doc.no 0707-5213-34.

meetings or functions scheduled to convene in Oregon.[113] Toole later reported that Becton had signalled his intention to make a full report of the situation to Urshan upon his return to St. Louis.[114]

4.9 The peculiar CBC board, 1981-82. *Back row, left to right:* Raymond Sirstad, Frank LaCrosse, Gary Gleason, C.H. Yadon. *Front row, left to right:* Winfred Toole, Don Fisher, Norman Rutzen, and Verneal Crossley

The scale of irony in this scenario is staggering. The Oregon District had formally withdrawn support for CBC eleven months earlier and the college continued to exist in Portland. Yet the Oregon District insisted and expected to be advised of college activities within Oregon. Moreover, it should be pointed out that both Winfred Toole and Gary Gleason continued to sit on the CBC board representing Oregon. It is difficult to imagine that the board was unaware of college functions or fundraising events, and if this is true than Toole and Gleason were also *au fait* with promotion and support efforts. Still, it appears that at least Toole expected to be consulted outside board meetings and perhaps in advance of board discussions. Such puerile policies bear closer scrutiny. When these private consultations and presumably requests from the college for permission to act within Oregon did not take place, the Oregon

---

[113] *Minutes*, CBC board meeting, 1 March 1982, p. 3.
[114] Winfred Toole, letter to the brethren of the Oregon District, 9 March 1982. FC, inv.doc.no 0707-5214-34.

District filed a protest with national UPC officials and Nathaniel Urshan commissioned C.M. Becton to travel to the west coast to hear Oregon leaders complain that they were being excluded by a college they had previously voted not to support. Don Fisher must have been disgusted and some board members were chagrined. CBC students later described the situation in the manner of an old wild west gunfight. "There was shooting from every direction and people being shot at from every direction."[115] The description is an apt metaphor of tensions which became ever more evident in the last days of CBC.

Toole's behavior is curious but not unprecedented. When his pastorate at First Church in Portland reached an impasse in 1976 and the church became mired in serious trouble, the Oregon District offered Toole the opportunity to work fulltime as district superintendent thereby providing a way for Toole to exit First Church gracefully. This plan was engineered by Lewis Davies and District Board member Albert Dillon. Toole accepted the option, announcing his resignation a number of weeks in advance. In place of several sermons he did not preach at all but simply mounted the pulpit and read chapters of the Bible to his congregation. At the last service, Toole announced to the congregation that he believed everyone needed to kneel and repent. While the congregation was praying, Winfred Toole walked off the platform and left the building without a word leaving the congregation in shock. He never returned to the church (ill.4.4, p. 155). A handful of people left with Toole, having been advised in advance but the majority of the church members were stunned.[116] He was succeeded by Lewis J. Davies, a generally progressive thinker, and subsequently by Leon Brokaw, who was the incumbent during the last days of CBC.

These factors, which clearly suggest ongoing dysfunction in the Northwest, raise several crucial questions about Fisher's election.

---

[115] Daniel R. Sirstad interview, 26 August 2013.

[116] Jerry Dillon interview, 19 April 2013, Ron and Wanda Calder interview, 9 August 2013, Darline (Kantola) Royer interview, 15 August 2013, Jan Smith interview, 24 September 2013, and Joe Sargent interview, 4 October 2013. All were church members and were present when Toole walked out. On the behind-the-scenes plan to ease Toole out of the church I am indebted to Lewis J. Davies interview, 19 August 2013.

One must wonder about the criteria advanced by Raymond Sirstad prior to Fisher's election. His appointment elsewhere has been characterized as a "mystery."[117] Had these area pastors originally backed Fisher only later to withdraw their support? Had his appointment been an unpopular hegemonic imposition? Had suppressed rumor, innuendo, and suspicion about Fisher drifted westward from Mississippi following his confirmation or had it been deliberately imported by express overnight service? It seems quite clear that what happened in Jackson followed Don Fisher to the west coast.[118] Had Fisher undertaken a severe and thorough house-cleaning upon arrival in Portland? Was Fisher responsible for the resulting alienation between the college and a large majority of Oregon pastors? Had power gone to Fisher's head? Now free from the "interference" or resistance of T.L. Craft – president of Jackson College of Ministries – was Fisher committed to making his mark on United Pentecostal Church higher education regardless of cost or consequence?[119] Had he determined to make CBC a fiefdom of "King Fisher"? Was he truly a follower of the notion that one should never hesitate to use power?[120] Alternatively, was Fisher a victim of a political power struggle in which he was out-manned and out-gunned from the outset? Was there an anti-Fisher conspiracy in the Oregon District in 1981? Was Don Fisher truly a heretic, and had he been, at long last, found out and cornered? Was there any justification for the financial stranglehold placed around the neck of CBC from 1981 onward which exacerbated the situation and unsurprisingly led to the collapse of the college two years later? Was there any evidential foundation to sustain the fear that a Fisher-led CBC was subverting UPC doctrine? Did an anti-CBC movement develop in the Northwest? Was the confrontation

---

[117] David Bernard interview, 16 April 1999.

[118] Thetus Tenney interview, 6 June 2013.

[119] Thomas L. Craft was the president of Jackson College of Ministries during Fisher's tenure. It appears that Fisher attended the day-to-day administering of the institution, but Craft retained ultimate power and authority. This resulted in varying degrees of conflict on several levels. Craft was likewise senior pastor of the college church. Some observers state that Fisher had conflict everywhere he worked on account of his inability to function as a subordinate. David Reynolds interview, 12 August 2013.

[120] Liddy, *Will*, p. 386.

at CBC the final showdown between the Yadon legacy and the "experts?" Were there secrets in Don Fisher's life which came to light only after he had been appointed? Each of these questions have been raised at one point or another in the last days of the college's existence and in the years which followed.

Paul Dugas alleged that Fisher's appointment was a violation of the usual normal appointment procedures and by consequence was

4.10  Ralph Reynolds, during his          4.11  Reynolds lecturing at CBC,
       second tenure at CBC, 1979                     May 1982

therefore illegal.[121] The allegation lacks evidential value. Ostensibly, there were no formal procedural rules in place for the election of presidents. Even those sitting on such boards were, in retrospect, quite uncertain of the process.[122] In terms of the 1981 process, while it is impossible to discover the record of a definite vote, it is highly likely that the support for Fisher was eight in favor (Rutzen,

---

[121] Paul Dugas interview, 25 January 1999. Dugas felt that Idaho promoted Fisher with support from Washington without regard for the wishes of Oregon. This was true but hardly illegal. Norman Rutzen interview, 24 July 2013.

[122] Enoch Hutcheson interview, 20 August 2013, was under the assumption that presidents were appointed by the tri-District Boards. This is certainly untrue.

Christensen, Kelley, Paul Yadon, LaCrosse, Denny, C.M. Yadon, and Hutcheson) and two against (Toole and Dugas). Normally, elections were conducted by secret ballot. Others asserted the anti-CBC faction "were just a bunch of carnal men."[123] It should be noted that when Ralph Reynolds resigned as college president in 1981 he made several recommendations (ill.4.10). These included the consideration of a number of candidates, that each applicant be interviewed, that each candidate present their policies, direction, and ideas for the future of the college, and that if necessary a special meeting of the board be convened to deal with the appointment.[124] The minutes of the board meeting wherein Fisher was elected do not reflect the suggested guidelines offered by Reynolds. Fisher's name was presented for consideration, it was moved and seconded that Fisher be accepted as the new president and the motion was carried.[125] No other candidates were discussed in that meeting. It should be noted that both Arless Glass and George Sponsler, representing the UPC Division of Education, were in attendance. Both supported a Fisher presidency with the former on record as affirming that "CBC needed someone of Don Fisher's calibre."[126] The president of CBC functioned as the chief executive officer and while he did not possess unlimited power, being answerable to the Board of Directors, he had considerable influence and power.[127] There were men uneasy with that authority in the hands of Don Fisher. Nevertheless, there could be no refuting the fact that Fisher had the confidence and support of United Pentecostal Church officials.[128]

The numerous questions surrounding Fisher's appointment do not lend themselves to easy, uncomplicated answers. The matter

---

[123] Harry Fisher interview, 13 July 2005.
[124] *Minutes*, CBC board meeting, 9 January 1981, p. 3. FC, inv.doc.no 0707-5192-34. It should be pointed out that Reynolds signaled his intention to resign as early as 8 February 1980 in a letter copied to Arless Glass and Winfred Toole. FC, inv.doc.no 0707-5186-34.
[125] *Minutes*, CBC board meeting, 8 April 1981, p. 2. FC, inv.doc.no 0707-5196-34.
[126] Arless Glass interview, 24 September 2013.
[127] *Corporate By-Laws, Conquerors Bible College*, 1967, Article 3, section 4, p. 3.
[128] David Reynolds, letter to CBC Alumni and Friends, 1 December 1981, p. 2. Reynolds strongly backed Fisher at the time but in retrospect considered his appointment a mistake.

constitutes a conundrum featuring a series of exceptionally complex
Gordian knots. What does seem plausible is that "when Don
[Fisher] came, lines were drawn no longer in the sand but chiselled
in rock."[129] Whatever optimism Fisher brought with him from
Mississippi quickly faded. After his first meeting with the College
Board following his relocation to Portland, Fisher came home
devastated.[130] There appear to be at least four plausible, general
theories to explain the demise of CBC. First, there was an organized
political plot among Oregon pastors to destroy Fisher and, if
necessary and unavoidable, CBC itself. Winfred Toole stoutly
denied this was the case.[131] However, Toole was prepared to act on
the basis of rumor and this stands in contrast to the posture he
assumed thirty years earlier when he acted quite differently.[132]
Second, the days of the Fisher administration constituted a vicious,
though bloodless war of religion fought silently behind closed
doors; a conflict which the college and its defenders lost. Such
episodes are also part of the histories of the Southern Baptists and
Missouri Synod Lutherans, with similarities evident at Fuller
Seminary. Third, the fall of CBC was merely the demise of a college
which had passed its prime and was already in institutional decline.
Fourth, the woes experienced on North Lombard were the direct or
indirect consequence of blatant administrative incompetence and
commensurate political blundering on the part of President Fisher.
Sorting out these four options is greatly complicated by a paucity of
documentation and for that which does exist there are large and
serious lacunae.[133]

Notwithstanding this, many of the participants in this drama
were still alive in the late 1990s and a rich and suggestive oral

---

[129] Jerry Dillon interview, 5 January 1999.

[130] Karissa (Fisher) Hopkins interview, 15 August 2013.

[131] Winfred Toole, letter to the Oregon District pastors, 23 February 1982. FC,
inv.doc.no 0707-5208-34. Contrary to this assertion, men close to Toole have
stated that rumors about Don Fisher were the central reason the Oregon District
withdrew support for CBC. Raymond A. Sirstad interview, 27 August 2013.

[132] Winfred E. Toole, letter to A.D. van Hoose, 7 September 1951. FC,
inv.doc.no 0707-1866-14. The letter demonstrates a Matthew 18 conviction.

[133] Whatever papers and files Don Fisher may have retained after 1983 are no
longer extant. Jesse Martin, letter to Thomas A. Fudge, 5 March 1999. FC,
inv.doc.no 0707-4748-32.

tradition continues to linger around the memory of CBC. It is important to point out that if the emerging mainstream in the Northwest, that is to say those standing outside the Yadon tradition, knew the details of the theological challenges presented under the Fisher administration at JCM especially between 1979

4.12 J.A.O. Preus, speaking at the General Convention
of the Missouri Synod, in New Orleans, 1973

and 1981, one can appreciate their anxiety over the likely direction of CBC.[134] It seems only fair to acknowledge that possibility. J.A.O. Preus and Paul Zimmerman in Missouri along with Adrian Rogers and Paige Patterson among the Baptists considered themselves defenders of the faith and guardians against the incursion of false doctrine and dangerous theological method. Preus' supporters considered him an honorable man and one of the "Synod's great heroes of the faith."[135] Less enthusiastic interpreters of the struggle

---

[134] Lewis, *The Journey Out*, pp. 21-44 provides a very thorough evaluation of the events in Mississippi from an insider point of view around the topic "what happened in Jackson."
[135] Zimmerman, *A Seminary in Crisis*, pp. 11, 65.

consider Preus a "master of duplicity."[136] Along with Barry King and Paul Dugas, these men were engaged on different fronts waging the Lord's holy war. Roman Catholic authorities asserted that every diocese should have oversight to seek out suspect ideas and teachings.[137] Men such as John R. Rice, Carl McIntire, Bob Jones, Sr., Wilbur Smith (1894-1976), and Charles Woodbridge (1902-1995) endeavored to preserve truth at Fuller and within the larger constituency of American Fundamentalism with militant opposition to every suggestion of compromise. In each of these movements, there was a definite commitment to the spirit of the seventeenth-century Lutheran theologian Abraham Calov who is reported to have prayed daily to be filled with hatred for heretics.[138]

The winds of change which began to sweep the Northwest in the 1970s produced success and failure as well as local church controversy. The specific situation at First Church in Portland is a microcosm of those conflicts. First Church gained numerical significance under the pastorate of Jim Roam between 1968 and 1973. Roam was a moderate, the son-in-law of C.H. Yadon, and a man whose approach appeared to be generally compatible with the PCI-influenced Northwest. That perception was not reliable. He was replaced, as we have seen, by Winfred Toole, who represented the newcomers. The unrest created by the importing of a more strident approach caused the size of the congregation to halve. Toole's turbulent tenure ended abruptly. Lewis J. Davies took over the pastorate of First Church in February 1977.

Davies was clearly within the Yadon tradition theologically but already, prior to his arrival at First Church, had begun to make strides along a theological trajectory which would prove antithetical to the direction the Northwest was heading. He was regarded within the UPC as a consistently liberal thinker and had begun teaching the ethics of the kingdom of God and focusing on the "sermon on the mount."[139] This radically changed his approach to ministry and precipitated a "huge spiritual metamorphosis" which

---

[136] Burkee, *Power, Politics, and the Missouri Synod*, p. 9.
[137] Pius X, encyclical *Pascendi domini gregis* in Sabatier, *Modernism*, pp. 340-341.
[138] Noted in Danker, *No Room in the Brotherhood*, p. 50.
[139] Dwain Hornsby interview, 3 October 2013. Hornsby attended First Church from 1961 to November 1977.

he intentionally introduced at First Church. Davies then proceeded into the theological emphases in the Pauline literature, especially that in Romans and Galatians. Thirty-five years later Davies noted facetiously that such an approach in the UPC was "a huge mistake." Many CBC students were attending First Church and it is reasonable to conclude that Davies was influencing those students. Other local pastors expressed concern especially when Davies introduced midweek open meetings at the church wherein questions were encouraged and open dialogue ensued. These developments became "the subject of a great deal of discussion."[140] UPC doctrines were subjected to biblical scrutiny and Davies refused to place limits on the nature of questioning. Soon a culture of open inquiry began to characterize First Church. Davies was influenced to some extent by a sermon C.H. Yadon had preached at First Church some years before, wherein an important distinction was drawn between the center and the circumference of the faith and Yadon had warned his hearers about confusing one with the other. Davies believed, as did Yadon and others, that Christ was the center while denominational doctrines and ideas constituted the circumference.[141]

If critics were already marshalled against C.H. Yadon, Jerry Dillon, and other heretics at or associated with CBC, the same concerns were flagged with respect to First Church. Davies began calling into question the UPC doctrine on the remission of sins, the presumed magical nature of the "Jesus name" formula, and his additional conviction that there was no specific New Testament baptismal formula.[142] He did not place any special emphasis upon the traditional standards of holiness and this caused immediate and growing concern within the increasingly strident Oregon District. Moreover, he taught that the baptism of the Holy Spirit as

---

[140] Lewis J. Davies, letter to Winfred E. Toole, 2 May 1978, p. 1.

[141] Lewis J. Davies, letter to Winfred E. Toole, 2 May 1978, p. 4.

[142] H. Leon White, letter to Thomas A. Fudge, 23 September 2013 who heard Davies on this point in 1978. FC, inv.doc.no 0707-5330-34. Explicated in Lewis J. Davies, letter to Thomas A. Fudge, 26 August 2013. FC, inv.doc.no 0707-5290-34. At this time, others were also questioning the characterization of "Jesus name" as a theological motif. Jerry Dillon interview, 19 April 2013.

articulated by the UPC had no relation to salvation.[143] We have already noted parallels at JCM occurring at roughly the same time.

Oregon District presbyter and pastor Joseph Dinwiddie (1938-2009) expressed his reservations about Lew Davies. Ex-pastor and then-current district superintendent Winfred Toole initiated contact to advise Davies that the District Board considered the situation at First Church to be "very serious."[144] The presbyter for Section One, Phillip Dugas, was called to investigate. Section One secretary Clyde Barlow was already suspicious of Davies. Paul Dugas registered his alarm and Barry King actually met with Davies to try and determine the extent of the danger posed by this new approach. Fred Scott (1916-2006) confronted Davies in the office at First Church and bombastically proceeded to charge Davies with "raping the people and destroying the church." Scott categorically refused to discuss his concerns in light of scripture. When challenged by Davies on this point Scott abruptly terminated the interview, left the office and for the next thirty years never again spoke to Davies. The bottom line for Scott was the authority of the UPC manual. Shortly thereafter, Davies was summoned to appear before the District Board to answer concerns but Superintendent Toole would not agree that the discussions should proceed on the basis of scripture alone.[145] Perceiving that he had already been judged and that there would be no proper forum for discussion or argument, Davies elected to avoid a predetermined inquisition and did not appear before the board.[146]

One of Davies' associates, former CBC student Steven Starcher, was warned by Winfred Toole, "if you hang around with a skunk long enough you'll start smelling like a skunk." The handwriting was definitely on the wall. Shortly thereafter, First Church elected overwhelmingly to disaffiliate from the UPC. Some members, wishing to remain within the fellowship of the UPC, left and a new

---

[143] Jan Smith interview, 24 September 2013.

[144] Lewis J. Davies, letter to Winfred E. Toole, 2 May 1978, p. 2.

[145] The Oregon District Board at that time (1978) consisted of Winfred Toole, David Johnson, Phillip Dugas, Fred Scott, David Knight, William Braddum, and Titus Duncan.

[146] Lewis J. Davies, letter to Winfred E. Toole, 2 May 1978, p. 2.

11509 Southeast 27th Avenue
Milwaukie, Oregon 97222

| Spiritual Encounter | Sunday | 2:30 p.m. |
| Living Concepts | Wednesday | 7:00 p.m. |
| Timothy Training | Saturday | 7:00 p.m. |
| Young People | Saturday | 7:00 p.m. |

| Care Line | 659-8095 |
| Share Your Prayer | 654-6419 |
| Ladies' Prayer and Share | Weekly |

Radio Ministry
| Spiritual Encounter | Sunday | 5:00 p.m. |
| Living Concepts | Daily | 1:25 p.m. |

FIRST UNITED
PENTECOSTAL
CHURCH

**Lewis J. Davies**
Pastor
(503) 654-6419

4.13  Advertisement for First Church, 1977

church was established under the leadership of Leon Brokaw. Doctrine was at issue along with controversy over standards of holiness. The latter conflict later sparked a split in the Puyallup church.[147] The ministerial licenses of Davies and Starcher were taken "under question" and Davies then decided to meet the board

---

[147] Gene Ziemke interview, 23 September 2013.

in an effort to resolve the "under question" classification.[148] In the summer of 1978, Davies and Starcher drove the seventy-five miles to Albany to attend a formally-scheduled Oregon District Board meeting but when they arrived at the venue discovered the meeting had convened elsewhere without notice. Davies and Starcher remained "under question" but Davies continued to serve as senior pastor of First Church until October 1982.[149] By that time, the energy of opposition by the "experts" against those "weak on the message" had intensified at CBC and Don Fisher was the new "skunk" in the crosshairs. The controversy at First Church is representative of conflict in the new Northwest and underscores similar unease at CBC. It is highly doubtful that Lewis Davies would have been called to account had C.H. Yadon still been superintendent of the Oregon District.

Indeed, Yadon had been much distressed and grieved over new directions in Oregon from 1975 on. While never arrogant or overly assertive, Yadon believed that a different leadership approach may have averted the collision of ideologies which resulted in the virtual loss of the largest church in the Oregon District. Yadon was a sorrowful eyewitness to the drastic changing of the guard in the Northwest.[150] After his resignation as superintendent of the Oregon District, the spirit of toleration and cooperation which he had endeavored to champion faded and during the clashes at First Church, there was little evidence of any remaining general or residual PCI influence.

Winfred Toole was not C.H. Yadon. Toole's theological emphases did not match with Yadon's. Yadon was a strong leader who could not be bullied into political showdowns. Toole was

---

[148] The background is enumerated in the five-page Lewis J. Davies, letter to Winfred E. Toole, 2 May 1978. The skunk comment also appears in Lewis J. Davies, letter to Thomas A. Fudge, 26 August 2013. "Under question" can imply action unbecoming a minister, or it can imply moral or theological irregularity. The qualification can only be removed if the minister in question has the matter resolved by the District Board which originally imposed it. Raymond A. Sirstad interview, 27 August 2013. Sirstad has served as the presiding officer for judicial procedure for the Northwest region of the UPC. See also *Manual* (2014), Article vii, section 7, point 21 (a), pp. 51-52.

[149] Lewis J. Davies interview, 19 August 2013.

[150] Norman Rutzen, letter to Thomas A. Fudge, 2 December 2013.

susceptible to manipulation. Yadon prized unity and was on public record as asserting that he had lived by the merger agreement. Toole considered doctrinal unanimity as essential and was more committed to what he and, by extension, the UPC believed to be truth than he was to theoretical considerations of the unity of the spirit. Toole believed that heresy suspects had to be confronted by direct intervention. Yadon did not fear heresy. Winfred Toole was determined either to force Lewis Davies into conformity with the new Oregon District or see him driven from the organization. C.H. Yadon was unprepared to destroy the building in order to deal with a so-called "rat" within. It is not possible to say for certain, but Toole's recent and bitter experience at First Church may have fuelled his personal determination to bring the brunt of the Oregon District's authority to bear on Lewis Davies.

4.14  R.V. Reynolds and Don Fisher in April 1981
during the transition in leadership at CBC

At the same time, the growing suspicion of compromise, though not entirely unprecedented at CBC, was sharply exacerbated in 1981. "With the retirement of Ralph V. Reynolds from the presidency, the mantle of leadership passed to Donald W. Fisher. Brother Fisher accepted the presidency knowing that he had been selected by the CBC board of directors to lead the college through a major SEASON OF CHANGE."[151] Ominous clouds gathering on the horizon only deepened the pall over what some regarded as the wasteland and hell of CBC.[152] The reality of affairs in the Oregon District in 1981 regarding CBC and the appointment of Donald Fisher as its president had ripple effects. A number of local churches, as already noted, withdrew their support forthwith. This had immediate implications. In the first instance, the pool of local church support in Portland had been abruptly reduced by more than half. While many faculty supported Fisher's appointment there were examples of conflict between Fisher and others of his staff. The senior ranking academic was Darline Kantola (ill.5.20, p. 292) who appears to have been deliberately marginalized by Fisher. Keys to administrative areas were taken from her, demeaning comments evidently were made to her publicly in staff meetings, some of her pedagogical methods were criticised, and Fisher once suggested she might consider going to the mission field, a comment Kantola took to mean Fisher would like to see her resign. At one stage Kantola was denied a proper office and on occasion staff meetings were held of which she was not advised. She endured effective demotion and came to believe that Fisher wanted her out of CBC. She found the situation quite hurtful and something of an enigma.[153] This however did not prevent her from remonstrating with students who made negative comments about Fisher, making it clear that such

---

[151] *Ensign*, vol. 29 (1982), p. 3.

[152] CBC "was a wasteland." Ronna (Fisher) Russell interview, 20 July 2013.

[153] Darline (Kantola) Royer interview, 15 August 2013. There was clear palpable tension between Don Fisher and Darline Kantola from the beginning of Fisher's appointment as president. The reasons for this are shrouded in indeterminate causes. Three possibilities have been suggested. First, when Fisher was an editor at Word Aflame Press, he turned down some of Kantola's work. Second, exception was taken in 1982 when Fisher abolished the deans of men and women and replaced these with a single college deanship and appointed Jerry Peden to that post. Third, Kantola had been at the college for such a long time (over twenty years) and in the course of that tenure had secured a fairly substantial influence. Fisher had no compunction in challenging her authority and he would simply not allow her to continue to have the free rein to which she had been accustomed. Jerry Dillon interview, 5 January 1999. Others perceive the issue as a personality conflict. April Purtell interview, 16 January 1999.

behavior was disrespectful and unacceptable. The guilty parties felt rebuked by Kantola.[154]

Several members of the-then-present faculty indicated they would not teach at CBC during the 1981-82 academic year. These included Clayton Brown, Anne Wilkins, Brent Nigh, Alma Lee King, and Dwylene Allen, despite the fact that contracts were offered to all faculty and staff at the request of president-elect Fisher.[155] There would have been a variety of reasons for these departures, including opposition to Don Fisher and the perceived direction of his administration. In the cases of Brown and Wilkins both were closely connected to Barry King and were influenced by him, so it seems reasonable to conclude their departures were linked in some sense to the arrival of the new president.[156] Fisher responded to this second challenge by bringing with him several individuals prepared to step in and teach and assume administrative responsibilities. Fisher himself taught several courses each term in addition to administrative duties. His wife Donna likewise taught and assumed other non-academic roles. Jerry and Esther Peden also joined the Fisher administration from a UPC pastorate in Berryville, Arkansas. With the departure of Clayton Brown, Jerry Peden was appointed as one of the deans and taught several courses.[157] Fisher especially wanted Peden to market and promote the college and Peden appears to have become Fisher's main confidant.[158] Esther Peden did some teaching but primarily assumed the affairs and daily

---

[154] Daniel R. Sirstad interview, 26 August 2013.

[155] Handwritten note on "Salary Committee Recommendations," 14 April 1981. FC, inv.doc.no 0707-5200-34. This committee consisted of Paul Dugas, Frank LaCrosse, and Winfred Toole.

[156] Darline (Kantola) Royer interview, 15 August 2013. Both Brown and Wilkins were unwilling to be contacted for the purpose of answering this query. Darline (Kantola) Royer, letter to Thomas A. Fudge, 22 August 2013. FC, inv.doc.no 0707-5281-34.

[157] Peden and Fisher met in the early 1960s in Jerome, Idaho. Fisher was an influence on Peden from that time on. Jerry Peden interview, 19 July 2002.

[158] Jerry Peden interview, 19 July 2002, said this was true to the extent that Fisher confided in anyone. Confirmed by April Purtell interview, 16 January 1999, and Donna Fisher interview, 3 January 1999. Donna Fisher thought her husband did not confide enough in her but admitted this may have been an attempt on his part to protect her from much of the developing nastiness which escalated after their relocation to Portland.

operations of the college business office. The other husband-wife appointment in 1981 was David and Barbara Wasmundt. David Wasmundt (ill.4.39, p. 238) was a music graduate of the highly-

4.15  John Klemin, Donna Fisher, Darline Kantola, Esther and Jerry Peden.
George Sponsler is in the background, 3 June 1982

regarded JCM music program led by the nationally known UPC award-winning song-writer and music personality Lanny Wolfe. Wasmundt immediately took up full responsibilities within the CBC music program while Barbara began her position as head of the kitchen staff. These appointments more than adequately solved the problem of faculty vacancies. John E. Klemin, Raymond A. Sirstad, Ruth Ann Brokaw, Darline Kantola, Stan and Lyn Johnson, and several others, continued on staff. The other concomitant problems were much more persistent and more difficult to solve.

The withdrawal of support in the Oregon District and the alleged hostility among local pastors produced further serious consequences for Fisher and CBC. The Oregon District in April 1981 expected that CBC might physically relocate out of the district by September of that same year. This was an unreasonable expectation and logistically impracticable.[159] The CBC board also took up the question of relocation and presented a resolution

---

[159] Recommendation of the Oregon District Board from its session in Portland, 8 April 1981. FC, inv.doc.no 0707-4803-32. See Appendix 7, p. 437.

wherein a new location be sought, preferably near the coast.[160] There is no evidence this was vigorously pursued. The Washington District countered, proposing a resolution at the same time which urged that the traditional tri-district oversight configuration continue.[161] Even though cooperation between the three districts was increasingly becoming unworkable, defenders of the college still thought it worth attempting to preserve.[162] A later five-point resolution passed by the Oregon District urged the removal of CBC from Oregon "as soon as possible."[163] There should be no doubt that Oregon actively wanted CBC out of its district. Senior faculty members at CBC considered the Oregon initiatives unjustified.[164] At a full CBC Board of Directors meeting on 28 August 1981, the proposals of the Oregon District were largely rejected though the college had no other recourse than to accept the withdrawal of Oregon.[165] C.H. Yadon made the motion against adopting the Oregon resolutions and a secret ballot vote carried the motion by a partisan four to two margin.[166]

At the same time pastors throughout Oregon and even further afield were actively discouraging prospective students from entering any of the several college programs offered at CBC. Even before Fisher's arrival this practice had begun. In 1978 two students, one of whom was Steve Hanson from Montana, were contacted by their district superintendent J.M. (John) Russell, who demanded they withdraw from the college forthwith on the grounds that CBC was not doctrinally viable.[167] "Come out from among them and be ye separate." Conquerors Bible College might well have been a UPC

---

[160] "School-Board Resolution (CBC)," 8 April 1981. FC, inv.doc.no 0707-5197-34, and FC, inv.doc.no 0707-5199-34.

[161] Washington District Resolution 1, 8 April 1981. FC, inv.doc.no 0707-4791-32.

[162] Raymond A. Sirstad interview, 27 August 2013.

[163] Oregon District resolution adopted at its conference at Turner, 30 July 1981, p. 1 and repeated on p. 2. FC, inv.doc.no 4805-32. See Appendix 10, pp. 442-443.

[164] Darline (Kantola) Royer interview, 15 August 2013.

[165] Response of the CBC Board of Directors to the Oregon District Resolution, *Minutes*, CBC board meeting, 28 August 1981. See Appendix 11, pp. 444-446.

[166] *Minutes*, CBC board meeting, 28 August 1981, pp. 1-2. Rutzen, Crossley, LaCrosse and C.H. Yadon doubtlessly were the nay votes while Toole and Gleason voted in support of the Oregon resolutions.

[167] Jerry Dillon interview, 5 January 1999.

school, but even there the truth of pure religious practice and doctrine seemed to have become adulterated with the arrival of Don Fisher.

Perhaps CBC might have been perceived as the lesser of evils if the only other alternatives had been the state universities and liberal arts colleges in Portland and the surrounding areas. But UPC pastors were able to direct their students south to California, where the UPC sponsored another college whose faculty were definite "experts" on vitally important holiness and theological matters. In Stockton, Christian Life College, formerly known as Western Apostolic Bible College, flourished under the presidency of Kenneth F. Haney (1937-2011). Unlike Fisher, Haney seemed well regarded by the majority of west coast ministers. Several pastors declined to have CBC representatives come to their churches to promote the college. The lack of support and enthusiasm for CBC among area churches contributed actively and significantly to dwindling student numbers at the start of the 1981-82 academic year. Though students had come from Alaska, Arkansas, Wisconsin, Texas, New Brunswick, and as far away as Germany, the student body experienced a massive shrinkage from sixty-seven in 1980-81 to only forty-eight in the 1981-82 academic year. This was an ominous development.

Meanwhile, before the end of the 1981 calendar year CBC declared its intention to operate outside of Oregon after the current academic year.[168] This led to the fourth and most dire of the complications caused by the anti-Fisher/CBC response in the Pacific Northwest: finances. The financial prospects of CBC following the Fisher appointment increasingly suggested imminent disaster. Income from tuition and student-generated revenue fell sharply. Outward signs indicated that Fisher's inaugural year was off to a rather stormy beginning and the future of CBC was perhaps already in serious doubt. It should be noted that the financial woes at the college were already a grave issue prior to the arrival of Don Fisher. Indeed, the future of the college was predicated on a solution to a serious financial problem, reflected in the college financial report for the first quarter of 1981, of which Fisher was

---

[168] C.H. Yadon proposal, *Minutes*, CBC board meeting, 10 November, 1981, p.1.

aware of before he came to Portland.[169] By 1980, the Oregon and Washington Districts had made loans to CBC, as had Frank LaCrosse. College officials noted that "The pressure of balancing the budget is constantly with us ... it would seem that we shall make it through the summer."[170] This was not a new situation. "The financial burden of the college is still weighing heavily on our hearts, and is a matter we cannot sidestep."[171] These comments made by former presidents R.V. Reynolds and John Klemin underscore the precarious existence of the college in the pre-Fisher years. That reality was left aside by others who proclaimed that the future of the college was "strong and bright."[172] There has been an almost deliberate attempt in several quarters to minimise the question of pre-existing financial problems and set it aside as a factor in the demise of CBC. The policies and practices of previous administrations are generally overlooked, while the contribution of local church politics to the difficulties experienced at CBC have often been subordinated to the simplistic explanation that "[Don Fisher] was the sole thing, that final ... straw that broke the camel's back."[173] Such claims fall victim to the danger of generalization and reductionism and betray a lack of acquaintance with the pertinent history and context surrounding the college.

During the 1981-82 academic year, options for the future of the college were discussed. The college administration decided to abandon any notion of refurbishing the old ten-acre campus on North Lombard (ill.2.4, p. 47). Structural damage had been noted as early as 1946.[174] Inasmuch as the CBC campus has wider historical significance, something should be said about its pre-college history.

During the Second World War, the American industrialist Henry J. Kaiser (1882-1967) contributed to the war effort by means

---

[169] Jerry Peden interview, 19 July 2002 and CBC quarterly report, 31 March 1981, 2pp which is a rather dismal summary. FC, inv.doc.no 0707-5193-34.

[170] R.V. Reynolds, letter to the CBC board, 6 June 1980.

[171] John Klemin, letter to the CBC board, 14 March 1975. The financial strain was noted elsewhere. "Pentecostal Bible school marks birthday" *The Oregonian*, 3 June 1978, p. 34.

[172] Raymond A. Sirstad, letter to the CBC board, 6 June 1980.

[173] Cleveland Becton interview, 14 April 1999.

[174] "School Seeks Yard Centers" *The Oregonian*, 27 March 1946, p. 12.

of shipbuilding. There were seven Kaiser shipyards owned by the Kaiser Shipbuilding Company. Four of these ship yards were in Richmond, California, on the east side of the San Francisco Bay north of Berkeley, while three others were created in the Portland area between January 1941 and July 1942. These were at Ryan Point on the north side of the Columbia River at Vancouver, Swan Island Shipyard in the Willamette River, and finally Oregon Shipbuilding Corporation which was developed at what is now Terminal 4 of the Port of Portland just west of North Lombard Street in St. Johns. Along with three other smaller shipyards, by late 1942 more than 92,000 workers were employed in the shipbuilding industry in Portland. Between 1941 and 1945, the Portland shipyards built more than 1,000 Liberty and Victory ships. In the fall of 1942, the SS Joseph N. Teal was built in ten days at the Oregon Ship yard.[175] President Roosevelt attended the celebratory launch. By 1944, Kaiser was the single largest shipbuilder in the U.S. Kaiser brought workers from all over the United States to work in the shipyards. To accommodate the massive influx of workers, Kaiser purchased 650 acres along the Oregon side of the Columbia River, and undertook to build a large wartime housing project. Vanport (a contraction of Vancouver and Portland) was designed by the Portland architectural firm of Wolff and Phillips to house 40,000 residents becoming the second largest city in Oregon. It was constructed on the Columbia Slough in ten months and included 10,000 housing units, stores, schools, a library, a theatre, post office, several fire stations, a hospital, social venues, a college, and was the largest housing project in the world. Kaiser developed Vanport using money from the U.S. Maritime Commission and it was completed and officially opened on 26 September 1943.

In distinction to other shipyards at the time, Kaiser employed women, and Oregon Ship became the first shipyard in the country to hire women to work in the yards. By 1943, women made up 65% of new hires in the shipyards and accounted for 30% of workers in the Kaiser shipyards.[176] As early as 1943, Kaiser employed as many

---

[175] The normal time was two months and the previous record had been twenty-four days. *Record Breakers* (Portland: Oregon Shipbuilding Corporation, 1945).

[176] Noted in "Kaiser goes east to ask improvements for workers" *The Oregonian*, 5 November 1943, p. 22.

as 12,000 women in his shipyards and 4,000 of them were mothers. Eleanor Roosevelt actively urged Kaiser to develop child care and educational facilities for these children at his Oregon shipyards.

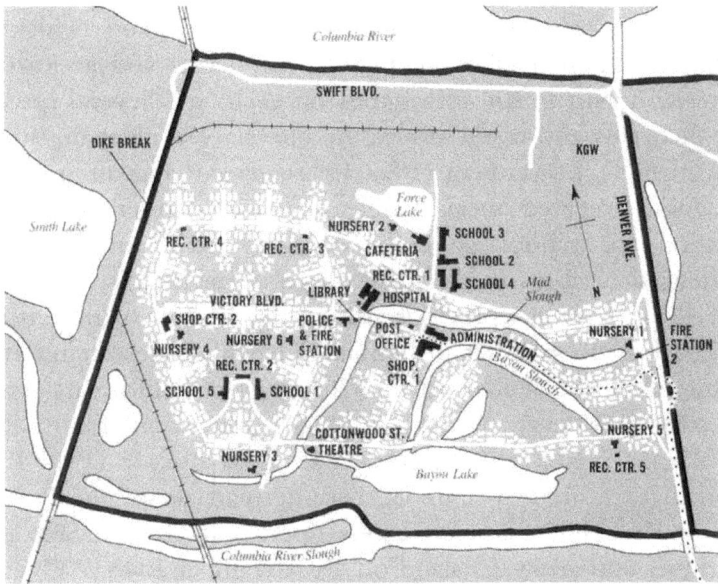

4.16   Map diagram of Vanport City, Oregon, 1943

Kasier had already built Vanport and made that town intimately connected to the shipyards. For example, Kaiser had arranged for bus routes to be set up which ran directly from the housing units past schools and on to the shipyards. Kaiser then responded positively to Roosevelt's suggestion and in 1943 developed a unique experiment in child care for working mothers. The Kaiser Child Service Centers, designed by Wolff and Phillips, were built by Charles Wegman & Son at a total cost of about $700,000 at Oregon Ship and on Swan Island (approximately four miles southeast of Oregon Ship) at the entrance to the shipyards.[177] A planned center

---

[177] Located in the Willamette River, north of the central business district, Swan Island was Portland's first airport, dedicated in 1927 by Charles Lindbergh. A photograph of the Swan Island center (Oregon Historical Society, #OrHi 78700) has been published in Garth S. Jowett and Victoria O'Donnell, eds., *Propaganda and Persuasion*, 5th edition (Los Angeles: Sage Publications, 2012), p. 309. "Child Centers Being Build" *The Oregonian*, 29 July 1943, p. 8.

at the Vancouver shipyard was abandoned.[178] The project manager
was Edgar F. Kaiser (1908-1981), son of the shipping magnate. The
staff included over 100 trained nursery and kindergarten teachers.
As an indication of the value Kaiser placed on education, the
teachers were paid salaries matching shipyard workers, which was
substantial. These facilities employed physicians and at least ten
registered nurses in the infirmaries on each site. Several qualified
child dieticians and cooks under the direction of chief nutritionist
Dr. Miriam E. Lowenberg (1897-1995), one of Benjamin Spock's
colleagues, prepared meals, while qualified instructors provided
education for school-age children. Each classroom had three
experienced teachers possessing college degrees. Lois Meek Stolz
(1891-1984), who had previously been the Director of the Institute
of Child Development at Columbia University, a researcher at the
Institute for Child Welfare at the University of California-Berkeley,
and past president of the National Association for Nursery
Education, served as the director. James L. Hymes, Jr. (1914-1998),
a student of Stolz at Columbia, became manager of the Portland
centers. The Child Service Centers opened at Oregon Ship on 8
November and at Swan Island on 18 November 1943.[179] Over the
course of the next two years over 4,000 children were served at the
Portland shipyards, operating twenty-four hours a day, seven days a
week. The facilities at Oregon Ship and Swan Island were identical
and had been constructed with children in mind. This included
child-sized chairs, tables, closets, toilets, sinks and bathing facilities,
large picture windows which came down nearly to ground level
(61% of wall area), and multiple outdoor play areas both enclosed
by the wheel-and-spoke design of the main building for security and
set up under covered porches to be of use even in the Oregon rain
and featuring a large open area within the building's circular
parameter. Each center covered an area equal to four city blocks.[180]

---

[178] "Child Centers Being Built" *The Oregonian*, 29 July 1943, p. 8, "Plan for Child
Care Center near Shipyard Abandoned" *The Oregonian*, 15 August 1943, p. 16.
[179] "Child Center Thrown Open" *The Oregonian*, 13 November 1943, p. 17 and
"Child Service Center Opens" *The Oregonian*, 19 November 1943, p. 10.
[180] Oregon Historical Society, #OrHi 80379 is a photograph of the Swan Island
courtyard published in Sonya Michel, *Children's Interests/Mother's Rights: The Shaping
of America's Child Care Policy* (New Haven: Yale University Press, 1999), p. 144.

All families were interviewed before their children were admitted to the Centers in order to tailor the program to meet special needs. There were additional features including laundry service, rental library for children's books, commissaries, grocery shopping for

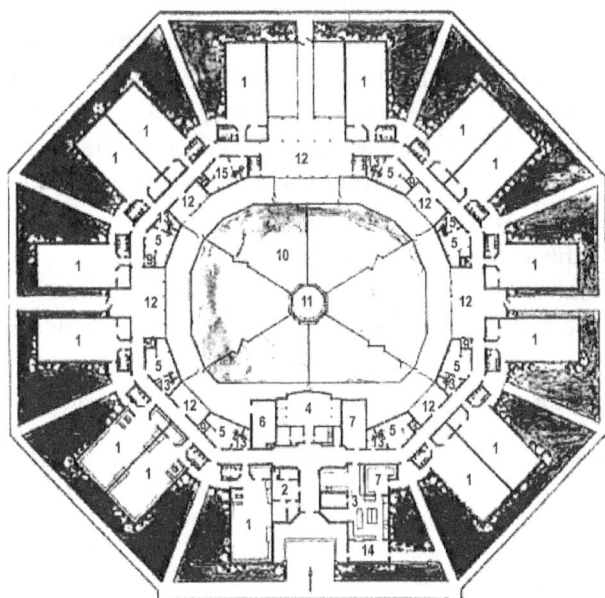

**Kaiser Child Service Centers Floor Plan**

| | | |
|---|---|---|
| 1 = Play room | 6 = Boiler room | 11 = Wading pool |
| 2 = Administration | 7 = Storage | 12 = Play porch |
| 3 = Kitchen | 8 = Bath | 13 = Teachers |
| 4 = Infirmary | 9 = Laundry | 14 = Home Service |
| 5 = Auxiliary | 10 = Play court | 15 = Teachers |

4.17 *Child Service Centers, Oregon Shipbuilding* (Portland: Kaiser, n.d.,) p. 1

workers, and hot meals to go for mothers, to pick up for the entire family, coming from the yards.[181] The Kaiser centers (in Portland and Richmond, California) had state-of-the-art facilities for children to play, eat, sleep, and be educated while their mothers worked in the shipyards. The Child Service Centers won the 1944 *Parents' Magazine* medal for outstanding service to children and published a bi-weekly newsletter.[182] When the war came to an end in 1945, Vanport was partially dismantled and the remains were destroyed

---

[181] "Food Service Due Mothers" *The Oregonian*, 4 January 1944, p. 10.
[182] "Edgar Kaiser Wins Award" *The Oregonian*, 18 December 1944, p. 5.

by a devastating flood in 1948. The Kaiser shipyard Child Service Centers were closed.[183]

The Swan Island facility was taken over by the Navy which signed a thirty year lease in 1948 at a cost of one dollar per year and thereafter undertook a half million dollar renovation. The site was used between 1948 and 1966 as a barracks and intake center, and a U.S. Navy-Marine Corps reserve training center.[184] The Oregon Shipyard facility became an emergency school to relieve over-crowding at the Sitton Elementary and George Middle schools. By 1948, the Portland School Board was involved in its control.[185] In due time, E.G. Moyer appeared. However, CBC was not the first college on the site. After the 1948 flood which destroyed Vanport, Vanport College (the predecessor of Portland State University) occupied the Lombard site before relocating to the city center.[186]

---

[183] On aspects of the history see Lois Meek Stolz, "The Kaiser Child Service Centers," in *Early Childhood Education: Living History Interviews*, 3 vols., ed., James L. Hymes (Carmel, CA: Hacienda Press, 1978-1979), vol. 2, pp. 30-33, 40-56, *Child Service Centers: Oregon Shipbuilding Corporation* (Portland: Kaiser Company Inc., 1945), MS C 414, Lois Meek and Herbert Rowell Stolz Papers 1917-1984, National Library of Medicine, Bethesda, MD. Box 6 contains materials on the Child Service Centers, Amy Kesselman, *Fleeting Oportunities: Women Shipyard Workers in Portland and Vancouver during World War II and Reconversion* (Albany: State University of New York Press, 1990), James L. Hymes, Jr., "The Kaiser Child Service Centers – 50 Years Later: Some Memories and Lessons" *Journal of Education* 177 (No. 3, 1995), pp. 23-38, Bill MacKenzie, "Caring for Rosie the Riveter's Children" *Young Children* 66 (No. 6, 2011), pp. 68-70, "The Nursery Comes to the Shipyard" *New York Times* (7 November 1943), "Nurseries Solve Big Problem for Mothers in Kaiser Shipyards" *New York Times* (17 November 1944), Charlotte Jean Anderson, "The Kaiser Child Service Centers: a brief report" *American Educational History Journal* 28 (2001), pp. 61-67 and "Kaiser Shipyard Child Care Center Collection," circa 1941-1945. Accession 26178, Oregon Historical Society, Research Library, Portland. Papers and photographs related to the center on Swan Island. See also Library of Congress, LOT 1810 (F) (M) [P&P], 36 photographs of the buildings, circa 1943.

[184] "Port of Portland, Navy Seek New Site for Reserve Centre" *The Oregonian*, 13 November 1965, p. 7 and "2000 Oregonians Now on Rolls of Navy and Marine Reserves" *The Oregonian*, 29 August 1948, p. 1.

[185] "Navy Takes Over Center at Island" *The Oregonian*, 22 December 1945, p. 7, "Lease Delay Irks Official" *The Oregonian*, 27 March 1946, p. 1, "School Seeks Yard Centers" *The Oregonian*, 27 March 1946, p. 12 and "Schools Set at Oregon Ship" *The Oregonian*, 5 April 1946, p. 1.

[186] "Vanport Lists Homecoming" *The Oregonian*, 31 October 1948, p. 29.

Having been built in 1943 by the government for housing the
children of shipyard workers as a response to needs generated by
World War II, the unique octagonal structure's life expectancy was
nearly expended when E.G. Moyer acquired it in 1953 at a cost of
$16,500 and began a Bible School within its walls.[187] The main
building of the former Kaiser Child Service Center at the entrance
to the former Oregon Shipbuilding yard, which became CBC,

4.18  Aerial view of the CBC campus, early 1970s

consisted of about 50,000 square feet on one level built around a
circular hallway with sixteen units extending outwards like spokes
from a central hub. These units were approximately twenty-eight
feet by sixty feet in dimension and were used as dormitories,
classrooms, a dining hall, chapel, library and other facilities. On the
inner side of the circular hallway were apartments, offices, smaller
classrooms, and rooms for other uses. Up to one hundred students
could be housed in the dormitories and there was additional space

---

[187] E.G. Moyer, *A Brief Autobiography and Collection of Articles* (Portland: By the
author, n.d.), pp. 9-10. See Appendix 1, pp. 401-403. *The Oregonian*, 13 November
1965, p. 7 and notice of sale *The Oregonian*, 28 June 1953, p. 43.

for couples to live on campus.[188] Reconstruction costs were rather prohibitive and were exacerbated by the financial difficulties CBC was now experiencing acutely. The old campus was located near a commercial section of Portland known as Rivergate Industrial District near the Willamette River and Terminal Four of the Port of Portland on its immediate north and west. To the south and the east the campus was bordered by one of Portland's lower income residential neighborhoods, where safety for women on the night streets was an ongoing concern.[189] During the second Reynolds administration, offers rumored to be up to two million dollars for the campus property had been tendered. Reynolds and/or the College Board of Directors declined to sell.[190] While the campus buildings were of little value, the property was desirable. With these factors in mind Fisher put the Lombard site on the real estate market and began immediately to seek a suitable campus elsewhere.

The intention was sound but more difficulties arose when the property failed to attract a buyer acceptable to the CBC board. There was an offer in the amount of $500,000 by Ed Ferris of Don Jones Realty to purchase the college but after David Sant of JA-SANT Corporation presented his package to the board and offered counsel on the offer, the board, following considerable discussion, directed Fisher to reject the offer.[191] What appeared to be a solution to the financial woes of CBC now took on the sense of a white elephant of gargantuan proportions. Voices complained of the now regrettable fact that Reynolds had not sold the campus when he had the opportunity. The handwriting was on the wall for CBC in terms of remaining at the Lombard Street site but relocation had already been contemplated earlier on account of numerous serious physical conditions of the main building.[192] Reynolds actively supported

---

[188] *Conquerors Bible College (Portland, Oregon) General Catalog 1979-1981*, p. 5.

[189] "Recommendation to Re-Locate Conquerors Bible College," (*c.* 1980), p. 1.

[190] I have been unable to find any evidence to substantiate this rumor and the sum of money offered for the campus seems highly unlikely.

[191] *Minutes*, CBC board meeting, 28 August 1981, p. 3. The board wanted a minimum of $650,000. Board constituency included Rutzen, Crossley, Toole, Gleason, LaCrosse, and C.H. Yadon. Fisher and Sirstad were also present.

[192] Harry B. Fisher, letter to the CBC board, 18 December 1979 and the undated document titled "Recommendation to Re-locate Conquerors Bible College." Noted in the CBC board executive committee meeting, 8 November 1979.

relocation and those interests were publically noted.[193] Various sites were considered especially the Holy Child Academy as well as the Portland Christian High School located at SE Market and 112th Street. As noted earlier, formal but unsuccessful offers were made for the former location.[194] Ralph Reynolds urged the college to a formal resolution to purchase the latter described as "an ideal property" and the "will of God" for CBC.[195] The investigation into relocation widened to include the metropolitan areas of the three districts. By the end of 1979, the College Board formally backed this initiative unanimously in a secret ballot vote though evidence suggests there had been efforts to sell the Lombard campus as early as 1974.[196]

At this point, the Idaho District expressed a keen interest in having CBC relocate within its borders. Even during the difficult years of the Fisher administration Idaho had remained largely a staunch supporter. College representation in local churches was encouraged, a significant percentage of the student body at the first and second year levels came from Idaho, and senior ministers actively and consistently supported the college financially and personally. Among the most prominent were Norman Rutzen, long-time district superintendent (1973-1988), along with C.H. Yadon, former president and later honorary presbyter of the UPC and scion of the large and historically important Yadon family. Rutzen and Yadon were easily the most powerful UPC men in the Idaho District and more importantly both were men with national connections at the UPC headquarters in St. Louis.[197] Rutzen defended the college "like a pit bull" and withstood the anti-CBC

---

[193] See especially, Ralph V. Reynolds, letter to Arless Glass, 8 February 1980, p. 1. FC, inv.doc.no 0707-5186-34. "Pentecostal Bible school marks birthday" *The Oregonian*, 3 June 1978, p. 34.

[194] John Klemin, letter to the CBC board, 6 June 1974.

[195] "Recommendation to Re-Locate Conquerors Bible College,"2 pp.

[196] R.V. Reynolds, letter to the CBC Board of Directors, 20 December 1979 and *Minutes* CBC board meeting, 6 June 1980. *Minutes*, CBC board meeting, 21 December 1979, p. 2.

[197] Rutzen was born in Minnesota but had come to the Northwest as a boy and his entire intellectual and spiritual formation therefore can be considered a product of the Northwest.

crowd of "experts" in Oregon.[198] He refused to comply with
Oregon district officials who requested that he not support certain
CBC activities.[199] Beyond being active supporters of CBC, both
Yadon and Rutzen were strong defenders of Don Fisher. Rutzen

4.19  Norman Rutzen, speaking in the CBC chapel, Fall 1981

was "severely criticised" for defending Fisher and was warned by
UPC national officials that he needed to exercise caution in who he
chose to support. The admonition centered around theology. UPC
Assistant General Superintendent James L. Kilgore told Norman
Rutzen directly and specifically that he should not support Don
Fisher based on the latter's stance in the troubling and protracted
theological controversies at JCM.[200] This warning was issued prior
to Fisher coming to Portland. C.H. Yadon had taught at Jackson
College of Ministries during Fisher's tenure there. Rutzen and
Fisher had known each other for nearly thirty years. Both had been
among the first students at CBC in the 1950s. Rutzen flourished in
the "liberal" Idaho District and might easily have been considered

---

[198] Jerry Dillon interview, 5 January 1999.
[199] Winfred Toole, letter to the brethren of the Oregon District, 9 March 1982.
[200] Norman Rutzen interviews, 8 February 1999, 24 July 2013, and 27 September
2013. The criticism of Rutzen was confirmed in George Sponsler interview, 12
February 1999.

the most "liberal" of all UPC district superintendents in the 1970s and 80s. Idaho must have seemed like a relatively safe haven for the embattled Don Fisher and his ailing Bible school. After all, as the Hot Springs meetings clearly revealed, he had previously considered establishing a theological training school in Boise. The chief deterrent blocking the relocation of CBC to Idaho was the failure of the old campus to sell and the related, perennial problem of cash shortage. As fate would have it, the Idaho District was in no financial position to pay for the expensive moving of a college more than four hundred miles.[201] Fisher had to look elsewhere.

Technically the college could not move outside the parameters of the Districts of Idaho, Oregon, and Washington. Constitutionally those districts owned CBC. Idaho was the logical choice, but it was too far away. It would have been precipitous to take the college deeper into hostile Oregon territory. Moving out of the Portland metropolitan area, to a location near the coast as noted earlier, would have created immediate employment difficulties for students, many of whom depended on jobs in the local area to finance their way through their studies. Moreover, there had already been an exhibited hostility toward Fisher and his vision for the college; a situation described by some as based upon "gossip-mongering."[202] Nothing could be gained from taking the college from Portland to another location in the Oregon District. Fisher turned north. The Washington District, while perhaps not as enthusiastic as Idaho, nonetheless cannot be said to have been in active opposition to the direction CBC was taking in 1982. Not only was there no evidence of deep, widespread, or sustained agitation against Fisher, the Washington District Board in November 1981 actually "gave a unanimous vote of confidence to Brother Fisher and a very strong vote of welcome to locate CBC in Washington state." Full-page advertisements to this effect were published.[203] The logical place for

---

[201] It is quite wrong to say that the Idaho District withdrew support from the college. Frank LaCrosse interview, 16 January 2001. Idaho firmly backed CBC to the end.

[202] Jerry Peden interview, 19 July 2002.

[203] Norman Rutzen, letter to the "Northwestern Brethren," 13 November 1981, p. 2. At the time, Rutzen was the chairman of the College Board of Directors. *CBC Jubilation* 15 (No.4, 1981), p. 1 featured a full-page welcome to Washington.

a college was the Seattle area.[204] The sky-rocketing costs of real estate in the Puget Sound area as well as the distance of at least one hundred and eighty miles made the possibility of relocation to the Seattle area as impractical as the aforementioned one to Idaho. The other city in the state of Washington large enough to accommodate a college with its need for student employment opportunities was Spokane. But at a distance of three hundred and fifty miles from Portland it was out of the question.

4.20  New CBC campus in Vancouver, Washington, 1982

Fisher then exercised the only option remaining to him and moved the college a short distance across the Columbia River into Vancouver, Washington. The new campus was located at 10621 NE Coxley Drive. The old decrepit Lombard dorms were replaced by modern apartments and an effort was made to replicate the CBC dining hall in a private room at the Kopper Kitchen restaurant a few blocks east of the campus. Some considered it a bold and courageous move to take the college out of the bellicose Oregon District.[205] Though still in sight of the contentious Oregon District, Fisher had solved one of his problems and staved off another. First,

---

[204] This was Fisher's thought. See, Don Fisher, letter to the "Ministers of Idaho and Washington," 1 September 1981, p. 1. See Appendix 12, pp. 447-448 and the recommendation of the Oregon District Board drawn up at a district meeting at Portland on 8 April 1981. Three properties were explored in the summer of 1981. *Minutes*, CBC board meeting, 28 August 1981, p. 3. FC, inv.doc.no 0707-5203-34.
[205] Jerry Dillon interview, 5 January 1999.

he was now operating in much friendlier territory, and second, by remaining in the Portland metropolitan area he had retained the best employment and resource market in the entire immediate region. No student technically had to give up a job on account of the campus relocation. The opening of the eight-lane Interstate 205 Glenn Jackson Memorial Bridge spanning the Columbia River, on 15 December 1982, greatly shortened the commuting time into downtown Portland. The new campus was considerably more efficient than the North Lombard location even if the facilities were measurably more compact.

4.21 *Seated front row:* Don Fisher, Doug Greer, Audrey Zapalac, Kerry Pavek, Cheryl Johns, Kim Simmons, Tressa Kantola, Rachel Lethin, Eric K. Loy. *Seated second row:* Heather Wasmundt, Jerry Peden, Dennis Spanner, Peggy Yelm, Carl Wopperer, Esther Peden, Donna Trumps, Karissa Fisher, Alice Blackshear, Joe Higgins. *Standing front row:* Melissa Reece, Collette Kilbourne, Donna Fisher, Melanie Poulsen, Patty Peffer, Cabot Peden, Ronna Fisher. *Standing back row:* Barb Wasmundt, Lisa Sanders, Stephanie Johnson, Lori Falwell, Peggy Faust, Dee Dee Beard, Doug Lethin, Mark Clayton, Thomas A. Fudge, Darline Kantola, Franz Bibfeldt(?), 17 March 1982

An institutional name change was introduced.[206] The acronym CBC was retained but the archaic "Conquerors" was dropped and "Cascade" was adopted more closely identifying the college with the nearby majestic Cascade Mountain Range which stretched from Canada to northern California.[207] In the summer of 1982, the newly dubbed Cascade Bible College appeared to shake off its past. The

---

[206] *Minutes*, CBC board meeting, 1 March 1982, p. 3. Several names were discussed. Fisher recommended Cascade Bible College which was adopted.

[207] *The Journal of Thomas A. Fudge, 1980-1985*, entries for 17 March and 25 April 1982. Several years earlier, John Klemin had contemplated a name change for the college but encountered a lack of enthusiasm among board members. *Minutes*, CBC board meeting, 28 January 1977, p. 2.

aging buildings at 10838 North Lombard were abandoned, the doors of the old campus closed for the last time, and a hopeful President Fisher led his troops across the river into a new future.[208]

There was of course a fair amount of nostalgia remaining for the old college campus.

> But CBC is not really a building, nor a street address. The time has come for the ministry of CBC to change locations, and the true CBC moves on in strength and purpose. As CBC moves, each one will retain memories from Lombard days. We'll smile when we think of Lake Lombard, leaky roofs, musical pipes, "missionary" showers, and a host of other unique characteristics of our Lombard home. All CBCers, past and present, will indeed remember 10838 N. Lombard.[209]

It was later suggested that Fisher took the college out of Oregon to suit his own ambitions and that his reckless disposal of property and inventory destroyed CBC.[210] The assumptions are specious. There was an upbeat mood. One student remarked, "This school year will be an excellent one."[211] Upon reflection, the transition out of Oregon marked the summit of the Fisher administration and the extent of his vision. Six months later it was effectively all over. Beneath the obvious swell of excitement, opposition continued to build against Don Fisher, the financial crisis was deepening, and the future looked bleak.[212] The history of CBC was drawing to a close.

The summer of 1982 saw four other developments of note. The first was the annual meeting of Christian higher education personnel of the United Pentecostal Church in Colorado. At that meeting, Nathaniel Urshan, the presiding General Superintendent of the United Pentecostal Church, and Don Fisher met in a private conference (ill.4.22). Urshan and Fisher had known each other on a

---

[208] National advertisement in *Pentecostal Herald* 57 (No. 6, 1982), p. 11 and *Ensign*, vol. 29 (1982), p. 124 (see ill.2.3, p. 43). The old corporation (Conquerors) was maintained in Oregon and E.G. Moyer was designated as the registered Oregon agent. Planning Session notes, CBC board, 2 March 1982, p. 2. FC, inv.doc.no 0707-5212-34. The registered Washington agent was Nathaniel Yadon. *Minutes*, CBC board meeting, 17 July 1982, p. 1. FC, inv.doc.no 0707-5218-34.

[209] *Ensign*, vol. 29 (1982), p. 123.

[210] Arless Glass interview, 24 September 2013.

[211] *The Journal of Thomas A. Fudge, 1980-1985*, entries for 14/22 September 1982.

[212] Darline (Kantola) Royer interview, 15 August 2013.

personal level since the 1960s. It was informal, non-programmic, unofficial, and an unminuted discussion of the situation in the Oregon District, and more importantly the future of CBC. Fisher apparently outlined to Urshan his personal theological leanings and

4.22 Nathaniel A. Urshan, late 1970s

4.23 Urshan and the author, Hazelwood, Missouri, 23 April 1999

his vision for CBC. Fisher later stated that Urshan expressed no dissatisfaction or concern with Fisher's theology and moreover pledged support for the newly named and relocated Cascade Bible College.[213] Urshan had been in Portland only weeks prior and had appeared officially as the commencement speaker for the formal CBC graduation ceremonies. On that occasion he delivered an idiosyncratic address which focused on the idea of a "dung gate" (Nehemiah 2:13, 3:14) which seemed a rather odd subject given the circumstances in Portland.[214] It was unclear if Urshan thought CBC

---

[213] This was the substance of Fisher's comments to the author in early February 1983 after the author met with Fisher in his office to discuss the future of the college. Fisher's comments were made in response to the direct query of where the UPC stood in relation to Fisher himself and CBC. *The Journal of Thomas A. Fudge, 1980-1985*, entry for 3 February 1983.

[214] Some openly characterized it as an exceptionally "idiotic" sermon. Jerry Peden interview, 19 July 2002.

was a dung gate within the UPC, or if the college needed to keep the excrement out. Nevertheless, Fisher returned from Colorado with renewed confidence and, in his mind, the personal support and endorsement of the highest ranking official in the sponsoring denomination.

4.24  Raymond Sirstad and Don Fisher, Fall 1981

The second development occurred after the 1981-82, academic year when there were several other faculty casualties. The most notable were Raymond Sirstad and John Klemin, both of whom had departed in the spring. Sirstad was pastoring a church in Hood River, Oregon a distance of sixty miles east of Portland. His new church building was dedicated on 1 May 1982. His departure was understandable and there was undeniable doctrinal incompatibility between him and Fisher.[215] Klemin was more of an enigma. He pastored the UPC church in Vancouver. There were suggestions that he had at long last withdrawn his support for Fisher, although this can only be inferred from his departure and lack of presence at any time on the new CBC campus. Other views were that he had not supported the college moving to Vancouver and starting a

---

[215] Michael Nigh interview, 18 August 2013, and confirmed in Raymond A. Sirstad interview, 27 August 2013.

church in the same city where he pastored.[216] Territorialism in the UPC has historically been quite common. Others suggest jealousy, while adding the caveat that jealousy was not characteristic of John Klemin. According to report, Klemin was initially prepared to fully support the idea of a college church, going so far as to make a verbal pledge to that effect, but then abruptly and inexplicably changed his mind.[217] Despite the fact that he had resigned from the college several years earlier, around 1981-82 Jerry Dillon was encouraging Klemin to join forces with CBC and a college church. Klemin was not receptive to these overtures. Dillon believed it made good sense for the Vancouver church to become the official CBC college church with Don Fisher as senior pastor. It is likely this latter point is what caused Klemin to have pause.[218] With all this as background, Klemin wrote a letter to the CBC board pleading that his feelings be taken into account should the college move to Vancouver and establish a college church. He asked that the college church not be within five miles of his own church, and expressed his fear that one key family in his congregation had indicated a desire to become involved in the CBC college church program. Klemin indicated that if his wishes were not taken into account he would file a formal objection with the Washington District.[219] Klemin's letter was read and discussed at the college-board level and it was determined that Don Fisher, Verneal Crossley, and Frank LaCrosse would meet with Klemin to vet all concerns.[220] This meeting must have been successful, for shortly

---

[216] Jerry W. Dillon, letter to John Klemin, 30 June 1980 [sic]. FC, inv.doc.no 0707-4788-32. Therein, Dillon announced his resignation from the Vancouver UPC church, noted the CBC move to Vancouver (which precludes a 1980 date), the establishment of a college church, and Dillon's intention to make himself available to Fisher for involvement. The telling statement is "I would have been delighted for us to have worked together; however, your decision in that matter has precluded that possibility." This suggests that Klemin had ruled out any partnership with Fisher and a college church. Fisher founded the college church with the permission of the Washington District Board. Donna Fisher interview, 3 January 1999. Dillon's letter should be dated to 1982.

[217] Jerry Peden interview, 19 July 2002.

[218] Jerry Dillon interview, 19 April 2013.

[219] John Klemin, letter to the CBC board, 26 February 1982.

[220] Notes from a Planning Session of the CBC board, 2 March 1982, p. 1.

thereafter Klemin offered his church as a temporary location for the college during its transition out of Oregon.[221] What can be stated with certainty is that whatever his motives were in 1982, John Klemin formally apologised to Fisher in a letter two years later.[222]

4.25  April Purtell at CBC,        4.26  Joseph H. Howell, teaching
        Fall term, 1982                          at JCM, 1980-81

The third issue is that in response to the loss of faculty members and a reluctance of any qualified persons in the area to assume teaching and administrative responsibilities at CBC, Fisher called upon his own legacy and imported a number of former students, mostly from JCM, to take up positions in Vancouver. Among those former students who answered Fisher's call were Rick McDonald, Kelvin Alexander, Naomi Yadon, and Sandi Derick.[223] Fisher also recruited April Purtell from Germany, where she was teaching at Schloß Freudenberg which housed the UPC Wiesbaden

---

[221] *Minutes*, CBC board meeting, 17 July 1982, p. 3. FC, inv.doc.no 0707-5218-34.

[222] The letter does not appear to be extant but Fisher communicated the contents verbally to the author in the spring of 1984. Ostensibly the letter stated that Klemin had harbored ill will toward Fisher but expressed remorse and asked forgiveness. Fisher was elated and said that regardless of past difficulties he regarded John Klemin as a man of integrity. Others were aware of the letter. Jerry Peden interview, 19 July 2002, and April Purtell interview, 16 January 1999.

[223] A troubled man, Alexander was later described by his first wife as a "prisoner of his own psychopathologies" but a man who esteemed Fisher and C.H. Yadon. Pamela Hatheway, letter to Thomas A. Fudge, 22 January 2003. Oregon pastor Jim Dillon apparently said he would not allow Alexander in his church. Jerry Peden interview, 19 July 2002. The reasons are unclear. Alexander had formerly served as interim pastor in Enfield, Connecticut.

School of the Bible led by a former Fisher colleague, CBC graduate, and heresy suspect, Wayne Nigh. She too was a JCM graduate, and became Don Fisher's secretary, assuming responsibility for teaching several courses. Fisher was not successful in persuading his brother-in-law, Dan Lewis, to join the faculty.[224] Lewis had attended CBC, later served on the faculty, and had been a prominent member of the innovative but controversial JCM theology program.[225] He was one of a very small handful of legitimate scholarly thinkers within the UPC at that time.[226] This assessment has been affirmed but with the nuanced caveat about Lewis, that "you can be a good teacher and teach the wrong thing."[227] It is surprising that Fisher did not actively attempt to recruit Joseph Howell to join the CBC faculty.

The work of Lewis and Howell in Jackson raises the question about proper theologians in the UPC in those days. The matter is complex. A theologian is an individual capable of independent, critical thought, who has formal advanced training in the area, is capable of producing a certain modicum of scholarship – subject to outside peer review (the only proper basis for academic or scholarly evaluation) – and engages in the dissemination of knowledge. In the UPC, practically anyone able to articulate a thesis in a classroom or from a pulpit with any degree of sophistication was often given the moniker of theologian. E.G. Moyer earned the equivalent of a Master's degree from Western Baptist Seminary in Portland but the degree was never conferred because he failed to meet entrance requirements in that he had never completed a properly accredited undergraduate program. At the time Don Fisher was heading up JCM and CBC, there were few if any men or women in the UPC possessing credible advanced degrees in the disciplines of theology, biblical studies, or church history. Fisher prompted within many of his students a type of disenchantment with the educational world of

---

[224] Technically this would have been insurmountably problematic since Lewis had officially left the UPC and had turned in his ministerial credentials. Lewis, *The Journey Out*, p. 11. Dan Lewis interview, 6 April 1999.

[225] Lewis, *The Journey Out*, p. 18.

[226] Lewis and Joseph Howell would be among the people Dan Scott had in mind when he told Fisher "I see the young men that were with you in Jackson have really opened up in that way." Dan Scott, letter to Don Fisher, October 1981.

[227] Thomas Craft interview, 20 April 1999.

the UPC, and a number of his students and faculty colleagues from both colleges later went on to earn PhDs from legitimate programs at accredited institutions. Fisher himself was not a theologian and neither was Peden, who made clear he was not an educator.[228] The closest candidate for a theologian at CBC in those days was C.H. Yadon. He qualified only in the narrow sense that he did possess independent judgment, read considerably wider than most of his UPC colleagues, and exhibited an element of critical thinking in teaching. However, he had no professional or systematic intellectual or academic formation. The extent of his formal studies took place at a school run by Harry Morse in Oakland, California. In 1967, Yadon was reluctant to accept nomination for president of CBC because of his "limited formal education."[229]

4.27  *Front row (left to right):* C.H. Yadon, Harry Morse, Ellis Scism, Fern and Harry Scism. Back row *(fifth from left):* Ruth Yadon, Ruby Martin and Marjorie Scism, Oakland, California, *c.* 1941

At JCM, there were men who might rightly be called theological thinkers of some sophistication. Dan Lewis and Joseph H. Howell should be considered the best examples. An examination of their course content, methodology, and desired outcomes reveals a unique approach to college-level education within the UPC. Jerry Peden directly utilised Lewis' materials for courses taught at CBC

---

[228] Jerry Peden interview, 19 July 2002. Not even possession of the venerable prayer bone altered this fact.

[229] C.H. Yadon, letter to Orion Gleason, 6 December 1967.

and Howell's booklist was circulated showing that JCM programs and emphases were transplanted at CBC. Unfortunately, although the UPC historically has consistently recognized the importance for

4.28  Jerry Peden, teaching in a CBC classroom during the 1982-83 academic year

4.29  The ever-humorous Jerry Peden with David Wasmundt following the closure of CBC

apprenticeship under properly qualified authorities in areas such as engineering, aviation, law, and medicine, it has not applied that same logic to theological students.[230] The posture is not anomalous for any group which considers itself already possessing absolute theological truth. Truth is not the same thing as opinion but the two ideas are often confused in the realm of religion. The Vatican ordered that all books not theologically compatible with Roman Catholic doctrine be forbidden to students.[231] Investigations at Concordia Seminary firmly concluded that faculty were teaching intolerable false doctrine.[232] During the crackdown in the Missouri Synod, the new Board of Control ordered faculty to submit course syllabi for examination. Had this been done at Jackson, it is hard to imagine who might have been expert enough in theology, historical method, or exegetical principle to evaluate the nature and content of education provided under the auspices of the Don Fisher administration. It seems impossible to identify a single individual

---

[230] Stanley W. Chambers, "The Value of Bible Schools" *The Pentecostal Herald* 61 (No. 2, 1986), p. 24.
[231] Noted in Pope Pius X, *Pascendi domini gregis* in Sabatier, *Modernism*, pp. 330-331.
[232] Tietjen, *Memoirs in Exile*, p. 154.

within the United Pentecostal Church around 1981 who, for example, possessed the necessary academic and intellectual qualifications to evaluate Howell's booklist. It is disingenuous to say that all of Fisher's enemies were anti-intellectual. Some undoubtedly were. Many were incapable of understanding the subtle points of doctrine.[233] This did not preclude them from harboring suspicions about the presence of a theological Trojan horse in their midst.

There were concerns expressed that Fisher might also try to recruit Jerry Dillon, who had graduated from CBC in 1964 and later served in teaching and administrative capacities at the college between 1969 and 1978.[234] The idea of Fisher, Lewis, and Dillon together on the same faculty caused considerable anxiety in some quarters and outright alarm elsewhere, especially since Dillon was thought to possess "anti-U.P.C leanings" and moreover had been admonished by senior pastors. "Bro. Dillon, I say this kindly, but you have a rebellious-tendency that needs to be overcome."[235] At a Washington District board meeting, C.M. Yadon informed his colleagues that he was absolutely opposed to a possible Fisher-Dillon collaboration around CBC and the Washington District Board agreed. It was left to John Klemin to inform Dillon that the district did not want him involved with Don Fisher either at CBC or at a future college church (ill.6.5, p. 325).[236] These concerns over Dillon's theological leanings and his influence were sufficient to deny him the standard "letter of transfer" usually supplied when leaving a UPC congregation. John and Ruby Klemin regretted Dillon's choices, while Loren Yadon was reportedly "extremely disappointed." Others continued to harbor deep suspicions about Dillon and the various "non-edifying friendships" he and his family maintained with UPC stalwarts.[237] There were questions about

---

[233] Burkee, *Power, Politics, and the Missouri Synod* pp. 69-70, 72, tends to characterize all of those opposed to Tietjen and the eventual Seminex group in this fashion.

[234] Edwin E. Judd, letter to Jerry Dillon, 3 February 1967, indicates that CBC had tried to hire Dillon even earlier. FC, inv.doc.no 0707-5130-34.

[235] John Klemin, letter to Jerry Dillon, 8 July 1982, pp. 1-2.

[236] Jerry Dillon interview, 5 January 1999, on the testimony of John Klemin who was at that meeting.

[237] John Klemin, letter to Jerry Dillon, 5 August 1982. The reference to Loren Yadon appears therein. FC, inv.doc.no 0707-4794-32.

Dillon's teaching at CBC years earlier, especially on taboo subjects such as the doctrine of the eternal sonship, but this was dismissed as a "misunderstanding" and the product of "false rumors."[238] Dillon himself has admitted that in the fall term of 1977 in his *Life of Christ* course, he began raising serious questions for Oneness theology in terms of defining a defensible Christology. Dillon was approaching the conclusion that Oneness doctrine could not be reconciled with the fourth gospel and saw no basis for saying God was made flesh.[239] We have already noted that C.H. Yadon took a similar view. Shortly after Fisher arrived in Portland, Dillon was found openly teaching Calvinist theology in the Vancouver church.

Oregon pastors asserted there were at least three well-known and definite heretics teaching at CBC: Jet Witherspoon, C.H. Yadon, and Jerry Dillon. Enough has been said already about Yadon and Dillon. In the 1970s, John Klemin was concerned about female students at CBC allegedly trimming the ends of their hair and he raised the issue in a faculty meeting. This was a matter of grave concern within the UPC since the practice is generally forbidden. Witherspoon responded to the effect that she had been

4.30    Jet Witherspoon, CBC faculty member, 1953-1975

engaged in that practice for years and wanted to know if that was a problem. Some of the faculty were quite appalled at the revelation that a pioneer Pentecostal like Witherspoon could be so cavalier

---

[238] Ted Tolstad, undated letter to John Klemin, FC, inv.doc.no 0707-4779-32, and Klemin's response, 18 December 1973. FC, inv.doc.no 0707-4780-32.
[239] Jerry Dillon interview, 19 April 2013.

about such a central article of holiness. John Klemin himself was shocked into silence.[240] On other occasions, Witherspoon openly stated in class that she did not think her Trinitarian friends were lost.[241] Some of her hearers were absolutely flummoxed. Eventually, Witherspoon was asked to retire.[242] She accepted this suggestion with graciousness. While proper institutions of higher learning were asking questions of gravity and developing great ideas, others within fundamentalist institutions and Bible colleges were, according to E.J. Carnell, arguing over trivialities such as when the rapture might occur.[243] Within the UPC, the kingdom of God and the preaching of the gospel were subordinated to questions about women cutting their hair and whether church members could own television sets. Fisher could not be bothered with such irrelevancies. In the end, neither Lewis nor Dillon were appointed to the CBC faculty.

In addition to this influx of former students who joined the CBC faculty and staff, Fisher also arranged to contract Dana P. Rowe, a talented musician from Columbus, Ohio, to support David Wasmundt and further bolster the CBC music program.[244] The aforementioned Nathaniel Yadon joined the staff, as did two others of the well-known Pacific Northwest Yadons, his cousin Roger and his eminent uncle C.H. Yadon. The presence of former president Charles Haskell Yadon on the faculty of CBC had two immediate

---

[240] Nevertheless, Klemin went on record concerning Witherspoon's "godly influence" on CBC students. See, for example, John E. Klemin, letter to Jet Witherspoon, 5 December 1972.

[241] Dan Satterwhite interview, 5 February 1999, Pendleton, Oregon. Similar views were confirmed about Dillon and Yadon. Paul Dugas interview, 25 January 1999, and Dan Lewis, letter to Thomas A. Fudge, 9 May 2013. FC, inv.doc.no 0707-5025-33. The three would have shared some common theological assumptions. Raymond A. Sirstad interview, 27 August 2013.

[242] *Minutes*, CBC board meeting, 13 December 1974, p. 3 citing her age and financial difficulties at the college though the question of her retirement had been raised two years earlier. *Minutes*, CBC board meeting, 14 December 1972.

[243] Marsden, *Reforming Fundamentalism*, pp. 172-173. Jet Witherspoon can be seen in ill.0.1, p. xviii. She appears in the fourth row, eighth from the left.

[244] He was actually hired by Jerry Peden, although Peden would not have made faculty decisions without the knowledge and consent of Fisher. Rowe had not previously known Don Fisher. Dana P. Rowe, letter to Thomas A. Fudge, 27 September 2013. FC, inv.doc.no 0707-5354-34. Rowe later became a New York based musical theater composer of some renown.

consequences: First, it silenced a number of waging tongues and second, it confirmed to others in the Oregon District that C.H. Yadon was just as "liberal" as Fisher, Norman Rutzen, and Wayne

4.31  Some CBC faculty and students, 1982-83: Dana Rowe, Sandi Derick, April Purtell, Roger Yadon, Kelvin Alexander, Naomi Yadon, Eric K. Loy, Donna and Don Fisher, Michael Nigh, Doug Greer, Thomas A. Fudge, Michael Fairservice, David Wasmundt

Nigh, all of whom seemed to enjoy a fraternal relationship. Yadon exerted a tremendous influence over men such as Fisher, Rutzen, Nigh, and also Edwin Judd. Former UPC ministers testified that Yadon's ruminations on the nature of truth became a catalyst for leaving the UPC.[245] At the time he returned to CBC, C.H. Yadon was already past his seventy-fourth birthday and had agreed to come to the college for the fall term only. Notwithstanding this

---

[245] Lewis, *The Journey Out*, p. 17. Others also influenced by Yadon continued to look to Fisher and under his influence also left the UPC. "Called Bro. Fisher and set up an appointment for tomorrow ... Bro. Fisher showed up at 10:00 [a.m.] and we had a very good meeting for 2 hours." *The Journal of Thomas A. Fudge, 1980-1985*, entries for 18 and 19 September 1983.

temporary appointment, the presence of C.H. Yadon was a positive sign. One of the grand old men of the movement had arrived to rejuvenate the flagging spirits at CBC. His appointment took on the

4.32  C.H. Yadon, CBC faculty member, Fall 1982

distinct air of formality when "by action of the Board of Directors" the college declared "we are pleased to announce the C.H. Yadon lecture chair" noting the college thought it important to preserve the philosophy he represented.[246] That implied the "no experts" doctrine. Presumably, the intention was to maintain a special and specific adjunct faculty appointment annually to occupy the "C.H. Yadon Lecture Chair." It would have been interesting to see a list of those chosen to give the Yadon lectures. One thinks immediately of men such as Wayne Nigh and James K. Stewart (ill.2.15, p. 77) but there may have actually been outsiders invited. When the senior class of 1981 at JCM voted to invite Donald Bloesch to deliver the

---

[246] *The Cascadian* 16 (No. 3, 1982), pp. 1-2. This had previously been approved. *Minutes*, CBC board meeting, 5 June 1982, p. 2. FC, inv.doc.no 0707-5217-34.

annual graduation address it nearly caused institutional apoplexy.[247] Bloesch was an ordained minister in the United Church of Christ and for thirty-five years was Professor of Theology at Dubuque Theological Seminary in Iowa.[248] As it turned out, Yadon himself was the first and the last to occupy the chair. Yadon's decision to join the CBC faculty at his advanced age must be attributed to the fact that "he had a great deal of regard for Don [Fisher]."[249]

In addition to these positive amendments, the fourth development was that Fisher decisively and dramatically eliminated the problem of local churches and student participation in congregations across the sprawling metropolitan area, by instituting for the first time in CBC history a college church. Historically, there had been friction between the college and local pastors. Prosaic entries in official documents conceal as much as they reveal. "During this term we had a very fine meeting with the local pastors, which I feel has helped to bring about a better understanding with them."[250] John Klemin was wrong and the situation only worsened. From the college point of view, local pastors wanted control of CBC, especially those pastors committed to a rigid, inflexible view of holiness and the new birth.[251] This factor caused one close observer to comment that "the college was a victim of a power struggle."[252] Houston Baptist pastor Kenneth Chafin concluded the struggle within the SBC could be boiled down to a power issue, while Tennessee editor Al Shackleford asserted the matter was one of control.[253] The situation at CBC was no different.

Men like Barry King taught an elevated doctrine of pastoral authority and expected students to put the local church first in order of loyalty and priority. Occasionally, absolute pastoral

---

[247] Lewis, *The Journey Out*, p. 41.

[248] A prolific author, Bloesch is best known for his previously-noted *Essentials of Evangelical Theology*, 2 vols and his seven volume *Christian Foundations* series (Intervarsity Press, 1992-2006).

[249] Jewel (Yadon) Dillon interview, 2 January 2001.

[250] See John Klemin, letter to the CBC board, 14 December 1973, p. 3.

[251] Norman Rutzen interview, 8 February 1999.

[252] George Sponsler interview, 12 February 1999. Also in Leon Brokaw interview, 29 January 2001, and in Darline (Kantola) Royer interview, 15 August 2013.

[253] Quoted in Shurden and Shepley, eds., *Going for the Jugular: A Documentary History of the SBC Holy War*, pp. 63 and 77.

autonomy exceeded even the hoary boundaries of scripture.[254] Fisher denied this point of view and preached that a leader in spiritual matters has no authority at all outside that mandated by scripture.[255] This was not something new. He was well-known for declaring that the formation of Christ in the believer was a world apart from the church or pastors and went on to conclude that ministers had no control in matters of salvation.[256] That sentiment did not resonate in the UPC. The perennial question among the strangers at the gate was, who is pastoring the students?[257] Area ministers considered themselves pastors while categorizing the CBC faculty as teachers and they often drew a fine line between the two, going so far as to effectively deny the faculty any pastoral role. Jerry Dillon dismissed the categories as untenable, noting that such men were "mistaken and distorted in their opinion of what a pastor is." Senior faculty at the college argued that CBC definitely had the capacity to provide pastoral oversight for all students.[258]

Some area ministers aggressively demanded student tithes from the CBC financial office and occasionally came to the campus demanding payment.[259] This was doubtlessly a major factor in the struggle for control. In 1975 the college proposed that students pay tithes to the college. That resolution was conveyed to the local churches. All but one opposed this idea.[260] The CBC board had entertained a resolution wherein one hundred percent of student tithes would be held to be used by the college and scheduled this to take effect at the beginning of 1981. The motion was brought by Norman Rutzen and seconded by Frank LaCrosse. A general discussion then ensued about the local-church relationship and eventually a secret ballot vote was taken. This resulted in a tie. The

---

[254] Jerry Dillon, "The Assassination of a Saint" *In Touch* 2 (No. 1, 1987), pp. 3-4.

[255] Don Fisher, "Leadership," sermon at Christ for the People Community Church, 2 November 1983.

[256] Don Fisher, "Let Christ be Formed in You," sermon at McCormick's Creek, Indiana, 1974, audio recording.

[257] Gary Gleason interview, 7 January 2000.

[258] Jerry Dillon interview, 19 April 2013, and Darline (Kantola) Royer interview, 15 August 2013.

[259] Harry and Freda Fisher interview, 8 December 2000. Freda Fisher kept the books and worked in that office.

[260] Noted in *Minutes*, CBC board meeting, 31 March 1976, p. 4.

motion was defeated when LaCrosse withdrew his second and the resolution died.[261] Later that year, C.H. Yadon again urged the implementation of a tithing policy wherein one hundred percent of the tithe remained with the college. This effort again foundered and the board handed Fisher the impossible task of appealing to local pastors to forfeit their share of student tithes.[262] The struggle for power and control was fuelled in part by financial interests. Conflict in schedules, travel, and events often forced students to decide whether to support the college or the church. Some area pastors appeared to schedule church functions to coincide with college events thus creating deliberate competition and then insisting upon loyalty to the local church.[263] CBC had mandated that the primary allegiance of the student was to the college not the local church.[264] Area pastors resented this stance. The establishment of a college church, which was in every respect compatible with the academic aims of the school and where all students would attend solved that problem.[265] By the time he left office in 1978, John Klemin had been defeated on the college church proposal. He wrote to the board "my recommendation at this time would be to drop the college church idea."[266] Long-time faculty members continued to advocate for a college church program.[267]

Don Fisher had first-hand experience at JCM of the troubles encountered when the direction of a college and that of a local church were dissimilar. With these factors in mind, and taking up the quest abandoned by Klemin, in August 1982, Christ for the People Community Church opened its doors for the first time from the rented facility of the Orchards United Methodist Church at 11000 N.E. Fourth Plain Road, a few blocks northeast from the new CBC campus and just over six miles from John Klemin's

---

[261] Recorded in *Minutes*, CBC board meeting, 9 January 1981, p. 2.

[262] Noted in *Minutes*, CBC board meeting, 28 August 1981, p. 3.

[263] Stan Johnson interview, 5 October 2013, who attended Barry King's church.

[264] See *Minutes*, CBC board meeting, 6 June 1974, pp. 1-2.

[265] Jerry Dillon interview, 5 January 1999, including the previous quotation. By comparison, at JCM all students were required to tithe to the college. *Jackson College of Ministries Catalogue*, p. 21.

[266] John Klemin, letter to the CBC board, 28 August 1978, p.1.

[267] Darline Kantola, "Reflections on Bible College Training," undated [1980], 2pp. FC, inv.doc.no 0707-5189-34.

church. Apart from Fisher's ministerial credentials, Christ for the People had no legal connection to the United Pentecostal Church. While affiliated with the college it was neither owned by the college nor, by extension, the Idaho, Oregon, and Washington Districts.

4.33   Orchards United Methodist Church, home of Christ
for the People Community Church, 1982-1987

The absence of the word "Pentecostal" in its name was conspicuous while the reference to Christ was deliberate. To men such as Barry King, this was both a revealing and troubling clue about the nature of doctrine and Christian identity practiced therein. That said, Fisher maintained a very clear Christological focus.[268] The church name and its logo were the creations of Fisher and appeared in the weekly bulletin. "Christ for the People ... our name and logo explain our understanding of God's reach for us through Jesus Christ. Jesus came as a servant to teach us (the towel and basin); as our Shepherd to lead us (the staff); in the power of the Holy Spirit to enable us (the dove); as the King of God's kingdom to share his glory with us (the crown)." Fisher also placed considerable emphasis on the kingdom of God and believed it was present in the world.[269] Don Fisher served as senior pastor and was

---

[268] This seems very clear from the testimony of those who heard Fisher teach and preach on a regular basis. See also Appendix 5, pp. 434-435.

[269] Harry Fisher interview, 13 July 2005 notes that Don once told him he believed the kingdom of God had come. Fisher said as much in his sermon "The Link" at Christ for the People Community Church, 11 November 1984, audio recording.

backed by a ministry team composed of Jerry D. Peden, Roger Yadon, Kelvin Alexander, and C.H. Yadon. All students from outside the local area were required to attend.[270] By late September,

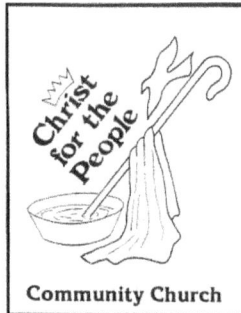

4.34  Christ for the People Community
Church, logo, 1982

attendance at the Sunday afternoon services had climbed to around two hundred. For United Pentecostal churches in the Portland area this was remarkable.[271] There is some evidence to suggest that this development was part of the rupture between Klemin and Fisher. Klemin's west Vancouver church had struggled for some time and its membership was less than fifty. Within weeks of setting up operations in east Vancouver, Fisher had quadrupled the membership of the old Vancouver church and moreover some of Klemin's parishioners had elected to join Christ for the People. No reliable evidence has emerged to support the claim that Fisher actively proselytized UPC church people in the Portland-Vancouver area, with perhaps the single exception of Jerry Dillon. However, Dillon was fairly well ensconced at the Beaverton Foursquare Church, in the west Portland metropolitan area, and in consequence was never an active part of Christ for the People during the Fisher years. Despite these mainly constructive developments in the college, the student body at CBC had slid to a paltry thirty three for the 1982-83 academic year. It appeared that the handwriting was on

---

[270] *Cascade Bible College 1982-1984 Catalog*, p. 47.
[271] Thomas A. Fudge, "A Short History of Cascade Community Church," unpublished paper, 2002, p. 1. FC, inv.doc.no 0707-4759-32. By the mid-1990s, after a dozen years, the church changed its name to Cascade Community Church. Ibid., p. 3. See ill.6.12, p. 346.

the wall for the college even though the college church seemed about to take Vancouver by storm. People came from all over the metropolitan area to share in the Sunday services. College students and faculty played a key role in the services, especially in preaching, leading worship, and music. Christ for the People Church was an electrifying experience even though it clearly lacked the obvious Pentecostal emphases as well as the distinctive UPC hallmarks. The music was exuberant, the preaching charismatic, but oddly undogmatic. Sunday services were preceded by a vibrant prayer session which convened on the mezzanine of the auditorium. Energy, excitement, and expectation are accurate descriptors of the mood surrounding Christ for the People. Don Fisher was the central personality. He had the innate ability to galvanize people and those in leadership at the church believed they were part of something deeply spiritual, purposeful, and Christ-centered.[272] Just before the worship service commenced, Fisher would gather the last of the people in the prayer-room together in close proximity, call attention to the energizing power of God, remind all those present why they had gathered, offer prayer, and would then lead those people into the church auditorium downstairs like warriors into battle. Those who were regular participants in those pre-service sessions often spoke of the sense of purpose and power.

On the matter of worship and its context, Fisher's approach might be described in this way. "Not a box of spiritual excitement in which we thrash around when the atmosphere is charged ... waiting for our time at the cargo air lift."[273] In other words, Fisher taught quite clearly that anything called worship which did not bring one's attention to Christ was therefore not really worship at all and should either be actively discouraged or disallowed. Fisher's congregation more and more came to resemble a mainstream evangelical church. Long hair on men, blue jeans, short hair and make-up on women became more and more evident. While these features were typical in mainstream Christian churches, the UPC actively mandated against such "worldliness," especially if the

---

[272] Michael Nigh interview, 18 August 2013.

[273] Included in "God's Greatest Gift Today: Hope," Christ for the People Leadership Seminar Notes, undated [1983 or 1984], in Fisher's handwriting.

persons in question took any active part in the services. At Christ for the People they did, and Fisher seemed not to notice or if he did remained blissfully unconcerned. But while the church was on the way up, CBC appeared to reach its nadir. Financial difficulties persisted and while student and faculty morale appeared high, an approaching storm, signalled by ominously dark clouds, began to gather on the horizon.

Don Fisher moved the college out of Oregon for several reasons but chiefly because the majority of ministers in the Oregon District elected not to support the efforts of CBC. Some ministers deny this.[274] From the very beginning, there were "serious questions" theologically about Fisher and as a result of that angst, Oregon withdrew on doctrinal grounds in opposition to Don Fisher.[275] Men like Barry King stated that Oregon forced the college out of its jurisdiction. This was considered a dire factor in the eventual demise of the college.[276] It is specious to argue that the Oregon District did not withdraw support. Unhappy that Washington and Idaho seemed to collude against the governmental wishes of Oregon and appeared to support the long-disdained idea of a college church, and having failed in its attempt to secure a single district control over CBC, Oregon signalled its intention to not support the college and then carried through with that resolve.[277]

The Idaho District continued to offer support from afar as it had consistently for many years, but Washington having opened its arms to Fisher and CBC now began to assume an increasingly aloof and then overtly hostile posture.[278] That unexpected stance had crippling consequences. It signalled a complete breakdown of local support for Fisher and the college. The influence of Barry King was considered in some quarters to be a major negative contributing

---

[274] Paul Dugas interview, 25 January 1999, claimed the explanation was a lie because everyone supported CBC. That position is difficult to reconcile with the formal withdrawal of support by the Oregon District in 1981 as noted.

[275] David Bernard interview, 16 April 1999, and E.W. Yadon interview, 25 July 2013.

[276] Edwin Judd interview, 10 April 1999.

[277] Resolution Number 1, Oregon District Conference, 25 April 1981, pp. 1-2. FC, inv.doc.no 0707-5201-34. See Appendix 8, pp. 438-439.

[278] R.V. Reynolds, letter to the CBC Board of Directors, 15 March 1979 notes the strong Idaho support.

factor.[279] Even those who agreed with King theologically thought he possessed a "very rotten spirit."[280] Throughout the fall of 1982, the support base for CBC in the Washington District was steadily eroded and was perhaps halved. This can be gauged in part from the decline in *Ensign* advertisements. The district ads fell from nine in 1982 to five in 1983, while church ads dropped from a total of seventeen in 1982 to eight in 1983. The numbers are sobering.

Elsewhere, Don Fisher was no longer in favor. In early 1982, he was under strong, active consideration as an invitee to conduct a seminar in France. The foreign missions division in St. Louis forbade the invitation from being extended on the grounds that in light of the "Jackson tragedy," American pastors would not look favorably upon Don Fisher speaking in a foreign missions context.[281] In light of Craft's letter of support for Fisher with its denial of doctrinal irregularity, this position assumed in St. Louis is inexplicable though potentially explainable especially in light of the Wayne Nigh controversy. The negative decision on the European seminar suggests the tip of the iceberg concerning opposition fomenting against Don Fisher in the UPC. College promotion efforts around the country became increasingly difficult. CBC was received well in Idaho, Hawaii, and in some churches in Indiana. Ohio was positively influenced to remain friendly to some extent by Fisher ally James K. Stewart, while Alaska District superintendent James Blackshear was supportive. Exceptions to the hostility in Oregon were churches pastored by George Sponsler, Leon Brokaw, and Albert Dillon. All of these latter supporters recommended students attend CBC.[282] The Tennessee District, historically very similar theologically to the Northwest, allowed the college to set up a promotional display at district functions but remained somewhat cool. By this time (1978), W.M. Greer had stepped down as district superintendent. The Arizona District would not permit CBC

---

[279] Jerry Peden interview, 19 July 2002. King has been called a "hard-nosed radical." Jerry Dillon interview, 5 January 1999. By contrast, Frank LaCrosse interview, 16 January 2001, suggests King had little to no influence.
[280] Clyde Barlow interview, 13 August 2013.
[281] Jim Wilkins interview, 1 May 1999. Wilkins was in France at the time and part of the decision to invite Fisher and by consequence had first-hand knowledge.
[282] Joe Higgins interview, 4 October 2013, reflecting especially on Blackshear.

advertisements or promotion. In Montana, District Superintendent J.M. Russell told Jerry Peden (in so many words) that he was not welcome. Even in Washington, while there was warm reception at a number of local churches, the college was not recognized at district functions.[283] This violated previous assurances to the College Board that CBC would be included in district conferences.[284]

By early 1983, the Fisher administration was increasingly isolated from any meaningful support network within the UPC. In an unprecedented portent, no new students were enrolled at the college for the winter term despite Fisher having made a direct plea to pastors. "Time is running out. Send us your students. We'll send them home rooted and built up in sound doctrine and strong in spirit."[285] The plea fell on deaf ears. No one responded. In fact, as previously noted, active recruitment efforts by the college were rebuffed to the extent that CBC was sometimes not permitted to engage in promotion at some district functions or make any public announcements about the college.[286] A ripple effect ensued. What was spoken in Oregon was heard in New York and the college suffered as a result.[287] Parents and pastors did not want to risk the security and salvation of their young people by turning them over to Fisher. They demanded that their young people be placed into the hands of proper "experts." They wanted assurances.

Southern Baptists demanded "experts" too and W.A. Criswell, Paul Pressler, and Paige Patterson (ill.4.35) were among the ones qualified to determine who the "experts" were. Jacob Preus and Herman Otten were the "experts" in the Missouri Synod and they were confident that the bulk of the Concordia Seminary faculty in the early 1970s were suspect. John R. Rice, Carl McIntire, and Charles Woodbridge were devoted "guardians" within American

---

[283] Jerry Peden interview, 19 July 2002, and Esther Peden interview, 7 October 2013, Douglas, Wyoming. Stewart and Fisher were close. The former was open-minded, thoughtful, and not at all certain that non UPC people were excluded from salvation. Mark Roberts interview, 5 May 1999.

[284] *Minutes*, CBC board meeting, 15 October 1982, p. 3.

[285] Don Fisher, "The Man and His Ministry" *The Cascadian* 16 (No. 3, 1982), p. 2.

[286] Esther Peden, quoted in Lewis, *The Journey Out*, p. 67. Jerry Peden interview, 19 July 2002, and Esther Peden interview, 7 October 2013.

[287] Darline (Kantola) Royer interview, 15 August 2013.

Fundamentalism. Umberto Benigni was the Vatican's "expert" who worked tirelessly to purge the church of her enemies. There were minority voices in the UPC suggesting that "security based upon ignorance, prejudice, illusions, misinformation and blind tradition is a false security."[288] Such opinions were routinely dismissed.

4.35  Paige Patterson, speaking at the convocation chapel service at Southwestern Theological Seminary, Fort Worth, Texas, August 2013

To compound matters, C.H. Yadon departed, though he clearly retained support for Fisher and the college right up to the bitter end. Nathaniel Yadon, suspected by some to be of unstable mind, began accusing Fisher of "stealing his church." The accusation, if it occurred, is specious. Yadon never had more than a handful of congregants at the time he decided to throw in his lot with Fisher. His courses at CBC were ridiculed by many students as simplistic, marginally competent, and utterly dogmatic when it came to the central tenets of the UPC. One of Yadon's courses was the *Acts of the Apostles* previously taught by Raymond Sirstad. By several testimonies Yadon was unable to teach the *Acts of the Apostles* beyond the second chapter where the doctrine of salvation in the United Pentecostal Church is firmly grounded. This posture was anomalous among the well-known and influential Yadon family of the Pacific Northwest. C.H. Yadon, the patriarch of the family,

---

[288] Marler, *Imprisoned in the Brotherhood*, p. 9.

consistently steered clear of the Acts 2:38 stance in terms of the new birth. At the end of his life he confessed he had never believed the text had any relation to salvation.[289] There were frequent whispers throughout the UPC questioning Yadon's orthodoxy. Assumptions that he remained in good standing with the organization to the end of his long life require nuance and qualification.[290] His nephew, Vern Yadon, caused waves when he began teaching the doctrine of justification while pastoring in Corvallis, Oregon. Some time later, he led his UPC congregation in Chattanooga, Tennessee through a two-year study of the book of Romans, became a Calvinist, embraced the doctrine of the Trinity, declared his non-acceptance of UPC theology, and voluntarily surrendered his ministerial license.[291] These may be two of the extreme examples, but strong adherence to the Acts 2:38 position

4.36　Vern Yadon and James G. Fudge discussing theology, Seattle, May 2009

among the Yadons was rare. They stayed attuned to the problem of the "foul ball," resisted pressure to conform theologically to the dominant trends within the UPC, and firmly adhered to the "no experts" doctrine.

---

[289] C.H. Yadon interview, 27 August 1997.
[290] Reed, *"In Jesus' Name,"* p. 290.
[291] Vern Yadon interview, 6 December 2000.

With the difficulty of contracting faculty members there was little the Fisher administration could do about Nathaniel Yadon even though both Peden and Fisher personally disagreed with his

4.37  Nathaniel Yadon, 1982, around the time
he attempted publicly to wash Don Fisher's feet

theological and pedagogical emphases. His inability to function as a balanced college instructor was exacerbated by bizarre behavior outside the classroom. During a Christmas service on 19 December 1982, at a time near the end of the gathering when Associate Pastor Jerry Peden was about to present President and Mrs. Fisher with a Christmas gift from the church, Nathaniel Yadon nearly stole the show. While Peden was making the transition from worship to the gift presentation, Yadon appeared at the rear of the church, shirt sleeves rolled to his elbows, towel draped over an arm, carrying a large basin of water in hand, and began making his way slowly up the central aisle to the left front pew where Fisher sat with his wife. The church was completely full. Upon seeing Yadon approach, Peden immediately called the congregation to prayer by asking all to bow their heads and close their eyes. Yadon remained undeterred. Reaching his target he placed the basin on the floor and informed Fisher that he wished to wash his feet. Fisher was visibly surprised and asked Yadon to repeat what he had just said. Fisher then slid the water basin under the pew with his left foot and instructed Yadon to sit down. Most of the congregation, thanks to Peden's shrewd intervention, remained oblivious to the aborted foot-washing ceremony.[292] What was Yadon thinking? There had been conflict between the two men. Yadon felt he had been directed by God to put Don Fisher to the test. That test was designed to demonstrate if Fisher was a man of God. If Fisher submitted to foot washing then he was *bona fide*. Yadon believed he had a divine mandate to act as he did and the outcome made clear who and what Fisher was. Don Fisher failed that test as clearly as he had flunked the examination at JCM during the Richard Heard crusade. The incident was proof to Nathanial Yadon that the program at CBC was contrary to the will of God.[293] Fisher's failure positioned him outside the safety of truth just as surely the purge within the LCMS was divine providence.[294] This episode, however, only illustrates the opposition that was continuing to mount against Fisher and CBC. Nathaniel Yadon's public attempt at humility underscored the serious conundrum presented by the Washington District's gradual withdrawal of support.[295] Still, no one could have known for certain that the dawning of 1983 was the last for CBC. The end was closer than anyone – with perhaps the exception of Fisher – could have imagined.

In late January, the mounting crisis reached fever pitch. Two events are instructive. First, the financial woes were now apparent to all, including the students. Clearly there was now considerable doubt that CBC could complete its thirtieth year. Limited but energetic and sustained promotion of the college had failed to elicit any measurable financial support. The Kopper Kitchen dining investment was not successful. It was rumored that members of the faculty went without pay. Fisher ostensibly put up a sizable amount of his own capital in a desperate but futile attempt to stave off the

---

[292] Supplemental details from Jerry Peden interview, 19 July 2002, and Michael Nigh interview, 18 August 2013.

[293] Nathaniel Yadon interview, 15 December 2000.

[294] Marquart, *Anatomy of an Explosion*, p. 78.

[295] Fisher was overheard, a few minutes later, at the end of service scornfully saying to Donna, "That crazy fool wanted to wash my feet!" All of those witnesses interviewed about this incident agreed unanimously that Yadon was simply trying to embarrass Fisher and create a public scene, though it is doubtful Yadon was conscious of that effect.

inevitable.[296] Some college detractors gloated as Fisher had earlier predicted. In asking for support for CBC Fisher noted that those who had no special regard for the distinctiveness of the college would rejoice in its demise.[297] Its fate now very much in the balance, some college students began approaching faculty and administrators voicing concerns about their collegiate future. The answers given were of course tentative and did little to allay the growing unease.

At the same time Fisher was increasingly and continuously besieged with letters and phone calls from UPC ministers hectoring him to clarify his position on any number of theological issues. Those letters and phone calls underscore the significant factor in the demise of CBC. One letter in particular asked him to state his position on water baptism. Evidently rumor suggested that Fisher had denied the fundamental teaching of the denomination.[298] This allegation was not new even though Thomas Craft had dismissed it in writing two years earlier as unworthy. An interview with Fisher in his office on 3 February 1983 witnessed signs of extreme agitation and possible despair at what he termed the "abandonment of long-time friends," the "unresponsiveness" of the UPC headquarters to the plight of the college, and the bitter sense of "betrayal" he felt especially from those in power particularly within the Washington District.[299] Though he did not make any further direct allusion or

---

[296] Jerry Dillon interview, 5 January 1999, claims to know this for a fact. Students were not fond of the Kopper Kitchen in terms of food quality or choices, especially the widely-ridiculed option number one "the basic burger."

[297] Don Fisher, letter "To the Friends of CBC," 14 December 1981.

[298] The UPC mandates baptism by total immersion and the formula to include "in the name of Jesus." The act remits sin though there is controversy within the UPC over the doctrine of baptismal regeneration. Immersion and the "Jesus name" formula are salvific and essential. All other forms, modes and formulas are invalid and lack efficacy. The letter asking Fisher to clarify his position is not extant but according to his testimony to the author in early February 1983, it represented an entire genre of communication. On that occasion, Fisher declared that neither his theological understanding nor practice of baptism had been modified since the 1950s. It is true that Fisher later publicly denied the efficacy and necessity of "Jesus name" baptism but during his tenure as president there is no evidence that he ever publicly questioned that theological tenet.

[299] The date is confirmed in *The Journal of Thomas A. Fudge, 1980-1985*, entry for 3 February 1983. The conversation with Fisher was unique. He did not often share such details with students.

offer to specifically identify any particular individual there is sufficient suspicion to suggest that he had Nathaniel Urshan in mind.[300] Less than six months had passed since Urshan had affirmed Fisher in Colorado and pledged continued support.

During the last days of CBC there is no evidence that Urshan made good his promise. The standard explanation that Urshan was constitutionally restricted by the by-laws of the districts in question and was therefore silent on the grounds of political restraint are not altogether convincing. Urshan had considerable moral influence and political clout which could have been used had he elected to do so. However, it was politically inexpedient for Urshan to come to Fisher's aid.[301] At least one Northwest official said that he begged Urshan to help.[302] On a separate occasion, at an Idaho District conference during the Fisher years, at which Urshan was present, C.H. Yadon made an "impassioned plea" for support on behalf of the college. In the same session, Jerry Peden publicly asked Urshan "Please do not let them close the school."[303] The generic reference to CBC's enemies included those within Oregon and Washington who had worked to undermine the college, who opposed Don Fisher, and who continued to allege that the school was "weak on the message." Much later Urshan was asked why he had not done anything to ameliorate the difficulties CBC faced. Astonishingly he replied that he had not been aware of the dire straits Fisher was enduring. "I was not aware ... I didn't know there was a crisis." He went on to say "I can't recall Brother Rutzen asking me to come out there."[304] A number of men, including Jerry Peden and Norman Rutzen, regarded that response as one lacking probity.[305] As noted

---

[300] Urshan says he sent Fisher a personal letter not long after CBC closed down. Nathaniel Urshan interview, 23 April 1999.

[301] Jerry Dillon interview, 5 January 1999. Such constraints did not prevent Urshan from involving himself in the Tennessee District when his son became enmeshed in controversy in Memphis.

[302] Norman Rutzen interview, 8 February 1999.

[303] Jerry Peden interview, 19 July 2002.

[304] Nathaniel Urshan interview, 23 April 1999.

[305] Jerry Peden interview, 19 July 2002, and Norman Rutzen interview, 2 January 2001. Former Urshan associates have commented publicly that Urshan was not above "bare-faced" lying. Robert A. Sabin, letter to the Oneness Pentecostalism Internet Discussion Group, 12 March 2005. FC, inv.doc.no 0707-4068-28.

earlier, the UPC headquarters, almost certainly upon the explicit direction or recommendation of Urshan, sent C.M. Becton to the Northwest. Becton achieved nothing and according to one source "absolutely turned his head" the other way.[306] Becton denied this, noting that the issues in Portland had nothing whatever to do with theology.[307] That statement is deeply problematic.

In the immediate aftermath of the closing of CBC there were men who drew attention to the need for theological fidelity should the college be revived. "Each person on the teaching staff would be expected to teach only the dostrines [sic] of the United Pentecostal Church or be dismissed."[308] A statement like this would never have been made were there not clear and certain grounds for concern that CBC had maintained a questionable doctrinal stance. The fact the admonition was formulated by a Northwest moderate only strengthens the assumption.

There were definite suspicions. Suspects had been identified. Theological issues had been enumerated. The list of errors included Don Fisher's disbelief in the fundamental UPC doctrine. Jerry Dillon taught Christological irregularities and was toying with Trinitarianism, eventually concluding that UPC doctrine of the Godhead was irreconcilably incompatible with the Gospel of John. Jet Witherspoon was notoriously "weak on the message" in a general sense. C.H. Yadon's doctrine of God was demonstrably inconsistent with UPC doctrine, he did not advocate an acceptable standard of holiness, and his concept of the new birth caused shudders among the missionaries who had come to convert the Northwest. Fisher, along with Peden, failed to advocate proper standards of holiness. These heretics were the usual suspects and so far as the "experts" were concerned such men and women could not be permitted to further contaminate the minds of young people. Heresy matters aside, from a legal point of view, the college came under the jurisdictional control of the three Northwest districts and Urshan could say with technical correctness that he

---

[306] Norman Rutzen interview, 8 February 1999.

[307] Cleveland Becton interview, 14 April 1999. Others concede that doctrinal issues did intrude. Raymond A. Sirstad interview, 27 August 2013.

[308] E.G. Moyer, letter to the District superintendents of Oregon, Washington, and Idaho, 11 March 1983, p. 2. FC, inv.doc.no 0707-5224-34.

was not empowered to intervene and that "radicals" were supposed to be dealt with at the district level.[309] Urshan did not speculate on how that was possible if the district leadership itself were made up of "radicals." The legal argument mounted to explain why Urshan did not and could not intervene in the destruction of CBC has some humorous antecedents. Biagio da Cesena, the sixteenth-century master of ceremonies in the Vatican, complained to the pope about Michelangelo's Last Judgment fresco in the Sistine Chapel claiming he was inappropriately maligned therein having been placed in hell wearing the ears of an ass. Pope Paul III declined to take up Biagio's cause, apocryphally claiming he had no jurisdiction in hell.[310] Is it possible that Urshan, known in some quarters as the "great persuader," simply did not wish to be seen on the politically disadvantageous side of Don Fisher and the "no experts" school?[311] The appearance of Cleveland Becton on 27 February 1982 to hear Oregon's "protest" was the sole official response by the national UPC. The Oregon District's formal request for a three or five member panel made up of members of the executive board of the organization to come to the Northwest to arbitrate Oregon's concerns over CBC did not materialize.[312] C.M. Becton did make an appearance before the College Board at their spring meeting that year, summarizing discussions he had been involved in with the Oregon District at their meeting two days earlier held at a hotel near the Portland airport. Norman Rutzen confronted Becton before the board challenging him on his support for Oregon action. Placed in a potentially embarrassing position, Becton had little choice but to declare his support for Toole and the Oregon District which he had already expressed to the Oregon ministers during a restricted meeting previously held at the Portland

---

[309] Nathaniel Urshan interview, 23 April 1999. Urshan independently introduced the term "radicals" into the conversation.

[310] Paola Barocchi, ed., *Giorgio Vasari: La vita di Michelangelo nelle redazioni del 1550 e del 1568*, 5 vols (Milan: Ricciardi, 1962), vol. 3, pp. 1297-1298.

[311] This was a moniker attached to Urshan in eastern Canada. Raymond A. Beesley interview 22 January 1998, Sussex, New Brunswick, and James G. Fudge interview, 19 September 2000, Saint John, New Brunswick.

[312] Resolution Number 1, Oregon District Conference, 25 April 1981, p. 2 and Winfred Toole, letter to the Oregon District pastors, 23 February 1982.

Airport Sheridan Inn. Rutzen expressed his disbelief.[313] All of this behind-the-scenes activity was concealed from the CBC faculty.[314] These events go some distance in shedding light on the Oregon opposition to CBC and on the effort to force Fisher into defeat.

If the impending financial crisis was a chronic condition, there was an incident that brought matters to a head. It was a social event on 22 January 1983. The entire college community had been invited to participate in a Christ for the People church-wide snow-tubing outing on Mt. Hood.[315] Winter outings to Mt. Hood were semi-regular occurrences at CBC, evidenced by photographs in various editions of the *Ensign*. This innocuous trip would have serious consequences for the fate of President Fisher, and by extension the entire community and future of CBC. The background can be stated briefly in the staunch position taken by the UPC on the doctrine of holiness. Simply stated, a particular, and some might say peculiar, understanding of holiness held very strongly within the UPC concerns the external appearance of men and women. Some of this was considered relative to salvation and there was plenty of one-upmanship on such matters. For example, in the 1970s, former Atlantic District Superintendent Ed Wickens was the Bible teacher at the Ludlow Falls camp meeting in Ohio. Wickens described the competitive outlook in these words:

> The problem was some of the people were getting what the Gospel is and set free from bondage and wondering why their pastor was not telling them this. You can well see how it would create a problem. The area had three different organizations[:] UPC, PCI, & PAJC ... They had their meeting while I was in the area. It was kind of amusing, and yet tragic as the various preachers would testify or give their speech of how they had better standard[s] of holiness. In the light of how Paul would see this, in Phil. 3 they were actually bragging of who had the bigger manure pile. Not a very solid foundation to depend upon for salvation.[316]

---

[313] *Minutes*, CBC board meeting, 1 March 1982, p. 3 (FC, inv.doc.no 0707-5211-34) and Norman Rutzen interview, 27 September 2013.

[314] Darline (Kantola) Royer interview, 15 August 2013. Other faculty were aware that the college was under attack. Stan Johnson interview, 5 October 2013.

[315] *The Journal of Thomas A. Fudge, 1980-1985*, entry for 22 January 1983.

[316] E.P. Wickens, letter to Thomas A. Fudge, 28 January 2013. The reference to the PCI is an error as it ceased to exist in 1945. FC, inv.doc.no 0707-4719-32.

In the culture of the UPC, facial hair on men is regarded as "worldly" and generally discouraged. Women are forbidden to cut their hair, or wear make-up or extravagant jewellery. Both sexes are discouraged from wearing shorts or any other article of clothing which is deemed to expose the body indecently.

While all of this is stated clearly in the manual of the UPC, none of this is relevant here.[317] But there is one point of the UPC doctrine of holiness and its application which came to bear critically on the CBC participation in the snow-tubing outing to Mt. Hood in late January 1983. That point is the conviction shared widely in the UPC that pants (slacks or trousers) on women is an egregious violation of the Deuteronomic injunction: "A woman shall not wear a man's apparel, nor shall a man put on a woman's garment; for whoever does such things is abhorrent to the Lord your God."[318] Despite the exegetical difficulties of maintaining such a novel interpretation of that text, the UPC steadfastly declares its adherence to that precise understanding. Any activity that demands that women wear trousers must be avoided. Popular preaching in many regions of the UPC take the view that if a woman is unable to appropriately participate in an activity while wearing a dress then she simply should not participate.[319] The emphasis upon outward appearances within the UPC is a major consideration and there is little appreciation for the possibility that in the service of God the disciple may learn that the appearance of things can deceive.[320]

Several female students at CBC approached Fisher to ask whether or not they would be permitted to wear ski pants for the

---

[317] *Manual* (2014), pp. 34-35, 160, 174-178.

[318] Deuteronomy 22:5. Dan Lewis, "Remarks on Deuteronomy 22:5," undated three-page typescript reflects accurately then-current Hebrew Bible scholarship. FC, inv.doc.no 0707-0063-01. The apodictic laws of Deuteronomy 22 focus in verse five on a technical practice of ritual transvestite behavior. Richard D. Nelson, *Deuteronomy* [Old Testament Library] (Louisville: Westminster John Knox Press, 2002), pp. 267-268. Its interpretation and articulation by the UPC is exegetically curious.

[319] Sermons, for example, by Arden Bustard, Senior Pastor of First United Pentecostal Church in Saint John, New Brunswick in the 1970s, and by Arnold Paisley (1941-2006), pastor of Revival Tabernacle (UPC) in Regina Saskatchewan in 1983-4 made this point in one form or another. The position is not anomalous.

[320] Way, *The Garden of the Beloved*, p. 22.

outing.[321] It ought to be stressed that several of the female students in question were from the Idaho District, where the so-called "standards of holiness" were not held at all or not as rigidly as elsewhere, even in the Caldwell church pastored by the District

4.38   CBC students snow-tubing on Mt. Hood, 22 January 1983, wherein college females were discovered wearing inappropriate attire

Superintendent, which included members of his own immediate family. For example, while televisions were generally banned within the UPC, district superintendent Norman Rutzen was not above renting a television set to watch particular broadcasts.[322] His wife (daughter of C.H. Yadon) did in fact cut her hair and numerous women at Valley Pentecostal Church in Caldwell (where Rutzen was pastor) openly wore make-up, cut their hair, and wore pants. Men wore long hair (by UPC standards) and beards. Rutzen did not impose sanctions nor did he preach about such matters from the pulpit. Several of the students in question were members of

---

[321] Peggy (Yelm) Dougherty interview, 27 July 2013, was among this group and remembers that Dean of Students Jerry Peden was approached on this matter. It is inconceivable that Peden would have acted on his own authority without consulting with Fisher.

[322] The author watched part of the Rose Bowl football game with Rutzen in his home in Caldwell. *The Journal of Thomas A. Fudge, 1980-1985*, entry for 1 January 1982, in which Washington defeated Iowa 28-0. As noted, at that time Rutzen was the United Pentecostal Church superintendent for the District of Idaho.

Rutzen's very "liberal" church, at least two of whom were alleged to have been involved in selling makeup in the female dorms at CBC.[323] The decision Fisher made regarding the CBC outing was in some ways trite yet his decision brought him to the final crossroads.

From the UPC point of view, the matter became the proverbial straw that broke the camel's back. Fisher granted permission to the female students to wear ski pants if they wished. However, he imposed the proviso that they must not wear the ski pants to or from the snow fields. Rather, they must wear their customary skirts or dresses, change into their ski pants at the actual site and then change back into their skirts and dresses for the trip back to the CBC campus. It appeared to be a sensible solution. Only one female from CBC did not wear pants. Even Donna Fisher (ill.5.10, p. 261) and Esther Peden wore ski pants.[324]

It should have been an inconsequential event. Fate intervened. On that same day, on that same snow-tubing slope called "Snow Bunny," also enjoying the winter recreation, were members of Paul Dugas' Portland UPC church.[325] Dugas had been one of those persistent and outspoken opponents of the Fisher administration. The Dugas women were snow-tubing also, but in good and faithful UPC fashion, wearing their dresses and skirts. These individuals reported back to Dugas their horror over the terrible stumbling-block that women from the Bible School were wearing pants on Mt. Hood. The forces of renewed criticism of Fisher and CBC were thus set in motion, this time with concrete and *prima facie* evidence. The youthful naïveté of the college girls might well have been excused. After all, many of them had come up under the "wishy-washy greasy grace" influence of the Yadons in Idaho and their supporters elsewhere. The blame for this outrage, however, could

---

[323] Females from Caldwell were described by hardliners as "hussies from Idaho." Kristi (Eld) Christensen interview, 4 October 2013, notes this and admits she was a Mary Kay consultant.

[324] Donna Fisher interview, 3 January 1999, and Audrey (Zapalac) Greer interview, 22 September 2013. The single exception was Renee Hills (1959-2000).

[325] Others believe the women were from Clyde Barlow's church in St. Helens, Oregon. Jerry Peden interview, 19 July 2002, and Donna Fisher interview, 3 January 1999. Paul Dugas interview, 25 January 1999, confirmed the group was from his church.

not be shifted from the man who had given them permission. He knew better. The action permitted at Snow Bunny on that winter day reflected either backsliders or individuals "weak on the message." Either scenario was insufferable in terms of a UPC Bible college. President Fisher had shown reckless disregard for the teachings of the church, the will and consensus of the Washington District, and by extension and implication the salvation and eternal welfare of his female students. The atrocities perpetrated at CBC had now gone much too far. The time had come for immediate and unequivocal sanctions.

4.39   CBC music group performing at a Washington District function, Seattle, 21 November 1981. *Left to right:* David Wasmundt (piano), Kendall Cobb, Thomas A. Fudge, and Gregg Calder

The first intimation of an official response was the banning of the CBC music group from performing at the Washington District conference in Seattle.[326] Don Fisher was informed by telephone on the morning of 11 February by Washington District Superintendent Verneal Crossley. When asked why the CBC contingent (with the exception of Kelvin Alexander) had been struck from the program, Crossley made reference to the incident at "Snow Bunny." Fisher

---

[326] Jerry Peden says this episode was sufficient for him to decide to resign. Jerry Peden interview, 18 July 2002.

then asked about the CBC choir which at that very moment was in the CBC chapel but prepared to make the trip to Seattle as planned. Crossley answered that the choir was not welcome at the conference and would in no case be permitted to sing. Don Fisher and the girls of CBC had violated one of the cardinal standards of holiness. By appearing clad in "that which pertaineth unto a man" the female CBC students, along with none other than "Sister Fisher" herself, had committed an insufferable abomination before the Lord. Crossley did not use the abomination language drawn upon Deuteronomy 22:5, but that phrase was commonplace in the UPC during that time. C.H. Yadon considered the entire affair inconsistent. Lecturing in a college classroom at JCM in the late 1970s, Yadon remarked that a preacher who forbade the wearing of a wedding ring while driving a Cadillac was a hypocrite. "There's a lot more metal on that car than around a finger."[327] The "experts" were unimpressed.

To the outsider such prohibitions and strictures surely seem ridiculous and perhaps grossly overstated and overemphasised in this account. While specific practices on this point do not always follow a uniform pattern within the UPC, one anecdote serves to illumine the lengths to which a doctrine can be interpreted and taken. One high-ranking UPC preacher is alleged once to have actually preached from the pulpit that women ought to wear a night dress to bed rather than pajamas in order not to violate the Hebrew Bible injunction.[328] This point of view constitutes a strict but quite accurate interpretation of the aforementioned Deuteronomic injunction within the prevailing UPC hermeneutic. In hindsight, the infraction at CBC was surely minor enough to warrant no more than a verbal reprimand and perhaps "official" warning to Fisher. Instead, the incident became a cornerstone in the UPC's case against the Fisher administration. For Fisher, the refusal of the Washington District to allow the CBC choir to sing because of the

---

[327] Jim Wilkins interview, 1 May 1999. Wedding rings were banned in Mississippi and other areas of the UPC in those days.

[328] This statement was made by Raymond Beesley (1927-2002), former district superintendent of the Canadian Atlantic District (1974-95), and was heard by Edwin P. Wickens, who preceded Beesley as district superintendent (1962-73). Wickens interview, 20 January 1998, Fredericton, New Brunswick.

Snow Bunny incident was, as previously noted, the proverbial straw which broke the camel's back. Don Fisher had had enough. He hung up the phone that Friday morning, went into the chapel, made his momentous announcement and seemingly with little hesitation, crossed his own Rubicon. He never looked back.

4.40 Division of Education (UPC), 1981-83. *Back row (left):* Arless Glass and Melvin Springfield. *Front row:* J.D. Langford, Hugh Rose, and George Sponsler

Washington District superintendent Verneal Crossley was seen in Vancouver two days later. Rumor began to circulate that George Sponsler might be installed as the next president of CBC at least on an interim basis.[329] Ten days after Fisher's announcement, on 21 February 1983, the CBC Board of Directors gathered on the college campus from around the Pacific Northwest, together with United Pentecostal Church DOE representatives from St. Louis, in the first of three lengthy *in camera* closed meetings to consider the future of CBC. The College Board had ultimate authority in college

---

[329] *The Journal of Thomas A. Fudge, 1980-1985*, entries for 13 and 14 February 1983. The first entry notes, "Father Crossley was there [Shilo Inn at Vancouver]. I wonder what he's here for." The latter entry notes "The story is Father George Sponsler is going to assume the presidency ... but nobody really knows what in the devil is going on."

affairs.[330] Don Fisher had been carefully watched, followed, and scrutinized (in a manner of speaking) from the moment he was appointed. Many of the details of that theological surveillance have been irretrievably lost. However, by an ironic twist of fortune arising from a student prank, which was centred in the Graphic Arts Department, we know considerably more about what occurred

4.41 CBC Graphic Arts Department. Stan Johnson (left) and Doug Greer. The dark room is in the rear.

in those closed meetings than we might otherwise. Of significance is the role theology played, that "quarrelsome old woman," in the last days of the college. The proceedings shed considerable light on the fundamental reasons behind the destruction of CBC and they reveal in unequivocal fashion that having come to Portland, Don Fisher discovered himself a stranger in the place he hoped to find a home. Instead of the silence of eternity, he encountered inescapable and relentless chaos, conflict, and controversy.

---

[330] *Corporate By-Laws, Conquerors Bible College*, 1967, Article 2, section 5, p. 1.

4.42  JCM faculty meeting, 1980. *Left to right:* Don Travis,
Dan Lewis, Don Fisher, Thomas L. Craft

4.43  Members of the CBC student council: David Brown, Peggy Yelm,
Thomas A. Fudge, Michael Nigh and Eric K. Loy meeting
with Don Fisher, October 1981

# 5

# Watergate on the West Coast

*Let not light be conquered by darkness,*
*Nor let truth flee from falsehood.*[1]

Confusion among students began to fester over the days following Fisher's dramatic resignation. What exactly were the "prevailing circumstances" Fisher alluded to when he publicly announced he would no longer continue as president of CBC? Officially, nothing concrete had been communicated concerning the details of Fisher's resignation and why the future of the college was in such grave jeopardy. Small groups of students discussed these issues and one plan was advanced that students ought to demand an explanation of the Board of Directors when they gathered. A number of belligerent students including Michael Nigh, Daniel Sirstad, James Paley, and Eric K. Loy suggested that a group of students simply force their way into the meeting and confront the board. That option, even if serious, came to naught when the dean Jerry Peden heard about it and warned the students that nothing good could come of such action, and that it might jeopardise Fisher's opportunity to obtain a fair hearing and elicit support from board members. He counselled the students to wait and see what the meeting might bring forth on its own. There was considerable grumbling among the zealots who perhaps had hoped for some tacit encouragement to force a confrontation.

As the week leading up to the board meeting passed slowly the grim reality began to set in firmly that the end had come and the Board of Directors was assembling only to supervise a perfunctory institutional post mortem. With direct intervention in the board meeting ruled out, two students, George C. Whalen and P.W.

---

[1] *The Odes of Solomon: The Syriac Texts*, ed., James H. Charlesworth (Chico, CA: Scholars Press, 1977), ode 18, verse 6, p. 79.

Maynard, approached a third student, Robert Manchester, in a hallway in the main campus building after lunch on 21 February and the three entered a small room which housed vending machines.[2] During the last two academic years at the college, male students were arbitrarily given ecclesiastical monikers. This was chiefly at the instigation of Jerry Peden. "Dr." Whalen and "Elder" Maynard had come up with a vaguely conceived plan whereby they hoped to discover exactly what was going on and wished to enlist the help of "Rev." Manchester in order successfully to execute their scheme. The plan was simple. They conspired to place the meeting room under audio surveillance and by this means surreptitiously record the proceedings. Without any apparent hint of hesitation. Manchester immediately and enthusiastically consented.[3]

The first problem was to determine where the meeting was to be held. The college by-laws made no provision for meetings to occur without a minimum ten day notification period.[4] A day earlier it was known only generally that "the board meets tomorrow to decide the fate and/or the future of the college."[5] Initially, it was

---

[2] George C. Whalen interview, 29 July 2013, St. Louis, Missouri, P.W. Maynard interview, 19 July 2013, Seattle, Washington, and Robert S. Manchester interview, 1 August 2013, Denver, Colorado. The names are pseudonyms and the interview details have been altered only to avoid overt identification. No effort has been made to protect against discovery. Whalen and Manchester had no compunction about being named in this book but Maynard expressed some reservation. An editorial decision concluded there was no advantage in identifying the students and there were grounds for being sensitive to Maynard. I agreed. All three spoke frankly and at length about the events described in this chapter.

[3] Robert S. Manchester interview, 1 August 2013. All three of the students were members of prominent UPC families. Each had a father who was an ordained minister, two of whom held or had held, important and highly visible positions. All three at the time of their clandestine meeting admitted the ethical question in what they were about to do. Notwithstanding that, none of the three initially seemed overly bothered by its moral implications. Consensus emerged that it was more important to learn the truth of what really happened behind the scenes and determine what Fisher had done to bring CBC to the brink of utter collapse. At least the two originators of the plan (Whalen and Maynard) thought it would be rather clever to actually pull off the prank. The third (Manchester) agreed but later stated the entire operation was a genuine effort to learn details which otherwise would never be known or communicated to the CBC community.

[4] *Corporate By-Laws, Conquerors Bible College,* 1967, Article 2, section 11, p. 2.

[5] *The Journal of Thomas A. Fudge, 1980-1985,* entry for 20 February 1983.

rumored that the board would assemble at the old campus site at 10838 North Lombard where their business might be carried out unobtrusively. Some suspicion was raised when the students began making inquiries but in the end their objective was gained when late in the afternoon board members began arriving on campus and it was revealed that the meeting would convene in the CBC college chapel. The three conspirators were ill-prepared to actually carry out their plot. In the first instance they did not have the necessary equipment. Coincidentally none of the three had a vehicle on campus that day. They enlisted therefore the help of two others. The new recruits, both of whom had cars, were dispatched in haste to procure the essential equipment. One was sent to a store to purchase several, high quality, long-running cassette tapes. The other was instructed to drive to the home of faculty member David Wasmundt and collect essential recording equipment belonging to Wasmundt to supplement and enhance the tools they had already confiscated from college inventory. Two of the students had specific connections to the Music Department and Wasmundt was telephoned by one of them on the pretext that they required some of his equipment to make some recordings for an unspecified special project. There is no evidence to suggest that Wasmundt suspected anything unusual.

By the time the equipment arrived on campus the Board of Directors' meeting was already in session, having started around 4:00 p.m. The immediate problem now was where to launch the bugging operation. Additional equipment, namely microphones and cables, had already been removed from the chapel before the meeting commenced and had been hidden in a closet. Three of the conspirators had connections to the Graphic Arts Department and the photographic unit, including the darkroom. The darkroom was situated immediately against the west wall of the chapel (ill.4.41, p. 241). These students announced to others in the photographic unit that they needed the dark room facilities for the evening in order to develop pictures for some urgent nonspecific college project. Within minutes the darkroom had been taken over, the uninvolved students summarily evicted, the door carefully secured, and the hastily-conceived conspiracy to record the proceedings of the closed board meeting was underway.[6]

Robert Manchester was assigned the difficult task of planting the recording microphone. He had been selected specifically on

5.1  George Whalen installing recording equipment in the ceiling above the CBC darkroom, Winter Term 1983

account of the likelihood that he would agree to participate, and also because of his agility in climbing.[7] Access to the fully-framed dropped ceiling was easily accomplished in the darkroom, and Manchester, with microphone in one hand, flashlight in the other, and about twenty-five to thirty feet of cable, was helped through the crawlspace hatch onto the joists above in the mechanical space.[8]

---

[6] Thirty years later, one student recalls being evicted from the area during that evening. Doug Greer interview, 22 September 2013, Morton, Washington.

[7] Both Whalen and Maynard agreed on this. George Whalen interview, 29 July 2013, and P.W. Maynard, interview, 19 July 2013.

[8] Robert S. Manchester interview, 1 August 2013. There are at least two photographs in existence of the plotting eavesdroppers engaged in their scheme

The students had estimated the distance between the darkroom wall and the center of the chapel where the board convened. Once Manchester was in the crawlspace, the ceiling entrance access was replaced in the event Darline Kantola or another faculty member happened by. Kantola's office was located immediately outside the dark room. Inasmuch as she was the faculty advisor for the *Ensign* project, it was altogether possible that she might be in the vicinity and might even wish access to the dark room. The recording apparatus was likewise placed in the ceiling so that nothing could actually be discovered without removing the entry panel into the mechanical space (ill.5.1). In spite of these precautions, at least two students later noted they saw a ladder in the darkroom where previously there had been none.[9] Once Manchester was in the ceiling, Whalen and Maynard remained in the dark room working with a radio turned on as a means of masking any sounds, which might inadvertently escape from the ceiling above.

Manchester's task in the crawlspace was difficult. There was at best two-and-a-half feet in height and it was necessary to balance one knee on the parallel beams – ceiling joists – in order to avoid falling through the sheetrock into the chapel. Manchester managed to avoid this by holding the microphone in one hand and a small flashlight clenched between his teeth, while using his free hand for balance in order to advance the necessary distance which involved moving laterally several feet to the left across the joists. The Board of Directors had already begun their proceedings while Manchester was above them planting the recording device and setting up the system. Manchester later recounted that any noise generated in the mechanical space was effectively masked initially by the loud prayers being offered up by the Pentecostal preachers as the meeting began. In the dimness, Manchester estimated when the center of the chapel had been reached by sound, following the volume of voices below.

The next challenge was to locate a suitable place in which to fix the recording device in order to obtain the best possible recording.

---

(both published herein) while a third picture (posed for at a later date) surreptitiously appeared in *Ensign*, vol. 30 (1983).
[9] Audrey (Zapalac) Greer and Doug Greer interview, 22 September 2013.

Once again, due to inadequate planning, Manchester had essentially to guess where to place the "bug" in order to best record the voices below. Had some advance planning gone into the operation, the space above the chapel could have been explored and a better system put into place. At length the microphone was placed into one of the sprinkler system heads directly above the men gathered in the CBC chapel. With this part of the mission accomplished, Manchester then retreated back to the darkroom where the others waited.[10] The first cassette was placed into the machine and the clandestine recording operation was underway. The students giddily congratulated themselves.

5.2  Robert Manchester emerging from the
mechanical space, 21 February 1983

Manchester, having been in the ceiling between fifteen and twenty minutes was now covered with dirt from the crawlspace and, on account of the heat, was sweating profusely. Continued

---

[10] Robert S. Manchester interview, 1 August 2013.

secrecy depended on the clothing not being so soiled as to raise suspicion upon exiting into the Graphic Arts Department, where other students and some staff were working, completely unaware of the conspiracy unfolding only a few feet away. Jerry Peden, who remained in the general area throughout the evening, may have suspected something going on, but on the several occasions when one or more of the three rogues in the backroom emerged they had elaborate stories concocted about what they were doing in the darkroom to deflect any suspicion and divert attention. This was complicated to some extent by the fact that Manchester had no justifiable reason for being in the darkroom. He generally stayed away from the scene but had regular updates from the others. A small alarm clock had been brought into the darkroom in order to time the recording going on in the ceiling. At each appropriate interval, the ceiling hatch was removed, one of the perpetrators entered the mechanical space where cassette tapes were replaced.

There was a collective sigh of relief when the first recording was placed into a cassette player in the darkroom and the students were able to eavesdrop on what had been said in the chapel. Manchester had been readmitted at this stage in order to witness firsthand the results of the initial efforts to eavesdrop on the College Board. The meeting went on for approximately four-and-a-half hours and while board members discussed the fate of CBC, three of its students, unbeknown to anyone else, were recording every word. When the meeting finally came to a conclusion, Manchester had to retrieve the microphone from the ceiling and was then given the assignment of taking all the cassette tapes back to the dormitory for safekeeping. What remained, after removing all traces of their deed, was to hear what the board members had said. What had gone on? What were the reasons for the college crisis? Why had Fisher really resigned? What were the "prevailing circumstances" behind the dramatic events at CBC? Who had said what? What had been decided? These were among the questions the plotters hoped the tapes would answer. The student conspirators had agreed that they would find a time in the coming days to get together and listen to the tapes. Manchester, however, was disinclined to wait. That very night, parts of the first tapes were played clandestinely behind closed and locked dorm room doors. The following day the trio of conspirators gathered secretly to listen to more of the recordings.[11] Maynard expressed some hesitation about the ethical implications of the operation but this did not deter the others.[12] Later evidence suggests that Maynard's pause was merely temporary.

The CBC College Board of Directors was comprised of equal representatives from the Washington and Idaho Districts.[13] Idaho was represented by its district superintendent Norman Rutzen from Caldwell, Wallace Leonard from Idaho Falls, the deacon Jay Craven (1918-1997) from Rupert, and C.H. Yadon. Both Craven and C.H. Yadon were absent. The latter was in St. Louis and unable to attend.[14] His son Elwin "Bud" Yadon, a District Board member pastoring at that time in Lewiston, attended in his father's place. Norman Dillon attended on behalf of Craven. (See ill.0.1, p. xviii. Dillon is in the front row, sixth from the left. He is Jerry Dillon's father. Craven appears in the fifth row, second from the right.) Washington had its district superintendent Verneal Crossley from Spokane, Frank LaCrosse from Tacoma, Leo O'Daniel from Richland, and C.M. (Charlie Moses) Yadon from the south Seattle

---

[11] *The Journal of Thomas A. Fudge, 1980-1985*, entry for 22 February 1983 mentions Whalen and Manchester but not Maynard.

[12] P.W. Maynard, interview, 19 July 2013.

[13] The Idaho District officials consisted of Norman Rutzen (Caldwell), Norman Dillon (Rupert), Wallace Leonard (Idaho Falls), E.W. Yadon (Lewiston), and Paul Yadon (Parma). Washington District leaders were Verneal Crossley (Spokane), Ronald Joseph (Walla Walla), Daniel Leslie (Yakima), Francis Mason (Everett), Ronald Seagraves (Longview), Brian Orffer (McCleary) and Keith Painter (Bremerton). Orffer served during 1981-82 and was replaced by Painter for the 1982-83 term. There is some uncertainty over Orffer and Painter inasmuch as a photograph of the Washington District Board for 1983 shows Orffer rather than Painter, *Ensign*, vol. 30, p. 105, while Painter is listed as the presbyter for Section Two in *Ensign*, vol. 30, p. 111, whereas in 1982 Orffer is noted in that position. *Ensign*, vol. 29, p. 129. The discrepancy is not significant. Orffer served from 1978 through April 1983. Brian Orffer, letter to Thomas A. Fudge, 26 November 2013. This means that he, not Painter, was the relevant board member.

[14] C.H. Yadon ostensibly was in St. Louis meeting with Nathaniel Urshan at the UPC headquarters concerning issues relating to CBC. Most regrettably, nothing is known or can be confirmed about that meeting. Yadon died on 9 December 1997. Urshan claimed to have no recollection. Nathaniel Urshan interview, 23 April 1999. Others say they recall this occurring. Jerry Peden interview, 19 July 2002, and Norman Rutzen, 8 February 1999. Craven was absent on account of illness. He had been active in CBC affairs since the 1950s.

area in attendance.[15] C.M. Yadon, the younger brother of C.H. Yadon, had been District Superintendent of Washington between 1965, when the old Northwest District was terminated, and 1981 when he was voted out of office.[16] He always operated in the shadow of C.H. Yadon.[17] As long-time district superintendent, C.M. Yadon had been under pressure from certain Washington ministers, especially those committed to the more extreme UPC doctrine, for it was during Yadon's tenure that the Washington District experienced serious theological change. In addition to these men the UPC Division of Education had commissioned two delegates, George Sponsler from Portland and Arless Glass from Pasadena, Texas, to attend the meeting and represent the organization.[18] David Reynolds was also in formal attendance on behalf of the Alumni Association.[19] It is unknown what if any decisions were made concerning the taking of minutes of the special proceedings. Ordinarily the board had a secretary whose responsibilities included keeping a record of proceedings. No official record of the meeting seems to exist which includes the protracted and important questioning of Don Fisher. The existing minutes are silent. Apart from scattered recollections of those present in the meeting, only the series of tapes produced by the students remained as a witness.

Former CBC Dean-Registrar George Sponsler chaired the bulk of the meeting. Prior to the last year of CBC's operations one of the district superintendents filled the role as chairman of the board. At the conclusion of the 1981-82 academic year that rule was formally amended.[20] During the 1982-83 academic year the president of the

---

[15] The constituency did not conform strictly to the *Corporate By-Laws, Conquerors Bible College*, 1967, Article 2, section 1, p. 1, but it did fulfill the rules governing quorum in article 2, section 4.

[16] Yadon was unhappy with this, having coveted the office, and was heard to remark bitterly, "I guess they want Tiny Crossley," a reference to the wife of his successor Verneal Crossley. Jerry Peden interview, 19 July 2002.

[17] Jerry Dillon interview, 5 January 1999.

[18] The latter has been described as an old friend of Don Fisher's. Donna Fisher interview, 3 January 1999.

[19] A recent motion ratified at board level invited the alumni president to attend meetings. *Minutes*, CBC board meeting, 15 October 1982, p. 2.

[20] *Restated Articles of Incorporation of Conquerors Bible College*, 7 June 1982 (notarized), Article 5, p. 2.

college chaired such meetings but this meeting had been called to consider the announcement made by the president of CBC one week earlier. It was, then, quite impossible for Don Fisher to have chaired this meeting at least in its entirety.[21] Indeed, the focus of the special meeting, in its early stages on 21 February, was almost exclusively on Don Fisher. Given the fairly strong disagreements between the Idaho and Washington districts it was felt that a neutral chairperson for this meeting was appropriate.[22]

5.3  George Sponsler, *c.* 1980, local pastor and member of the DOE

5.4  Sponsler addressing the graduating class, 6 June 1980

A word must be said about the tape recordings which form the bulk of what follows. The quality of the tape-recording was in fact marginal and required specialized filtering and enhancement. The contrived plot to record had been thrown together in haste and was

---

[21] It is inaccurate to say that Fisher should not have chaired these meetings. *Corporate By-Laws, Conquerors Bible College*, 1967, Article 2, section 6, p. 1 does specify that the chairman of the board be one of the district superintendents. However, the *Restated Corporate By-Laws* (1982), Article 2, section 5, p. 1 mandates that the chairmanship of the board shall be filled by the college president. Additionally, the College Board was to be replaced by a Board of Regents consisting of two members from both Idaho and Washington, two roving members from outside those districts, and the college president as permanent chairman. Planning Session notes, CBC board, 2 March 1982, p. 1.

[22] Norman Rutzen interview, 24 July 2013.

based upon a serious lack of exploratory intelligence. Due to the challenges of recording under the unique circumstances and despite enhancement efforts, some statements and dialogue on the tapes proved altogether indecipherable and the identity of the speaker was a subject of debate in certain instances. This is related to where each member of the board was actually seated in the chapel in relation to the microphone installed overhead.[23] What was clearly unambiguous was the division of opinion reflected in the meeting.

5.5 Arless Glass with C.H. Yadon, undated photograph

The first item on the lengthy printed agenda was Don Fisher's resignation. Arless Glass begged off early from taking an active role in the deliberations, by stating that he was there in an official capacity, representing the UPC generally and the DOE specifically,

---

[23] Because of these challenges, I have elected to limit verbatim quotations from the proceedings. Those statements which are cited directly were matters of limited common knowledge at the time among the conspirators who repeated the statements to each other. The dialogues, given here and elsewhere in this essay, are paraphrased reconstructions. Notwithstanding this handicap, the nature, structure, and direction of statements and arguments are accurate, even if actual wording and sentence structure have been condensed. There is an essential qualification to note. A good number of the statements are substantially accurate. Those which are verbatim statements are enclosed within quotation marks. The reconstruction does not impair the accuracy or the integrity of what transpired in the proceedings and conversations recorded here.

and expressed his desire to listen to the proceedings rather than be a formal and active participant. He had little to say of substance in the course of the discussions though initially he earnestly begged Don Fisher to reconsider his resignation.[24] The posture assumed by Glass clearly reflects a continuing modicum of support for Fisher at the national level which may be set in contrast against elements which conspired to eliminate his candidacy from the European seminar scheduled in France noted earlier. George Sponsler had plenty to say in his role as chair, but once again very little of actual substance in terms of taking sides in the ensuing discussions and debates. It is fair to state that Sponsler's attitude throughout the meeting was one of measured neutrality. He agitated neither for nor against Fisher and conducted the meeting in a fair, efficient, and balanced manner. Whalen and Manchester agreed on this. A parallel might be drawn to the even-handedness of Paul Zimmerman during the inquiries into heresy in the Missouri Synod a decade earlier, or the position adopted by Harold Ockenga (1905-1985) during the Fuller Seminary disputes. Wally Leonard, Leo O'Daniel, Norman Dillon (1920-2003), and Bud Yadon said very little.[25] The same might be said for Frank LaCrosse. David Reynolds did not contribute to the discussion. That left Rutzen, Crossley, and C.M. Yadon to carry much of the argument and dominate this aspect of the conversation on the floor. In general terms, Rutzen spoke on behalf of Fisher while Crossley and Yadon were adamantly opposed to the Fisher administration and the direction that CBC had taken under him. Verbal confrontations and clashes punctuating the meeting underscore the ideological differences.

Don Fisher initially chaired the meeting and a printed opening statement set the stage for the ensuing discussion.[26] Fisher noted

---

[24] David Reynolds interview, 12 August 2013, confirmed in Arless Glass interview, 24 September 2013.

[25] Leo O'Daniel interview, 23 September 2013, Richland, Washington, suffers from Alzheimer's disease and has no recollection of the meeting. According to the *Minutes*, CBC board meeting, 21 and 22 February 1983, pp. 1-3 he was active on several motions ratified by the board. None of these related to Fisher.

[26] *Opening Statement*, Don Fisher to the CBC Board of Directors, 21 February 1983. FC, inv.doc.no 0707-5221-34. The full text appears in Appendix 17, p. 455. Noted in *Minutes*, CBC board meeting, 21 February 1983, p. 1. FC, inv.doc.no 0707-5222-34.

the important debt to posterity. He underscored the severe financial constraints and the repeated reminders made to the board and college constituency. It appears that Fisher disagreed with the rejection of the 1981 cash offer for purchase of the Lombard campus noted earlier. Fisher then shifted gears and underscored the "great exception" taken by the Washington District Board (ill.5.12, p. 267) to the recent church outing to Mt. Hood and connected this incident to the rejection of CBC participation in the district youth conference earlier that month, and to his own subsequent summons to appear before the Washington District Board. Fisher stated directly that "the intensity of feelings regarding this situation, as well as the general climate in the Washington District in regard to both me and the college" has made impossible his continuing tenure as president. Fisher then read his brief formal letter of resignation to the Board.[27] A general discussion followed.

With these preliminaries concluded, Don Fisher then turned the chairmanship of the meeting to George Sponsler and left the room, leaving the board to deliberate. C.M. Yadon spoke, "Well, I say we vote for his [Fisher's] resignation." As chair, Sponsler immediately responded, "What's the use of that? He's already resigned." The meeting then seemed undecided as to which way to go. Finally Sponsler brought the blurred focus to the matter of whether or not the board should accept Fisher's resignation. This gave rise to a protracted debate between Rutzen on one hand, and Crossley and C.M. Yadon on the other. Rutzen opposed accepting Fisher's resignation. Such response would send a clear message to the constituency that the CBC board backed its president. Crossley and C.M. Yadon opposed that idea vigorously. Aggravated allegations, theological concerns, and heated statements indicated that neither Crossley nor C.M. Yadon were open to discussion on the matter. They believed Fisher's departure was necessary. The sense of the recordings was that the Idaho contingency tacitly supported Rutzen, though no clear statements were made, while the position held by Frank LaCrosse cannot be determined. His virtual silence cannot be interpreted one way or the other though he recalls that

---

[27] Don Fisher, letter to the CBC board, 11 February 1983. FC, inv.doc.no 0707-5221-34. The text appears in Appendix 16, p. 454.

the proceedings amounted to a "very heavy discussion."[28] It was decided that Fisher ought to be re-summoned to the meeting. Fisher was in his office across the parking lot from the chapel in

5.6 Verneal Crossley, c. 1980, around the time he was elected Washington District superintendent

expectation of being called. Indeed, this was to be the first of several calls that evening. Fisher offered to remain as president of CBC, until a successor could be found. He refused to withdraw his resignation. He refused to remain as president until the end of the academic year in mid-May. He did confirm his willingness to remain in office if the board wished through the conclusion of winter term (11 March).[29] Fisher was quite clear that he did not wish for any student or course of study to be unnecessarily disrupted by his resignation. However, he would in no case countenance remaining as president of CBC beyond the conclusion of winter term. This reinforces his letter of resignation wherein he quite firmly stated he would not remain in office beyond 18 March. That firm and unequivocal stance ended the debate. Arless Glass had met with Fisher in a lengthy private meeting prior to the board session and had failed to convince Fisher to withdraw his resignation.[30] In light of all this, the board then moved to accept Fisher's resignation

---

[28] Frank LaCrosse interview, 1 October 2013.
[29] David Reynolds interview, 12 August 2013.
[30] Arless Glass interview, 24 September 2013.

effective 18 March. It is significant that the motion was made and seconded by members of the Washington District.[31]

Fisher was pressed by both sides of the floor to explain why he had resigned in the first instance after less than two years as president and furthermore why he was so adamant that he would not consider remaining as president of CBC. Fisher's reply was frank and unambiguous. He stated his conviction that the United Pentecostal Church was not serious about CBC and furthermore that the Districts of Oregon and Washington were opposed to his appointment and continuance as its president. He intimated that in his view the UPC was incapable of forward motion or reform.[32] Crossley objected. Fisher then demanded to know why the Washington District, having ratified the relocation of CBC to Vancouver, had appeared to turn so quickly and dramatically away from that support. Crossley insisted that Washington continued to support CBC as an institution and its presence in their district.[33] To this, Fisher replied that he wished to know why churches seemed unreceptive to having CBC students visit on weekends for preaching and music (ill.5.7), why the district seemed not to actively promote the college at the district level and why his leadership had been increasingly under attack. More to the point, why had the college been stricken from the district conference program a scant ten days earlier? Astonishingly Crossley denied that Fisher was under attack or the college under a great cloud of suspicion. Fisher responded by demanding to know why he was receiving letters and telephone calls asking for clarification of various doctrinal positions.[34] This was nothing new inasmuch as Fisher's fidelity to

---

[31] *Minutes*, CBC board meeting, 21 February 1983, p. 1.

[32] April Purtell interview, 16 January 1999 reveals that it was evident from comments he made to her that Fisher no longer believed he had any role left to play in the UPC.

[33] Frank LaCrosse interview, 16 January 2001 refuted this saying the Washington District would not work with Fisher.

[34] At the time of his appointment, Fisher publicly solicited communication from "pastors, parents, alumni, or interested students." Open letter from Don Fisher, "We're Coming Home!" *Ensign*, vol. 28 (1981), p. 127. See Appendix 6, p. 436. It is doubtful that Fisher anticipated the sorts of contacts he referred to during his appearances before the College Board two years later.

5.7  Promotional advertisement distributed to area churches, 1982-83 academic
year. *Left to right:* Mike Fairservice, Jeff Peden, Thomas A. Fudge,
Rick Frandin, Rick Mann, and Jay Nacino.

UPC doctrine had been under challenge almost from the time he was elected president of CBC.[35] Fisher had even addressed these allegations publicly and in print. "Since assuming the office of President of CBC ... some have inquired regarding my personal doctrinal positions."[36] A year later the CBC Alumni Association felt it necessary to question Fisher about doctrine at the college.[37] All of this underscores the matter of theology as a key element in the declining support for CBC.

5.8  Masked faculty member at CBC, 1976,
one of Barry King's "spiritual creeps"

Much later, solicited local opinion remained uncompromising. Drawing on the New Testament book of Jude, Fisher and his associates were denounced by Barry King as "spiritual creeps" who were among "those certain men who crept in unawares" and brought with them ruin. "They crept in then. They're still creeping

[35] Norman Rutzen, letter to Northwestern Brethren, 13 November 1981, p. 1.
[36] Don Fisher, "A Point of Interest to Those Who Care" *CBC Jubilation* 15 (No. 4, 1981), p. 2.
[37] Noted in the *Minutes*, CBC Alumni Officers meeting, 27 September 1982, p. 1.

in. I call them spiritual creeps and that's what they are. They get by boards. They're not detected. God allows it to happen to test the fabric and the framework of everything else. And he is still doing it. And that man [Don Fisher] took the Bible School out of Portland, moved it across the river into Washington because Oregon forced it."[38] Barry King's "spiritual creeps" is a parallel to W.A. Criswell's characterization of both moderate and liberal Southern Baptists as "stinking skunks" who are a terrible curse on the church and the cause of innumerable heresies.[39] Elsewhere, others worried about "evil geniuses" and their influence infiltrating the Missouri Synod.[40] Rome identified its dissenters as "enemies of the Church."[41] At Fuller Seminary, Edward J. Carnell, Paul Jewett, and some of their colleagues were considered traitors to the truth and Bob Jones, Sr. asserted that disloyalty was the unpardonable sin.[42] In all four cases, there was reason to suspect a theological Trojan horse. In Portland, Don Fisher was unofficially condemned on grounds of heresy.

There was some pause over Fisher's vehement characterization of the opposition to him personally and the college generally. Verneal Crossley asserted that he did not know why there continued to be questions about Fisher's orthodoxy. (The protest is not compelling. After all, it was Crossley who interrogated CBC faculty member Roger Yadon about Don Fisher when the latter was asked to answer questions which might be characterized as a search for evidence to justify the Washington District's animosity towards Fisher and the college.)[43] Fisher went on to state that he believed there was no substantial base of support for him within the constituency of the UPC and that there were more profitable things he might do with his life and ministry. He asserted that the pressure of running the college against such insurmountable odds had begun

---

[38] Barry King interview, 20 January 1999.
[39] Shurden and Shepley, eds., *Going for the Jugular: A Documentary History of the SBC Holy War*, p. 235.
[40] Marquart, *Anatomy of an Explosion*, p. 138.
[41] Pius X, encyclical *Pascendi domini gregis* in Sabatier, *Modernism*, p. 233.
[42] This is noted in Quentin Schultze, "The Two Faces of Fundamentalist Higher Education," in Martin E. Marty and R. Scott Appleby, eds., *Fundamentalisms and Society: Reclaiming the Sciences, the Family, and Education* (Chicago: University of Chicago Press, 1993), p. 503.
[43] Roger Yadon interview, 8 October 2013.

to have an adverse effect on his family, some members of which were also being openly criticised for their ostensible failure to mirror properly the aims of the UPC.[44] Family members insist that

5.9  Esther Peden, in the CBC business office, 1982

5.10  Donna Fisher, in the CBC library, 1982

the suspicion and criticism levelled against Fisher contributed to the tendency to critique his own family and he once went so far as to tell his youngest daughter she had ruined his career by trimming her

---

[44] Fisher had been married to Donna Lewis since 1959 and they had three daughters. Two of their daughters, Karissa and Ronna, lived with their parents in Vancouver. Their eldest daughter Susan was married to Skip Paynter, a graduate of JCM, who at the time was serving as youth pastor at a UPC church in Lancaster, Ohio. It does not appear that Donna Fisher was actively criticised prior to her appearance at the snow-tubing outing wearing "that which pertaineth unto a man." Karissa and Ronna were regarded as "worldly" on account of their failure to conform sufficiently to UPC standards of appearance for women. This was little more than general, idle gossip, though based on Fisher's testimony on 21 February these comments had come to his attention more than once. A number of years later he made similar statements. Similar complaints against Fisher's daughters arose at Jackson. Thetus Tenney interview, 6 June 2013, and Ronna (Fisher) Russell interview, 20 July 2013.

hair.[45] It is entirely probable the comment did not reflect considered opinion. Don Fisher told the CBC board that he was unprepared to subject his family further to the "malicious gossip of carnal people."

Fisher's comments reflect one of the historic consequences for those maligned as heretical. The suspect "is not always put to the test of a formal trial, but he [or she] undergoes multiplied pain in informal trials which also result in devilish penalties."[46] The pages of church history provide frequent examples, including the purges within the LCMS and the SBC. At this stage, Fisher was dismissed in order for the board to deliberate privately on the information gathered thus far.[47] The views expressed by Fisher were later mirrored by his wife even more succinctly.

> The need for control was already at Jackson, too. In time it became evident that the virus was alive and at work in the educational effort. There, it took the form of seeing education as indoctrination, not learning. We could see that if we stayed, we must play the game by their rules. We left. Then, we met the same kind of power in our beloved Pacific Northwest. We saw that the same kinds of capitulation had taken place there, also. My husband repeatedly was called before District Boards to answer and satisfy petty questions and the inquisition grew very tiring. Though the questions were always answered, we seemed to remain on the list of suspicious characters. 'They' were always looking for something over which to accuse us, rather than seeking ways in which we could have fellowship. We realized that if we were to continue to grow personally, we had to move toward the light God had given us. We made the journey out. Actually, we didn't come out, we were compelled to leave. We did attempt to turn in our fellowship card [ordination credential], but it was rejected. 'They' preferred, rather, to put us out 'under question.' That way, we were not welcome among them. It was another power and control ploy. It seemed that our goals at the Bible college in Portland were doomed all too quickly.[48]

---

[45] Ronna (Fisher) Russell interview, 20 July 2013. The incident occurred at CBC.

[46] Shriver, *American Religious Heretics*, p. 14.

[47] Nathaniel Yadon interview, 15 December 2000 said that at a meeting in McCleary, Washington, Fisher was able to sway critics (temporarily) to his side with the argument that his family was under harsh and unfair criticism. Yadon thought it was a tactical means of avoiding real issues which he saw as mainly doctrinal in nature. Once again, suspicions of theological irregularity intrude.

[48] Quoted in Lewis, *The Journey Out*, pp. 57-58. Other details in Donna Fisher interview, 3 January 1999 and also Donna Fisher, letter to Thomas A. Fudge, 18

Power and politics were dominating factors in the last days of CBC. This is not contestable. It appeared that repeated requests for Fisher to appear to answer inquiries were based on the sense that the various boards were prepared to believe rumors lodged informally against the college. The rumors appear to have been limited to concerns about doctrine and the direction the college was taking. Questions might be answered on one occasion, only to be raised again shortly thereafter and tabled at yet another board meeting. There was a history of such procedures at CBC following the influx of missionaries who migrated into the Northwest in an effort to counteract the "no experts" doctrine. If C.H. Yadon was thought to be theologically dangerous, then his disciple Don Fisher was considered toxic. Such men had to be eliminated from positions of influence. Similar policies within the SBC, especially those consistently exercised by Paul Pressler and Paige Patterson, were unequivocally denounced as the "unscrupulous use of power and manipulation."[49]

More than a dozen years prior to the Fisher administration the college found itself locked in a protracted struggle with area pastors. "We met with the local pastors this past Thursday to discuss with them matters of mutual concern ... we feel it vital ... to always maintain a harmonious relationship with ... local pastors."[50] These efforts ultimately appear to have achieved little. CBC students later characterized these ongoing conflicts as another manifestation of "ministerial mudslinging."[51] By the late 1970s, it was rumored that certain CBC faculty did not believe UPC doctrine. "The issues began to really roil in 1977."[52] That spring a meeting of the College Board was scheduled to convene on campus and the Portland area pastors were asked to attend. Norman Rutzen took charge of the

---

March 2013, p. 2. *Manual* (2014), Article vii, section 7, point 21 (a), pp. 51-52 enumerates the "under question" clause as a "flagrant violation of the Manual."

[49] Roy Honeycutt, "To Your Tents O Israel," convocation sermon at Southern Seminary, Louisville, Kentucky, August 1984, in Shurden and Shepley, eds., *Going for the Jugular: A Documentary History of the SBC Holy War*, p. 132.

[50] President's report (John Klemin) to the CBC board, 15 December 1973, p. 2.

[51] Daniel R. Sirstad interview, 26 August 2013.

[52] Jerry Dillon interview, 19 April 2013. Others admit suspicions of doctrinal weakness at the college lay at the root of opposition. Darline (Kantola) Royer interview, 15 August 2013. Kantola sees no validity in the assumption.

meeting and asked for specific identification of those faculty members who were "weak on the message." After much hesitation on the part of the ministers and considerable prodding by Rutzen, Jerry Dillon was nominated as a member of the faculty holding suspect theological positions. Rutzen then summoned Dillon to the meeting. Rutzen informed Dillon what the specific concern was and asked if he would be prepared to address the matter. Dillon said he would be delighted to do so and also pointed out that this was the first time he had ever been given opportunity to address theological concerns. Faculty colleagues later noted that "guns were

5.11 Jerry Dillon, *c.* 1977, around the time he addressed the College Board and area pastors over theological concerns and allegations of doctrinal irregularities lodged against him

pointed towards Jerry" Dillon and he was seldom provided an opportunity to reply to his mainly anonymous critics.[53] On this occasion, once Dillon concluded his statements addressing various concerns over the doctrine of God, the image of God, and the Christological difficulties for the Oneness position as presented in the Gospel of John, Rutzen asked if there were any questions. Not a single comment or question for further explanation or clarification was raised. Rutzen then pressed the gathering if all

---

[53] Darline (Kantola) Royer interview, 15 August 2013.

those present were satisfied with Dillon's statements. There were no dissenters. Unwilling to leave hostages to fate, Rutzen then went around the room asking each and every minister personally and individually if they were satisfied with Dillon's expressed doctrinal positions. Every one of them declared they had no qualms with his explanations and harbored no lingering theological concerns. Dillon was dismissed from the meeting and it appeared the accusations of heresy, against Dillon at least, had been asked and answered. Uncharacteristically, college critic Barry King said such discussions were both good and useful because while there were theological clashes, dialogue promised clarification rather than destruction.

King's comment was a hope which was never fulfilled. At the next meeting of the Oregon District Board, Jerry Dillon and suspicions of heresy once again became a subject of discussion.[54] Understandably, Dillon was outraged and felt it necessary years later to apologise to at least seven ministers for "anger, bitterness and resentment" which these conflicts had created in him. Only one of the seven acknowledged the letter.[55] While the minutes of meetings never underscore the concern, Dillon's views of the Godhead were generating some anxiety. He articulated his evolving position some years after he left CBC when he declared he would "rather be part of a Trinitarian church that is Christ centered than a oneness church that is not."[56] Area pastors who supported Dillon noted he was well ahead of the curve and was distrusted by the UPC establishment, "always looked at with suspicion" on account of his assumed liberal stance and the fact that "he was not dependable on the message."[57] Students were aware that Dillon remained a heresy suspect and occasionally pastors were informed by college students of certain things Dillon taught. This generated more ill-will towards Dillon specifically and CBC generally with rumors and rumblings

---

[54] Norman Rutzen interview, 8 February 1999. Dillon's view of the Godhead was problematic. Phillip Dugas interview, 23 January 1999, Portland, Oregon. There were further reflections on this meeting in Jerry Dillon interview, 19 April 2013.

[55] Jerry Dillon, letter to Paul Dugas, Barry King, Clyde Barlow, David Johnson, C.M. Yadon, Winfred Toole, and Phillip Dugas, 10 December 1983. Only Johnson responded. David Johnson, letter to Jerry Dillon, 16 February 1984.

[56] Stated in Jerry Dillon, letter to John and Ruby Klemin, 8 January 1984, p.1.

[57] Lewis J. Davies interview, 19 August 2013.

still reverberating in Oregon.[58] The next year the College Board again attempted to placate the Portland-area pastors and invited them to meet in session. Only three pastors responded positively.[59] It would appear that the majority of local pastors were disinterested in dialogue with the college. They desired either control, wherein CBC followed their specific dictates, or complete withdrawal of support. By 1981, that second option was formally exercised.

In terms of the Fisher administration six years after the Dillon interrogation (ill.5.12), some of the "inquisitioning" was as prosaic as questions on whether Fisher's wife dyed her hair. Evidently, the main thrust of the regular questioning centered on issues of such triviality that Fisher was disgusted and disheartened.[60] John Zapalac, a 1963 CBC graduate, often sent farm products to the college. In that last year he donated some home-brewed cider. Informants to the Washington District Board alleged it was alcohol and Fisher was again forced to defend himself.[61] Wearied by the incessant and occasional puerile badgering, Fisher became "disillusioned."[62] This is understandable, inasmuch as "there was nothing but criticism that came his way."[63] Some of this was so sweeping that Fisher was blamed for the fact that a female student at JCM lost her virginity while at the college.[64] Evidently, his failure to adequately enforce standards of holiness was blamed for the sexual trysts of college students. Such causal connections were rather inventive.

Don Fisher's appearance before the College Board on Monday, 21 February 1983 constituted his final appearance before UPC boards of inquiry, groups he eventually considered "scribes, Pharisees, hypocrites" (Matthew 23:13-39). He had often been fond of publicly saying "measure your need, then measure your God." It is unknown how he considered that philosophy at the end. What is

---

[58] Dale Royce interview, 24 August 2013.

[59] *Minutes*, CBC board, 10 March 1978. FC, inv.doc.no 0707-5180-34.

[60] Donna Fisher interview, 3 January 1999, testified she did not dye her hair but wondered what the point was if she had.

[61] Audrey (Zapalac) Greer interview, 22 September 2013.

[62] April Purtell interview, 16 January 1999.

[63] Norman Rutzen interview, 8 February 1999.

[64] An Oregon minister communicated this to some CBC faculty upon Fisher's appointment. Stan Johnson interview, 5 October 2013.

manifestly clear is that Fisher was no longer prepared to remain imprisoned in the brotherhood. If John Tietjen was suspended and forced from office, Don Fisher went on his own initiative. The former was found guilty of "holding, defending, allowing, and fostering false doctrine."[65] The latter was never formally charged as such, but a similar cloud of suspicion persisted. It is quite wrong to assume that the College Board either removed Fisher from office or forced him to resign.[66]

5.12 The Washington District Board (1982-1983) that presided over repeated interrogations of Don Fisher. *Back row, left to right:* Daniel Leslie, Francis Mason, and Brian Orffer. *Front row, left to right:* Ronald Seagraves, Verneal Crossley, and Ronald Joseph

Having answered the questions put to him, Fisher left the meeting. Sponsler then put the query to the floor about whether they ought to rule on the continuation of a functioning college through the end of the academic year. It was reiterated that there would need to be an interim president for any prospective spring term since Fisher would not countenance remaining beyond 18 March. During the subsequent discussion it became fairly clear, to the satisfaction of the board, that CBC in all probability did not have the resources to actually complete the academic year. It was

[65] Tietjen, *Memoirs in Exile*, p. 242.
[66] Joe Higgins interview, 4 October 2013, is one who was under the impression this was the case.

reconfirmed, without dissent that Fisher would be asked to oversee the college through the end of the present term which, was at that point already half completed.

The discussion returned to Fisher's theological positions. Opinion was expressed forcefully by Crossley and C.M. Yadon that Fisher was "weak on the message." Once again, this buttresses the claim that doctrine was at issue in the last days at CBC. Yadon then brought up the matter of his son, Nathaniel. "Yeah, he [Fisher] told me that my boy needed to see a doctor, that he wasn't right in the head. I didn't appreciate that very much. I didn't appreciate that very much at all." Several CBC faculty members regarded Nathaniel Yadon as being of unsound mind as well as the curious incident wherein he attempted to wash Fisher's feet just two months earlier. C.M. Yadon was very sensitive to and protective of Nathaniel on account of the latter's diabetes and the dire effects it ultimately had on him resulting in his premature death.

One further anecdote might be told which goes some distance to establishing at the very least questionable practices. Nathaniel Yadon's congregation met in 1981-82 in the rented facility of the Methodist Church located at the corner of Southeast 164th Avenue and Mill Plain Boulevard in east Vancouver at 3:00 p.m. on Sundays.[67] On 4 April 1982, several CBC faculty including David Wasmundt and Jerry Peden, neither of whom were regular attenders, visited Yadon's church. Everyone was obliged to wait in the parking area, on account of the fact that the church doors were shut and locked. Yadon did not arrive until 3:15 to open the building. He offered no explanation for his tardiness and began the service by asking everyone to kneel where they were and pray. This went on for about fifteen minutes. After everyone took their seats again, Yadon stood in the pulpit and following a series of rambling disconnected comments solemnly announced that he felt it was "God's will" to dismiss, leave the building, and for all to return to their homes. The congregation was mystified. The students and CBC faculty who had come that Sunday for worship had spent

---

[67] This nineteenth-century structure was pulled down in 1997 and converted into a pub in the architectural design of a traditional church. That business later failed and was subsequently replaced by a restaurant.

approximately thirty minutes driving the eighteen miles from the Lombard campus in order to attend.[68] The incident was deplored by those present. Doubtlessly, it was later reported to Fisher who would have considered the entire affair insufferable.

The meeting in the chapel continued. At the request of the board, Fisher appeared in the proceedings several times. Some occasions lasted only as long as it took to answer a single question, other appearances lasted up to a quarter of an hour. His main appearance before that body went beyond a half hour as they questioned him on doctrine. This fact absolutely and conclusively establishes that theology constituted a central issue in the Fisher administration of CBC, and a key factor in its demise. This also throws doubt on C.M. Becton's earlier claim that theology played no role whatever in the downfall of CBC. This was the point of contention at Jackson, and suspicions about Fisher's doctrinal orthodoxy remained at issue in Portland. While Rutzen attempted somewhat unsuccessfully to temper the nature of the questions and to moderate the importance of Fisher's answers, Crossley and C.M. Yadon appeared intent on forcing Fisher into a corner where he would have no recourse but to reveal himself as the heretic they suspected him of being. If Fisher was in fact "weak on the message" his appearance before the board was designed to confirm that. Be that as it may (and here the intentions can only be surmised on the basis of the questions asked and the manner in which they were put), the interrogation itself was reasonable. The questioners did not attempt to bully Fisher, and they permitted him time and opportunity generally to answer as thoroughly as he chose. It should also be noted that Norman Rutzen persisted in ameliorating the nature of the exchanges and George Sponsler maintained order. One can only speculate on the moderating influence that C.H. Yadon may have brought to the discussion had he been present. It is likely that Crossley would have been deferential to C.H. Yadon and it is also certain that C.M. Yadon would have been far less vocal. Unfortunately, C.H. Yadon was absent. However, his presence would not have altered the basic fundamental fact of Fisher's resignation.

---

[68] *The Journal of Thomas A. Fudge, 1980-1985*, entry for 4 April 1982.

The interrogatories began with the UPC's *Fundamental Doctrine*. Crossley asked Fisher what his message was and whether he had changed the basic thrust of his doctrine. Fisher answered that his

5.13 C.M. Yadon, Auburn, Washington, 11 December 1999

doctrine was the same as it had always been. The answer might be construed as evasive. C.M. Yadon then asked if he believed in the "one God, Acts 2:38 gospel." Fisher answered that his message had not changed. Once again, Fisher neither admitted to anything improper nor provided the Board with any ammunition. Rutzen then interrupted to query the nature of the questions and to ask what the relevancy was. After all, Rutzen stated, had Fisher's theology not been scrutinized prior to his appointment as president of CBC? Since Fisher had just affirmed his doctrine as unchanged what was the point, to use a legal reference, of badgering the witness? Moreover, Thomas Craft had put into writing his opinion that rumors about Fisher's lack of regard for the *Fundamental Doctrine* of the UPC had no merit. Don Fisher then asserted his belief in the centrality of the cross and made clear that he believed the blood of Christ was sufficient for salvation.[69] This statement

---

[69] David Reynolds interview, 12 August 2013. A decade earlier Fisher had asserted he did not have to earn anything for the work was Christ's. Don Fisher, "Let Christ be Formed in You," sermon at McCormick's Creek, Indiana, 1974, audio recording.

was construed as a denial of any water and Spirit doctrine and a commitment to justification by faith.[70] Contrary to UPC theological claims, it is impossible to maintain a finished work of the cross theology while simultaneously promoting an Acts 2:38 doctrine. Fisher's declaration had taken him onto dangerous ground. Verneal Crossley and C.M. Yadon pounced. Fisher did not flinch. The garbled exchange which followed was agitated but effectively indecipherable. When clarity returned to the recording, Sponsler had intervened and taken control of the deliberations, and Fisher was now being pressed specifically about his doctrine and understanding of holiness. Fisher's answer was a carefully measured doctrinal response. It seems pertinent to digress at this stage to introduce two points which bring the necessary nuance to Fisher's reply, and which also sheds light on the divergences of doctrine on the matter of holiness. During Fisher's tenure at JCM, several like-minded faculty members, including Dan Lewis and Joseph Howell, wrote what would remain an unpublished book on the doctrine of holiness.[71] Fisher submitted the manuscript to the UPC's Word Aflame Publications for consideration, noting his pleasure at the overall quality of the work. The authors acknowledged Fisher's encouragement of the project. Of note is that the proposed book was dedicated to C.H. Yadon.[72] The UPC publishing house unsurprisingly declined to print the work, and its circulation or use in the college was never sanctioned. The "official" response to the book concluded that the approach in the proposed volume was unhelpful and likely to cause confusion. References to people such as Martin Luther and John Wesley were critiqued as suggesting "approval of the spiritual life of these men." Neither, of course, could pass the holiness exam set down by the UPC. Wesley's hair

---

[70] Years earlier, Fisher had publicly declared his adherence to the doctrine of justification by faith. Note his "Evangelization of the Subconscious," sermon at McCormick's Creek, Indiana, January 1975, audio recording.

[71] Joseph H. Howell, Daniel Lewis, Mark Roberts and James Wilkins, *A Call to Holiness*, unpublished 154 page book manuscript, 1981.

[72] Don Fisher, letter to James Hall, 5 January 1981, pp. 1-2. FC, inv.doc.no 0707-4789-32. Howell said Fisher wrote a forward. Joseph Howell interview, 21 April 1999. However, the typescript does not contain anything from Fisher. The reference to Fisher's encouragement appears on p. iv.

was too long, while Luther drank beer and frequently used colorful language. Both men promoted doctrines that were incompatible with UPC orthodoxy. Moreover, the study was adjudicated as being of little assistance to pastors facing decisions on weighty matters concerning women cutting their hair, social drinking, men with long hair, wearing jewellery and makeup, and so on. It also retained dangerous "echoes of higher criticism."[73] Fisher's answer to the

5.14 Jim Wilkins with former CBC student Paul Cowell, Kingston, Tennessee, 4 May 1999 and (5.15) with Skip Paynter, Vancouver, WA, December 2000. Wilkins co-authored the rejected holiness book. See also ill.2.12, p. 70

College Board followed the general argument elaborated by his JCM colleagues in their book. Effectively, the JCM writers had defined holiness as separateness unto God and empowered commitment for service. Little was said explicitly about dress codes or specific practical application of unique holiness principles. From the UPC organizational perspective, a book such as this might be defined as helpful as far as it goes, but as a reflection of true Biblical holiness was "weak on the message." Clearly it had not been written by "experts." Unlike former JCM faculty member Jim Wilkins, who was "infinitely sacrilegious" and openly critical about holiness standards, Don Fisher had little to say publicly on the matter.[74]

---

[73] The reply was composed by J.L. Hall, at the time editor-in-chief of the UPC publications industry. The three page letter was sent to Don Fisher in early 1981 but is unaddressed, undated, and unsigned. FC, inv.doc.no 0707-4789-32. I rely on Dan Lewis interview, 6 April 1999. For Lewis' reflection on this episode see Lewis, *The Journey Out*, pp. 34-35.

[74] Joseph Howell interview, 21 April 1999.

Nevertheless, Fisher had preached entire sermons on sanctification wherein he never once referred to holiness standards.[75] Silence on such important issues was itself a serious indictment. The other point is the incident involving C.H. Yadon in a CBC classroom during Fall term 1982. Pressed by a student on whether a woman who wore pants or cut her hair was committing sin, Yadon replied that there was only one standard of holiness, which was Christ.[76] Fisher certainly supported the views of his colleagues as expressed in the proposed book on holiness and he embraced the Yadon doctrine. That position deeply concerned the holiness "experts," providing additional fuel to the fire designed to purge CBC of heresy. There were antecedents. Donna Fisher's wedding ring was airbrushed out of a JCM photograph in 1976 to avoid scandalizing church members. In 1981, Barry King warned CBC student Gregg Calder to get a haircut if he wanted to accomplish anything for God. Pressure in Washington caused the Dean, Jerry Peden, to ask two CBC music students to remove their rings during a district function in Seattle in the Fall of 1981. They declined.

Meanwhile, the board, especially Crossley and C.M. Yadon, were unsatisfied with the response on what was considered the all-important matter of holiness. Fisher's answer was thought to be too strictly theological, he had not addressed the practical implications or application of the doctrine. Neither Crossley nor C.M. Yadon could be regarded as theologians but they were not so benighted as to overlook the fact, that while Fisher's reply theoretically could not be impugned, it revealed nothing about specific belief or practice. Fisher asked rhetorically what exactly they were driving at. Crossley then asked Fisher to affirm or deny that CBC girls had been given permission to participate in a snow-tubing outing on Mount Hood wearing ski pants (see ill.4.38, p. 236). This was the crucial issue. This was the crux of the holiness debate. Fisher was now backed into a corner. Yes or no? Had the women in his charge been holy or had they been "worldly" on that Saturday afternoon in the snows on Mt. Hood? It was a simple question, demanding a simple,

---

[75] Don Fisher, "The Will of God is Sanctification," sermon at McCormick's Creek, Indiana, 1975, audio recording.
[76] *The Journal of Thomas A. Fudge, 1980-1985*, entry for 18 November 1982.

unequivocal answer. The tape recording reveals that Fisher did not hesitate for a moment in acknowledging that female students from CBC had indeed worn ski pants during the event in question. In anger, C.M. Yadon immediately and indignantly demanded to know on whose authority such reckless permission had been granted. Fisher declared that it had been given on his authority as pastor of the church and president of the college. Crossley then asked Fisher how he could possibly reconcile that decision with the Biblical teaching of holiness.[77] The exchange which followed underscored Fisher's clear lack of commitment to denominational positivism.

Fisher:      The Bible teaches modesty and so do I.

Crossley:    "But Brother Fisher, the United Pentecostal Church takes the position that women wearing pants is not holiness."

Fisher:      I don't think what the UPC says is material here. We are talking scripture.

Crossley:    Brother Fisher, the Washington District does not approve of women wearing pants.[78]

Fisher:      I am not interested at the moment with what the Washington District Board approves. I am not answerable to the Washington District Board.[79] I am answerable to God.

Crossley:    But Brother Fisher ...

Fisher:      Please let me finish.

---

[77] UPC districts sometimes mandated precise rules. See, *The Oregon District Apostolic Accent* 23 (No. 6, 1986), p. 9 where jewelry, makeup, beards and the like are prohibited for church leaders. This questioning is among three sets of exchanges from the tape-recordings which are herein presented. I have presented these in summary outline form.

[78] The membership of that board, which was the same board that summoned Fisher repeatedly to appear to answer questions, consisted of Daniel Leslie (Yakima), Francis Mason (Everett), Brian Orffer (McCleary), Ronald Seagraves (Longview), Ronald Joseph (Walla Walla), and Verneal Crossley (Spokane). A photograph of this board was published in *Ensign*, vol. 30 (1983), p. 105. One change from the previous year was that Seagraves had replaced Robert Stark (Scatter Creek) representing Section Four of the district. (See ill.5.12, p. 267).

[79] Fisher was technically correct, being accountable to the CBC Board.

C.M. Yadon:    You should listen Brother Fisher.

Fisher:    "I believe Scripture clearly teaches holiness as modesty. In my opinion a dress on a ski slope is not modest. As long as I am the president of this college and the pastor of this church we will preach biblical holiness. A dress, brethren, is not modest sliding down a hill on a tube."[80]

Yadon:    Maybe those girls shouldn't be up there then if they're so immodest in their dresses and skirts.

Fisher:    That's ridiculous.

Crossley:    Brother Fisher, the United Pentecostal Church and the District Board do not approve.[81]

Fisher:    Look, the United Pentecostal Church and the Washington District Board can do anything they like.[82] However, I have a personal responsibility to the college, the church and to God. This was a local church social event to which the college community, as part of the church, was invited to participate in. It was not in any sense an official college function. And as long as I am here —

C.M. Yadon:    Well, maybe you shouldn't be here.

Rutzen:    Now wait a minute Brother Yadon.

Fisher:    I won't be here much longer. The point is, I don't come into your church and tell you what to preach, why are trying to tell me what to teach and practice here?

---

[80] Fisher's detractors would find this argument incompatible with the historic claim of the college to "its high standard of holiness." CBC advertisement in *The Pentecostal Herald* 37 (No. 5, 1962), p. 15, or the declaration of John Klemin who stated that "in a day when standards are falling, CBC is making every effort to hold them high." CBC advert in *The Pentecostal Herald* 53 (No. 6, 1978), p. 22.

[81] This exchange mirrors rather closely the argument outlined in Lewis J. Davies, letter to Winfred E. Toole, 2 May 1978, pp. 2-5 wherein Toole refused to allow a doctrinal matter to be settled on the basis of scripture alone.

[82] Statements such as this convinced UPC officials that Fisher no longer believed in aspects of UPC theology. Arless Glass interview, 24 September 2013.

Crossley:        While the college does answer to you as its president, you are directly accountable to us as the College Board of Directors and we answer to headquarters. We send our young people to you. We must know what you're teaching them. There is far too much liberalism already in this district. We must hold the line on the truth and for the message.

Crossley's remarks were not dissimilar to those expressed during an earlier SBC pastors conference wherein James Robison insisted that toleration of any form of liberalism made one the enemy of God.[83] In response to Crossley's comments, a general and fairly heated, discussion ensued, with Rutzen attempting to support Fisher and modify the arguments C.M. Yadon and Crossley were advancing. To borrow insider terminology, considerable carnality began to dominate the meeting. George Sponsler was forced to intervene repeatedly to bring order to the session.[84] At length Fisher was dismissed. The controversy over issues of modesty within the UPC have often turned on curiosities. In 1980, a similar issue arose at JCM when the college sponsored a variation of donkey basketball. Instead of deploying real donkeys, students were permitted to ride each other, as it were, with the person being carried shooting the basketball. The females, being carried by male donkeys, were not permitted to wear either trousers or divided skirts on the explicit orders of President Craft. There were definite modesty issues when these girls were bucked off or fell off their donkeys.[85] It appeared that the fleeting exposure of thighs, crotches, and buttocks was considered less problematic than a violation of the Deuteronomic injuction. Fisher was disgusted.

Fisher supporters elsewhere placed a fine point on the developments which had led the eighth president of CBC to stand down and turn in his ministerial credentials.

---

[83] See James Robison, "Satan's Subtle Attacks," sermon at the SBC pastors conference, Houston, Texas, 10 June 1979, in Shurden and Shepley, eds., *Going for the Jugular: A Documentary History of the SBC Holy War*, pp. 24-38, at p. 31.

[84] C.M. Yadon interview, 11 December 1999.

[85] Dan Lewis, letter to Thomas A. Fudge, 24 May 2013, p. 3. FC, inv.doc.no 0707-5036-33.

I just heard from Don Fisher, I called him. It looks like 'they' got him. I find no way in the knowledge of God and the Word, how this nasty action can be justified. Whats [sic] happening to us? And I wonder who 'thye' [sic] are? And what is the motive? Are we developing a race of 'super Pharisees' of some sort?[86]

Others opined that it was difficult to avoid the conclusion that UPC officials in Oregon and Washington were set on getting rid of Don Fisher once and for all.[87] Reflecting on several events at the college, some of the students were certain that either organizational officials or church ministers were against Fisher.[88] The college dean, Jerry Peden, provided his own perspective on the Fisher affair.

Theological questions were raised, and Don Fisher, the new president, was compelled to meet the District Board so often that it bordered on the ridiculous. Nathaniel Urshan, the General Superintendent, was asked to intervene on our behalf. Our belief was that, since we were in good standing with the denomination and since our college was endorsed by the UPC's Department of Education, such antagonistic behavior would not be tolerated. No help came. Eventually, the District Superintendent of Washington [Verneal Crossley] smugly handed me a letter directing me to meet with the District Board. No mention of any charges were made in the letter, so from a legal standpoint, there was no way the Board could take any ecclesiastical action against me. However, I had already seen what this same board had done with innuendo and conjecture to Don Fisher, and I knew that I did not have the stamina to face such a 'meat-grinder.'[89]

Peden never responded to the summons. He also apparently never filed a letter of resignation with the college.[90] He was too disgusted to bother doing either.

Accusations, allegations, examinations, and questions of the genre which Fisher faced at CBC were nothing new in the history of Christianity once the urge-to-purge mentality settled into the

---

[86] Wayne Nigh, letter to Jerry Dillon, 15 February 1983. FC, inv.doc.no 0707-4795-32.

[87] Lewis, *The Journey Out*, p. 57.

[88] Cheryl (Johns) Crousser interview, 1 October 2013.

[89] Quoted in Lewis, *The Journey Out*, p. 65. Also Jerry Peden interview, 19 July 2002.

[90] Noted in *Minutes*, CBC board meeting, 21 March 1983, p. 1. FC, inv.doc.no 0707-5227-34.

fabric of the faith following the rise of Constantinianism in the fourth century. Such procedures were driven by politics and designed to eliminate differences and it rarely mattered who actually came under suspicion. The result was often the same. It was hard to kick against the pricks. Those within the Roman Catholic Church who sought to initiate reform, such as the priests Alfred Loisy and George Tyrrell, were denounced as attackers whose efforts cut deeply at the roots of the faith.[91] (See ills.1.5 and 6.18, pp. 36 and 374.) Ministers working among the Missouri Synod Lutherans and Southern Baptists found themselves on the horns of a dilemma. They had either to conform to dominant trends or find themselves censured and expelled. Calls to give up attempts to establish forced uniformity fell on deaf ears.[92] The idea of being forced to join the dominant point of view can be traced to the fifth century when Augustine used Luke 14:23, which speaks of compelling people to come in so that the house would be filled, as a proof-textual basis to justify the use of force (*cogite intrare*) against stubborn heretics whom he believed should be compelled to conform.[93] On trial for heresy at the town of Carcassonne in southern France in the fourteenth century, the Franciscan Bernard Délicieux noted ruefully that if SS Peter and Paul were to come under the same unrelenting scrutiny he had, they would certainly be found guilty of heresy![94]

The rest of the board meeting constituted an animated debate over aspects of the Fisher administration, with Rutzen maintaining firm support for Fisher and for the college. C.M. Yadon and Crossley were equally adamant that Fisher should never have been appointed in the first place and that it was impossible for him to continue as president and the matter of his resignation ought to be considered. Sponsler again interjected with the comment that Fisher had already resigned, and asked his colleagues to remain focused. Yadon and Crossley continued to underscore their conviction that Fisher was essentially and now evidentially "weak on the message" and a liability to the spirituality and salvation of young men and

---

[91] Pius X, encyclical *Pascendi domini gregis* in Sabatier, *Modernism*, pp. 232-234.
[92] Dilday, *Higher Ground: A Call for Christian Civility*, pp. 134-137.
[93] Augustine, Letter 93.2.5 in *Corpus Scriptorum Ecclesiasticorum Latina*, vol. 34.2, ed., A. Goldbacher (Vienna: Tempsky, 1898), pp. 445-496 at pp. 449-450.
[94] Paris, Bibliothèque Nationale MS Lat. 4270 fol. 139r-v.

women at the college and throughout the UPC. According to some sympathetic local pastors, the chief issue used to leverage Don Fisher out of CBC was the accusation that he promoted a teaching which insisted that one should only be held to what had been revealed to or understood by the individual. This was known as "the light doctrine."[95] The point is speculative. Fisher's allegiance to the PCI perspective was at the root of the hounding which he was forced to endure.[96]

Following this long discussion about Don Fisher and these several theological issues, which sheds light on the specific "prevailing circumstances," Sponsler then convened a dialogue amongst the board over a recent proposal advanced by Gene Ziemke, who had expressed interest in securing the college charter and continuing to operate CBC.[97] Ziemke was a CBC graduate who pastored a church in Puyallup, Washington, between 1966 and 1986, which was among the largest United Pentecostal churches in the entire Pacific Northwest. By the early 1980s, Ziemke's church had a congregation of more than 700 members.[98] Moreover, Ziemke had for several years been thinking about a college sponsored by his church.[99] The board passed a motion to invite Ziemke to appear to discuss his interests. Following this, Sponsler returned the chairmanship of the session to Fisher who recessed the meeting for supper at around 5:30 p.m. Following the break, a variety of business items were then discussed. The one item of note to occur was the decision to name Darline Kantola as office manager to serve in that capacity through the end of June.[100] The

---

[95] Leon Brokaw interview, 29 January 2001. On this see Fudge, *Christianity without the Cross*, pp. 74, 152-153, 172-174, 187-188.
[96] Roger Yadon interview, 8 October 2013.
[97] Noted in *Minutes*, CBC board meeting, 21 February 1983, p. 1. FC, inv.doc.no 0707-5222-34.
[98] Jim Roam in Portland and Ziemke were in competition in the drive to establish the largest church in the Northwest. It has been suggested that Roam resorted to inflating attendance figures. Ron and Wanda Calder interview, 9 August 2013. On attendance figures, Gene Ziemke interview, 23 September 2013.
[99] Jerry Dillon, letter to Gene A. Ziemke, 11 January 1976, p. 3 (FC, inv.doc.no 0707-5132-34), and Gene Ziemke interview, 23 September 2013.
[100] *Minutes*, CBC board meeting, 21 February 1983, p. 2. FC, inv.doc.no 0707-5222-34.

meeting then recessed at about 9:00 p.m., scheduled to reconvene the next morning.

At the reconvened board meeting, Gene Ziemke and his church business manager, Joseph Horan, met with the board. The minutes of the meeting do not reveal details but the board did resolve to pursue the possibility that Ziemke might assume operation of the college including the purchase of its inventory. A secret ballot vote was called for and passed by an eight to one margin.[101] That summer Ziemke attended the annual DOE retreat in Colorado and his forward-planning ideas met with approval by long-time CBC faculty.[102] The church pastored by Ziemke in Puyallup was regarded in certain quarters of the Washington District as a "renegade" church and it is possible that for this reason there was sufficient opposition to CBC coming under the control of another man deemed insufficiently loyal to the increasing dominant trends in the Northwest.[103] While the specific reasons remain unknown, the Ziemke initiative ultimately failed and we later learn that the CBC charter went back to the UPC Division of Education with a recommendation from the Washington and Idaho Districts that the college remain in the Northwest. The motion was carried by a seven-to-one margin.[104] This special and significant two-part board meeting concluded after calendaring a subsequent session to discuss the future and financial situation of the college. The upshot was that Don Fisher's days at the college were numbered and among the central issues were questions about theology.

---

[101] *Minutes*, CBC board meeting, 21 February 1983, pp. 2-3. FC, inv.doc.no 0707-5222-34.

[102] Darline (Kantola) Royer interview, 15 August 2013.

[103] Gene Ziemke interview, 23 September 2013.

[104] *Minutes*, CBC board meeting, 21 March 1983, p. 2. FC, inv.doc.no 0707-5227-34. An undated typed summary of a General Board resolution, communicated to the CBC board by telephone by C.M. Becton, required the charter to revert to the Division of Education. The typescript bears the handwritten date "1983." FC, inv.doc.no 0707-5229-34. The current whereabouts of the charter is unknown. Daniel Batchelor, letter to Thomas A. Fudge, 9 October 2013. FC, inv.doc.no 0707-5379-34. Batchelor is the current superintendent of the DOE. There is uncertainty over whether there is any meaningful distinction between the charter and the endorsement. Arless Glass, letter to Dan Batchelor, 9 October 2013. FC, inv.doc.no 0707-5383-34. It is unknown if there was ever a written charter.

The idea of being "weak on the message," which was both implied and asserted in the 21 February board meeting should be placed into context. In the UPC this specifically means a lack of robust enthusiasm for the *Fundamental Doctrine*. In the Missouri Synod Lutheran Church and among the Southern Baptists it could be gauged from any support, however slight, for the principles of biblical criticism or opinions which appeared at variance with the Lutheran Confessions or the *Baptist Faith and Message*. At Fuller Seminary, those who did not firmly subscribe to a doctrine of strict inerrancy were suspect. Edward J. Carnell's failure to press the famous Swiss theologian Karl Barth (1886-1968) on the matter of inerrancy and his damaging admissions to Barth in the face of the latter's erudite arguments at a seminar in Chicago in 1962 were damning proof.[105] National officials within the United Pentecostal Church noted that some people think a person is "weak on the message" if they detect any semblance whatever of diverse doctrinal understanding.[106] That comment has much to commend it. Don Fisher, Jerry Peden, and C.H. Yadon, to name three of the principal actors in the twilight of CBC, were Northwest men and by extension products of the PCI tradition. That body merged with the PAJC in 1945 to form the UPC but did not, generally, hold to a water and spirit doctrine as the main thrust in salvation. The PCI believed that salvation occurred at repentance. Water and spirit baptism followed as a result of being saved. The PAJC held generally to a three-step doctrine which regarded salvation as occurring after (and as a result of) repentance, baptism and spirit infilling. This was a serious theological difference. The various theological views around such issues created a fault line running beneath the merger, giving rise to seismic activities in 1945, 1973, and 1992. The merger agreement stipulated that no one was to contend for their particular views to the point of disunity. Between the formation of the *Fundamental Doctrine* and its revision in 1973, a movement coalesced which culminated in the contentious Westberg Resolution of 1992, wherein the organization sought to eliminate doubts, clarify the unity of the faith, and establish a definitive

---

[105] See Nelson, *The Making and Unmaking of an Evangelical Mind*, pp. 111-112.
[106] Nathaniel Urshan interview, 23 April 1999.

doctrine for all time. The PAJC tradition overwhelmed the PCI point of view.[107] The epicentre of theological discourse occurred around the central doctrines of the organization (namely the new birth and notions of holiness); there were fractures caused by theological movement and these several shifts created significant displacement. JCM and CBC exposed various nuances of this fault line. Residual PCI inclinations and educational efforts like those engineered by Fisher clearly threatened to disrupt the process of unanimity, which gathered in strength between 1973 and 1992. Lewis, Howell, and others sought intellectual freedom. To some extent, they had UPC constitutional protection. Until the Westberg Resolution of 1992, ratified by the General Conference in that year and enforced from 1993, the idea of salvation as held by Fisher, Peden, and Yadon could not be impeached as false, erroneous, or heretical. According to the merger agreement, this was perfectly acceptable, even if by the early 1980s, men who held that view were maligned as "weak on the message."

In other words, Don Fisher's notional concept of the new birth was not at variance with historic UPC doctrine.[108] If there was any basis whatever to the accusation of being "weak on the message," its only validity was on account of omission to the extent that Fisher did not emphasize those particular doctrines.[109] A case can be made that those attacking Fisher were in violation of the spirit of the merger agreement, which admonished all ministers not to contend for their own points of view to the disunity of the body of Christ. Notwithstanding, as early as the spring of 1978, Paul Dugas' disciple Clyde Barlow called for a purging of CBC, "a bastion of liberal theology," by suggesting the entire faculty should resign because not one of them was sufficiently strong on the message. That included the sitting president John Klemin and the senior academic Darline Kantola.[110] The allegation is extraordinary and an

---

[107] Thetus Tenney interview, 6 June 2013, and Raymond A. Sirstad interview, 27 August 2013.

[108] Fudge, *Christianity without the Cross*, pp. 75-112 and on details surrounding the Westberg Resolution, see pp. 200-275.

[109] April Purtell interview, 19 January 1999.

[110] Jerry Dillon interview, 5 January 1999. The meeting was convened at the college campus with the eight Portland area pastors along with the administrative

infuriated Norman Rutzen objected. It should be noted that in calm reflection, Barlow judged that during those days he was "full of baloney" and asserted that most of his opinions about CBC were

5.16 John H. Tietjen, on the conference floor at the General Convention of the Missouri Synod, in New Orleans, 1973

flat wrong.[111] However, in 1978 Barlow's opinion constituted a fine example of making arguments based on negative assumptions. It is almost certain that Barlow was in the meeting at the college in the spring of 1977 when Jerry Dillon, at the behest of Norman Rutzen, addressed theological concerns to the satisfaction of every area pastor. "The chief of sinners," John Tietjen, had been warned and when he continued to support his faculty and failed to invoke the wishes of Jacob Preus and the Board of Control he was summarily

council of CBC which consisted of John Klemin, Ray Sirstad, and Jerry Dillon. Clyde Barlow interview, 13 August 2013.

[111] Clyde Barlow interview, 13 August 2013, expressing a one-hundred-and-eighty degree change of opinion. Former colleagues have been astonished by Barlow's change of heart. Raymond A. Sirstad interview, 27 August 2013.

removed and in his wake Missouri was purged.[112] When Russell
Dilday failed to align and identify himself closely enough with the
conservative resurgence movement, he was promptly dismissed by
the "carnal conservatism" that was sweeping his denomination.[113]
At Fuller Theological Seminary, Edward J. Carnell and Paul Jewett
were quite unwilling to support the full gamut of fundamentalist
theology. These men were all "weak on the message" as espoused
and taught by their respective churches and theological movements.
In one sense, they were no different than men such as Marcion,
Peter Abelard, and Jan Hus of previous eras. The results were
almost always the same. Suspects were labelled "putrid frogs."[114]

Regardless of Gene Ziemke's controlling interest in the college
and the hopes that operations might be resumed in the future, it
was far too confident to state that CBC would be open for fall
term.[115] A firm decision was made during the board meeting that
CBC could not continue beyond its winter term, which concluded
on 11 March. That decision was publicly announced two days later
on 23 February. Reactions were mixed. One wrote, "the news is the
academic year ends 03/11/83. No spring term. There will be a year
book, etc. Mental Pollution ... What a supreme crock."[116] It was
likewise decided that the future of the college was very much in
doubt. This hinged, of course, on a careful analysis of the actual
financial situation, which was to come under close scrutiny over the
next month. Because of these factors no effort was ever made to
find a suitable successor to Don Fisher to assume the presidency of
CBC. The last days of the college fairly bristled with heretics and
politics as CBC slowly wound down. Efforts were made to relocate
the college back to the Lombard campus with necessary repairs to
enable the old location to continue under its original name and
organizational structure. Nothing ever came of this initiative. It was
altogether impracticable and impossible, and to include the Oregon

---

[112] Danker, *No Room in the Brotherhood*, pp. 43-44.

[113] Dilday, *Higher Ground: A Call for Christian Civility*, pp. 115-127.

[114] According to the twelfth-century Augustinian theologian, Walter of St-Victor,
"*Le Contra quatuor labyrinthos Franciae de Gauthier de Saint-Victor*," ed., by Palémon
Glorieux. *Archive d'histoire doctrinale et littéraire du moyen-âge* 19 (1952), p. 201.

[115] Arless Glass, letter to George Sponsler, 4 March 1983.

[116] *The Journal of Thomas A. Fudge, 1980-1985*, entry for 23 February 1983.

District in the proposal demonstrated a failure to understand one of the key problems leading to the demise of CBC.[117]

5.17  Final chapel service, 11 March 1983. *Left to right:* James Paley, Eric Loy, Jerry Peden, Michael Nigh, April Purtell, Fred Scott, Donna Fisher, George Sponsler, Sandi Derick, Arless Glass and Don Fisher

The last term was a study in protracted death. Students came and went as usual, lectures were given, examinations held, papers marked, chapel services attended, as the college rolled on inexorably towards its inevitable end. The college community of CBC gathered together in the chapel for the last time on 11 March. Special guests included the aforementioned Arless Glass, George M. Sponsler, Northwest pioneer minister Fred Scott, and former faculty member Jerry Dillon. Glass had been a stalwart defender of education.[118] Don Fisher preached his last CBC sermon before an emotional audience. The college ensemble sang "with his word, comfort one another, be a keeper of your sister and your brother. Share his love, be forgiving with each other, and be one, until he comes." Fisher also presided over a celebration of the eucharist (see ill.0.5, p. 18).

---

[117] E.G. Moyer, letter to the District superintendents of Oregon, Washington, and Idaho, 11 March 1983, pp. 1-2. FC, inv.doc.no 0707-5224-34.

[118] Darline Kantola, letter to Arless Glass, 20 September 1984. FC, inv.doc.no 0707-5237-34.

The CBC singers brought the academic year and the formal history of CBC to a close with a song which included the words, "protect us as we go our way, o'er shadow us both night and day. Lead and guide us, stay thou beside us, in Jesus name we pray."[119] When the music faded away and Don Fisher's final "amen" was heard, the last student body in the thirty-year history of CBC was dismissed.[120]

5.18  Wayne Nigh and Hans Petermann, 1982

5.19  R.V. Reynolds during his last CBC visit

Three students were in their senior year and had been due to graduate in May. Provisions were made for those students to be engaged in directed study for their final term, following which, on 18 May 1982, seniors Michael Nigh, Daniel R. Sirstad, and Audrey Zapalac were presented with graduation certificates 349, 350, and 351. These were the last ever to be issued by CBC. Appropriately enough, the commencement speaker for the final official act in the history of CBC was a long-time Fisher ally and suspected heretic, Wayne Nigh.[121] Don Fisher did not attend the last convocation. He

---

[119] The group included Peggy (Yelm) Dougherty, Belinda Trevino, Angel Vestal, Thomas A. Fudge, Jay Nacino, and Michael Fairservice.

[120] "It was quite a chapel service." *The Journal of Thomas A. Fudge*, entry for 11 March 1983. Four photographs feature on a full-page layout of this final service in *Ensign*, vol. 30 (1983), p.106. These feature Glass at the podium addressing the student body, the CBC ensemble singing, and two images of Fisher celebrating Holy Communion. Glass apparently reported to the national headquarters that everything at CBC was being worked out and everything was being taken care of. Nathaniel Urshan interview, 23 April 1999.

[121] *Minutes*, CBC board meeting, 21 March 1983, p. 3, but noting a scheduled commencement date of 28 May. FC, inv.doc.no 0707-5227-34.

called graduating seniors earlier in the day to tell them he would not be present but offered congratulations and wished them well.[122] Former college president R.V. Reynolds handed out the graduation diplomas to the last class.[123]

There had been efforts to counter the rising tide of change in the Northwest and rein in the radical element. At an Oregon District conference in the 1970s, convened at the Killingsworth Street church in Portland, C.H. Yadon wept publicly and pled with ministers to leave off bickering and dissension. Refraining from referring to them as brethren, he addressed them rather less gently as "you men" and implored them to unite.[124] At the end of his life, Yadon reflected with considerable regret on the destruction of the college, the situation at First Church, and the changes in the Northwest. He lamented the impossibility of turning back time in order to do what should have been done and what needed to occur. He also wondered publicly if he had somehow personally failed. While acknowledging that he could not change history, he declared that it was not over and that the events of 1983 were not the end of the story. "Men of dust" appeared to have prevailed, but in God's time eternal outcomes would emerge.[125] He did not elaborate but it is clear that he wished he had been a stronger influence against the missionary "experts" who had invaded the region seeking to save the lukewarm and backslidden UPCers from their eternal fate; those who had supposedly been misled and deceived by the Dillons, the Yadons, and the Fishers. Most of the Dillons, Yadons, and Fishers were firm subscribers to the false "no experts" doctrine. What was needed was a proper "hell-fire and damnation" approach.[126] The UPC conceived a solemn duty to withstand "spiritual creeps" like the Fishers, the Yadons, and the Dillons, just as the Missouri Synod and the Southern Baptist Convention had to expel the "stinking skunks" and "evil geniuses" like John Tietjen and Russell Dilday

---

[122] Michael Nigh interview, 18 August 2013.
[123] Audrey (Zapalac) Greer interview, 22 September 2013.
[124] Wallace Leonard interview, 3 August 2013.
[125] C.H. Yadon, sermon "Now and Then," Valley Pentecostal Church, Caldwell, Idaho, 22 June 1997, audio recording. FC, inv.doc.no 0707-3156-22.
[126] This is how one pastor retroactively described himself and his ministry in the 1970s. Clyde Barlow interview, 13 August 2013.

from their respective offices as seminary presidents. The supposed
malignancy within these Trojan horses could not otherwise be
contained. Don Fisher's rejoinder was that anything which stood
against the freedom to learn had to be set aside.[127] The ideological
collisions which followed were severe and irresolvable. CBC fell
victim to internecine church politics and doctrinal disagreement. It
was another manifestation of the old PCI and PAJC theological
conflict.[128] Walter of St-Victor's twelfth-century "putrid frogs"
could be heard croaking once again.

After 11 March, faculty began moving out of their rooms,
equipment began to be stored, students departed. On 17 March,
Don Fisher, George Sponsler, and Darline Kantola met to discuss
remaining issues connected to the transfer of college leadership.
The following day Fisher turned over all aspects of CBC leadership
to Sponsler, expressing deep personal regret for the atmosphere of
hostility and volatility in which the transition was taking place.[129]
Robert Manchester, who had climbed into the mechanical space in
the ceiling and planted the recording device during the first board
meeting, was travelling in Nevada over the spring break, arriving
back on campus on 21 March, was met by one of the two original
conspirators (Maynard) who had been plotting and planning yet
another episode of clandestine surveillance. "Today was the day for
the board meeting so [Maynard] and [Manchester] conspired to bug
[the] meeting. [Manchester] did the dirty work again."[130] Manchester
was informed that the CBC Board of Directors were convening
once again that afternoon in the library. A cordial invitation was
extended to consider reprising the deeds of the previous month.
The willingness of Maynard to once again become involved in the
surreptitious activity stands in sharp contrast to that individual's

---

[127] Bach, *Jonathan Livingston Seagull*, p. 83.

[128] Roger Yadon interview, 8 October 2013.

[129] Don Fisher, letter to the CBC board, 18 March 1983.

[130] *The Journal of Thomas A. Fudge, 1980*-1985, entry for 21 March 1983. The
meeting originally had been scheduled to convene in Pendleton, Oregon. *Minutes*,
CBC board meeting, 21 February 1983, p. 3. FC, inv.doc.no 0707-5222-34. It is
unknown why the venue changed. Thirty years after the episode, Maynard had
only vague recollection of the second secret eavesdropping and tape-recording.
P.W. Maynard, interview, 19 July 2013.

remorse a month earlier. Notwithstanding this fact, the invitation
was warmly accepted by Manchester. A complete repetition of the
events which transpired on 21 February occurred. "[Whalen] and
[Manchester] went back to the graphics room and did some more
taping."[131] This means that all three of the original tape-recorders
were involved to one extent or another in the second round of
activity in the ceilings of the CBC campus. This time the bugging
was done well in advance, with a microphone planted in an air
conditioning and heating duct immediately above the table around
which the board members sat. Manchester once again climbed
through the ceiling and crawled an even greater distance through
the mechanical space in order to organize the necessary recording
equipment. This time Arless Glass was not in attendance, but
Darline Kantola had been invited to attend, representing the
interests of the college and the faculty. Kantola had been one of the
deans and was the longest tenured member of staff, having served
continuously on the faculty of CBC since 1961 (ill.5.20, p. 292).
During this meeting she was appointed corporation secretary, with
authorization to sign all legal documents. George Sponsler was
appointed Acting President.[132] Once again E.W. "Bud" Yadon
represented C.H. Yadon, but Jay Craven was able to attend this
meeting and therefore Norman Dillon did not reprise his
appearance of 21 February. The recordings made on this occasion
were of considerably better quality than the first set and were in fact
excellent. Unfortunately, for our purposes, these tapes have limited
relevance. The board proceedings during the 21 March meeting
were entirely financial, with discussions of records, assets, severance
pay for faculty and staff, considerations of property, legal matters,
and the like. The four hour meeting made perfectly clear in its

---

[131] *The Journal of Thomas A. Fudge, 1980-1985*, entry for 21 March 1983.
[132] *Minutes*, CBC board meeting, 21 March 1983, p. 1. FC, inv.doc.no 0707-5227-
34. Kantola was later confirmed in these continuing appointments until either she
took other employment or until all CBC matters were finalized. *Minutes*, CBC
board, 12 September 1983, p. 6. FC, inv.doc.no 0707-5230-34. She was later
appointed treasurer of the corporation. *Minutes*, CBC board meeting, 6 March
1984, p. 1. FC, inv.doc.no 0707-5231-34. It is important to note that Sponsler
and Kantola played important roles in the administration of CBC after March
1983. David Reynolds interview, 12 August 2013.

conclusions and summary statements that CBC was no longer financially viable, and for all intents and purposes was insolvent.

The often-stated opinion that CBC was effectively and essentially a financial casualty, that money constituted the central factor which brought the school down, has already been refuted in print.[133] Financial woes, though a serious matter, were a secondary causal factor in the destruction of CBC. Heretics and politics were the salient factors behind the financial crisis. Men such as Clyde Barlow were convinced this was absolutely the case. Surviving documents suggest that the essence of the matter was doctrinal. If the several factors of decline and destruction are considered, the root cause which emerges is theological.[134] It is arguable that if the heretics and the politics had been properly eliminated, then the insurmountable financial issues would never have grown to such gargantuan proportions. The real issue was theology, doctrinal deviance based upon the methodology of historical and theological criticism, biblical exegesis, and a commitment to critical thinking which refused to stop short of examining established UPC doctrine. Ranking officials within the denomination recognized that there were "doctrinal differences" between Don Fisher and the UPC.[135] It may be argued that had Fisher been successful in making the college financially independent and solvent that he would thereby have positioned himself in a much stronger vantage point from which to resist the various challenges of his detractors. Had the college been a going concern, might Fisher have been able to weather the storms? The idea is intriguing but one has only to look to the situation at JCM to conclude that Fisher could not for long have withstood his many detractors in the Northwest. JCM was financially strong and solvent, and was also considerably larger than CBC. Notwithstanding this, Fisher reached his Rubicon there early in 1981 and resigned. It is doubtful that CBC could have survived financially and institutionally without endorsement and no college within the UPC could retain that recognition for long under the shadow of heresy accusations and suspected doctrinal weakness. A

---

[133] Thomas A. Fudge, "A Place to Stand: An Open Response to Chuck Parrish" *In Touch* 3 (No. 2, 1989), p. 6.
[134] Clyde Barlow interview, 13 August 2013.
[135] Nathaniel Urshan, letter to Don Fisher, 18 July 1995. See Appendix 20, p. 458.

growing financial crisis did bring CBC down but that crisis was chiefly created and sustained by matters of theology. Inasmuch as Fisher was now effectively no longer president of the college, he was neither called nor specifically discussed apart from rather mundane business decisions. At the conclusion of the meeting, the student conspirators concealed their tracks again, collected the cassette tapes, removed all traces of their activity, returned borrowed equipment to its proper place, and entrusted the tapes once again to the safekeeping of Manchester, who had again done the real "dirty" work.[136] That individual, in keeping with earlier practice, returned to the dormitory and promptly listened to the entire second set of recordings, which consisted of four, one-hour long cassette tapes, while the fifth tape was retrieved later. The material prompted one direct response: "things proved to be very interesting. There are lots of questions that need to be answered."[137] Those queries were never addressed. Meanwhile, considerable discussion was generated in the dorms among some students and at least on one occasion doctrinally objectionable material originating from JCM was circulated.[138] It is notable that of the three principle conspirators, Maynard heard very little of the two sets of recordings once they were removed from the CBC campus. In the course of listening to the surreptitious recordings, Maynard felt that the eavesdropping had been inappropriate and concluded it was wrong to listen to the tapes. Whalen heard parts of the first set, but no sustained hearing. Manchester listened to every discernible word on both sets of recordings, a point confirmed by Whalen.[139]

---

[136] The fifth and final tape was actually retrieved from Maynard two days later when Manchester made a final entry into the crawlspace to collect the recording equipment from the ceiling. *The Journal of Thomas A. Fudge, 1980-1985*, entry for 23 March 1983. Manchester listened to the final tape immediately.

[137] *The Journal of Thomas A. Fudge, 1980-1985*, entry for 21 March 1983.

[138] The pseudonymous essay Joseph D. Siwell, "Escape from History: An Exploration into Oneness Pentecostal Roots and Being" (May 1981), actually written by Dan Lewis, was distributed by CBC staff member Rick McDonald (former JCM student). *The Journal of Thomas A. Fudge, 1980-1985*, entries for 25 and 27 March 1983. On the first date, a two-and-a-half hour discussion ensued. Lewis' essay later formed a chapter in his *The Journey Out*, pp. 85-119.

[139] Robert S. Manchester interview, 1 August 2013, and George C. Whalen interview, 29 July 2013. Maynard later calculated that roughly less than 5% of the

The student prank and conspiracy to surreptitiously infiltrate those closed board meetings would have passed silently and without trace into history had the eavesdroppers not exposed themselves with their own careless handling of incriminating evidence. During the first taping session, Maynard took two photographs in the darkroom. One photograph revealed parts of the recording system being installed by Whalen in the ceiling, complete with microphone, cables, and monitors. The second picture showed Manchester emerging from the crawlspace (i.e. mechanical space) in the ceiling looking rather dishevelled and dirty (see ill.5.1 and ill.5.2, pp. 246 and 248). Fatefully, and by sheer chance, those two photographs later fell into the hands of CBC college authorities and during the following month the entire covert operation was exposed.

5.20   J. Darline Kantola, during the        5.21   "DK" teaching in a CBC
       last years of CBC, c. 1982                     classroom, 1982

In late April, the conspiracy was uncovered. The sleuth who cracked the case was none other than the ubiquitous Darline Kantola. The details of how this came about remains something of a mystery. Manchester admitted to being "curious as to how she uncovered the plot."[140] There are three possibilities. The first is that Maynard, having been "convicted" of the clandestine activities, or

---

recordings were heard before conscience would not allow further indulgence. P.W. Maynard, interview, 19 July 2013.

[140] *The Journal of Thomas A. Fudge, 1980-1985*, entry for 26 April 1983.

"getting a conscience," in the words of Whalen, confessed to Kantola directly.[141] It is unknown what specific factors may have prompted such action and the individual in question later did regret involvement in the affair and expressed remorse. (Maynard accepts this explanation as possible but unlikely, and prefers a different version of events.) What is more certain is that Maynard was acting quite "antsy" and did indiscreetly tell another student during the recording operation what was going on. That student conveyed the information directly to Darline Kantola who initially downplayed the suggestion and did not take the information seriously.[142]

There is a second possibility. Robert Manchester had recently photographed various areas in the Columbia River Gorge, and on 22 April Kantola asked if she could see the pictures. Three days later, Manchester loaned Kantola an album of photographs. The two incriminating pictures were inadvertently included in that collection. The second scenario is rather more pedestrian but it requires a great deal of shrewdness on the part of Darline Kantola. Once having seen the photographs, Kantola did a splendid job of putting two and two together and actually coming up with four.[143] Former faculty members recall Kantola attempting to locate Manchester, intimating that there was trouble in which Manchester was implicated and stressing the importance of locating that individual as soon as possible.[144] Those efforts were unsuccessful. Failing to locate Manchester but armed with her own suspicions, she approached one of the original student plotters, Maynard, and evidently confronted that individual with her suspicions. Of the three perpetrators, Maynard had the most to lose. Given apparent ministerial aspirations and psychological weakness, Maynard broke down entirely and confessed what had in fact been done. Maynard later recounted how angry Kantola was over the secret operation; and was taken aback at the negative significance she attached to the affair. Maynard likewise recalls legal ramifications which Kantola presented in unequivocal terms. Kantola wanted to know who was involved in the taping operation and made clear that she wanted the

---

[141] George Whalen interview, 29 July 2013.
[142] Audrey (Zapalac) Greer interview, 22 September 2013.
[143] *The Journal of Thomas A. Fudge, 1980-1985*, entries for 25 and 26 April 1983.
[144] April Purtell interview, 13 April 2013.

tapes turned over to her immediately, assuming that Maynard had copies. Maynard denied this was the case. Ruminating on this explanation, Whalen does not think it plausible that Kantola could have, unaided, uncovered the recording scenario based upon the existing photographs, a position maintained even after thirty years.

It seems most likely that the revelation of the tape-recording consisted of yet a third scenario, in which Kantola viewed the photographs, and asked innocent questions about what Whalen and Manchester were actually engaged in. When Maynard demonstrated discomfort with the photographs, Kantola raised further questions, resulting in the confessions which did occur. In this sense, Maynard did not approach Kantola (as suggested by Whalen) and Kantola did not independently connect the photographs to the activities which took place in the mechanical space of the dropped ceiling on campus (as assumed by Manchester). This third explanation is most probable. Be that as it may, the next day, on 26 April, Manchester who had loaned the photo album to Kantola returned to her office to collect the book. The following conversation took place.[145]

Kantola: Do you know anything at all about some tape recordings of board meetings?

Manchester: What do you mean?

Kantola: Do you have any information about students tape-recording a board meeting recently on this campus? [Sensing that Manchester was unlikely to volunteer information, Kantola continued.] Look, you should know I have already spoken to one of the students involved and got a pretty honest statement about the situation.[146]

Manchester: Well, yes, I seem to have heard something about that.

Kantola: Were you involved?

Manchester: Yes.

---

[145] Robert S. Manchester interview, 1 August 2013.

[146] It is now certain that by this date Kantola had also spoken with both Maynard and Whalen.

Kantola:      Which of the board meetings was taped?

Manchester:   Both of them.

Kantola:      Both of them? Are you aware of how unethical this sort of thing is? This is exactly the kind of thing that drove Richard Nixon from office. Why would you get involved in such a thing? Whose idea was it in the first place?[147]

Manchester:   I don't really remember whose idea it was.[148]

Kantola:      Who all was involved?

It was quite clear that Maynard had already named the other two members of the plot to record the board meetings. Manchester identified Whalen and Maynard as the principle conspirators but omitted referring to the others who had assisted them. Manchester noted the extraordinary linkage between Watergate and CBC and further remarked that Kantola's evaluation seemed rather strained and decidedly overwrought.[149] Kantola did not respond to that expressed opinion but instead wondered if the students had been encouraged.

Kantola:      Does Brother Fisher know about this?

Manchester:   Definitely not.

Kantola:      Where are the tapes?

Manchester:   I have them.

Kantola:      Who all has listened to them?

Manchester:   I am the only one who has actually listened to all of the tapes.

---

[147] Kantola's unmistakable surprise indicated that Maynard had failed to reveal this fact. It is certain that at this stage, Kantola thought only one of the sessions had been clandestinely recorded.

[148] In retrospect, both Whalen and Maynard remember it was their idea and so that question cannot be resolved. George Whalen interview, 29 July 2013, and P.W. Maynard, interview, 19 July 2013.

[149] Ironically, the term "Watergate" was used at least twice with reference to the recording operation prior to Kantola's comments. *The Journal of Thomas A. Fudge, 1980-1985*, entries for 21 February and 23 March 1983.

| Kantola: | (incredulous) You listened to all of them?[150] |
|---|---|
| Manchester: | Yes. |
| Kantola: | Have any copies been made of any of those tapes from the meetings? |
| Manchester: | No. Not that I am aware of. |
| Kantola: | Why did you tape the meetings anyway? |
| Manchester: | Well, I can't speak for the others. Part of it was a joke. Just to see if we could get away with it. But, for my part, I really wanted to know what was happening and why the college was in such trouble. I spoke to Brother Fisher not too long before the first meeting. He indicated a number of factors concerning rumors and suspicions regarding his theology, what was being taught, about pastors no longer supporting the school. If the UPC has plenty of money, why don't they save the college? It just doesn't make sense to say that the problem with CBC is financial. There seems to be much more to the problem. |
| Kantola: | I don't think this is something for you and I to decide. We should accept what the Board of Directors decide and say. Brother Fisher is no longer president and I think it was extremely rash for you (students) to have done this sort of thing. It just makes everything worse. Look, this is a very serious matter but I have no wish to make this incident public. This could cause a great deal of embarrassment both to you and the college. I think it would be best if the matter was handled quietly without a lot of fuss. If you |

---

[150] There was clear genuine surprise that the tapes had been heard in their entirety. They consisted altogether of more than eight hours of conversation and deliberation, and required a great deal of patience and enhancement to decipher the complete discussion. Ostensibly, Maynard had openly declared to Kantola no substantial knowledge of the contents of the tapes, which was quite true. P.W. Maynard, interview, 19 July 2013.

bring me all of the tapes with your word that there are no copies then we'll just forget about this whole thing.

Manchester agreed with this proposal but neglected to ask Kantola the all-important question of what she intended to do with the tape recordings once they were in her possession. Manchester left Kantola's office and spoke to Maynard who had confessed. Maynard was extremely sullen and did not want to discuss the matter at all declaring the entire affair had been "pretty stupid."[151] Manchester registered sharp disagreement. Several other comments were in every way indicative that Maynard wanted nothing more to do with the unfortunate incident and recommended that both Whalen and Manchester, already implicated in the recordings, comply with what Kantola suggested to avoid serious trouble. The next day Whalen contacted Manchester by telephone to reveal that Kantola had already made contact and was, as with Maynard, "quite angry." Kantola had specifically wanted to know how many sets of tapes existed. There was further interrogation about who had been involved. While no names were advanced by Kantola, Whalen was under the impression that the nature of the questions around that subject appeared to implicate either Jerry Peden or Don Fisher, or both. The suggestion was denied. Whalen would later opine that Kantola did not appear to believe the version of the story related to her by any one of the perpetrators. Kantola had repeatedly asked Whalen to turn in copies of the recordings and seemed unsatisfied with the rejoinder that no tapes were in that individual's possession. Whalen impressed upon Manchester that the tapes must not yet be turned in and asked that the second set be withheld until such time as they could be collected. Manchester agreed but insisted that whatever was going to happen to the tapes (especially any planned copying) should not be communicated in order that when all the tapes were handed over to Kantola an unequivocal statement could

---

[151] Many years later Maynard continues to maintain that the recordings had been unethical and a matter of continued personal regret. However, there was acknowledgement from Maynard that the undertaking had been a lot of fun. P.W. Maynard, interview, 19 July 2013. Other comments from the time characterize the episode as worthwhile and "probably a first in the history of CBC." *The Journal of Thomas A. Fudge, 1980-1985*, entry for 26 April 1983.

be made that no copies existed. The matter was agreed.[152] The
following evening Manchester, who had been storing the tapes,
handed over the first set of tapes to Kantola via former faculty
member David Wasmundt. Kantola insisted upon this transaction
by means of a telephone call that afternoon stressing urgency. The
second set of tapes was hidden inside a Bible case and handed off
to Whalen's representative (Karissa Fisher) in front of Wasmundt
without his knowledge. Wasmundt was instructed to convey to
Kantola that the second set would be forthcoming and was also
told, when pressed, that Whalen had the tapes. Two days later the
second set of tapes was scheduled to be handed over to Kantola.[153]
The matter of the west coast Watergate episode was at an end.

Don Fisher by this time had vacated his CBC office and was
never again seen on the campus. As previously noted, he did not
attend the final convocation of the college marking the end of its
thirty-year life. Being confined in a fairly rigid system caused Fisher
to develop bitterness and resentment. Ultimately he could not live
with the restrictions of the United Pentecostal Church.[154] Despite
murmuring among certain UPC individuals, he continued to serve
as senior pastor of Christ for the People Community Church.
Rumor suggested that the Washington District of the UPC was
planning to step in and take over the church. Fisher anticipated that
possibility by directing his secretary to remove from the college
offices all papers and files relating to the church.[155] No takeover
was ever attempted. Faculty members who continued to support
the organization, among them Darline Kantola, ceased attending
the college church and went elsewhere. The bulk of the church
congregation supported Fisher strongly but attendance declined
with the departure of most of the students, who returned to their
hometowns and a number of the faculty who also left the area.

---

[152] *The Journal of Thomas A. Fudge, 1980-1985*, entry for 27 April 1983.
[153] *The Journal of Thomas A. Fudge, 1980-1985*, entry for 27 April 1983. Kantola no
longer has copies of any of the tapes in her possession. Darline Kantola, letter to
Thomas A. Fudge, 30 August 2013.
[154] Thetus Tenney interview, 6 June 2013.
[155] Roger Yadon had been the church secretary. Upon his resignation, Fisher
appointed April Purtell, who carried out the directive. April Purtell interview, 16
January 1999.

Nonetheless, the church remained a strong community. CBC was not quite dead. Its doors had been closed and locked, the tapes had been confiscated, and Fisher was gone.

One evening, Manchester, who had turned the tapes in, received a telephone call. It was from one of the other perpetrators, Whalen, the individual who had requested the second set of tapes. Whalen had disturbing news for Manchester. Kantola had not kept her word about maintaining silence over the recording operation. Having the critical set of cassette tapes in her possession, she raised the alarm on 27 April. Whalen later reported that Kantola had conveyed in a telephone conversation that she could not sleep with the knowledge of what had gone on and had to tell someone possessing more authority than she did. Manchester took the view that Kantola had been duplicitous, planning all along to expose the matter once the tapes were safely in her possession. Issues of motivation cannot be explained and remain conjecture.[156] What can then be established is that Kantola approached George Sponsler who was apparently called at 1:00 a.m. on 27 April. He was aroused to tremendous wrath and being outraged at the news was reported to have breathed a series of threats including the vow that the conspirators would face criminal prosecution: "We'll take them to court! We'll sue them!"[157] It was also rumored that Wayne Nigh, the UPC missionary in Germany was also contacted. This was untrue.[158] Norman Rutzen, however, was taken into confidence, either by Kantola or Sponsler but certainly by the former, and briefed about the clandestine recordings.[159] Presumably other board members were likewise notified, though this cannot be confirmed. At the home of faculty member April Purtell, following a Bible study, Whalen and Manchester discussed the various possibilities and Whalen shared with Manchester what Kantola had said about the

---

[156] Kantola has admitted that this narrative bears the suggestion of duplicity but also insists her recollection of what happened is unclear. Darline (Kantola) Royer interview, 15 August 2013.

[157] It is neither apparent why Kantola should have made a telephone call at that inconvenient time, nor why the time of call should have been known to Whalen who communicated those statements to Manchester.

[158] Wayne Nigh interview, 25 July 2013.

[159] *The Journal of Thomas A. Fudge 1980-1985*, entry for 28 April 1983.

developing affair.[160] The students advised each other to be prepared
for contact from board members, while the clearly fearful Maynard,
who was advised of these developments the next day, counselled
the others to be frank and repentant, bewailing the consequences
should the story reach the ears of Maynard's very visible father. He
mournfully enumerated his fate should his father be informed.
There is no indication that either Whalen or Manchester were
concerned by these developments. Kantola later admitted that if
this series of events is correct as reported she should have informed
the students, especially Manchester, of her revised thinking.[161]

On the morning of 29 April, around 7:30 a.m. Manchester –
who had done the "dirty" work, kept all the tapes, listened to all of
them, and eventually turned them in – was awakened by a long-
distance telephone call from Idaho District Superintendent Norman
Rutzen (ill.4.19, p. 200).[162] Though a keen supporter of the Fisher
administration throughout the collapse of CBC, Rutzen nonetheless
was openly annoyed with the covert operation carried out by the
students. He saw no humor in it whatsoever, stated that clearly,
deplored the intentions and motivations of the students, and came
right to the point.

Rutzen:       I understand you and some other fellows taped
              the board meetings.

Manchester:   Yes, that's correct.

Rutzen:       Do you understand the seriousness of all of this
              situation?

Manchester:   Yes, I think so.

Rutzen:       You are here in the country on a student visa.
              This could be grounds for deporting you from

---

[160] *The Journal of Thomas A. Fudge, 1980-1985*, entry for 28 April, 1983, notes that
Whalen informed Manchester of the following: "DK raising a big stink. [She]
Called Georgie and Rutzen. Rutzen is going to call [the perpetrators]."
[161] Darline (Kantola) Royer interview, 15 August 2013.
[162] Robert S. Manchester interview, 1 August 2013. Rutzen had called Manchester
the previous day (28 April) but was unable to make contact. The message was
then relayed to Manchester who anticipated the call on 29 April. *The Journal of
Thomas A. Fudge, 1980-1985*, entries for 28 and 29 April, 1983. The second entry
contains the laconic sentence "DK sure has a cavernous mouth."

the country. I don't think you would like to see that happen. "Now, I have received information that you boys planned to duplicate these tapes, mass produce them, and send them around the country."

Manchester: Well, that's ridiculous. There was never any such plan, at any time. Who told you that?

Rutzen: That's not important.[163]

Manchester: I think it is important. Whoever told you that doesn't know what they are talking about and are spreading lies.

Rutzen: Well, I am not going to say. Did you duplicate those tapes with the intention of circulating them?[164]

Manchester: I already told Sister Kantola we had not.

Rutzen: But I'm asking you.

Manchester: The answer is still the same.

Rutzen: I am not sure I like your attitude and I am not entirely convinced you understand how serious this situation might be. You were involved in something illegal and immoral and the only way you can help yourself now is by being honest and open with me.

Manchester: Look, I've already said there are no copies of any of those tapes to the best of my knowledge. I have certainly not made any, nor do I have any knowledge that anyone else has. At no time was

---

[163] Thirty years later Rutzen could neither accurately nor definitively recall the source of that information. Norman Rutzen interview, 24 July 2013. However, in April 1983, Whalen told Manchester that Kantola admitted she had called Rutzen. *The Journal of Thomas A. Fudge, 1980-1985*, entry for 28 April 1983.

[164] Comparing notes much later, Whalen noted how closely Kantola had interrogated this point during the previously-mentioned telephone call. George Whalen interview, 29 July 2013.

there ever a conversation about duplicating them. I am not going to answer that again.

Rutzen:       Alright, I'll take your word about that. But let me say that if copies turn up somewhere down the road there could be trouble.

Manchester:   I said there are no copies. How many times do I have to say that? You get me out of bed at this hour of the morning and accuse me of lying. There are no tapes![165]

Rutzen:       I am not accusing you of lying. I just want to make sure that you are telling me everything. "Now then, we have been informed that you boys were paid to do this taping. Is that true?"

Manchester:   No, that isn't true. That's absolutely crazy. Who told you that?

Rutzen:       I am not going to say who told us that. You were not paid to tape the board meetings?

Manchester:   No.

Rutzen:       "We have also received further information that Brother Fisher put you boys up to taping the sessions."[166]

Manchester:   Oh, come on. That is ridiculous!

Rutzen:       Well, we have a pretty good source. We have this information on good authority. This is very important. "Did Brother Fisher put you boys up to tape the meetings?"

---

[165] Several months later it was discovered that copies of some of the tapes had been made and preserved. *The Journal of Thomas A. Fudge, 1980-1985*, entry for 21 October 1983. This fact was not known to Manchester during the critical period between February and May.

[166] All three students were specifically asked by Kantola if Don Fisher had any involvement or if someone had put them up to their activities in the college ceiling mechanical space. George Whalen interview, 29 July 2013, P.W. Maynard, interview, 19 July 2013, and Robert S. Manchester interview, 1 August 2013.

Manchester: Look, I am getting really getting tired of being asked the same questions over and over again. Brother Fisher doesn't know a single thing about any of this. He was never involved. If he had known, he would probably have crucified us. The answer is no to any knowledge on Fisher's part. We did it ourselves because we wanted to. We wanted answers and no one was willing to give answers. Even now all we hear is that CBC has been shut down because of money. That's ridiculous and you know it. And I know it too, because I heard every word that was spoken in those meetings. The point is, the UPC has it in for Fisher, they think he's too liberal and won't harp on some of the stuff they want.[167]

Rutzen: Do I understand your comments to mean that Brother Fisher knows nothing about this taping operation?

Manchester: That's right.

Rutzen: Alright. I will take your word on it, but really if you're not being truthful you could be in a lot of trouble. You are a very bright young man and I would hate to see you ruin your future over an incident like this.

Manchester: You make it sound like a federal case and that I might wind up in prison.

Rutzen: Well, you never know. I am going to ask you to do something important. I would like for you boys involved in this business to write a letter of apology to the board stating what you did and apologising.

Manchester: I'll think about it.

---

[167] Other CBC students felt it was wrong for the college to close with such little explanation. Cheryl (Johns) Crousser interview, 1 October 2013.

Rutzen:          You need to do more than think about it. I want
                 you to write a letter of apology to the board for
                 your actions. Address it to Brother Crossley.
                 He's the chair.[168]

Despite being told that the others would also be contacted,
neither Whalen nor Maynard were never officially or unofficially
approached apart from their exchanges with Darline Kantola.
Manchester, following the protracted conversation with Norman
Rutzen, resolved to apologise neither to the board nor to anyone
else. In Manchester's mind there was nothing to apologise for.
Whalen later concurred on this point noting there was nothing to
regret on the part of the students and nothing to apologise for. No
apology was ever offered. Maynard expressed deep remorse almost
immediately but Whalen expressed opinion thirty years later that
the recordings were entirely "justified." Three decades on, Maynard
expressed his conviction that the CBC "Watergate" episode had a
quite profound and lasting negative effect both on Whalen and
Manchester.[169] Notwithstanding this, the information which had
reached Rutzen was seriously flawed, filled with grave errors, and
alarmingly false. The presumption that Don Fisher may have
orchestrated and financed the west coast "Watergate" break-in of
the *in camera* CBC board meetings was a matter far too serious to
ignore or to leave unchallenged. Thirty years later Darline Kantola
believes she may have thought at the time that Don Fisher had put
the students up to their clandestine activities, but does not think she
had any part in conveying those ideas to Norman Rutzen, either
directly or indirectly. When pressed on specific details about her
involvement in the CBC "Watergate" episode, Kantola suggested

---

[168] Rutzen was incorrect on this point. During the 1982-3 academic year, the
college president had been chair of the board. Once Fisher resigned, George
Sponsler was appointed acting-chair. *Minutes*, CBC board meeting, 21 February
1983, p. 3. FC, inv.doc.no 0707-5222-34. He was definitely filling this role at this
time. George Sponsler, letter to April Purtell, 29 March 1983, is signed as "Acting
Chairman, Board of Directors." FC, inv.doc.no 0707-4811-32. See Appendix 18,
p. 456. Since Sponsler had been elected Acting President, according to the CBC
by-laws, he was by virtue of that position chairman of the board. *Minutes*, CBC
board meeting, 21 March 1983, p.1. FC, inv.doc.no 0707-5227-34.
[169] P.W. Maynard, interview, 19 July 2013.

"maybe God doesn't allow us to have recall on some things."[170] Thirty years after the fact, Whalen and Manchester remain skeptical.

5.22 Norman Rutzen with the author, Caldwell, Idaho, 18 May 2012

The allegations advanced by Norman Rutzen, which had been presented to him "on good authority," were serious and significant. Each of the three students involved in the recording affair emphatically denied any validity whatever to the charges. What were the bases for such conjecture, and who should be held responsible? During the last week of April there were a total of nine identifiable individuals possessing knowledge of the tape-recording episodes. These included the three principle perpetrators, their two fellow CBC student associates, Karissa Fisher, Darline Kantola, George Sponsler, and Norman Rutzen. Prior to Rutzen's telephone call to Manchester, the three original conspirators spoke of the affair only with Kantola. Neither of the students who assisted the three eavesdroppers, nor Karissa Fisher, spoke to anyone about the tapes during the spring of 1983. On no occasion, then or thereafter, did Whalen or Maynard ever speak with Sponsler or Rutzen about the recordings. There are four possibilities for the dissemination of disinformation concerning the tapes. Option one is that Maynard either manufactured those details or made suggestive statements to Kantola which then caused the latter to arrive at the conclusions presented to Robert Manchester by Norman Rutzen. Maynard has strenuously denied any such culpability. Option two is that George Sponsler communicated those details to Rutzen in one fashion or

---

[170] Darline (Kantola) Royer interview, 15 August 2013.

another. But one must wonder on what basis? Sponsler is deceased and cannot be questioned on the matter but it seems highly unlikely that Sponsler would have alleged such charges on his own. If he was the one who communicated those statements to Rutzen, who had informed him to that end? The only surviving knowledge on this matter is that Darline Kantola did in fact alert Sponsler to the surreptitious tape-recordings. All three of the students in question discount any possible active role played by Sponsler. Option three is that Norman Rutzen concocted the allegations on his own initiative in an effort to pry loose from Manchester suspected hidden or hitherto undisclosed details. It seems uncharacteristic and highly unlikely that Rutzen would have done this. Option four is that Darline Kantola either presented these suspicions to Rutzen as suggestions or conveyed them to him as serious probabilities. The fourth option is the most persuasive. Kantola did initiate contact with all three of the perpetrators. However it was accomplished "DK ... solved the Watergate case."[171] Kantola did communicate the matter to George Sponsler. Kantola did have in her possession all of the original tapes. Kantola questioned all three of the students about additional copies of the tapes. Kantola did question Whalen and Manchester about the possible involvement of others behind the scenes. Kantola did acknowledge years later that at the time she may have entertained thoughts that Don Fisher was behind the clandestine affair. Kantola did not appear to believe the version of the students' motivation as described by Whalen. During the last week of April, at least two of the conspirators believed that Kantola was responsible for the content of Rutzen's concerns: According to Manchester, he "had to get up at 7:30. Rutzen was on the phone. He gave [Manchester] the same as [Whalen]."[172] According to the latter, upon the foundation of her own comments to Whalen, Kantola had conveyed information to both Sponsler and Rutzen. Whatever she told Rutzen was sufficient for him to make an almost immediate telephone call to Manchester that same day. Whatever she communicated to Rutzen was considered "a big stink" and was thus characterized as such by Whalen and Manchester. Why did the

---

[171] *The Journal of Thomas A. Fudge, 1980-1985*, entry for 26 April 1983.
[172] *The Journal of Thomas A. Fudge, 1980-1985*, entry for 29 April 1983.

only written contemporary account of the matter note that DK had a "cavernous mouth?" Where did Whalen obtain this information? Whalen was absolutely certain that the only communication about the tapes occurred with, and at the initiation of, Darline Kantola.

However, the matter actually unfolded, Kantola was the link between the illicit tapes made by the students and the information which reached Sponsler and Rutzen. Regardless of how Rutzen received his briefing, the transmission appears to be an attempt to further impugn the reputation and integrity of Don Fisher. Records set down during the last week of April 1983 indicate that Kantola did in fact contact Rutzen. There is no extant evidence to challenge or refute that testimony. She is the only person connected to the affair known to have spoken with Norman Rutzen prior to the disclosures made to Manchester on 29 April. Philosophically, the various suggestions communicated to Rutzen occurred when a "person's obligations or opportunities to speak about some topic exceed his [or her] knowledge of the facts that are relevant to that topic."[173] All of this said, there is insufficient available evidence to conclude definitively that Darline Kantola was intentionally involved in manufacturing or conveying deliberate falsehood. However, it seems certain that she was in some sense the active connection between the explanations offered by the three students and the allegations which reached Norman Rutzen. Given her lack of recall on the specifics of the episode, and her final statement on the subject – that perhaps God does not allow the exercise of memory on certain subjects and that further "comments would be imaginary" – means that the matter remains shrouded in mystery.[174]

Manchester later spoke with both Darline Kantola and P.W. Maynard at the college but there is no record that the topic of the tapes came up.[175] However, with the incident out in the open and the egregious allegations about the intentions of the eavesdroppers and the involvement of Don Fisher having reached stunning proportions, Manchester decided to write a letter of clarification to the CBC Board of Directors. On 13 May 1982, a letter was drafted

---

[173] Harry G. Frankfurt, *On Bullshit* (Princeton: Princeton University Press, 2005), p. 63.

[174] Darline (Kantola) Royer, letter to Thomas A. Fudge, 8 October 2013.

[175] *The Journal of Thomas A. Fudge, 1980-1985*, entry for 11 May 1983.

and addressed to the board in general. The letter contained neither apology nor remorse. Instead, it stated what had happened while quite specifically and categorically denying the allegations of mass duplication of the tapes for national distribution, the suggestion that some unidentified person or persons provided payment to the students for their efforts and, most importantly, of any direct or indirect involvement of Don Fisher in any aspect of the affair before, during, or after the actual taping. The letter denied explicitly that Fisher had any knowledge of the "bugging" operation.[176] The others were not consulted and the letter did not reveal their identities.[177] Manchester then left the country the next day to take up an appointment at a UPC church in Canada for the summer.

The actual document was handed to Darline Kantola by a CBC student, Peggy (Yelm) Dougherty, in a sealed envelope upon the direction of Manchester. Yelm later reported that Kantola opened the envelope despite the fact that it was addressed to the CBC board. Her response, after skimming its contents was, "Oh, this isn't for me."[178] There was never any response to that letter from the CBC Board of Directors. Perhaps curiously, the matter was never minuted in a subsequent CBC board meeting and no trace of the letter has come to light in the UPC archives. It was the final episode in the immediate events surrounding the power struggles and politics in the last days of an American Bible college. Don Fisher and his supporters in the Yadon school of thought had found it hard to kick against the pricks. Politics had intervened.

---

[176] In the early 1990s, some eight to ten years after the actual events, Don Fisher was told about the tape recording escapade by his daughter Karissa, who had been taken into confidence by Whalen after the recordings had been made. It is reported that at the revelations Fisher laughed and shook his head in mock disgust, exclaiming, "Oh, those guys!" but otherwise had no comment. Karissa (Fisher) Hopkins interview, 15 August 2013. Others said that "he probably loved it." Ronna (Fisher) Russell interview, 20 July 2013.

[177] Letter to the CBC board, 13 May 1983. A copy of the letter is reproduced in Appendix 19 (p. 457) in its entirety save for the name of the author (Manchester).

[178] There was no lasting animosity between Kantola and Manchester as may be evidenced by a report that Kantola sent a friendly letter several months later and Manchester later called her. *The Journal of Thomas A. Fudge, 1980-1985*, entries for 15 September and 1 October 1983. The details of the letter transfer have been confirmed in Peggy (Yelm) Dougherty interview, 27 July 2013.

"Experts" had prevailed. Heretics were expelled. After thirty years, having run its course, Conquerors Bible College became part of the history of Pentecostal higher education in the United States and joined the list of those which failed.

5.23  Main CBC campus entrance, during demolition, March 1985

As late as 1984, there was still expressed hope that CBC might be revived, though certainly not at the old campus site.[179] This never eventuated. Its demise was as thorough as the purging of the Missouri Synod Lutheran Church and the removal of liberal thinkers from positions of authority and influence within the Southern Baptist Convention. Together, Toole, King, and Dugas had seen Fisher, Yadon, and Dillon marginalized. Preus and Otten had gotten rid of Tietjen. Criswell, Pressler, and Patterson had constructed an agenda whereby Dilday could be fired. E.J. Carnell (ill.1.3, p. 34) came under such intense pressure that he suffered a psychological breakdown and later died of a drug overdose in an Oakland, California hotel.[180] What was paramount were particular understandings both of theology and scripture as codified in the

---

[179] *Minutes*, CBC board meeting, 6 March 1984, p. 4 (FC, inv.doc.no 0707-5231-34), and Darline Kantola, letter to the CBC board, 13 September 1984, pp. 1-2.

[180] Verdict of the Coroner, Alameda County, California, pointing out that death may have either been accidental or suicidal. Noted in Nelson, *The Making and Unmaking of an Evangelical Mind: The Case of Edward Carnell*, p. 120.

*Fundamental Doctrine*, the Lutheran Confessions, and the *Baptist Faith and Message*. What is of importance is that none of these theological positions can be said to be founded on the Bible, but instead on a particular tradition of interpretation of the Bible. The distinction is crucial. It is clear that hermeneutics definitely shape and preserve institutions. The *Fundamental Doctrine*, the Lutheran Confessions, and the *Baptist Faith and Message* preserve the institutional identities of the churches which subscribe to those articles of faith.

As the college was in the last stages of dissolution, there were efforts on the part of districts no longer involved with CBC to obtain some benefit from the final distribution of assets. It is not surprising that the Oregon District was the first to make such a request.[181] On behalf of CBC, George Sponsler said the request would be considered by the board and was careful to point out that it would be the entire board, not any one individual, who would make official decisions on the final disposition of assets.[182] The British Columbia District made a similar advance with a much more detailed application referring specifically to the dissolution of the old Northwest District in 1965, the establishing of the British Columbia District, the support for CBC especially by the New Westminster church, and verbal undertakings made by C.M. Yadon.[183] Sponsler replied with essentially the same counsel to British Columbia as he had to Oregon.[184] What would prove critical to these claims for consideration in the proceeds from the final dissolution of the college, is the unavoidable fact that the articles of incorporation of CBC mandated that all assets be divided equally between the Washington and Idaho Districts without any reference to other claims.[185] The requests were taken under advisement by the CBC board but were dismissed with reference to the corporation papers filed in Oregon, which made no consideration for interested parties outside the Idaho and Washington Districts. The revised articles of incorporation made null and void a majority secret ballot vote taken by the CBC board nearly three years earlier which

---

[181] Winfred Toole, letter to George Sponsler board chairman, 30 August 1984.

[182] George Sponsler, undated letter to Winfred Toole.

[183] Paul V. Reynolds, letter to George Sponsler, 18 February 1985.

[184] George Sponsler, letter to Paul V. Reynolds, 23 February 1985.

[185] *Restated Articles of Incorporation* (1982), Article 3, pp. 1-2.

allowed for some consideration for the Oregon District.[186] There was no motion made on the matter in 1985, but it appears that the requests made by Oregon and British Columbia were denied.[187]

The distribution of assets again draws attention to allegations earlier that Fisher recklessly divested CBC of its inventory. Extant records utterly refute these claims. The sale of the college library has already been noted. The Lombard campus was sold, but not by Fisher and not until long after he left the college. The topsoil project sale – wherein soil from the Lombard property was sold – was authorized by the board, not secretly coordinated by Fisher.[188] When the college relocated to Vancouver, all equipment not required at the new campus was stored, not sold or given away by Fisher.[189] Once the college ceased operations, existing inventory was to be sold in consultation, not with Don Fisher but with George Sponsler.[190] A mutual understanding concerning all CBC equipment was reached between Fisher, Sponsler, and Darline Kantola.[191] Fisher did not act alone. Once Fisher's presidency ceased, all inventory was turned over to the supervision of Sponsler.[192] Inventory items were authorized for sale by the board, not by Don Fisher, to Sponsler, Verneal Crossley, and David Reynolds.[193] As late as March 1984, we find evidence that the major inventory items of the college, including classroom furniture, remained in the possession of CBC.[194] A variety of items, including light fixtures, chapel pews, desks, and carpets, were later sold.[195] This evidence destroys the argument that Don Fisher pilfered the assets of CBC, recklessly gutted college inventory, acted unilaterally

---

[186] "… in the event the college should be dissolved in the future, the Board of Directors now go on record as being willing to give the Oregon District's request consideration regarding the disposition of the assets not to exceed 1981 value (which is approximately $500,000)."*Minutes*, CBC board, 28 August 1981, p. 2.

[187] Discussion not recorded. *Minutes*, CBC board meeting, 8 April 1985, p. 1.

[188] *Minutes*, CBC board meeting, 10 November 1981, p. 2.

[189] *Minutes*, CBC board meeting, 5 June 1982, p. 2. FC, inv.doc.no 0707-5217-34.

[190] *Minutes*, CBC board meeting, 21 February 1983, p. 3.

[191] Typed statement attached to the board meeting records, dated 17 March 1983.

[192] Don Fisher, letter to the CBC board, 18 March 1983.

[193] *Minutes*, CBC board meeting, 12 September 1983, pp. 5-6.

[194] Noted in *Minutes*, CBC board meeting, 6 March 1984, p. 4.

[195] Darline Kantola, letter to the CBC board, 13 September 1984, p. 2.

in his own personal interests, or administered the property of the corporation to the detriment of the college's future. Such charges can only be sustained if evidence is produced to invalidate the facts contained in official documents surviving among the CBC records. Board members have pointed out that the financial pressure was so severe Fisher would have been justified in doing whatever he had to do to meet his responsibilities as president.[196] But the fact remains, Don Fisher was falsely accused of financial mismanagement, gross misappropriation of college property, and unauthorized business dealings. The accusations are malicious and specious.

Within church history, the wheat is always accompanied by the tares and there has never been agreement on which is which.[197] Both could be found flourishing within the CBC garden. The particular episodes forming the history of the college illuminate a larger story of transformation, theological conflict, and reform, characteristic of Christianity. This is evident in Roman Catholicism, the LCMS, SBC, at Fuller Seminary, and the UPC. The plight of the separatist and the attempt to engage with the historic stream of Christianity is part of the foundation of this story. On a prosaic level, "a very good school" failed because it was hobbled by an unresolvable internecine leadership struggle.[198] That is only a partial explanation. It is more accurate to say that Don Fisher attempted to capture the intellect of his students in such a way as to transform their thinking about God, life, church, and religious experience. He believed that it was intellectual betrayal to surrender to easy answers, insisting that the primary obligation must always be to truth. He sought to create a paradigm to enable them to understand faith and its practice in a profoundly new way. He inculcated the conviction in his students that one must never argue towards a predetermined conclusion, but instead follow the truth wherever it led. Along with a number of his colleagues, Fisher eschewed teaching that did not encourage intellectual progress but instead reinforced a form of emotional conviction. The dissenters believed that creative transformation was required in order for faith to be

---

[196] Norman Rutzen interview, 27 September 2013.
[197] Marsden, *Reforming Fundamentalism*, p. 261.
[198] Frank LaCrosse interview, 16 January 2001.

more than loyalty to ideas of the past. Area pastors and denominational officials considered such philosophy dangerous and incongruous with the faith once delivered to the saints, now articulated and defended by the UPC. Equally alarming was the fact that Joseph Howell's booklist was circulated at CBC and there were students who began building personal libraries based on Howell's list. Some of these same individuals concluded that the dominant UPC tradition constituted an escape from history.[199] Don Fisher's philosophy of education, Dan Lewis' essay "Escape from History," and Howell's booklist, combined with the teaching themes of C.H. Yadon and Jerry Dillon, were seeds that, once planted in the soil of JCM and CBC, produced a diverse crop and must be considered part of the legacy of college education in the UPC.

5.24 Norman Rutzen with Nathaniel Urshan, Portland, Oregon, 5 June 1980

5.25 Rutzen at the controversial CBC banquet, Salem, Oregon, 1 March 1982. See Appendix 15, p. 453

Two years after Don Fisher resigned the presidency, Norman Rutzen presented a formal motion to the CBC College Board that

---

[199] "Escape from History: An Exploration into Oneness Pentecostal Roots and Being," "wasn't intended to be distributed. I shared a copy with a couple of JCM faculty members who were friends (Joe Howell, Jim Wilkins, Mark Roberts), and a copy went into a vertical file in the JCM library, where we tended to put things we had written but not published as a collection point primarily among ourselves as theology faculty. I believe students discovered this file, and copies were made." Dan Lewis, letter to Thomas A. Fudge, 17 April 2013.

the board "go on record that no one can now or hereafter resurrect Conquerors Bible College and that the CBC board of directors have and do hereby permanently retire Conquerors Bible College with all honors due its great history." The board passed a motion that the CBC corporation be dissolved not later than 30 June 1985.[200] By that time all that was left was memory and rubble. What remains now, is to return to the larger picture of the roiling drama which surrounded Don Fisher and CBC and subject both topics to critical evaluation.

5.26  Remains of the original CBC campus, March 1985, looking north

---

[200] *Minutes*, CBC Board of Directors meeting, 8 April 1985, pp. 2 and 3.

# 6

# Chronicles of Destruction

*It is the path we all must take,*
*over the Bridge of Sighs into Eternity.*[1]

From some insider perspectives, the taking down of Don Fisher constituted nothing less than a "vicious and personal" vendetta which seemed to begin as soon as he reached Portland.

> We immediately were confronted with a well organized and unethical opposition. Vindictiveness was directed at us because we happened to be related to those already branded as heretics, Don Fisher and Dan Lewis. The next months were some of the most stressful and heartbreaking of our entire lives. As Jerry [Peden] attended meeting after meeting with Don Fisher and watched the inquisition, he determined that he would never allow himself to be subjected to such torture. Heresy charges were made but unsubstantiated ... When we traveled to represent the college for student recruitment our 'sins' had gone before us. We were refused access to camp meetings in some states. In other areas, we were deliberately not recognized though other Bible colleges were recognised. Insinuation and innuendo followed our recruitment efforts.[2]

Others agreed. "I really feel that a lot of it was a personal vendetta against Don Fisher by some of them. In fact I know in one case it was."[3] Fisher confided that the degree of pressure on him was enormous.[4] Some of the CBC faculty were aware of the magnitude

---

[1] Kierkegaard's journal for 1837, quoted in Joakim Garff, *Søren Kierkegaard: A Biography*, trans., Bruce H. Kirmmse (Princeton: Princeton University Press, 2005), p. 115.

[2] Esther Peden, quoted in Lewis, *The Journey Out*, pp. 66-67, and Esther Peden interview, 7 October 2013.

[3] George Sponsler interview, 12 February 1999. Heresy issues predominated.

[4] E.W. Yadon interview, 25 July 2013. This disclosure came at the same time Fisher preached on grace during the Idaho camp meeting in 1981.

of the forces marshalled against him.[5] The grim politics of power triumphed. Heresy hunters found what they were looking for and the witch-hunters prevailed. Don Fisher was finally removed from every place of persuasion and evicted from the several education programs sponsored by the UPC. Within the Southern Baptist

6.1   Paul Pressler at the Southern Baptist Convention Annual Meeting, in Houston, Texas, June 2013

Convention, Paul Pressler publicly announced in September 1980 that the fundamentalists were "going for the jugular" in their campaign to expel liberals.[6] That sentiment was evident in Portland. Hopelessly weak on the essential message and seemingly beyond all resuscitation, the death sentence was pronounced and the history of CBC came to a close.

Some were satisfied. "Because of the way it was going, I have said all along I was glad it was closed."[7] The UPC was better off for

---

[5] Roger Yadon interview, 8 October 2013.

[6] Shurden and Shepley, eds., *Going for the Jugular: A Documentary History of the SBC Holy War*, pp. 4 and 56.

[7] Barry King interview, 20 January 1999. King specified doctrinal issues.

the departure of Don Fisher. In the minds of the radicals it was the will of God for CBC to close. The LCMS felt that the Seminex episode only strengthened Missouri claims to truth and divine blessing.[8] The movement birthed by Paul Pressler and Paige Patterson to drive liberals from the SBC was a fulfilment of divine commandment and the election of Adrian Rogers as the will of God.[9] There were alternative views expressing that the demise of CBC was "a great loss."[10] Some thought the college had been "very important" for the Northwest region, while others concluded "the school was very, very important to the entire fellowship."[11] Men who had long ceased to support the college regarded its demise as "a tragedy and a half" and said they felt "terrible" about the whole thing.[12] Long-time faculty members described the closure of the college as the most traumatic event in their lives.[13]

There are always terrible costs to be sustained by the institution that suppresses internal dissent. Mixed feelings also characterized the closing of ranks within other Christian denominations. As regrettable as it seemed to some, the majority of Missouri Synod Lutherans believed those who formed Seminex needed to go. Southern Baptist ministers and professors who refused to subscribe to inerrancy were considered corrosive to the faith and had to be removed. In reflecting on the days of crisis within the Southern Baptist Convention, Albert Mohler concluded that the needed reform of his denomination was achieved "at an incredibly high cost."[14] In the days leading up to the housecleaning in Missouri, suspected heretics suggested that Jacob Preus used the fear of false doctrine as a weapon to consolidate power, and later writers suggest

---

[8] Zimmerman, *A Seminary in Crisis*, pp. 139-141.

[9] Shurden and Shepley, eds., *Going for the Jugular: A Documentary History of the SBC Holy War*, pp. 163 and 271.

[10] Nathaniel Urshan interview, 23 April 1999, and Enoch Hutcheson interview, 20 August 2013.

[11] Edwin Judd interview, 10 April 1999, and Ralph V. Reynolds interview, 13 December 1999.

[12] Paul Dugas interview, 25 January 1999.

[13] Darline (Kantola) Royer interview, 15 August 2013.

[14] Albert Mohler, "The Southern Baptist Reformation—A First-Hand Account" (2006). The text is available at http://www.albertmohler.com/2006/06/14/the-southern-baptist-reformation-a-first-hand-account/

this was connected to a politically-driven agenda which was then related to larger social anxieties of the 1960s and 70s.[15] Reflecting on the holy war within the SBC, journalist and former White House press secretary Bill Moyers described Paul Pressler as a "secular politician who has infected this Christian fellowship with the partisan tactics of malice, manipulation, and untruth."[16] Within the UPC it is difficult to see language about truth, faith, and theology as anything other than a cover-up for uses of power. Defenders of tradition appear to have won the main battles within the UPC, the Southern Baptist Convention, and the Missouri Synod. Roman Catholicism also successfully pushed back the modernists and it is questionable to claim that the second Vatican Council allowed the heretics to ultimately claim victory especially in light of negative curial decisions in the 1970s and 1980s concerning Charles Curran (1934-), Edward Schillebeeckx (1914-2009), Hans Küng (1928-) and even more recent suspects in the conflict between established authority and new ideas. After all, the decretal *Lamentabili* made unflinchingly clear that the Vatican claimed the papal office alone possessed the authority to determine both theological truth as well as the proper interpretation of scripture. That was in 1907. Nothing thereafter suggested otherwise. The situation at Fuller Theological Seminary ended differently. Under the administration of David Hubbard the institution moved even farther away from its roots.

Many saw the action against Fisher as necessary, even desirable. Still others regarded his treatment at the hands of the various boards as persecution and "reprehensible."[17] In 1977, a Christian company produced a short film called *John Hus* starring Rod Colbin (1923-2007) in the lead role.[18] At the initiative of Dan Lewis, this film was shown at JCM in the spring of 1981 and apparently created

---

[15] Tietjen, *Memoirs in Exile: Confessional Hope and Institutional Conflict*, p. 26, and Burkee, *Power, Politics, and the Missouri Synod: A Conflict that Changed American Christianity*, p. 59. See the outline on pp. 9-10.

[16] Quoted in Shurden and Shepley, eds., *Going for the Jugular: A Documentary History of the SBC Holy War*, pp. 242-243.

[17] Michael Nigh interview, 18 August 2013.

[18] Faith for Today, Vision Video, and Gateway Films are associated with the production. It was awarded "best film of the year" distinction by the Christian Film Distributors Association, and Colbin received the best actor award.

a sensation. Jan Hus (1371-1415) was a late medieval Czech priest who became the target of numerous heresy accusations. Hus was excommunicated multiple times, tried, and then burned as a heretic.

6.2 The burning of Jan Hus. Prague, National Museum Library MS IV B 24, fol. 38ᵛ. (Jena Codex)

6.3 Jan Hus at the Luther Monument, Worms, Germany. Designed by Ernst Rietschel, 1868

Parallels between Hus and Fisher were drawn at Jackson. Thomas Craft was unhappy that Hus was portrayed as a genuine Christian, since he clearly was not baptised in Jesus' name, never received the Holy Ghost with evidence of speaking in other tongues, remained committed to the doctrine of the trinity, and did not adopt standards of holiness compatible with truths espoused by the UPC. Some of the JCM students began comparing the aggressive members of the Council of Constance who destroyed Hus with Craft himself.[19] The same film was screened at the CBC winter retreat at Camp McGruder in Rockaway, Oregon on 30 January 1982, and then again during the next academic year.[20] The second occasion was held at the Public Utility District (PUD) building at the Fort Vancouver Way and East Mill Plain Boulevard intersection

---

[19] Lewis, *The Journey Out*, p. 37. Dan Lewis, letter to Thomas A. Fudge, 6 February 2013. FC, inv.doc.no 0707-4721-32.

[20] *Ensign*, vol. 29 (1982), p. 101, and *CBC Jubilation* 16 (No.1, 1982), p. 4.

near downtown Vancouver, before a large gathering comprised of college staff and students and the Christ for the People Community Church membership. While there were no overt comparisons drawn at CBC as there had been at Jackson, the Hus trial later figured into characterizations of what had happened to Fisher.[21]

There are ironies. Many Northwest pastors had no wish for their young men and women to be exposed to Don Fisher, CBC "worldliness," and the corrupting liberal emphases at the college.[22] Area churches supporting the college, especially those pastored by Sponsler and Brokaw, were regarded as too worldly.[23] But if the majority of the Portland pastors were opposed to CBC, Fisher likewise did not want students coming under the influence of men like Barry King and Paul Dugas, since he believed that the doctrine and attitudes of such men were counter-productive to his vision at CBC. This stance was regarded as an example of Fisher simply "defying all of them."[24] Fisher took no note of such opinion and faculty colleagues suggested that Fisher "was not intimidated by the wolves in the UPC."[25] Within the Missouri Synod, John Tietjen was formally charged with disobedience.[26] That was predicated upon the assumption that he refused to recognize any human authority.[27] The

---

[21] The Hus film had been privately previewed at CBC before it was shown. *The Journal of Thomas A. Fudge, 1980-1981*, entries for 3 December 1981, 30 January 1982, and 26 February 1983. Elsewhere, Thomas A. Fudge, letter to Harry Scism (copied to Edwin Judd, Robert Rodenbush, J.S. Leaman, Robert McFarland, and Nathaniel Urshan), 13 August 1985, pp. 3-4, where the treatment of Fisher and Wayne Nigh was compared to the fate of Hus. "Peggy [Yelm] called at night. She told me the story about the continued persecution against W. Nigh. Therefore I took it upon myself to write a 4 page letter to the men in St. Louis decrying such ... nonsense." *The Journal of Thomas A. Fudge, 1980-1985*, entry for 13 August 1985.
[22] George Sponsler interview, 12 February 1999, confirmed the perceived idea that CBC was liberal and that this perception remained a prevalent assumption among pastors in Portland. Clyde Barlow interview, 13 August 2013.
[23] Cheryl (Johns) Crousser interview, 1 October 2013 attended Neighborhood Church, pastored by Sponsler, since age twelve and knew the church's reputation.
[24] Cleveland Becton interview, 14 April 1999. Others characterized Fisher as a rule-breaker. Karissa (Fisher) Hopkins interview, 15 August 2013.
[25] Stan Johnson interview, 5 October 2013.
[26] Tietjen, *Memoirs in Exile*, pp. 175-176, and Zimmerman, *A Seminary in Crisis*, p. 110.
[27] Burkee, *Power, Politics, and the Missouri Synod*, p. 143.

Board of Control considered Tietjen's posture a "relentless attack" on the integrity of the church.[28] Don Fisher never learned to accept the politically expedient limited achievement. It was all or nothing.[29] He appeared as one prepared to buck the tide and go against the grain almost as a matter of principle.[30] Shortly after the cessation of CBC, Fisher commented that the buying and selling of loyalty limited opportunities for ministry.[31] Concerned conservatives were keen to marginalize the "spiritual creeps," "stinking skunks," "evil geniuses," and "putrid frogs." Even before the advent of Fisher, certain area pastors did little to disguise their contempt for the college. For example, Barry King (ill.3.9, p. 123) was invited to address a group of senior students at a retreat on the Oregon coast. King brought with him a CBC catalogue, and holding it up as he spoke, proceeded to ridicule education, castigating it as being of little value. Rather than college education, King promoted the local church and pastoral authority.[32] Fisher's open memorandum stated that education "has always been an integral part" of the work of God.[33] Certain elements in area churches tended to subvert the emphases being advanced at the college. This was the historic reasoning behind the urge to establish a single college church.[34] So while the men of the old PCI persuasion in the Northwest looked askance upon the militant missionary mentalities which infiltrated the pastoral culture of toleration, the missionaries were appalled by the rank compromisers and the insufferable "backsliding" they discovered in the Pacific Northwest and they were determined to counter those dangerous elements which were above all things

---

[28] Board of Control, *Exodus from Concordia: A Report on the 1974 Walkout*, p. 61.

[29] Thetus Tenney interview, 6 June 2013.

[30] It was said of Canadian Prime Minister John G. Diefenbaker (1958-63), show him the grain and he'll go against it. Commentators referred to this propensity frequently on the occasion of Diefenbaker's death in 1979.

[31] Reference in Don Fisher, sermon at Christ for the People Community Church, 20 November 1983.

[32] Jerry Dillon interview, 5 January 1999.

[33] *Cascade Bible College 1982-1984 Catalog*, p. 10.

[34] Paul Dugas interview, 25 January 1999, denied that area churches or pastors created problems for the college. Confirmed in Phillip Dugas interview, 23 January 1999. The minutes of CBC board meetings suggest another perspective.

"weak on the message."[35] The "breakdown of regional identities" can be traced to the newcomers who had no roots, no traditions to defend, and whose presence caused great change from the previous non-dogmatic methods and approach in the Northwest.

6.4   C.H. Yadon, Don Fisher, Edwin Judd, and Ellis Scism
at a Missions Conference at CBC, Autumn 1982

UPC colleges might have avoided some of the factionalism that later developed had the idea of national colleges prevailed. This would have meant that the colleges would have enjoyed national endorsement and theoretically been free of local machinations. This concept, however, was rigorously opposed by S.G. [Stuart Green] Norris and C.P. [Clairborne Price] Williams (1898-1979) and never gained traction.[36] It was the divisiveness of doctrinal differences and a lust for power and control which produced an internecine conflict

---

[35] In the late 1970s, neither Winfred Toole nor C.M. Yadon expressed interest in Jerry Peden when the latter contacted them about church ministry possibilities in the Northwest. Jerry Peden interview, 19 July 2002. Clyde Barlow interview, 13 August 2013, thinks the missionary impulse explanation is "100% accurate."
[36] Edwin Judd interview, 10 April 1999.

which destroyed CBC. "Some people want a legacy regardless of the cost."[37] The college "was brought to a conclusion by men who were not Northwest brethren, who were not supportive, and who did not have the same Northwest vision that we had in 1953 when we began that school" (see ill.0.1, p. xviii).[38] Mindful of these transformations, Fisher was warned not to return to Portland.[39] The ultimate fate of the old Northwest, however, according to other interpretations, should be assumed in large measure by CBC itself. The strong missions emphasis increasingly fostered by the college failed to place CBC-trained ministers in the Northwest. This ran counter to its original purpose. As a result, the alumni were scattered. Churches were increasingly pastored by outsiders hostile to the PCI tradition. The children were not close to the mother. Had this trend been reversed, had CBC held to its original purpose, a stronghold for the PCI could have been maintained.[40] That emphasis on foreign missions was fostered especially by Presidents Reynolds, Judd, Klemin and Fisher himself. Others identify Edwin Judd, Darline Kantola, and Wayne Nigh as the central figures in shifting the original college mission of training men and women for work in Northwest churches to overseas missionary activity.[41]

If Barry King was pleased to see the end of CBC, there were others, including R.V. Reynolds himself, who went on record as saying that the college would have continued had he remained as president.[42] The claim is suspect, and questioned even by long time college supporters who believe Fisher inherited a near-hopeless situation.[43] The dire financial crisis which doomed the Fisher administration was well in place under the rule of Reynolds, despite claims that Don Fisher effectively bankrupted the college.[44] Such assertions are mitigated by the fact that on the eve of Fisher's

---

[37] Nathaniel Yadon interview, 15 December 2000.
[38] Wayne Nigh interview, 4 January 2000, Caldwell, Idaho.
[39] Freda Fisher interview, 13 July 2005.
[40] Loren Yadon interview, 3 January 2000, Boise, Idaho.
[41] Loren Yadon interview, 26 July 2013.
[42] Ralph V. Reynolds interview, 13 December 1999.
[43] George Sponsler interview, 12 February 1999, and E.W. Yadon interview, 25 July 2013.
[44] Nathaniel Urshan interview, 23 April 1999, and Thomas Craft interview, 20 April 1999.

appointment, CBC had less than six hundred dollars on hand.[45] Certainly, Reynolds would have had more support in the region than Fisher, but how did Reynolds propose to reduce college debt and return the institution to solvency? Near the end of his administration a financial struggle persisted.[46] During the Reynolds years, CBC indulged in the curious practice of extending financial loans to students already in debt to the school. Many outstanding accounts were never collected. Some of these were held by students who had gone on to ministerial positions in the UPC. Some of those men were utterly hostile to efforts by the college to make good on those loans.[47] More than a decade earlier, a formal effort was inaugurated to try and recover student debt.[48] Harry Fisher voluntarily gave up his salary in order to help the college financially but that contribution was allocated to increase the salary of a particular member of the college administration.[49] There is local testimony that during the Reynolds years, the college experienced significant decline.[50] The tenuous nature of the existence of CBC at the time Fisher came to the helm meant that without a substantial reversal in fortune, the failure of the college itself was inevitable, especially since Fisher had insufficient time to build a significant national support base. It is almost certain that had Ralph Reynolds

---

[45] Financial statements reflect $593.52 on hand at the time. CBC Quarterly Report, 31 March 1981, p. 1. This sum is negated in the same report (p. 2) by accounts payable totaling $3,972.70 and outstanding debts (loans) of $12,700.00.

[46] Ralph V. Reynolds, letter to the CBC board, 9 January 1981.

[47] Esther Peden assumed responsibility for the college book-keeping and this paragraph is based upon her comments made on tape during the Jerry Peden interview, 19 July 2002, and Esther Peden interview, 7 October 2013.

[48] Jerry Dillon was instructed to develop a strategy, which he did. *Minutes*, CBC board meeting, 14 December 1972 and his *pro forma* letter dated 10 April 1973 which he proposed sending to the student, the parents, local church pastor, and the relevant district superintendent. *Minutes*, CBC board meeting, 8 June 1973, p. 3. The process was adopted but also met with limited success.

[49] Harry and Freda Fisher interview, 8 December 2000. Freda Fisher was the college bookkeeper and in a position to know that a member of the college administration's salary was immediately increased to the precise amount as a result. Inasmuch as there may be relevant factors unknown to the Fishers and to the author, I have chosen not to identify the staff member.

[50] Paul Dugas interview, 25 January 1999.

remained as president the college is unlikely to have survived more than one to two further years.

By the late 1970s, the prevailing climate in the Northwest was so acrimonious that a continued cooperative initiative around the college itself was no longer possible.[51] George Eads (1912-2000) expressed alarm. (See ill.0.1, p. xviii. Eads is in the fifth row, sixth from the left.) The history of CBC might have turned out differently had there been an alternative philosophy of leadership, though the argument remains conjecture. In 1978, Jerry Dillon left CBC because he was convinced the college was doomed. This assumption was based upon the fact that for several years previous to 1978, there had been a "steady and increasing resistance towards the college" and an erosion of support. President John Klemin was a man of integrity whose character was above reproach. Unlike many of the Portland area pastors, Klemin was not afraid of inquiry and encouraged it. But even his staunchest supporters felt he could

6.5  John E. Klemin, while     6.6  Klemin and E.G. Moyer in the CBC
president of CBC, 1977            chapel, Winter 1982

have fought harder against the anti-CBC coalition. Unfortunately, Klemin did not possess the necessary stamina to stand against the

[51] Noted in Norman Rutzen interview, 24 July 2013, and Darline (Kantola) Royer interview, 15 August 2013.

vocal outsiders and the missionaries who had been dispatched to save the Northwest. Klemin exercised a passive form of leadership and was not forceful with either the College Board or the local pastors. John Klemin failed CBC by not taking a firmer hold of the reins and moving the college forward. Unlike Fisher, Klemin was not fast on his feet and this might help to explain his numerous changes of heart on various issues already noted. By 1976, Dillon was considering leaving the college and by 1978, he believed that CBC no longer had a viable future.[52] Far too many enemies had marshalled at the college gates.[53] Critics of the college perceived Dillon as a definite problem, who allegedly caroused with students, participated in boxing with them, allowed students to fire guns from the back doors of dorms, and was generally permissive. In terms of theology, his name became a lightning rod: "Well, now! I liked him but I know he went wild."[54] Had a more forceful and decisive leader been appointed after C.H. Yadon resigned in 1971, the history of CBC may have been quite different, but Yadon recommended John Klemin, who was unanimously elected on the nominating ballot.[55] Don Fisher regretted Yadon's resignation as Oregon District Superintendent in 1975 because it meant a decrease in the "stabilizing influence which [Yadon had] so capably given over the years."[56] A variety of relatively minor factors might have caused CBC to attain a significant presence in the Northwest generally and in Portland specifically. Some thought it regrettable that Edwin Judd had not remained in the president's office.[57]

In a historical irony, the CBC Board of Directors contacted Don Fisher in 1971 about the presidency. Fisher declined. Had he come to Portland ten years earlier, before the ethos of the old Northwest essentially vanished, his tenure at the college would

---

[52] Jerry Dillon, letter to Kenneth Haney, 6 January 1976, wherein he states he is ready for a change of ministry. FC, inv.doc.no 0707-5120-34.

[53] Jerry Dillon interview, 19 April 2013.

[54] Paul Dugas interview, 25 January 1999. The assertion about the use of firearms is questionable, inasmuch as the college had banned their presence on campus. *Minutes*, CBC board meeting, 3 June 1971. FC, inv.doc.no 0707-5154-34. The alleged incidents in question may have occurred prior to that date.

[55] *Minutes*, CBC board meeting, 3 June 1971. FC, inv.doc.no 0707-5154-34.

[56] Don Fisher, letter to C.H. Yadon, 18 April 1975. FC, inv.doc.no 0707-3087-21.

[57] Jerry Dillon interview, 5 January 1999.

doubtless have been different. But Fisher did not respond to the opportunity and John Klemin was appointed. A second effort was made to bring Don Fisher back to CBC. When Arlo Moehlenpah resigned as Dean-Registrar in March 1976, M.D. Padfield, Wendell Gleason, Phillip Dugas, Rich Mincer, and Don Fisher were advanced as candidates. While he did come to Portland that same year (see ill.8.1, p. 464), Fisher declined.[58] Mincer's candidacy was thwarted early on when Nathaniel Urshan wrote to John Klemin alleging a breach of ministerial ethics and complaining of a slight to his pastoral authority, inasmuch as he had not been consulted about options being considered at CBC. Jerry Dillon's response to the matter was marked with irritation.[59] Mincer was unaware of these developments until 1979.[60] A third attempt was made later that year when John Klemin indicated he wished to step down. Don Fisher, Allen Ellis, and J.R. Ensey were considered, in that order of preference. Once again, Fisher decided not to return to the west coast.[61] It appeared that Don Fisher's name came up whenever there were crises at CBC in the 1970s, and he was frequently perceived as the proverbial savior, with the lament "if only Don Fisher were here." During this third period of consideration over bringing Fisher to Portland, Klemin changed his mind anyway and decided to remain as president.[62] Around the same time, Klemin told Jerry Dillon that he could envision Dillon as the next president of CBC. As noted earlier, others thought the appointment should have fallen to Raymond Sirstad.[63] In the end, neither man was ever seriously considered at board level. Despite his mounting and ultimately insurmountable frustration and interest in leaving the college, Jerry Dillon testified more than twenty years later that "the

---

[58] *Minutes*, CBC board meetings, 31 March 1976 (FC, inv.doc.no 0707-5175-34), and 11 June 1976.

[59] Jerry W. Dillon, letter to Nathaniel Urshan, 22 December 1976. FC, inv.doc.no 0707-5134-34. Klemin approved the letter.

[60] Rich Mincer interview, 27 September 2013. Mincer was later sought after by JCM for a similar position during the Fisher years but Urshan likewise concealed this expression of interest from Mincer.

[61] *Minutes*, CBC board meeting, 5 November 1976, p. 1.

[62] John Klemin, letter to the CBC board, 21 January 1977. FC, inv.doc.no 0707-5178-34. This is another example of Klemin's vascillation.

[63] David Reynolds interview, 12 August 2013.

very finest years of my life were spent at CBC."[64] His eventual letter
of resignation prompted an overwhelming appeal for Dillon to
remain at CBC including board approval, a student petition, and a
personal appeal by John Klemin.[65]

Criticism of men like Dillon, Fisher, Howell, and Lewis often
centred on the accusations that they violated the trust placed in
them by the college and the UPC and that their teaching was not
only subversive but also unethical. There were similar concerns
openly expressed within the Missouri Synod Lutheran Church, the
Southern Baptist Convention, and at Fuller Seminary. The rejoinder
to that general accusation has been that failing to teach the truth as
they understood it was in effect to frustrate the grace of God.[66]
Detractors admitted the possibility of "sincere motives" on the part
of Fisher, Lewis, and Howell, but ideological collisions were
unavoidable. Dan Lewis "was a heretic ... Joe [Howell] was a heretic
too." Mark Roberts was influenced quite a bit by Fisher, so "he's a
heretic too." Jim Wilkins "was with them but he had a different
frame of mind." Others at JCM such as Carl Adams, Gene Dillon,
Jewell (Yadon) Dillon, and Darrell Johns, while not teachers of
theology, were regarded as sympathetic to Fisher's approach and
from time to time were suspected of less than solid loyalty to UPC
doctrine. Johns later changed his mind and put his support behind
Craft. Don Fisher, of course, was the ringleader of the heretics,
who rode into Jackson inside a theological Trojan horse. What he
was trying to do was "absolutely, one hundred percent, one

---

[64] The second half of this paragraph is based upon Jerry Dillon interview, 5
January 1999.
[65] Jerry Dillon, letter (of resignation) to John Klemin, dated 11 May 1978. FC,
inv.doc.no 0707-5126-34. Klemin tried to dissuade Dillon from leaving the
college and the CBC board refused to accept Dillon's resignation by a vote of
seven in favor, one opposed, and one abstention. John Klemin, letter to the CBC
board, 8 June 1978, p. 1 (FC, inv.doc.no 0707-5181-34), and *Minutes*, CBC board
meeting, 8 June 1978, p.1. FC, inv.doc.no 0707-5183-34. A student petition
circulated dated 7 June 1978 and signed by at least thirty-six students. FC,
inv.doc.no 0707-5127-34. A few weeks after Dillon departed, Klemin also
tendered his resignation. John Klemin, letter to the CBC board, 28 August 1978.
FC, inv.doc.no 0707-5184-34. Klemin's comment about a Dillon presidency
never advanced to board level.
[66] Dan Lewis interview, 6 April 1999.

hundred and eighty degrees different from what the organization was ... [Fisher] had an agenda that was adverse to anything in the United Pentecostal Church." Thomas Craft ruefully reflected on the "Jackson tragedy," admitting "I made some mistakes by getting the wrong faculty."[67] These were the occupants of the Trojan horse.

Some of those criticised for undermining UPC doctrine point out that while they were aware of some of the implications of their theological inquiries, they had sought counsel on the matter from others. For example, at CBC, Jerry Dillon actively sought out Oregon District superintendent Winfred Toole, Oregon District secretary David Johnson, and college president John Klemin to take their advice on his theological direction. None of these men suggested he cease his doctrinal investigations and each admitted there was value in what he was doing. Naturally, these were private admissions and whispered admonitions. Publicly, some of these men participated in character assassinations. Dillon felt betrayed by the lack of frankness and the duplicity which followed.[68]

Which is more important in college life and education, leaders or guards? Leadership implies the provision of direction when exploring new territory. Remaining on familiar ground requires no leadership. It seems that guards would be a more useful designation for those in authority in the UPC. Guards protect, but leaders take people where they have never been before.[69] Tradition does not encourage curiosity. It does not require faith. Instead, it demands blind obedience. It is useful to ponder the perspective that it is illegitimate to teach contrary to the articles of faith in a UPC college. Don Fisher and his colleagues were accused of doing just that. According to UPC national officials, Bible colleges have three

---

[67] Thomas Craft interview, 20 April 1999. Craft's assessment of Wilkins is quite wrong. I used the "heretic" nomenclature in the interview and by it both Craft and I meant deviance from UPC doctrine. There was absolutely no rancor on Craft's part in the use of the word. Roberts has distanced himself from Lewis and Howell in terms of theological acumen during the JCM era, noting they were well ahead of him in terms of their own thinking and development. Mark Roberts interview, 5 May 1999. The term "Jackson tragedy" or "Jackson disaster" seems to have been a common phrase to describe the college during the Fisher era. Larry Snyder interview, 5 May 1999.
[68] Jerry Dillon interview, 19 April 2013.
[69] Marler, *Imprisoned in the Brotherhood*, p. 17.

objectives: first, to provide sound basic Bible training, second, to train men and women for specific ministries, and third, to broaden the educational and intellectual capabilities of the student. Each of

6.7  The author, C.H. Yadon, James G. Fudge, and Norman Rutzen, Middleton, Idaho, June 1993, around the time Yadon and Rutzen left the UPC

these must be undertaken with a specific view towards UPC doctrines. The Fisher program appeared to focus only on the third. Can this be justified? It is possible that Fisher and his colleagues discovered themselves on an intellectual journey and it is equally possible they did not realize precisely when they moved beyond UPC orthodoxy or just how far they departed from that tradition.[70] If they did know where they were situated, was their conduct indefensible? It is also possible that the departures of men such as Dan Lewis and Joseph Howell in the spring of 1981, indicated they knew they had reached a place where they could no longer teach at JCM with integrity.[71]

---

[70] Sandra Blevins interview, 11 April 1999.

[71] On issues of legitimacy and the role of Bible colleges, I rely upon David Bernard interview, 16 April 1999. Dan Lewis left the UPC in 1981, but two years earlier had departed mentally and spiritually. *The Journey Out*, p. 11.

The Westberg Resolution of 1992 within the UPC might be regarded as a parallel. Even among many ministers who signed the affirmation, there was conviction that it violated either the spirit of

6.8   Leonard E. Westberg, Junction City, Kansas, 24 April 1999

the merger or the merger agreement itself. Robert A. Sabin (ill.6.13, p. 348) and Raymond A. Beesley were two leaders who assumed outspoken opposition to the Westberg initiative. C.H. Yadon and his colleagues were effectively "forced out" of the church, while Kenneth Haney was absolutely wrong to fire Loren Yadon from the faculty of Christian Life College.[72] C.H. Yadon declared that he had lived by the merger agreement and his refusal to sign the Westberg Resolution was a decision consistent with the spirit of the merger. Near the end of his long life, he publicly affirmed that he was glad he had nothing to do with an initiative that only divided

---

[72] Arless Glass interview, 24 September 2013, made strong affirmations on both Yadons and told Haney personally how he felt about Loren Yadon. Glass supported the controversial sermon preached by Loren Yadon in 1993. On the matter of Yadon's termination from Christian Life College, George Sponsler advised Yadon "not to get a Christian attorney, but one who was the dirtiest, and meanest, who would sue these fellows [Haney and his lieutenants] for all their worth." Loren Yadon, letter to Thomas A. Fudge, 15 June 2005, p. 2, reflecting Sponsler's verbal admonitions. FC, inv.doc.no 0707-4105-28.

and destroyed.[73] No one could contest that ministers had the right in the UPC to preach a three-step plan of salvation predicated upon Acts 2:38. That conviction had been part of the PAJC perspective in 1945. By the same token, ministers had every right to teach a

6.9  Don Fisher and CBC students, 1982-83 academic year. *Back row:* Renee Hills, Fisher, Joe Higgins, Michael Nigh, Thomas A. Fudge, Daniel Sirstad, Audrey Zapalac. *Front row:* Jay Nacino, Deborah Beaulieu, Peggy Yelm, Lori Falwell, Eric K. Loy

doctrine of salvation which placed water and spirit baptism *after* salvation. That was a point of view espoused by the PCI in 1945. Both ideas were sanctioned by the merger agreement. For one school of thought to force the other either to conform or leave the fellowship altogether appears to be a serious breach of historic UPC principles. Perhaps it would have been more ethical for those supporting the Westberg Resolution to have left the organization rather than to have remained, contending for their views to the disunity of the body of Christ and in so doing acting against the

---

[73] C.H. Yadon, sermon "Now and Then," Valley Pentecostal Church, Caldwell, Idaho, 22 June 1997, audio recording. FC, inv.doc.no 0707-3156-22.

articles of faith. If Fisher, Lewis, Howell, Roberts, Dillon, the Yadons, and their supporters were engaged in illegitimate teaching activities, it is also fair to say that Leonard Westberg (1925-2001), David Gray (1917-1996), and Paul Price (1922-), together with their followers should also be censured. That suggestion, however, carried no weight within the UPC. Collisions were unavoidable between those who strove for unity and those who identified doctrinal purity as the main objective.[74]

Finally, on the idea that certain members of the JCM and CBC faculties were betraying the trust placed in them by parents and pastors who sent young people to those colleges, it is important to point out that the students in question were not children. They were adults. Admittedly young adults, in most cases, but adults nonetheless. They were old enough to own and drive cars, hold down employment, live away from home, marry, have children, and exhibit certain levels of independence. To suggest they needed protection from ideas is absurd. That type of approach fosters only a regrettable eternal childhood of the believer mentality. Individuals requiring that type of protective custody would be better served by living at home with their parents and remaining in their local church Sunday School. Fisher and some of his colleagues, at Jackson and later in Portland, tried to advance critical thinking. They were viewed with distrust by their denomination.[75] It is quite possible that Fisher was prepared to run the risk of being viewed as subversive or dishonest, believing as he did that the end justified the means.[76] He likewise taught that sometimes the things which frighten most can bring the pilgrim to the place of greatest safety.

There is another angle to be considered. The stream of thinking within the UPC which had been shaped by the PAJC tradition tended to regard truth as settled and unassailable. There were others who believed there was clear precedent in the movement for a considerably broader and more evangelical statement of Christian

[74] Reed, *"In Jesus' Name,"* p. 363.
[75] Men like Loren Yadon and T.F. Tenney thought that what was happening at JCM was dishonest, and Yadon once expressed his concern to Dan Lewis and also attended a seminar at JCM wherein Fisher appeared to challenge UPC doctrine. Loren Yadon interview, 26 July 2013.
[76] Liddy, *Will*, pp. 383-384.

theology, particularly as it came through the avenue of the PCI
influence. Fisher, Lewis, Howell, Dillon, and many of the Yadons
considered this was certainly a historically verifiable aspect of the
movement's history, though that was generally denied by those who
adhered to the PAJC persuasion. CBC stood in the PCI perspective
and Fisher imported that into JCM. Fisher and his colleagues did
not see any disjunction in identifying with this part of UPC history,
and in particular with people like Howard A. Goss and C. H.
Yadon. This could not be construed as subversive or disloyal.
Instead, the attempt to revise UPC history by expunging certain
parts of that history as though it had never existed was itself
dishonest. Lewis and Howell in particular recognized this. Lewis
warned about attempting to escape from history and Howell saw
the limitations of a hermeneutic which failed to take into account
the breadth of its own context. Beyond this, C.H. Yadon, Jerry
Dillon, Don Fisher, Dan Lewis, and Joseph Howell believed that
ideas of truth had to take clear precedence over denominational
preference for particular (PAJC) points of view. Goss and his
colleagues in the 1940s had discussed this and concluded there was
sufficient common ground that they were prepared to tolerate
existing differences. That approach was adopted both at JCM and
at CBC. To suggest that Fisher and certain members of his faculty
were being dishonest with respect to the expectations of pastors
and parents who sent their young people to those colleges
presupposes that all pastors and parents were loyal to the PAJC
point of view. This is untrue. An argument can be mounted and
sustained that what Fisher was doing was historically honest in the
face of concerted revisionism.[77]

In spite of these arguments, there was fear that the Fisher
philosophy would lead students astray. This suggests a basic
insecurity in the UPC beliefs system. Ministers worry about their
young people facing unbearable pressure and criticism of their
beliefs in secular institutions where faith is thought to be assailed by
humanism and atheism. "The number of young people who lose
their faith while attending secular colleges is a problem of major

---

[77] This paragraph is based partially on comments in Dan Lewis, letter to Thomas
A. Fudge, 10 August 2013. FC, inv.doc.no 0707-5266-34.

concern to thoughtful pastors."[78] Don Fisher shared the perspective that "we seem afraid that our ideas and beliefs cannot stand the test of these new ideas."[79] Jonathan Livingston Seagull had no fear of learning and Fisher cultivated that attitude.[80] However, the question of ethics and integrity in the educational programs at Jackson and Portland should be carefully scrutinized. Lingering fears of contamination persisted. In the 1970s, the CBC board passed a motion allowing students to simultaneously take courses at secular colleges and universities. That motion was later challenged on the grounds that such exposure to "ungodly instructors" might send students down a wrong road ending only in "charred ruins" and "disgrace."[81] What is patently clear is that the core philosophy of education espoused by Don Fisher was an approach with few built-in safeguards. That reality cannot be ignored. Albert Schweitzer underscored the danger. "If thought is to set out on its journey unhampered, it must be prepared for anything, even for arrival at intellectual agnosticism."[82] I do not believe that Fisher found this possibility threatening. After all, he claimed to believe in the work of the Holy Spirit in the life of the believer and he was committed to the principle that the strongest faith was the examined faith. He urged his students to pay attention, to think critically, to use their mental faculties, to take responsibility for their lives and faith, to pursue truth and if necessary to change their viewpoints. He refused to encourage people to remain trapped by expectations of what their lives ought to be as determined by men and women who considered themselves "experts" on such matters. Above all, he

---

[78] Arless Glass, "The Value of a Bible College Education" *The Pentecostal Herald* 62 (No. 4, 1987), pp. 2-3 and also Glass, "A United Pentecostal Education" *The Pentecostal Herald* 61 (No. 2, 1986), p. 3.

[79] Marler, *Imprisoned in the Brotherhood*, p. 31.

[80] Bach, *Jonathan Livingston Seagull*, p. 60.

[81] *Minutes*, CBC board meeting, 31 March 1976, p. 1, for the motion (FC, inv.doc.no 0707-5175-34) and John Klemin, letter to CBC board, 21 May 1976 for the challenge. The college later attempted an evening program. Advertisement in *The Oregonian*, 1 October 1977, p. 22. Several years later Norman Rutzen suggested that students be permitted to live on campus but attend other colleges part-time. *Minutes*, executive meeting, CBC board, 6 November 1980.

[82] Albert Schweitzer, *The Decay and Restoration of Civilization*, pt 1: *The Philosophy of Civilization* (London: A&C Black, 1923), p. 104.

emphasized trust in the work of the Holy Spirit. His views were neither new nor original.

Fisher utilized a variety of means to encourage higher-level thinking. Around 1977, while preaching in the JCM chapel, he utilised Tony Campolo's provocative illustration about values. Campolo sometimes told audiences that thousands of children had died the previous night around the world from hunger and many Christians really did not give a damn. "In fact some of you are more upset that I said 'damn' than you are that thousands of kids died of hunger last night."[83] Some feared their sons or daughters might become heretics by means of education. Addressing such concerns, reformers long before Fisher had this to say: "well, you have to take that chance ... Young and tender trees are more easily bent ... and some may break in the process."[84] The ethos at CBC seemed less concerned with that possibility and more focused on the pathway of faith and learning. After all, the strongest faith was the examined faith. That conviction characterized CBC classrooms. Don Fisher never wearied of making that point. Inevitably, there would be unforeseen or unintended outcomes. For example, John Henry Newman (1801-1890) converted from the Church of England to Roman Catholicism in 1845 and was later made a cardinal. What prompted such a journey? He was a scholar who had spent years carefully studying Greek texts in the library. This discipline and commitment became the foundation for theological decisions.

Don Fisher was a man easily glorified or vilified. He was a polarizing figure who inspired admiration and loyalty on one hand, while on the other he seemed able to elicit loathing and hatred. The paradox is not especially unusual. Cliff Mitchell (1954-2012) came to CBC from South Dakota in the fall of 1981. "He fell in love with Don Fisher ... and never once regretted his decision ... it was that decision that not only changed him but challenged him."[85] That

---

[83] April Purtell interview, 13 April 2013. The word "damn" was sometimes replaced with a stronger expletive to draw an even finer point on the argument.

[84] Martin Luther, *Eine Predigt dass man Kinder zur Schulen halten solle* (A Sermon on the necessity of educating children), in WA, vol. 30, pt 2, pp. 517-588 which dates to 1530.

[85] Paula G. Mitchell, letter to Thomas A. Fudge, 6 March 2013. FC, inv.doc.no 0707-4949-33.

process of being changed and challenged was one that many JCM and CBC students experienced. Whether it was the presence of the Holy Spirit, or Fisher's passion for Christ, or personal charisma, some regarded Fisher as a latter-day St. Paul.[86] Other students testified "we almost worshipped Don."[87] There were many times in CBC classrooms when his passion for Christ and the kingdom of God would cause Fisher to be almost in tears as he taught.[88] Some faculty colleagues admitted they were mesmerized by Fisher.[89] Some family members considered him a "benevolent dictator."[90]

He was regarded by others as the devil incarnate. Fisher could be kind, generous, and patient but paradoxically he also had a propensity for running "roughshod" over those he perceived to be in the way of his vision.[91] According to close associates, he could be "pushy" or "harsh," perhaps even manipulative; he was "hot-tempered" and sometimes displayed a "rough edge."[92] Mood swings and a certain propensity towards being highly-strung was supposed by one colleague to be a result of hypoglycaemia.[93] Fisher possessed an unpredictable temper that was often triggered by mysterious causes and produced violent outbursts which terrified his children.[94] He could be magnanimous when one expected dismissal or punishment, but inexplicably in other circumstances he could be severe even to the point of inhumanity. Fisher could be short-fused and even rude to those he found difficult to tolerate.[95] His years in

---

[86] April Purtell interview, 13 April 2013.

[87] Jim Wilkins interview, 1 May 1999. Some former CBC students continue to consider their connections to Fisher significant. For example, Michael Nigh interview, 18 August 2013.

[88] Lori (Falwell) Callan interview, 23 September 2013.

[89] Jewel (Yadon) Dillon interview, 24 July 2013.

[90] Susan (Fisher) Paynter interview, 26 August 2013, Vancouver, Washington.

[91] Testimonies to this include Donna Fisher interview, 3 January 1999, and Darline (Kantola) Royer interview, 15 August 2013.

[92] Jerry Peden interview, 19 July 2002, and Jim Wilkins interview, 1 May 1999. Susan (Fisher) Paynter interview, 24 January 1999, agreed that her father could be manipulative. Freda Fisher interview, 13 July 2005 noted he could be a bit sharp with his own parents from time to time.

[93] Thomas Craft interview, 20 April 1999. This was never medically confirmed.

[94] Ronna (Fisher) Russell interview, 20 July 2013.

[95] April Purtell interview, 16 January 1999.

the south seemed to have left him with a "hard spirit."[96] Those who worked with Fisher in Oregon and previously in Mississippi noted differences in him which might be put down to the toll exacted from him as a result of protracted conflict and acrimonious controversy.[97] From time to time he was an absent, negligent, and abusive father who engendered fear in his family.[98]

There were also inexplicable peculiarities in certain of his decisions. For example, he brought David Wasmundt to CBC in the summer of 1981, to head the Music Department in the wake of Walter Nigh's departure, the last full-time music director who had departed a year earlier. There were few music majors at the time. Late in the 1981-82 academic year, it was rumored that the music major might be eliminated.[99] Two months later Dana Rowe was contracted and added to the music faculty. There were even fewer music students in the final year of CBC's existence and having two full-time staff was quite unnecessary. Wasmundt was baffled by this development, and had every reason to believe his position at the college was being undermined without cause or explanation. Moreover, Wasmundt, who was the music director at CBC, had not been advised of Rowe's appointment until the latter arrived.[100] This is all the more puzzling since Fisher appeared intent on cutting back some of the music offerings.[101] Budgetary constraints also made the addition to the music program a questionable decision. In sum, the appointment of Dana Rowe made no more sense than appointing Paul Dugas as professor of theology (see ill.3.11, p. 127). An effort to extract an explanation from Fisher over Rowe's appointment failed to produce any satisfactory reply.[102]

"Don Fisher was an innovative and aggressive leader, intellectual, progressive, efficient and sometimes abrasive."[103] When

---

[96] Harry and Freda Fisher interview, 8 December 2000. Apparently, Don Fisher admitted this. Harry and Freda Fisher interview, 13 July 2005.
[97] April Purtell interview, 13 April 2013.
[98] Ronna (Fisher) Russell interview, 20 July 2013.
[99] *The Journal of Thomas A. Fudge, 1980-1985*, entry for 13 May 1982.
[100] David Wasmundt interview, 3 October 2013.
[101] *The Journal of Thomas A. Fudge, 1980-1985*, entry for 23 September 1982.
[102] Barbara Wasmundt interview, 3 October 2013.
[103] Lewis, *The Journey Out*, p. 36.

Fisher took over the CBC presidency he attempted to make sweeping changes. Naturally, this incurred staunch opposition.[104] He possessed a rock-star persona which set him apart within his denominational context.[105] Students were often intimidated by him, even those who were otherwise drawn to him. Fisher was thus an enigma who was equally loved and feared.[106] He had his favorites, was subject to his own vanities, and at times exhibited unusual vitriol towards women. There were exceptions, but he could be utterly unreasonable and scathing when it came to dealing with females. Incidents involving JCM students Cindy Blake and Bonnie Fox were unnecessarily harsh, disproportionally offensive, and unprofessional. Fisher's conduct was indefensible. There were other instances. "He was not real kind to women" and neither favored female faculty members specifically nor women in ministry generally.[107] He was from time to time verbally and psychologically abusive to women. One of his former students noted that Fisher's ideas about women were not nearly as progressive as his views on theology, while colleagues could not understand his point of view noting there was no consistency in interpretation.[108] He was also harsh with students struggling with issues of sexuality and there are one or two notorious examples, including a rather stark exchange with JCM student Mitchell Nickens (1957-1987) wherein Fisher's angry and insensitive shouts from his office could be heard by general staff through closed doors.[109]

---

[104] David Reynolds interview, 12 August 2013.

[105] Ronna (Fisher) Russell interview, 20 July 2013.

[106] Larry Snyder interview, 5 May 1999.

[107] Dan Lewis interview, 6 April 1999, Thomas Craft interview, 20 April 1999, Larry Snyder interview, 5 May 1999, and Jim Wilkins, letter to Thomas A. Fudge, 7 May 2013. FC, inv.doc.no 0707-5022-33. Apart from family and among others, Fisher enjoyed significant and mainly positive relations with Thetus Tenney, Jewel (Yadon) Dillon, April Purtell, Carol Roberts, Sandi (Derick) Nelson, and Sharon Graham. For the Blake and Fox incidents I rely upon the eye-witness testimony of Dan Lewis.

[108] Sandra Blevins interview, 11 April 1999. Blevins is a now an Indianapolis-based attorney. *The Diary of Jewel (Yadon) Dillon*, entry for 7 July 1980.

[109] Jewel (Yadon) Dillon interview, 24 July 2013. On the other hand we find evidence wherein he showed compassion to those struggling with such issues. Karissa (Fisher) Hopkins interview, 15 August 2013.

Fisher could be cutting, authoritarian, and utterly unreasonable, yet he was eminently capable of effective diplomacy if he chose that approach. He did not abide fools gladly, one might go further and assert he did not abide them at all, and did not suffer any challenge to his authority. Those who attempted to do so were usually met with stiff counter resistance. This was not gender specific and at times he used harshness when addressing college students.[110] Some perceived him as exercising a typical "my way or the high-way" policy.[111] Even close friends did not shrink from characterizing his ruthlessness with a capital "R."[112] He possessed an "ego bigger than the sky" and from time to time there were manifest traits of both selfishness and arrogance in his conduct.[113] His sophistication was distrusted by many UPC people.[114] Some of the older ministers resented Fisher because he was young and undeniably bright and it is also apparent that he did not consistently give them sufficient respect.[115]

He was a charismatic leader and a man of considerable power and charm. "He was imposing, formidable, in a lot of ways."[116] Some of his students regarded him as a genuine "fireball" capable of stimulating critical thinking.[117] Ministerial colleagues noted that Fisher "was a smart man, too smart for the rest of them."[118] This concerned the denomination. Critics of liberals in the Southern Baptist Convention characterized their plight in terms of being "held captive by a coterie of slick religio-political 'denomicrats.'"[119] Don Fisher consistently exercised independence of thought and seems to have been relatively immune to the tyranny of the majority which helps to explain his resistance to the various boards which

---

[110] *The Diary of Jewel (Yadon) Dillon*, entries for 27 and 28 February 1980.

[111] Thomas Craft interview, 20 April 1999, and David Reynolds interview, 12 August 2013.

[112] Thetus Tenney interview, 6 June 2013.

[113] Ronna (Fisher) Russell interview, 20 July 2013, David Reynolds interview, 12 August 2013, and Karissa (Fisher) Hopkins interview, 15 August 2013.

[114] Mark Roberts interview, 5 May 1999.

[115] Jewel (Yadon) Dillon interview, 24 July 2013.

[116] Karissa (Fisher) Hopkins interview, 15 August 2013.

[117] Joe Higgins interview, 4 October 2013.

[118] Frank LaCrosse interview, 16 January 2001.

[119] Patterson, *Anatomy of a Reformation*, p. 4.

sought to bring him into line with their own ideas.[120] Some who worked for him characterized Fisher as a "great moral leader" and a "Renaissance man in the UPC."[121] He earned a reputation for being the type of individual that people listened to.[122] Fisher had taught at JCM and CBC that the only ministry one ever has is the ministry people give them. Young men and women in Mississippi and Oregon willingly gave Don Fisher a ministry. Fisher also suggested that the best means of determining whether one was a leader was to look behind and see if anyone was following. Once again, there were men and women, especially in the colleges, who followed Fisher and considered him teacher, mentor, and leader. Within the UPC, in the realm of leadership and education, he was a towering figure; an iron giant with feet of clay.

After the destruction of CBC, Don Fisher turned his attention to the role of senior pastor at Christ for the People Community Church. Fisher's dynamic and charismatic ministry attracted many and the church remained a vibrant community.[123] Part of his vision, put into place at Jackson and then CBC, was carried on at the church. The explicit philosophy appeared in writing. "One must be educated to the level of his spiritual experience or he will when under pressure revert to his original faith."[124] Fisher continued to emphasize balance. Moreover, he taught that "fear is the greatest enemy of the truth."[125] Following his departure from CBC it was suggested that "Brother Fisher has also declared his intention ... to open a training program in connection with the church which he is

---

[120] The "tyranny of the majority" is a phrase found in John Adams, *A Defense of the Constitutions of Government of the United States of America*, 3 vols, third edition (Philadelphia: William Cobbett, 1797), vol. 3, p. 291.

[121] Joseph Howell interview, 21 April 1999.

[122] Former Texas District Superintendent E.L. (Ernest Lee) Holley (1927-1995) characterized Fisher this way. Harry Fisher interview, 13 July 2005.

[123] The Christ for the People Community Church directory contains the names of 145 people. This undated directory is clearly from the post-CBC era. FC, inv.doc.no 0707-5418-34.

[124] Don Fisher, sermon at Christ for the People Community Church, 4 March 1984 and Fisher, "The People of the Covenant," handwritten three-page teaching outline, 9 May 1984, p. 2. FC, inv.doc.no 0707-5421-34.

[125] Christ for the People Community Church, Leadership Seminar #3, undated handout, probably 1984. FC, inv.doc.no 0707-5422-34.

currently pastoring."[126] If true, this never took place. However, one of the more successful and vibrant outgrowths of the church, and an extension of the college, was a Sunday evening discipleship class

6.10   Discipleship class, Prune Hill, Spring 1984. *Left to right:* April Purtell, Chuck Parrish, Don Fisher, Skip Paynter, Susan (Fisher) Paynter, two unidentified individuals, Donna Fisher, Wilma Herr, James Paley, Lori Falwell, Elizabeth Purtell, Ronna Fisher, Gregg Calder, and Karissa Fisher

which convened regularly at the Fisher residence at 1906 SE 130th Avenue in Vancouver. Quite a number of former CBC staff, faculty, and students were regular participants in these robust and intellectually challenging sessions.[127] Among a variety of texts used were the works of the prominent British evangelical thinker John R.W. Stott (1921-2011). Joseph Howell's booklist appeared now and again. On one occasion, Fisher took the entire discipleship group to a Portland synagogue to hear Elie Wiesel, a prominent but

---

[126] Arless Glass, letter to George Sponsler, 4 March 1983. FC, inv.doc.no 0707-5223-34.

[127] These included Donna Fisher, April Purtell, Sandi Derick, Thomas A. Fudge, Elizabeth Purtell, Michelle Kelley, Michael Nigh, Gregg Calder, Doug Greer, James Paley, Audrey Zapalac, Lori Falwell, Wilma Herr, Karissa and Ronna Fisher, among others.

morally compromised Jewish political activist and holocaust-industry apologist.[128] Reactions to Wiesel were mixed.

The book of Galatians and its central themes became a prominent study point in the discipleship sessions wherein Fisher taught that salvation was by faith alone. At this stage, Fisher had openly and unambiguously embraced the teachings of St. Paul along with Martin Luther on topics such as justification by faith. He also took occasional points of departure from the writings of Dietrich Bonhoeffer.[129] Prior to this, with CBC as his base, Don Fisher had hoped to recover the lost PCI heritage in the Northwest and this hope must be factored into his guiding vision for the college.[130] That fragmented and fading vision, however, was now marked off from the heritage Fisher had always known. What was left to Fisher was the former college church and the discipleship program. He continued to take an interest in young people and sometimes visited the facilities of *Youth Outreach* in Vancouver where a number of former CBC students worked.[131]

CBC faculty members wishing to retain contractual status with the college beyond the official closure date of 18 March 1983, were obligated, by formal advice, to cease attending Christ for the People and affiliate with a church pastored by a UPC licensed minister.[132] At this stage, all college faculty and staff remaining in the immediate area had to make that choice. Some area pastors imposed harsh sanctions. Raymond Woodson, who succeeded John Klemin at the Vancouver UPC church in December 1982, forbade former CBC student Libby (Thompson) Langel, for example, from having any contact whatever with Barbara Wasmundt so long as the latter attended Christ for the People and maintained connections to Don

---

[128] *The Journal of Thomas A. Fudge, 1980-1985*, entry for 4 March 1984.

[129] Bonhoeffer is noted in Don Fisher, "The Will of God is Sanctification," sermon at McCormick's Creek, Indiana, 1975, audio recording.

[130] Dan Lewis interview, 6 April 1999.

[131] Doug Greer interview, 22 September 2013. *Youth Outreach* was a residential treatment program for teenagers operating several facilities in Vancouver, Washington. *Youth Outreach* had been founded by Ron Hart, senior pastor of Walnut Grove Community Church in Vancouver. Greer, Eric K. Loy, Thomas A. Fudge, Sandi Derick, among others from CBC, were employed.

[132] George M. Sponsler (Acting Chairman, Board of Directors, Cascade Bible College), letter to April Purtell, 29 March 1983. See Appendix 18, p. 456.

Fisher.[133] Such unyielding uses and abuses of pastoral authority created serious issues for those "imprisoned in the brotherhood."[134]

The church settled into its post-CBC existence, but Fisher was not particularly well-suited for parish ministry. He had often said that "pastoring was not his forté."[135] His was a life best lived on the cutting edge of higher education. He was a man with a vision, an innate ability to challenge, inspire, and motivate. In some ways his work at JCM and CBC was altogether successful. He produced a rare breed of students within the UPC. Many of them ultimately left the denomination, though their reasons varied. JCM, and by extension the UPC, lost a lot of young people on account of Don Fisher and his agenda.[136] His detractors noted with disdain that "he influenced a pile of kids not only at CBC, but at Jackson College of Ministries."[137] With defections like those of Stephen Graham to Roman Catholicism, Jim Wilkins to the Episcopal Church, and numerous other students to a variety of non-Pentecostal Trinitarian churches, that influence has often been characterized as the destructive outcome of the Trojan horse which had been brought into the vineyard of the Lord. It was a different sort of "foul ball" altogether and there were other unintended consequences. Some students elected to leave the Christian faith altogether. Some of Fisher's closest colleagues later testified to the loss of purpose in the aftermath of CBC. There were men whose commitment to education and transformation proved difficult to replicate or replace and moving heavy equipment did not compare with moving hearts and minds towards critical thinking, authentic spirituality, intentional religious practice, and ultimately God.[138]

---

133 Barbara Wasmundt interview, 3 October 2013.

134 See the work of former JCM student, Nelson Lewis Paynter, "Authority and the Pastor: An Examination of the Nature of Power and Authority for Church Leaders," Master of Religion thesis, Warner Pacific College, 1987.

135 Donna Fisher interview, 3 January 1999. Others do not believe that Fisher wanted to be a pastor. April Purtell interview, 16 January 1999. Skip Paynter interview, 24 January 1999, does not think Fisher had a pastoral calling.

136 Thomas Craft interview, 20 April 1999.

137 Barry King interview, 20 January 1999.

138 Jerry Peden made these comments around 2001, just prior to the diagnosis of a brain tumor which later killed him, noting he no longer knew what to do with his life. April Purtell interview, 13 April 2013.

The last student body president of CBC was told to "come out from among them and be separate" when it was discovered he was attending an Assemblies of God congregation following the closure

6.11 Don Fisher preaching in the pulpit of Christ for the People Community Church, Fall 1982

of CBC.[139] Former colleagues were warned that "students need to be in a United Pentecostal Bible College" rather than remaining under the influence of Don Fisher.[140] It has been suggested that there were CBC students during the Fisher years whose lives were ruined by their college experience.[141] By contrast, others have testified that CBC during the Fisher years was "one of the most significant times of my life," while still others described their time at the college as being an "awesome experience."[142] It is doubtful

---

[139] Eric K. Loy interview, 17 July 2005. The admonition had been given by Ray Sirstad.

[140] Arless Glass, letter to George Sponsler, 4 March 1983.

[141] David Reynolds interview, 12 August 2013.

[142] For example, Michael Nigh interview, 18 August 2013, and Joe Higgins interview, 4 October 2013. Kristi (Eld) Christensen interview, 4 October 2013 described CBC as a "wonderful experience." Stan Johnson interview, 5 October 2013 referred to CBC as an "enriching time of life."

that Fisher had any regrets about his influence. After all, he
consistently claimed to believe in the work of the Holy Spirit in the
lives of all believers. "He marked his generation with the gospel.
You can't be in charge of leadership in schools, forming the lives of
people, without indelibly marking history and the kingdom of God.
Those students that were under his teaching" learned much of
value from him.[143]

6.12  Jerry and Kris Dillon at the 20th anniversary of their pastorate of the
former Christ for the People Community Church, 29 August 2004

In the summer of 1984, just two years after he founded Christ
for the People, Don Fisher somewhat abruptly announced his
resignation as senior pastor and declared his intention of accepting
a ministerial leadership position as administrator at Christ the King
Community Church, pastored by Paul Adams, in Sacramento,
California.[144] In August he was succeeded as senior pastor by Jerry
W. Dillon, a position Dillon would fill for over twenty years until

---

[143] Paul Adams interview, 16 August 2013.
[144] *The Journal of Thomas A. Fudge, 1980-1981*, entries for 8 and 25 August 1984.
The work party on the latter date consisted of Don Fisher, Jerry Peden, Jerry
Dillon, and Thomas A. Fudge "while Blair Crumpacker watched ... from the
shade." Paul Adams interview, 16 August 2013, for details on Fisher's assignment
in Sacramento.

October 2004. In some ways, Dillon continued the basic premises emphasized by Don Fisher, indicating that he was prepared for continued theological exploration as well as the discoveries which accompany every honest quest for truth. He articulated, in writing, that the ministry of the church was predicated upon the principles of love, acceptance, and forgiveness, while pointing out that "it is possible to become so dependent on our previous experiences and understandings of God that we actually become closed to any new discoveries."[145] While he may not personally have agreed, it is likely Fisher would have chortled at the fact that during his tenure as senior pastor of Christ for the People Community Church, Dillon embraced both Calvinism and Trinitarianism. After all, Fisher seems to have approved of Jan Hus, who once said "from the very beginning of my studies I made it a rule that whenever I encounter a sounder opinion to happily and humbly surrender the one previously embraced. For I am quite certain [...] that what we know is considerably less than what we do not know."[146] Between 1985 and 1987, the discipleship program established by Fisher was fully integrated into the church program and directed by two of Fisher's disciples, who during Dillon's tenure were appointed associate pastors at Christ for the People Community Church. The ongoing discipleship program played a significant role in the life of the church and continued to provide a venue for serious theological reflection and continuing education. Joseph Howell's booklist remained a guiding principle.[147]

Dillon and his ministerial colleagues continued to move steadily farther away from their doctrinal and faith roots. The history of the former CBC college church bears this out in unequivocal detail. Two unprecedented events in the immediate aftermath of CBC

---

[145] Jerry Dillon, "Statement of Purpose (partial)," Christ for the People Community Church, February 1985. FC, inv.doc.no 0707-5432-34. See also Dillon, "The Problem of Growth" *In Touch* 1 (No. 3, 1986), p. 1.

[146] Hus, *Defensio libri de Trinitate* in Jaroslav Eršil, ed., *Magistri Iohannis Hus Opera omnia*, vol. 22 (Prague: Academia, 1966), p. 42.

[147] Skip Paynter and Thomas A. Fudge both left Christ for the People in 1987. The former went to a position at Longview Community Church in Washington State while the latter assumed the pastorate of the Church of Our Redeemer in Beaverton, Oregon. Thomas A. Fudge, "A Short History of Cascade Community Church," pp. 1-2. In the 1990s, the church assumed its new name.

were contributing factors. The first was an academic conference convened at Harvard University in the summer of 1984.[148] The second was the televised debate between Walter Martin and UPC representatives in the autumn of 1985.[149] Both events confirmed to

6.13   Oneness theologian Robert A. Sabin,
St. Paul, Minnesota, 10 July 2000

the ministry team at Christ for the People their serious theological misgivings about their religious heritage. It seems evident that Jerry Dillon was quite determined not to build monuments to previous experience and understanding. As noted earlier, Dillon had deep roots in the UPC, was a graduate of CBC and had served on the faculty during the Yadon and Klemin administrations, from 1969 until 1978. Dillon had maintained some loose connections with

---

[148] "The First Occasional Symposium on Aspects of Oneness Pentecostalism" (5-7 July 1984) at Harvard University featured nineteen speakers including Joseph Howell, Dan Lewis, Stephen Graham, Rod Loudermilk, James Brandyberry, and Larry Snyder. Each of these had formerly been affiliated with JCM or JCM faculty. J.L. Hall, David Bernard, Tom Weisser, and William Chalfant spoke for the UPC. Don Fisher and Nathaniel Urshan were invited but did not attend. There is a published overview in Donald W. Dayton, "Oneness Pentecostals Meet at Harvard" *The Christian Century* (3 October, 1984), pp. 892-894.

[149] *The Trinity or 'Jesus Only': What do the Scriptures Teach?"* The John Ankerberg Show (Chattanooga, TN), hosted by John Ankerberg. Walter Martin and Calvin Beisner debated Nathaniel Urshan and Robert Sabin. Several programs were aired. The complete transcript of the recordings amount to eighty-seven single-spaced pages and 232 minutes of video. Sabin held his own but Urshan was hopeless, and the moderator, John Ankerberg, clearly favored the Martin/Beisner duo granting them unfair and disproportionate air time.

Fisher and the former college church.[150] Even his old ministerial colleague, John Klemin, wrote to him shortly before he took up the pastorate of Christ for the People to say "we do see the hand of God in your life ... and I don't think you have to belong to [the] UPC to be saved."[151]

Don Fisher's stay in Sacramento was brief, even shorter than his presidency of CBC. Less than one year after taking up his appointment he resigned from the staff of the church, relocated to Los Angeles where he entered the secular business world. For more than ten years he worked as a dynamic and successful businessman. Never again did he hold any ministerial or educational position. Occasionally he returned to the Portland area and engaged in preaching ministry.[152] His last sermon at Christ for the People Community Church was delivered in 1986. His final appearance in a pulpit was a guest sermon preached in the Chapel of the Good Shepherd at the Glendale City Seventh-Day Adventist Church in Glendale, California during Easter 1995. Provocative to the end, Fisher's address "The Resurrection" on 15 April was remembered for its content and for its capacity for making people think.[153]

Tom Fred Tenney apparently had urged Fisher not to go to another UPC college and others were very surprised that he did go to Portland.[154] Whether he regretted taking the helm at CBC cannot be determined though it is certain that the trajectory he was on prior to coming back to Portland would have taken him out of the UPC sooner or later. Fisher did not adapt to the UPC and close friends were not surprised that eventually he left.[155] Had the approaches championed by Don Fisher, John H. Tietjen, Russell H. Dilday, E. J. Carnell, George Tyrrell, and Alfred Loisy succeeded,

---

[150] *The Journal of Thomas A. Fudge, 1980-1985*, entry for 7 December 1983, notes that "Jerry Dillon preached" that evening at Christ for the People.

[151] John Klemin, letter to Jerry and Kris Dillon, 4 February 1984, p. 2.

[152] "Went to church in Oregon City where Bro. Fisher was preaching." *The Journal of Thomas A. Fudge, 1980-1985*, entry for 10 March 1985.

[153] Jesse Martin interview, 17 August 2013 and service bulletin.

[154] Noted in Thomas Craft interview, 20 April 1999, and Jewel (Yadon) Dillon interview, 24 July 2013.

[155] Thetus Tenney interview, 6 June 2013. Donna Fisher interviews, 3 January 1999 and 7 October 2013 notes she had no regrets about her marriage to Don Fisher or about their return to the Northwest.

those several respective denominations would have been radically transformed and the United Pentecostal, Missouri Synod, Southern Baptist, and Roman Catholic churches would have evolved along rather unlikely trajectories. That point alone accounts for why such men garnered powerful enemies and why those churches strove to minimise their influence.

What sort of man was Don Fisher? While he may have been an iron giant with feet of clay, he strove for balance. How does his life compare with that goal? His career in its latter UPC stages might be dissected under three headings: pride, power, and position. Fisher was a proud man, though this need not imply he was guilty of one of the medieval capital sins. He went about his work with pride and took pride in his accomplishments. Fisher knew very well that pride can blind and this can result in great harm in that it causes people to fear God but not necessarily love God.[156] It is possible that pride prevented Fisher from ever being completely honest about the emotional agony he lived much of his life with.[157]

He was also not immune to power and its effects. It has long been axiomatic that power tends to corrupt and absolute power corrupts absolutely.[158] It would be facile to dismiss all suggestion that Fisher was immune to the corrupting influence of power. As much as he eschewed the politics of power and the administration thereof (especially in its southern manifestations), like most men, Don Fisher enjoyed power.[159] This should not be taken to mean that he was drunk with its influence or that he abused power. However, he did become locked in a power struggle with Thomas Craft in the last years at Jackson.[160] This fact was known even at the national levels.[161] He was forced into similar bellicose engagements with the Oregon and Washington District Boards, the CBC Board of Directors, and local pastors in the Portland area who considered

---

[156] Way, *The Garden of the Beloved*, p. 71.
[157] Lori (Falwell) Callan interview, 23 September 2013.
[158] Lord Acton, letter to Bishop Mandell Creighton, 5 April 1887, published in John Neville Figgis and Reginald Vere Laurence, eds., *Historical Essays & Studies* (London: Macmillan, 1907), p. 504.
[159] April Purtell interview, 16 January 1999 thinks that Fisher loved power.
[160] Dan Lewis interview, 6 April 1999.
[161] Nathaniel Urshan interview, 23 April 1999.

him heretical. His own perception of power can be shown in an incident when Fisher addressed the entire student body at JCM over some relatively minor disciplinary issue and asserted that if students continued to make life difficult for him he would simply resign.[162] It was an intentional power play predicated upon Fisher's own perception of his popularity among the student body and a gamble based on a subjective measure of their loyalty to him. One faculty member at JCM observed the politics of power philosophy. "Don started abruptly on 'sheep' mentality. Bro Craft (our pastor/shepherd) came in. A tense moment. Sometimes I think Don is unconscious of his thirst for power."[163]

Many of his admirers among the student bodies of JCM and CBC, to say nothing of some of his peers, put Fisher on a pedestal and there is evidence to suggest that he willingly stepped up on the pedestal with confidence. It is not necessary to see Don Fisher as arrogant, though he was sometimes taken as that, but he was a man capable of assertiveness and considerable confidence. It is possible that pride, power, and his position upon a pedestal not only supported his iron will and determination, but also contributed to the clay which made up his feet and which ultimately could not support the weight he was called upon to bear.

What manner of man was Don Fisher? Is there merit to the suggestion that clues can be found by considering the life story of G. Gordon Liddy? After three years of struggle in Jackson, some observers suggest that something changed. Along with one or two colleagues, Fisher attended a secular leadership training seminar, around the college spring break in 1980, in which he was exposed to Machiavellian ideology and the dynamic and subtle use of power. Ostensibly, Fisher seized upon the philosophy with enthusiasm and began to implement its use at JCM. This changed his leadership approach as well as his personality. His goals for the college required more power and after this seminar he was prepared to engage in the uses of power for what he thought best for the program. Fisher explained to at least one colleague who Niccolò

---

[162] Susan (Fisher) Paynter interview, 24 January 1999.
[163] *The Diary of Jewel (Yadon) Dillon*, entry for 8 October 1980. The incident took place during a faculty meeting wherein Fisher took sharp exception to Craft's previous public statements about the shepherd and the sheep.

Machiavelli (1469-1527) was and the basic thrust of his thought. The dangers of power, pride, and corruption loomed not just for Fisher but for others at JCM. The stark divisions which resulted tarnished all of those involved and none were blameless.[164] It does not seem legitimate to categorize Don Fisher as Machiavellian in the pejorative sense of deceitfulness or manipulation for personal advantage, nor yet as a political figure prepared to do anything – by foul or fair means – in pursuit of policy or practice aimed at satisfying himself. Still, there is possible justification for seeing Machiavelli as an element in Fisher's personality.

About five years after Fisher resigned from CBC and withdrew from the UPC, he gave away copies of a book called *The Knight in the Rusty Armor* to a number of people, including former students, friends, and young people he had once known. This small book provides a clue, however modest, to his thinking and to part of his own journey.[165] The story that Robert Fisher (no relation) tells is of a knight who wore his armor to impress, and to conceal, but wound up isolating himself from all meaning in life. The armor was worn so long and so often that at length the knight could not take it off. The hard struggle with this self-imposed prison caused the knight to disadvantage and alienate his own family, create widespread disillusion, and ultimately bring the knight to the brink of death. A series of circumstances takes him on a long and arduous journey of self-discovery which enables him finally to get rid of the armor. Along the way he discovers truth and the meaning of authentic life. *The Knight in the Rusty Armor* is a parable which underscores that everyone has armor which keeps the true self concealed and the rest of the world at a safe and comfortable distance. Some forms of armor are much easier to see than others, but people in general carry various forms of protection.

*The Knight in the Rusty Armor* takes the "path of truth," and this journey requires him to pass through the castles of "Silence," "Knowledge," and "Will and Daring." This is a journey of learning

---

[164] Jewel (Yadon) Dillon, *Annals of God's Grace* (Caldwell, ID, 2012), pp. 24-6. Other details in Jewel (Yadon) Dillon interview, 24 July 2013 and various entries in *The Diary of Jewel (Yadon) Dillon*, 1980 forms the basis for this summary.
[165] Robert Fisher, *The Knight in the Rusty Armor* (North Hollywood, CA: Wilshire Book Company, 1987).

who one truly is and through that discovery an understanding of truth. The realization of his predicament becomes clear along the journey when the knight realizes, "we set up barriers to protect who we think we are. Then one day we get stuck behind the barriers and can't get out."[166] Did Don Fisher create barriers to protect what he thought he was, what he desired to be, how he wanted people to perceive him, and at some point became trapped by his own image and protections? In the "Castle of Silence," the knight is compelled to listen to his heart, to the inner light (as the Quakers call it), and to the still small voice. Listening to these deep voices of truth, *The Knight in the Rusty Armor* is rather like Siddhartha listening to the river, but the silence enables the knight to move from one room to the next in the castle.[167] The silence and the loneliness helps him to see and to understand how his armor has adversely affected others, especially those who loved him most. The armor begins to rust and weaken from his tears of remorse and enlightenment and it slowly begins to fall off. What was Don Fisher's armor?

At the "Castle of Knowledge" the knight encounters a sign which asks the pilgrim "have you mistaken need for love?"[168] Within this castle the knight comes to realize that he needed people and effectively used them, but also that he had not properly loved them because the armor got in the way and prevented him from being real.[169] The knight comes to the understanding that until he can love himself, without his protective shield, he cannot truly love others. He also realizes that he has lived his entire life in a deliberate manner hoping that others might like him. But the armor was essentially a false impression.[170] At the "Castle of Will and Daring," the knight finds his forward progress obstructed by the dragon of fear and doubt. After much timidity, he realises he does

---

[166] Fisher, *The Knight in the Rusty Armor*, p. 48.

[167] Hermann Hesse, *Siddhartha*, trans. Hilda Rosner (New York: MJF Books, 1951), pp. 121-122.

[168] Fisher, *The Knight in the Rusty Armor*, p. 63.

[169] A number of years earlier at CBC, Fisher had emphasized the differences between "need-love" and "gift-love" as articulated in a course text. Claypool, *The Preaching Event*, pp. 55-81.

[170] Fisher, *The Knight in the Rusty Armor*, pp. 64-65, 68. Similar themes expressed in Fisher, "Evangelization of the Subconscious," sermon at McCormick's Creek, Indiana, January 1975, audio recording.

not have anything to prove and is confronted by the fact that perception is not the same thing as reality. "God gave man courage. Courage gives God to man."[171] The journey of discovery along the "path of truth" helps the knight to see and understand that self-knowledge destroys the dragons of fear and doubt which are, in the end, only illusions. At the end of the journey to the top of the mountain, the previously self-sufficient knight accepts the importance of trust (in God) and finally experiences the truth that one must let go of one's own armor and self-reliance in order to be free. When the knight is finally able to trust in a higher power and let go, the remaining bits of rusty armor fall away and the knight is finally liberated from the prison of his own security. This book, considered important by Don Fisher, is an extension of themes noted earlier which were evident and developed in the sermons at McCormick's Creek (ill.3.15, p. 138), in the moving tale of *The Velveteen Rabbit*, in the resolve of *Jonathan Livingston Seagull*, and along the journey narrated within the pages of *The Garden of the Beloved*, wherein the eyes of the heart are opened.[172] These were stages in Fisher's thinking about redemption, salvation, and transformation. These were themes that Joseph Howell, Dan Lewis, and Jerry Dillon also explored but they did so principally through scholarship and academic inquiry. Fisher found valuable clues in the particular genre of literature just noted. *The Knight in the Rusty Armor* is also a tale of salvation, one which clearly resonated with Don Fisher and which may reflect aspects of Fisher's own struggle for truth, authenticity, and redemption. More than fifteen years before his death he confided to a colleague that he had a lot of questions about himself.[173] Did he slay the dragons of fear and doubt, or did they destroy him? Did he succeed in exorcising the demons which surely came his way, or did the demons overpower him? These are questions for which there cannot be firm answers. E.J. Carnell once spoke of the "demonic uncertainties" in the life of the Christian.[174] It is certain that Fisher ultimately understood what Carnell feared. All of these considerations aside, Robert Fisher's book generated

---

[171] Fisher, *The Knight in the Rusty Armor*, pp. 80-81.
[172] Way, *The Garden of the Beloved*, passim.
[173] Jewel (Yadon) Dillon interview, 24 July 2013.
[174] Noted in Marsden, *Reforming Fundamentalism*, p. 258.

conversation among a number of Don Fisher's former students and inspired at least one minor publication.[175]

In the years remaining to him after he left the ministerial fellowship of the United Pentecostal Church, Don Fisher could not often be drawn into conversation about CBC. It was a chapter in his life he preferred not to revisit, and he never spoke to family members about what had happened.[176] He had no interest whatever in "esculating [sic] an ecclesiastical 'Cold War.'"[177] It is noteworthy that among his closest confidants during the CBC years, we find an expression of Fisher's attitude towards the UPC. "He never publicly and rarely privately made any negative statements against the UPCI. His hope until he resigned was that there was a progressive movement within the organization that would eventually become the dominant voice."[178] There are multiple verifiable examples that Fisher encouraged people not to leave the UPC.[179] This contrasts with other views which characterized Fisher as holding "anti-U.P.C. leanings."[180] Some former students and colleagues noted that Fisher never gave a straightforward answer if it would contradict UPC doctrines.[181] By 1984, Fisher did openly question the traditional understanding of the necessity of baptism in Jesus' name during a Sunday sermon in the pulpit of Christ for the People Community Church (noting that baptism had no salvific value, and the formula is significant only in the sense that it reflects the work of Christ for salvation).[182] That sermon reflected a PCI theological orientation

---

[175] Thomas A. Fudge, "The Tarnished Knight" *In Touch* 3 (No. 1, 1989), pp. 1-2.

[176] Karissa (Fisher) Hopkins interview, 15 August 2013. "We sat around at Fishers and laughed about the good old days at CBC." *The Journal of Thomas A. Fudge, 1980-1985*, entry for 6 November 1983. It cannot be said with any certainty that Don Fisher was part of this conversation.

[177] The phrase is Jerry Dillon's, from an editorial in the publication *In Touch* 1 (No. 1, 1986), p. 1.

[178] Jerry Peden, letter to Thomas A. Fudge, 27 September 1999 (FC, inv.doc.no 0707-4828-33), and Peden interview, 19 July 2002.

[179] April Purtell interview, 13 April 2013.

[180] John Klemin, letter to Jerry Dillon, 8 July 1982, p. 1. FC, inv.doc.no 0707-4793-32. Klemin suggests that it was Dillon who made the inference about Fisher. Also V. Arlen Guidroz interview, 15 April 1999.

[181] Jim Wilkins interview, 1 May 1999.

[182] Don Fisher, "Water Baptism," sermon at Christ for the People Community Church, 12 February 1984. This sermon generated significant discussion between

but also exceeded that tradition by some margin. Some argued that
Fisher and some of his colleagues like C.H. Yadon, Joseph Howell,
Dan Lewis, and Jerry Dillon became less and less UPC and more
and more Christian. Others countered by characterizing Fisher's
career as a slow eroding of the faith once delivered to the saints and
an example of irreversible backsliding. Men such as Alfred Loisy,
Russell Dilday, John H. Tietjen, Edward Carnell, Don Fisher, Jerry
Dillon, and C.H. Yadon may have been seen by their adversaries as
dangerous heretics or doctrinally deviant, but they remained
thoroughly Christian in their thinking and in their ideas. The clash
seems to have centered in the fact that these men were more
committed to being Christian than they were to being Roman
Catholic, Southern Baptist, Missouri Synod Lutheran, or UPC.

Outwardly, Don Fisher appeared to get on with life. He later
expressed bitterness about attacks on his family and stated that had
the pressure been against him alone, he might well have ignored
persistent personal criticism and remained at CBC. Ultimately, he
was unprepared to do that in light of the detrimental effects on his
family. Family members later stated that the constant surveillance,
climate of suspicion, and false accusations were both "frightening
and unjust." The church environment cultivated that atmosphere,
and after Fisher went to Jackson, he brought that pressure to bear
in his own home. The results were entirely negative.[183] He was also
equally bitter about the lack of support among those he previously
numbered among his friends. His principal mentor worried about
bitterness taking root in him.[184] That fear seems to have been
realized. "I'm afraid Don let bitterness destroy him."[185] His
experiences over the ten-year period between 1966 and 1976 at the
UPC headquarters were regarded by some as exposure which

---

former faculty member April Purtell and former student Thomas A. Fudge with
the latter questioning if Fisher had not gone too far. Within a year, Fudge
declared that Fisher had not gone far enough. *The Journal of Thomas A. Fudge,
1980-1985*, entry for 12 February 1984.

[183] Ronna (Fisher) Russell interview, 20 July 2013.

[184] C.H. Yadon expressed this concern to the author during a conversation in
Caldwell, Idaho around 1989.

[185] Edwin Judd interview, 10 April 1999, Donna Fisher interview, 3 January 1999,
and Thetus Tenney interview, 6 June 2013, are three examples of a host of
friends and colleagues who confirm that Fisher was bitter.

"helped to make him a bitter man."[186] Religious prophets are always martyred by their religious peers rather than by those outside the community.[187] For many years Don Fisher took theology more seriously than politics but by the time CBC closed "he had gotten so sick and bitter that he ceased to care about theology."[188] It is entirely possible to argue that before the end of his life, Fisher relinquished his preoccupation with balance.

By 1983, Fisher essentially was abandoned both at the national and local levels. He found rejection very difficult, especially by those he thought were his friends.[189] David Johnson and Verneal Crossley were men Fisher previously regarded as friends.[190] Neither supported his work at CBC. It has been reported that something occurred at JCM which prompted Johnson to turn against Fisher.[191] Determining the particulars has proven elusive. Hugh Rose and Fisher had been close and Fisher had supported Rose in an earlier conflict in Ohio. Yet when Fisher left the UPC, Rose abruptly ceased communication. Family members took sharp exception to such behavior.[192] From his Mississippi days, he seems to have retained little regard for Tom Fred Tenney, and alluded to betrayal, though he could not be drawn on the matter.[193] Tenney was a man of national prominence capable of progressive thinking but those qualities remained largely in the shadows as he cautiously sought out a politically expedient pathway within the UPC. Fisher may have regarded this as hypocrisy and inconsistency. Some sectors

---

[186] Freda Fisher interview, 13 July 2005.

[187] Reinhold Niebuhr, *Leaves from the Notebook of a Tamed Cynic* (New York: Willett, Clark & Colby, 1929), pp. 100-101.

[188] April Purtell interview, 13 April 2013.

[189] Jerry Peden interview, 19 July 2002, and Donna Fisher interview, 3 January 1999.

[190] Fisher and Johnson were ordained together during the same service. Donna Fisher interview, 3 January 1999.

[191] Edwin Judd interview, 10 April 1999.

[192] Karissa Fisher wrote a Rose a strongly-worded letter taking the latter to task. Karissa (Fisher) Hopkins interview, 15 August 2013. There was no response.

[193] Fisher told April Purtell in June 1995 that he had no use for Tom Fred Tenney. April Purtell interview, 16 January 1999. It has been suggested that it was Fisher who severed his relationship with Tenney. Thomas Craft interview, 20 April 1999. Tenney was later uncomfortable speaking about Fisher. Tom Fred Tenney interview, 20 April 1999.

within the UPC blamed Tenney for what happened at JCM because it was considered in the deep south that Tenney had protected Fisher for years and had served as a buffer between him and his

6.14   Tom Fred Tenney, Tioga, Louisiana, 20 April 1999, and (6.15) in 1969

enemies. Alternatively, Don Fisher came to believe that Tom Fred Tenney had colluded with T.L. Craft against him. Fisher had been warned to slow down the pace of change and reform but his retort was to the effect that he had been slow enough and that the emphasis upon education in the UPC had been too slow for far too long. Tenney remarked that one could not turn a large ship in the same fashion one might turn a canoe. Fisher wanted to turn the ship without delay. Tenney believed that one had to take into account the fact that one served a larger constituency and that it was improper to offend one party on account of the liberty of another group. Tom Fred Tenney may have provided an essential balance until at length Fisher no longer paid attention to Tenney's point of view.[194] Over time Fisher's relationship with Tenney deteriorated, but the reasons for this are obscure. Even strong supporters thought that Fisher was moving too far, too fast.[195]

---

[194] Thetus Tenney interview, 6 June 2013. T.F. Tenney's moderation of Fisher, especially during the latter's tenure in St. Louis has been confirmed in Arless Glass interview, 24 September 2013.
[195] Jewel (Yadon) Dillon interview, 24 July 2013.

In terms of CBC, only Jerry Peden stood with Fisher right up to the bitter end, though he was supported by individuals such as Norman Rutzen, Wayne Nigh, C.H. Yadon, and others from their respective places. Nigh even had Fisher preach at the UPC Schloß Freudenberg in Wiesbaden, Germany after leaving CBC and the UPC (ill.4.2, p. 150). Daryl Rash was particularly incensed and Nigh came under increased criticism for having Fisher on his platform and for involving him in European UPC affairs.[196] According to Nigh, Fisher was an exceptionally positive influence in Germany, France, Austria, and Serbia.[197] Tom Fred and Thetus Tenney were criticized for their relation with Don Fisher on the grounds that they should have had a higher level of discernment.[198] The truth in the fable of the seagull (which Fisher knew only too well) was very clear in this matter: speaking truth in the face of the majority and

6.16 Don Fisher and the author in Los Angeles, 7 August 1992

contrary to tradition results in the creation of the outcast. Those remaining in the group are instructed to ignore those expelled, and those who fail to observe that warning soon become outcasts as

---

[196] Jerry Peden interview, 19 July 2002.
[197] Wayne Nigh interview, 25 July 2013. Only James Stewart was thought to rival Don Fisher in effectiveness.
[198] Thetus Tenney interview, 6 June 2013.

well.[199] From the standpoint of ministry, when Fisher resigned from the UPC he was informally declared to be *vitandus*, that is shunned, one to be avoided, by those remaining true to the faith. This was the consequence of backsliding. Though Fisher neither said so nor overtly intimated, there was a sense in which he felt betrayed both by Nathaniel Urshan, whom he described as "the consummate politician," and by others who affirmed their allegiance and support privately but when the time came to stand and be counted never made an appearance.[200] Urshan discounted that perspective. "That's interesting to me because I have never been afraid of a situation. It didn't matter what it put me in. Never ... I have always responded when I could to anything dangerous or [to what I] thought might be harm[ful]."[201] Urshan was a "very complicated character" whose life, thinking, and leadership was always challenging.[202]

There was considerable speculation that a number of pastors and organizational officials were prepared to leave the UPC if someone of national stature and respect were to lead an exodus. With seventeen years of experience as a national figure Don Fisher potentially was that man. Fisher privately revealed that countless ministers within the UPC had confided to him that they were prepared to withdraw, but when he took a stand, the number who followed him was negligible.[203] The general apathy had little to do with people being ignorant of what had transpired at CBC and there are parallels elsewhere.[204] Fisher was disappointed to realize that he had made the steep and difficult ascent only to discover he was alone on the top of the mountain. That reality "must have been devastating."[205] He had aspired to be the next C.H. Yadon and in

---

[199] Bach, *Jonathan Livingston Seagull*, pp. 61 and 78.

[200] Donna Fisher interview, 3 January 1999, also characterized Urshan as a politician, while Norman Rutzen interview, 8 February 1999, noted that Urshan too often was politically influenced.

[201] Nathaniel Urshan interview, 23 April 1999. During this interview, Urshan did wonder if Fisher numbered him among his betrayers and was informed that Fisher did consider him among that number.

[202] Thetus Tenney interview, 6 June 2013.

[203] Arless Glass interview, 25 September 2013 was aware of that rumor. Norman Rutzen interview, 8 February 1999, regretted not leaving the UPC sooner.

[204] Tietjen, *Memoirs in Exile*, p. 252.

[205] Ronna (Fisher) Russell interview, 20 July 2013.

that aspiration perhaps cultivated an "over-developed sense of destiny."[206] Nevertheless, it was widely known that "C.H. Yadon was his hero."[207] Some would opine that at the time he abandoned his religious heritage he had hatred in his heart towards the UPC. That assessment might be too strong.[208] When asked how he felt about the demise of CBC and the failure of many friends and colleagues to stand with him and whether this was not difficult to deal with, Fisher made this rhetorical riposte: "Don't you think I would not just like to tell everyone to go to hell?"[209] In response to another direct question about why he resigned the presidency of CBC and left the UPC, Fisher replied with a clear trace of bitterness in his voice, "I got tired of getting my ass kicked."[210] Judged on the historical merits of the last days of CBC, it is difficult to dismiss those comments as lacking substance or being entirely unwarranted.

After he decided to resign from the presidency of CBC and relinquish his ministerial credentials, Don Fisher set his face to a future apart from his religious heritage and never looked back. He was especially devastated at the collapse of the college and regarded its destruction as a personal failure.[211] Christian leaders before him also felt that sting. Martin Luther died at Eisleben, Germany on 18 February 1546. Though gravely ill, he successfully mediated a dispute between feuding magistrates and preached his final sermon three days earlier in the Andreaskirche (Church of St. Andrew).[212] Only five people attended. Luther is said to have lamented the failure of reform. Luther had the good fortune of dying, but Fisher had to live. He found it extremely difficult to deal with failure.[213] His detractors of course placed the blame squarely on his shoulders. His supporters refused to accept that. "It is not right nor is it true

---

[206] Joseph Howell interview, 21 April 1999.

[207] Karissa (Fisher) Hopkins interview, 15 August 2013.

[208] Arless Glass interview, 24 September 2013.

[209] April Purtell interview, 16 January 1999. The comment was made in 1984.

[210] Comment made during a conversation the author had with Fisher over lunch in Los Angeles on 17 November 1989.

[211] Donna Fisher interview, 3 January 1999, also said "it was not in his nature to look back." He never spoke of his career at CBC. Doris (Fisher) Newman interview, 20 August 2013.

[212] WA, vol. 51, pp. 187-194 on Matthew 11:25-30.

[213] Susan (Fisher) Paynter interview, 24 January 1999.

to shoulder him with the demise of the Bible School."²¹⁴ Don Fisher felt he had somehow betrayed the CBC tradition and on one occasion was heard to say "what will Ernie Moyer say about me now?" The vision he had embraced and articulated in Hot Springs and attempted to bring to fruition at Jackson and later at CBC was irretrievably gone. He lost that vision entirely and gave it up in the aftermath of the shattering experience of CBC. Close associates describe him as "shocked" and "disillusioned" over the drastic changes in the Pacific Northwest and the stranglehold of disunity, noncooperation, and incessant rumor-mongering which convulsed the once unified, cooperative and peace-loving districts of Oregon, Washington, and Idaho, and which resulted in an almost total inability to operate a college based on principles of proper higher education.²¹⁵ Fisher was absolutely rocked by the ferocity of the forces which arose against him in Portland.²¹⁶ The destruction of CBC was also in one sense the destruction of Don Fisher. It is absolutely specious to suggest that Don Fisher was a charlatan masquerading as a minister of the gospel while engaged in the deliberately subversive activity of corrupting young minds, or worst still, to present him as a wolf in sheep's clothing. Such tactics reflect the classic *ad hominem* method of attack. They contribute nothing.

Some of his detractors have attempted to establish that Fisher was engaged in immoral conduct with the insinuation that his enthusiasm for young people and education was a front for another sort of passion which was neither salutary nor sanctified.²¹⁷ Not a shred of evidence has ever been produced to sustain such rumors

---

²¹⁴ Norman Rutzen interview, 8 February 1999. Others asserted, "I do not fault Don Fisher for the demise of the college." E.W. Yadon interview, 25 July 2013. Similar comments in Wayne Nigh interview, 25 July 2013, and Wallace Leonard interview, 3 August 2013.

²¹⁵ Jerry Peden interview, 19 July 2002. "Should you choose to write about the 'fallout' of the closure of the college I trust that you will give a fair treatment to the effect that it had upon Don's dreams, how they were shattered and how it destroyed him personally." Jerry Peden, letter to Thomas A. Fudge, 27 September 1999. Confirmed in April Purtell interview, 13 April 2013.

²¹⁶ Karissa (Fisher) Hopkins interview, 15 August 2013.

²¹⁷ Asserted in Paul Dugas interview, 25 January 1999. Others believe the rumors to be true and allege that the truth was not told by JCM officials when Fisher came to the Northwest in 1981. Wallace Leonard interview, 3 August 2013.

which are nothing more than vulgar innuendo based on third-hand hearsay. What seems evident is that such gossip was known in the Northwest in 1981 when Fisher was considered for the presidency of CBC. The Washington and Idaho Districts were unwilling to make decisions based on rumor and innuendo. Oregon was prepared to act on that basis.[218] This helps to explain the lines of demarcation evident in the spring of that year in the voting for Don Fisher. There is in fact evidence which mitigates against such allegations. For example, Thomas Craft, president of JCM, although admittedly happy to see Fisher leave in 1981, also testified, without hesitation or qualification, that he knew of no immoral impropriety on Fisher's part during the years he served on the faculty and administration of Jackson College of Ministries. Craft asserted, with some confidence, that if such allegations had any basis in fact, he would have known about it.[219] Nevertheless, Don Fisher was homosexual. This is not a fact for dispute. What has hitherto been uncertain is when Fisher began to practice that sexual orientation. Thomas Craft says it could not have been in Mississippi. Fisher told Jerry Dillon in 1988, in reply to a direct question, that while he was a licensed minister in the UPC, he had not had any sexual contact outside his marriage.[220] Unless one is prepared to argue that Don Fisher was a liar, there seems to be no compelling reason to assume otherwise. Some disagree, and cite the New Testament passage where it alludes to those who, because they did not love the truth, fall prey to falsehood and therefore perish.[221] This is a possibility, of course, but it is difficult to see Fisher as anything other than a man of principle, integrity, and honesty through the time he served the

---

[218] Raymond A. Sirstad interview, 27 August 2013. Oregon simply did not trust Don Fisher. Arless Glass interview, 24 September 2013.

[219] Thomas L. Craft interview, 20 April 1999. Without naming the source, Dugas' allegation was presented to Craft who dismissed it as untenable. Reconfirmed in Thomas L. Craft interview, 25 September 2013, Terry, Mississippi. Others do not believe the Dugas claim. Arless Glass interview, 24 September 2013.

[220] Jerry Dillon interview, 4 January 1998, Vancouver, Washington, and also expressed during the Harry and Freda Fisher interview, 8 December 2000. Fisher had nothing to gain by lying and nothing to lose by telling the truth. Fisher made the same confession. Ronna (Fisher) Russell interview, 20 July 2013, and shortly before his death. Susan (Fisher) Paynter interview, 24 January 1999.

[221] Wallace Leonard interview, 3 August 2013 referring to II Thessalonians 2:10.

UPC and despite intensive research, no evidence to the contrary has come to light. Former colleagues remain unbowed by such rumor and have noted that among the great joys of their lives was team-teaching with Don Fisher at the New Life Pentecostal Church in Bridgeton, Missouri, pastored by Guy Roam (1918-1994).[222]

This strong declaration of defence for Don Fisher, however, cannot be extended to cover the remainder of his life. Sometime after Fisher left CBC, and the UPC, he radically changed course and his values took on a different focus. It would be remiss to ignore or overlook the contradictions which were manifested in the last years of his life. To sidestep these more difficult matters would be disingenuous. In the post CBC era, there is one case of possible financial impropriety occurring at Christ for the People Community Church. The details are unimportant but a sizeable contribution to the church does not appear to have been properly recorded or handled according to regular procedures. At the very least, this leaves a door open for doubt or serious questions of irregularity in terms of bookkeeping, transparency, and accountability.[223] It must be stressed that the incident has not been established as theft or other unbecoming conduct. It simply remains as an unresolved question with potential integrity implications.

Rumors and revelations of Don Fisher's homosexuality led to considerable scandal, resulted in his temporary ostracization by some family members, lasting rejection by some of his longstanding friends, and widespread gossip and innuendo. Sometime after March 1983, late in that calendar year or early 1984, Fisher began a homosexual relationship which spanned the remainder of his life. This relationship did not involve anyone with previous connections to CBC, JCM, the UPC, or Christ for the People Community Church.[224] A careful investigation reveals several factors which should be taken into account. The man Fisher spent the last ten

---

[222] Thetus Tenney interview, 6 June 2013.

[223] April Purtell interviews, 16 January 1999 and 13 April 2013. Purtell was Fisher's secretary at CBC and at the church and had responsibility for financial records. In Purtell's opinion, the matter was irregular in its handling, not theft.

[224] It has been rumored that Fisher had a homosexual relationship with a CBC student while president. Arless Glass interview, 24 September 2013. Based upon the specific details contained in the allegation this is verifiably impossible.

years of his life with moved from Tennessee to the Portland area in August 1982. He had no previous connection to Don Fisher. He did not meet Fisher until the following summer during a routine business transaction. By this time Fisher's CBC and UPC career was some months in the past. The friendship between the two men did not advance to a physical level until several months thereafter, some time during the autumn of 1983 at the earliest. There is every indication this was Fisher's first homosexual experience. It is his partner's considered opinion that Fisher had not previously been involved sexually with anyone outside his marriage.[225]

In 1984, Fisher left the Portland area and went to Sacramento to take up the previously mentioned church position, after several attempts by Paul Adams to secure Fisher's services. Working with

6.17  Sharon, Paul and Carl Adams, and the author,
Palm Springs, California, 17 August 2013

senior pastor Paul Adams and associate minister David Shebley (1933-2010, see ill.0.1, p. xviii, Shebley is fourth from the right, in the back row), Fisher was the administrator at Christ the King Community Church and the head of a Bible college which he started under the auspices of the church. In a brief space of time between sixty and seventy students were studying with Fisher.[226] A public incident in California prompted Fisher to resign from the church and abandon traditional Christian ministry forever, entering secular employment. The Bible college program in Sacramento did not continue once Fisher left the area. He moved to Los Angeles in

---

[225] Jesse Martin interview, 17 August 2013.
[226] Paul Adams interview, 16 August 2013.

1985, and for the next decade worked for Colonial Life Insurance. For about two years, Fisher's sexual reorientation was not widely known. During that time, he deceived his wife, and one might argue, with considerable justification, misled his family and friends and treated his wife and daughters in a manner that simply cannot be defended or condoned.[227]

There is staggering irony in this situation. Fisher firmly told the Washington District and CBC Boards that he would no longer countenance the abuse or mistreatment of his family at the hands of his enemies. Fisher had been well-known for his firm family-centered orientation.[228] Within two years, Fisher was engaged in conduct unbecoming a man who claimed to love his family. It is easy to stand in judgment and reduce complicated situations to facile categories. Clearly, Don Fisher found himself in an untenable situation, was stalling for time in an effort to stumble upon a happy ending for all concerned, and being caught on the horns of a dilemma handled a difficult situation even more badly than might have been. His behavior in this particular instance was absolutely and inexplicably inconsistent with the balance, honor, principles and integrity that previously marked his life. Why this should have been defies simplistic explanation. We shall never know for certain. His life was a study in contrasts. He garnered the love and affection of many students yet sacrificed members of his own family on the altar of his own ambitions. Ronna lived in fear of her father her entire life. Reflecting on his demise she commented that, "it was a relief to me when he died. And I have never missed him. Not for a second. Not once. No missing."[229] Karissa considered his death meaningless to the extent that by the time his life ended there was no longer any meaningful relationship.[230] Susan was also relieved when he died and felt that her grieving process had already been experienced years earlier.[231] Fisher had once taught that if one had a

---

[227] "I also do not disparage his life. I take comfort in knowing that still today many are stronger because of his influence in their lives." Donna Fisher, letter to Thomas A. Fudge, 28 September 2006. FC, inv.doc.no 0707-4349-30.

[228] David and Barbara Wasmundt interview, 3 October 2013.

[229] Ronna (Fisher) Russell interview, 20 July 2013.

[230] Karissa (Fisher) Hopkins interview, 15 August 2013.

[231] Susan (Fisher) Paynter interview, 26 August 2013.

proper vertical relationship (with God) than one's horizontal relationships (with family and friends) would also be positive and proper. The failure of meaningful connection to his family in the last ten years of his life is one of the deepest tragedies of this story.

For most of his professional and ministerial career, Don Fisher emphasized balance in every aspect of human life and faith. There is considerable evidence that he practiced that philosophy. For many years, especially during his time at JCM and CBC, he gave himself selflessly to young men and women. He was devoted to his students. He encouraged discipleship, not of himself but of Jesus Christ (ill.6.10, p. 342). He rarely missed opportunities for ministry and was tireless in his efforts to make Christ real and to cultivate the work of the Holy Spirit in the lives of believers. He became an important mentor to countless young men and women. He was selfless, giving, and balanced. Between 1966 and 1983, Don Fisher encountered a series of obstacles and setbacks in his professional life. He endured deep disappointment, struggled with mounting opposition, and even had to face persecution at the hands of former friends and his brethren. This intensified at JCM after 1979 and reached fever pitch in Portland. The clash between heretics and politics during the last days of CBC reflect aspects of that struggle. After fighting to the limit of his endurance, he walked away. After he left CBC and forsook the UPC, resentment began to fill up the empty spaces of his life and a root of bitterness took hold of Don Fisher. He began thinking less about the needs of others and started to focus on his own needs. Bitterness turned to selfishness. Perhaps Fisher reached a point where he felt entitled. After years of sacrifice and working for the good of others, he decided to focus on himself. Though entirely understandable, that decision was perilous. After 1985, Don Fisher openly embraced his own needs. Selfishness and a lack of balance were the results. He paid for those choices with his life.

There is yet another matter which should be brought to bear the weight of inquiry. In June 2004, Mickey Friend (senior pastor of the former ABI college church) while discussing CBC in general and the matter of Don Fisher specifically wondered "did we kill him?"[232] The "we" referred to the UPC, even though Friend had long ceased affiliation. The immediate answer is that there is no relation between Fisher's UPC ministry and his later life and untimely death. A more thoughtful reply requires a broader frame of reference, some nuance and of course considerable conjecture. This enables some basis for interpretation which is not the same thing as explanation. There are those *au fait* with the situation who believe the UPC had contributory responsibility in Don Fisher's death.[233] Such opinion requires expansion. Matters of human sexuality cannot easily be reduced to simplistic explanations. Those who attempt to do so are either dishonest or terribly uninformed. Sexuality is among the more complex factors of human identity.

While ultimately unprovable, it is probable that Don Fisher had latent homosexual tendencies from a young age. Nonetheless, there are good grounds for seeing Don Fisher's sexuality and his eventual struggle for authenticity as not something exceptional.[234] Being raised in a particular cultural and religious environment which took the firm view that homosexuality was sin, would have led Fisher to suppress any latent tendencies he may have had.[235] Thus he married, had a family, committed himself to ministry, and kept his sexuality within the boundaries of his marriage. Had Fisher encountered sexual temptation in his life, particularly same gender attraction, to whom could he have turned for counsel or support? The church

---

[232] Mickey Friend interview, 15 June 2004, St. Paul, Minnesota. Others wondered the same thing. Wayne Nigh interview, 25 July 2013.

[233] Jerry Dillon interview, 5 January 1999, takes this position.

[234] Mel White, *Stranger at the Gate: To Be Gay and Christian in America* (New York: Simon and Schuster, 1994), John J. McNeill, *Both Feet Firmly Planted in Midair: My Spiritual Journey* (Louisville: Westminster John Knox Press, 1998), Michael Ford, *Wounded Prophet: A Portrait of Henri J.M. Nouwen* (New York: Doubleday, 1999).

[235] Susan (Fisher) Paynter interview, 24 January 1999, thinks his betrayal and bitterness gave him an excuse to make the lifestyle choices he did. Fisher did say in June 1984 that he was sick and tired of trying to live his life to please others. Susan (Fisher) Paynter interview, 26 August 2013. Ronna (Fisher) Russell interview, 20 July 2013, believes her father was biologically homosexual his entire life. In 1995, Fisher said he believed he had been born homosexual. Jewel (Yadon) Dillon interview, 24 July 2013. Fisher told Donna late in his life that he had homosexual inclinations from age four. As a result of her own recent training as a medical practitioner Susan Paynter now believes that her father was born with homosexual tendencies. Susan (Fisher) Paynter interview, 26 August 2013.

has been described as the only army that shoots its wounded. All too often throughout its tumultuous history, the church has subjected to cruel and unusual treatment those of its members found in situations of compromise, or even those who were brave enough to confess weakness or problems in an effort to find help.[236] The fourth-century historian Ammianus Marcellinus noted that in the year 361 the anti-Christian emperor Julian the Apostate considered Christians their own worst enemies noting that experience taught him that "no wild animal is such an enemy of humanity as most Christians are in their deadly hatred of each other."[237] The opinion was also reflected by some Christians. "We have behaved like wild animals toward each other, oblivious to the grace of divine love for humankind."[238] The Cathars endured two decades of relentless violence at the hands of the church before suffering virtual annihilation. Hussite blood was spilled in the Czech lands during five crusades proclaimed by ecclesiastical preachers. Those who found themselves forced out of the Missouri Synod Lutheran Church and the Southern Baptist Convention believed they had been unfairly treated by their brethren. Protests to the contrary, apart from murder and literal bloodshed, such realities have also been part of the fabric of the UPC and ministers therein have spoken of the importance of concealing the reality of one's inner life. Such masks are effective only temporarily.[239]

It is likely that for some time before 1984, Fisher lived in denial of his primary sexual orientation. Theologically, he held to the notion that such proclivities were sinful. Had he turned to his UPC brethren there is every reason to believe he would have been rejected, exposed, and banished. Fisher must have been certain that even if he were so inclined, the outcome would have been fatal. Compassion, support, and confidentiality are not virtues public figures can rely on. In such matters, no one has ever characterized the UPC as merciful. Turning to professional therapists would have

---

[236] Note Fisher's 1975 comment about homosexuality in Appendix 2, p. 420.
[237] The *Res Gestae* 22.5.4 records this stinging observation. The critical edition is Wolfgang Seyfarth, ed., *Ammiani Marcellini rerum gestarum libri qui supersunt*, 2 vols (Leipzig: Teubner, 1978), vol. 1, p. 256.
[238] Maximus the Confessor, Letter 14, in Migne, PG, vol. 91, col. 541. (*c.* 630s).
[239] Carmont, *The Naked Mentor: One Man's Journey, One Man's Journal*, pp. 137-139.

been virtually unthinkable for Fisher, and if he was in denial this would have required him to face his own sexuality. Beyond this, counselling psychology was generally frowned upon within the UPC. If Don Fisher struggled with issues of sexuality he kept that to himself, poured himself into his work, and directed his energy in that direction. The popular idea that such issues can be resolved with sufficient prayer and fasting is questionable. The pervasive UPC "come to the altar and pray through and make a new start" approach has all too often resulted in dismal failure. Fisher's energetic commitment to the work of running a college program at Jackson and later in Portland may have insulated him from other preoccupations. Such strategies, however, were temporary.

There were instances of Fisher uncharacteristically breaking down emotionally. There was a definite occurrence at McCormick's Creek in 1975, in a classroom at JCM in 1976, and at the Vancouver church during the CBC 1981-82 academic year. On each occasion the subject of transformation was at issue. One cannot speculate with certainty on whether Don Fisher felt guilt for having brought persecution upon his family and thereby transferring disgrace upon them. In his gay relationship, Fisher found someone who did not judge his past and had not been part of his earlier life. One may surmise that Fisher found an emotional refuge in this relationship.

"Did we kill him?" The Don Fisher who kicked off the academic year at CBC on 21 September 1981 was a man filled with enthusiasm, vision, determination, and what appeared to have been a total commitment to a rare and fulfilling opportunity. A tide of oceanic proportions was clearly against him from the start. Fisher not only lost the contest, he lost badly. What Fisher lost in his last stand was more than a job, more, even, than the presidency of CBC. There would be no place else to go within the educational orbit of the UPC. He lost his ministerial credentials.[240] That meant he could no longer function in ministry within his own church organization. Any pastor who dared bring Fisher on staff and use him in any capacity would have been called to account before the relevant District Board and censured. Don Fisher could easily have

---

[240] Even had he retained his ministerial credentials, there was no place within the UPC for a man like Fisher to go. Thetus Tenney interview, 6 June 2013.

maintained a hold on Christ for the People Community Church but he had no track record of being a church builder and only slightly more as a pastor. By the time he resigned his pastorate, Christ for the People Community Church was "literally falling apart."[241]

Outside the UPC, he was an unknown entity. The man was well suited for the academic world. But outside the UPC he had no identity, no experience, no qualification. He applied at the highly regarded independent liberal arts Reed College in Portland but was turned down.[242] By 1983, Fisher was a middle-aged man possessing an undergraduate degree from Cascade College. That qualification did not even register on the scale of calibration in the academic world. The fact is, the UPC pummelled Don Fisher into submission and then when he was down, kicked him repeatedly. In the midst of his persecution at the hands of his own brethren, Fisher found himself isolated, frustrated, and vulnerable. "I kind of wonder if he just gave up."[243] Family members later perceived Fisher as being extremely vulnerable after he left CBC and gave up his ministerial credentials.[244] He did have the opportunity to assume significant administrative involvement with the newly formed "Global Network of Christian Ministries," founded by L.H. Hardwick in 1986, but by the time Hardwick's new fellowship took shape, it was already too late. He had some initial connection with the new organization but it was short-lived. Beyond this, Hardwick had invited Fisher to take up a ministerial position at Christ Church in Nashville, but by the time that opportunity presented itself, Fisher had established himself as a secular businessman in Los Angeles.[245]

At the age of sixteen, Fisher wrote that "the closer you are living to the Lord the more temptations you will naturally have."[246]

---

[241] Jerry Dillon interview, 5 January 1999.
[242] Jerry Dillon, letter to Robert J. Mansueto (Reed College), 18 June 1984, offered a strong recommendation for Fisher. FC, inv.doc.no 0707-5129-34.
[243] Skip Paynter interview, 24 January 1999.
[244] Susan (Fisher) Paynter interview, 26 August 2013.
[245] An undated brochure for Global Christian Ministries, Inc., (*c.* 1986) lists a nominated sixteen member "Steering Committee," together with L.H. Hardwick as "Moderator," and Don Fisher as "Administrator." FC, inv.doc.no 0707-4669-31. Dan Lewis, letter to Thomas A. Fudge, 24 May 2013, p. 4. FC, inv.doc.no 0707-5036-33. Confirmed in L.H. Hardwick interview, 22 August 2013.
[246] Don Fisher, "Temptation" *Pentecostal Northwestern News* 9 (No. 7, 1955), p. 3.

Was this conviction part of the foundation upon which Don Fisher attempted to construct a serious program of holistic education in Mississippi and Oregon? Was the struggle between temptation (of every description) and spirituality a factor in the themes revealed at McCormick's Creek, in the pages of *The Velveteen Rabbit*, in the spiritually coming of age described in *The Garden of the Beloved*, in the trials and triumphs of *Jonathan Livingston Seagull*, and emphasized in the several tests endured by *The Knight in the Rusty Armor*? Perhaps in his post-CBC isolation, Fisher yielded to opportunity and circumstantial temptation which had previously been suppressed. Latent tendencies now proved more difficult to resist. Others suggest that Don Fisher was a wicked sinner, a reprobate, a pervert, who not only gave up everything he had worked for up to 1983, but also turned himself over, willingly, to the lusts of the flesh joining, the company of the "lewd fellows of the baser sort" (Acts 17:5).

One may argue that Fisher's sexual preferences and his life after 1983 onwards were chosen and fostered. Those sympathetic to him regarded his persecution within the UPC as unjust. The pressure "drove him to a place of discouragement and I think the devil got him when he was in his weak moment and took him off."[247] By 1983, Don Fisher found himself in the midst of "the perfect storm of failure which he was not used to" brought about by the demise of CBC, the loss of his professional identity, and the silence of his former friends.[248] That this perfect storm happened to occur in the Northwest made the situation more traumatic. These factors are important to consider for a man with homosexual tendencies who fought these inclinations successfully for decades, but encountered vulnerability in the aftermath of deep personal failure, gave up the fight against his inner demons, and embraced his natural urges.

On the other hand, regardless of why he did what he did after leaving CBC, no one is an island. Don Fisher had been born into, nurtured by, and shaped according to the particular culture of the UPC. Can they be held responsible for his choices and life? No. Fisher had to live with and die with his own choices and decisions and their inevitable consequences. "Did we kill him?" The UPC

---

[247] Harry Fisher interview, 8 December 2000.
[248] Karissa (Fisher) Hopkins interview, 15 August 2013.

must bear some responsibility for the choices and decisions which Fisher made, for he was in some sense a product of its unique environment.[249] There is a hint of parallel with a pre-Christian text of ethical teaching in which it is noted that when an influential or powerful person speaks, everyone is silent and they revere whatever is said. But if a poor man speaks, they say "who is this fellow?" and if he stumbles they conspire to destroy him.[250] Some assessments of this are rather pointed. "One of these days, Jesus Christ is going to ask some people right around here, 'where were you when Don Fisher was in prison? You didn't visit him. When he was bound, you didn't minister. When he was hungry, you didn't feed him. What you did was kick him out and say good riddance! And as much as you've done it unto him, you've done it unto me.'"[251] The manner in which the UPC treated him must be numbered among the salient influences which came to bear upon latent personality characteristics, perhaps linked to a sense of inadequacy related to his small stature and combined with his driving sense of mission. Don Fisher did not choose his personality, and he grew up believing that truth was paramount and that human achievement was important. It is certain that Fisher believed that the human spirit had been created to unfold, not to be folded or twisted into something like a paper crane – perhaps beautiful but twisted and distorted. This basic conviction perhaps lay at the root of Fisher's discontent with the UPC. Beyond these considerations, the witch-hunting that closed ranks around CBC between 1981 and 1983 was a function and an outgrowth of UPC thinking and culture. Fisher bears unavoidable personal responsibility but the UPC cannot be excused from sharing part of the burden. Unfortunately, in matters of moral failing, it has been customary within the UPC to find condemnation rather than restoration as the principle response.

Heresy hunters were after Don Fisher for a number of years before the final showdown finally came at CBC. Defenders of UPC orthodoxy pursued him relentlessly. This is understandable from a history of ideas perspective, in which people operate within an

---

[249] Donna Fisher interview, 3 January 1999, stressed that regardless of how the UPC treated Fisher, the more crucial issue was his own personal responsibility.

[250] *Ecclesiasticus, or The Wisdom of Jesus son of Sirach* 13:23.

[251] Jerry Dillon interview, 5 January 1999 appropriating Matthew 25: 31-46.

inquisitorial mentality devoted to defending God and truth from every possible taint of impurity. Fisher believed one thing, his detractors believed another. Fisher adopted a particular philosophy and approach to ministry and education while many of his denominational colleagues followed another path. There was bound to be serious conflict. The whale and the elephant are two creatures so unlike they cannot possibly live together.[252] The struggles within the UPC, the Missouri Synod, the Southern Baptist Convention, at Fuller Seminary, and earlier within Roman Catholicism were not simply political. They were also predicated upon attempts to sustain the traditional beliefs and historical continuity of those respective communities of faith. These issues were considerably more serious than simple controversy.[253] What is striking is the raw lust of that pursuit within the Church which dogged Fisher's footsteps. That lust, that pursuit, was clearly a manifestation of the madness of theology. Within the Missouri Synod, Jacob Preus and Herman

6.18 Fr. George Tyrrell, rare, undated photograph, early 20th century

6.19 Tyrrell's grave in the Parish Church of St Mary, Anglican cemetery at Storrington, West Sussex

Otten represented an insatiable hunger that is part and parcel of the madness of theology – which requires enemies in order to flourish

---

[252] Karl Barth described he and Rudolf Bultmann, and later Emil Brunner, in this sense. Eberhard Busch, *Karl Barth: His Life from Letters and Autobiographical Texts*, trans. John Bowden (Philadelphia: Fortress, 1976), p. 449.
[253] Dilday, *Higher Ground: A Call for Christian Civility*, pp. 2 and 39.

and survive.[254] "Evil geniuses" were toxic. W.A. Criswell believed that "stinking skunks" should not remain among the Southern Baptists. When George Tyrrell died at age forty-eight he was denied burial in a Catholic cemetery. Father Henri Brémond made the sign of the cross over Tyrrell's grave and was disciplined by the church, *suspensio a divinis* meaning he was forbidden to exercise his ministry until further notice.[255] Ministers within the UPC were determined, figuratively, to kill Fisher and the "spiritual creeps" who supported him. His basic philosophy of education, theological proclivities, and position on the teachings of holiness and the *Fundamental Doctrine*, threatened and frightened men so much they conspired to kill the man who incarnated that perceived threat to their own security. The "putrid frogs" had to go. The treatment of Don Fisher was first degree theological homicide. The malice that drove the opposition amounted to murder. They determined that Fisher should be silenced and driven from the fellowship. Murder took hold of them.

Men such as Barry King and Paul Dugas were vociferous in their condemnation of Fisher but there were men in the UPC, such as Norman Rutzen and C.H. Yadon, who defended Fisher with all their might and even recommended him for ministry positions after his tenure ended at CBC.[256] Rutzen went so far as to tell both C. M. Yadon and Verneal Crossley to their faces that their opposition to Fisher was both inconsiderate and unfair.[257] Others affirmed that "he had been mistreated by powerful men who envied him."[258] Some CBC staff members were called before the Washington District Board (ill.5.12, p. 267). One faculty member told that committee he believed Fisher was the subject of a witch-hunt.[259] Between these two camps were chameleons biding their time; men who supported Fisher until it was politically inexpedient and then

---

[254] Burkee, *Power, Politics, and the Missouri Synod* pp. 178-179.

[255] This was in accordance with the Code of Canon Law, lib. VI, pars I, tit. iv, cap. 1, canon 1333 §1. *Codex iuris canonici* [Pontificia Commissio Codici Iuris Canonici Authentice Interpretando] (Vatican City: Libreria Editrice Vaticana, 1989), pp. 416-417. This is not the same thing as being defrocked.

[256] L.H. Hardwick interview, 22 August 2013 notes that Yadon and Rutzen advanced him to Hardwick as a candidate.

[257] Norman Rutzen interview, 24 July 2013.

[258] Dillon, *Annals of God's Grace*, p. 25.

[259] Roger Yadon interview, 8 October 2013.

switched to the other side. Others perpetually remained steadfast in the wishy-washy valley of indecision, afflicted by the paralysis of analysis, unwilling or unable to take sides, unwilling or unable to declare themselves for or against. It is difficult to say anything constructive about temporizers when the existence of a college is at stake, when the uncertain futures of young men and women hang in a precarious balance, and when the life and ministry of one of their own colleagues awaits a fateful verdict.

The process by which Don Fisher was publicly tried, excoriated, and ultimately condemned to denominational death and murdered in the name of God and in defence of absolute truth claims is not especially different from heresy hunting within the history of the Church. Medieval Cathars, Hussites, and Waldensians, early modern Anabaptists, and Quakers, modern Lutherans and Baptists, and many others have walked that path of terror and faith throughout much of Christian history. Men and women have always been expendable when they have clashed with agendas foreign to the gospel, kingdom principles, and the ethics of Jesus. Too often in the history of religion, when heretics and politics collide, the latter wins. The chameleons are always accomplices. Sebastian Castellio hit the nail on the head in the sixteenth century when he wrote that to kill a man is not to defend a doctrine, it is to kill a man.[260] "Did we kill him?" There is evidence for concluding that Don Fisher was hurt more profoundly by the betrayal of the temporizers (some of whom he thought were his friends) than he was by those who openly declared him heretical and called for his removal. *Ex post facto* explanations and defences have seldom been persuasive. The posture and fate of those stranded in the middle is not anomalous. It has been estimated that at least 950 congregations within the Missouri Synod were sympathetic to Seminex and its *raison d'être* but their support was essentially silent.[261]

Rightly or wrongly, Don Fisher has been excoriated chiefly because he was gay. His illness and death were regarded by some of his old detractors as divine retribution for his heresy, and his

---

[260] Sebastian Castellio, *Contra libellum Calvini in quo ostendere conatur haereticos iure gladii coercendos esse* (Holland, 1612), unpaginated but #77. No modern edition. The book was written in 1554.

[261] Tietjen, *Memoirs in Exile: Confessional Hope and Institutional Conflict*, p. 269.

demise was thought to invalidate his work at JCM and CBC.[262] As he lay dying, he received messages from former UPC colleagues which have been characterized as "horrible letters," condemning and judgmental, uttering terrible things, to the extent of declaring satisfaction at his condition and smugly pronouncing a verdict of hell and damnation.[263] This is not unusual. During the Lutheran Seminex controversy, John Tietjen began receiving hate phone calls at home.[264] When former CBC faculty member David Wasmundt was diagnosed with multiple sclerosis in 1987, Joan Dillon, wife of Albert Dillon and sister of Barry King, asserted that the illness was God's punishment on Wasmundt for having left the UPC.[265] It is unknown what Joan Dillon's thoughts were when her own husband was diagnosed with terminal cancer and died in 2007.

As recently as 2013, it was still being alleged that the heart of the conflict at Jackson between 1976 and 1981 was homosexuality, noting specifically the person of Don Fisher.[266] The assumption is without merit. There were those who lost no time enthusiastically commenting on Fisher's sexual orientation and the manner of his dying.[267] It is true that Fisher remained in a homosexual relationship to the end of his life. There is nothing to suggest that Fisher ever considered his later lifestyle to be sinful. Thus, he seems to have

---

[262] Jim Wilkins interview, 1 May 1999, and Stan and Sandra Blevins interview, 11 April 1999, reflecting gossip. Paul Dugas interview, 25 January 1999 claims the Washington District discovered the truth about Fisher's sexuality. This explains his resignation. The statement is specious.

[263] Fisher refused to allow these letters to be preserved. Susan (Fisher) Paynter interview, 26 August 2013.

[264] Tietjen, *Memoirs in Exile*, p. 117. Australian heresy suspect Samuel Angus received hate mail. S. Angus, *Alms for Oblivion* (Sydney: Angus and Robertson, 1943), p. 183.

[265] Barbara Wasmundt interview, 3 October 2013.

[266] These were among the remarks made by O.C. [Oscar Calvit] Marler when asked to comment on the JCM situation. Reported in Don C. Marler, letters to Thomas A. Fudge, 20 and 24 January 2013. FC, inv.doc.no 0707-4711-32.

[267] Examples include Raymond Woodson interview, 17 January 2001, Vancouver, Washington, Barry King interview, 20 January 1999, and Cleveland Becton interview, 14 April 1999, who brought Fisher up and made pointed comments. King said "he was A gay!" To his credit, Becton later withdrew the comments and apologized for introducing remarks which he admitted were irrelevant for discussions concerning Fisher's work at JCM and CBC.

died unrepentant. Is the question of his sexual orientation a matter of sin and salvation? For many people, it clearly is. There is some preference for the words spoken by C.H. Yadon during a raucous board meeting at which the salvation of non-UPC people was being discussed. Someone turned to Yadon and asked him for his opinion. He replied that the matter was not within his purview for elsewhere it had been written "I have the keys of death and hell" (Revelation 1:18). Christ may have given to Peter the keys of the kingdom, but the keys of death and hell had been given to no one. The price one pays for freedom, in many cases, is the consequences of one's action and the non-involvement of God. A twenty-minute tryst in a hotel room on a December afternoon in 1980 was not, despite the hue and cry of men such as John Ankerberg, Jimmy Swaggart, and Jerry Falwell, the sum and substance of the sin of Jim Bakker.[268] Sin and transgression on any level are not matters to be taken lightly but it is altogether unfortunate when issues of sexuality are assigned a higher premium and considered more egregious than everything else. Passing judgment on this aspect of Fisher's life, assigning or denying salvation, or even essaying an opinion on the question of homosexuality is not relevant in this context. That will please some and dismay others. The one without sin may cast the first stone. That admonition disqualifies most people, and opinion on the matter is neither germane to this study nor significant. As C.H. Yadon noted, no one has been given the keys of death and hell. Trusting in the mercy of God appears to be the best option.[269]

What is more salient than sexuality and sexual behavior is ethics. Two weeks before he died Fisher expressed regret for all of the pain he had caused his family.[270] In 1989, he declared "I have always loved Donna and I always will. Nothing can change that."[271] Where it is quite impossible to avoid condemning Don Fisher is over the enormous gulf that separates his words from his actions, especially as he neared the end of his life. Don Fisher did not die suddenly. He had plenty of time to think, to reason, to imagine, to

---

[268] Jim Bakker, *I Was Wrong* (Nashville: Thomas Nelson Publishers, 1996), pp. 13, 20, 49, 63, 73.
[269] Thetus Tenney interview, 6 June 2013.
[270] Harry and Freda Fisher interview, 13 July 2005.
[271] The comment was made over lunch in Los Angeles on 17 November 1989.

deliberate on his life, to review his conduct, and prepare himself for the cessation of human life. In his last months, former students had opportunity to visit with him on several occasions. According to some opinion, "he did not have a deeply spiritual lifestyle," while others suggested he eventually abandoned Christianity altogether.[272] As a counterpoint, Fisher provided assurances that he had put his house in order, was in a proper relationship with God, one he characterized as more profoundly right than at any other time in his life, was unafraid to die, and was at peace.[273] A few days before he lapsed into a state of unconsciousness, which characterized his last days, he telephoned former CBC student Audrey Zapalac and confirmed he was at peace with God and quite prepared to die. He told Zapalac that the song which meant the most to him at that particular moment was the well-known 1882 Fanny J. Crosby hymn, "Redeemed." She sang the first verse to him. "Redeemed how I love to proclaim it! Redeemed by the blood of the Lamb; Redeemed through his infinite mercy, His child, and forever, I am." His last words to her were "that's the one."[274] Fisher argued that his ministry had not ended in 1985, and that during the last ten years of his life he had led many people to Christ. Family members consider that perhaps in his later life Fisher's faith finally became real.[275]

In those last weeks when he knew he could not recover and death was coming, for reasons that have always puzzled and perplexed many of his former students and colleagues, he never made a gesture to his wife Donna, whom he claimed to always love. Why? Thirty-seven years earlier he had written to his parents about falling in love with the young Donna Lewis, noting he had never imagined love could be so wonderful. At the end there was not a word. Had he forgotten? That does not seem possible. This behavior may be considered as the unforgiveable sin in his life.

---

[272] Arlen Guidroz and David Bernard interviews, 15/16 April 1999.

[273] Essentially the same assurances were communicated to his parents in late November 1995. Harry and Freda Fisher interview, 13 July 2005.

[274] Audrey (Zapalac) Greer interview, 22 September 2013, and letter to Thomas A. Fudge, 24 September 2013. FC, inv.doc.no 0707-5334-34.

[275] Those who heard this directly from Fisher include Paul Adams interview, 16 August 2013, and his niece Vonnie Lewis interview, 28 August 2013, Vancouver, Washington. Ronna (Fisher) Russell interview, 20 July 2013.

Such unfathomable neglect can only be rightly characterized as inexplicable, insufferable, and unacceptable. It tends to subvert or at least call into question all of the goodness he did in his lifetime, all of the sound discipleship he engaged in, all of the principles he stood for and defended, and the teachings he left with his many students and followers. Don Fisher dishonored himself and his life more with this sin of omission than by any sin of commission.[276]

The end of the story leaps forward in time, a dozen years after the decline of CBC had reached its nadir and the destruction of the college was complete. The tale largely played out on public stages in Jackson and Portland reached the last act in southern California.

> *I have a journey, sir, shortly to go.*
> *My master calls me, I must not say no*
> *The weight of this sad time we must obey*
> *Speak what we feel, not what we ought to say*
> *The oldest hath borne most. We that are young*
> *Shall never see so much, nor live so long.*[277]

In early December 1995, Don Fisher sent a letter to his friends expressing great thankfulness for meaningful relationships and wishing his friends richest blessings.[278] One week later, on an early Tuesday morning, 12 December, at the age of fifty-six, Don Fisher died as a result of AIDS in Los Angeles far, far away from the storms of theological controversy and political conflict which had swirled around him in Jackson, Mississippi and Portland, Oregon. He died nearly forgotten by the United Pentecostal Church, an organization he had served for more than twenty-five years. The oversight cannot be condemned.[279] Some who felt they had been

---

[276] The only communication was a telephone call, by Donna, wherein she confessed no ill will towards him. It may be supposed that he no longer had any emotional connection to his former wife. Ronna (Fisher) Russell interview, 20 July 2013. Former colleagues were puzzled by his detachment. Jewel (Yadon) Dillon interview, 24 July 2013. Close friends have been unable to shed any light on this matter, but note that in contrast, Donna sent Don's partner a condolence card when her former husband died. Jesse Martin interview, 17 August 2013.

[277] King Lear, Act V, Scene III.

[278] Don Fisher, letter to his friends, 5 December 1995. See Appendix 21, p. 459.

[279] It would be indefensible to ignore gestures of good will extended to Fisher in his last days. On 12 June 1995, Fisher received the author and April Purtell in

harsh in attitude to Fisher went to see him, asked forgiveness, hugged his neck and kissed his cheek.[280] For much of his life "he was a tormented person."[281] At the end he was calm. Whatever bitterness had taken root in him years earlier was no longer evident. Those who were with him in the last days have testified that Don Fisher seemed to be at peace. In the hours before he died, hymns of the faith from his youth and from his past were sung to him by his friend and recording artist Jesse Martin. The last hymn sung to him was "Great is Thy Faithfulness," one of Fisher's favorites.[282]

6.20 Fisher's grave at the Deschutes Memorial Gardens, Bend, Oregon. *Left to right:* John H. Newman (Fisher's nephew) and Don Fisher, both died in the autumn of 1995, and Fisher's parents, Harry and Freda Fisher, who died in May 2013

He was interred at the Deschutes Memorial Gardens in Bend, Oregon. Ironically, the Oregon District that so badly wanted to get rid of Don Fisher, and went to extraordinary lengths to achieve that objective, wound up with his mortal remains in perpetuity. It had

---

Los Angeles. He related the reception of letters from old "friends" and former colleagues. Near the end of August 1995, Fisher visited Portland for the last time. On that occasion, he spoke of a letter he had received from Nathaniel Urshan. Appendix 20, p. 458. According to Fisher that letter was a magnanimous gesture. Although Fisher remarked that it was "only about twenty years too late," it was clear he was moved by its contents.

[280] Paul Adams interview, 16 August 2013.
[281] Ronna (Fisher) Russell interview, 20 July 2013.
[282] Jesse Martin interview, 17 August 2013.

been his personal desire to be laid to rest in Bend. A few months before his death, he had come for the last time to the city of his birth. During that last visit to the Pacific Northwest he made a special point of making a visit to the cemetery to see the setting. While there he inspected the plot of ground where he would lie at the end of his earthly pilgrimage.[283] He could not have been unaware that his journey was nearly through and that he was about to pay the common debt of humanity.

Did Don Fisher think of himself at the end as *The Knight in the Rusty Armor?* Had he finally rid himself of the barriers which bound him to a form of slavery to false security, to "need-love" only, and which had prevented him from becoming all that he was meant to be? Had he reached the end of the "path of truth," or was he about to embark on that momentous journey? Only Don Fisher could say for sure. Among the last words he wrote to the CBC board, more than twelve-and-a-half years earlier, was "we will all see the glory of God revealed in His time."[284] Where is the glory of God in the last days of CBC? The answers are legend. Former colleagues suggested the last judgment would vindicate Don Fisher. There would be rewards and penalties but these were not about salvation.[285]

The twelfth-century Suger, Abbot of the Priory of St. Denis outside Paris, died in January 1151. His epitaph might be applied to Fisher. "Small of body and family, constrained by a two-fold smallness, he refused, in his smallness, to be a small man."[286] Don

---

[283] Harry and Freda Fisher interview, 13 July 2005. During his illness, Fisher talked on a weekly basis with his parents, and in August 1995 had recovered sufficiently to make that final visit to Portland. During that time he spent a few days in Bend. The exhaustion of the trip sent him to bed for two weeks upon his return to Los Angeles. After Thanksgiving, Harry and Freda went to visit and spent a day and a half with him. They would not see him again.

[284] Don Fisher, letter to the CBC board, 18 March 1983. FC, inv.doc.no 0707-5226-34.

[285] Jewel (Yadon) Dillon interview, 24 July 2013.

[286] "Corpore, gente brevis, gemina brevitate coactus, in brevitate sua noluit esse brevis." Noted in Erwin Panofsky, ed. and trans, *Abbot Suger: On the Abbey Church of St.-Denis and its Art Treasures*, second edition (Princeton: Princeton University Press, 1979), p. 33. Others disagree finding in Fisher the Napoleon complex. "Don was a man of small stature, physically, and he had a small man stature syndrome." Tom Fred Tenney interview, 20 April 1999. Agreement in Jewel

Fisher will always remain linked to the history of an insignificant American Bible college. The paradoxical significance of his work at the colleges in Jackson and Portland should not be underestimated.

6.21 Don Fisher addressing the CBC community on the occasion of his appointment as President, April 1981

No matter how the outcomes of the Fisher experiments at JCM and CBC are assessed, George Sponsler's observation is both sobering and challenging: "Education will be our salvation."[287] Put another way, the character of a society is not gauged according to revenue, fortification, or the beauty of its civic works, but instead by its culture, education, and enlightenment.[288] Don Fisher strove to bring all three in greater measure to the United Pentecostal Church and to the young men and women who chose to share their lives and spiritual journey with his. Eternity will reveal the measure of the man.

---

(Yadon) Dillon interview, 24 July 2013, and David Reynolds interview, 12 August 2013.

[287] George Sponsler interview, 12 February 1999.

[288] From Martin Luther's 1524 address to the civil leaders in German cities advocating the establishment and maintenance of schools. *An die Radherrn aller Stedte deutsches lands* in WA, vol. 15, p. 34.

6.22   Hallway running south past the CBC chapel,
Lombard campus, Winter 1982

# Afterword

*Evil is easy, and has infinite forms.*[1]

7.1 Demolition of the CBC campus, March 1985, looking west

After several years of lingering frustration and futility, the long-abandoned old Lombard campus, a relic of World War II, finally sold. In the fall of 1984, the Port of Portland purchased most of the campus (just under eight acres) for $400,000. Mike Moyer, the son of CBC founder E.G. Moyer, bought the remainder of the property (just under two acres) for $100,000.[2] In March 1985, the CBC buildings were pulled down, the small hill situated on the southwest corner was flattened, excavators and bulldozers obliterated the

---

[1] Blaise Pascal, *Penseés*, p. 129 (no. 408).
[2] *Minutes*, CBC board meeting, 15 May 1984. FC, inv.doc.no 0707-5233-34, and also in Darline Kantola, letter to the CBC board, 13 September 1984. FC, inv.doc.no. 0707-5236-34. The campus property occupied a total of 9.6 acres. The Port of Portland bought 7.77 acres and Moyer took the remaining 1.83 acres.

entire campus.[3] Today, its former location houses a mainly vacant automobile import yard, and is once again available for purchase. There is no evidence that an institution of higher learning ever existed on that site. Nothing remains to indicate that over 1,000 students once studied there. There are no monuments to any of the personalities who devoted their lives to the college. There is no hint of the drama which produced the heretics and politics which once dominated this ordinary piece of land. C.H. Yadon, Don Fisher, and most of their colleagues are dead. The silent empty spaces at 10838 North Lombard Street contain nothing of their memory. For all of the excitement and activity, only largely-forgotten ghosts now prowl the dimly lit corridors of memory. The briefly occupied Vancouver campus was absorbed into office buildings late in the spring of 1983. CBC vanished without visible trace.

7.2 Destruction of the CBC campus

C.H. Yadon's story, told in the Prologue, about a troublesome rat in an Idaho barn was retold from an Oregon point of view. The lone farmer was now a group of determined "experts." Once they acquired their target in the sights of their multi-barrelled shotguns,

---

[3] "We took a ride over by the old school. It's just about all torn [down]. A pretty sad sight actually." *The Journal of Thomas A. Fudge, 1980-1981*, 24 March 1983.

they were just as careless in their eagerness as the erstwhile Idaho farmer. When the firing ceased, and the massive explosion died away, some of the gunmen were dazed and dismayed but they declared they had won the war. They got rid of the rat, all right, but at the cost of destroying a college. And all that remained were smoked-filled skies and charred rubble and ruins. Even some of Fisher's detractors reflected grimly on the carnage and the loss of a once productive Bible college.

In the aftermath, the General Superintendent of the United Pentecostal Church Nathaniel Urshan, formally requested that the CBC library be loaned to the UPC headquarters. This request was taken under advisement and considered at some length but ultimately declined by the College Board.[4] Instead, the library of more than 9,000 volumes was housed in the facilities of Valley Pentecostal Church in Caldwell, Idaho, under the leadership of Norman Rutzen. Several years later, the library was sold to the United Pentecostal Church-sponsored Indiana Bible College in Indianapolis. It was shipped there in 1990 and incorporated into the existing IBC collection which was subsequently renamed the E.G. Moyer Library in honor of the founder of CBC.[5] Even in the days following its closure, controversy continued to plague the college. Nathaniel Urshan says he saved the old campus from an intended underhanded sale orchestrated by at least two anonymous and unscrupulous individuals who proposed disposing of the property for the sum of $142,000. Urshan objected to this proposed business deal and asserted that he personally intervened at the last moment and borrowed that precise amount of money from a bank and thereby averted the transaction. He claimed that the lion's share of the eventual proceeds from the sale of the property ($695,000) was seized by the Idaho District in clear violation of the College statutes.[6] The claim lacks merit and accuracy. In fact, after clearing outstanding indebtedness, the proceeds were split evenly between

---

[4] See *Minutes*, CBC board meeting, 6 March 1984, p. 4.
[5] The naming of the CBC library was a result of a motion by the CBC College Board. *Minutes*, CBC board meeting, 8 April 1985, p. 2. On the transfer details, David Brown, letter to Thomas A. Fudge, 13 August 2013.
[6] Nathaniel Urshan interview, 23 April 1999. This has been refuted. Norman Rutzen interview, 24 July 2013.

the Idaho and Washington Districts in strict accordance with the college *Articles of Incorporation*.[7] The asking price for the Lombard property had certainly once been $695,000 but that is not what the campus sold for in 1985.[8] Ironically, the final selling price in 1985 was exactly the sum of the cash offer made four years earlier which the College Board had perhaps unwisely rejected. As noted above, most of the physical structure of the campus was completely destroyed. However, the large wooden CBC sign, formerly situated in the parking lot near the Lombard Street entrance did survive the destruction. It remains in the possession of college graduate, CBC defender, and Alumni Association president, David Reynolds.[9]

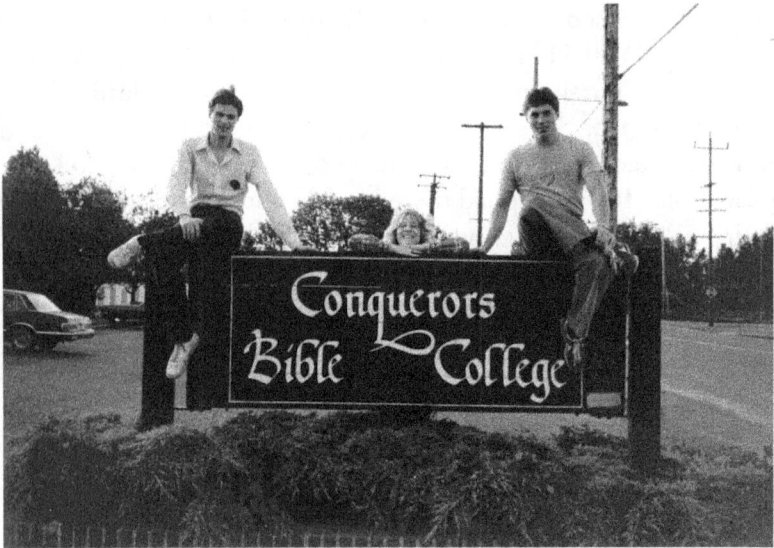

7.3   CBC students Thomas A. Fudge, Peggy Yelm and Gregg Calder at the main campus sign on North Lombard Street, Spring 1982

On a separate note, a unique remnant of the college survived its physical demise being pulled literally from the wreckage. During the demolition of the old Lombard campus, a model of the school was discovered in the CBC attic where it had lain undisturbed for an

---

[7] *Restated Articles of Incorporation* (1982), Article 3, pp. 1-2.
[8] On the formal asking price, *Minutes*, CBC board meeting, 21 March 1983.
[9] David Reynolds interview, 12 August 2013.

indeterminate number of years. A beige-colored wooden hinged case, featuring old-fashioned suitcase latches obviously made for the model, approximately three feet in length, three feet in width, and perhaps ten to twelve inches deep, with a carrying handle, was retrieved from the attic as the walls were being torn down. Its existence, as well as the details surrounding it, had either been forgotten or virtually unknown. Observing the demolition, Jerry Dillon rescued the historical artifact from the bulldozers and heavy equipment which were reducing the last physical remnants of CBC to dust and rubble. Seven months after Dillon acquired the model from the ruins of the campus it was personally turned over to Norman Rutzen at Valley Church in Caldwell, Idaho. Dillon believed the model should remain with the CBC library and other college materials which had already been sent to Caldwell.

Further investigation reveals that the model was built in 1967 by Stephen H. Judd, the teenage son of the then-CBC president Edwin Judd, and thereafter was taken to the General Conference in Tulsa, Oklahoma that same year, where it was displayed at the CBC promotional booth. The model had been constructed for that specific promotional purpose and was built on a blueprint of the floor plan of the main CBC building which had been discovered at the college sometime earlier. The blueprint was pasted to the foundation board and the model was built on top of it. The model was built to scale and accurately reflected the campus as it looked from the air or indeed from any angle. This included a black parking lot and walkways, a green lawn, the white central building and black roof. The case was constructed specifically to house the model for its shipment by train to the General Conference. Neither its builder nor prominent college personalities from the 1960s were aware that the model had been stored at the college and preserved.[10] For a short period of time in the late 1960s, the model had been publicly displayed in the hallway near the front entrance of the college. On an indeterminate date, the model disappeared from

---

[10] I am grateful to Jerry Dillon interview, 19 April 2013, for the details about the discovery of the model during the CBC campus demolition and to Edwin Judd, letters to Thomas A. Fudge, 19 and 20 June 2013 (FC, inv.doc.no 0707-5071-33 and FC, inv.doc.no 0707-5073-33), for additional and pertinent information on the model's origin and construction.

Caldwell, Idaho. Details are obscure. Its ultimate fate or current whereabouts is unknown.[11]

History is the story of men and women and their acts. The names of five men from this bellicose history, namely Don Fisher, C.H. Yadon, Dan Lewis, Joseph H. Howell, and Jerry Dillon have appeared frequently and repeatedly in this book. Each of them played vital roles in a variety of ways in the narrative which makes up the story of heretics and politics at Jackson College of Ministries in Mississippi and at Conquerors Bible College in Portland, Oregon.

7.4  Don Fisher and April Purtell during Fisher's final visit to Portland, late August 1995. He died sixteen weeks later

They were certainly not the only important actors in the last days of CBC and one might argue why they have been championed when the contributions of others have not been as carefully scrutinized. Fisher, Yadon, Lewis, Howell, and Dillon left their mark in the histories of higher education in the United Pentecostal Church.

---

[11] It is regrettable that Norman Rutzen has no recollection of the CBC model. Jerry Dillon, and Michael Nigh interview, 18 August 2013, recall its display. According to John Smelser it does not appear to have been stored at the UPC archives in St. Louis and according to David Brown, IBC Director of Library Services, it was not included with the CBC library which was purchased by Indiana Bible College. David Brown interview, 4 August 2013.

Where are they now? Chapter six outlined the main contours in Fisher's life from the time he left Portland in the summer of 1984 until his untimely death eleven years later in southern California. For better or worse, it was Don Fisher who emerged in the eye of the storm of controversy at JCM, and even more prominently at the college in Oregon. As we have learned, during the last days of CBC, he took decisive action. He surrendered his ministerial credentials and left the UPC. He made no effort to continue either with his ministerial or teaching career. He died on 12 December 1995.

7.5 C.H. Yadon, Caldwell, Idaho, 27 August 1997. He died fifteen weeks later

C.H. Yadon continued to teach part time in UPC colleges as an esteemed elder statesman. In 1984, he was made an honorary member of the General Board of the United Pentecostal Church. He was deeply saddened by the events which led to the closure of CBC and was grieved by the way Don Fisher had been treated by his enemies. He expressed keen disappointment in the new strident leadership approaches in the Northwest.[12] His reputation remained

---

[12] Norman Rutzen, letter to Thomas A. Fudge, 2 December 2013.

unchanged, but grave suspicions of heresy and doctrinal irregularity persisted. Though generally respected within the UPC, by 1992, he stoutly refused to support the controversial Westberg Resolution. Despite pressure from church officials to the contrary, he made a formal representation to the General Board in an effort to persuade his colleagues to oppose the initiative. When this failed, he was forced out of the UPC, along with several hundred other ministers. He was formally recognized as an honorary elder by the Global Network of Christian Ministries. His last pastoral appointment was to the staff of Valley Church in Caldwell, Idaho. His active ministry stretched from 1927 to 1997. He died on 9 December 1997.

7.6  Dan Lewis, Troy, Michigan, 16 December 2013

One of the persistent lightning rods at JCM, Dan Lewis left the college in the spring of 1981 and shortly thereafter relinquished his ministerial credentials with the UPC. Later that same year, despite efforts by the Michigan District of the United Pentecostal Church to keep him out of Michigan, he assumed the pastorate of the non-denominational, conservative evangelical Troy Christian Chapel in Troy, Michigan. He has served as Senior Pastor from the autumn of 1981 to the present. He has announced his formal retirement for April 2015. C.H. Yadon has been a guest preacher in his pulpit. Lewis was numbered among the featured presenters at the 1984 symposium on Oneness Pentecostalism which convened at Harvard University. Lewis earned degrees from William Tyndale College, the University of Detroit, and also studied at St. John's Provincial Seminary. In addition to pastoral work, he has taught at William Tyndale College and continues to be active in scholarly endeavors which includes regular lecturing at international venues.

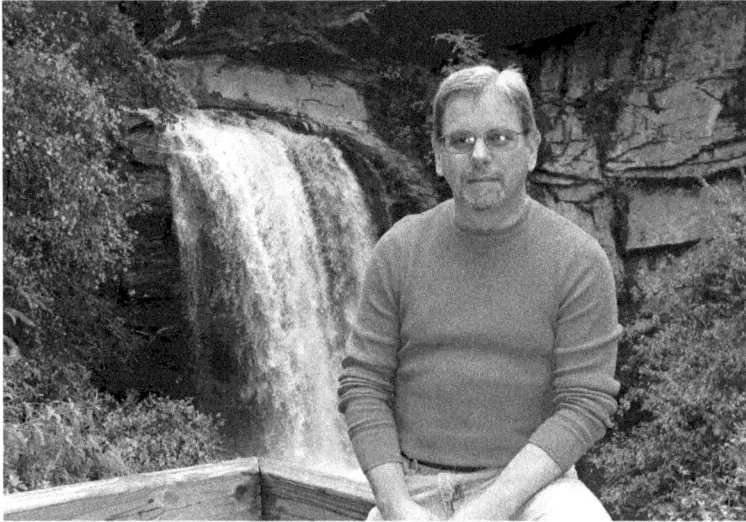

7.7 Joseph Howell, Looking Glass Falls,
Brevard, North Carolina, November 2013

Joseph Howell left Jackson College of Ministries in 1981 near the time Don Fisher and Dan Lewis departed. He too surrendered his ministerial license shortly thereafter and did not maintain any affiliation with the United Pentecostal Church. Widely regarded as the intellectual stimulus behind the attempted theological reforms at JCM, Howell should be acknowledged as the most sophisticated and accomplished theological thinker, without predecessor or peer within the UPC at that time. Along with Lewis, he presented one of the major papers at the Harvard symposium in the summer of 1984. Following that event, he earned his PhD from Florida State University in 1985 producing a highly regarded dissertation on Oneness Pentecostalism which can be ranked among the most important studies of its genre and which continues to be cited in the scholarly literature. Thereafter, Howell subsequently worked at several colleges in Florida. He has published in the areas of bioethics, and educational technology. Howell now lives in Georgia and identifies himself as a United Methodist.

7.8   Jerry Dillon, Camas, Washington, 23 August 2013

After twelve years at CBC, and in spite of robust attempts to persuade him to remain, Jerry Dillon resigned from the college in the spring of 1978. He remained a licensed minister with the United Pentecostal Church until around 1982. During that time, he held ministerial positions at churches in Salem, Oregon and Vancouver, Washington while maintaining connections to CBC. After his formal departure from the UPC, he was briefly associated with a Foursquare Church congregation in Beaverton, Oregon. Thereafter he succeeded Don Fisher as Senior Pastor of Christ for the People Community Church and served in that capacity from August 1984 until October 2004. He was thereafter affiliated with a Lutheran congregation. Over many years, his continuing studies eventually caused him to embrace Reformed theology, historically rooted in the thought of John Calvin. He now lives in Camas, Washington and currently serves as an elder in the Presbyterian Church USA.

From the United Pentecostal Church denominational point of view, these men – Fisher, Yadon, Lewis, Howell, and Dillon – were the heretics. These were men whose lives both informed and were

7.9  CBC students and staff, 1981-82: *Back row:* Cheryl Johns, Kim Scott, Gregg Calder, Carl Wopperer, Peggy Yelm, Kristi Eld, and Bob Bowker. *Middle row:* Donna Trumps, Kendall Cobb, Ruth Caldwell, Collette Kilbourne, Cliff Mitchell, Debbie Sirstad, Lisa Sanders, Melissa Reece and Marcia Johnson. *Front row:* Joe Higgins, Cheryl Stallard, Ruth Brokaw, Kim Simmons, David Wasmundt and Eric K. Loy.

shaped to some extent by the politics which coalesced during the last days of CBC. Lewis and Howell were not there in the flesh, but the mark they made at Jackson was evident philosophically and theologically in Portland. These men were among the major players in a minor story but their influence was certainly not limited to the classrooms and chapels during the controversial days of the schools. Altogether, these five men touched the lives of thousands in ways beyond the calibration of time and human language. There may have been theological Trojan horses, there was a "foul ball," "experts" clashed with "spiritual creeps" and the last days of CBC were indelibly marked by heretics and politics.

Winston Churchill once described the Soviet Union as "a riddle wrapped in a mystery inside an enigma."[13] The fall of CBC is less puzzling. When the Czech heretic Jan Hus reached the end of his five-year legal ordeal in 1415, legal provisions for mercy were ignored. Criminal procedure within medieval church law permitted latitude when dealing with those straying from the well-worn paths of institutional certainty. "There are many to be corrected, like Peter; many to be tolerated, like Judas; and many who are unknown, until the Lord comes, who will bring to light the hidden things of the darkness."[14] Ignoring these admonitions, the church turned this priest over to the secular authorities to be burned alive. Why? Convictions of divine mandate and claims to absolute truth form the common denominator motivating medieval church courts along with the ministers and boards that adjudicated the last days of CBC.

More than five and a half centuries after Hus, Don Fisher was considered unworthy of being included with Peter, or numbered among the unknowns, or categorized with Judas. He was not to be corrected, he was not to be tolerated, and it seemed imprudent to wait for the coming of the Lord to shine light in the dark places. These are among the consequences of absolute truth claims and the madness of theologians. It came down to theology, power and perception. The last days of CBC were all too predictable. Radicals, committed to particular interpretations of doctrine, never ceased to seek out others "weak on the message." Moderates, frightened by the implications of such accusation, sometimes took a more rigid stance in hopes of avoiding suspicion. The efforts sometimes failed.

Some years after the closing of CBC, Phillip Dugas, pastor of the UPC congregation near the old CBC campus arrived for a Sunday morning service to discover that he and his congregants had been shut out of their own church (see ill.3.12, p. 127). The locks had been changed and a prominent sign had been posted which read: "Followers of Phillip Dugas not welcome here." Police were summoned while frustrated church members gathered in the parking lot. Holed up inside the church was Paul Dugas who had changed the locks, posted the sign, and was determined to make a

---

[13] BBC radio broadcast, 1 October 1939 and in print *The Times*, 2 October 1939.
[14] C.2 q.1 c.18 *Multi corriguntur*, in Friedberg, *Corpus iuris canonici*, vol. 1, col. 382.

stand for Truth. Peering out the window at the confusion below, he was utterly convinced that his own brother, Pastor Phillip Dugas, was "weak on the message."[15] The history of the church provides ample evidence from its own records and archives that toleration has often been considered a vice and those "weak on the message" must be expelled forthwith from the brotherhood. "Putrid frogs," "evil geniuses," "stinking skunks," and "spiritual creeps" were all targeted by "experts" and regardless of cost or consequence were made either to conform or were excluded. The last days of CBC bear witness. The "quarrelsome old woman," theology, was both constructive and destructive.

In many cases, when a book fails to satisfy the fascination or preoccupation with particular subjects, it can sometimes be attributed to the fact that readers either wish to find within the pages support for their own views, or that they have come to the text seeking reassurance more than history. Alfred, Lord Tennyson completed his poem "In Memoriam A.H.H." in 1849. One stanza is relevant. "Our little systems have their day; they have their day and cease to be: They are but broken lights of Thee, and thou, O Lord, art more than they."[16] In reflecting upon the bellicose history of CBC, perhaps monuments of stone and mortar are not the proper measure after all. "The institution lives on in the lives of the people it served."[17] The legacy of CBC, now more than sixty years in length, and the controversial influence of Don Fisher, C.H. Yadon, Jerry Dillon and others, survives faintly in the memory of those who, having once studied within its humble walls, are now scattered around the world.[18]

---

[15] I am grateful to Vivian Dugas (sister-in-law of the Dugas brothers) for details. Leon White, letter to Thomas A. Fudge, 19 December 2013.

[16] Alfred, Lord Tennyson, *In Memoriam A.H.H.*, second edition, ed., Erik Gray (New York: W.W. Norton, 2003).

[17] Edwin Judd interview, 10 April 1999. Confirmed in Darline (Kantola) Royer interview, 15 August 2013.

[18] "I have met so many fine people that were under your ministry in Jackson that I felt I just must write and thank you for the contribution you have made to the kingdom of God." Dan Scott, letter to Don Fisher, October 1981. FC, inv.doc.no 0707-4790-32. Dan Lewis interview, 6 April 1999, nominated the most influential men in his life as Clarence Lewis (his father), C.H. Yadon, Joseph Howell, and Don Fisher.

7.10  The last students leave the CBC, Lombard Street, campus, June 1982

# Appendices

Almost all of the twenty-two appendices which follow are specifically linked to arguments, conclusions or aspects of the book. The importance of many of these will be readily apparent to the reader. However, a brief comment will situate these documents in context.

The first two appendices (Moyer, pp. 401-403 and Fisher, pp. 404-427) have an explanatory comment at the head of the document (pp. 401 and 404) to which the reader may refer.

Lewis J. Davies' official resignation letter from the United Pentecostal Church (2 May 1978) may seem out of place. However, events at First Church in Portland, during and prior to his pastorate, shed important light on developments in the Northwest (especially the Oregon District) and also mirrors some of the drama unfolding at CBC. Some of that story is related in chapter four. In contrast to Don Fisher's letter of resignation (11 February 1983), Davies outlines cogently and in sufficient detail a number of salient issues, pp. 428-432. An article in *The Oregonian* (the Portland-based largest newspaper in the state) on the occasion of the silver anniversary of the college (p. 433) is the only substantial coverage of CBC in the public media.

Two brief documents written by Don Fisher (1979 and April 1981) indicate, in the first instance, a dominant theological orientation, pp. 434-435 (which might be compared with his sermon text in appendix two, pp. 404-427), while the second provides details surrounding his return to the Northwest following a fifteen year absence in Missouri and Mississippi, p. 436.

Appendices which contain official information and documents from the administration of the Oregon District (8 April, 25 April, and 30 July 1981, pp. 437-438, and 442-443) outline some of the differences between the college and the Oregon District. The CBC board meeting minutes (28 August 1981) indicate the response of the college to Oregon, pp. 444-446.

The letter from Thomas L. Craft (29 April 1981) goes some distance in refuting unfounded but persistent claims, echoed all the way to the national level of the United Pentecostal Church, that the CBC Board of Directors did not diligently investigate and obtain proper references for Don Fisher while at the same time actively and wilfully ignoring a number of grave rumors originating or fomenting in Mississippi. The written recommendation of Fisher from his immediate prior superior, and esteemed UPC minister, is a problematic document for those who continue to insist that the CBC board either ignored or was completely unaware of theological concerns about Don Fisher, pp. 440-441.

Four additional appendices, namely two letters written by Don Fisher (1 September and 14 December 1981, pp. 447-448, 451-452), one composed by Norman Rutzen (13 November 1981, pp. 449-450), and one from Winfred E. Toole (23 February 1982, p. 453), underscore aspects of the conflict which existed prior to Fisher's arrival in Portland and which served to mitigate any serious hope of the continued cohesion and effectiveness of CBC during the Fisher administration.

Fisher's resignation letter (11 February 1983, p. 454), along with the formal opening statement read at the special meeting of the College Board on 21 February 1983, p. 455 supplement some of the narrative of chapter five.

The official College Board letter to all CBC faculty and staff, signed by the acting chairman George M. Sponsler (29 March 1983, p. 456), as well as the only slightly redacted letter by a student to the College Board (13 May 1983, p. 457) are documents which highlight aspects of college operations in the days immediately following the closure of CBC.

The final three documents – Nathaniel A. Urshan letter to Don Fisher (18 July 1995, p. 458), a general letter written at Don Fisher's behest (5 December 1995, p. 459), and the pages of his subsequent funeral bulletin (April 1996, pp. 460-463) – are from the last days of Fisher's life. There are a number of chronological errors which appear in Appendix 22 on pages 462-463.

## APPENDIX 1: Notes on the Foundation of CBC

This extract provides details of the acquisition of the Lombard
Street property and the establishment of CBC. Lombard used to be
Burgard Street, The building on the property was approximately
50,000 square feet. E.G. Moyer, *A Brief Autobiography and Collection
of Articles* (Portland: By the author, n.d. [*c*.1990]), pp. 8-10.

[8] It was while I was in the school there [PBI, in Tupelo,
Mississippi] that I had a vision for a Bible School in Oregon.[1]

Upon returning to the Oregon District, I discussed the
possibility with the men on the District Board of opening a Bible
School. Brother C.H. Yadon was superintendent then and also
pastored a church in Twin Falls Idaho. The brethren were all in
favor with the idea and gave me the go-ahead to try to bring it
about. At this time we were living with my wife's [9] parents. As I
had some additional college work I wanted to finish, I enrolled in
classes at Portland State.[2] I also kept my eyes open for any property
suitable for a Bible School which might become available. It was
while in one of these classes I became acquainted with a professor
who advised me of a building on Lombard St. which would be up
for sale the following year. It had been built by the government
during the war for housing the children of shipyard workers during
the day. I looked at the property with greedy eyes wondering how
much it would cost. There were ten acres of ground and the
building looked suitable for our purpose. I knew it would take a
miracle, but my faith was not in the little amount we might have to
offer, but in the ability of God to do it for us. The professor also
gave me the name of the authority in San Francisco for the

---

[1] Moyer was in Mississippi from the summer of 1951 through the spring of 1952
temporarily replacing Edwin Judd (Dean of the Faculty at PBI) who was on a
year's leave of absence during that period completing a degree in Education and
Psychology at Cascade College in Portland. Edwin Judd, letter to Thomas A.
Fudge, 13 December 2013.
[2] The college began as the Vanport Extension Center in 1946 and until the
devastating flood of 30 May 1948 operated in Vanport itself. From 1948 to 1953,
Vanport College was headquartered in the converted buildings at the Oregon
Shipyard. In 1953, it was moved to its current location in downtown Portland. In
1955, it became Portland State College and in 1969 attained university status as
Portland State University.

information I would need. I wrote for and received first-hand information on the property and notified the district board about it. We came together for the purpose of finding the best way to raise money. It was in my mind to sell shares to any one who was interested, one hundred dollars a share, either cash or in payments. It caught fire and before long I was on my way within the district of five states, selling people on the idea and selling shares. Within six months time we had $11,500. cash on hand. Some had given more, including myself.

When the time came to submit our bid some were a little skeptical as it seemed so little for so much. As for me, I had prayed through and told many that God was going to give it to us.

I am sure that some felt that Brother Moyer meant right, but he was too worked up about it. We placed the bid for what we had and prayerfully waited for several days. When we received the report we had bid $500. more than a steel company which was also interested in the property. Because we were high bid we had first chance. The government, however, turned both bids down, asking for an additional $5000.

I remember one brother called me and said, "Too bad, Brother Moyer, but your bubble has burst." I tried borrowing from banks for the additional amount needed, but with no success. [10] I called Brother Yadon asking if I might see my attorney. This man was a fine Christian man and had sold us the property on Killingsworth.[3]

---

[3] Moyer refers to 1552 North Killingsworth Street in Portland, which was one of the early locations of First Church. That congregation had been established by Fred K. Scott on East Burnside Street in 1943 and Scott pastored the church until 1946. Around that time, Scott went to Wisconsin. He was succeeded by Moyer, who initially was utilizing a wartime housing project in southeast Portland. After the war, and under Moyer's leadership, the congregation met in a rented hall on North Interstate Avenue. During Moyer's pastorate, in 1946 or 1947, the Killingsworth Street property was acquired and that building remained under construction for several years. For some time, the congregation met in the basement and only later was the actual church constructed. This may not have been completed until the late 1950s. By 1949, J.A. (Arthur) Johnson, had taken up the pastorate of First Church and continued in that role until late 1953 or early 1954. At that stage, C.H. Yadon, assumed the leadership. Yadon pastored until 1958 or 1959 when R.V. Reynolds took over. His pastorate lasted less than two years. Reynolds was definitely the pastor in the fall of 1959 when the young Raymond Sirstad enrolled as a freshman at CBC. By 1960, John Klemin was

I really wanted his advise [sic] about our problem. Told him what I was there for he said, "Don't worry Brother Moyer, I will have the amount you need in 15 minutes." He not only got the loan for us, but handled all the legal work at no charge. What do you know![4]

Within a week I walked on the property, into the building, and it was ours. Can you imagine my feeling? What a day of rejoicing for the district. That very fall we opened the doors for students. After thirty three [sic] years of operation several hundred students were turned out into Christian work all over the world. Although the school has run its course and is now closed, the work goes on.

---

ensconced as senior pastor and remained as such until 1967 when he resigned to take up an overseas missionary appointment in Argentina. He was succeeded in 1968 by Jim Roam, who served until 1973. Winfred Toole was pastor until 1976. Lewis Davies filled that position between 1977 and 1982. I am grateful to Edwin Judd, Wanda Calder and Daniel Sirstad for advice on the history of the church. Edwin E. Judd, letter to Thomas A. Fudge, 13 December 2013. FC, inv.doc.no 0707-5525-35, Wanda Calder, letter to Thomas A. Fudge, 4 January 2014. FC, inv.doc.no 0707-5548-35, and Daniel R. Sirstad, letter to Thomas A. Fudge, 21 January 2014. FC, inv.doc.no 0707-5602-35. Ambiguity about Johnson's tenure as pastor at First Church has been clarified to some extent by a public notice in the Portland media that he was still in that position in late 1953. "Conference set for Pentecostals" *The Oregonian*, 31 October 1953, p. 24.

[4] The original mortgage was paid off in October 1966. *Conquerors Bible College (Portland, Oregon) General Catalog 1979-1981*, p. 8.

## APPENDIX 2: Evangelization of the Subconscious

> The following is a transcript of a sermon preached by Don Fisher
> during a campus ministry retreat at McCormick's Creek, Indiana in
> January 1975. This transcription was made by April Purtell in May
> 2013 and corrected in August. Parenthetical comments such as
> "hallelujah" and "praise the Lord" which often punctuate
> preaching in Pentecostalism have been omitted. Otherwise this
> version of an oral text has been left unaltered. Explanatory notes
> have been added. This address preached before Fisher began his
> seven-year career as an educator and college administrator provides
> a summary of one of the great themes of his vision.

I appreciate what I feel here tonight. It's time for us to talk a little
together. I feel God's got us right where He wants us for just a little
while. I come to these Advance [Retreat] meetings with a great
spirit of expectation. How about you? Because I know God is more
anxious to minister to us than we are to be ministered to. And I feel
tonight we have moved into the area right now where God wants to
begin to speak to us.

I have never addressed anyone on this subject before in my life.
I have never heard it preached among us. But it's time we hear it.
And I want to hear it. And I want God to do it in my life. You
don't know what it is, but how many of you want it? About a
month ago, it was over the Christmas holidays that I heard a tape
by Dr. Seamands entitled "Damaged Emotions."[1] Maybe some of
you have heard this tape. But it was while I was listening to this
tape that God spoke to me about "Advance 75." Do you believe
that? In days gone by we've talked a lot about what to do and we've

---

[1] David A. Seamands, *Healing for Damaged Emotions* (Wheaton, IL: Victor Books,
1981). The material in this book circulated in audiotape form years before
publication. Seamands (1922-2006) was a United Methodist scholar, missionary
in India (1946-62), pastor of the Wilmore, Kentucky United Methodist Church
(1962-84), Professor at Asbury Theological Seminary (1984-92), and following
retirement, Emeritus Professor at Asbury. His wife Helen Davis Seamands (1922-
2013) partnered with him in his work as a pioneer in the field of Christian
counseling. One of the main emphases in Seamands' work was the healing of
memories. I am grateful to my colleague Irv Brendlinger, former professor of
church history and theology at George Fox University in Newberg, Oregon, for
discussion about Seamands, a man Brendlinger knew personally for many years.

talked about why to do it, but not very often have we addressed ourselves to the subject of how to do it.

Why and what, but not how. I approach this subject tonight, and my subject is the evangelization of our subconscious minds. We have evangelized our emotions for years. We have evangelized our feelings. We have evangelized everything on the surface. But there have been too many spiritual calamities among us which makes me to know in the deep part of my heart that there are some areas that have never been evangelized, and they've got to meet Christ too. And I don't want them to. I don't want them to. Because that's where I live – I live deeply. That's where you live. That's where you really live – is deep. And if that deep part of us – the inside levels of us – become evangelized this world will be shaken; by a few men and women that have been changed inside. Let's ask God to help us. Doctrine is of little or no value until it makes a difference in your life. I didn't say your speech. I said your life. I have seven pages of notes. I usually come with just a few statements or a scripture. I don't know how I'm going to handle this. I want to share everything I have on my notes. I hope you're not in any hurry. I may stay with them, and I may not. But I hope I handle the subject.

Brother [Nathaniel] Urshan said some wonderful and powerful things to us this morning.[2] He skirted this subject; he touched it. All day, and I think by the time you lay your head on your pillow tonight, if you've been with us all day, you'll see the hand of God building, building, building until now. God wants to complete something in our hearts. I'm here tonight hungry for God. I've had enough of everything else. I am sick of everything else. I've had too much of it, but I haven't had enough of Him. Holy Ghost power does a lot of things for us, and it has. And I thank God for everything He's done among us. For years I've thanked God for what I've felt, and I thank God for what I've seen Him do. I thank God for what I know I feel in my spirit that He's going to do. And the Holy Ghost will deal with some other areas of our life if we'll

---

[2] Urshan was General Superintendent of the UPC between 1978 and 2002. At the time the McCormick's Creek meetings convened, Urshan was senior pastor of Calvary Tabernacle, one of the largest UPC churches, located in Indianapolis, Indiana. Urshan held that pastorate for thirty years.

let Him. The Spirit will dig us out – if we'll ask Him to. That's where I get fearful. Because I know He will. And I want Him to. And yet I don't want Him to, because it hurts.

I rather apologize tonight for dealing with the vessel. We like to talk about the oil. But the oil cannot be of much value apart from the vessel. And the condition of the vessel determines the blessing of the oil. We sang a chorus a while ago, "God picked up the pieces of my broken heart," and those pieces are what I'd like to talk about tonight. We sang the song, "I'm praying for you." I thank God for each of you. I really do. As I was sitting there a while ago, listening to the testimonies, I was just astounded again, as I am so often of the way God does a great personal work among us. Each of us are so different. We are so complex. We're so mystical. People are very, very complicated. And God has such a wonderful way of reaching each of us – reaching into our hearts, reaching into the deep parts of our hearts and speaking to us. It isn't what we see in one another that really counts. The measure of a man isn't what we measure one another to be. But God can get down into the deep part of us and help us and minister to us. And the world is hurting tonight. And the church is hurting. We're hurting because we've never dealt with our subconscious level effectively.

That's why we can't stand under pressure if we don't feel God. That's why we lose faith, when we can't see it being lived out in the lives of those who have such beautiful, glowing testimonials. And I believe that God wants to be Lord of my entire life. All of it.

Cliff Readout put his finger on it tonight.[3] It's the sin question. We're here tonight, again, wielding a death blow to sin in our lives. That's what this is all about. And that's an indication of how far we've swung away from the principles of Christ.[4] We have gotten

---

[3] Clifford H. Readout, Jr, was converted to Christianity through the campus ministry initiatives in Indiana, coordinated by Tom Hare, Pat O'Pelt, and Rich Mincer. Readout was particularly influenced by Tom Hare, Pat O'Pelt, and Kirby Tiller. He has pastored the Apostolic Church in Enfield, Connecticut since 1978. He was formerly superintendent of the Connecticut District,

[4] The balance of Fisher's teaching and preaching ministry reveals that "the principles of Christ" are codified in the Sermon on the Mount and in the kingdom principles summarized in Matthew chapters 5-7. This emphasis is apparent both at JCM and at CBC.

so carried away with the evangelization of the world, until we have forgotten to deal with the sin at the lower levels of our lives, and God will do it tonight.

There are people here tonight with deep-rooted emotional damage in their lives. Sin, once acknowledged sin, but we have said that once you have found Christ, there is no sin of this nature in your life. And they knew it was there; it had never been dealt with effectively. And when you've got sin in your life and it isn't dealt with because of the priorities of the church, or the opinionated gospel of the bigot, you repress your desire to repent, and when you repress these things, deep things happen in us. Yes. I don't have to tell you tonight that I am no psychologist, or psychiatrist. I'm not approaching this subject as a professional. I'm approaching this subject as an evangelist wanting it to be evangelized by the power of the Holy Spirit. My subconscious. I firmly believe that the ministry of the Holy Spirit is to bring healing and wholeness. I must be a whole man! Paul dealt with this in the church. After many years of having a knowledge of Christ, he said you are still sucking the bottle. Let's face the fact. The person who has serious emotional problems and personality difficulties is not automatically healed by either regeneration or sanctification.[5]

---

[5] Fisher did not subscribe to the UPC doctrine that in order for an individual to be saved that person had to keep him or herself in a state of grace. "A Christian must walk with God and keep himself in the love of God (Jude 21) and in the grace of God." *Manual* (2014), p. 35. This formulation was taken over from the PCI. *Discipline –The Pentecostal Church Incorporated* (St. Louis: Pentecostal Publishing House, 1945), p. 17. The Greek verb translated "build up" in Jude 20 implies a structure upon a pre-existing foundation. Verse 21 is neither grammatically nor theologically a passage about salvation in the sense of regeneration or justification. It presupposes salvation and addresses the mature, proper, response to that divine work. The person who is diligent about salvation possesses the certainty and the security of redemption. The negligent individual may forfeit divine blessing and benefit. The Greek construction has two clauses concerning eternal life: remaining in God's love, and waiting for God's mercy. How does Jude understand the former? There are several indicators in the text. These include 1) keeping in mind apostolic doctrine (v. 17), 2) building up one's faith (v. 20), 3) praying (v. 20), 4) remaining in the love of God (v. 21), and 5) relying upon God's mercy (v. 21). The first three constitute the fourth point, and each of nos. 1-4 are undertaken with a view towards no. 5. The fact that the UPC *Fundamental Doctrine* nowhere makes mention of divine grace or faith, and indeed

The Holy Ghost does not cleanse all of our emotional complexities. We have taught, you have heard it preached for years – some of you, as if it was a panacea for all time. The initial, infilling of the Spirit [hear me tonight – stay with me]. I am a firm believer in the centrality of the plan of salvation. Brother Duane one, two three; I believe in the infilling of the Holy Ghost and the initial signs.[6] But I'm saying that the emotional infant is not made emotionally mature by the infilling of the Holy Ghost. What problems does this create to the new convert? Who very soon finds out this too. When they come in and we say, "you want to get high – a real high?" I don't want to hear it again from any of you. Someone called it *cheap grace*.[7] Cheap grace is no grace at all. God in

---

the *Manual* treats "the grace of God" as a separate topic from the doctrine of salvation, implies a lack of theological connection between the two. UPC officials note that it is "interesting" that the articles of faith do not contain explanations of subjects such as grace, faith, and the atonement, but suggest this is so because the UPC holds such theological concepts in common with other major Christian groups. David K. Bernard, *Understanding the Articles of Faith: An Examination of United Pentecostal Beliefs* (Hazelwood: Word Aflame Press, 1998), pp. 16-17. Keeping oneself in the grace of God in UPC theology and practice is understood as fulfilling the three-step formula of Acts 2:38, adhering to holiness standards as determined by the denomination (outlined in part in the sections "Holiness," and "Public School Activities"), regular church attendance, paying tithes, and submission to pastoral authority. The UPC denies that the section on grace implies salvation by works. Bernard, *Understanding the Articles of Faith*, pp. 22-23. All of this is assumed to be non-negotiable truth. The philosophy can be traced to pre-UPC understandings. For example, "Our Creed, Discipline, Rules of Order and Doctrine is the WORD of God." *Ministerial Record Book –The Pentecostal Assemblies of Jesus Christ* (Basil, OH: The Miller Press, 1945), p. 5. Don Fisher did not agree with this interpretation of remaining in grace. Further, he neither supported the idea that outward standards of appearance had any relation to spirituality, nor did he subscribe to the popular belief that "praying through" could normally be regarded as sufficient for challenges in one's life. Evidence of these convictions were increasingly demonstrated during his tenure at JCM and CBC.

[6] At the time, Duane Flemming had association with James K. Stewart. Flemming is the senior pastor of Christian Community Church North, in Columbus, Ohio, a church he founded in 1979.

[7] Fisher is referring to the famous 1937 text by Dietrich Bonhoeffer, *The Cost of Discipleship*, revised edition, trans. Reginald H. Fuller (London: SCM Press, 1964). The book is a classic of Christian thought based on the Sermon on the Mount. In the book, Bonhoeffer elaborates what he believes it means to follow Christ. The

the Spirit – He is a Spirit – we must invite Him in to the deep part of our lives for a total rejuvenation. A creation of God. And when we tell someone, and there may be people here tonight who have never received your initial baptism in the Spirit, let me tell you it is a beautiful experience. It is a Bible salvation experience. And you don't have much hope – if any – without the baptism of the Spirit.[8] God is a Spirit. If you want God, you must be filled with the Spirit. Being filled with the Spirit is being filled with God. You'll never make another kingdom in yourself, and in the energy of the flesh. It's going to take a baptism of the Spirit.

We're going to do it, Jerolyn.[9] She's laughing at my cufflinks. I know I threw them in my suitcase, but I couldn't find them. I am truly wired up tonight. It's not humility, it's necessity.[10]

But for those of you who have just received the Holy Ghost, or those of you who are hungry for it, or those of you who will be hungry for it. I must warn you that there are other things involved in being a disciple of Jesus Christ than having an initial baptism of excitement and power from heaven. And when we wake up some cold, dark, gloomy, depressing Monday morning after having spoken in tongues in a rip-roaring Sunday night meeting, and discover that we still carry a little load, you must acknowledge that there is more to this than that. And when it isn't dealt with, repression occurs.

---

book was published during the rise of Nazi power in Germany and the application of its ideas led to Bonhoeffer's death in 1945

[8] Considered within the overall theology of Don Fisher, this is a questionable statement. He certainly did not defend this position as president of CBC. Fisher did subscribe to a doctrine of salvation which embraced an understanding of justification by faith which preceded water and spirit baptism. This was a general PCI point of view though many of the PCI brethren clearly did not fully understand the doctrine of justification. However, Fisher could place emphasis upon spirit baptism without actually articulating that within the initial evidence doctrine which demanded tongues as the essential component despite his earlier allusion to this. It is also possible that in early 1975, Fisher had not yet fully thought through the implications of the UPC doctrine of salvation.

[9] Jerolyn (Chambers) Kelley was the youngest of three daughters of the-then UPC General Superintendent Stanley W. Chambers (1915-2004).

[10] Fisher was wearing paper clips as cufflinks.

And those of you who know more about this subject than me, know that repression is denying that we even have the problem. We say, "I'm not supposed to feel this way, therefore I don't. But I really do." And so we keep repressing, pushing it down, and under, and out, and away from us. But problems pushed under don't stay there. It's like a balloon you're trying to sink. Repressed emotions always reappear, but never in the form in which it was repressed. It disguises itself, and it returns. And so some of us have not effectively and completely dealt with our sub-level of living in the gospel.

I better stop here. I want to make sure that you are with me. I guess what I'm saying is that too many of us live off of the top of our heads and call it Christ.[11] We can get excited when the drums are beating, and the organ's a trumping but when it comes down to good old hard rock living for Jesus we ain't got it. Now you're with me. That's where I'm starting from tonight. Now let's go from there and start digging. How many want to dig with me?

And so, instead of dealing with the problem, we repress it. We say we shouldn't have this – surely a born-again son of God doesn't feel this way, and so we say it doesn't exist. I'm really not thinking these thoughts. This truly isn't me. This can't be happening to me. And so it comes up another way, and we have health problems. We have unhappy marriages. We have broken homes. And we have nervous breakdowns, which are nothing more or less in many instances – a reoccurrence – a reappearance – a surfacing – if you please – of some subconscious level sins that need to be dealt with.

Life, itself, not theology, is the great evangelizer. It's often said, "If this doesn't match your theology, it will match your experience."

---

[11] C.H. Yadon earlier had drawn a clear line of demarcation between Christianity and Christ. The former consisted of the structures (including the UPC) which had been built around Christ. The latter was essential and indispensable, while the former was nothing more than a means of accessing divine mystery and meaning and might be set aside. The ideas were developed in sermons. "Presenting Jesus Unobstructed," sermon at Valley Church, Caldwell, Idaho, 15 April 1981, and "The Unobstructed Christ," sermon at New Life Pentecostal Church, Bridgeton, MO, 6 March 1983. His "The Unobstructed Christ," undated, unpublished, twenty-page typescript outlines the same point in detail with the summary statement, "Christianity is Christ, not the structure men build around him" (p.1).

It's like I was told when I was in college, and they were trying to teach us how to understand children, and I'm finding this out that was classroom and now I'm experiencing it. By the time you know how to raise them [children], you're out of business. Isn't that right Brother Sleeva?[12] He doesn't know. But because many times our message doesn't match our living, people become disillusioned, and even lose their faith.

I'd like for you to turn with me to the thirteenth chapter of the book of Luke, verse eleven. Luke chapter thirteen and I'd like to read verses eleven, twelve, and thirteen. And this of course is following the ministry of the Lord Jesus, I'll tell you I enjoyed and appreciated what Brother Tiller had to say this afternoon.[13] That was tremendous. I got about six messages this afternoon, Brother Tiller, beautiful, that was beautiful. And the gospels are full of things that are totally exciting – that's life in Christ. You can have your mysteries of the book of Revelation, let me try to keep step with the man on the shore.[14]

"And, behold, there was a woman which had a spirit of infirmity eighteen years, and was bowed together, and could in no wise lift up herself. And when Jesus saw her, he called her to him, and said unto her, woman, thou art loosed from thine infirmity. And he laid his hands on her: and immediately she was made straight, and glorified God." This woman was not demon possessed. But her spirit affected her body. Now, relax, I'm not a Christian Scientist. One time, a number of years ago, back when I was in college, one of my classmates played the organ. She was not a Christian Scientist, but she played the organ for them on Sunday morning. So this one Saturday, she was in bed on her back with flu.

---

[12] Jim Sleeva graduated from Gateway College in St. Louis. He was briefly on staff at JCM and was close to Fisher. He also worked as a missionary pastor in Heidelberg, Germany for fifteen years (1973-1988) and has been on the staff of IBC since 1989. Sleeva visited CBC during both years Fisher was president.

[13] Kirby C. Tiller (1916-2007) was a pastor in Indiana between 1945 and 1983 and served as a district presbyter for fourteen years. He graduated from ABI. Tiller left the UPC in 1985.

[14] This is a statement indicating Fisher's lack of enthusiasm for the end-time, so-called "prophetic" emphases current in the UPC in the 1970s. This comment can be compared with Fisher's attitude about the Richard Heard crusades at JCM during the late 1970s and early 1980s.

The real old genuine flu. She was sick. So she called, and she said, "I'm sorry, but I won't be there in the morning. I can't make it in the morning." And a couple of weeks later when she was back at the organ, she was informed very politely, that she should have been there, for she wasn't really sick at all. She just thought she was. That must demonstrate the power of the mind. And the Scripture says, "Let this mind be in you, which was also in Christ Jesus. Walk not after the flesh, but after the Spirit."[15]

This woman that Jesus ministered to was a woman who had an infirmity for many years. It had affected her back. She was bowed down low. Her back was physically bent. Do you believe that? She was not in a car accident. She was not born this way. The Bible says she had a spirit of infirmity. Jesus Christ must deal with my spirit at the lower deep levels of my life, or it's going to affect me as a whole man. I'm going to come back to this, but let me digress a moment. Jesus said, the Scripture said rather, Paul in his instruction regarding communion, what does he say? He says some of you have partaken of this unworthily. Therefore some of you are ill in your bodies, in fact, some even sleep.[16] Now that's an interesting passage. Have you ever dissected that before? There is a direct correlation between the evangelization of our deep spirits, call it what you will – subconscious or otherwise – but that too must be evangelized. And I'm here to tell you that once it is evangelized it brings about a total revolution in the life of the believer.

These areas of weak personality have been used by Satan among us. I said the weak areas of our personalities – our damaged emotion areas – have been used as an instrument of the Satanic forces of the world to drive a wedge in our hearts, to keep us from full spiritual maturity. Some of us are blubbering idiots in the spirit simply because we have never dealt a death blow to the deep parts of us. Why is there carnality in our life? Why is there worldliness? Why are we so easily deterred from a direct course into the presence of a God that changes and transforms us? Because down underneath where you live, sir, is an area that you have never dealt with in the spirit.

---

[15] A conflation of Philippians 2:5 and Romans 8:1.
[16] 1 Corinthians 11:27-30.

That's why Paul had a beautiful perspective on life. If I covet anything, I believe that it is within the will of God for me to covet the kind of relationship and dedication and commitment that Paul had to Calvary. There wasn't anything he had touched in life, there wasn't anything he had ever had a hold of, that still had a hold of him. He said, "I come to you, not with enticing words of men's wisdom, but in power and demonstration of the Spirit."[17] But more beautiful words were never spoken or written. What was he saying? He was saying I have understood my ministry. And I may come to you with all kinds of words, but that's not the secret. The secret is my touch with God. And I go back and I refer you again – the oil, and the ministry, and the blessing, the relationship of the oil is directly related to the vessel. And that's why some of us are not strong witnesses. That's why some of us are up and down, in and out, cold and hot. Because we have never really come to God at all levels.

And the devil delights in using these weak areas of our emotions and our personalities. He delights in using them against us. And notice how Jesus ministered to the woman. He said, "woman thou art loosed from thine infirmity." He dealt with her spirit. Not with her body. Because he says in the next verse. Then he laid hands on her. Didn't he? He laid his hands on her and immediately she was made straight and glorified God. Oh, I'll tell you, this subject eats me up. To realize that if I can ever get myself, the whole man, committed to the Christ, get out of my way!

That's why Jesus took just a handful of men, and you've heard it in this place today, and they, not him but they, turned the world upside down.

I use my conscious will and mind to come to God in repentance and in commitment. Let me say it another way, I consciously, I am aware of what I am doing. I kneel at an altar of prayer, and I say, "Lord if I know my heart, I'm yours." And I mean it. And you mean it. But that's from the top of us. And we say, "Lord, and I've heard it here tonight, and I pray to God it's true, Lord, whatever it takes. Be careful. Whatever it takes. Lord, I have no choice. Paul, I know in whom I have believed. That's the

---

[17] 1 Corinthians 2:4.

deep part, and I am persuaded that neither death nor life, nor principalities, nor powers, nor things present, nor things to come, or heights or depths, famine, poverty, inconvenience, nakedness, starvation, tribulation and persecution, ridicule, hatred, jealousy, pride. Name it all, will you please, because he had it under the blood, he was committed. Nay, in all these things, we are more than conquerors through Him who loved us and gave, that's the secret of it all, and gave.[18]

We come to God at this level. All of us have imperfections. We really do. We're all human. We all have a weak spot and that's why the old saying is so popular, I guess, familiarity breeds contempt. The closer you work with me the more human I become. What causes some of these damaged emotions that have a relationship and direct bearing on my Christ life? You can go back into your early childhood. I am crushed tonight because we have a generation on our hands of people with damaged emotions.

Several of you are school teachers here tonight. I taught school myself a number of years ago, and many times I wept for my children in my classroom. I would tell them goodbye for the day and sit at my desk and weep because I knew they didn't have a chance to be a whole man or a whole woman unless God Almighty wrought miracles in their lives.[19]

And we have a generation on our hands tonight that we are trying to bring to God and many of us who have come from these areas of life ourselves, and there are some who are sitting here tonight that have come from broken homes. Perhaps physical impairments; no father image; a dominating mother figure. Tragedy, emotional immaturity as a lifelong example. You have an uphill fight to be whole, but I'm telling you there's healing in the Spirit tonight. There is healing for you at the low levels of life where you're living and where you're hurting. And we've got a whole world out there tonight that's hurting and hurting badly.

---

[18] Romans 8:35-39.
[19] Fisher taught fifth grade in Hoonah, Alaska between 1961 and 1964. Inasmuch as Fisher's degree was not in education, he undertook the required additional training during summers in Anchorage. Donna Fisher, letter to Thomas A. Fudge, 13 December 2013. FC, inv.doc.no 0707-5518-35.

The biggest problem, and the biggest hurt, is not a pain in the body. It's not a broken back; it's not a hurting leg; it's not arthritis; or sugar diabetes, but it's the area of the damaged emotions – cracked and warped personalities. And we've got to bring these to Christ too. Sometimes I get furious. I'll tell you sometimes our services make me furious. You come to church and you say "Are there any prayer needs tonight?" We spend twenty minutes talking about arthritis and sugar diabetes. And never one time do we hit it on the head. And we'll conclude, because there is a twinge of guilt and conviction, and we've asked for so many things for the body, we say, "oh yes, and please do pray for them because they're unsaved." Thank God. Once in a while we see a flicker of light.

Paul too had this body. That's why I'm telling you I don't like what I'm preaching, because it hurts. I'm selfish; I'm greedy; I'm egotistical; I'm self-centered. And my world is the whole world. But not so in Christ. We talk about sacrifice; we don't know what we're talking about. We fall in love with couches – would you believe it? I have the privilege of sitting on the foreign missions board, and we meet next week, and I hope you'll pray for us. We've got a world out there to touch. We've got a world out there of almost four million [sic] people with damaged emotions; empty stomachs; hungry hearts, and we've got to touch their lives, and we've done such a poor job of preparing. After so many years, we've got such a feeble crew. I don't mean feeble in strength, but feeble in number. God's got to help us. And I don't know how to relate this, but on occasion, I've heard men say, "it's been tough coming to a decision like this. To present myself for foreign missions involvement. We just built a new home. We just filled it full of nice furniture – you don't impress me! Get out of here! That's what my heart says. There's the door. You're not ready for this. Because everything we have we love. And so do I. But when are we going to allow God? When are we going to come to Him in totality? In commitment? And count it as dung that I might win Christ.[20]

Paul had his head on straight. Friend, I'll tell you he did. Oh, God. I'm hungry for this. I tell you I'm hungry for this. I've got to know God in this dimension or I'll die. I've got to wrestle myself to

---

[20] Philippians 3:8.

the ground in these areas. And if you'll be honest with me, I'll have some company.

What am I talking about? Brother Fisher, can you be specific? I think I can. What are damaged emotions? I would suggest one of them are some deep feelings of inferiority. Why have we for so many years been [dis]couraged – "You're Pentecostal; you're apostolic. Lift your head up. Square your shoulders." I liked what Brother Urshan shared with us today about Brother [W.T.] Witherspoon years ago.[21] When he came out of his corner in a positive note, declaring that he knew God in the power of the Spirit and in the tongue-talking experience also. But some of us will never be powerful witnesses because we are too inferior. We think of ourselves as not worthy, and it's false humility. It's a rationalization that you don't have the goods. We say, "I'm not worthy." We ought to say, "I'm not being honest." Deep feelings of inferiority, and I'm not talking about the other spectrum either. But I get so tired of trying to explain everything I preach. Some of us, that's the trouble with us. We've got to apologize for saying something truthful. Because there are so many among us who have such little brains; they give you no tolerance and no latitude.[22]

Continuous anxiety and fear. Always fearful. Always afraid. Calamity. Problems. Negative. I think we ought to be realistic. The world is a terrible place out there. Now that we've acknowledged it; let's go on. The top of the head says, "I believe." I thank God for that time when I was flat on my back and speaking in other languages, and I felt the impact of the Holy Ghost for the first time in my life. I thank God for that glorious feeling of being clean – for the first time. Oh, do you remember? Cleansed by His blood. "I'm redeemed by what? Love divine." Beautiful. Powerful, but then on moments of reflection, there's something that gnaws away at unbelief. And deep scars of doubt must heal to be full of faith.

---

[21] William Thomas Witherspoon (1880-1947) had been the General Chairman of the PAJC from 1938 to 1945 and was one of the main proponents of the 1945 merger which formed the UPC.

[22] The comment provides a glimpse into the contempt Fisher increasingly felt for the lack of formal education and critical thinking within his denomination. The commitment to producing a different generation marked his tenure at JCM and later at CBC.

Another area is the ghastly perfectionist complex. I can never please. I'm always feeling guilty for not doing enough or doing it right. I will never succeed. I'm always reaching and if I don't do it just right God is going to hit me on the head. Because you know He is a terrible tyrant. He demands perfection. Does He? No, He doesn't. For God knows us, all too well. He expects us to work into perfection. He expects us at any moment to be perfect in that particular relationship with Him. Not perfect, now and for always. I am perfect in my spiritual development at this point in time. But He knows, He must have known, I was human, and I was frail because He made an alternate plan back. He said, "If you sin."[23] He must have known me. He must have known that I was going to need a way back. We must go back to the days of Luther and be justified by faith.[24] "Stand or fall, dear God, here I am."

The supersensitive. Some of us will not be effective because we have damaged areas here. We are supersensitive. In my life I've called it creativeness. Reaching for affection. Easily, deeply hurt. Suspicious. We compensate by many things. And all of these can be rationalized. And some of you may not be seeing yourself at all tonight. Because you've worked them out so many times so well. It's such a beautiful explanation. Fearful of failure. Some of us are so afraid of failing.

I've dealt with a backslider. You've dealt with a backslider. Come to God with a full faith, and a renewed commitment to what you know in the deep part of your heart. I've said it, so what? Come to God in wholeness and power. And be saved. You say, "I can't. I've tried it before and failed."

Spectators – always and forever looking on. They won't play the game because they don't want to lose. It's like a man buying a car.

---

[23] I John 1:5-10 and I John 2:1-2. Fisher was fond of quoting this passage and pointing out that a remedy for sin had already been established.

[24] Luther's lectures on Romans and Galatians are pertinent here. See also Thomas A. Fudge, "Saints, Sinners and Stupid Asses: The Place of Faith in Luther's Doctrine of Salvation" *Communio viatorum* 50 (No. 3, 2008), pp. 231-256. I think it might be too generous to claim that either Don Fisher or C.H. Yadon fully understood the doctrine of justification by faith as articulated by Luther. This is a conclusion held both by Dan Lewis and Vern Yadon. Dan Lewis, letter to Thomas A. Fudge, 15 November 2013 and Vern Yadon interview, 6 December 2000, Bothell, Washington.

He doesn't really want to buy a car, he's just a tire kicker, just checking it out. A little boy prayed a prayer, "Dear God. What is it like when you die? Nobody will tell me. I just want to know. I don't want to do it." God, what would it be like to be totally committed? What would it be like to be able to stand in the presence of God, and say from the deep part of everything in you, "I count it all as nothing, that I might know Him."[25]

These are areas which God will deal with effectively. What are the consequences? How can we, if we have an area that is not dealt with in the Spirit, how can we – be honest with me – how can we if we are not totally dealt with in the Spirit, launch out into a full, mature, apostolic ministry? Believe in God. Moving out from this place to help others when we ourselves are in pathetic shape. If we don't face ourselves; we cannot be an effective tool of the Spirit. Is God interested in this? Some may be saying, "oh, Brother Fisher, really, I can't believe this. I just can't believe you're spending your time here." Can't you really? Yes, you can. There are areas that need to be dealt with. And God will minister to us.

Is God interested in this? You say, "Let's keep it spiritual." Let's do, shall we? Let's look at First Corinthians. You don't have to turn in the Scripture, you can if you wish, but Paul opened his dissertation to these precious believers with many imperfections. I hate to repeat myself. I say some things only once, and I do hope you get them. I said Paul addressed himself to believers with many imperfections. But, oh, Brother Fisher, you say, this is what he said. This is what he said, "for I am determined not to know anything among you save Jesus Christ, and him crucified."[26] Then why in the world are you meddling? Because, my dear neighbors, I've read the rest of the book. And from that point when Paul – the good man of God; the apostle; the saint of the church – when he said, "I declare unto you I am determined." Paul was ... If I was an artist I would draw Paul, and it would be with a set jaw. "I am determined to know nothing among you save Jesus Christ and him crucified." And from that point he went into a long dissertation. He talked

---

[25] Philippians 3:10 which was one of Fisher's oft-quoted texts and which should be regarded as a key text for understanding his theological approach.
[26] I Corinthians 2:2.

about quarrels, party splits, court cases, property disputes, incest, prostitution, premarital relationships, marital relationships, post-marital relationships, widowhood, divorce, dieting, vegetarianism, drunkenness at the communion table, the communion table itself, speaking in tongues, funerals, and taking up offerings. But he began by saying, "dear friends, I am determined to know nothing among you save Jesus Christ and him crucified."

I am convinced that Jesus Christ is interested in me at this level. And some of us have been so spiritual we have never been honest with ourselves. We can lead a praise service. We can even try to preach, and we are so insecure, and so filled with self-deficiencies, and acknowledged personal fleshly desires and appetites. Sometimes we come that close to getting head-over-heals in trouble, and I'm telling you they need to be dealt with. And we've been raised in a generation that has fed on this stuff. We have been weaned on indiscipline, sensuality, and license. Dr. Seamands put it this way, "Pablum, Playboy, and the Pill." We must deal with our damaged areas. Guilt. Constant defeat. Condemnation. They must be taken to the cross. But we get so excited, and we have talked about it for years. We have our little line, and we really handle them well. Smoking, and drinking, and movies, and dances, but we sure back off of reality. They must be taken to the cross, and I'm here to tell you how they're going to the cross. They are going not emotionally. You have already gone that route. We're going to take these things to Calvary with understanding – not with emotion.

You can relax. I am. I know I'll not be invited to preach this at General Conference. But we say, "The Holy Ghost will make a difference in your life." You better believe He will. But He doesn't make enough difference, because there aren't enough leading the way into these areas of commitment. I've got to believe that the Holy Ghost can minister at this level. I've got to believe that the Holy Ghost can meet people's needs that have severe problems. I've got to believe that the Holy Spirit can heal damaged emotions. I've got to believe that the Holy Ghost can go back into the early days of childhood. I've got to believe that He can go into the womb prior to conception, and He can begin to heal the broken, damaged tissues that have been put there by a drug-, a cigarette-sucking, a dope-taking mother. Don't you sit there and tell me that our relationship with Jesus Christ is not affected by these things – it is and it has been. Some unfortunate relationship in the home, and he comes out a homosexual. We sure enough back away from that one, don't we? What kind of Holy Ghost have you got any way? Can it only deal with cigarettes? Or dare we ask him to come into the picture and deal with some deep-rooted problems?[27]

I'm here to tell you that I believe that God can do it. Tonight, He can do it! Oh, we line them up to pray for their headaches. I'm not even going to say the next thing. Because you know it's true. "Pray for this lady, she's hurting, Lord." Why don't we say, "Lord, in this congregation tonight, are people who have been struggling almost from birth with some damaged areas that have kept them from being the kind of an effective power in the Spirit that they would like to be. And Lord, let us lead them tonight into a knowledge of the visitation of the Spirit and we take control of that situation. In the name which is above every name." Is it? Does it? Do we? Will we? Hurting bodies, and anything more serious than that – we close shop.

Romans chapter seven and chapter eight now we've talked about some of the problems. I have tried to expose some areas. I've tried to help us do some thinking and get some understanding and begin to appropriate the power of the gospel of Jesus Christ into some areas that heretofore have been off limits. Can God do this for us? I want to hear it tonight. Can He do it for us? Romans seven has all kinds of problems of the flesh and the devil. Romans eight is a passage of power and victory and it begins by saying, "There is therefore now no condemnation to them which are in Christ Jesus, who walk not after the flesh, but after the Spirit. For the law of the Spirit of life in Christ Jesus,"[28] and this is from the man who says I am coming before you, ladies and gentlemen, with no enticing words of men's wisdom, but brother listen to him. "For what the law could not do, in that it was weak through the flesh, God sending his own Son ..."[29] Did you hear that? "Weak in the

---

[27] This entire section of the address underscores Fisher's conviction that the life of a mature and balanced Christian went well beyond the Acts 2:38 experience and commitments to particular life styles and dress codes.

[28] Romans 8:1.

[29] Romans 8:3.

flesh, God sending his own Son in the likeness of sinful flesh, and for sin." That is the issue tonight. The evangelization of the world does not depend on our ability. The evangelization of the world does not depend on our finance. The evangelization of the world does not depend on our physical plants. It does not depend on our organizational approach and our promulgation of programs. The evangelization [of the world] – I'm here to tell you tonight – depends upon the evangelization of me!

Sanctification. The infilling of the Spirit is not glorification. The whole – look at verse eighteen – "For I reckon that the sufferings of this present time are not worthy to be compared with the glory which shall be revealed in us." What are you sitting around crying about spilled milk for then? So many troubles, Dear God. We're full of it. Because we're full of ourselves – our nasty, dirty flesh that has never been consecrated at Calvary, and it's sin. The whole earth – look at verse twenty-two – "For we know that the whole creation groaneth and travaileth in pain together until now." And if Paul, my God in heaven, if Paul could say it to the Romans, what would he say about today? You can't say it any more completely than he said it. The whole; the whole creation groaneth. He had excellent insight into our generation, didn't he? Travaileth in pain together until this very moment. Everything is damaged. Everything is damaged. Everything is damaged. I'm preaching a gospel of wholeness and completeness in Christ Jesus the Lord. Verse twenty-three – "And not only they, but ourselves also ..." Paul, you've got to be kidding me. We've cast him in bronze so long, it's hard to believe that he puts himself in the groaning category. He said, "And not only they, but ourselves also, which have the first-fruits of the Spirit, even we ourselves groan within ourselves, waiting for the adoption, to wit, the redemption of our ..." What? If he had said Spirit, I don't quite know how I would have handled it here. But he said, "For the redemption of our body." He's addressing himself to the vessel. We've got a little work to do on the vessels. We talk about revival. Revival's not our problem. We're our problem. When we get an opportunity and take it, of looking at ourselves, as a man with imperfections in the body and in the flesh, coming to a Christ who is full of power and victory and dominion and grace and glory, and recognize that we fall into His presence as mere men, and He

addresses himself to our problems as a man. Then we can bring
wholeness and healing all the way through.[30]

Just being filled with the Holy Ghost does not mean perfect
personality functioning.[31] It is not the will of God. We've got so
much garbage in the will of God. It is not the will of God that I be
a powerful witness, He wants me to be a silent one. It is not the will
of God that I go "there" to take the message of truth. He wants me
to keep the home fires burning. It is not the will of God for me to
do "that." Or say "that." Because it would mean my political skin.
It would cut me out. It would alienate me. I haven't crucified the
flesh, I'm not willing to go "there." I wouldn't see Mama for four
years. Rationalization. Never dealing with it. Always repressing it.
Always pushing it down under. Hoping to ignore it and it will go
away. It's gone away hasn't it? It hasn't, has it?

We'll be healed through contact with our God. I'm not going to
psych you into victory tonight. If you've got problems, you're going
to have to go to Calvary and take them with you. And He'll meet
your need. How can we get help? How can you get help? If you're
here tonight, and you know, and you know that God could do
something with you if you would just bow yourself to committal.
How can you do that? I told you a while ago, you can do it tonight.
How can you? Number One – you have to face yourself tonight.
You say, "Lord not here. How about in a bigger crowd?" Just keep
playing your games. Keep playing your games. Quit repressing it.
Quit saying, "Lord, that isn't me. But it sure fits him." You've got
to be honest, and you've got to acknowledge that it's there. You
told yourself long enough, "It's gone." It isn't gone; it's still there. If
it hasn't been dealt with at Calvary. It's still there. But you say, "But
it hasn't bothered me for three days." Wonderful. That's really
some Christ, isn't it? "Praise God, I've had three days of victory."

---

[30] Fisher frequently emphasized the incarnation and his understanding of God
was consistently expressed in terms of a Christology.

[31] This sentence is the central thesis statement of Fisher's sermon. The
Pentecostal experience is not the apex of the Christian life. This was a theme
which marked Fisher's teaching and preaching at CBC and at Christ for the
People Community Church. Within the UPC, such doctrine prompted suspicion
and accusations of heresy.

Some of you that would be for eternity. Three days of total victory! I can't believe it.

Face your own responsibility. Face it. Sure. You were hurt. You say, "Brother Fisher, you weren't hurt like I was hurt, or you wouldn't be saying that that damaged area could be repaired tonight." You were hurt because you responded to the knife. You're all choked up because you watched the bleeding. You do have a responsibility. The Scripture says, "All we like sheep have gone astray."[32] That's the universality of sin. We have chosen our willful ways. That's individual responsibility. We've got to acknowledge our sin and our need. And here's the clincher. You've got to really want to be delivered. Some of us wouldn't know how to act if we couldn't come crying all the way through testimony service. If we have to throw our crutch away, we wouldn't have anything to talk about. Where would we get our sympathy? And what would be the source of our attention?" It just could be that we then would have time to look on the harvest, for the fields are white – already to harvest. And the only prayer He told us to pray was, "Pray ye therefore the Lord of the harvest, to send for laborers."[33] Not pretty daisy pickers. Not pansies. Not hybrids. Laborers – men and women – that know that labor includes dirty hands and sweaty brows, and long hard hours in the fields.

Do we really want to be healed? It would change the whole complexion of our witness. It's like the leaning Tower of Pisa. For 795 years she's been leaning. It's a tourist attraction. Everyone goes to the city to see the leaning tower. But a few years ago they discovered it was leaning too much. And if it kept leaning too much it would lean too much. And it would no longer bring attention to itself, and so they decided they must halt the leaning – slow the leaning – but the commission that designed the corrective measures made sure she still leaned.

Augustine prayed, "Make me pure, oh, God. But not entirely."[34] Halt the tilting, Lord, but don't straighten me up. Check the

---

[32] Isaiah 53:6.
[33] Luke 10:2.
[34] Fisher is referring to the famous line from Augustine's *Confessions* wherein he prayed, "Lord, give me chastity, but not yet" (8.17). *Saint Augustine Confessions*, trans., Henry Chadwick (Oxford: Oxford University Press, 1991), p. 145.

imbalances, God. But don't correct it totally. Leave me an out for
the flesh – if I need it. Jesus said, "Woman, you are freed from your
infirmity!" She was free from it, because she wanted to be! And
then He laid hands on her. He dealt with the problem, and then, He
straightened her back. Her back was not her problem. We've prayed
prayers that God can't answer. He must first deal with the real
problem. Some of you are wasting your prayers. And now, comes
the moment of truth. Dare we ask the Holy Spirit to speak to us?
And as the Psalmist said, "Cleanse me," even from what kind –
presumptuous.[35] Lord, cleanse my heart. Reveal to me tonight. I'm
telling you tonight can be a night of great truth and illumination in
your life. There is someone here tonight. There are many here
tonight with areas that are deeply damaged that have kept you from
a full, dynamic, powerful, apostolic ministry.

But if you will ask God, through the Spirit, to show you your
problem – to isolate it for you – if you've got the courage to do
that, He will minister to you. The Scriptures say, "We receive not,
because we ask not."[36] Jesus Christ will not rudely come into your
life and deal with these areas. Any more than He will come at initial
conviction without an invitation from an open heart. He will not
tread on your holy ground neighbor. I don't care how long you've
had the Holy Spirit. At the surface level. He'll not come deeper.

Oh, Brother Tiller, you blessed me today. That lesson on Mary
and Martha. Where does Jesus sit in your life? At the first seat by
the door? Just in case He becomes embarrassing, and He can make
a quick exit at your invitation. Or have you moved Him up so far
into view that it's obvious that He's Lord?

We receive not, because we ask amiss.[37] "Lord, heal my back."
Lady, that's not your problem. It's your spirit. "Lord, please heal my
back. My back's killing me, God. I can't see the stars. I know
nothing of the glow of the sun. I know nothing of the beauty of the
tops of the trees. Please, heal my back." It's your spirit that's
damaged. Be free! You are healed. You are whole. Spirit and body –
functioning. A sign of God. We need other people's help. The

---

[35] Psalm 19:12-13.
[36] James 4:2.
[37] James 4:3.

Scripture says in James 5:16, something that is wonderful. Now I am in left field, aren't I? The Bible says James 5:16, "Confess your faults one to another, and pray one for another, that ye may be healed." Have you ever heard it on that wise? We've reversed the order a bit. We've confessed our faults for one another, and we've prayed at one another. The Bible says, "Confess your faults one to another, and pray one for another." The Catholics have made confession mechanical. We completely eliminate it, and we are both wrong.[38]

One of the gifts of the Spirit is discernment. Have we ever had the courage – I want to hear it tonight – to ask God the Spirit, to say, reveal to me my imperfections.[39] Illuminate the Body of Christ. My brother in my behalf, discern in me my area of weakness. Oh, God, speak to me, and help me to know wherein I am not whole and need healing. Do we really believe that the spirit of discernment could function on this wise? It's not nearly as dramatic as saying, I discern there is a woman on the left side of this congregation tonight who has a dreaded disease in her body. You see the games we play in the Spirit? God can heal us. I said, God can heal us. But He will not, He will not, He will not violate my self. I must bring it to Him. I must bring it to Him. It has been said that we should pray

---

[38] For a survey of medieval practice, see Henry Charles Lea, *A History of Auricular Confession and Indulgences in the Latin Church*, 3 vols (New York: Greenwood Press, 1968), and for its understanding in the European Reformations, see Ronald K. Rittgers, *The Reformation of the Keys: Confession, Conscience, and Authority in Sixteenth-Century Germany* (Cambridge, MA: Harvard University Press, 2004). Within the Anglican tradition, confession and absolution are ordinarily constituent elements within corporate worship. This is generally the case at services featuring Holy Eucharist. Within this liturgical setting, congregants are invited to repentance by the priest. A period of silent prayer follows during which participants are invited to confess their sins silently. This is followed by a form of general confession which is spoken by all gathered. A general absolution is announced by the priest, frequently accompanied by the sign of the cross. Many Protestant churches avoid formal confession and Pentecostalism knows nothing of it.

[39] Phrases such as "God the Spirit," unpopular and virtually never heard within the UPC, formed part of the basis of accusations of Trinitarianism which followed Fisher over the course of his UPC career.

for the healing of our memories. That's beautiful, isn't it? Pray for the healing of our memories.[40]

The evangelization of the subconscious mind. If anything is going to happen to me tonight of a significant dimension in the Spirit in this area, I am going to have to acknowledge that it's there, and I'm going to have to desperately want deliverance and empowerment. I must bring it to God. I must bring it to God. Oh, how my heart hungers that the Spirit would speak to me, and say, here, this area.

Steve, I want you to come and be ready to lead us in that chorus again, about picking up the broken pieces.[41] The song talks about our vessel. And that's what we're working on tonight. We're working on the vessel. It's a whole lot more fun to talk about the oil. It's a whole lot more invigorating than discussing revival. Great sweeping moves of the Spirit among hungry people everywhere, and it's happening. But it's happening through the lives of men who have gone to Calvary.

And my heart tonight is so full of anticipation of what God will do through some of you in the next little while. I know what God wants to do, if I can read the signs and signals in the Spirit, we're headed for a challenge. The old church is headed for a challenge. I'm headed for a challenge in the Spirit. And I'm going to have to have my whole body committed. We've all played these games. Some of us are still playing games. Falling in love with things. Falling in love with ourselves – you pretty little thing. You're in trouble. It's time you got your head on straight. The Lord's about to come. He's coming, and He's not coming after these pretty little things, He's coming after a people who have made themselves ready. I liked what Brother Flemming said today, he got a personal revelation of what it meant to work out your own salvation.[42] The Scripture says that He is coming after a people that have made

---

[40] The healing of memory was among the dominant and central themes of Fisher's ministry. This emphasis appears to be without antecedent or peer within the UPC.

[41] The reference is to Steve Richardson (1947-2012), musical composer, singer, and songwriter, for many years involved with Calvary Tabernacle in Indianapolis, and a member of the Calvary Four Quartet.

[42] An allusion to Philippians 2:12-13.

themselves ready!<sup>43</sup> Some of us have been around a long time and we're not ready. But we can get ready tonight. Lord, I've been proud. I have been egotistical. I have been supersensitive. I have been jealous. My God, He hates it. We talk about so many trivial things. We get hung up on so many just junky little things and stuff. Because it keeps our measly little minds busy. The devil has used this triviality to take away the concentration on the facts of basic Christianity which is a renewed Spirit.<sup>44</sup> "Create in me, O God, a right Spirit."<sup>45</sup> The love of God. Oh, that we would love one another as Christ loved the church, and he gave himself for it.

I don't have anything on you tonight. I want to love you. I want to love you. I want to love you. But it hurts to love. I open myself for hurt, and I'm not going to do that unless this old flesh has been taken to Calvary, and some of us are so proud of us.<sup>46</sup> We think we've got it made. We are fooling ourselves. Oh, that we could love. I want to love each of you. I've got to love you. I am not to judge you. I don't want to judge you. I don't know your heart. All I know is what I get from God in the Spirit. That's all I know. I'm not smart. I haven't been [. .].<sup>47</sup> The more I learn the more I know I don't know...

---

<sup>43</sup> Perhaps a reference to Revelation 19:7.

<sup>44</sup> Fisher has in mind the madness of the theologians and its destructive effects upon the church and the spiritual pilgrimage. Elsewhere, Fisher grimly remarked on theology (in the same sense that Erasmus had) as a "quarrelsome old woman" who had become so bloated with pride that she needed to be taken back to the fountainhead of faith and reformed.

<sup>45</sup> Psalm 51:10.

<sup>46</sup> It is both notable and revealing that in this sermon Fisher refers seven times to Calvary, three times to the cross, three times to crucifixion, and twice to blood. Fifteen allusions in a single sermon (which is not especially devoted to atonement) reinforce the idea that Fisher was a preacher and theologian of the cross. Fisher also placed a high premium on the New Testament epistles. In this sermon we find 19 references to the epistles, and Paul is mentioned by name 15 times. This contrasts with three allusions to the Hebrew Bible, two references to the gospels, and two passing comments on Revelation. Emphases on Christ, the epistles, and Calvary can be consistently located in Fisher's preaching and teaching.

<sup>47</sup> There is a single word which cannot be identified. The audio recording appears to have come to an end as Fisher was making concluding remarks.

# APPENDIX 3: Lewis J. Davies, letter to Winfred E. Toole

May 2, 1978

Rev. Winfred E. Toole
10726 93rd Ct.
Portland, Oregon 97266

Dear Bro. Toole,

I have enclosed my license and fellowship card with the United Pentecostal Church, and am accompanying them with this letter of resignation from the U.P.C.I.

The circumstances which have precipitated this action are well worth recording. As is quite generally known, myself along with First Church of Portland have been the subject of a great deal of discussion. Those who have found time to speak about us number in the thousands; those who have found time to inquire as to what we are preaching and doing can be numbered on one hand. Because there is no forum within the UPCI in which I can speak, I must use the only means available to me to vindicate my action.

On Monday evening, April 24, 1978, you, Bro. Phil Dugas, and myself met for a discussion of our situation; to "talk things over", as you put it. During that discussion, I laid to rest some of the ugly rumors that have been circulated about us. I personally felt the meeting was productive, and enjoyed sharing my position on the scriptures very much. At that meeting, Bro. Toole, you told me that the District Board may wish to talk to me, but that there would not be time during this year's District Conference. I informed you that I had other commitments and would be unable to attend anyway. We discussed other things, then the meeting ended.

On Thursday afternoon, April 27, 1978, at 4:30p.m., you called me from Roseburg to convey the message that the Board would like me to come and talk with them. I was, of course, taken completely by surprise because you had already informed me that they were't going to have time during this conference.

- 2 -

I mentioned that I had other commitments previously scheduled and didn't think I would be able to attend. I asked you if the Board was willing to wait until their next scheduled meeting, or if they would have a special meeting to discuss the matter. You mentioned that they would prefer to do it now. I agreed to see if I could break my other commitments and call you at your motel on Friday morning.

Friday, April 28, 1978, at 7:45 a.m. I called you in Roseburg, and we talked until almost 9:00 a.m. I mentioned that it would be impossible for me to come at that time because I had other obligations, and the Board was only giving me one day notice. During this conversation you told me the Board considered our situation to be, "very serious", and would not view it to kindly if I refused to come. I mentioned that they could view it as a refusal if they so desired, but that they should consider the fact of the distance, the short notice, and the fact that you told me there wouldn't be time anyway.

During this Friday conversation you told me that coming would be the honorable thing to do. I mentioned that honor works two ways, and some of the men who had been speaking about our position on certain doctrines, etc., should have contacted me long before if they were worried about me. The Biblical way would have been for them to attempt to restore me. Instead, it was brought to an official Board of the UPCI which had already decided my case was, "very serious". I told you that if they considered it "very serious" prior to hearing my side of the story, that it appeared I had been pre-judged, and any effort on my part to vindicate myself would be fruitless.

To me, however, the most significant part of the whole thing is that I tried desperately to get you to agree that the Board confine its deliberations, in my case, to the Bible alone. If they wanted to know where I stood with regard to certain doctrines; that I be examined in the light of the Scriptures alone. You could not agree to do that, Bro. Toole. That, I think is the root of many of the problems the UPCI is presently experiencing. I don't really have much of a problem with the Articles of Faith of the UPCI, but the way some of them are applied is wrong. It is, in other words, not what they say, but rather what men make them say, that gives me the greatest problem. I refused then, as I ever shall, to be judged by what is, "traditionally acceptable," or "generally considered to be". The Bible itself, and by itself, is God's revelation to man. It must remain the distinctively authoritative rule of the church in all matters of faith and practice. It alone must be our guiding rule and standard for judgement. To teach and practice otherwise is cultish; believing that we must have other documentation in order to explain the scriptures. God's word stands alone, and I am more than happy to submit myself to its teaching, its doctrines, and rules.

- 3 -

I am equally happy to submit myself to the brethren so long
as I don't have to compromise my stand on the Scriptures as
God's only revelation to man, to do it.

You should consider by resignation an act of submission to
the brethren. As I indicated to you, it is not my desire to be
a disruptive influence in the section, or district. We have
not sown discord, we have not promulgated disharmony. We have
paid our tithes to the district, we have supported the district,
the brethren, and the programs of the UPCI. But I have been
called names to my face and it has been highly recommended to
me to "just get out", and all of this by a man who is now a
member of the district board. I am aware that we have not
been appreciated, nor welcome in the meetings and councils.
Therefore my resignation is an effort to create peace.

Prior to Monday, April 24, 1978, neither you, nor any other
man in any official capacity, had spoken to me about the
situation. I have been in town, my telephone is listed, the
address has not changed. Why, Bro. Toole, did not those who
have considered our case "very serious", call to reconcile me
if they felt I was wrong?

I want to speak out of my heart as a younger man. We
often hear of our "Pentecostal heritage". I have never known
anything but exactly what we have. I grew up in UPCI churches,
and went to the camps and conferences. But as a young man I
plead with you as an Elder; do not just hand us a heritage,
complete, enclosed, with all the answers for all situations.
I respect highly all those who have passed before; they brought
this to us, and without them we would not have it. But the
nonbiblical items that they discussed, fought for, and championed;
those things for which there were no scripture, yet were wrong;
those things cannot morally be placed beside scripture. If the
arguments for or against those things are valid, they will stand
up under scrutiny. We don't want a tradition, we want an opportunity. This is ground that must be won by every generation for
itself. The unwillingness of the Oregon District Board, and the
entire UPCI to open up its doctrines to question, and to discuss
them on the basis of the Bible alone should make one shudder
with fear. Why should anyone be unwilling to discuss doctrine
on the basis of the Bible alone? In Acts chapter 15, the
apostolic fathers gave the extent of what was to be required
of gentile converts. What right do we have to come and add
more to what they purposely limited? This is not to say that
we cannot agree that certain things must not be named among us,
but when we begin adding things to the Bibical lists of prohibitions, we come dangerously close to adding to the Book. We
have not been willing, as Paul was, to make the distinction
between what is sin, and what is not expedient. We have come
now to the place where men are vilified, and ostracized because
they can't conform to all the expediences. We have made a
whole host of non-biblical requirements, the criteria for
fellowship.

- 4 -

At First Church I have not been completely explicit with
regard to outward things. My reasons are legion. I see Jesus
stressing that it isn't what goes into a man, but that which
comes out that counts. I see Him teaching that outward murder
or adultry is no worse in the eyes of God than inward hatred,
or lust. He taught us that if the disease is truly cured, all
its symptoms disappear. This does not mean that God does not
care what we look like or how we act, but it means that we
must get first things first, or the remainder has no meaning.
Most of the holiness preaching in our movement today centers
around the symptoms, and the disease goes untreated. If I may
be condemned for preaching absolute surrender to Jesus Christ;
that He is to dominate our every thought, motive, and attitude,
and be the center of our life, then I stand condemned. If I
may be condemned for preaching that when Jesus is the center
of our life everything will flow from Him, and He will affect
our habits, our dress, our conversation, the places we frequent,
the company we keep; then I stand condemned. I believe that
when one is truly consecrated and totally submitted, every
facet of his life will reflect Jesus Christ. I further believe
that putting on a pentecostal exterior has no merit at all
unless it is in response to the Voice of the Spirit, and it
is done gladly to reflect Jesus. I maintain that there is a
distinct difference between Pastor-controlled saints, and
Spirit-controlled saints. I believe that the reason some men
want to tell the saints every move to make, and demand behavior
that isn't mentioned in the scriptures, is that they are afraid
that the Spirit may tell the saint something different than
they want to tell him.

We have grown to the place where so much emphasis is
placed on the exterior that certain roles must be played in
order for one to be considered saved. If these roles are not
played - even though they may not be taught in scripture at
all - one becomes an outcast. The words of Paul to Galatia
(3:1-3) need to be read, pondered, and obeyed, "You foolish
Galatians, who has bewitched you, before whose eyes Jesus Christ
was publicly portrayed as crucified? This is the only thing I
want to find out from you: did you receive the Spirit by the
works of the Law, or by hearing with faith? Are you so foolish?
Having begun by the Spirit, are you now being perfected by the
flesh?" As I have mentioned, I don't have a problem with our
Articles, but the way they are coming to be applied is wrong.
We begun in the Spirit of renewal early in this century, and
now we talk about flesh all the time. We lay restrictions on
people that are the commandments of men, but we call them doctrines of God, and force people to comply. We will never
become perfected in this manner. This is not to say that our
behavior should not be chaste, and right in every way, but it
does mean that this does not save us.

I said earlier that there was no forum in which I could
speak. That is true. No man is permitted to question our

- 5 -

traditions. Everyone is expected to accept them without
question. The manual explicitly states that we cannot write or
speak against our Articles. Every minister I know or have ever
known very well in the UPCI lives with fear that someone may
discover that he differs from the "accepted practice". Asking
questions about certain things is tantamount to committing
suicide in the UPCI. Therefore, at our conferences and
councils, we get a steady diet of the same thing: everyone has
to evidence the fact that he isn't apostate - he knows his a,
b,c"s. I truly believe most men do it out of fear of imtimi-
dation rather than by choice. It will narrow us down, Bro.
Toole. Not only that, it's wrong Biblically.

Why could we not agree on the great themes of scripture,
and have liberty on the matters about which scripture is silennt?
Why can't men voice their opinions and yet keep the unity of
the Spirit until they all come into the unity of the faith?

I could write, Bro. Toole, for a month. Time doesn't
permit me to refer to the remainder of Galatians, or Romans 1-8,
or Colossians chapter 2. Then there is I Corinthians 8, and
10, Romans chapter 14 giving guidance on Christian maturity.
My requests are simple, and they are Biblical; they may not,
however, be traditional. I urge you to encourage the brethren
to do as the Christians at Bearea did; they received the word
with great eagerness examining the Scriptures daily to see
whether these things were so.

My love and prayers are with the brethren and the churches
of the UPCI. We will continue to support the efforts of the
UPCI; we ask for continued fellowship. We will not contend for
our individual view to the disnuity of the body. We intend to
cooperate in every way with the churches in the area. Let it
be a matter of public record that I have the highest regard
for you as a man, and a man of God. May the grace of the Lord
Jesus Christ be with your spirit.

Warm Christian regards,

Lewis J. Davies

LJD/bd

## APPENDIX 4: CBC Silver Anniversary Announcement

*The Oregonian*, 3 June 1978, p. 34

# Pentecostal Bible school marks birthday

By VELMA CLYDE
of The Oregonian staff

Conquerors Bible College is celebrating its 25th anniversary this year, but there are many Portlanders still unacquainted with the school, which started in 1953.

On the far west end of North Lombard Street, the founder, the Rev. E.G. Moyer, found 10 acres and some former government buildings for $16,000 back in 1953. There were three graduates in 1954; this year there will be 31 graduates and one intern.

Commencement service will be at 10 a.m. Saturday, June 10, in the First Baptist Church of St. Johns, 7535 N. Chicago. A silver anniversary banquet will be in the Hilton Hotel Ballroom, Friday, June 9.

Operated by the United Pentecostal Church, the school is better known in other states and areas for its Bible training of young people than it is in its home town. The 89 members of the student body come from many parts of the United States.

The comparatively small pentecostal denomination, with an estimated 350,000 members in 2550 churches, traces its history to the Azusa Street Mission in Los Angeles, where in 1906 the pentecostal movement was born. The particular branch responsible for Conquerors Bible College flourished in the south, and its current president, John E. Klemin, came to Portland from the mission field. He was a missionary in Argentina, and after moving to Portland served as pastor of a United Pen-

JOHN KLEMIN

tecostal Church at 1552 N. Killingsworth St. Klemin is the sixth president of the Bible college, which primarily trains young people for missionary work or Christian education, or as associates of pastors.

Sometimes the school graduates what they call four-year interns, and these students, usually young men, are ready to be associate pastors. Three-year students are licensed by the church for various kinds of work, but more study and experience are required by the denomination for ordination.

The United Pentecostal Church, formed in the merger of two pentecostal bodies in 1945, differs from other Pentecostal denominations in that it baptizes only in the name of Jesus and does not believe in the Trinity as three distinct persons in one Godhead. The adherents hold to Scripture, and most of the classes at the three- or four-year school are concerned with Bible and religion. They also have a strong music department.

Klemin led a visitor down the school's halls to the library of 10,000 books, many of which were gleaned from Cascade College's religious library when that school closed.

The president said the 12-member board, made up of two ministers and two laymen from each of the three districts in the Northwest, would like to move to an area where they would have more natural exposure, but with the property and buildings paid, for the financial strain would immediately increase if a new location were found.

As to the school's finances, Klemins nodded when asked if it were supported through the usual worry and prayer.

"We depend on tuition, board and room and individual donors interested in the college, and people in our churches. The Northwest region includes Oregon, Idaho and Washington.

"More and more, everyone is realizing the importance of trained workers for all types of Christian work, and our three-year program is a strong beginning," Klemin said. He said they were having no problems placing students

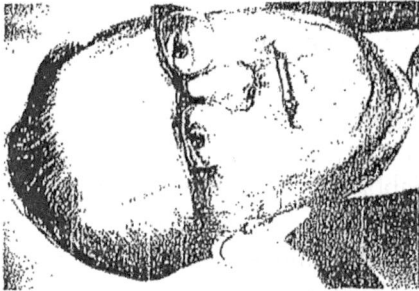

and have had requests from comparatively distant places.

The first three graduates of 1954 are still in Christian work. One is a missionary in Guatemala; another is serving in a Bible college in Jackson, Miss., and the third is a district superintendent for the church in Idaho.

The school has its own graphic arts department and produces its own yearbook.

A radio broadcast over Radio Station KPDQ from 9:30 to 10 a.m. each Saturday is produced by students and faculty in the school chapel. "The students handle all of the technical parts of the broadcast," Klemin said.

Conquerors was the name of the United Pentecostal Church's young people's group when the founder and the newly formed board picked the name in 1953. It is taken from the Bible. "We are more than conquerors through him who loved us." (Rom. 8:37).

Present enrollment is 89, and the school has a capacity for 125. But unlike reports from many Eastern schools, placements remain high, and President Klemin said as far as he knows each graduate already has a job.

"We want to remain in the Portland metropolitan area," he said, "since nearly all of our students work and we have planned our class schedule from 7 a.m. to noon to accommodate their needs. But we would like to have a little more visibility than this address at 10838 N. Lombard St. gives us," he said.

## APPENDIX 5: Don Fisher, "Our Lord"

The following text was written by Don Fisher and published in the
*Pentecostal Herald* 54 (No. 4, 1979), p. 19.

The announcement was no cause for celebration;
From the beginning, a world of questions.
The birth of Jesus Christ was on this wise ...
He never seemed to come at the proper time.
Born of a virgin, in a humble home;
So out of character for a classic.
The object of a proud man's search for death;
Inconveniencing everyone, sorrow for many from the start.
Raised in an obscure village;
Will there ever be an opportunity to be proud?
His grand opening;
Wine flowed at last!

... And Mary pondered these things in her heart.

The handpicked staff began to travel;
Such a gangly entourage it was.
Galilee today, Samaria tomorrow;
Was there no plan of action at all?
Widows, cripples, curious and children;
Were there no bigger game?
Arguments, Sabbath hassles, polarization.
When would the unity push begin?
Miracles, truly amazing things were happening!
Now, that's more like it.
Crowds, interest, lessons to be taught;
The campaign was finally rolling.

... And the disciples pondered these things in their hearts.

Get ready Jerusalem!
We're on our way to the capitol.
The sound of laughing and shouting;
Happy men, palm branches and victory.

Let's get together for supper;
A sop, a basin and a towel.
A brief escape in prayer, a kiss from a friend.
What's going wrong here?
Soldiers, bitter accusations, lanterns and a long walk;
An angry atmosphere – there's no mistake.
Judgment, sentencing, crucifixion;
And it was night.

... And Peter pondered these things in his heart.

What, He is not here!
Where have you taken him?
Peter, John, Thomas!
Amazing, indeed.
Instructions – Ascension – Jerusalem.
Promises to keep . . .
Wind, fire, power.
People everywhere!
Strong men, full of passion;
Men on their knees.
Washed, cleansed, forgiven and empowered;
A people called by His name.

... And men everywhere ponder these things in their hearts.

## APPENDIX 6: Don Fisher, Open Letter

# We're Coming Home!

*From the Desk of Donald W. Fisher*

*Life has a way of taking a person full circle. And though that circular route may take one to regions beyond, it is most gratifying as it winds its way back home.*

*Our roots are in the great Northwest--from my first memory of an encounter with God, at age 7 in Idaho Falls, Idaho . . . to water baptism and Spirit infilling at the Bend, Oregon Camp Meeting at age 12 . . . to Bible College graduation from CBC in 1958 (and my wife's in 1959) . . . to my first ministry and administrative responsibilities as well as ordination, coming in the time frame and fellowship of the Northwest District. Our first two daughters (Susan and Karissa) were born in Oregon and Alaska, respectively.*

*I thank God for my parents who often sacrificed to get us to fellowship meetings, camp meetings and Bible college. These experiences put me in contact with so many mighty men and women - people who formed character, instilled truth, with love and respect for God's Word. The host of friends who most lovingly shaped my life and ministry are too numerous to mention by name. But they know who they are . . . and we're coming home to be among them.*

*A great honor has been bestowed upon me to serve Conquerors Bible College as President. I assume this responsibility heavily depending on the Lord Jesus and my friends for love, counsel and support. Our area - the great Districts of the Northwest - genuinely need a strong Pentecostal Training center. CBC will be just that as we blend our hearts, minds and finance . . . for the purpose of training our sons and daughters to serve God and His church.*

*These 16 years away have been filled with the purpose of God. And to be coming home, in His will, is most satisfying. Already the staff and student body at the college have been so very thoughtful and loving. The college Board of Directors, as well as President Reynolds, have made this transition a pleasant one. Deep thanks to everyone!*

*And now the exciting task of building the future of the college lies before us. It will take some quality students. They are out there . . . in churches in Oregon, Idaho, Washington, Alaska, Montana, Wyoming and Utah; the Dakota's, the Southwest, and beyond! There won't be a more exciting campus this fall . . . come to CBC . . . and let the Holy Spirit and the Word of God prepare you for service to the world for which Christ died!*

Yours for an expanding future,

Donald W. Fisher
President Elect

*P.S. I would be delighted to receive personal calls from pastors, parents, alumni, or interested students regarding our program in Bible education.*

## APPENDIX 7: Oregon District Recommendation on CBC

Portland, Oregon   April 8, 1981

Recommendation from the Oregon District Board to the Washington, Idaho, and Oregon district boards in joint session.

Inasmuch as the returns from recent questionaires sent to all Oregon pastors indicate that a large majority feel a decided change should be made in the operation of CBC,

And inasmuch as they express a strong desire for the continuance of the Bible College in the Northwest region;

We recommend that CBC be re-located preferably near the coast with suggestion of the Seattle area. The college shall be under the direction of the District board where it is located.

The Oregon District would be willing to leave it's monetary assets with the college so long as it remains a college in it's present sense and true to the fundamental doctrines of the UPCI.

In the event the college should be discontinued all assets would be distributed as provided in the present charter.

The Oregon District desires to see the college grow and prosper under God, and will continue to feel a part of this worthy cause encourageing support throughout the district.

If this recommendation is accepted it is hoped that the above change be implimented by fall term.

## APPENDIX 8: Oregon District Conference Resolution

# OREGON DISTRICT
# United Pentecostal Church

DISTRICT SUPERINTENDENT
Winfred E. Toole
10726 S.E. 83rd Ct.
Portland, OR 97266

DISTRICT SECRETARY
David Johnson
Box 805
Albany, OR 97321

April 25, 1981

Oregon District Conference
Resolution Number 1

CONQUERORS BIBLE COLLEGE
Whereas Conquerors Bible College, founded in the city of Portland and in the state of Oregon in 1953, has remained in it's present location for approximately twenty-eight years experiencing a great deal of success during this time, and

Whereas it is the strong opinion of our ministerial brethren that the present governmental structure of Conquerors Bible College is not based on a right principle in that, representation on the board from three districts makes it impossible for any one district to have control of the Bible College in any situation, and

Whereas the Oregon District ministry in the past several years has not had an effective voice in the administration of the school with their vote being nullified by a close affinity of the Washington and Idaho Districts whose beliefs and concerns regarding school administration do not harmonize with those of the Oregon District: therefore these two districts now completely dominate present school policy, and

Whereas the board of directors of Conquerors Bible College at it's board meeting April 8, 1981 passed a resolution to have the school remain under a three district government, and this in complete disregard for the results of the survey sheets submitted by our pastors, and

Whereas the same resolution, passed by the school board, also calls for the relocation of the school outside the state of Oregon if so desired by the board, and

Whereas at this time plans are underway to move the school to the state of Washington, and

Whereas the current plan is to have the new school a church operated school, and

Whereas the Oregon District not only opposes these concepts, but the district board has already refused to endorse a church school:

# OREGON DISTRICT
# United Pentecostal Church

DISTRICT SUPERINTENDENT
Winfled E. Toole
10726 S.E. 93rd Ct.
Portland, OR 97266

DISTRICT SECRETARY
David Johnson
Box 805
Albany, OR 97321

Resolution Number 1
Page 2

Therefore be it resolved that we the Oregon District, declare the said school board resolution to be unacceptable to our district by nullifying any and all action taken to affirm or exact it's directives, and

Be it further resolved that the Oregon District appeal to the executive board of the United Pentecostal Church International for a three or five member panel from that board to come to our district before the end of the current school year to hear testimony and arbitrate the problem of governing the school.

Be it further resolved that should the present property be sold or the school start to move the Oregon District consider the Oregon incorporation dissolved and call for the distribution of the assets as stated in Article III of the articles of incorporation. This would include not only the property but all other assets such as furniture, college machines, library etc.

# APPENDIX 9: Thomas L. Craft, Recommendation Letter

Jackson College **JCM** of Ministries

**THOMAS L. CRAFT**
PRESIDENT

**DONALD W. FISHER**
EXECUTIVE VICE PRESIDENT

April 29, 1981

Rev. C. M. Yadon
6006 Northeast 97th Avenue
Vancouver, Washington  98662

Dear Brother Yadon:

Christian greetings. I enjoyed our conversation the other day on the telephone. This letter is my written statement in regards to the things we discussed.

In Brother Fisher's leaving Jackson College of Ministries and going to Conquerors Bible College, many rumors have been flying. It is a shame rumors have been so prevalent in this time of transition. We are our brother's keeper. If I can help these rumors to be laid to rest, I would like to.

It has been rumored that Brother Fisher does not believe in the inspiration of the scriptures. This could not be farther from the truth! That has never been questioned nor even discussed as a problem at JCM. Why would a man give his whole life to teaching the word of God if he did not believe it was divinely inspired, every word of it in its original text.

It was also rumored that he does not believe in the fundamental doctrine of the United Pentecostal Church which states:

"The basic and fundamental doctrine of this organization shall be the Bible standard of full salvation, which is repentance, baptism in water by immersion in the name of the Lord Jesus Christ for the remission of sins, and the baptism of the Holy Ghost with the initial sign of speaking with other tongues as the Spirit gives utterance."

This is absolute falsehood. As far as I know, he teaches and preaches the essentiality of this message.

1555 BEASLEY ROAD — JACKSON, MISSISSIPPI 39206 — 601-981-1611

Rev. C. M. Yadon                  Page 2                  April 29, 1981

I am happy that Brother Fisher is getting to return home. This is the part of the country that he loves. I pray God's rich blessings on you, the Fisher family, and CBC.

Sincerely,

Thomas L. Craft
President

TLC:bc

## APPENDIX 10: Oregon District Conference Resolutions

# OREGON DISTRICT
# United Pentecostal Church

DISTRICT SUPERINTENDENT
Winfred E Toole
10726 S E 93rd Ct
Portland, OR 97266

DISTRICT SECRETARY
David Johnson
Box 805
Albany, OR 97321

Oregon District Conference,  Turner, Oregon    July 30, 1981

Inasmuch as the resolution adopted relative to Conquerors Bible College
in the last Oregon District Conference was presented to the Board of
Directors, then referred back to the Oregon District for clarification,
we present the following resolution to more clearly state our position.

#1
We recommend that the constitution and by-laws be changed to provide
that the college be operated under the authority of the Oregon District
Conference with ownership and interest in assets continuing to be shared
by the three Districts.  The Oregon District would seek to re-locate
the college in a more suitable location inside Oregon.

#2
If recommendation #1 is unacceptable, we recommend that the constitution and by-laws be changed to provide that the college remain a tri-
district owned college located outside Oregon but operated under the
authority of the District Conference of the District where the college
is located.

#3
If recommendations #1 or 2 are not acceptable to the Board of Directors,
the Oregon District requests release from the college directorship and
ownership with the college moving outside the Oregon District and a
reasonable settlement being negotiated for Oregon District's share of
the present assets.

The Oregon District shall retain its position on the Board of Directors
until the above is finalized.

#4
If recommendations #1, 2, or 3 are not acceptable to the Board of Directors of Conquerors Bible College, the Oregon District will withdraw
from the directorship of the college and relinquish it's interest in the
assets.

a.  The college shall re-locate outside of Oregon as soon as possible.

b.  A contract shall be drawn up and agreed upon that shall renew
    Oregon's interest and rights to assets in the event the college
    should be dissloved in the future.  Said contract and agreement
    shall not be subject to change by the Board of Directors.

I

# OREGON DISTRICT
## United Pentecostal Church

DISTRICT SUPERINTENDENT
Winfred E Toole
10726 S E 93rd Ct
Portland OR 97266

DISTRICT SECRETARY
David Johnson
Box 805
Albany, OR 97321

Page 2

#4 (continued)

    c. The Oregon District shall retain it's position on the Board of
       Directors until the above is finalized.

#5
If none of the above recommendations are acceptable to the Board of
Directors of Conquerors Bible College, the Oregon District moves to
withdraw from the directorship of the college and relinquish it's
interest in the assets of the college.

    a. The college shall re-locate outside of Oregon as soon as possible.

    b. The Oregon District shall retain it's position on the Board of
       Directors until the above is finalized.

    c. In the event the college should be dissolved in the future the
       Oregon District would like to go on record as desiring our share
       of the assets at such a time.

2

# APPENDIX 11: CBC Board Meeting Minutes

Meeting Minutes
Board of Directors
Conquerors Bible College
August 28, 1981

Members Present: Norman Rutzen, Chairman    Gary Gleason
                  Verneal Crossley         Frank LaCrosse
                  Winfred Toole           C.H. Yadon

Administration:    Donald W. Fisher, President
                 Raymond A. Sirstad, A.D.

The meeting was called to order by the chairman, Norman Rutzen, at 2:02 p.m. Proverbs 16 was read by the chairman. Brother Toole led in prayer for the blessing of God upon the meeting.

The minutes of the previous meeting were read and accepted as read.

OREGON DISTRICT RESOLUTION:

Whereas the Oregon District met in official conference session on July 30, 1981, in Turner, Oregon, for the purpose of making a decision regarding their continuing legal and official relationship with Conquerors Bible College, and

Whereas the following resolution was adopted by the Oregon District Conference in session:

#1  We recommend that the constitution and by-laws be changed to provide that the college be operated under the authority of the Oregon District Conference with ownership and interest in assets continuing to be shared by the three Districts. The Oregon District would seek to re-locate the college in a more suitable location inside Oregon.

#2  If recommendation #1 is unacceptable, we recommend that the constitution and by-laws be changed to provide that the college remain a tri- district owned college located outside Oregon but operated under the authority of the District Conference of the District where the college is located.

#3  If recommendation #1 or 2 are not acceptable to the Board of Directors, the Oregon District requests release from the college directorship and ownership with the college moving outside the Oregon District and a reasonable settlement being negotiated for Oregon District's share of the present assets.

The Oregon District shall retain its position on the Board of Directors until the above is finalized.

#4  If recommendations #1,2, or 3 are not acceptable to the Board of Directors of Conquerors Bible College, the Oregon District will withdraw from the directorship of the college and relinquish its interest in the assets.

a. The college shall re-locate outside of Oregon as soon as possible.

b. A contract shall be drawn up and agreed upon that shall rι ew Oregon's interest and rights to assets in the event the college should be dissolved in the future. Said contract and agreement shall not be subject to change by the Board of Directors.

c. The Oregon District shall retain its position on the Board of Directors until the above is finalized.

#5 If none of the above recommendations are acceptable to the Board of Directors of Conquerors Bible College, the Oregon District moves to withdraw from the directorship of the college and relinquish its interest in the assets of the college.

a. The college shall re-locate outside of Oregon as soon as possible.

b. The Oregon District shall retain its position on the Board of Directors until the above is finalized.

c. In the event the college should be dissolved in the future the Oregon District would like to go on record as desiring our share of the assets at such a time.

*Following* Thorough discussion, Brother C.H.Yadon moved and Brother V. Crossley seconded that the following resolution be adopted: Motion carried by a vote of 4 for and 2 against by secret ballot.

"Be it resolved that points number 1,2,3, and 4 be rejected and that point number 5 be adopted as follows:

"The college Board of Directors receives the withdrawal of the Oregon District from involvement in the directorship of the college; said involvement to terminate as soon as the college operation relocates outside the state of Oregon, and

"Further, the college Board of Directors receives the relinquishment by the Oregon District of any and all interests in the assets of the college, and

"Further, in the event the college should be dissolved in the future, the Board of Directors now go on record as being willing to give the Oregon District's request consideration regarding the disposition of the assets not to exceed 1981 value (which is approximately $500,000)."

TOP SOIL PROJECT
Brother Fisher gave a report on the progress of the Top Soil Project. In view of a pending sale of the College property, the Administration was instructed to renegociate the contract with Chuck Holmes in order to set the expiration date to coincide with the possession date of a buyer (ie: July 1, 1982).

PARTNERS IN EDUCATION
Brother Fisher gave a report on the P.I.E. picture. Contributions show a marked increase.

STUDENT CHURCH ATTENDANCE
Brother Fisher presented the enclosed "Working Agreement". Brother
LaCrosse moved to adopt this policy. C.H.Yadon seconded. Motion carried.

BIBLE AND PRAYER CONFERENCE
Following discussion, it was decided to postpone this type of meeting
until a later time.

PROPERTY LISTING
Brother Fisher have a summary of listing the property with the JA-SANT
Corporation.

1981-82 BUDGET PROJECTIONS
Brother Fisher presented the Budget projections for the coming Academic
year. Following discussion, Brother Crossley moved and Brother Toole
seconded to express the Board's appreciation for the effort and work put into the projections and to receive the report. Motion carried.

MID-WEEK SERVICE ON CAMPUS
Brother Crossley moved and Brother LaCrosse seconded that a mid-week
service on campus be provided for students who are unable to attend a
local church because of work hours, etc., and further that this item
be included in a cover letter sent to local pastors along with  the
"Working Agreement." Motion carried.

TITHING POLICY
Brother C.H.Yadon suggested that 100% of the student tithes be left in the
college instead of 50% going to the local churches. Brother LaCrosse moved
that the policy be changed to the preceeding. The motion died for lack
of a second. The Board then directed Brother Fisher to appeal to the
local pastors to forfeit their portion in view of the financial need of
the college.

CASH OFFER
Mister Ed Ferris of Don Jones Realty presented an offer to purchase the
college property in the amount of $500,000. After David Sant of JA-SANT
Corporation presented his package to the board and offered counsel on the
proposed cash offer,Brother LaCrosse moved and C.H. Yadon seconded to
reject the offer. Motion carried.

After much discussion on the matter, Brother Yadon moved and Brother
Crossley seconded, that the Board direct Brother Fisher to contact
Ed Ferris concerning the Boards' rejection of the offer and to further
convey to him the Board's openness to consider a $650,000 or higher
offer, and to further establish the credability of the proposed
buyer's financial status. Motion carried.

RELOCATION
Brother Fisher gave a summary of the Board's exploratory trip to
Seattle in search of suitable properties. The Board viewed three school
properties in the Seattle area which were available for lease. It
was the consensus of feeling that our present facilities would first
need to be disposed of before we could secure a new facility.

Brother LaCrosse moved and Brother Crossley seconded that the meeting be
adjourned. Carried.

Respectfully Submitted,     *Raymond A. Fisher*

## APPENDIX 12: Don Fisher, Letter to Idaho and Washington

### Conquerors Bible College

10838 North Lombard, Portland, Oregon 97203 [503] 286-5788

Memo to:  Ministers of Idaho and Washington
Date:      September 1, 1981

Dear Brethren:

Christian greetings from the CBC campus!

This is a very busy time here. . .the Fall Term begins in two weeks. Your interest and prayer support in our behalf is greatly appreciated. We are asking the Lord for "a very special year" at CBC.

As you know, some very important decisions have been made recently regarding the future of the college. We look at the end result as a very positive direction for the future!

Enclosed is a copy of the Oregon District action. The response to that recommendation by the college Board of Directors is enclosed. I am sharing this action with you at the request of the Chairman of the Board. We feel you deserve the right to know the status of the college directorship and her immediate future.

Our plans call for operating at this location for this academic year (September to June). We trust our relocation can be affected in early summer 1982. . .so we will be "ready" in our new home (most likely in the greater Seattle area) for the Fall Term of 1982. Please pray with us for a sale and for a purchase.

Our campus is presently listed with an industrial realtor who has made some very excellent contacts already. The prospects for sale look good. The board turned down a purchase offer last week because it was felt to be too low.

—"Christian Education for Worldscope Ministries"—

Brethren, we look to the future with much faith. Together we can continue to provide our children with excellent Bible training in the tradition of the great Northwest. It is an heritage worth sharing! We solicit your support. . .in interest, prayer and finance. May I encourage you and your congregation to join us monthly through PIE (Partners in Education). This regular giving is very important. . no **one** else is going to do it for us.

Thank you for standing by the college and its purpose. I believe that CBC will be in good hands. . .those of the Idaho and Washington brethren! Please don't hesitate to contact me at any time should you have a question or suggestion.

Your friend,

Donald W. Fisher
President

## APPENDIX 13: Norman Rutzen, Letter to Northwest Pastors

*Conquerors Bible College*

10838 North Lombard, Portland, Oregon 97203 (503) 286-5788

Dear Brethren,

    Christian greetings!

    As chairman of the College Board of Directors, and in the best interests of the college, I feel that the enclosure will give you a better insight into the facts regarding our "large majority selection" of Brother Fisher as our president. This letter was written just two weeks before the close of the last academic year very near the time Brother Fisher's resignation was effective in Jackson. It was addressed to Brother Yadon, who was serving as Chairman of the Board at that time. This was the status at that time, which was of course also known by many of us prior to the April meeting of the Board of Directors.

    Just two weeks ago I personally talked with Brother Craft on the phone. He contributed nothing to change this April 29 statement regarding Brother Fisher.

    Further, Brother Craft's recorded statement at Graduation in Jackson, on May 15, in the presence of several hundred people, highly praised Brother Fisher's work, his contribution to the college and the fact that he would be welcome to stay and continue his service there.

    Brethren, the time has come--is long overdue--for men to behave as Christian gentlemen. Sordid and twisted unnuendos regarding a fellow minister's doctrine is unbecoming to men of God. Not one shred of evidence has been produced to even imply any doctrinal irregularities, either to me or our General Superintendent. A generous letter of high recommendation from Brother Urshan was sent to all pastors of the Northwest earlier. It was felt at the time that this enclosed letter was not necessary to be shared. However, since the innuendos continue, we felt your receiving it at this time would be helpful in making known to you the facts.

    An Apostolic approach to our ministry includes much more than just the heart of the Gospel message; it also includes our relationship to each other, our attitudes and our spirits. The facts are evident. Let's get on with the business of the church and Bible training in the Northwest, in unity of spirit and purpose.

*"Christian Education for Worldscope Ministries"*

Northwestern Brethren          Page 2          November 13, 1981

Our board has just completed its Fall meeting. We had a good meeting. The college is enjoying a very beautiful year . . . chapel, classes and the entire atmosphere among both students and staff are just tremendous! A genuine move of the Holy Ghost is obvious on campus. We have a really fine quality evident among the student body this year. To God be the glory!

Winter Term begins January 5 . . . your young people would be greatly blessed by spending time at CBC! Give the college a call and request information packets for the eligible young people in your church. A generous offering (<u>investing in our youth</u>), would be gratefully received, as well.

It will interest you to know that the Board of Directors has just voted to relocate the college outside the State of Oregon in the summer of 1982. Lord willing, Fall '82 classes will convene at the new location.

Also, the Washington District in conference this week gave a unanimous vote of confidence to Brother Fisher and a very strong vote of welcome to locate CBC in Washington state.

Join with me, please, in asking God for the sale of our present property and the opening of facilities for our big move. The future belongs to those who possess it!

Your brother in Christ Jesus,

Norman Rutzen, Chairman
Board of Directors

## APPENDIX 14: Don Fisher, Letter to CBC friends

# Conquerors Bible College

10838 North Lombard, Portland, Oregon 97203 (503) 286-5788

December 14, 1981

Dear Friends of CBC!

Warmest Christmas greetings. . . .and may our Lord's love bring us ever closer together! "By this shall all men know that ye are my disciples, if ye have love one to another" John 13:35.

Let me bring you up-to-date: We are just concluding a very excellent term. The atmosphere on campus is splendid! It has been a very profitable time in the Word and in the Spirit.

We are gearing up for Winter Term, which begins January 5. Your prayer support is eagerly sought!

As you know. . . .this is a year of transition. I accepted the presidency of the college knowing her existence was being challenged (at the April meeting) all the while believing men would be honest, ethical and Biblical in their approach to solving the difficulties of the past.

As the last few months have evidenced, some have chosen to disassociate themselves because they have no spirit or desire to cooperate, only to control. This unfortunate move was initiated by men who have no love-roots in the Northwest; no rich heritage in the struggle which gave birth to our college; neither do they share our perspective.

CBC has a long history in this fellowship for being centrist. She has never been "radical" or "extreme." Her tradition has always been one of balanced theology and stewardship. At no time has she ever been political in nature or partisan in ethics. She is loved and respected for this moderate Biblical philosophy. The Gospel has always been her message, Christ her theme. That has always been enough.

It is no different today. Her objective is the same. Her doctrine is the same. Her motive is the same. In this hour of "great wide swings" she is needed in our fellowship more than ever. Her clear, peaceful, temperate and sustaining influence is really needed as we look to the future.

"Christian Education for Worldscope Ministries"

We're in a peculiar position. We are sitting on a valuable piece of real estate (over $500,000). This, as well as all of our furnishings and equipment, are debt free. But you can't pay electric bills or buy groceries and pay salaries with real estate. Our present student body cannot generate enough cash flow to operate. No small private college can. (You will appreciate the fact that all present students are now current on their accounts.)

We have a lot of exciting plans for the future! We plan to sell our Oregon facility this year and relocate in Washington state. We plan no huge indebtedness in relocation. But to get to the future we must handle this year of transition. It is crucial. You who love the college and genuinely believe in her ministry. . . must appreciate our situation. Those who don't respect this distinctiveness would rejoice at her demise. Her survival depends on you. And we must hear from you now. It will take all of us. Some generous gifts are needed, but no gift is too small. None is insignificant. Everyone who cares will do something.

One brief visit to this campus; just one chapel service; just one day with the current staff and student body. . .would make a believer out of anyone who was genuinely concerned about training young men and women for Gospel work in a positive atmosphere.

Friends, the time has come to be counted. Does the CBC family wish their college to continue to train young men and women for God's work? I cannot do it alone. Our staff is presently sacrificing. . .but they can't carry the load alone. CBC has always been the "special ministry" of the great folk in Idaho, Oregon and Washington. She still needs that same expression of affection from people who care throughout the entire Northwest. I believe you care!

In the fear of God, and in the name of our Lord Jesus. . .your response is invited. Simply ask God what He would have you do now. . .to help meet our need of approximately $50,000 (in order to complete this year of transition in peace).

Special thanks to so many of you who have already written, called and/or sent a love gift. Your prayers, and love are all deeply appreciated.

Let me conclude by appealing for the future of our youth. They are a worthy investment. I believe in the work of the Holy Spirit in them! Thank you for joining me in this expression of support.

In Christ's Name,

*Donald W. Fisher*
President

P.S. Enclosed is a commitment return form and envelope. Say "yes" to the future!

## APPENDIX 15: Winfred Toole, Letter to Oregon Pastors

# OREGON DISTRICT
# United Pentecostal Church

DISTRICT SUPERINTENDENT
Winfred E. Toole
10726 S.E. 93rd Cir.
Portland, OR 97266

February 23, 1982

DISTRICT SECRETARY
David Johnson
Box 805
Albany, OR 97321

Oregon District Pastors,

Christian Greetings!

I am writing concerning a meeting called to discuss the relationship of the Oregon District with Conquerors Bible College.

To bring you up to date from the passing of the Oregon District resolution at the Camp Meeting, we presented it to the next C B C Board meeting. Proposals 1, 2, 3, & 4 were rejected and number five was accepted. This means that the Oregon District would no longer be involved with the school, the campus would be moved as soon as possible, and our representatives would sit on the school board until the campus was moved out of Oregon. In the event the school was ever dissolved our portion of the assets would be considered on the honor of the brethren on the school board at that time. No promises was made otherwise.

In the light of our resolution and their action concerning it, at our November meeting of the District Board we recommended that no scholarships be offered from the District Departments, and no Ensign ads be purchased by the District or the Departments. We felt this was consistent with the District position in the resolution.

This places the Oregon District in the same relationship with all Bible Schools. We do not offer scholarships to any other Bible Schools, nor do we purchase ads in their annuals. We are not trying to destroy C B C in doing this any more than we are trying to destroy any Bible School.

We feel it is entirely up to the local churches and pastors to decide if they wish to support the school and send students there.

In spite of our taking a clear position concerning the school there is a continual attack made upon the District Brethren and District Board charging that we are trying to destroy the school. This is absolutely not true. Letters have been sent to the laymen and alumni with derogatory statements concerning the ministry. This is unethical and has created much confusion. The Fund Raising Dinner in Salem on March 1 has been organized and promoted without the proper ethical principles used. Every notice and every letter by all involved parties reached me second hand when I should have been the first to be consulted and notified.

I have appealed to Brother Urshan and he is sending Brother Becton to listen to our protest. A meeting with him is to be held on February 27 at 2:00 P. M. at the Airport Sheraton Inn. I am urging all Oregon District ministers to be present. If you have ministers in your church please let them know of this meeting.

Sincerely,

*Winfred E. Toole*
Winfred E. Toole

# APPENDIX 16: Don Fisher, Resignation Letter

February 11, 1983

Board of Directors
Cascade Bible College
Vancouver, Washington


Dear Brethren:

In view of prevailing circumstances it is in the best interest
of the college, my family, and my ministry to offer this letter of
resignation as president of the college.

This resignation is effective at the will of the Board of
Directors, but not to extend past March 18, 1983.

Thank you for every kindness that you have shown to us.

Sincerely,

Donald W. Fisher
President


DWF/ap

Cascade Bible College • P.O. Box 1887 • Vancouver, Washington 98668

# APPENDIX 17: CBC Special Board Meeting

CASCADE BIBLE COLLEGE

To:    CBC Board of Directors

Date:  February 21, 1983

From:  The President

### Opening Statement

For posterity's sake, as well as for your own understanding, it is imperative that the reasoning for this session be explained.

As you well know, the financial condition of the college has been treacherous for years, and especially so since the days of economic crunch and limited enrollment. This board, as well as the college constituency, has been repeatedly reminded of the need for funding. You took action on two fronts in recent months which, at the time, appeared to be short-term solutions to long-range conditions . . . namely, the turning down of the cash offer purchase of the Lombard site and the securing of a credit line to remain operational. Time was needed. The marketing and sale of the property were essential to survival. Everyone knew that. Decisions were rendered in good conscience and with hope of survival.

Time is running out and the inevitable has to be faced. Are you interested in buying more time? If so, how? Thus, I called a meeting for February 28.

In the meantime, great exception was taken by the Washington District Board over learning that some of the college ladies had dressed in ski pants while attending a church "tubing" function on Mt. Hood. The students were scheduled to sing at the Washington District Youth Convention, Friday, February 11. Because of the above, this engagement was cancelled and I was personally summoned to meet the Washington District Board.

The intensity of feelings regarding this situation, as well as the general climate in the Washington District in regard to both me and the college, made it mutually advisable that this earlier meeting be held. We have come today to look at the facts regarding the existence of CBC, not to debate the issue. And as the first order of business I would like to read the following letter to you, respond to any questions you may have in regard to it, turn the chair to the representative from the Division of Education, George Sponsler, and allow you to render a decision.

**Cascade Bible College • P.O. Box 1887 • Vancouver, Washington 98668**

## APPENDIX 18: CBC Board, Letter to Staff

CASCADE BIBLE COLLEGE

P.O. BOX 1887  VANCOUVER, WASHINGTON 98668

March 29, 1983

Dear Sister Purtell,

The entire staff of Cascade Bible College is to be congratulated for being willing to serve the college even though all of you were aware of the many difficulties being faced by the school. The college board joins with you, as well as a host of alumni and friends, in regretting the decision to close Cascade, at least for the present.

Traditionally, the closing of any school renders all staff contracts with that school null and void. However, the board is offering you the opportunity to continue your contract with the college. This is based on your willingness to agree to the following conditions:

    1. That service be performed for the college under the direction of the college board.

    2. That you be willing to attend a church whose pastor is licensed by the parent organization of the college, the United Pentecostal Church International. This latter request would be in harmony with the general intent of the Division of Education policy of the UPCI.

We of the board sincerely hope that you will give the matter your careful consideration. Should you desire to retain your contract, please indicate your willingness by April 5. A failure to notify in writing will indicate your desire to cease your association with the college. Some of your colleagues are continuing their employment, and you are invited to join them. A great deal of work will need to be done to consumate the school's closure.

Enclosed you will find your March salary check for the eighteen days of operation prior to the official closure date of March 18. Your severance benefits and earned vacation pay (should you desire to conclude your service with the college as of the March 18 closure) will be paid to you just as quickly as the college can obtain the funds.

Yours in Christ,

George M. Sponsler
Acting Chairman, Board of Directors
Cascade Bible College

# APPENDIX 19: Student Letter to the CBC Board

958 NE 91st
Portland, OR 97220

May 13, 1983

Cascade Bible College
Board of Directors

Gentlemen:

This letter is one of statement intended to clarify the purpose behind the recording of the CBC Board of Directors meeting of February 21, 1983 and March 21, 1983, at Cascade Bible College.

Certain allegations, which have been voiced by certain individuals such as that Brother Fisher or some other individual(s) paid us to do the recordings, are completely untrue. Other statements, of complete absurdity, include that we had purposed to reproduce the tapes and distribute them for any number of devious reasons, and that I had supposedly made the statement that before I turned the recorded material in, my intentions were to duplicate them for my own purposes.

Two other gentlemen, along with myself, engineered and carried out the entire recording sessions. No other individual was involved at any time, and to the best of my knowledge, no other individual had knowledge of our actions at the particular time in which they were being carried out. Again, I stress the point that Brother Fisher had neither knowledge nor approval of what had taken place.

In regard to the exact purpose of motivation, we simply undertook this operation just for the sake of doing it. I did realize that this sort of thing was definitely unethical when I took part; however, there was never a time when we planned or even considered to cause a scandal with the distribution of any of the taped material.

Also, I was the only one who heard the recorded material in their entirety.

I sincerely trust that this problem can be resolved without any unnecessary reverberations. The above statements are true and the entire recorded material has been turned in. I trust this letter will clarify this situation to a clear understanding.

Sincerely,

# APPENDIX 20: Nathaniel Urshan, Letter to Don Fisher

NATHANIEL A. URSHAN          CLEVELAND M. BECTON          JAMES L. KILGORE          JESSE F. WILLIAMS
GENERAL SUPERINTENDENT      GENERAL SECRETARY           ASSISTANT SUPERINTENDENT   ASSISTANT SUPERINTENDENT

UNITED PENTECOSTAL
CHURCH INTERNATIONAL

July 18, 1995

WORLD EVANGELISM CENTER

Mr. Donald W. Fisher
3372 Rowena Avenue, #8
Los Angeles, CA 90027

Dear Don:

It has come to my ears that you are very ill and that you are in a state of physical suffering. I wanted to write you and to tell you that we are praying that God will help you in this hour of trouble and physical illness.

I've personally thought of you many times and the great contributions you made to the United Pentecostal Church while you were with us. Even though there are disparities that developed in doctrinal positions at a later date, we cannot overlook what you gave to us, both at the World Evangelism Center and Jackson College of Ministries.

I pray to Almighty God through Jesus Christ, that He will ease your suffering and pain, and it is always possible for Him to heal from any kind of disease.

Some of our mutual friends told us about your sickness and suffering and asked me if I would pray, which we have done, and am sending you this personal letter to let you know we pray the compassion of Jesus Christ will overflow in your mind and heart and you will be at ease in His presence.

Sincerely in Christ,

Nathaniel A. Urshan
General Superintendent
United Pentecostal Church International

NAU:db

## APPENDIX 21: Don Fisher, Letter to Friends

December 5, 1995

Dear Friends,

Over the past few months, I have been over-whelmed with the kindness and concern of people like you who have been a part of my life.

Although I'm unable to answer each of you indi-vidually, please know that I deeply appreciate you and your thoughtfulness. It is *wonderful* to have friends who come through when you need them most!

I am receiving the best medical care available, as well as being surrounded by friends and family who are making my illness more tolerable. In addi-tion, I am strengthened by the knowledge that many of you are praying for me.

God's richest blessings to you and your family this holiday season.

Love,

*Don passed away peacefully on December 12. When we last saw him on Thanksgiving weekend, he requested that we write this letter to you. As his daughters, we add our sincere thanks for your expressions of love.*

*Susan Paynter    Karissa Hopkins    Ronna Russell*

**APPENDIX 22: Don Fisher Funeral Bulletin**

IN MEMORIAM

DONALD WAYNE FISHER

1939-1995

## DONALD WAYNE FISHER
### FEBRUARY 16, 1939 - DECEMBER 12, 1995

| | |
|---|---|
| 1939-1943 | BORN TO HARRY & FREDA FISHER IN BEND, OREGON |
| 1943 | PORTLAND, OREGON |
| 1943-1947 | ATTENDED 1ST & 2ND GRADE<br>IDAHO FALLS, IDAHO |
| 1947-1948 | ATTENDED 2ND & 3RD GRADE<br>SALMON, IDAHO |
| 1948-52 | ATTENDED 4TH - 8TH GRADE<br>POCATELLO, IDAHO |
| 1952-54 | LEFT HOME AT AGE 14 TO ATTEND C.B.C. HIGH SCHOOL<br>PORTLAND, OREGON |
| 1954-1955 | COMPLETED HIGH SCHOOL IN ONE YEAR WITH 4.0 GPA<br>SALMON, IDAHO |
| 1955-59 | ATTENDED CONQUEROR'S BIBLE COLLEGE<br>EDITOR OF SCHOOL NEWSPAPER<br>GRADUATED IN 1959, PORTLAND, OREGON |
| 1958-1960 | ATTENDED CASCADE COLLEGE<br>SPIRITUAL LIFE CHAIRMAN, 1958<br>GRADUATED IN 1960, PORTLAND, OREGON |
| 1960-61 | ASSISTANT PASTOR, SECTIONAL YOUTH LEADER<br>JEROME, IDAHO |
| 1961 | ASSISTANT PASTOR, UNITED PENTECOSTAL CHURCH<br>SALEM, OREGON |
| 1961-1964 | HOME MISSIONARY & TAUGHT 5TH GRADE<br>EDITOR, ALASKA DISTRICT NEWSLETTER<br>HOONAH, ALASKA |
| 1964 | ASSISTANT PASTOR, FIRST PENTECOSTAL CHURCH<br>PORTLAND, OREGON |
| 1964-1965 | PASTOR, UNITED PENTECOSTAL CHURCH<br>INSTRUCTOR, CONQUEROR'S BIBLE COLLEGE<br>VANCOUVER, WASHINGTON |

| | |
|---|---|
| 1966-1968 | DIRECTOR OF PROMOTIONS & PUBLICATIONS<br>YOUTH DIVISION, UPCI<br>INITIATED NATIONAL BIBLE QUIZ PROGRAM<br>ST. LOUIS, MISSOURI |
| 1968-1970 | FOUNDER & EDITOR, WORD AFLAME PUBLICATIONS<br>ST. LOUIS, MISSOURI |
| 1970-1976 | DIRECTOR OF OVERSEAS MINISTRIES<br>FOREIGN MISSIONS DEPARTMENT, UPCI<br>COORDINATED FIRST INTERNATIONAL CONVENTION,<br>JERUSALEM (1976). ST. LOUIS, MISSOURI |
| 1976-1981 | EXECUTIVE VICE PRESIDENT<br>JACKSON COLLEGE OF MINISTRIES<br>JACKSON, MISSISSIPPI |
| 1981-83 | PRESIDENT, CASCADE BIBLE COLLEGE<br>PORTLAND, OREGON |
| 1983-1984 | PASTOR & FOUNDER<br>CHRIST FOR THE PEOPLE COMMUNITY CHURCH<br>VANCOUVER, WASHINGTON |
| 1984-1985 | ADMINISTRATIVE PASTOR<br>CHRIST THE KING COMMUNITY CHURCH<br>SACRAMENTO, CALIFORNIA |
| 1986-1995 | INSURANCE AGENT, COLONIAL LIFE INSURANCE<br>LOS ANGELES, CALIFORNIA<br>"VIP," 1985<br>REPRESENTATIVE FOUNDER'S AWARD, 1986<br>PRESIDENT'S CLUB AWARD, 1987<br>PRODUCTION CLUB WINNER, 1987<br>PRESIDENT'S CLUB AWARD, 1995<br>MEMBER, GLENDALE CHAMBER OF COMMERCE, 1986-1995 |

DIED DECEMBER 12, 1995
LOS ANGELES, CALIFORNIA

INTERMENT, DESCHUTES MEMORIAL GARDENS
BEND, OREGON

### At Conquerors Bible College
PORTLAND, OREGON     JUNE 9 - 12, 1976

# Northwest Bible Conference
# &
# CBC's Twenty-third
# Annual Commencement

**BIBLE TEACHER**
**DAVID GRAY**

**COMMENCEMENT SPEAKER**
**BIBLE TEACHER**
**D. W. FISHER**

**BIBLE TEACHER**
**C. H. YADON**

## Bible Conference

**JUNE 9**

7:00 p. m. — Opening Worship
First UPC (Milwaukie)
8:00 p. m. — DAVID GRAY, Bible Teacher

**JUNE 10**

8:30 – 9:00 a. m. — Devotions
9:00 – 9:55 a. m. — C. H. YADON, Bible Teacher
10:05 – 11:00 a. m. — D. W. FISHER, Leadership Seminar
DONNA FISHER, Ladies Seminar
11:05 – 12:00 a. m. — DAVID GRAY, Bible Teacher
12:00 — Lunch ($1.75)
1:30 – 3:00 p. m. — Discussion Period: Christian Home
and Family (Moderator - Jerry Dillon)
7:00 – 8:00 p. m. — CBC SINGSPIRATION (First UPC)
8:00 p. m. — DAVID GRAY, Bible Teacher

**JUNE 11**

8:00 – 9:00 a. m. — FINAL CHAPEL & COMMUNION
(For CBC Students Only)
9:00 – 9:55 a. m. — DAVID GRAY, Bible Teacher
10:05 – 11:00 a. m. — D. W. FISHER, Ministry of the
Holy Spirit Seminar
11:05 – 12:00 a. m. — C. H. YADON, Bible Teacher
12:00 — Lunch ($1.75)
1:30 – 3:00 p. m. — Discussion Period: Discipleship
(Moderator - Arlo Moehlenpah)
7:00 – 8:30 p. m. — DRAMA: "The Final Treatise
(Freshman Class)
8:30 p. m. — DAVID GRAY, Bible Teacher

DAY SESSIONS at Conquerors Bible College
EVENING SERVICES at First United Pentecostal
Church, 1725 27th Street, Milwaukie

## CBC's Twenty-third Annual Commencement

● **JUNE 12 – 10:00 A. M.**
First Baptist Church of St. Johns
7535 N. Chicago - Portland, Oregon

SPEAKER: REV. D. W. FISHER
Overseas Ministries Director
United Pentecostal Church International

*— featuring growth in God's Word —*

8.1    Advertisement in the *Voice of Idaho*, May 1976

# Bibliographical Essay
## with a Comment on Sources

The nature of the research required to write this book negates the traditional standard bibliography one expects in academic books. There are a variety of books, essays, and other sources listed in the footnotes on aspects of church history, theology, and education. Though an historical investigation, predicated upon scholarly principles, *Heretics and Politics* could not draw upon a plethora of previous studies nor yet upon a well-defined and accessible body of research materials. There are no studies of any nature dealing with CBC, Don Fisher, or anything remotely related in terms of the UPC. The historian, then, must turn to a variety of less conventional sources in order to study the last days of CBC. All of the materials utilized in this book have been cited or referred to in the footnotes. For purposes of convenience, the following is an outline of the main categories of resources upon which this study has been constructed.

**CBC Files** Following the closure of the college in 1983, selected documents were extracted from existing materials and sent to the UPC headquarters in Hazelwood, Missouri for storage and preservation. It is unknown the nature of the documents which were not considered useful to preserve. The CBC collection is housed in four filing cabinets under the immediate purview of the *Center for the Study of Oneness Pentecostalism*. However, the collection technically is under the administration of the Division of Education. There is no established system for referencing the materials in the collection and indeed there is no catalogue of its holdings. Despite having been shipped to the denominational headquarters in late 1984, there is no evidence the files have been utilized for research purposes prior to 2013. The materials constituting the collection have been arranged in several categories which include the confidentially-restricted Student Records, college publications such as the *Ensign* and the *CBC Jubilation* (and its successor *The Cascadian*), back issues of college catalogues, and general files. This latter category appears to have been ordinarily filed in chronological order, though there are some anomalies. Contained within these files are minutes of the meetings of the CBC Board of Directors, but not the minutes of regular faculty meetings. These latter minutes appear not to be extant. The articles of incorporation and College By-Laws, along with their revisions are available. No charter document or record of endorsement has been located in the files and there does not appear to be a mission statement outlining the direction for the college as conceived by the founders. Another notable absence is any document detailing the process by which a president was elected or appointed. There are considerable financial records stretching across the duration of the college's history. Appearing at regular intervals in the materials are reports made by the respective presidents and academic deans to the College Board. These are normally appended to or filed with the minutes of the meeting at which these reports were made. Throughout the general files there are miscellaneous notes and papers addressing a myriad of issues including financial concerns, planning sessions, campus maintenance, and other day-to-day business. There are further a variety of correspondence from presidents, deans, the College Board, district superintendents, district boards, and other persons. There are legal and real estate documents among the collection. For this book, I took very little note of the extensive financial reports except to determine the financial state and viability of the college prior to the Fisher administration. The minutes of many board meetings were useful and, as the footnotes reveal, were drawn upon extensively. There are limitations. In keeping with the minuted meetings from virtually every other corporation, considerations surrounding weighty issues were either summarized briefly or given a perfunctory annotation. For example, the *Minutes* of the special board meeting convened on 21 February 1983, to discuss the resignation of the president and consider the future of the college, has this entry. "Agenda was read. Opening statement by the president, followed by his letter of resignation. Discussion followed; then the chair was turned to G. Sponsler" (p. 1). The two words "discussion followed" is the sole official record we have of a protracted discussion, interrogation, question-and-answer exchange, argument, and detailed deliberation. If the minutes of this particular meeting constituted the sole source of information there would be no reason to conclude that anything other than a brief straightforward conversation ensued. As chapter five details at some length, quite the opposite occurred. Within these College-Board *Minutes*, points of view expressed were rarely connected to a particular board member. There is every reason to believe that the minutes of board meetings conceal as much as they reveal. All thirty volumes of the *Ensign*, the college yearbook, were taken into consideration. The same may be said with respect to the surviving issues of the *CBC Jubilation* and *The Cascadian*. The lacunae are significant. Volumes 1-11 of the *CBC Jubilation* are not among the collection, nor are numbers 1-4 and 6 of volume 12. Volume 15, number 3 is also missing. Obviously, *The Cascadian* succeeded the *CBC Jubilation* in 1982 but there is only a single extant issue (vol. 16, no. 3), meaning that either volume 16, number two, was never produced or not preserved. The Oregon District opposition to CBC is fairly well-documented in terms of conference resolutions and recommendations and correspondence from the-then district superintendent, Winfred Toole. These documents have been closely scrutinized.

**Oral Sources** No fewer than 105 individuals were interviewed in relation to CBC and relevant aspects of its history. These included Carl Adams, Paul Adams, Clyde Barlow, C.M. Becton, Raymond Beesley, David K. Bernard, Sandra Blevins, Stan Blevins, Leon Brokaw, David G. Brown, Ron Calder, Wanda Calder, Jim Christensen, Kristi (Eld) Christensen, T.L. Craft, Cheryl (Johns) Crousser, Lewis Davies, Bev Davies, Mickey Denny, Gene Dillon, Jerry Dillon, Jewel (Yadon) Dillon, Kris Dillon, Peggy (Yelm) Dougherty, Paul Dugas, Phil Dugas, Lori (Falwell) Callan, Donna Fisher, Freda Fisher, Harry Fisher, James G. Fudge, W.M. Greer, Arless Glass, Gary Gleason, Doug Greer, V. Arlen Guidroz, L.H. Hardwick, Jeff Herbig, Joe Higgins, Harold Hodge, Karrisa (Fisher) Hopkins, Dwain Hornsby, Joseph Howell, Enoch Hutcheson, Stan Johnson, Edwin Judd, Darline Kantola, George Kelley, Barry King, Ruby Klemin, Frank LaCrosse, Wallace Leonard, Clarence Lewis, Dan Lewis, Vonnie Lewis, Eric K. Loy, Jesse Martin, Rich Mincer, Allene Moyer, E.G. Moyer, Doris Newman, Esther Nigh, Mike

Nigh, Wayne Nigh, Leo O'Daniel, Skip Paynter, Susan (Fisher) Paynter, Esther Peden, Jerry Peden, April Purtell, David Reynolds, Ralph V. Reynolds, Mark Roberts, Dale Royce, Ronna (Fisher) Russell, Norman Rutzen, Ruby (Yadon) Rutzen, Joe Sargent, Dan Satterwhite, Daniel Sirstad, Raymond Sirstad, John Smelser, Jan Smith, Larry Snyder, George Sponsler, T.F. Tenney, Thetus Tenney, I.H. Terry, Nathaniel Urshan, Barbara Wasmundt, David Wasmundt, Ed Wickens, Grace (Yadon) Wiens, Jim Wilkins, Raymond Woodson, Bud Yadon, C.H. Yadon, C.M. Yadon, Hack Yadon, Loren Yadon, Nathaniel Yadon, Roger Yadon, Vern Yadon, Audrey (Zapalac) Greer, and Gene Ziemke. The use of oral history supplements our knowledge gleaned from written sources. The obvious drawbacks and challenges of memory-based evidence can be balanced by accessing more than one independent witness. Of the main players in the last days of CBC, only Winfred Toole (†1985) and Verneal Crossley (†1996) were not interviewed. The materials in the CBC files and the interviews constitute the essential sources undergirding the arguments and conclusions in this book.

**Correspondence** Some correspondence may be accessed from the CBC files. Others must be obtained from private sources. I am especially grateful to Susan (Fisher) Paynter, Lewis Davies, and Jerry Dillon for sharing letters from their personal files. The letters of Winfred Toole, written in his capacity as superintendent of the Oregon District, are especially important. I have also enjoyed unrestricted access to the papers of C.H. Yadon.

**Journals and Diaries** Access to these are complicated by lack of knowledge of their existence and by a general reluctance on the part of their owners to make public the details of private reflection. There are doubtlessly more of these than I was able to uncover. There are particular challenges in using one's own journals but in this case unavoidable for they provided information not available elsewhere. I had a certain advantage in writing this book, having been a student at CBC during the last years, having subsequently worked closely with Don Fisher, having established long-term personal relationships with key figures such as C.H. Yadon and Jerry Dillon, as well as numerous members of the Fisher family, and having been privy to unique bodies of primary-source information.

**FC (The Fudge Collection)** This is a private collection of materials in the possession of the author. It constitutes more than 5,600 documents collected between 1998 and 2014 consisting of thirty-five file-boxes spanning 122.5 inches or 10.2 linear feet, currently housed in the School of Humanities (E11, G53), at the University of New England in New South Wales, Australia. The contents have been inventoried in a 137 page catalogue. The FC includes various miscellaneous documents, publications, recordings, correspondence, photographs, recorded interviews, a variety of unpublished materials, a considerable collection of letters to and from the author, notes on sermons, audio recordings of sermons, news-clippings, interview notes, and copies of some early Oneness publications (i.e. *The Apostolic Call*, *The Apostolic Herald*, *The Apostolic Faith*, *Pentecostal Herald*, *Meat in Due Season*, *The Pentecostal Outlook*, *Pentecostal Testimony*, and the *Pentecostal Northwestern News*). The collection has been culled from various public and private sources and for convenience assumed the FC designation. In the late 1990s, the collection was assigned a specific reference in New Zealand. For example, FC, inv.doc.no 0707-5233-34 should be understood as a collection number (0707), followed by a particular document number (5233), and finally a reference to the box number in which the document is stored (34).

**Recorded Materials** The central source for the narrative of chapter five rests upon a series of illicit tape-recordings. While ethical and legal issues come to bear upon these materials, their usefulness cannot be overestimated. They provide a unique, unequivocal, unbiased, account of the proceedings of an *in camera* meeting at which a number of salient issues concerning significant factors in the last days of CBC were revealed, discussed, and made abundantly clear. Inasmuch as no official or approximate parallel source exists, these tapes were considered too valuable to ignore. They do constitute the most unique source of historical evidence available for any aspect of the investigation into events and decisions at CBC in the last years.

**Sermons** Within a predominantly oral culture such as Pentecostalism, sermons and public addresses are a valuable source of information. In this book I have accessed many of the sermons of Don Fisher and C.H. Yadon and have used these recordings as a basis for determining points of theological understanding, doctrinal emphases, educational perspectives, along with occasional commentary on contemporary events. In the absence of audio recordings, there is a collection of about 150 pages of notes taken during these sermons in the period between 1983 and 1985 (FC, inv.doc.no 0707-0072-01). Though not as reliable as the recordings, they are still important.

**District Publications** Efforts to access copies of the Oregon District *Apostolic Accent* met with limited success. Past and current editors were unable to account for the period between 1975 and 1985. The current district superintendent was also unable to be of assistance. *The Washington Word* does not have archived copies prior to 2004. In both cases, there does not appear to be an official collection of either publication. These resources have not been fully accessed or utilized and are probably limited in usefulness to brief editorial comment about CBC. The older publication of the Northwest District, *The Pentecostal Northwest News*, was consulted but the useful applicability for this study was restricted.

**Pentecostal Herald** The official organ of the UPC is of limited value for projects such as *Heretics and Politics*. There are some articles dealing with education from a general point of view. Otherwise, there are only various announcements about the college and CBC advertisements. One would not expect to find comment on specific colleges.

**Christ for the People Community Church** The files and materials from the early days of the church's existence (during and immediately following the demise of CBC) have some relevant records. These are generally limited to tape recordings of sermons preached by Don Fisher, leadership seminar notes, and the publication *In Touch* (1986-1990). All of these have some value for assessing Fisher and aspects of the legacy of the college.

**Don Fisher's Library** Following his death, Fisher's books and private papers were either scattered or destroyed. There are no reliable means of ascertaining what he may have retained from his JCM and CBC administrations, or the nature and content of files he may have amassed. It is pointless to speculate. That said, there was certainly substantial correspondence from his critics during the last days of CBC which he once referred to. It has been noted earlier, that various documents were destroyed at Fisher's direction near the end of his life. Close associates such as Dan Lewis recall that Fisher kept duplicate copies of numerous memoranda while at Jackson College of Ministries. There is no reason to believe he abandoned this practice when he went to Portland. Donna Fisher has confirmed that he maintained a voluminous filing system pertinent to his work and that periodically he revised these holdings and sorted them. However, the exact nature of these files was not something to which she was privy. However, Fisher had a reputation for being both exact and meticulous. Several books which Fisher owned have been identified in this volume as significant for understanding aspects of his life and ministry. These include G. Gordon Liddy, *Will: The Autobiography of G. Gordon Liddy* (New York: Dell Publishing Company, 1980), Robert Fisher, *The Knight in the Rusty Armor* (North Hollywood, CA: Wilshire Book Company, 1987), Richard Bach, *Jonathan Livingston Seagull – A Story* (New York: MacMillan, 1970), Margery Williams, *The Velveteen Rabbit* (New York: Avon Books, 1975), and Robert E. Way, *The Garden of the Beloved* (Garden City, NY: Doubleday, 1974). Each have been analyzed and contextualized. Fisher seems to have written very little. The absence of a memoir is regrettable.

**Writings by Others** In this category I refer specifically to Jerry Dillon, C.H. Yadon, Dan Lewis, and Joseph H. Howell. Dillon's writings are limited to letters and these have been taken into account. There are illuminating exchanges with John Klemin, for example, and indications of political maneuvering in the Oregon district and commentary on the volatile relation between the college and local pastors. Yadon edited one book and wrote numerous short articles. Few of these publications have any direct bearing on any of the subjects contained in this book. For a bibliographical listing see, Fudge, *Christianity without the Cross*, pp. 369-371. Of much importance is Dan Lewis, *The Journey Out of the United Pentecostal Church* (Troy: MI: By the author, 1994), especially the author's first-hand ruminations on what happened at JCM during the Fisher years. Some of Lewis' JCM course syllabi are extant and have been used. A number of essays from the late 1970s through the early 1980s were also quite pertinent. These include "Is Your Faith Balanced?," "Escape from History," "Leadership, Laity, and the

Priesthood of Every Believer," "The Theology of the Baptism of the Holy Spirit in the United Pentecostal Church," and "A Call for Biblical Preaching." Joseph Howell also wrote a number of essays in the same period which reflect aspects of the ethos at JCM. These include "Theology and the Serious Pentecostal" (coauthored with Lewis and Mark Roberts), "Roots of American Fundamentalism," "The Righteousness of God: A Study in the Development of a Concept," and "Essentials of Faith." Howell's doctoral dissertation is also of some value in this context. Joseph H. Howell, "The People of the Name: Oneness Pentecostalism in the United States" Ph.D. dissertation, Florida State University, 1985. Finally, his widely circulated "Suggested Booklist for Theological Students," (1981), 20pp is a helpful reference. Of additional note is Joseph H. Howell, Daniel Lewis, Mark Roberts and James Wilkins, *A Call to Holiness*, unpublished book manuscript, 1981; a 154 page typescript. One might usefully add to this list Don C. Marler, *Imprisoned in the Brotherhood: A Search into the Fundamentalists' Web of Tradition* (Jericho, NY: Exposition Press, 1973) which partially illuminates aspects of UPC thinking and attitude by a then-member.

**Books on Pentecostalism** Though there is an increasing volume of historiographical material devoted to aspects of Pentecostalism, many of these are not explicitly pertinent to the themes under consideration in this book. Those that were of some use include Grant Wacker, *Heaven Below: Early Pentecostalism and American Culture* (Cambridge, MA: Harvard University Press, 2001), David A. Reed, *"In Jesus' Name": The History and Beliefs of Oneness Pentecostals* (Blandford: Deo Publishing, 2008), and aspects of my previous work assembled in Thomas A. Fudge, *Christianity without the Cross: A History of Salvation in Oneness Pentecostalism* (Parkland, FL: Universal, 2003). Of more general applicability, I would add Arthur L. Clanton and Charles E. Clanton, *United We Stand*, revised edition (Hazelwood: Word Aflame Press, 1995), David K. Bernard, *Understanding the Articles of Faith: An Examination of United Pentecostal Beliefs* (Hazelwood: Word Aflame Press, 1998), J.T. Pugh, *The Wisdom and the Power of the Cross* (Odessa, TX: By the author, 1998), Ethel E. Goss, *The Winds of God: The Story of the Early Pentecostal Movement (1901-1914) in the Life of Howard A. Goss* (Hazelwood: Word Aflame Press, rev. edn, 1977), Harvey Cox, *Fire from Heaven:*

*The Rise of Pentecostal Spirituality and the Reshaping of Religion in the Twenty-First Century* (New York: Addison-Wesley Publishing Company, 1995), Stanley M. Burgess and Eduard M. van der Maas, eds., *The New International Dictionary of Pentecostal and Charismatic Movements*, revised expanded edition (Grand Rapids: Zondervan, 2002), various tape-recordings and printed essays from "The First Occasional Symposium on Aspects of Oneness Pentecostalism" (5-7 July 1984) at Harvard University, the various monographs published in the *Journal of Pentecostal Theology Supplement Series* (edited by John Christopher Thomas for Deo Publishing, formerly published by Sheffield Academic Press/Continuum), and David Bundy, "Documenting 'Oneness' Pentecostalism: A Case Study in the Ethical Dilemmas Posed by the Creation of Documentation" *ATLA Summary of Proceedings* 53 (1999), pp. 162-163.

**Comparative Studies** Throughout *Heretics and Politics* I drew parallels or comparisons to several other denominations or expressions of Christianity. Recommended resources include, but are not limited to, the following:

**Southern Baptist Convention**: Walter B. Shurden and Randy Shepley, eds., *Going for the Jugular: A Documentary History of the SBC Holy War* (Macon, GA: Mercer University Press, 1996), Paige Patterson, *Anatomy of a Reformation*, 2$^{nd}$ ed (Fort Worth: Seminary Hill Press, 2004), Paul Pressler, *A Hill on Which to Die: One Southern Baptist's Journey*, revised edition (Nashville: Broadman & Holman, 2002), and Russell H. Dilday, *Glimpses of a Seminary Under Assault* (Macon, GA: Smythe & Helwys, 2004).

**Missouri Synod Lutheran Church**: Frederick W. Danker, *No Room in the Brotherhood: The Preus-Otten Purge of Missouri* (St. Louis: Clayton Publishing House, 1977), Kurt E. Marquart, *Anatomy of an Explosion: Missouri in Lutheran Perspective* (Fort Wayne: Concordia Theological Seminary Press, 1977), John H. Tietjen, *Memoirs in Exile: Confessional Hope and Institutional Conflict* (Minneapolis: Fortress, 1990), James C. Burkee, *Power, Politics, and the Missouri Synod: A Conflict that Changed American Christianity* (Minneapolis: Fortress Press, 2011), places emphasis on politics, while Paul A. Zimmerman, *A Seminary in Crisis: The Inside Story of the Preus Fact Finding Committee* (St. Louis: Concordia Publishing House, 2007), stresses theological issues.

**Fuller Theological Seminary**: George M. Marsden, *Reforming Fundamentalism: Fuller Seminary and the New Evangelicalism* (Grand Rapids: Eerdmans, 1987), and Rudolph Nelson, *The Making and Unmaking of an Evangelical Mind: The Case of Edward Carnell* (Cambridge: Cambridge University Press, 1987).

**Roman Catholicism**: Lester R. Kurtz, *The Politics of Heresy: The Modernist Crisis in Roman Catholicism* (Berkeley: University of California Press, 1986), Joseph F. Kelly, *History and Heresy: How Historical Circumstances can Create Doctrinal Conflicts* (Collegeville, MN: Liturgical Press, 2012), Gabriel Daly, *Transcendence and Immanence: A Study in Catholic Modernism and Integralism* (New York: Oxford University Press, 1980), Otto Weiß, *Modernismus und Antimodernismus im Dominikanerorden: zugleich ein Beitrag zum "Sodalitium Pianum"* (Regensburg: Friedrich Pustet, 1998), and Émile Poulat, *Intégrisme et catholicisme intégral: un réseau secret international antimoderniste: La "Sapinière" (1909-1921)* (Paris: Casterman, 1969).

**Alfred Loisy**: Alfred Loisy, *Mémoires pour server à l'histoire religieuse de nôtre temps*, 3 vols (Paris: Émile Nourry, 1930-1), Loisy, *My Duel with the Vatican*, trans, Richard W. Boynton (New York: Greenwood Press, 1968), Francesco Turvasi, *The Condemnation of Alfred Loisy and the Historical Method* (Rome: Edizioni di storia e letteratura, 1979), and Harvey Hill, *The Politics of Modernism: Alfred Loisy and the Scientific Study of Religion* (Washington, D.C.: Catholic University of America Press, 2002).

**George Tyrrell**: Oliver P. Rafferty, ed., *George Tyrrell and Catholic Modernism: A Reassessment* (Dublin: Four Courts Press, 2010), Nicholas Sagovsky, *On God's Side: A Life of George Tyrrell* (Oxford: Clarendon Press, 1990), and M.D. Petre, ed., *Autobiography and Life of George Tyrrell*, 2 vols (London: Edward Arnold, 1912).

**Heresy hunting in Australia:** My research also discovered the notorious cases of Samuel Angus (1932–1943) and Peter Cameron (1993). See Michael S. Parer, *The Angus Case: Australia's Last Heresy Hunt* (Sydney: Wentworth, 1971), Susan E. Emilsen, *A Whiff of Heresy: Samuel Angus and the Presbyterian Church in New South Wales* (Kensington: New South Wales University Press, 1991), and Peter Cameron, *Heretic* (Sydney: Doubleday, 1994). Though clear parallels exist, I was unable to incorporate the Angus and Cameron cases, both of which concerned the Presbyterian Church.

# Index

*There are no comprehensive notations for entries including, but not limited to, the United Pentecostal Church (UPC), Oneness Pentecostalism, Portland, Oregon, Conquerors Bible College (CBC), Jackson College of Ministries (JCM), or Don Fisher as these are topics which pervade the text and are extremely numerous. For convenience, entries on leading personalities (Jerry Dillon, Don Fisher, C.H. Yadon, et al), important entities (like CBC, the College Board, or the Oregon District), or major themes (such as heresy, education, and theology), have been subdivided. The names of female students have generally been entered as they were in those days. The index is a guide to the contents of this book for those interested in particular subjects. However, it has not been conceived as an exhaustive summary of the contents. Entries include footnotes, appendices and illustration captions.*

liberal reputation, 49, 86, 120-
121, 127, 145-146, 153, 158,
180, 226-227, 281, 287, 320,
321-322
*See also* "Experts;" Pentecostal
Church, Incorporated;
missionaries; "Weak on the
message;" Yadon, C.H.
Noth, Martin, 99
Nowacki, Jean-Claude (John), 147,
148

O'Daniel, Leo, 250, 254, 467
O'Daniel, Thomas R., 165
Oakland, California, 210, 309
Ockenga, Harold, 254
*See also* Fuller Theological
Seminary
Offiler, W.H., 130-131
Oggs, Allan, 97-98
Oklahoma, 152, 389
O'Pelt, Pat, 92, 406
Oregon District, 46, 50, 160, 175,
202, 265, 310-311, 381, 428-
432, 437, 438, 442-443, 453
desire to control CBC, 158, 161,
442, 451, 453
excluded from CBC assets, 310-
311
initiative to revive the college
charter, 163
opposed to college church idea,
165, 166, 219, 223, 438
opposition to CBC, 157, 158,
161, 162, 163, 172-173, 178,
186, 223, 233-234, 453, 467
radical element in, 154, 157, 181,
287, 451
*See also* "Experts;" Missionaries;
Northwest District; Toole,
Winfred; Yadon, C.H.
*Oregonian, The* (newspaper), 39, 44,
105-106, 191-197, 335, 399,
403, 433
Orffer, Brian, 250, 267, 274

Otten, Herman, 29, 225, 309, 374

Padfield, M.D., 73, 109, 327
Painter, Keith, 250
Paisley, David Arnold, 235
PAJC (Pentecostal Assemblies of
Jesus Christ), 49, 86, 120, 132,
159, 234, 288, 408, 416
theology of, 281-282
triumph over PCI, 282, 333-334
Paley, James, 243, 285, 342
Parrish, Chuck, 290, 342
*Pascendi domini gregis* (papal decree),
36-37, 180, 211, 260, 276
Pastoral authority, 32, 86, 95, 98,
140-141, 161, 165, 217, 218,
219, 224, 321, 327, 344, 408
Craft, Thomas and, 140-141, 175
King, Barry and, 217, 321
Urshan, Nathaniel and, 75, 327
Patterson, Paige, 32, 157, 179, 225,
226, 263, 309, 317
*See also* Southern Baptist
Convention
Paul St, 7-8, 16, 17, 139, 141, 181,
234, 278, 337, 343, 407, 412-
413, 415, 418, 421, 427
Pavek, Kerry, 203
Paynter, Skip, xx, 12, 69, 76, 117,
261, 272, 342, 344, 347, 467
Paynter, Susan. *See* Fisher, Susan
PCI (Pentecostal Church,
Incorporated), 49, 61, 69, 86,
120, 146, 148, 153, 159, 234,
288, 321, 323, 334
considered liberal, 69, 120
doctrine of salvation, 65-66, 129,
281-282, 332, 335-336, 407-
408, 409
regional strength, 49, 86, 114,
145, 146, 153, 157, 180, 281,
321, 343
*See also* New Brunswick;
Northwest; Tennessee
Peden, Cabot, 203

# ABOUT THE AUTHOR

PHOTO CREDIT Trish Wright

Canadian by birth, Dr. Thomas A. Fudge, B.A. (Religion), *summa cum laude*, Warner Pacific College; Master of Divinity (Reformation history and theology), *summa cum laude*, The Iliff School of Theology; PhD (medieval history), University of Cambridge; PhD (theology), Otago University in New Zealand, undertook his initial formal studies at CBC, where he was influenced both by Don Fisher and C.H. Yadon. He is a church historian and an historical theologian with a principally defined specialization in the later medieval and early reformation periods. He is widely considered an international authority on matters relating to the Czech reformer Jan Hus and fifteenth-century Hussite history. Initially appointed to a fully-tenured university level professorial chair in 2003, his teaching and research is now based in the School of Humanities at the University of New England in New South Wales, Australia, where he is also a member of the Research Committee.

He is the author of eight previous books: *The Magnificent Ride: The First Reformation in Hussite Bohemia* (Ashgate, 1998), *Daniel Warner and the Paradox of Religious Democracy in Nineteenth-Century America* (Edwin Mellen Press, 1998), *The Crusade against Heretics in Bohemia, 1418–1437: Sources and Documents for the Hussite Crusades* (Ashgate, 2002), *Christianity without the Cross: A History of Salvation in Oneness Pentecostalism* (Universal, 2003), *Jan Hus: Religious Reform and Social Revolution in Bohemia* (I.B. Tauris, 2010), *The Memory and Motivation of Jan Hus, Medieval Priest and Martyr* (Brepols, 2013), *The Trial of Jan Hus: Medieval Heresy and Criminal Procedure* (Oxford University Press, 2013), and *Heresy and Hussites in Late Medieval Europe* (Ashgate-Variorum, 2014).

He has also written more than sixty-five book chapters, essays in scholarly journals, and articles in many academic reference works. These include Cambridge University Press, Oxford University Press, Scribner's, MacMillan-Palgrave, *Mediaevistik: Internationale Zeitschrift für Interdisziplinäre Mittelalterforschung, Journal of Pentecostal Theology, The Sixteenth-Century Journal, Central European History, Fides et Historia, Parergon, Communio viatorum, Canadian Journal of History,* and the *Journal of Religious History.* His numerous book reviews have appeared in more than fifteen learned journals including *Speculum, International History Review, Catholic Historical Review, Religious Studies Review,* and *Pneuma: The Journal of the Society for Pentecostal Studies.* He has held ten contestable research grants over the past twenty years together with formal commendations and awards for excellence in teaching. He is the previous holder of the Elizabeth Iliff Warren Research Fellowship, the Crosse Theological Fellowship, and the Lightfoot Research Grant, within the Faculty of History and the Divinity School at Cambridge University. He is a co-founder (1992) of the biennial international symposium *The Bohemian Reformation and Religious Practice* convening in Prague during even numbered years.

Thomas A. Fudge has held academic appointments in the United States, New Zealand, and Australia, and formerly taught college-level courses in the Texas State prison system at Gatesville. He can be contacted at UNE or at thomas_fudge@yahoo.com

www.ingramcontent.com/pod-product-compliance
Lightning Source LLC
Chambersburg PA
CBHW060746100426
42813CB00032B/3411/J